SNOWSHOE
ROUTES
WASHINGTON

SNOWSHOE
ROUTES
WASHINGTON

THIRD EDITION
DAN A. NELSON

MOUNTAINEERS
BOOKS

Mountaineers Books is the publishing division of
The Mountaineers, an organization founded in 1906
and dedicated to the exploration, preservation, and
enjoyment of outdoor and wilderness areas.

**MOUNTAINEERS
BOOKS**

1001 SW Klickitat Way, Suite 201, Seattle, WA 98134
800.553.4453, www.mountaineersbooks.org

Printed in the United States of America
Distributed in the United Kingdom by Cordee, www.cordee.co.uk

Third edition, 2015

Copy editor: Paula Thurman
Design and layout: Jennifer Shontz, redshoedesign.com
Cartographers: Jerry Painter and Jennifer Shontz
Cover photograph: ©iStock.com/Onfokus
Frontispiece: *A happy snowshoer kicks up his heels in the soft snow.*
All photographs by the author unless otherwise noted.

Library of Congress Cataloging-in-Publication Data

Nelson, Dan A.
  Snowshoe routes, Washington / Dan A. Nelson.—Third Edition.
    pages cm
  Includes bibliographical references and index.
  ISBN 978-1-59485-919-9 (trade paper)—ISBN 978-1-59485-920-5 (ebook)
1. Snowshoes and snowshoeing—Washington (State)—Guidebooks. 2. Trails—
Washington (State)—Guidebooks. 3. Washington (State)—Guidebooks.
4. Natural history—Washington (State) I. Title.
  GV853.N45 2015
  796.9'209797—dc23

                                                              2015011036

ISBN (paperback): 978-1-59485-919-9
ISBN (ebook): 978-1-59485-920-5

CONTENTS

LEGEND

🛡70	Interstate highway	**2**	Route number
(2)	US highway	⅄ N	North
(36)	State highway	Ⓣ	Trailhead or route start
272	County or Forest Service road	Ⓟ	Parking area
———	Paved road	❇	Sno-Park
═══	Unpaved road	⊃⊂	Bridge
═══	Unpaved road continues (not shown)	⌣	Pass
- - - - -	Snowshoe route	⌒⌒	Mountain peak
··········	Alternate or other route	⌒	River or creek
•—•—•—	Powerline	⟶	Falls
▲	Campground or campsite	⬭	Lake or pond
⎪⎪⎪	Picnic area	⁂	Marsh
▯	Tower		
■	Building or site		
≡	Avalanche chute		

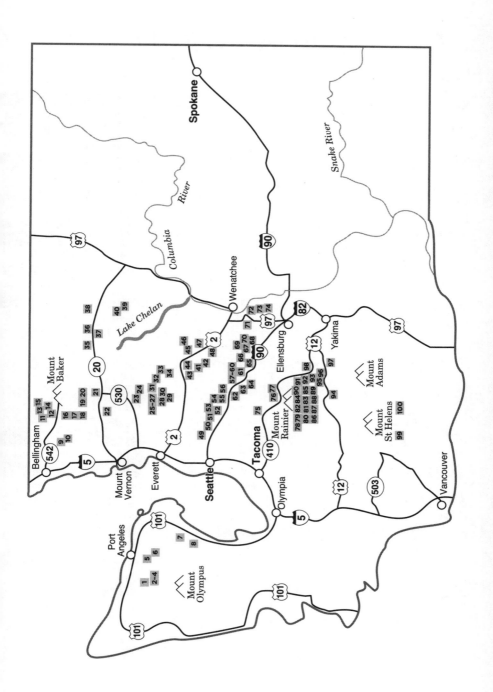

ROUTES AT A GLANCE

ROUTE NUMBER AND NAME	RATING	AVALANCHE POTENTIAL*	BEST SEASON
OLYMPICS			
1 Hurricane Hill	Easiest+	Moderate	Dec–Mar
2 Mount Angeles	Backcountry	Moderate	Dec–Mar
3 Eagle Point	Most difficult	Moderate	Dec–Mar
4 Klahhane Ridge	More difficult	High	Jan–Mar
5 Lake Angeles	More difficult	Low	Jan–Mar
6 Blue Mountain & Deer Park	More difficult	Low	Jan–Mar
7 Mount Townsend	Most difficult	Moderate	Dec–Mar
8 Lena Lake & Valley of Silent Men	Backcountry	Low	Jan–Feb
MOUNT BAKER HIGHWAY			
9 Coal Pass	More difficult	Moderate	Jan–Mar
10 Coleman Glacier	Moderate+	Moderate	Jan–Feb
11 White Salmon Creek	Easiest	Low	Dec–Mar
12 Razor Hone Creek	More difficult	Low	Dec–Apr
13 Goat Mountain Approach	More difficult	Moderate	Dec–Apr
14 Silver Fir Campground Ramble	Easiest	Low	Dec–Apr
15 Welcome Pass	Backcountry	High	Dec–Apr
16 Bagley Lakes	Easiest	Moderate	Jan–Apr
17 Artist Point	More difficult	Low	Dec–Apr
18 Table Mountain	More difficult	Moderate	Jan–Apr
19 Middle Fork Nooksack River	Backcountry	Low	Dec–Feb
20 Schriebers Meadow	More difficult	Moderate	Jan–Mar
NORTH CASCADES—WEST			
21 Sauk Mountain	Backcountry	High	Dec–Feb
22 Iron Mountain	Backcountry	High	Jan–Mar
23 Rat Trap Pass	More difficult	High	Dec–Feb
24 Crystal Lake	Backcountry	Moderate	Jan–Feb
25 Mount Pilchuck	Easiest+	High	Jan–Feb
26 Heather Lake	More difficult	Moderate	Jan–Feb
27 Lake Twentytwo	Backcountry	High	Jan–Feb
28 Boardman Lake	More difficult	Moderate	Dec–Feb
29 Bear Lake	More difficult	Low–moderate	Jan–Feb
30 Mallardy Ridge	More difficult	Moderate–high	Jan–Mar
31 Marten Creek	Backcountry	Moderate	Dec–Feb
32 Kelcema Lake	More difficult	Low–moderate	Jan–Feb
33 Coal Creek	More difficult	Low	Jan–Mar
34 Big Four Ice Caves Viewpoint	Easiest	Low	Jan–Mar

* NOTE: EVERY slope is a potential avalanche slope. The ratings merely compare the

ROUTE TIME	ELEVATION GAIN	PERMITS/ FEES	FAMILY FRIENDLY	DOG FRIENDLY	PANORAMIC VIEWS	WILDLIFE VIEWING	CAMPING OPTIONS	SNO-PARK/ PARKING
4 hrs	800'	•	•		•			•
6 hrs	600'	•			•	•		•
7 hr+	2500'	•			•	•	•	•
6 hrs	1500'	•	•		•	•		•
6 hrs	2300'	•						
6 hrs+	2500'	•			•	•	•	•
7 hrs+	2500'	•			•	•	•	
6 hrs	2000'	•	•	•		•		
6 hrs	2400'	•	•		•			•
1–2 days	4500'	•			•	•	•	
6 hrs	300'	•	•					•
2.5 hrs	500'	•	•	•		•		•
3 hrs	400'	•		•				•
2 hrs	100'	•	•	•				•
9 hrs	3200'				•		•	•
2 hrs	150'	•	•		•			•
4 hrs	1200'	•	•		•			•
2 hrs	300'	•	•		•			•
5 hrs	900'	•	•	•		•		
1–2 days	1200'	•	•		•	•	•	
8 hrs	3500'				•	•		
8 hrs	1800'				•	•		
6 hrs	1900'				•	•		
1–2 days	2800'				•	•	•	
10 hrs	2600'				•			•
4 hrs	1100'	•	•		•	•	•	
4 hrs	1200'	•			•	•		
1–2 days	1800'					•	•	
6 hrs	1400'		•			•		
6 hrs	1900'				•	•		•
5 hrs	1300'	•	•			•		•
6 hrs	1600'		•			•		•
4 hrs	900'		•					•
3.5 hrs	250'	•	•					•

relative risks of each route. You must evaluate the actual risks on any given day for yourself.

ROUTE NUMBER AND NAME	RATING	AVALANCHE POTENTIAL*	BEST SEASON
METHOW VALLEY AREA			
35 Silver Star View	More difficult	High	Dec–Mar
36 Upper River Run	Easiest	Low	Dec–Mar
37 Cedar Falls	More difficult	Low	Dec–Mar
38 Paul Mountain	Easiest+	Moderate	Jan–Mar
39 Lookout Mountain	More difficult	High	Dec–Mar
40 Eagle Creek	Backcountry	Low–moderate	Jan–Mar
STEVENS PASS			
41 Surprise Lake	Backcountry	Moderate	Dec–Apr
42 Lake Susan Jane	More difficult	Moderate	Dec–Apr
43 Skyline Lake	More difficult	Moderate	Dec–Apr
44 Lake Valhalla	More difficult	Moderate-high	Dec–Mar
45 Lanham Lake	More difficult	Low–moderate	Dec–Mar
46 Wenatchee Ridge	Easiest+	Low	Jan–Feb
47 Chiwaukum Creek	More difficult	Moderate–high	Dec–Mar
48 Eightmile Creek	Backcountry	High	Dec–Mar
SNOQUALMIE PASS			
49 Mount Teneriffe	Most difficult	Low–moderate	Dec–Feb
50 Taylor River	More difficult	Low–moderate	Dec–Feb
51 Talapus Lake	Most difficult	Moderate–high	Jan–Mar
52 Ira Spring Approach	Easiest	Moderate	Jan–Mar
53 Denny Creek Campground	Easiest	Low	Jan–Mar
54 Snow Lake	Backcountry	High	Jan–Mar
55 Commonwealth Basin	Backcountry	High	Jan–Mar
56 Kendall Peak Lakes	More difficult	Moderate	Jan–Mar
57 Gold Creek Pond Loop	Easiest	Low	Dec–Feb
58 Upper Gold Creek Valley	Easiest	Low	Jan–Mar
59 Mount Margaret	Easiest+	Moderate	Dec–Feb
60 Keechelus Ridge	More difficult	Moderate–high	Jan–Feb
61 Amabilis Mountain	Most difficult	Moderate–high	Jan–Feb
62 Twin Lakes	Easiest	Low–moderate	Dec–Feb
63 Windy Pass & Mount Catherine	Most difficult	Moderate	Dec–Feb
64 Keechelus Lake & John Wayne Trail	Easiest	Moderate	Dec–Feb
65 Kachess Campground Loops	Easiest+	Low	Dec–Feb
66 Hibox Approach	More difficult	Low	Dec–Feb
EAST & CENTRAL CASCADES			
67 Hex Mountain	More difficult	Moderate	Dec–Mar
68 Sasse Ridge	Backcountry	High	Dec–Mar
69 Salmon la Sac Creek	Most difficult	Moderate	Dec–Mar

* NOTE: EVERY slope is a potential avalanche slope. The ratings merely compare the

ROUTE TIME	ELEVATION GAIN	PERMITS/ FEES	FAMILY FRIENDLY	DOG FRIENDLY	PANORAMIC VIEWS	WILDLIFE VIEWING	CAMPING OPTIONS	SNO-PARK/ PARKING
3 hrs+	700'		•					•
4 hrs	500'	•	•			•		•
5 hrs	800'		•			•		
5 hrs	1500'	•	•					•
5 hrs	2100'		•		•			•
4 hrs+	4900'				•	•		•
6 hrs	2300'	•			•	•		
3.5 hrs	1200'		•			•		•
2 hrs	1100'							•
5.5 hrs	1700'		•			•		•
3 hrs	1100'	•	•			•	•	•
7 hrs	2000'		•		•			•
6 hrs+	1200'					•	•	
1–2 days	2600'				•	•	•	
8 hrs	3800'	•		•	•	•	•	
6 hrs	650'	•		•		•		
7 hrs	1600'	•			•			
5 hrs	100'	•	•	•				
3 hrs	100'	•	•	•				
7 hrs+	2000'	•		•	•	•	•	•
7 hrs	2300'					•		•
7 hrs	1700'	•	•		•			•
2 hrs	100'	•	•	•		•		•
5 hrs	1200'	•		•		•		•
6 hrs	2800'	•	•					•
5 hrs	2100'	•			•			•
6 hrs	2100'	•		•	•	•		•
5 hrs	400'	•	•			•		•
7 hrs	2300'	•	•					•
3 hrs	200'	•	•					•
3 hrs	400'	•	•	•			•	•
8 hrs+	600'	•		•		•	•	•
6 hrs	2600'				•	•		•
2 days	2700'				•	•	•	•
5 hrs	1300'	•				•	•	•

relative risks of each route. You must evaluate the actual risks on any given day for yourself.

ROUTE NUMBER AND NAME	RATING	AVALANCHE POTENTIAL*	BEST SEASON
EAST & CENTRAL CASCADES cont.			
70 Cooper River	More difficult	Low–moderate	Dec–Mar
71 Indian Creek	Easiest+	Low	Dec–Mar
72 Swauk Forest Discovery Trail	Easiest	Low	Dec–Mar
73 Haney Meadow Loop	More difficult	Low	Dec–Mar
74 Wenatchee Crest	Easiest	Low	Dec–Mar
MOUNT RAINIER & SR 410			
75 Sun Top	More difficult	Moderate	Jan–Feb
76 Bullion Basin	Backcountry	High	Dec–Mar
77 White River	Easiest	Low	Dec–Feb
78 Copper Creek Hut	More difficult	Low–moderate	Dec–Apr
79 Busywild Overlook	Easiest	Low	Dec–Mar
80 Snow Bowl Hut	More difficult	Moderate	Dec–Apr
81 High Hut	More difficult	Moderate–high	Dec–Apr
82 Kautz Creek	More difficult	Low–moderate	Jan–Mar
83 Eagle and Chutla Peaks Trail	Most difficult	Moderate	Jan–Mar
84 Rampart Ridge	More difficult	Low–moderate	Jan–Mar
85 Wonderland Trail	Easiest	Low–moderate	Dec–Apr
86 Reflection Lakes	More difficult	Low–moderate	Dec–May
87 Pinnacle Saddle	Most difficult	High	Dec–May
88 Glacier Vista	Easiest	Low–moderate	Dec–May
89 Panorama Point	Most difficult	Low–moderate	Dec–May
90 Mazama Ridge	More difficult	Low–moderate	Dec–Apr
91 Camp Muir	Most difficult	High	Feb–May
92 Silver Falls & Grove of the Patriarchs	More difficult	Low	Jan–Mar
93 Olallie Creek	Most difficult	Low	Jan–Mar
SOUTH CASCADES			
94 Packwood Lake	Most difficult	Low	Jan–Mar
95 Sand Lake	More difficult	Low	Dec–Mar
96 Cramer Lake	Most difficult	Moderate	Dec–Mar
97 Tieton River Meadows	Easiest	Low	Dec–Mar
98 American Ridge	Backcountry	Moderate–high	Dec–Mar
99 Mount St. Helens Summit	Backcountry	High	Dec–Feb
100 June Lake	More difficult	Moderate	Dec–Mar

* NOTE: EVERY slope is a potential avalanche slope. The ratings merely compare the

ROUTE TIME	ELEVATION GAIN	PERMITS/ FEES	FAMILY FRIENDLY	DOG FRIENDLY	PANORAMIC VIEWS	WILDLIFE VIEWING	CAMPING OPTIONS	SNO-PARK/ PARKING
6 hrs	400'	●	●	●		●	●	●
2–10 hrs	1300'	●	●		●	●		●
2–5 hrs	450'	●	●			●		●
8 hrs+	1600'	●	●	●		●	●	●
5 hrs	400'	●	●					●
7.5 hrs	3000'	●			●	●		●
4 hrs	1500'				●	●	●	●
3 hrs	400'	●	●					●
5 hrs+	1000'	●	●				●	●
4 hrs	900'	●	●		●		●	●
7 hrs+	2000'	●	●		●		●	●
7 hrs+	2400'	●	●		●		●	●
7 hrs	2800'	●				●		●
6 hrs	2900'	●			●	●		●
5 hrs	1200'	●	●		●	●		●
5 hrs	1300'	●	●			●		●
3 hrs	560'	●			●	●	●	●
5 hrs	1400'	●			●	●	●	●
3 hrs	700'	●	●		●	●	●	●
4 hrs	1300'	●			●			●
5 hrs	900'	●	●		●	●		●
9 hrs+	4400'	●			●		●	●
2/3.5 hrs	200/400'	●	●			●		●
7 hrs+	1800'	●				●		●
7 hrs+	500'	●	●	●		●	●	
5 hrs+	900'		●	●				●
7 hrs	800'		●			●		●
8 hrs	350'	●	●	●		●		●
5 hrs	2600'	●			●	●		
9 hrs	5700'	●			●			●
3 hrs	500'	●	●					●

relative risks of each route. You must evaluate the actual risks on any given day for yourself.

View from the trail up Mount Margaret (Route 59)

PREFACE

In the mid-1990s, the age-old activity of snowshoeing began to boom as a winter sport. As the new millennium dawned, the sport kept growing. Through the first decades of the 21st century, snowshoeing continues to flourish, growing faster than any other winter sport in the Pacific Northwest—and throughout the northern states. Part of the reason for that is the tremendous popularity of hiking in the Pacific Northwest. Summer hikers are loath to give up their favorite pastime simply because the seasons change. So, come winter, hikers have two options—step onto a pair of cross-country skis or strap on snowshoes. In the past, skis have been the preferred choice for backcountry enthusiasts. But not everyone wants to take the time, or make the considerable effort, needed to master the art of cross-country skiing in mountain country. Snowshoeing has become a popular alternative.

Probably the main reason for this trend is the ease with which beginners can become accomplished snowshoers. Anyone who knows how to walk knows how to use snowshoes—just strap them on and walk, it's as simple as that. Another reason snowshoes are increasingly popular is that hikers can get to the same areas in winter that they hike to in summer. They can move easily through thick forests and up steep slopes. Skis, on the other hand, are more difficult to maneuver on forest trails, and uphill slopes pose tougher challenges for novice skiers (although the downhill run is undeniably more fun on skis).

Although hikers can travel many of the same trails on snowshoes that they can in the summer, more often than not the trailheads for those trails are inaccessible by car. Fortunately, the surge in interest in cross-country skiing in the 1970s prompted Washington to build and maintain a series of Sno-Parks throughout the state. These facilities are merely parking lots that are kept cleared of snow and access roads that are kept plowed during the winter. More than one hundred Sno-Parks are maintained for winter recreationists, with no fewer than fifty devoted solely to nonmotorized recreationists.

Cross-country skiers and snowmobilers have utilized these Sno-Parks for nearly four decades. Many of the facilities also feature groomed ski trails, groomed snowmobile trails, and a few even have tracks set for skiers who prefer that mode of skiing.

While the skinny skis and screaming snowmobiles crowd the groomed roads and wide trails leading out of these parking areas, snowshoers can take advantage of the solitude found on the forest trails that angle away from the roads. These snow-laden paths are impossible—if not illegal—for snowmobilers to negotiate and too difficult for the majority of skiers to attempt. But a hiker wearing a pair of modern snowshoes can climb the snowy trail as easily

The author (far left) and friends enjoy a rest on a ridge top.

as a hiker can trudge up switchbacks in summer. In fact, snowshoers have a decided advantage over their summer colleagues simply because they can often walk right over the top of many difficult obstacles—thick brush, fallen logs, treacherous talus fields, and so forth. A heavy blanket of snow can level the most difficult field so that in winter, hikers feel like they are hiking through an open meadow, whereas in summer, hikers may find the same area to be an impassable slope of slide alder.

Unfortunately, that blanket of snow can also make finding a specific trail next to impossible. That's where this book comes in. I have put together one hundred of my favorite winter hikes around Washington and present them here as a means of helping other hikers find the beauty of the winter backcountry without the hassle of trying to pick and choose a route. Of course, the routes I describe here are not as easy to follow as a snow-free summer trail, nor should snowshoers think they have to follow my exact footprints. Part of the mystique and wonder of snowshoe hiking is the ability to explore anywhere—a route is limited only by a snowshoer's physical and mental limits, tempered with a heavy dose of common sense and avalanche awareness.

Special thanks to Erik Swanson, co-chair of the Snowshoe Committee of the Seattle Branch of The Mountaineers. Erik provided invaluable field research and review for several routes included in this book.

A Note About Safety

Please use common sense. This book is not intended as a substitute for careful planning, professional training, or your own good judgment. It is incumbent upon any user of this guide to assess his or her own skills, experience, fitness, and equipment. Readers will recognize the inherent dangers in snowshoeing and mountain or backcountry terrain and assume responsibility for their own actions and safety. Changing or unfavorable conditions in weather, roads, trails, etc., cannot be anticipated by the author or publisher but should be considered by any outdoor participants, as routes may become dangerous or slopes unstable due to such altered conditions. Likewise, be aware of any changes in public jurisdiction, and do not access private property without permission. The publisher and author are not responsible for any adverse consequences resulting directly or indirectly from information contained in this book.

—*Mountaineers Books*

Looking east toward Mount Baker from the Mount Baker Highway as it climbs north toward Glacier

INTRODUCTION

Snowshoes are the earliest-known means of making travel on snow easier. The best archaeological evidence suggests these early "foot extenders" originated in central Asia about 4000 B.C. Further evidence shows that without this mode of winter transportation, aboriginal people would not have been able to journey to what is now North America via the Bering Strait. Snowshoes are a natural for modern-day winter trekking, as more and more people are coming to realize. With a little planning and preparation, you can embrace the beauties of the backcountry year-round. Definite benefits are derived by supplementing warm-weather hiking with snowshoeing come winter. In addition to the readily apparent payoffs of summer hiking—escape from the mechanized, hectic world, if only for a short time; strenuous, healthy workouts in beautiful surroundings; the thrill of accomplishment after hiking a long trail or climbing a steep peak; communion with the natural world—winter wilderness rambling offers its own rewards. The landscape is more serene, covered in a sound-absorbing carpet of snow. No irritating swarms of bugs gnaw on your exposed skin, and far fewer humans compete for a spot in the quiet wilderness.

Of course, there are other winter recreation considerations, most notably the weather—the cold weather. This factor influences all the benefits—and dangers—of exploring a snow-shrouded wilderness.

The lower temperatures of winter make snow recreation more intense than its warmer-season counterparts. The planning and preparation of a trip takes more time and thought. More equipment and clothing are needed for winter camping. The discomforts of a poorly planned trip are more acute. But the pleasures of a good outing are more profound.

STEPPING OUT INTO THE SNOW
The most visible change from summer to winter is your method of locomotion. When the snow flies, it's no longer possible to merely lace up your sturdy boots and head up the trail—try doing that after a deep pack of Cascade concrete has filtered down on the hills, and you'll find yourself exhausted in the first 100 yards. That's where snowshoes come in. Snowshoes are the easiest way to get acquainted with winter wilderness. The basics of snowshoeing are simple—it's just like walking, but with bigger feet. Of course, there is a bit more to it than that, but essentially, any other techniques are simply variations of walking strides.

Snowshoes themselves come in a variety of forms. Traditional shoes are made with wooden frames and rawhide laces for decking. These range in shape from round "bear paws" to long, tapered "Yukons," which feature a lot of surface area and extended tails that drag in the snow to help keep the shoes pointed forward. You can still find wooden shoes, although the lace decking is usually made with strips of neoprene rubber these days, but the best bet for any general-use winter hiking is the "modern" design. This is essentially a narrow bear paw. It features an aluminum or rigid plastic oval frame with a solid decking of synthetic fabric. Several shoes are now available that are made from extruded plastic. Some of these solid plastic shoes are lightweight, affordable, and for the most part, very effective. Regardless of the type, make sure the shoes have ice spikes—called crampons, or cleats—under the forefoot and heel plates.

The size of your snowshoes depends on a number of factors, primarily your weight (including the weight of your pack) and the kind of snow in which you'll be trekking. In the Cascades, the general rule is to plan on heavy, wet snow. Most people under 180 pounds can wear snowshoes in the 8-by-25-inch category. Larger folks, or hikers who will be carrying heavy packs, should consider shoes in the 9-by-30-inch range. Given the dense, wet snow common to the Pacific Northwest, few people will ever need shoes larger than 30 inches. The smaller the snowshoe you use, the better—smaller means lighter and less cumbersome. If you plan to snowshoe in areas where the snow is generally lighter and fluffier, you'll need to move up a step in shoe size. Before buying a pair of snowshoes, it's a good idea to rent several different pairs to get a feel for which model you prefer and which size is best for you.

Snowshoers huddling up for a safety talk before heading out

FOOTWEAR

Unlike cross-country skiing, there are no specific boots that must be worn with snowshoes. Regular hiking boots, mountaineering boots, heavily insulated "pac" boots, or even cross-country ski boots can be worn with the easy-to-use bindings found on most quality snowshoes. Ideally, you want boots that provide the type of ankle and foot support found in regular hiking boots, but which also keep your feet warm and dry.

Many hiking boot companies have begun to work with snowshoe makers to design insulated hiking boots specifically for snowshoe trekking. The best option now is to use all-leather hiking boots that are large enough to comfortably allow you to wear a thick layer or two of insulated socks, and then cover the boots with waterproof gaiters. Just don't pack too much wool into your boots, because too tight of a fit will make your feet feel even colder than if there were no insulation.

CLOTHING

In addition to snowshoes, you'll need to carry several layers of bulky clothing in your pack for winter excursions. Avoid anything made with cotton. Instead, you'll need multiple layers of synthetic or wool clothing.

By layering your clothing, you can easily make adjustments when you start to heat up (and you will heat up, as walking in snowshoes is a better aerobic workout than walking on a dry trail) or cool down—just add or subtract a layer or two. Working from the skin out, start with a good base layer of silk, wool, or synthetic (polypropylene, Capilene, Thermastat, etc.) long johns. These will form a thin insulating layer next to your skin, but more importantly, they will pull moisture away from your body. Without that wicking action, the moisture could end up freezing on your skin, causing almost instant hypothermia.

Over the base layer, add a thin insulating layer, like a wool or synthetic fleece sweater and pants. On very cold days, or if you generally get cold easily, cover this layer with a thicker insulating layer—a fleece jacket or vest. When the wind is blowing or moisture is in the air, top off the whole outfit with a sturdy waterproof parka and pants. This layer will cut the wind and prevent any external water from soaking through.

The idea behind building an insulation shell in layers is that you can then easily adjust your clothing to the conditions. When getting started each day, take into consideration not only the weather but also the type of snowshoeing you'll be doing. A lot of climbing early on means you'll be working hard, and if you have too many layers, you'll quickly work up a sweat. To avoid that, adjust the layers to the point where you can just feel a chill as you start out, knowing that within a few steps you'll be warmed up enough to be comfortable, but not overheated.

OTHER GEAR

Every time you venture more than a few yards away from the road on a snowshoe outing, you should be prepared to spend the night under the stars (or under the clouds, as may be more likely). Winter storms can whip up in a hurry, catching you by surprise. What was an easy-to-follow trail during a calm, clear day can disappear into a confusing world of white in a windswept snowstorm. Therefore, every member of the party should have a pack loaded with The Mountaineers Ten Essentials, as well as a few other items that aren't necessarily essential but are good to have on hand in a winter emergency.

The Ten Essentials: A Systems Approach

1. **Navigation (map and compass).** Carry a compass and a topographic map of the area you plan to be in, and know how to use them.
2. **Sun protection (sunglasses and sunscreen).** While necessary for most high-alpine travel, sunglasses are absolutely essential for snow. Snow blindness (sunburn of the eyes) can render you immobile and helpless.
3. **Insulation (extra clothing).** This means more clothing than you would wear during the worst weather of the planned outing. If you get injured or lost, you won't be moving around generating heat, so you'll need to be able to bundle up. (See Clothing above.)
4. **Illumination (headlamp or flashlight).** If caught after dark, you'll need it to follow the trail. If forced to spend the night, you'll need it to set up emergency camp, gather wood, etc. Carry extra batteries and bulb.
5. **First-aid supplies.** Nothing elaborate is needed—especially if you are unfamiliar with some of the uses. Make sure you have adhesive bandages, gauze bandages, pain-relief medicine, etc. A Red Cross first-aid training course is recommended.
6. **Fire (firestarter and matches/lighter).** An emergency campfire provides warmth, but it also has a calming effect on most people. Without it, the night is cold, dark, and intimidating. With it, the night is held at arm's length. A candle or tube of firestarting ribbon is essential for starting a fire with wet wood. Pack matches in a waterproof container and/or buy the waterproof/windproof variety. Book matches are useless in wind or wet weather, and disposable lighters are unreliable.
7. **Repair kit and tools (including knife).** There are a multitude of uses for a knife; some come easily to mind (whittling kindling for a fire; first-aid applications), while others won't become apparent until you find you don't have a knife handy. A multitool is an even better option because the pliers can be used to repair damaged snowshoes. My repair kit contains a 20-foot length of nylon cord, a small roll of duct tape, some 1-inch webbing and extra webbing buckles (to replace any that might break on snowshoe bindings), and a small tube of fast-bonding glue.

8. **Nutrition (extra food).** Pack enough so that you'll have leftovers after an uneventful trip. (Those leftovers will keep you fed and fueled during an emergency.)
9. **Hydration (extra water).**
10. **Emergency shelter.** (See Camping, below.)

In addition to these essentials, I add my emergency survival kit, which holds a small metal mirror, an emergency Mylar "blanket," a plastic whistle, and a tiny signal smoke canister—all useful for signaling to search-and-rescue groups, whether they are on the ground or in the air.

Other items you might want to carry with you on your snowshoe outings include a small compactable snow shovel and ice saw. Both tools are extremely useful when setting up a camp in the snow. Even when you are only out for the day, a shovel comes in handy for notching out benches or seats during rest stops and lunch. Most snowshoers find ski poles very helpful—if not essential. This is especially true when climbing or descending hills. Finally, some campers prefer to pull their gear on a sled rather than pack it on their backs.

A snowshoer high-steps her way through deep snow.

SNOWSHOEING TECHNIQUE

As I stated at the outset, if you can walk, you can walk on snowshoes. Generally, that is true; however, a few special techniques can help in tricky situations. Heading up and down hills, for instance, can be a problem unless you alter your hiking technique to accommodate the snowshoes.

To climb a hill, kick your toe into the hillside to dig the forefoot cleats into the snow, and then step down, putting weight on the toe so that the cleats get a good, solid bite into the slope. To go back down the hill, bend your knees, lean forward slightly, and plant your whole foot solidly on the surface of the snow. This engages the entire surface of the snowshoe on the slope, and by leaning forward, you distribute your weight evenly on all the cleats. If, however, you lean back and keep your weight more on your heels (as you generally would do when hiking), you'll disengage the cleats on the front half of the snowshoe and slide forward.

Also, if you find you need to back up, the first thing you'll notice is the back of the snowshoe drags under your foot and trips you up. Counter this by using your trekking poles to push down on the front of the snowshoe, forcing the back to lift as you lift your foot. This is also the easiest way to turn around on snowshoes.

Perhaps the biggest difference between walking and walking on snowshoes is the distance between your feet. With snowshoes, you'll need to walk a bit straddle-legged so that the shoes don't overlap or hit your legs as you stride.

CAMPING

There is nothing like spending a night in a snowy wilderness setting. The cold, clear sky and quiet forest are unlike anything you'll experience in the summer. But winter camping has different requirements than camping in the other three seasons. In terms of gear, you'll need a cold-weather sleeping bag (something rated to 0 degrees at least, or an insulation liner for your three-season bag) and a four-season tent. Here in the wet Northwest, the best bets for sleeping bags are those with synthetic fill, or insulation layers. Synthetic fills are (relatively) inexpensive, work even when wet, and have evolved to be nearly as efficient and compressible as goose down. Goose down is a wonderful insulator and compresses well to fit into a stuffed backpack, but if it gets wet, it's no good at all. Down is also expensive, and if you add a waterproof shell to a down bag (a necessity in Washington's climate), you drive the price through the roof.

For shelter, you can build snow caves, stay in backcountry huts (found on some maintained ski-trail networks), or pitch a tent. A tent is the best option, but it must be sturdy enough to withstand potentially violent winter winds and heavy snowfall. Most backpacking tents are sold as three-season tents and don't have the stability needed to stand up to the extreme abuses of winter. Four-season tents are built sturdier, with more poles, steeper walls (to shed

The copper-toned bark of ponderosa pines in the Swauk Pass area adds some welcome color to the stark white landscape.

snow), and heavier flies. All that extra engineering is necessary to make them snow-safe, but it also drives up their price. Fortunately, four-season tents can be rented, so you won't have to invest in a new fabric home if you camp only a few times a year.

When setting out on a winter backpacking trip, keep in mind the short daylight hours of winter and the longer amount of time you will need to set up camp. Plan carefully, and err on the side of caution—it's better to cut a trip short than to push on to a planned destination after darkness has fallen.

Setting up a winter camp is different from setting up a summer camp. You'll want to do it when you still have plenty of daylight! Remember that the cold weather will slow you down, and you will be setting up your tent wearing mittens or gloves. But before the tent goes up, clear a place for it. Brush off loose snow and/or stomp down a flat pad for the tent floor. If time allows, build a "wind wall" on the windward side of the tent. Do this by packing snow into a thick, semicircular wall up to 4 feet high. This wall deflects the worst of the night's wind around the tent, keeping the tent warmer and more secure.

While you are setting up camp, "make" water by melting snow. This can take a long time (and burn a lot of stove fuel, so pack extra).

Once your basic camp is set up, if you still have daylight left, you can spiff up the place by building a camp kitchen. Excavate a trough roughly 2 feet wide and 2 feet deep. Cut seats into one wall of the trough and a table into the other. Step into the trough, and you can then sit down to do your cooking and eating. If any of your camp setup included digging a snow cave or other undercut or hidden structure, please make sure you collapse the roof or overhang before leaving so as not to leave a hidden danger for other recreationists in the area.

DETECTING AVALANCHE DANGER

Winter recreation has some risks inherent to the season. Cold temperatures and wet conditions are the obvious ones, and proper clothing and preparation are essential to help you deal with the cold and wet. But as harsh as the weather conditions can be, it's the snow that poses one of the biggest threats to winter recreationists, especially in the mountains. The danger of avalanche is found anywhere there is a slope with snow on it. Sometimes the danger is minimal, sometimes a slide is inevitable, and frequently you won't be able to tell the difference by looking at the hillside. Knowledge of current snow conditions, recent weather patterns, and future weather forecasts are all necessary to help you understand and evaluate the avalanche danger on a given day, in a given area.

One of the best resources available to winter recreationists is the Northwest Avalanche Center (NWAC), which keeps detailed records on weather and snow patterns and conditions and makes its findings available to the public via a recorded message line. Every time you plan to venture out into the snowy mountains, you should first call the Avalanche Center, check its website (see

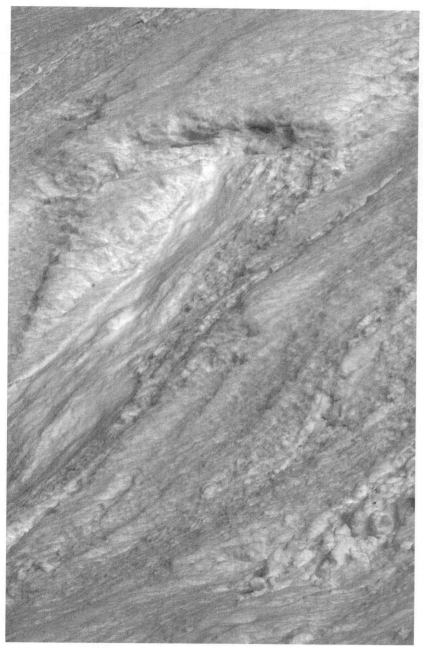

When snow sloughs off slopes like this, it indicates potential avalanche danger.

Snowshoers traverse a steep hillside after determining the avalanche danger was low.

Resources & Land Managers), or use the NWAC app (available for both Android and iOS devices) to get the avalanche danger report for your area of interest. Or failing that, purchase and use a weather radio. These radios tune in special FM frequencies not normally found on home radios. These frequencies, 162.4 to 162.55 megahertz, are reserved for use by the National Oceanic and Atmospheric Administration (NOAA), so they can broadcast ongoing weather reports and conditions. Frequent mountain weather reports, which include avalanche condition reports, are broadcast on the Northwest weather radio.

In addition, you should learn to recognize the clues of avalanche danger. All avalanches start with unstable snow—snow that isn't bonded to the hillside. Avalanches are of two primary types: slab avalanches occur when large solid sections of snow break away at once, and loose snow avalanches occur when unattached snow crystals slide down a slope, dislodging more and more snow as they go.

A quick study of the slope ahead of you can reveal clues to avalanche potential. First, estimate the steepness of the slope. Avalanches are most common on a slope of 30 to 45 degrees, but they can and do release on slopes as gentle as 25 degrees or as steep as 65 or more degrees. Second, take note of the profile of the slope. A slope with a convex profile—that is, it bulges out a bit—is more likely to slide than a concave slope. Third, look at the exposure of the slope. A north-facing slope may be slower to stabilize than other slopes because it doesn't receive as much direct sunlight, and therefore the snow doesn't settle and compact as quickly. A leeward slope tends to become wind-loaded with unstable snow more often than a windward slope, since a windward slope generally has less snow, and what is there is more compacted by the wind. Wind is a major contributor to avalanche hazards, and the higher and more prolonged the wind, the greater the threat of avalanche.

Other visible clues to avalanche danger include the following:

- Sticky snow, which indicates the surface snow is warmer than the snow below.
- Evidence of recent avalanches. If you see a slope that has apparently slid in the last 24 hours or so (rough, disturbed surface of slope, large snowballs or piles of loose or clumped snow at slope base), consider it a good indication that snow conditions are unstable.
- Hollow drumming or "whomping" sounds coming from the snow underfoot indicate slab conditions and a high potential for release.
- Rime ice on trees. This build-up of ice and frost suggests there were high winds during a recent storm, and therefore chances are good that leeward slopes are highly wind-loaded and likely to slide.
- Broken limbs and/or snow plastered to the uphill side of trees shows past avalanche occurrence. A slope that slides once will slide again after the next storm.

Understanding and recognizing these signs aren't all there is to know about avoiding avalanche danger. This discussion simply serves as a brief primer on the subject. More detailed information is readily available in a number of excellent books, including *Avalanche Essentials: A Step-by-Step System for Safety and Survival* by Bruce Tremper (Mountaineers Books). Tremper's *Avalanche Pocket Guide* is a handy reference to keep with you in the mountains.

FROZEN LAKES

Unless you have a desperate need to cross a frozen lake, it's always better to skirt the lakeshore rather than risk the ice. The combination of generally mild winters and the volcanic nature of the Cascade Range makes all lake ice suspect. Even if temperatures are cold enough long enough to freeze a lake solid, the geothermal activity below the mountains creates a lot of warm and hot springs, some of which can spout out of the ground in the middle of a lake, keeping it warmer than you might expect. In effect, these unseen warm springs sometimes melt the surface ice from underneath.

FINDING A DESTINATION

This book details one hundred snowshoeing routes in Washington. That is by no stretch a complete inventory of the possible snowshoe outing destinations. The goal of this book is to show some of the better areas to explore and to encourage backcountry enthusiasts to get out in the cold months and enjoy the beauty of the snowbound mountains.

There are hundreds, if not thousands, of routes available for snowshoe trekkers in this state. The best way to find them is to utilize your library of hiking guidebooks, your inventory of topographic maps, and your growing knowledge of what makes a good winter hike. Plan a snowshoe hike using these tools, as well as current information on snow and weather conditions.

If you are new to snowshoe hiking, start slow. Pick a short hike for your first outing to get a feel for the sport and your abilities. And above all, be flexible. You may find a trip in these pages that sounds like a perfect outing for you, but if the weather is unfavorable, or avalanche dangers are high in that region, choose a different trip. You can hike your first choice another time. It's better to explore a different location than to risk getting caught in an avalanche's path.

Exercise good judgment and basic common sense, take advantage of the knowledgeable rangers and avalanche forecasters, and learn to evaluate avalanche potentials and determine snow conditions, and you will have a good outing. Like all outdoor adventures, winter hiking has its dangers, but planning and precaution can mitigate most of them. Be prepared, and you will be safe.

SNO-PARKS

Most of the hikes in this book originate from state Sno-Parks (indicated by a snowflake symbol on route maps). These facilities are parking areas maintained throughout the winter exclusively for winter recreationists. Many are open for multiuse by skiers, snowmobilers, dog mushers, snowshoers, and sledders, although nearly half are set aside for nonmotorized sports. Even if a Sno-Park is open to snowmobilers, there is no reason to pass it by. Typically, snowmobilers will stick to the groomed roads and trails leading away from the Sno-Park, leaving plenty of untracked areas for snowshoers to explore.

Permits are required to park in these facilities, and the permit fees are used to keep parking spaces plowed, bathrooms clean and maintained, and ski and snowmobile trails groomed and maintained. Washington State Sno-Park permits are available by the day, by the week, or for an entire season, and thanks to a cooperative recreation program, the Washington permit is also accepted in Oregon and Idaho (and permits from those states are accepted here). Sno-Park permits are available at U.S. Forest Service ranger stations, outdoor retailers, and online from Washington State Parks (see Resources & Land Managers).

When parking—whether in a Sno-Park or a less maintained area—you should always try to park with your vehicle pointed in the direction you need to travel to leave. By turning around and pointing "out" at the start of the day, you avoid potential problems at the end of the day should more snow fall or conditions get icy. It's always easier to drive forward in the snow and ice than backward, so if you set yourself up in the morning, you'll avoid headaches in the afternoon.

The Gold Creek Pond Loop (Route 57), cradled in the lower Gold Creek valley near Snoqualmie Pass

USING THIS BOOK

The route descriptions in this guide are self-explanatory. But keep a few things in mind as you browse through the book, looking for that perfect outing.

Rating the Trails

The rating system for the hikes is subjective, and not everyone will agree with every rating. The individual ratings are based on the following guidelines:

Easiest: No previous snowshoe experience is required. These are great trails for first-timers who want to get a feel for the sport. Generally, elevation gain and loss are small and avalanche dangers are minimal at all times. These are good routes for groups with children or when campers are pulling loads of gear on sleds.

More difficult: Some previous snowshoe experience is helpful, and some winter survival skills are recommended (i.e., basic knowledge of avalanche slope evaluation, emergency shelter construction, etc.). A bit more climbing is required, as these trails feature more elevation gain, but for the most part, elevation gain is less than 1000 feet or, if more, the slope is gradual and relatively stable at all times. Routes may include forest trails, narrow logging roads, or moderate-slope climbing.

Most difficult: Hikers should have good experience and familiarity with snowshoes. These routes feature sections that will need to be evaluated for avalanche safety every time. The trails climb considerably and may include climbing to ridge tops. Traverses across forested or open slopes may be required. An ability to self-arrest with an ice ax or trekking pole is recommended.

Backcountry: These routes follow topography rather than trails or roads, so skill with a map and compass is essential. A variety of conditions may be encountered along backcountry routes, including steep elevation gains and losses. These routes require complete competence in winter survival skills, avalanche and snow condition evaluation, and some basic mountaineering skills.

Round Trip

Because snow levels vary so widely from year to year—and month to month—round-trip distances listed here are not absolute. Some of the routes begin at formal Sno-Park areas, and are therefore fairly consistent in their trip mileage, but others begin wherever the snow line is encountered, so the distances can increase or decrease by several miles based on snow accumulation. The starting points for the mileage are calculated from the average base point.

Hiking Time

Everyone moves at different speeds, but a general rule of thumb is to estimate that when walking on snowshoes, you'll be moving 30 to 50 percent slower than you would walking on a bare trail. So if you generally hike at a rate of

The view from the Crystal Lake basin

3 miles per hour, figure you'll be doing 1.5 to 2 miles per hour on snowshoes. Several factors play into this reduced rate of speed. First and foremost, when snowshoeing, you are lugging around big, broad, heavy items on your feet. You are also moving on a surface that creates a lot more friction, so you work harder to move those big, high-friction snowshoes forward. Snow may also accumulate on your snowshoes, further increasing their weight. Bottom line, the snowy environment adds up to make your travel more difficult, and therefore slower.

And that slower rate, combined with short winter days, means you should plan on doing fewer miles than you would if you were hiking bare trails in the summer. In fact, you should plan to cut your hiking mileage by the same 30 to 50 percent. For example, if you generally take summer day hikes of 10 to 15 miles, plan to take snowshoe hikes of 6 to 10 miles.

Elevation Gain
Starting from the base starting point, this number is the accumulated total elevation gain from the trail's start to its high point. The total will vary if snow levels force you to start above or below the starting point listed.

High Point
This is the elevation of the highest point on the route, not necessarily the end point.

Best Season
There is only one accurate answer to the question "When is the best time to snowshoe each route?" That answer is "It depends." But since that's not too useful, I have put myself on the line and offered an estimate of when you'll find the best conditions for each route. Bear in mind, though, that first answer. The best time to snowshoe any given route is when the snow is stable, yet deep and fluffy; when the weather is clear and calm; and when the route is free of avalanche danger. While a trail may be great one December, it could be bare of snow the next. I have snowshoed some trails in June that I had hiked the previous June with no snow in sight. So, again, I have estimated a range for the "average" year and ask that you be open-minded with your interpretation of that range.

Maps
Not enough can be said about the importance of carrying and using good topographic maps on every outing. Winter hiking isn't like summer hiking—the trail isn't always visible. In fact, more often than not, the "trail" doesn't exist anywhere but on the map. It is your responsibility to make sure that you are on course.

The maps in this book are not designed to be used for routefinding. They are intended as locator maps to assist you in visualizing the hike and to help you locate the route on a topographic map.

Powdery snow makes for soft landings, so have fun!

To help you find the maps you need, I have also listed the Green Trails and/or Custom Correct maps covering the hiking area. Green Trails and Custom Correct maps are commercially produced. While many snowshoers may have and use U.S. Geological Survey (USGS) maps—they are available for the entire state—I have found the commercially produced maps, when available, are more beneficial to recreationists because they are revised regularly, with updated trail and road information. USGS maps are not updated regularly. Many of the Washington maps haven't been revised for more than twenty years, so the roads and trails listed on them may be outdated, although the geographic information is still highly accurate.

Custom Correct offers detailed topographic maps for the Olympic Peninsula. The maps are not based on a grid system like USGS maps, but instead are designed to cover entire river valleys and/or trail networks. As such, the Custom Correct maps have a lot of overlap, but their strength is the fact that for any given hike, only one map is needed. Green Trails maps, on the other hand, are based on a grid system covering the Olympic Peninsula and the entire Cascade Range through northern Oregon.

Who to Contact

In addition to calling the Northwest Avalanche Center (NWAC) hotline, it is a good idea to contact the local land manager to get current information on the specific area you plan to visit. To make it easier for you to do that, I have included the name of the agency in charge of the land traversed by each route. Addresses and phone numbers are provided in the Resources & Land Managers section at the back of this book.

Permits, Passes, and Fees

The routes described here make use of a variety of public lands, managed by several different state and federal agencies. And in this time of "pay-to-play" public funding processes, snowshoers face a dizzying array of permits, passes, and fees. Depending on the route being explored, you might need a Washington State Discover Pass (required at Washington State Parks and Washington Department of Natural Resource lands) or a Washington Sno-Park Permit (required at all state-maintained Sno-Park facilities). In 2015, the cost of a Washington Sno-Park Permit was $20 per day or $40 annually. A Washington State Discover Pass cost $10 per day or $30 annually. Due to ever-changing policies, it's possible you may need a Washington State Discover Pass and a Washington Sno-Park Permit to legally park at some areas. Check online at www.parks.wa.gov/130/Winter-Recreation.

To park at official trailheads on National Forest lands, you need a Northwest Forest Pass, which cost $5 per day or $30 annually in 2015. Access National Park Service areas by paying a fee at the park entrance ($15–20 per car) or using an America the Beautiful Pass ($80 annually).

Finally, several local and private groups have implemented fees and permit requirements for the private lands they manage. You can find the details of who to contact on each route description and all the required contact information for those agencies in the Resources & Land Managers section.

Opposite: The winds that inspired Hurricane Ridge's name sculpted snow into these graceful whorls.

OLYMPICS

1 Hurricane Hill

Rating: Easiest to more difficult
Round trip: 6 miles
Hiking time: 4 hours
Elevation gain: 800 feet
High point: 5760 feet
Best season: Late December through early March
Maps: Green Trails: Mount Olympus No. 134, Mount Angeles
      No. 135; Custom Correct: Hurricane Ridge
Who to contact: Olympic National Park
Permits/fees: National park entry fee required

Hurricane Ridge is the preeminent destination for folks who want to see the beauty of Olympic National Park any time of the year. When winter rolls in and the broad, sweeping meadows of the ridge are blanketed in snow and the high jagged peaks of the Bailey Range swaddled in white, the area is unbelievably beautiful.

Directions: From Port Angeles leave US Highway 101 near milepost 249, following Race Street south 1.2 miles to Hurricane Ridge Road (Heart o' the Hills Parkway) and passing the Olympic National Park Visitors Center and Wilderness Information Center.

Route: Hurricane Ridge, and the snowshoe hike to Hurricane Hill, offers the best views in the park of majestic Mount Olympus. The peak so captivated early explorers with its beauty that the mountain was deemed worthy of being home to the gods. All the best—and some of the worst—aspects of snowshoeing are found here: wide, wonderful panoramic views; alpine meadows of rolling snowdrifts; frosted evergreens and dark, brooding forests; and occasionally frigid, scouring winds that blind all visitors with whiteout conditions.

Heading west from the lodge, snowshoe along the roadway as it rolls around the flank of the Hurricane Ridge meadows. The road soon enters forest and drops gently with the ridge for nearly a mile. The trail levels out along a high saddle, passing a broad picnic area near the end of the road. A brief climb from the picnic area takes you to the end of the road at 1.5 miles. At this point the real snowshoeing work begins. If you are just looking for a quiet stroll, turn back here and explore the trailside meadows on your return trip; but if you are looking for more of a challenge, continue toward Hurricane Hill.

Following the general path of the small hikers' trail west from the end of the road, snowshoe steeply up an exposed ridgeline to the top of Hurricane Hill. The trail stays on the west side of the ridge, passing under two tricky avalanche

Cougar and snowshoe hare tracks cross in the snow.

chutes. Snowshoers will do better to merely stick to the narrow (sometimes, knife-edged) ridge crest all the way to the top. If the snow is heavily crusted or icy, even snowshoes with heavy cleats will not be enough to ensure safe footing, so come prepared to turn around before reaching the true summit of Hurricane Hill.

Even if the top isn't reached, the views are spectacular all along the trail. To the north, the Strait of Juan de Fuca is a dark blue ribbon between the Olympic foothills and the far shore of Canada's Vancouver Island. Northeast, the San Juan Islands are seen cradled in the calm, blue waters of upper Puget Sound, with Mount Baker rearing its icy head beyond. To the east, Mount Angeles and McCarthy Peak jut up at the far side of the Olympic Mountains. To the south, Mount Olympus reigns supreme, dominating the impressive Bailey Range.

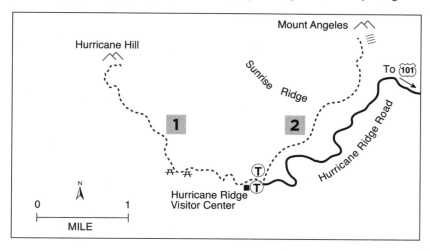

There is beauty to behold in every direction. But there is also the possibility of danger. Weather on Hurricane Ridge is unpredictable and prone to rapid changes. Come prepared for a variety of conditions—sunny days can quickly fade into heavy fog and frigid temperatures. Calm weather can give way, in just minutes, to heavy winds and whiteout conditions. Be ready for extreme conditions, and be willing to turn back the moment the weather starts to turn foul.

2 Mount Angeles

Rating: Backcountry
Round trip: 6 miles
Hiking time: 6 hours
Elevation gain: 600 feet
High point: 5900 feet
Best season: Late December through early March
Maps: Green Trails: Mount Angeles No. 135;
     Custom Correct: Hurricane Ridge
Who to contact: Olympic National Park
Permits/fees: National park entry fee required

Although little elevation gain occurs along this route, a lot of work is necessary for snowshoers planning to play here. But with the hard work come ample rewards. Mount Angeles and Rocky Peak loom large, and all around the trail are picturesque scenes of winter loveliness—open meadows, frosted evergreens cradled by rolling snowdrifts, and icicles hanging like crystal fingers off rocky ledges on the mountain face.

Directions: From Port Angeles drive 17 miles up Hurricane Ridge Road (Heart o' the Hills Parkway) to the Hurricane Ridge Visitor Center. Park near the lodge, and sign in with the rangers at the center.

Route: The trail starts high and stays high as it skirts steep ridges and traverses around the flanks of towering mountains. From the visitor center, snowshoe right around the downhill ski area and turn north to climb to the ridge crest above the rope tow. Snowshoe out along the ridge crest with Mount Angeles towering dead ahead. The trail is fairly level as it pierces small stands of forest and crosses open meadows.

At 1.8 miles, the route rolls under the nose of Sunrise Ridge, which stretches off to the left. The trail stays high on the narrow ridge as it passes Sunrise and crosses above a wide, open basin on the left. This pretty, forested alpine valley nestles between Sunrise Ridge and Mount Angeles. On the east side of the trail, the slope drops steeply to the Cox Creek valley. Stunning views of Elk

Mountain, Maiden Peak, and Blue Mountain lie to the southeast. The road to Hurricane Ridge is occasionally seen directly below the trail.

At 2.7 miles, the trail curves right across the steep flank of Mount Angeles. Continue north, leaving the trail route, and climb 0.25 mile to the top of a wide bench on the southern flank of the mountain. Here, at 5900 feet, enjoy views of the mountain while avoiding the avalanche-prone east side of Mount Angeles—the area to which the trail leads.

Plenty of opportunities are available for scrambling around the flanks of the mountain, but you will find that the slopes are steep and avalanche danger is high throughout the area when the snow isn't completely stable. Make good use of the Northwest Weather and Avalanche Center, and the avalanche information posted at the Hurricane Ridge Visitor Center, before venturing out on this trail.

A ball of snow clings to a treetop along the Mount Angeles route.

3 Eagle Point

Rating: Most difficult
Round trip: 9 miles
Hiking time: 7 hours to 2 days
Elevation gain: Up to 2500 feet
High point: 5500 feet
Best season: Late December through early March
Maps: Green Trails: Mount Angeles No. 135;
     Custom Correct: Hurricane Ridge
Who to contact: Olympic National Park
Permits/fees: National park entry fee required

With the sweeping line of white mountains that ends at glacier-capped Mount Olympus stretching before them, snowshoers may wonder why they ever bothered visiting this area in the summer.

Directions: From Port Angeles drive 17 miles up Hurricane Ridge Road (Heart o' the Hills Parkway) to the Hurricane Ridge Visitor Center. Sign in at the center (required for all users), and then drive back down the road 0.5 mile to the trailhead parking area near the first bend in the road.

Route: This hike begins with a short, steep descent and then wanders over fairly level terrain—just a few rolling hills—as the trail stretches east under the flank of jagged Steeple Rock and Eagle Point. Snowshoers will find great views of the distant peaks of the Bailey Range and look down into the dark Lillian River valley.

Start the hike from the last switchback on Hurricane Ridge Road. You will need to hike a few hundred yards back from the parking area and then drop off the road end, descending a steep hill for about 100 yards before reaching the

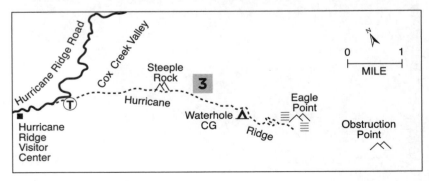

Snowshoe trekking on the Eagle Point route

fairly level, wide trail leading off to the east. You'll be in high subalpine forest with frequent breaks with views south to Mount Olympus and the Lillian River valley and northwest to Mount Angeles.

The trail skirts along a windswept sidehill meadow on the flank of Steeple Rock. Be careful here, as the fierce winds can load up avalanche chutes and create hazardous conditions occasionally. But if the winds are calm and the weather is clear, this is also the best place to find truly grand views of the entire Bailey Range of the Olympic Mountains. Steeple Rock is passed at just under 2 miles from the parking area.

In another 1.5 miles, you'll pass a broad, sheltered forest clearing known as Waterhole Camp. This is a great place to camp, or just to stop and catch your breath, taking in the scenery. Snowshoers looking for a gentle outing (or if the snow is icy) can pitch their tents here. For a more strenuous trek, push on past Waterhole to reach the flank of Eagle Point, a 6247-foot summit towering over the trail.

This last leg is treacherous in inclement weather, so pay attention to weather reports and current conditions. If a storm threatens, make camp at Waterhole and save the ascent to Eagle Point for another time, or do it the next morning as a pre-breakfast blood-warmer if the air is clear and calm.

This route makes a fine outing for novice winter campers. The trail is level enough that carrying winter camping gear isn't too difficult, and the distance is short enough to be doable but not long enough to get you out into a true wilderness camp.

4 Klahhane Ridge

Rating: More difficult
Round trip: 4 miles
Hiking time: 6 hours
Elevation gain: 1500 feet
High point: 6080 feet
Best season: January through early March
Maps: Green Trails: Mount Angeles No. 135;
    Custom Correct: Hurricane Ridge
Who to contact: Olympic National Park
Permits/fees: National park entry fee required

Klahhane Ridge towers over Hurricane Ridge Road, providing outstanding views of Mount Angeles and the long sweep of Hurricane Ridge. The trail climbs steeply, but once the work is done, snowshoers can trek along the long ridge stretching between Mount Angeles and Rocky Peak.

Directions: From Port Angeles drive 15 miles up Hurricane Ridge Road to the broad plowed area signed Third Peak Parking Area. (This parking lot is about 2.5 miles from the Hurricane Ridge Visitor Center.) Hike about 0.25 mile up the road (heading toward Hurricane Ridge) to a hairpin turn in the road. The route begins in a creek basin on the north side of the road.

Route: During warm summer months, the trail switchbacks back and forth steeply up this narrow drainage, covering more than 1.6 miles before ascending the ridge top. With a thick blanket of snow, however, snowshoers can kick step a more direct route to the top, cutting the climbing distance to about a mile. The downside is that although the route is just a mile long, it climbs more than 1400 feet in elevation. You can either gasp your way through a straight ascent or sweat yourself through a more moderately angled and less grueling, but longer, route up.

For the best views and the clearest route, stay on the right flank of the creek basin and angle east toward the Klahhane Saddle. Once in the saddle, you can turn left and stomp through the wind-stacked snowdrifts along the ridge to the flank of Mount Angeles. Or, for a more leisurely and more scenic trek, turn right and stroll east

The winds on Hurricane Ridge sculpt the snow into unique forms.

along the ridge. Be aware that several sections of ridgeline have cornices—big overhanging drifts of snow—so you need to stay to the center of those sections to avoid collapsing a cornice and starting an avalanche.

From this open ridge, you can peer south across the Cox Creek valley to Hurricane Ridge. The rocky spire of Steeple Rock is due south, and the high summit of Obstruction Point anchors the east end of Hurricane Ridge. Follow the ridge east as far as you care to and then retrace your steps, taking care to descend slowly and carefully.

5 Lake Angeles

Rating: More difficult
Round trip: 7.5 miles
Hiking time: 6 hours
Elevation gain: 2300 feet
High point: 4169 feet
Best season: January through early March
Maps: Green Trails: Mount Angeles No. 135;
   Custom Correct: Hurricane Ridge
Who to contact: Olympic National Park
Permits/fees: National park entry fee required

This popular summer hiking trail also works well for a snowshoe outing. The route explores dense forest and leads into a scenic lake basin.

Directions: From Port Angeles drive 5 miles up Hurricane Ridge Road toward the entrance to Olympic National Park. Just before reaching the park entrance booth, turn right (west) into a large parking area. This trailhead parking area is seldom plowed, but generally the snow depth is minimal. If the parking area is inaccessible, do not park along the road—forgo this route and opt instead for one of the routes higher up in the park where parking is available.

Route: When the snow line descends toward Port Angeles, the need to drive all the way to the top of Hurricane Ridge diminishes. A good close-in option for these conditions is the Lake Angeles route. Deer frequently roam the lower reaches of the trail, browsing in the thinner snowpacks, while birds flit along the entire route, often providing trilling accompaniment for your trek.

From the trailhead, the route climbs rapidly along the Ennis Creek valley, gaining elevation and snow depth as it ascends. If the snow is thin

Snow melt refreezes into graceful ice sculptures.

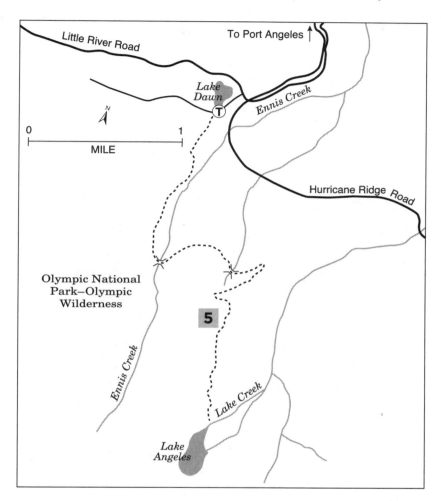

enough at the trailhead, you might start out with your snowshoes strapped to your pack, but within the first mile you'll certainly want them underfoot.

The trail crosses Ennis Creek and veers to the left (east), rounding a ridge face and running up a creek valley. After ascending this valley, cross the creek a couple of times on narrow bridges. Be very careful on these crossings—in deep snow accumulations, you might need to kick or dig the crest off to ensure you have a stable track on which to cross without sliding. The trail leaves the creek near the 2-mile mark and ascends toward the ridgeline. At 3.5 miles, the route traverses into the cirque holding Lake Angeles. Be sure to evaluate avalanche conditions and if there is a risk, stay clear of the cirque and open chutes. Stop well back from the lake basin to avoid potential slide zones.

6 | Blue Mountain & Deer Park

Rating: More difficult
Round trip: Up to 14 miles
Hiking time: 6 hours to 2 days
Elevation gain: 2500 feet
High point: 6000 feet
Best season: January through early March
Maps: Green Trails: Mount Angeles No. 135;
      Custom Correct: Hurricane Ridge
Who to contact: Olympic National Park
Permits/fees: National park entry fee required

> This route offers a bit of human history as well as a glorious exploration of natural history, in the form of deep old forest and an abundance of wildlife.

Directions: From Sequim, drive west on US Highway 101 toward Port Angeles. At the very edge of Port Angeles—you'll see a movie multiplex theater on the left—turn left (south) onto Deer Park Road. Follow this road 9 miles to the Olympic National Park boundary. The road may be gated here (elevation 2000 feet). If the gate is open, continue up the road another 2.8 miles to a second gate at 3500 feet (or as far as the snow allows). If the first gate is closed, park there (do not block the gate) and start your trek. If the road is snow-free, you'll need to hike to the snow line before donning your snowshoes.

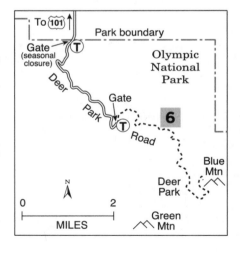

Route: From the second gate (the most likely starting point), the road wanders east and south, climbing 5 miles along the long ridge on the north flank of Blue Mountain. The road rolls through shadowy, gray-green forests for the first few miles before breaking out into occasional clearings and hillside meadows. Snowshoers can branch off to the east through the larger of these clearings to climb to the ridge crest if they want broad views without going all the way to the top.

A narrow track marks the route to Deer Park.

Among the cedars and firs, snow trekkers can wander, luxuriating in the snow-flocked beards of moss that drape the trees. Martens and fishers (or at least their tracks) can often be seen scampering between the trees. Bobcats and cougars also roam these woods and hillsides, as do blacktail deer and the odd mountain goat, so watch for their tracks.

The human history of Deer Park Road is less obvious. The road, which climbs to the Blue Mountain summit, once led to a rope-tow ski area. The tow rig now resides on Hurricane Hill, but skiers still frequent this road, so be prepared to share the route. Don't stomp on the ski tracks, and be cautious rounding curves since skiers like to blast down the slope on their return run.

Those who want to push on to the end of the road, though, can continue south along the roadway to find the sweeping meadows of Deer Park (5300 feet) at about 5 miles from the second gate. Great campsites can be found along the edges of the meadows. For an extended adventure, push up through the open expanses of Deer Park, edging east, before turning north and climbing the southern flank of Blue Mountain, reaching the summit ridge about 7 miles from the second gate. Be alert to avalanche conditions and if there is any chance of slides, stay clear of the mountain's flanks—hold to the road near the lower reaches of Deer Park.

7 Mount Townsend

Rating: Most difficult
Round trip: 10 to 13.5 miles
Hiking time: 7 hours to 2 days
Elevation gain: Up to 2500 feet
High point: 5500 feet
Best season: Late December through early March
Maps: Green Trails: Tyler Peak No. 136;
    Custom Correct: Buckhorn Wilderness
Who to contact: Olympic National Forest, Hood Canal
    Ranger District
Permits/fees: Northwest Forest Pass required

Starting with a road walk, this snowshoe trek leads through steep clearcuts, virgin forest, and up to some near-vertical alpine meadows, but throughout it all, one aspect is constant: incredible, staggering views.

Directions: From Quilcene drive north on US Highway 101 for 1.5 miles to Lords Lake Road on the left (west). Continue up Lords Lake Road for 3 miles before turning left (south) onto Forest Road 2909 and driving 3.5 miles. At a wide road junction, turn left (the sharpest left of two possible left turns) onto FR 2812 (Little Quilcene Road) and follow it through a loop curve to the west. Continue west on FR 2812 to the point where the snow is deep enough to impede your progress, generally near the head of the Little Quilcene River valley at 3000 feet.

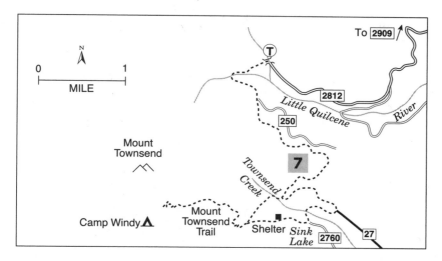

Route: The vistas from the road and trail along this route include sweeping views of Mount Rainier, upper Puget Sound, lower Hood Canal, and all of the eastern Olympic peaks. Snowshoers can scatter out and explore untouched snow in meadows and forests well off the trail, or they can stick to the assigned path and make a nice, quiet day hike of it. Or they can do both and spend a night or two and explore the possibilities of the slopes of Mount Townsend. The mountain itself is more of a long ridge. The summit stretches north to south and, although it's difficult to get to the top thanks to a slew of avalanche chutes, there is no shortage of scenic overlooks on which snowshoers can pause and admire the long mountaintop.

To find the best snowshoeing options, cross the Little Quilcene River via the FR 27 bridge and snowshoe up the road as it climbs steeply up through broad meadows (clearcuts), traverses around to the south side of the valley, and rolls south to a low saddle at 2 miles (3700 feet). The pretty views of the first leg of the trek are supplemented here with stunning panoramas sweeping from Mount Townsend over the Quilcene River valley, east to Puget Sound, and beyond to Mount Rainier.

The road drops from the saddle, rolls south around the nose of the ridge and, at 3.5 miles, encounters a small side road on the right. Follow this narrow, brushy road southwest for 1 mile to intercept the well-signed Mount Townsend Trail at 4.5 miles. This forested hiking path climbs steeply from its trailhead for 0.25 mile before turning west on a long, climbing traverse to the base of the steep walls of the upper reaches of Mount Townsend.

Stop your climb before breaking out of the trees near the 4500-foot level if there is even a whisper of a chance of avalanche. If the snow is extremely stable, continue to snowshoe up the trail to reach the ridge crest (5500 feet) at 6 miles.

Since Mount Townsend is outside the national park, it's a great place for snow-loving dogs to play.

When the avalanche danger is moderate or higher, a better alternative for winter camping is to turn left when you encounter the Mount Townsend Trail and descend along it for 0.5 mile to reach, at mile 5 from your car, one of the small, three-sided shelters that were so common in the Olympic Mountains in the middle half of the twentieth century.

Return the way you came or, to complete a loop, hike another 0.5 mile down the trail from the shelter to a trailhead on FR 27. Turn left on the road, and hike 1.5 miles up it as it curves northwest to reach the point where the spur road took off to join the upper trail.

8   Lena Lake & Valley of Silent Men

Rating: Backcountry
Round trip: Up to 10 miles
Hiking time: 6 hours
Elevation gain: 2000 feet
High point: 2800 feet
Best season: Mid-January through late February
Maps: Green Trails: The Brothers No. 168;
      Custom Correct: The Brothers–Mount Anderson
Who to contact: Olympic National Forest, Hood Canal
      Ranger District
Permits/fees: Northwest Forest Pass required

The Lower Lena Lake Trail doesn't offer panoramic vistas, but a pretty forest surrounds the route, with a nice creek basin to cross and the beautiful lake to enjoy. Beyond the lake, a short excursion to the Valley of Silent Men leads snowshoers into a cathedral-like forest of massive trees, flanking a clear, tumbling stream in a narrow valley.

Directions: From Hoodsport drive 13 miles north on US Highway 101 to a junction with Hamma Hamma Road (Forest Road 25). Turn left (west) onto Hamma Hamma Road, and continue west 8 miles to the Lena Lake trailhead parking area on either side of the road. The trail is on the right (north) side of the road.

Route: This is an unusual snowshoe outing in that, except in periods of heavy snow, the lower section of the trail may require hikers to strap their snowshoes to their backs while they hike a mile or two up to the snow. In

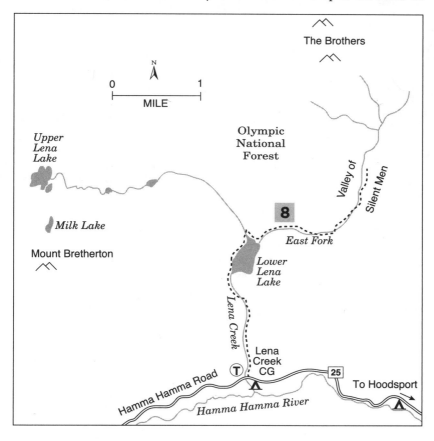

Ice forms along the Lena Lake Trail

heavy snow years, a thin layer of snow may be found at the trailhead (800 feet), but generally you will have to leave your 'shoes on your packs and start up the trail in your boots. The trail climbs steeply though, and shortly after crossing Lena Creek at 1.5 miles the snow deepens. When it is too deep, or too slick, to hike in boots, strap on the snowshoes and continue.

The trail tapers into a gentle climb at 1.6 miles and a quiet, serene forest surrounds the route. At 3 miles, the trail rolls along the west side of Lower Lena Lake (2050 feet). Follow the lakeshore north, and turn right to cross the first inlet stream at the north end of the lake. Head east along the second inlet, East Fork Lena Creek, as it climbs into the lush ancient forest of the Valley of Silent Men. The trees sport drooping beards of emerald green lichens and mosses, and the stream is lined with a lacy network of ice.

Trail signs indicate this is the climbers' route to The Brothers, but generally you won't be going that far. Snowshoe up the bottom of the valley, following the trail corridor as it weaves through the trees, for up to 1.5 miles from the lake before turning back.

The valley makes a great place to stop for a leisurely picnic. Sit and enjoy the soft music of the stream tumbling over icy rocks. Listen to the songs of the birds flitting through the branches of the trees above: gray jays, as always, dominate the air when there is any chance they can beg—or steal—a meal from hikers. Relax in the soothing peace that covers all visitors to these cathedral forests, which are made all the more peaceful by the quiet of winter.

Opposite: Dark clouds and deep snow are hallmarks of the Mount Baker region.

MOUNT BAKER HIGHWAY

9 Coal Pass

Rating: More difficult
Round trip: 10 miles
Hiking time: 6 hours
Elevation gain: 2400 feet
High point: 4500 feet
Best season: January through early March
Map: Green Trails: Mount Baker No. 13
Who to contact: Mount Baker–Snoqualmie National Forest,
    Mount Baker Ranger District
Permits/fees: Northwest Forest Pass required

For those snowshoers who like to just get out and walk for miles without worrying about the intricacies of routefinding in deep snow, the Coal Pass trek is a great option. The route follows a wide roadbed as it climbs from the forested Glacier Creek valley to the open views in Coal Pass.

Directions: From Bellingham drive east on State Route 542 (Mount Baker Highway) to the town of Glacier and continue another 0.7 mile, passing the U.S. Forest Service Public Service Center, before turning right (south) onto Forest Road 39 (Glacier Creek Road). Drive to the snow line, usually found near a road junction with FR 3940 (gated) just past Coal Creek, about 5.2 miles from Mount Baker Highway.

Route: Strap on your snowshoes, and start the trek by following FR 39. The road weaves through many forest clearings and crosses several creek basins before reaching its end at the 4500-foot pass separating the twin peaks of Lookout Mountain. Snowmobilers and skiers also use this road, so stick to the side to avoid being run down by motorists and to avoid tromping on the carefully laid tracks of skiers.

The road climbs along Lookout Creek before crossing the creek and traversing south above the deep cut of Glacier Creek Gorge. In 2 miles, go right at the fork onto FR 36. (The left fork leads to Route 10, Coleman Glacier.)

The road traverses through young second-growth forest, clearcuts, and steep alder slopes before banking to the left and crossing the upper Lookout Creek basin near the 4500-foot level, 2 miles from the start of FR 36. Across Lookout Creek basin, the road loops north, and then flips through a wide switchback to reach another road junction. Stay right (on FR 3610), and climb steeply through a short series of switchbacks and a 0.5-mile-long traverse to reach Coal Pass, just a touch over 5 miles from the Coal Creek parking area.

Pausing during the climb to Coal Pass

Views to the southeast sweep over Mount Baker's northwest flank, from Chowder Ridge to Lincoln and Colfax Peaks, with the sprawling ice of Coleman

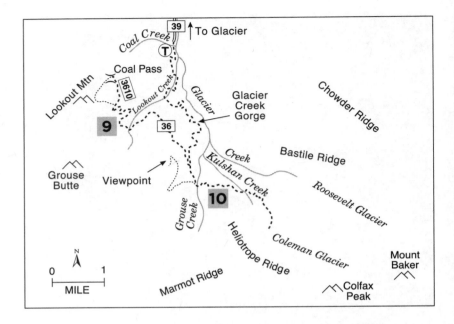

and Roosevelt Glaciers in between. Soak up the sights, enjoy a leisurely lunch, and then decide whether to head back or extend the outing.

For more adventures, leave Coal Pass and climb to the left (south), ascending the main peak of Lookout Mountain (5021 feet). There is no formal trail, but climbing through the trees and meadows is easy with snowshoes. Pick the path of least resistance. The best bet is to climb steeply, but angle just a bit to the left on the ascent to avoid the steepest pitches. The summit is about 0.5 mile from the pass. To cut the return trip mileage, drop to the east from the summit to rejoin the road about 0.5 mile down from the pass.

10 Coleman Glacier

Rating: Moderate to backcountry
Round trip: 9 miles
Hiking time: 1 to 2 days
Elevation gain: 4500 feet
High point: 6000 feet
Best season: January through February
Map: Green Trails: Mount Baker No. 13
Who to contact: Mount Baker–Snoqualmie National Forest, Mount Baker Ranger District
Permits/fees: Northwest Forest Pass required

Starting with an easy stroll along a wide trail in a narrow creek valley, this trek offers a taste of all the best winter has to offer. The trail climbs away from the valley bottom after a few miles and presents two choices: a modest climb along a wide road to a high promontory with great views of Mount Baker, or a longer, more strenuous climb along the narrow, forested path on Heliotrope Ridge.

Directions: From Bellingham drive east on State Route 542 (Mount Baker Highway) to the town of Glacier and continue another 0.7 mile, passing the U.S. Forest Service Public Service Center before turning right (south) onto Forest Road 39 (Glacier Creek Road). Drive to the snow line, usually found near a road junction with FR 3940 (gated) just past Coal Creek, about 5.2 miles from Mount Baker Highway.

Route: Novice snowshoers will find plenty of excitement and enjoyment on the Mount Baker view trek, while more experienced backcountry snowshoers will find the Heliotrope Ridge Trail puts their skills to good use. Both provide

Looking east from the Coleman Glacier route

wonderful views and a good stretch of the legs in deep snows, but snowshoers must share the road with skiers and snowmobilers, while the Heliotrope Ridge Trail is quiet and usually untracked. But this also means the trail is considerably more difficult to follow than the wide roadbed.

Beginning at the snow line, follow FR 39 upvalley. Snowmobilers and skiers also use this road, so stick to the side to avoid being run over by motorists and to avoid tromping on the carefully laid tracks of skiers. The road climbs through thick, young forest for the first 0.5 mile before crossing Lookout Creek and leveling out somewhat. A few small clearcuts offer modest views and the first opportunity to step off the track and practice some deep-snow travel techniques.

In 2 miles the track forks. Stay to the left on FR 39 (the right fork leads to Route 9, Coal Pass), and in about 0.5 mile the road curves sharply to the right. The Heliotrope Ridge trailhead is found at this corner. Turn left into the forest, and follow the trail corridor east, crossing Grouse Creek almost immediately and climbing through the shadowy woods. The trail may be difficult to find in places, so follow the widest corridor between the dark tree trunks. The route climbs steadily for 0.5 mile before tapering into a long, ascending traverse along Heliotrope Ridge's north side.

About 1.5 miles after leaving the road, cross the upper reaches of Kulshan Creek. This is the best place to establish camp if you plan to spend the night. The trees offer shelter from the wind and weather, while the views are found less than 0.5 mile away. To get to those views, turn right on the west side of the Kulshan Creek draw, and climb uphill to break out of the trees and enjoy views of Coleman Glacier and upper Heliotrope Ridge.

For a less strenuous outing, stick to FR 39 at the trailhead and climb to the right along the roadway for another 1.5 miles. The road ends at a high viewpoint above clearcut meadows. The view of Mount Baker's northwest side, with its sprawling Coleman and Roosevelt Glaciers, is unmatched. Enjoy the view over lunch, and then if you want a change of pace, abandon the road as you start the return trip. Point the tips of your snowshoes toward Mount Baker and drop downhill, angling slightly to the right, through the meadows and trees for a little off-trail snowshoeing before rejoining the road in 0.25 mile or so.

11 White Salmon Creek

Rating: Easiest
Round trip: Up to 10 miles
Hiking time: 6 hours
Elevation gain: 300 feet
High point: 2400 feet
Best season: December through early March
Map: Green Trails: Mount Shuksan No. 14

Who to contact: Mount Baker–Snoqualmie National Forest,
    Mount Baker Ranger District
Permits/fees: Washington State Sno-Park Pass required.
    You may also need a Washington State Discover Pass;
    check www.parks.wa.gov/130/Winter-Recreation.

Bring the whole family to this beautiful river valley. The wide track, with plenty of open meadows and forest glades for exploring, offers great snowshoeing for folks of all abilities, as well as appealing scenery.

Directions: From Bellingham drive east on State Route 542 (Mount Baker Highway) to the town of Glacier and continue another 13.5 miles to the large Salmon Ridge Sno-Park parking area on the left just after crossing the North Fork Nooksack River.

Route: When venturing out this way, be sure to call the district ranger first to get a current snow report. This is a fairly low-elevation trail, and although some years 3 or 4 feet of snow may be along the trail, mild winters can find the track snow-free for much of its length. Of course, one of the conveniences of snowshoes is that regular hiking boots can be worn when walking on them. That means when the snow is thin, you just stash the snowshoes and take a winter hike.

Deep snowdrifts line the route along White Salmon.

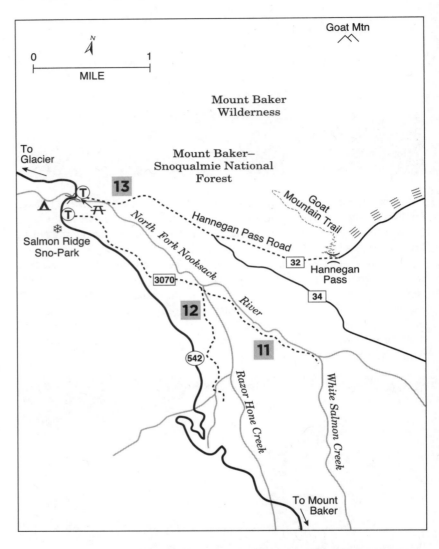

From the Sno-Park, you can simply ramble out into the open glades along the Nooksack River, but to get in a full day of snowshoeing, head out along Forest Road 3070 as it parallels the picturesque river upstream. As you hike up the valley, be sure to stay off the groomed ski tracks. Volunteers groom this trail for cross-country skiers, and there is no faster way to irritate skiers than by tromping their tracks into a series of deep snowshoe depressions. But plenty of room is available for all, and in several areas you can take off through open meadows to get well clear of the ski tracks and be off on your own.

The views begin with the glorious winter landscape around the trail—picture dark, shadowy evergreens flocked with heavy white snow set beside a clear mountain river—but soon all eyes are drawn to the vista beyond. This is a narrow valley, and the mountains flanking it soar straight up into the sky. From Goat Mountain to Mount Sefrit and the Nooksack Ridge, the peaks form a ragged skyline far above the valley floor.

Angle off to the left in the first mile or so to get down to the river for some water views. But stay back from the edge because weak snow may be overhanging the water. As you move up the valley, veer to the right to climb onto the foot of the valley wall and enter the dark cedar and hemlock forest. At 2 miles, turn sharply to the right (south) and climb a small bench for good, open views of Goat Mountain to the north.

Then traverse around the lower edge of the bench and enter the White Salmon Creek basin. Pick a path through the trees to the edge of the creek. For an extended outing, push on upstream and continue until the trees get too tight or your legs get too tired. To keep the trek modest, turn downstream and follow the White Salmon for 0.25 mile back to the main track, which ends where the White Salmon empties into the Nooksack.

12 Razor Hone Creek

Rating: More difficult
Round trip: 5 miles
Hiking time: 2.5 hours
Elevation gain: 500 feet
High point: 2500 feet
Best season: December through April
Map: Green Trails: Mount Baker No. 13
Who to contact: Mount Baker–Snoqualmie National Forest, Mount Baker Ranger District
Permits/fees: Washington State Sno-Park Pass required. You may also need a Washington State Discover Pass; check www.parks.wa.gov/130/Winter-Recreation.

Very few snowshoe routes in the Cascades offer stunning views with minimal elevation gain, but this is one of them—and one of the best. The route parallels the North Fork Nooksack with scattered views of the river and skyline peaks of the towering mountains of this valley.

Directions: From Bellingham drive east on State Route 542 (Mount Baker Highway) to the town of Glacier and continue another 13.5 miles to the large

Two- and four-legged snowshoers enjoy the Razor Hone route.

Salmon Ridge Sno-Park parking area on the left just after crossing the North Fork Nooksack River.

Route: The route heads east along Forest Road 3070, a wide road, as it meanders up the North Fork valley. The broad, nearly level route starts under forest canopy and within the first 0.5 mile, after sweeping to the southeast, the track nears the Nooksack River itself, providing good views of the braided channels of this wandering river. See the first four paragraphs of the route description for Route 11, White Salmon Creek, for details.

The trail continues in and out of the forest, with broken views of the river and the North Cascades peaks, for 1.5 miles before reaching a fork. Stay on the road to the right as it climbs moderately to a junction with the Razor Hone Creek basin. This route weaves through trees, and at times it can be difficult to follow in heavy snow, as huge drifts drop off the towering firs leaving mounds of snow to scramble up and over.

The route climbs gradually for more than a mile from the junction before encountering Razor Hone Creek. This is a great place to turn around and descend back to your starting point.

13 | Goat Mountain Approach

Rating: More difficult
Round trip: 5 miles
Hiking time: 3 hours
Elevation gain: 400 feet
High point: 2450 feet
Best season: December through April
Map: Green Trails: Mount Baker No. 13
Who to contact: Mount Baker–Snoqualmie National Forest,
    Mount Baker Ranger District
Permits/fees: Washington State Sno-Park Pass required.
    You may also need a Washington State Discover Pass;
    check www.parks.wa.gov/130/Winter-Recreation.

Goat Mountain is a steep, scenic hike in the summer, but it's not a summit you'll likely reach come winter. However, the approach to the summit is a worthy snowshoe route that offers a mix of easy forest trekking and modest climbing with some wonderful woodland views in a winter wonderland.

Directions: From Bellingham drive east on State Route 542 (Mount Baker Highway) to the town of Glacier and continue another 13.4 miles to Hannegan Pass Road on the left (found just before crossing the North Fork Nooksack River bridge). If Hannegan Pass Road (Forest Road 32) is snow-free, turn left and continue up the road as far as is safe before snow stops you or until you reach the trailhead at 2.4 miles. Most likely, though, snow will block the road, in which case you should continue up SR 542 another 200 yards past Hannegan Pass Road, and just after crossing the river, turn left into the Salmon Ridge Sno-Park. To start your hike from here, carefully walk the highway shoulder back to Hannegan Pass Road.

Route: During normal snow years, you'll start trekking Hannegan Pass Road from its junction with SR 542. From the Salmon Ridge Sno-Park, hike back across the North Fork Nooksack River bridge (always being mindful of traffic) and head east up Hannegan Pass Road as it runs alongside the river, crossing Swamp Creek before veering slightly upward at about 0.5 mile. The forested road swings well away from the river for the next 0.5 mile or so before coming back to the braided channel of the Nooksack.

At 1.4 miles, the road forks. Stay left to start climbing along FR 32. From here, the route moves upslope away from the river into denser forest. The distance views disappear, but the snow-laden forest presents its own wild beauty to enjoy. At 2.5 miles, the Goat Mountain trailhead is encountered. Snowshoers

Gnarled old firs along the Hannegan Pass route

may opt to try ascending this steep summit trail, but it is difficult to find in the snowy forest, where heavy drifts between the moss-laden trees obscure all signs of an official trail. The better option is to turn back here. If you still have a little lift in your step, you may continue up the road past the trailhead for another mile or so, but at that point the route encounters several avalanche chutes and further travel is not recommended.

14 Silver Fir Campground Ramble

Rating: Easiest
Round trip: 1.5 miles
Hiking time: 2 hours
Elevation gain: 100 feet
High point: 2100 feet
Best season: December through April
Map: Green Trails: Mount Baker No. 13
Who to contact: Mount Baker–Snoqualmie National Forest,
    Mount Baker Ranger District
Permits/fees: Washington State Sno-Park Pass required.
    You may also need a Washington State Discover Pass;
    check www.parks.wa.gov/130/Winter-Recreation.

Sometimes kids just want to run and jump and play in the snow—
regardless of whether the kids in question are three or eighty-three years
old. The Silver Fir Campground Ramble offers a no-stress day in the snow
for families with kids of all ages. Explore the wonders of snow-laden mossy
forests, natural ice sculptures along a blue-green river, and drifts of snow
that make ideal obstacles on which to learn snowshoe trekking skills.

Directions: From Bellingham drive east on State Route 542 (Mount Baker
Highway) to the town of Glacier and continue another 13.5 miles to the large
Salmon Ridge Sno-Park parking area on the left just after crossing the North
Fork Nooksack River.

Route: To explore the Campground Ramble, carry your snowshoes out
of the Sno-Park parking lot and cross SR 542. After crossing the highway, get

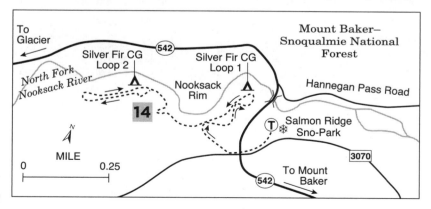

Some of the firs that inspired the name Silver Fir Campground

well away from the road and strap on your shoes before starting west along the Silver Fir Campground access road. This route leads west back toward the river. In just a few hundred yards, the route splits; head right to start and explore the forested loop nestled between the Nooksack River and the highway (Loop 1). Energetic kids can ramble up into the woods, while more sedate adventurers can simply stroll (as much as anyone can stroll on snowshoes) along the access road as it loops through a few campsites.

Head back out of this loop, and after passing the road you hiked in on, continue west toward the main campground loop (Loop 2). Scramble up into the woods to fully enjoy the brilliant colors of the winter forest: shimmering silver white snow glistens around emerald green mosses that drape the area's boulders and trees. Deep russet tree trunks add a rich earthen hue to the mix.

Explore the entire campground loop, pressing on westward past the end of the camp if you desire for another 0.25 mile or so, before heading back to the trailhead.

This route may be combined with Route 10, Coleman Glacier, or Route 11, White Salmon Creek, to add richness to the day.

15 Welcome Pass

Rating: Backcountry
Round trip: 7 miles
Hiking time: 9 hours
Elevation gain: 3200 feet
High point: 5200 feet
Best season: December through April
Map: Green Trails: Mount Baker No. 13
Who to contact: Mount Baker–Snoqualmie National Forest, Mount Baker Ranger District
Permits/fees: No parking pass required

If you want a workout, you are *welcome* to it here. The route starts overly easy, climbing along the access road from the highway to reach the true trailhead where the work begins in earnest. You'll gain nearly 1000 feet per mile with the rewards of outmatched views and burning thigh muscles!

Directions: From Bellingham drive east on State Route 542 (Mount Baker Highway) to the town of Glacier and continue another 12.5 miles to a junction with Forest Road 3600 on the left. This small, poorly marked road is usually blocked by snow just a few yards in. Pull in and park clear of the road itself. (If you reach the Department of Transportation work center, you have driven too far. FR 3600 is found just 0.25 mile west of that center.)

Route: Hike up Welcome Pass Road (FR 3600) as it gradually climbs away from SR 542, and in 0.75 mile (about 450 feet of elevation gain) look for the

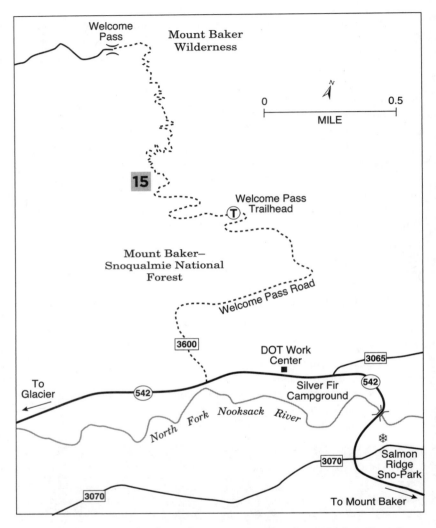

summer parking area for the Welcome Pass trailhead at 2450 feet. From here, the trail climbs to the north, growing increasingly steep as it ascends. The heavy snow-dumps off the trees that surround the trail make routefinding challenging at times. A GPS track log can be a valuable tool to have in hand here. The route climbs steeply through trees for 2.7 miles before reaching a break in the forest at Welcome Pass.

If you succeed in reaching the pass, you'll find jaw-dropping panoramic views sweeping before you. Mount Tomyhoi towers above and an array of peaks sprawl across the northern horizon.

View from the Welcome Pass route

16 Bagley Lakes

Rating: Easiest
Round trip: 2 miles
Hiking time: 2 hours
Elevation gain: 150 feet
High point: 4300 feet
Best season: January through early April
Map: Green Trails: Mount Shuksan No. 14
Who to contact: Mount Baker–Snoqualmie National Forest,
   Mount Baker Ranger District
Permits/fees: Northwest Forest Pass required

Bagley Lakes draws far fewer recreationists than nearby Artist Point (Route 17), which is a great reason to visit here. The snowshoeing is equally easy, the winter scenery is stunning—although the views aren't quite as grand—and the route is far less crowded.

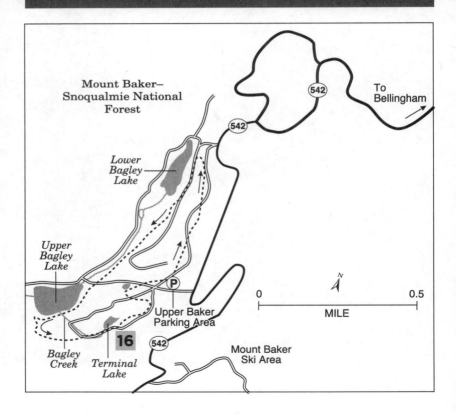

Looking northeast from Bagley Lake toward Mount Sefrit and Nooksack Ridge

Directions: From Bellingham drive east on State Route 542 (Mount Baker Highway) to the road end, about 55 miles to the upper parking lot of the Mount Baker Ski Area, signed Bagley Lakes trailhead.

Route: Mount Baker offers some of the most beautiful alpine scenery in the world, and for snowshoers, it offers the added enticement of alpine adventures with little elevation gain. By starting high, snow trekkers can explore glorious snow-laden meadows above timberline with little climbing required. That is an incredible benefit when the adventurers in question tend to be sea-level dwellers and the meadows they want to explore are nearly a mile above sea level.

From the west end of the parking area, angle off to the right (west) to descend a gentle slope to Lower Bagley Lake. This open snowfield is a great place to practice your downhill snowshoeing skills, whether you are a novice looking to perfect your balance or an experienced snowshoer looking to learn some speed-descent skills. The slope is gentle and well contoured, so fun can be had by all.

At Lower Bagley Lake, less than 0.25 mile from the parking lot, start working uphill to the left, climbing the shallow valley toward the Upper Bagley Lake basin. Staying to the east side of the lakes (avoid crossing the lakes—as with all Cascade Mountain lakes, the ice cover should never be trusted with your weight), continue to climb around the upper lake basin and, about 1 mile out, veer southeast to traverse over to the ridge holding Terminal Lake. Continue to turn east and then north to complete a loop down the spine of this open ridge to return to the trailhead.

17 Artist Point

Rating: More difficult
Round trip: Up to 5.5 miles
Hiking time: 4 hours
Elevation gain: 1200 feet
High point: 5200 feet
Best season: December through April
Map: Green Trails: Mount Shuksan No. 14
Who to contact: Mount Baker–Snoqualmie National Forest,
    Mount Baker Ranger District
Permits/fees: Northwest Forest Pass required

Artist Point may have earned its name because of the oft-captured image of the broad meadows filled with summer wildflowers, backed by the towering rock summit of Mount Shuksan and the glacier-crowned Mount Baker, but many feel the area is even more beautiful and worthy of reproduction on film or canvas when shrouded with snow.

A view of Tomyhoi Peak from Artist Point

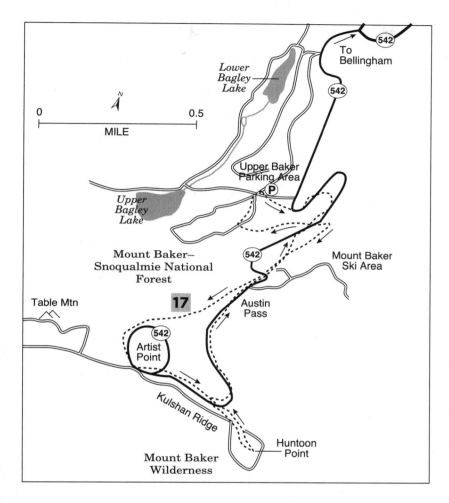

Directions: From Bellingham drive east on State Route 542 (Mount Baker Highway) approximately 55 miles, to the upper parking lot of the Mount Baker Ski Area.

Route: The namesake of this trail is a high viewpoint between the two great peaks of Mount Shuksan and Mount Baker. All around the point are ancient forests, and come winter, the deep green trees are cloaked in shrouds of white as wind-driven snow and hoarfrost cling to the evergreen limbs. On overcast days, the area becomes a world of black and white, with many shades of gray. But on clear, calm days, the world is blue and white: white snow, white peaks, blue-tinted evergreens, and sapphire blue skies.

To start the trip, leave the south (upper) end of the ski area parking lot and edge along the flank of the downhill area along the access road leading to Austin Pass, or choose the steeper, straight-up route followed by the summer hiking trail.

Just past the ski runs, the route turns upward and you begin a long, steady climb to the pass. Stay off to the right of the road to avoid cross-country skiers who are heading for the deep backcountry bowls beyond Artist Point. The track covers 500 feet of elevation gain from the parking area to 4700-foot Austin Pass, but that gain is easily accomplished on snowshoes—it's the side-stepping cross-country skiers who will be sweating this section.

From Austin Pass, the road sweeps out to the left in a long switchback. Keep right, and climb the open meadows ahead to cut across the neck of this loop, rejoining the road in a few hundred yards at the road end at the lower end of Kulshan Ridge, just past the 2-mile mark. A final 0.25 mile of hiking to the left along this ridge gets you to the impossibly beautiful views at Artist Point.

Soak in the views of Mount Shuksan to the east and Mount Baker to the west, and to the southwest Coleman Pinnacle towers seemingly just beyond reach. Backcountry telemark skiers are often seen playing in the steep, deep bowls along Ptarmigan Ridge, which stretches between Artist Point and Coleman Pinnacle. This ridge is filled with dangerous avalanche chutes, so before deciding to trek out along it, be sure of the current avalanche conditions.

A better option for an extended trek from Artist Point is to the left (east) along the more stable snow of Kulshan Ridge. A half mile of hiking along the deep snow on the ridge crest leads to Huntoon Point, a high knob on the upper end of Kulshan. From this lofty observation point, look out over the expanse of the Mount Baker Wilderness to the west and south, North Cascades National Park (which encompasses Mount Shuksan) to the east, and the ragged line of Shuksan Arm—reaching out from Shuksan—to the north.

18 Table Mountain

Rating: More difficult
Round trip: 1.5 miles
Hiking time: 2 hours
Elevation gain: 300 feet
High point: 4300 feet
Best season: January through early April
Map: Green Trails: Mount Shuksan No. 14
Who to contact: Mount Baker–Snoqualmie National Forest,
    Mount Baker Ranger District
Permits/fees: Northwest Forest Pass required

Looking east from Table Mountain toward Mount Shuksan

The scramble to the summit of Table Mountain is best left to summer hikers, but careful showshoers can explore the flanks of the broad flat-topped mountain, provided that avalanche conditions allow it. Grand views and sweat-popping workouts await eager explorers here.

Directions: From Bellingham drive east on State Route 542 (Mount Baker Highway) about 55 miles to the upper parking lot of the Mount Baker Ski Area, signed Bagley Lakes trailhead.

Route: From the uppermost parking area, head west along the ridge above Bagley Lakes basin. This ridge leads to the sweeping rock snout of Table Mountain in a bit over a quarter-mile. The long, narrow mountain runs west away from the parking area, and snowshoers should restrict their travels to the slope leading up to the long broad mountain.

Instead of attempting to scramble up that craggy face, stay right and work your way through a long, looping 180-degree turn around the upper end of the

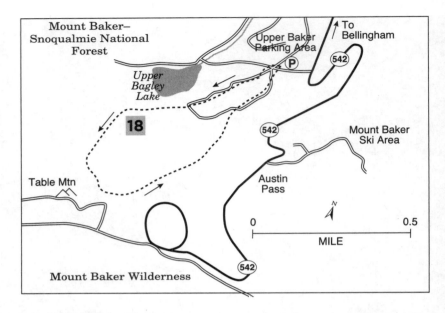

ridge to head back northeast along the crest of the cirque that cradles Bagley Lakes. Follow this cirque crest east for up to 1 mile toward Austin Pass, enjoying the fantastic imagery presented by the hulking mass of Mount Baker to the east, before veering right to gain the ridge crest. From here, circle back to the southwest to close out the long, narrow loop at the trailhead.

19 Middle Fork Nooksack River

Rating: Backcountry
Round trip: 7 miles
Hiking time: 5 hours
Elevation gain: 900 feet
High point: 3000 feet
Best season: December through early February
Map: Green Trails: Hamilton No. 45
Who to contact: Mount Baker–Snoqualmie National Forest, Mount Baker Ranger District
Permits/fees: Northwest Forest Pass required

This trail follows the Middle Fork Nooksack River upstream in the very shadow of majestic Mount Baker. When you tire of the view of that big volcano, glance right and soak in the beauty of Loomis Mountain.

A snowshoer and her dog explore the hard-packed snow along the Middle Fork Nooksack.

Directions: From Bellingham drive east on State Route 542 (Mount Baker Highway) for 18 miles before turning right onto Mosquito Lake Road (about 2 miles north of the junction of Mount Baker Highway and State Route 9 at Deming). Drive 5 miles east on Mosquito Lake Road, and then turn left (east) onto Forest Road 38. Continue 11 miles east on FR 38 to a junction with a small spur road (elevation 2000 feet) on the right, signed as the access to Elbow Lake Trail. Depending on snow levels, park here, or in light snow years continue up the main road another 1.5 miles to a switchback. The Middle Fork Nooksack trailhead is found at the apex of this switchback corner. Most years, the snow is at or below the Elbow Lake trailhead parking area.

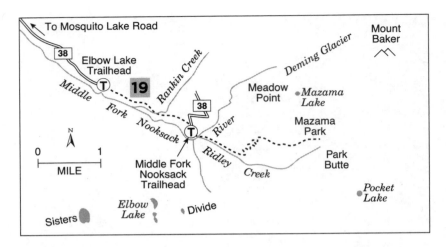

Route: The most difficult part of this snowshoe hike is getting to the snow. Once the network of roads has been safely navigated, the fun can begin in earnest. This is a largely untouched winter wilderness setting, and finding solitude amid such staggering beauty is remarkable.

From the Elbow Lake trailhead, hike the 1.5 miles up FR 38 to the Middle Fork Nooksack trailhead. Relax and enjoy the scenery along this road, which is nearly level and well graded. Mount Baker dominates the northeast horizon, and the wide bed of the Middle Fork Nooksack River is a constant source of entertainment to your right. The river weaves in and out of gravel bars and small forested islands, and the snow-lined banks provide a crisp edge to the tumbling waters of the river.

At the first hairpin turn in the road, go straight to find the trail at the point of the switchback. The trail continues to follow the river upstream, while the road climbs the hill away from the river. The trail is narrow, and if the snow isn't deep, there may be a few downed trees to scramble over. This trail is seldom maintained, and fallen trees are nearly always present. However, the trees are more a hindrance to skiers than to snowshoers, and they help to ensure solitude on this beautiful trail.

The next 1 mile of trail parallels the river, and the views remain largely unchanged: where the forest is open, Mount Baker, Loomis Mountain, and Park Butte dominate the skyline; where the forest canopy closes in, the beautiful old-growth forest and sparkling river will captivate you.

At about 3 miles (3200 feet), the trail begins to climb toward Mazama Park on the southwest flank of Mount Baker. The trail, though, is difficult to follow as it traverses several avalanche slopes and dips into areas of dense forest. Better to just enjoy the views, and turn back when the trail turns vertical.

On the return trip, Mount Baker is at your back, but the twin towers of Sisters Mountain loom ahead. In the midst of all this mountain scenery lives an array of wild creatures for snowshoers to quietly observe. Snowshoe hares, ptarmigans—large, grouse-like birds that turn snowy white come winter—martens, weasels, foxes, and blacktail deer thrive in this valley. Of course, with all those prey animals living here, predators are close at hand. Bobcats, lynx (one of the last population of lynx in Washington), cougars, coyotes, and possibly even wolves roam these woods. These critters pose little danger to healthy adult humans, and any encounter with them should be counted as a blessing.

20 Schriebers Meadow

Rating: More difficult
Round trip: 11 to 14+ miles
Hiking time: 1 to 2 days
Elevation gain: 1200 feet
High point: 5200 feet
Best season: January through March
Maps: Green Trails: Hamilton No. 45, Lake Shannon No. 46
Who to contact: Mount Baker–Snoqualmie National Forest,
    Mount Baker Ranger District
Permits/fees: Washington State Sno-Park Pass required.
    You may also need a Washington State Discover Pass;
    check www.parks.wa.gov/130/Winter-Recreation.

This route is a jewel for winter enthusiasts. The great white cone of Mount Baker looms over the trail to the north, while the broad, undulating snowfields of Schriebers Meadow beckon one and all out into the untracked expanses for a moment of wintry solitude.

Directions: From Sedro-Woolley drive east on State Route 20 (North Cascades Highway) for 14 miles before turning left (north) onto Forest Road 11 (Baker Lake Road). Drive north on FR 11 for 12.5 miles, and then turn left onto FR 12. Continue on FR 12 for 3.5 miles to the Mount Baker NRA Sno-Park at the junction with FR 13. If snow conditions permit, turn right and drive up FR 13 to the snow line (typically about 3 more miles, near the 2500- to 3000-foot elevation).

Route: Depending on the starting snow elevation, this may be a wonderful day hike in wide meadows or a long, overnight trek through forests before reaching those alpine clearings. If the snow is heavy, park at the Sno-Park and

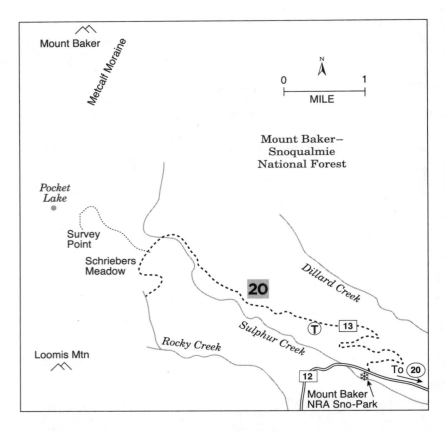

begin a 5-mile trek along the wide, forested corridor of FR 13. This leads up a pair of switchbacks before tapering in a long, climbing traverse along the hillside above Sulphur Creek. The road ends at a broad parking area marking the trailhead for the Schriebers Meadow–Park Butte Trail. This road section provides a good stretch for the legs without an excessive workout, leaving you with plenty of energy for snowshoeing through the wondrous meadows above.

Expect to share the road and trail with cross-country skiers and probably a few snowmobilers, although midweek or after mid-January (after the typical holiday rush to the hills) finds the setting tranquil and uncrowded. But even if others are along the route, there is plenty of wild country and beautiful scenery for all to share.

At the road end, the route jumps onto the narrow trail, crossing Sulphur Creek before climbing in a short 0.25 mile to the lower edge of Schriebers Meadow. This world of white is a paradise of winter recreation. Skiers are sure to be found slashing down the slopes flanking the meadows, and on busy

Drifting snow along Schriebers Meadow

Saturdays in January, expect to hear the whine of a few snowmobiles too. To find solitude, angle off into the untracked reaches of the meadows. To the south, climb up a moderate slope for 0.25 mile or so to reach a basin with three or four ice-covered alpine tarns. Here the views of Mount Baker are at their ultimate best, and good campsites are found in this area, too. Just pick a spot big enough for a tent on the leeward side of the hill, with a glade of trees flanking your site for added shelter from storms in February.

Another alternative is to push on for a longer snowshoe trek to Survey Point, by crossing the flat meadows to the northwest and then starting a gradual climb between two long rocky ridges. These ridges are lateral moraines—rock piles that were pushed aside by flowing glaciers. Climb this wide trough, and in about 1.5 miles from the end of the road, cross the upper reaches of Rocky Creek. Use care here because the many seemingly solid snow bridges may be weak and unsafe, especially late in the season or after periods of unusually warm weather. After you cross the creek, the climbing is steep and steady for another 0.5 mile. Then bear left (west), and traverse a long, open slope to reach the top of the ridge of the left-hand moraine for stunning views of Mount Baker, the sprawling white blanket of Schriebers Meadow, and the high peaks of Park and Black Buttes to the west.

Opposite: Snowshoers climbing through the trees

NORTH
CASCADES—WEST

21 Sauk Mountain

Rating: Backcountry
Round trip: 11 miles
Hiking time: 8 hours
Elevation gain: 3500 feet
High point: 5500 feet
Best season: Late December through early February
Maps: Green Trails: Darrington No. 78, Lake Shannon No. 46
Who to contact: Mount Baker–Snoqualmie National Forest, Darrington Ranger District
Permits/fees: No parking pass required

Although this snowshoe trek makes use of a road for much of its length, the way is steep, generally icy, and the upper section follows narrow, avalanche-prone hiking trails. But when conditions are good, the physical exertion needed to tromp up this steep-sloped peak is richly rewarded with stunning views of the jagged crests of a multitude of North Cascade peaks.

Directions: From Sedro-Woolley drive east on State Route 20 (North Cascades Highway) to the town of Concrete. Continue east another 6.5 miles, and turn left (north) onto Sauk Mountain Road (Forest Road 1030). If you pass Rockport State Park, you have gone too far. (Turn around, and drive 200 yards west of the park to find the Sauk Mountain Road junction.) Drive north on Sauk Mountain Road to the snow line—generally about 1.5 miles up the road, near a junction at the 1400-foot level.

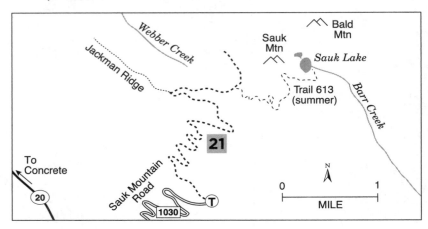

Route: After turning around and parking well off the main road, continue up the roadway on snowshoes. The road repeatedly switchbacks as it climbs relentlessly for another mile through open clearcut meadows and thin patches of second-growth forest. The road continues to climb, now in heavy second-growth timber, until, near the 4-mile mark, views reveal stunning peeks down into the perpetually mist-laden Sauk River valley and southwest toward Glacier Peak.

The peak dominates the horizon to the southeast, but the landscape closer at hand is just as lovely. Because of the frequent, frigid winds, the vegetation of exposed meadows on the upper slopes of Sauk is usually glazed with frilly ice lacing. Hoarfrost, formed by wind-driven moisture and cold air temperatures, creates delicate icy ornamentation on limbs, leaves, and—when they stand still too long—snowshoers.

These snowshoers know to stay well back from cornices.

Keep hiking along the windswept road as it rolls along the flank of Sauk Mountain to a final switchback corner at about 4.5 miles. Here Puget Sound comes into view. From this point, near 3600 feet, the road climbs back toward the west to a point directly below the summit of the mountain. This stretch crosses several avalanche chutes and should be attempted only when avalanche danger can be confirmed as minimal.

On days when the snow is stable, push on the last mile to the end of the road and the start of the summer hiking trail to the summit of Sauk (Trail 613). The summit should be approached only by advanced winter mountaineers because the upper slopes are icy, steep, and prone to rock- and snowslides.

When avalanche dangers are moderate or higher, turn around at the last switchback, or to add a couple of miles to the outing, bear northwest on a small spur road that leads out onto Jackman Ridge. This partially logged ridge is largely unremarkable, but the trail along its crest is mostly level for its 1-mile length, and some excellent views of the upper Puget Sound basin are found along the way.

22 Iron Mountain

Rating: Backcountry
Round trip: 9 miles
Hiking time: 8 hours
Elevation gain: 1800 feet
High point: 4000 feet
Best season: January through early March
Map: Green Trails: Oso No. 77
Who to contact: Mount Baker–Snoqualmie National Forest,
    Darrington Ranger District
Permits/fees: No parking pass required

This area won't be looked at twice by wilderness seekers in summer months, but when blanketed in snow, the narrow logging roads and gentle slopes are magically transformed into a pristine wilderness.

Directions: From Sedro-Woolley drive south on State Route 9 across the Skagit River Bridge and immediately turn left (east) onto South Skagit Highway. Drive east along the South Skagit Highway as it parallels the river upstream. In about 12 miles, turn right (south) onto Forest Road 17 and follow it south as it climbs the Cumberland Creek valley. Drive to the snow line, usually at least 5 miles up the road, near the 2000-foot level.

Looking out from Iron Mountain

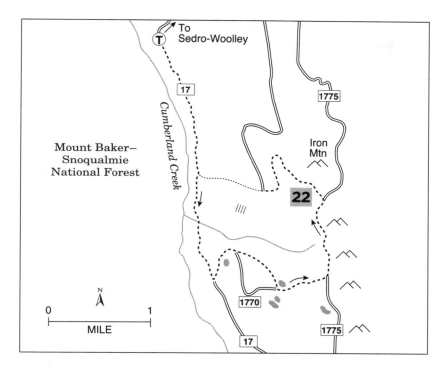

Route: This route offers no awesome views of high peaks over beautiful wilderness rivers, but the scenery is lovely and very enjoyable. Just trekking through a quiet forest blanketed in a heavy quilt of snow is reward enough for this snowshoer.

Snowshoers with excellent routefinding skills can cut cross-country through forest and meadow to climb high onto the flanks of Iron Mountain. Less experienced winter travelers can stick to the roadway for several miles. Bear in mind that snowmobilers frequent the roads in the area on weekends, so weekdays may be the best time to visit. Also, although snowshoers hiking cross-country will find the climb to Iron Mountain quiet and snowmobile-free, snow machines may be encountered near the summit because a long, looping road leads nearly to the top of the mountain.

Start up FR 17 as it climbs gradually but steadily for the next 2.5 miles. The route slices across a few small clearcuts and pierces some dense, second-growth forest before reaching a junction with FR 1770 on the left. Snowshoe up this short spur road as it curves north and then turns back to the east. After a mile on this road, 3.5 miles from the start, the road curves back to the north. Leave the road here, and climb through the young forest, angling up the slope. There is no trail here, so simply pick the path of least resistance while always going up and slightly to the left (north). The forest here is mixed, with some young second-growth among thinner, old forests and open meadows.

About 1 mile of snowshoeing from the end of the road, after gaining about 450 feet in elevation, cross the wide path of FR 1775 at the top of the ridge. This road meanders for several miles along the ridge crest. Turn left and follow it north as it approaches the high peak of Iron Mountain. About a mile up the ridge, 5.5 miles from the start of the hike, the road forks. The left fork slants out along the southwest side of the mountain; the right fork, the main road, curves around the eastern flank of the peak. There is no easy approach to the summit proper, but this junction is a good turnaround point. Enjoy the views from the ridge, including some nice views west toward Puget Sound, before heading back.

Time and distance can be saved with some effort by dropping off the road and heading west through the forest immediately. This means dropping down the slope at a steeper angle than where it was climbed, but the main route, FR 17, is directly downhill from FR 1775. No matter where you drop off, just head straight downhill, being careful to avoid rocky promontories and tight thickets of brush, to catch FR 17.

23 Rat Trap Pass

Rating: More difficult
Round trip: 7.5 miles
Hiking time: 6 hours
Elevation gain: 1900 feet
High point: 3500 feet
Best season: December through February
Map: Green Trails: Sloan Peak No. 111
Who to contact: Mount Baker–Snoqualmie National Forest, Darrington Ranger District
Permits/fees: No parking pass required

This little pass bridges the gap between the Crystal Creek valley to the south and the Straight Creek valley to the north. Come summer, the area is a bleak little saddle scarred by clearcuts and a narrow dusty road. But dump several feet of snow on the pass to mask the ugly logging scars, and Rat Trap Pass becomes a stunning little alpine world. High, rocky cliffs cradle snow-filled meadows and picturesque groves of juvenile fir and hemlock.

The author and a friend pause along the Rat Trap Pass route.

Directions: From Darrington drive southeast on State Route 530 (Mountain Loop Highway) for 9 miles before turning left (east) onto Forest Road 23 (White Chuck River Road). Continue east on FR 23 for 5 miles before crossing the White Chuck River. Drive another 0.3 mile after the river crossing to the junction with FR 27 and turn left. Park in the broad area near the road junction, or drive north along FR 27 to the snow line.

Route: The climb to Rat Trap Pass is pretty enough to make the journey enjoyable, if not overly remarkable, but it's the destination that makes this snowshoe hike one to remember. By mid-December, the pass offers snowshoers a wide world of snowy exploration. Climb through open fields of snow to find secluded little playgrounds blocked off from other pass visitors by the rolling landscape and remnant stands of forest. Enjoy a midday repast with stunning views of the wintry landscape all around. White Chuck Mountain towers over the pass to the west, while the eastern skyline is punctuated by the craggy tops of Circle Peak and Meadow Mountain.

From the junction of FR 23 and FR 27, hike up FR 27, staying clear of the ever-present ski tracks, as it climbs north up a secondary valley above the White Chuck River. In less than a mile, the route crosses Crystal Creek and climbs in another 0.5 mile to the first clearing. Here, look southwest for an open view of the snow-crowned monolith of Glacier Peak. Stick to the roadway for another 2 miles, passing Crystal Creek Road (FR 2710)—see Route 24, Crystal Lake—

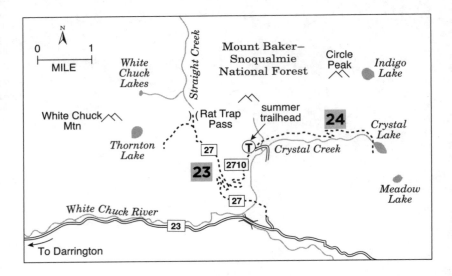

at 2.5 miles from the parking area, to gain the lower reaches of the meadows surrounding Rat Trap Pass. Along this stretch, the route climbs a long traverse with periodic open views of White Chuck Mountain in front of you on the left.

Once at the meadows of the pass, angle off to the left for the best views and thinnest crowds. A small road cuts up the moderate slope, but pick a destination on the opposite side of the snowy fields and angle toward it. Climb the slopes, slicing through the few stands of mature forest and around the jumble of juvenile trees scattered here and there until reaching a suitable spot for lunch. Your picnic spot may be just beyond the main trail leading into the pass, halfway up the hillside on the western wall of the pass, or at the farthest, along the narrow draw that holds the frozen waters of Straight Creek at the far northern edge of the Rat Trap Pass meadows.

24 Crystal Lake

Rating: Backcountry
Round trip: 13.5 miles
Hiking time: 1 to 2 days
Elevation gain: 2800 feet
High point: 4485 feet
Best season: January through February
Map: Green Trails: Sloan Peak No. 111
Who to contact: Mount Baker–Snoqualmie National Forest, Darrington Ranger District
Permits/fees: No parking pass required

With its many open views back toward Pugh Mountain, this trail offers an exceptional weekend outing in the winter wilderness.

Directions: From Darrington drive southeast on State Route 530 (Mountain Loop Highway) for 9 miles before turning left (east) onto Forest Road 23 (White Chuck River Road). Continue east on FR 23 for 5 miles before crossing the White Chuck River. Drive another 0.3 mile after the river crossing to the junction with FR 27 and turn left. Park in the broad area near the road junction, or drive north along FR 27 to the snow line.

Route: This route begins gently enough, climbing along a wide, moderately pitched road. It then turns up a secondary valley and crawls along a narrower, steeper road. Finally, the route becomes a narrow, winding single-track trail in a dark, old forest. This section is not for the fainthearted, nor for untested navigators. The trail is often hard to find, and snowshoers have to trust their

Snowshoers skirting Crystal Lake

skills with map, compass, and common-sense navigation to wend their way up the valley to the pretty little alpine lake lying between Circle Peak and Meadow Mountain.

Those who expend the considerable effort to hike the trail are amply rewarded. Along the way, the views and local scenery are magnificent: from sweeping panoramas that take in Pugh and White Chuck Mountains to up-close and personal encounters with the deep gray-green forest of old fir, hemlock, and cedar wrapped in a cloak of snow and frost. Snowshoers will leave most of the ski traffic behind as they peel away from the main track to Rat Trap Pass (see Route 23, Rat Trap Pass) and angle up the side valley of Crystal Creek and its headwaters at Crystal Lake. With fewer folks crowding the route, wildlife is more visible—the ever-present whiskey jack whistles all along the route, while weasels, ptarmigans, and even a few sly foxes have been spotted as well.

From the junction of FR 23 and FR 27, hike up FR 27 as if heading toward Rat Trap Pass. The first 2.5 miles offer some nice views of Glacier Peak, Pugh Mountain, and the White Chuck River valley from a gentle trail. At the junction of FR 27 and the smaller FR 2710, go right onto FR 2710 to begin the climb up into the Crystal Creek valley. The road switches back a time or two, climbing some 500 feet in less than 0.5 mile before rolling into a long traverse up the valley. The road stays well above the creek itself, but the steep sidewalls above the road provide their own problems. Snow conditions must be scrupulously checked before entering this valley, because a high degree of avalanche danger can exist.

The road forks 1.5 miles from the FR 27 junction. Stay left to remain on the north side of Crystal Creek—the right fork slants down across the valley and then rolls out into a long, looping traverse above the White Chuck River. The route to Crystal Lake becomes narrower at the fork, but it holds fairly level as it continues to traverse upvalley to the road end, nearly 1.5 miles past the last fork.

The summer trailhead of the Crystal Lake Trail is found at the road end. The trail is a faint, seldom-maintained path that is difficult enough to find in August. Come winter, the path is visible only as an often-indistinct corridor through the trees. If the trail is lost below the snow, just pick the path of least resistance through the trees, staying on the north side of the creek while climbing gradually to the 4400-foot level.

In about a mile, at 4400 feet, the creek turns right as it drops over a modest falls. At this point the trail is down close to the creek banks, but it remains on the north side of the water until right before the lake is reached—about 0.25 mile above the falls. Crystal Lake is at 4485 feet, and from its shores, Circle Peak, Meadow Mountain, and the crown of White Chuck Mountain are visible. The lake basin offers plenty of fine sites for camping. Crystal Lake is seldom frozen solid enough for safe travel across it, so stick to the shorelines to avoid an unwanted plunge into the icy waters.

25 Mount Pilchuck

Rating: Easiest to more difficult
Round trip: 11 miles
Hiking time: 10 hours
Elevation gain: 2600 feet
High point: 4000 feet
Best season: Late January through late February
Map: Green Trails: Granite Falls No. 109
Who to contact: Mount Pilchuck State Park
Permits/fees: No parking pass required

Mount Pilchuck offers several miles of gently climbing trail that follows the winding road leading to the summer trailhead parking area. Farther up the trail, adventurous snowshoers can forsake the roadway and hike up through the trees or along the wide runs of an abandoned downhill ski area.

Directions: From Granite Falls drive east on the Mountain Loop Highway 1 mile past the Verlot Public Service Center, and turn right (south) onto Mount Pilchuck Road (Forest Road 42). Continue up the road 1.6 miles to reach the winter closure gate. Park in the wide areas near the gate, but do not block the main road or any side access (private) roads.

Trekking through the trees on the flank of Mount Pilchuck

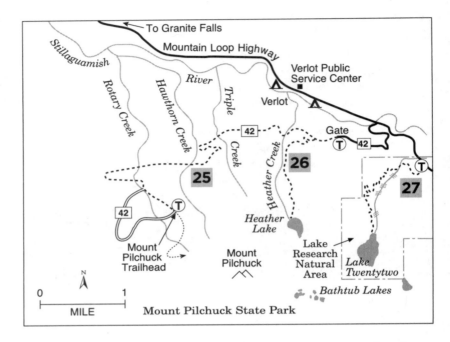

Route: The vehicle gate marks the end of all legal motorized traffic, so after snowshoeing around it, you enter a world of default wilderness. The road climbs steadily but not too steeply along its first 2 miles. Off-road rambling isn't recommended in this early stage, but about 3.5 miles up the trail—just after crossing Triple Creek—there is an opportunity in heavy-snow years to angle up through the trees to the left, cutting across the neck of a wide switchback. This will require some routefinding skills because there is no true trail. However, the trees are widely spaced enough that, if the undergrowth is buried in enough snow, you can simply climb between them.

If you prefer to keep things simple and serene, continue around on the road. At just over 4 miles, the road switches back to the left. A half mile farther up the route, the road turns back to the right, but if the snow is stable and avalanche dangers are minimal, a better option awaits. From the corner of the second switchback, head straight out toward the southeast in a climbing traverse of the snowy slope on the flank of Pilchuck.

In less than 0.5 mile, you will encounter the first open run of the old ski area. Alpine skiers swarmed here in the 1970s, but the resort failed after just a few years, leaving broad slopes for snowshoers to climb and telemark skiers to swoosh down. Climb up this wide trail, sticking to the edge near the trees to avoid a nasty confrontation (i.e., collision) with backcountry skiers practicing their telemark turns on the open slopes.

By using this steep, direct approach, the climb to the top is more of a work-out, but it cuts nearly 1 mile off the road distance. It will also get you to the top before the crowds of skiers can kick their way up the road. That means more time at the top—the end of the road and the site of the old ski lodge—to enjoy the views alone and uninterrupted. The lodge is long gone, but the views of the Stillaguamish River valley—including the deep, dark cut of Robe Gorge—and the high, serrated ridges above it are as beautiful as ever.

If you have a mountaineering background and advanced avalanche-recognition skills, you might consider climbing partway up the Mount Pilchuck Trail. The route is steep and difficult to find as it winds its way up through forests, rocky slopes, and dangerous avalanche chutes. This added adventure isn't for the fainthearted or the untested—summer hikers often get lost here.

26 Heather Lake

Rating: More difficult
Round trip: 4 miles
Hiking time: 4 hours
Elevation gain: 1100 feet
High point: 2440 feet
Best season: Early January to late February
Map: Green Trails: Granite Falls No. 109
Who to contact: Mount Pilchuck State Park
Permits/fees: Washington State Discover Pass required

The Heather Lake Trail can be a wonderful route for snowshoers as it climbs just 2 miles—gaining more than 1000 feet—through thick second-growth forest to arrive at a stunningly beautiful alpine lake nestled in a deep rock cirque on the north face of Mount Pilchuck.

Directions: From Granite Falls drive east on the Mountain Loop Highway 1 mile past the Verlot Public Service Center and turn right (south) onto Mount Pilchuck Road (Forest Road 42). Continue up the road 1.6 miles to reach the winter closure gate. Park in the wide areas near the gate, but do not block the main road or any side access (private) roads.

Route: This trail is heavily traveled in the summer, but winter visitors will find the crowds thin and the forests even more beautiful when blanketed in soft white. Around the lake are several excellent campsites, each with its own charm and glorious view of Mount Pilchuck or the Stillaguamish Valley. The short distance makes this a great destination for first-timers in the art of winter camping.

Trekking into the Heather Lake basin

The Heather Lake Trail leaves the left side of the parking area near the gate and immediately begins climbing through the dense young forest, switching back a time or two before traversing west into the Heather Creek valley. The trail climbs steadily alongside the creek, gaining more than 1000 feet in the 2 miles to the lake.

After nearly a mile of climbing, notice how the surrounding forest begins to age. Old, stout trees of massive size are mingled with the young, crowded stands of second-growth fir and hemlock. At the 1.2-mile mark, the forest is entirely old growth, with ancient hulks towering over the trail and long-dead trunks lying scattered about the forest floor. The decaying fallen trees provide just the rich nourishment seeds need to sprout and grow into young, upstart trees. In this way, the dead trees, or nurse logs, hold the roots of a new generation, closing the circle of forest life. Even buried under snow, these nurse logs are evident. Just look for the long rows of young trees, and imagine them all rooted in one long, straight log.

The trail reaches the Heather Lake basin at just above 2400 feet and breaks out of the forest and into open views of the towering summit of Mount Pilchuck beyond. The lake is at a low enough elevation that at no time should you attempt to cross its ice; the ice is seldom thick enough to support an adult, and even then, it is likely riddled with cracks and fissures, which could open and send you into a quick bout of hypothermia.

Campsites can be found around the perimeter of the lake, and the best are on the eastern shore where the slope is most gradual and the view most splendid.

27 Lake Twentytwo

Rating: Backcountry
Round trip: 5 miles
Hiking time: 4 hours
Elevation gain: 1200 feet
High point: 2440 feet
Best season: Early January to late February
Map: Green Trails: Granite Falls No. 109
Who to contact: Mount Baker–Snoqualmie National Forest,
    Darrington Ranger District
Permits/fees: Northwest Forest Pass required

This showshoe hike is a workout, but the rewards are phenomenal. The trail follows a beautiful tumbling creek as it rushes down a narrow gorge. Along the way, the creek drops over no fewer than four pretty waterfalls, with each successive one sporting larger and more intricate ice mantles.

A frozen stream below Lake Twentytwo

Directions: From Granite Falls drive east on the Mountain Loop Highway 1 mile past the Verlot Public Service Center and continue east 2 miles to the Lake Twentytwo trailhead on the right (south) side of the highway.

Route: Although the snow is frequently thin at the base of this trail, the route climbs quickly and snowshoes are needed not only for flotation but also for traction on the steep slopes. If the snow is thin at this low-elevation trailhead, strap your snowshoes on the back of your pack and hike up the trail until the snow deepens. The trail climbs gradually for 0.25 mile and then turns straight up the creek valley and rolls through a long series of switchbacks. Frequently, even if the snow isn't deep, snowshoes will be required simply because the beefy crampons on their base afford a sure grip on the slick trail.

The first waterfall is passed 0.5 mile up the trail, and then more are seen at 1 mile, 1.2 miles, and 1.5 miles. Just past the third waterfall, the trail levels out (relatively speaking) as it rolls west along the hillside for several hundred yards before turning back toward the creek. It passes through a couple of these longer, more moderate switchbacks before making a long, straight traverse back to the creek at the fourth falls. From there, it's a 0.25-mile climb to the lakeshore.

This trail is steeper and the lake more remote than the nearby Heather Lake route (Route 26), but it is also less visited in winter months. Some of the open slopes above the trail, especially on the upper reaches, are prone to slide in moderate to high avalanche conditions, so use caution.

28 Boardman Lake

Rating: More difficult
Round trip: 11.6 to 11.9 miles
Hiking time: 1 to 2 days
Elevation gain: 1800 feet
High point: 3000 feet
Best season: Late December through late February
Map: Green Trails: Silverton No. 110
Who to contact: Mount Baker–Snoqualmie National Forest, Darrington Ranger District
Permits/fees: No parking pass required

The best way to enjoy this scenic wonderland is by spending the night beside the high mountain lake. By taking at least two days to complete the trek, you can enjoy the views and scenery to their utmost.

Directions: From Granite Falls drive east on the Mountain Loop Highway 4 miles past the Verlot Public Service Center and turn right (south) into the wide area near the junction with Forest Road 4020 (Schweitzer Creek Road). Park here, and start hiking up the heavily visited Schweitzer Creek Road.

Route: Loads of recreationists are usually on the Schweitzer Creek Road system: Skiers love it because of the scenic beauty of the area. Snowmobilers like it because of the wide roadways and loop possibilities. Snowshoers will love it because of the opportunities to share the beauty on the gentle trails before leaving the hordes behind and venturing into the seldom-visited splendor of the narrow trail to the lakes.

Ice floes on Boardman Lake

To begin the snowshoe trek, walk up the gently climbing Schweitzer Creek Road as it ascends a ridge face above its namesake creek. The road pierces the old, moss-laden forests of the valley bottom and climbs into increasingly young second-growth forest. After 2.5 miles, the scenery picks up and the views increase. The forests give way to open meadows (i.e., clearcuts) that spread like downy white quilts upon the hillside. Beyond these pillowy white meadows stretch the ragged crests of the Mountain Loop peaks: Three Fingers, Big Four, and Vesper Peak all scratch the sky on the far side of the Stillaguamish Valley to the east.

The road splits at just over 2.5 miles. Stay left on the main road as it rolls east around a small, rounded hilltop. (A right turn leads to Route 29, Bear Lake.) The route along this section pierces second-growth forests of Douglas fir, with occasional breaks of sunshine as it crosses clearcut meadows. Stay to the edges of the road along here, as snowmobilers tend to increase their speed on the long, straight stretches.

Five miles from the parking area at the base of the hill, the road sweeps right around a hairpin corner. A couple hundred yards past the apex of the turn, find the Boardman Lake trailhead on the left. This hiking trail climbs gently for just under a mile, passing Lake Evan after a mere 100 yards, before continuing on into increasingly old forest. The trail climbs steadily from Lake Evan but gains just 200 feet along the way. The trail is fairly easy to follow, even in heavy snow years, but if you lose it in the trees, simply head due south, climbing straight up the slope to reach the northern end of Boardman.

The trail crosses the lake's outlet stream immediately upon reaching the lake. This area can be a bit tricky because of the jumble of logs clogging the neck of the outlet stream. The debris allows you to keep your feet dry while

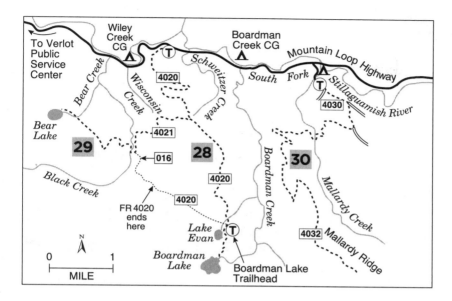

crossing, but the odd angles of the many logs can make footing precarious at times. Use care when stepping over the logs, and the crossing can be accomplished without undue difficulty.

Once across, enjoy the views of the ice-covered lake and distant vistas. To the east, Mallardy Ridge lines the sky. To the north, Boardman Creek leads down into the Stillaguamish Valley, and beyond that are the high peaks of Three Fingers, Big Bear Mountain, and Liberty Mountain. To the south, Bald Mountain rises over the lake basin.

Good campsites are located along the eastern shore of the lake for those planning to stay. Spending the night gives you several hours in this beautiful area after all the hotshot snowmobilers and speedy skiers are headed for home. Best of all, though, a two-day trip means watching the sun set in a blaze of midwinter glory and, come morning, watching it rise anew over the orange-dappled peaks of the North Cascades.

To return home, head back down the narrow forest trail to its junction with the road. From there, go right to retrace your steps, or head left and make a loop of the trip. Going this way, the road descends more than a mile, crossing a clearcut and young stands of second-growth timber. About 1.25 miles from the Boardman Lake trailhead, the road banks right—a blue-diamond blaze on the trees nearby indicates a trail. Continue straight ahead along this connector trail to reach the narrow bed of FR 4021. Stay right on this new road, and follow it down 2 miles to a junction with FR 4020. Go left and walk the last 2 miles out to the junction with the Mountain Loop Highway.

29 Bear Lake

Rating: More difficult
Round trip: 10 miles
Hiking time: 6 hours
Elevation gain: 1400 feet
High point: 2775 feet
Best season: January through late February
Map: Green Trails: Silverton No. 110
Who to contact: Mount Baker–Snoqualmie National Forest,
      Darrington Ranger District
Permits/fees: No parking pass required

This trail is largely ignored by skiers and snowmobilers despite its glorious wilderness-like atmosphere and stunning scenery.

Directions: From Granite Falls drive east on the Mountain Loop Highway 4 miles past the Verlot Public Service Center and turn right (south) into the wide area near the junction with Forest Road 4020 (Schweitzer Creek Road). Park here, and start hiking up heavily visited Schweitzer Creek Road.

Route: On its way to a pretty little alpine lake amid young forest, this route crosses some old clearcut meadows, which provide ample opportunity for snowshoers to bask in the midwinter sun before ducking back under the green canopy of forest that shades most of the route. The bulk of the climbing is taken care of in the first few miles, leaving a leisurely hike over the last couple miles. That's as it should be because the best views, prettiest forests, and most enjoyable snow lie along the upper sections of the trail.

Expect to share the route with skiers and snowmobilers for the first 2.5 miles, as it climbs popular Schweitzer Creek Road (FR 4020). The road ascends a ridgeline above the creek. The first 0.5 to 0.75 mile of road ambles through a thick rainforest-like environment—trees heavy with moss and lichen shade the road. But as the route starts to climb the ridge, the forest changes to young second-growth and occasional small clearcuts.

At 2.5 miles, as it crosses the head of Schweitzer Creek, the road splits. This is the start of the Schweitzer Loop—one road eventually leads back to the other. Loopers are best served by going left (also the way to Route 28, Boardman Lake), but to access Bear Lake, turn right onto FR 4021 and hike across a generally flat forest and meadow area. The road curves south, providing some nice views east toward Big Four Mountain, Vesper Peak, Sperry Peak, and Little Chief.

Near the 4-mile mark, the road splits again. Most of the ski and snowmobile tracks will head off on the left fork (FR 016). FR 4021, the right fork, is the road

Snowshoers approaching Bear Lake

less traveled, but it is also the road to Bear Lake. So, hooking sharply to the right, cross Black Creek and hike west up a very gentle slope. The road meanders and wanders a bit, but when the snow is heavy (covering the underbrush), straighten out the course by heading cross-country across the necks of the looping turns. Just bear west-northwest, and recross the road in a few hundred yards.

A half mile farther, at 4.5 miles, the road makes a big swing south, and then hooks abruptly northwest. Near the 5-mile mark, a small trail leads due west from the roadway. Hike along this forest path about 200 yards to find Bear Lake at 2775 feet.

30 Mallardy Ridge

Rating: More difficult
Round trip: 10 miles
Hiking time: 6 hours
Elevation gain: 1900 feet
High point: 3500 feet
Best season: Late January through early March
Map: Green Trails: Silverton No. 110
Who to contact: Mount Baker–Snoqualmie National Forest,
   Darrington Ranger District
Permits/fees: No parking pass required

Mallardy Ridge is a spectacular wild area that is seldom enjoyed by summer hikers because there are few true trails and no protection from motorized recreationists. Come winter, the old logging roads become de facto trails as the snow drifts over and around them, turning this heavily roaded area into a wild, scenic wonderland.

Directions: From Granite Falls drive east on the Mountain Loop Highway 7.4 miles past the Verlot Public Service Center, and just before crossing the Red Bridge, turn right (south) into the wide parking area near the junction with Mallardy Ridge Road (Forest Road 4030).

Route: Follow Mallardy Ridge Road for an easy, carefree outing with the family, or go cross-country to make the journey more difficult and more adventurous. No matter how the ridge is explored, there is plenty of enjoyment for all. In addition to the simple beauty of the snowy playground immediately at hand, the views of the high, craggy peaks of the Mountain Loop region are astounding. From various points along the snowshoe trails, enjoy views of Three Fingers and White Horse Mountains to the north; Big Four, Sperry, and Vesper Peaks to the east; and Bald Mountain to the south.

Nearing the crest of Mallardy Ridge

Snowshoe along Mallardy Ridge Road (Forest Road 4030) as it glides through the ancient cedar forests along the valley bottom. Soon, however, the road tilts upward and begins the long, steady climb up the side of the ridge. If you are looking for a short day trip, consider taking one of the spur roads encountered along the first couple of miles, but bear in mind these side trails lead nowhere (except into pretty snow-painted forests).

To make the most of the trek, continue up the main road to the first major road junction at 1.5 miles. Go right onto FR 4032—the smaller and generally less well-traveled of the two options—to access Mallardy Ridge. The road rolls up and down for 1 mile, crossing Mallardy Creek, before the long, southbound ascent of the ridge. The crest is reached at the 5-mile mark and makes an excellent place for a leisurely lunch before turning back.

From the crest, enjoy sweeping views of Bald Mountain—seemingly just an arm's length away, just west of Boardman Creek—as well as the more mammoth hulks of Little Chief Peak to the east and Liberty Mountain to the north.

31 Marten Creek

Rating: Backcountry
Round trip: 7.5 miles
Hiking time: 5 hours
Elevation gain: 1300 feet
High point: 2800 feet
Best season: Late December through early February
Map: Green Trails: Silverton No. 110
Who to contact: Mount Baker–Snoqualmie National Forest,
    Darrington Ranger District
Permits/fees: Northwest Forest Pass required

Marten Creek Trail is an oft-overlooked route in summer months that is virtually forgotten come winter. That is a blessing to those who know about, and take advantage of, the beauty of this secluded forest valley.

Directions: From Granite Falls drive east on the Mountain Loop Highway about 9 miles past the Verlot Public Service Center, and just past Marten Creek Campground (closed in winter), turn around and park in the narrow parking area on the left (north) side of the highway at the Marten Creek trailhead.

Route: The crowds skip over this trail because there are no high, wind-swept ridges to explore and no deep alpine lake basins in which to camp. But there is a narrow, winding trail that is loads of fun to follow on snowshoes, a rich forest ecosystem to explore, and a host of wildlife to view and appreciate.

In low-snow years, it may be necessary to carry snowshoes on the lower section of trail, but the upper valley is generally deep in snow by mid-December. From the Mountain Loop Highway, the trail climbs steadily, staying well above Marten Creek for the first mile. The views are limited to the local forest scenery, but that is rich enough to hold anyone's attention. Of course, you don't always have the opportunity to gawk; this narrow, under-maintained trail is rough

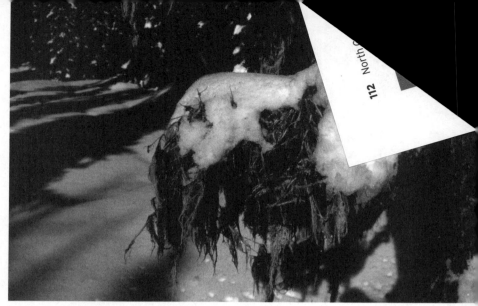

Mossy snow near the start of the Marten Creek route

and, with a blanket of snow on it, avoiding snowshoe-tearing branches and toe-grabbing logs sometimes requires undivided attention.

At other times, however, the trail is open and easily followed. These stretches—especially past the 1-mile mark—are where the views can be best appreciated. After the initial 1.5 miles, the trail stops climbing and rolls into a long traverse of the ridge wall above the creek, dipping at times to water level before angling back up into the open forest above. Around 2.5 miles, the trail angles left toward the head of the valley. It continues another 0.8 mile before the formal trail peters out.

It's possible, when the snow is stable, to continue up the valley for another 0.5 mile to get right under the shadow of the near-vertical headwall. Just don't get too close, as avalanches aren't the only danger here. Rockfalls are much more common than snowslides, and just as deadly. If the weather is warming, or the avalanche danger is moderate or great, don't push past the end of the formal trail.

Because the creek valley is relatively wide-bottomed with plenty of lush undergrowth for forage, it's common for deer to be found in this area. And where there are deer, there are cougars. Count yourself lucky if you see one of these big, elusive cats. Usually the only proof that mountain lions exist in these woods comes in the form of deep, clawless tracks pressed into the snow.

Big animals aren't the only inhabitants here. Grouse roost in the trees near the creek, snowshoe hares scamper through the underbrush along the trail, and at least one great horned owl glides silently between the trees looking for a midwinter meal of rabbit, vole, or marten. Yes, the creek is aptly named—martens have also been seen along this pretty trail.

32 Kelcema Lake

Rating: More difficult
Round trip: 10 miles
Hiking time: 6 hours
Elevation gain: 1600 feet
High point: 3182 feet
Best season: January through February
Map: Green Trails: Silverton No. 110
Who to contact: Mount Baker–Snoqualmie National Forest,
    Darrington Ranger District
Permits/fees: No parking pass required

This route climbs steadily, but at a gentle enough rate that snowshoers of all abilities will enjoy this outing. The route offers beautiful old forests to explore, open clearcut meadows to play in, and high, craggy ridges and peaks to admire.

Directions: From Granite Falls drive east on the Mountain Loop Highway about 12 miles past the Verlot Public Service Center to the end of the plowed road. Park in the cleared pullout area on the north side of the highway.

Route: Explore this pretty forest valley and deep lake basin in snowmobile-free splendor, since the route is maintained for nonmotorized winter recreation only. The road is frequented by cross-country skiers, but if snowshoers just think of skiers as fellow snowshoers who prefer long, skinny snowshoes, they will have no problem sharing the trail. After all, there is plenty of wonderful country and splendid scenery here for everyone to enjoy.

This route follows a small road that parallels Deer Creek on its way up the valley to the Kelcema Lake trailhead. Find the start of Deer Creek Road (Forest Road 4052) near the eastern edge of the parking area and start snowshoeing up the road. The lower section is frequently crowded with families sliding on inner tubes and sleds. Be careful not to trudge across their line of descent, as they are more often than not plummeting downhill, out of control. Also, as a matter of courtesy, while trekking up the road try to avoid stomping down the twin grooves carved by cross-country skis.

As the road climbs through the first thick grove of second-growth forest, the views are limited to the roadway itself. After just a mile, the road slowly banks west, following the course of the creek, and you can catch a few glimpses north of the crown of Bald Mountain. Gradually, the views increase in quantity and quality. The narrow road continues to roll upstream, as the thick second-growth forest gives way first to small clearcuts and then to older, more mature forests.

Snowshoers gearing up for a trek up the Kelcema Lake route

Near the 2.5-mile mark, stop for a breather and you will find the increasingly pretty views before you are nothing compared to the scenery at your back. Turn around and look down the valley to see a skyline punctuated by Big Four Mountain, and Sperry, Vesper, and Little Chief Peaks.

At 3.5 miles, the trail crosses Deer Creek—stay to the center of the bridge to avoid sloughing snow—and climbs out of the valley bottom. The road gains elevation steeply for the next mile as it sweeps west before switching back to climb toward the headwaters of the creek. At 4.5 miles, the road recrosses the creek and runs into the Kelcema Lake trailhead.

The road continues west for another 0.25 mile, and most cross-country skiers will follow it out. With wide snowshoes you have a decided advantage over

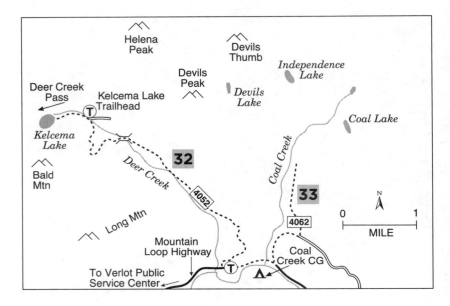

skinny skis on forest trails, so turn left just after crossing the creek and climb the Kelcema Lake Trail. This narrow path weaves through old second-growth forest—with a few ancient giants left to inspire the younger trees—for 0.5 mile. The trail climbs gently along this stretch, and because the trail corridor is fairly wide, the route is easy to follow. The lake is met near the outlet stream, and some nice campsites are scattered along its shores as well as plenty of places to sit and enjoy a quiet lunch while soaking in the beauty of the region. Bald Mountain, to the south, towers over the lake basin, and Devils Peak is visible across the valley to the east.

33 Coal Creek

Rating: More difficult
Round trip: 6 miles
Hiking time: 4 hours
Elevation gain: 900 feet
High point: 2400 feet
Best season: January through March
Map: Green Trails: Silverton No. 110
Who to contact: Mount Baker–Snoqualmie National Forest, Darrington Ranger District
Permits/fees: No parking pass required

The Coal Creek valley is the first large valley leading north away from the Mountain Loop Highway, and it offers outstanding opportunities to trek through untouched meadows, open stands of forest, and along clear, sparkling creeks.

Directions: From Granite Falls drive east on the Mountain Loop Highway about 12 miles past the Verlot Public Service Center to the end of the plowed road. Park in the cleared pullout area on the north side of the highway.

Route: The snow-covered sections of the Mountain Loop Highway are open to anyone and everyone with the means to enjoy the snow—be it via cross-country skis, snowshoes, inner tubes, dogsleds, or snowmobiles—but the side valleys leading away from the main road are often ignored by all of these recreationists. That's a mistake that snowshoers can quietly take advantage of.

From the parking area, follow the Mountain Loop Highway up the Stillaguamish River valley for nearly 1 mile. Look for the Coal Creek Campground on the right. Just past the campground, cross Coal Creek via a small bridge, and then bear left onto a tiny spur that leads north. This road ends in just a few hundred yards, but a faint skier and snowshoer trail—marked with blue-diamond blazes—climbs up the Coal Creek valley.

The trail pierces a stand of old second-growth forest. The blazes, sporadically placed, are sometimes difficult to see. If the next blaze is out of sight, just continue a gentle climb, going straight up the face of the thinly forested hill while staying well above the creek itself. In less than a mile, the trail encounters FR 4062. Turn left and follow it as it traverses and gently climbs the valley wall on the east side of Coal Creek. The road ends in another mile, offering picturesque views down the valley to the Stillaguamish River valley and beyond to Hall and Marble Peaks.

Frosty trees alongside Coal Creek

34 Big Four Ice Caves Viewpoint

Rating: Easiest
Round trip: 7 miles
Hiking time: 3.5 hours
Elevation gain: 250 feet
High point: 1800 feet
Best season: January through March
Map: Green Trails: Silverton No. 110
Who to contact: Mount Baker–Snoqualmie National Forest,
   Darrington Ranger District
Permits/fees: Northwest Forest Pass required

Want a walk through a gorgeous winter wonderland without a sweaty climb up a steep trail? This route offers all the beauty and majesty found in the wintry mountains without the strenuous workout usually required to see such splendor. It is perfect for taking the family on a gentle snowshoe stroll or for introducing newbies to the joys of snowshoeing.

Directions: From Granite Falls drive east on the Mountain Loop Highway about 12 miles past the Verlot Public Service Center to the end of the plowed road. Park in the cleared pullout area on the north side of the highway.

Route: The trail is wide—actually, most of the "trail" is on a section of the unplowed Mountain Loop Highway—and flat, so first-timers can get the feel for walking on snowshoes without having to worry about climbing, crossing, or descending steep slopes. But despite its mild nature, this trail accesses some truly wild country. Trekking up to the base of Big Four Mountain, snowshoers can gawk in awe at the towering peak before them. The granite monolith of Big Four, with its long icicle fingers and snowy cap, captivates most visitors, but it's definitely not the only natural wonder found here. Huge ancient trees, a clear, ice-rimmed river, and hordes of animals—big and small—are here to enjoy as well.

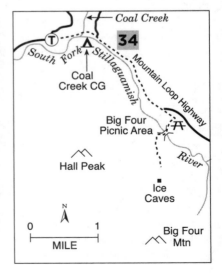

Icicles dangling off a stub of limb

Leave the parking area and trek up the snowbound Mountain Loop Highway as it follows the Stillaguamish River upstream. The road is lined with towering cedar and fir trees—many of which sport long, flowing beards of green. At 0.5 mile, cross the sparkling waters of Coal Creek as it rushes in from the north to empty into the Stillaguamish. Follow the road more than 2 miles until a small side road veers away to the right. This is the entrance to the Big Four Picnic Area and the trailhead for the Big Four Ice Caves Trail.

The ice caves themselves are typically blocked by early December—heavy snowfall and continual avalanches keep the caves capped tight throughout the winter—but the 1-mile trail from the picnic area is worth exploring. The trail leads to the base of Big Four and, along the way, offers outstanding views of the giant rock face of the mountain. Though it may be tempting to snowshoe right up to the jumbled pile of snow at the mouth of the ice caves, resist that temptation. That pile of snowballs is what remains of the devastating avalanches that flash down the side of the mountain after every snowstorm and after most sunny mornings. The bright sun on the rock face weakens the snow and ice, sending it crashing down on the trail below with absolutely no warning.

Opposite: Looking up toward the Early Winters Spires from the Silver Star route

METHOW
VALLEY AREA

35 Silver Star View

Rating: More difficult
Round trip: 4 to 20 miles
Hiking time: 3 hours to 2 days
Elevation gain: 700 feet
High point: 3500 feet
Best season: December through early March
Maps: Green Trails: Washington Pass No. 50, Mazama No. 51
Who to contact: Okanogan–Wenatchee National Forest,
    Methow Valley Ranger District
Permits/fees: No parking pass required

> This route provides the unique opportunity to snowshoe up the middle of one of the most popular highways in the state.

Directions: From Winthrop drive west on State Route 20 (the North Cascades Highway) to the end of the plowed road. Park in the wide parking area.

Route: Come summer, SR 20 is swarming with tourist traffic, but in December the road is snowbound, and it stays that way until June or July most years. That means snowshoers and cross-country skiers can play in the road

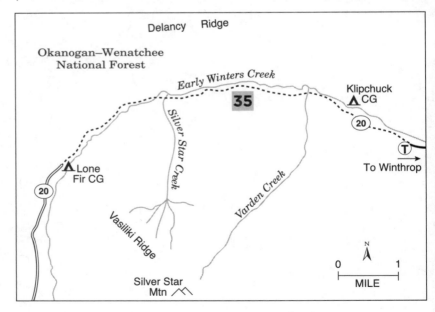

Exploring the lower section of the Silver Star route.

without fear. Of course, there is still a danger of being run over—the danger comes not from cars and trucks but from sliding snow. Avalanche chutes line the upper section of the highway as it approaches Washington Pass, so recreationists are well advised to stick to the lower areas and avoid the route altogether when avalanche dangers are moderate or higher.

Strap on your snowshoes, and trek up the highway, staying to the side of the road to avoid tromping on skiers' tracks and to avoid collisions with the snowmobilers who occasionally zip along this route. The road parallels the Methow River upvalley, making a long, gradual curve to the left, and offers great views of the many high peaks that mark the North Cascades crest.

Snowshoeing up the first 2 miles, the view is straight ahead toward The Needles—a collage of rocky spires towering up to 8140 feet. As the road curves to the southwest, the magnificent crown of Silver Star Mountain comes into view on the left, directly above the road. As beautiful as this mountain is, it is also highly dangerous. Many of the avalanches that keep the road unplowable (and therefore open only to snow recreationists) are spawned on Silver Star.

Just past the Silver Star Creek crossing at around 6 miles, all the Washington Pass peaks are visible on clear days. With Silver Star Mountain on the left and The Needles on the right, look for Tower Mountain, Cutthroat Peak, Whistler Mountain, and Liberty Bell Mountain (partially obscured by Silver Star) in between.

Because of the risk of avalanches caused by changing conditions, overnight camping is discouraged. For a quiet day outing, snowshoe up the road until lunchtime, and then return home. Speedsters might work their way up the valley as far as Lone Fir Campground, but that makes a long day—it is more than 10 miles beyond the end of the plowed road.

36 Upper River Run

Rating: Easiest
Round trip: 7 miles
Hiking time: 4 hours
Elevation gain: 500 feet
High point: 2800 feet
Best season: December through early March
Map: Green Trails: Mazama No. 51
Who to contact: Okanogan–Wenatchee National Forest,
     Methow Valley Ranger District
Permits/fees: Methow Valley Trails Pass required, $5 per day
     for snowshoers

Nothing beats an easy snowshoe stroll through the world-renowned winter wonderland of the Methow Valley. Rolling meadows of snow, nestled amid the tall, willowy aspen trees, sturdy pines, and towering firs, offer a wonderful playground for snowshoers, and the River Run Trail system is the way to experience these wonders.

Directions: From Winthrop drive west on State Route 20 (the North Cascades Highway) to the Mazama turnoff and continue on SR 20 another mile before turning left (south) into the Early Winters/Arrowleaf property. Stay left and follow the signs to Jacks Cabin 0.25 mile down the road. (If you reach the Freestone Inn at the end of the 0.5-mile road, you have gone too far.) Purchase a trail pass at Jacks Cabin.

Route: Although created with cross-country skiers in mind, the flat trails alongside the Methow River are just as enjoyable for snowshoers. They can hike along and soak in the beautiful scenery around the trail and exult in the inspiring views of high ridges and towering peaks that surround the valley. From young kids to seasoned veterans, snowshoers of all abilities will enjoy the easy trails of River Run.

Because these trails are heavily used by skiers, snowshoers will be asked—sometimes told—to stay to the extreme edges of the trails, and when possible, to stay off the groomed track completely. Also, the trails cross private property occasionally, so visitors shouldn't wander far from the actual trail corridors.

From the parking areas, hike west, passing Freestone Inn and, in 0.25 mile, several small cabins—the original Early Winters Cabins—alongside Early Winters Creek. Angle toward the highway, and cross the creek via the SR 20 bridge. Then cross the highway and pick up the trail system on the north side of the road.

Frozen fog coats a pine on the upper River Run route.

The trail turns right and leads away from the highway. A few hundred yards later, it veers left and follows the Methow River upstream. In the next 0.5 mile, several trail junctions are passed—one leads right, crosses the river, and ends at the North Cascades Basecamp property. Others merely cross meadows and create an intricate network of loops. The trails extend about 3.5 miles upstream from the highway crossing, for a trip of more than 7 miles. But shorter trips can be had by making use of the many connectors and cutoff trails.

A full loop is best done by sticking to the River Run Trail as it follows the river upstream. At the upper end of the route, stay left and cross the wide valley bottom to access Jacks Trail at the base of the western valley wall. Return to Jacks Cabin via this trail.

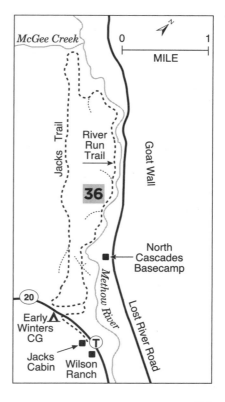

37 Cedar Falls

Rating: More difficult
Round trip: 5.6 miles
Hiking time: 5 hours
Elevation gain: 800 feet
High point: 3600 feet
Best season: December through early March
Map: Green Trails: Mazama No. 51
Who to contact: Okanogan–Wenatchee National Forest,
    Methow Valley Ranger District
Permits/fees: No parking pass required

Snowshoes make easy work of this trail, climbing gently as it does through deep, dry-side forests to end at the site of a pretty little waterfall. The cascade is rather unspectacular in summer months, but cloaked in snow and ice, the falls becomes a wonderful work of water art.

Directions: From Winthrop drive west on State Route 20 (North Cascades Highway) to the Early Winters Campground. Continue west 2.3 miles to find Forest Road 200 on the left. Park in the wide space (room for only one or two cars most of the time) at the base of this road, staying well clear of the traffic lanes of SR 20.

Route: This trail represents one of the best chances for snowshoers to escape the ever-present hordes of skiers who clog the tracks and trails of the Methow Valley. While the occasional skier may struggle up the narrow trail, the route is mostly ignored simply because so many other trails are better suited to their long skis.

The hike begins with a gentle snowshoe walk up FR 200 to its end, about 1 mile up the valley. At that point, the true trail begins. It is a narrow hikers' path following the valley wall high above Cedar Creek. The trail is easy to follow even in heavy snow, although it is slow going at times as the route weaves up and down, in and out of tree wells.

Massive ponderosa pine, aspens, larch, cedar, and fir all fill this valley and provide habitat to an array of birds and animals. Chittering, begging camp-robber jays flit through the limbs, woodpeckers hammer on the trunks, and grouse and ptarmigan scurry around the roots of the big trees. Great horned owls are frequently seen hunting in this valley, which has plenty of prey animals for them to consume. Aside from the grouse and ptarmigan, the owls feast on the resident martens, weasels, mice, chipmunks, squirrels, and other small mammals.

At 1.8 miles out, the trail angles down toward the creek and the last mile is right alongside the waterway. Views are limited, although periodic peeks open up of Sandy Butte to the east, and Driveway Butte can be seen to the north from the lower sections of the trail (it's best viewed on the return trip, when you're facing north).

At 2.8 miles, find a nice view of Cedar Falls, a small cascade on this little creek. The icy crust and snowy mantle that surround the falls give it a fairy-tale appearance that is worthy of a photo or two before you return home.

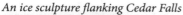

An ice sculpture flanking Cedar Falls

38 | Paul Mountain

Rating: Easiest to more difficult
Round trip: 7 miles
Hiking time: 5 hours
Elevation gain: 1500 feet
High point: 3360 feet
Best season: January through early March
Map: Green Trails: Doe Mountain No. 52
Who to contact: Okanogan–Wenatchee National Forest,
   Methow Valley Ranger District
Permits/fees: Washington State Sno-Park Pass required.
   You may also need a Washington State Discover Pass;
   check www.parks.wa.gov/130/Winter-Recreation.

A gentle road walk provides excellent opportunities to see and experience the snowy ponderosa pine forests that line beautiful Eightmile Creek. Along the way, and from the trail climbing the flank of Paul Mountain, there are stunning views of Buck Mountain and Paul Mountain itself.

Directions: From Winthrop leave the north end of town on East Chewuch River Road. Nearly 7 miles out of town, turn left across the river and then go right onto the West Chewuch River Road (Forest Road 51) as it continues north. About 2.6 miles after crossing the river, turn left into the Eightmile Sno-Park at the base of Eightmile Road (Forest Road 5130).

Route: This is a trek that can be tailored to any snowshoer: from an easy, flat walk perfect for families and first-time 'shoers, to a strenuous climb along a well-graded road for more adventurous sorts, or to a full-on snowshoe scramble to the top of a gnarly peak for snowshoe mountaineers. Generally, the best bet is to stick with the initial riverside

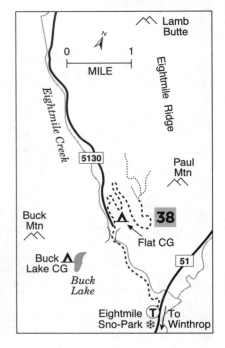

A light snowpack covers the lower approach of Paul Mountain.

walk and maybe add a short snowshoe up the flank of the mountain to attain a better view of the glorious valley below. Leave the mountaineering to those fanatics who use snowshoes merely as tools to get to the top rather than as a specific form of recreation separate and complete in itself.

Many snowshoeing options are available upon leaving this Sno-Park, but for this trail, head straight up the wide track of Eightmile Road (FR 5130). This route follows the pretty, tumbling waters of Eightmile Creek and provides countless opportunities to walk along its edge and listen to the gentle music of its water splashing over ice-crusted rocks. Generally in midwinter, several arching snow bridges span the small creek. As tempting as it may be to point your snowshoes across one of these, resist that urge, as the delicate bridges seldom are strong enough to bear the weight of a small animal, let alone a plodding snowshoer.

As the road approaches Flat Campground at 2 miles, it crosses the one truly safe bridge—one made of iron and wood—over the creek. Now on the north side of the creek, wander through the campground, enjoying the views of Paul Mountain (4210 feet) and the long crest of Eightmile Ridge that leads north away from the peak's summit.

To find a better view of Eightmile Valley, follow the road a few hundred yards farther up the valley to a small road leading off to the right. This route climbs steeply up the flank of Paul Mountain, and as it passes through increasingly thin forests, it offers many views along the length of Eightmile Valley and across it to Buck Mountain (4490 feet). The road continues for nearly 2 miles before it divides into a maze of spur roads, but from the first of these multiple road junctions at 3360 feet, the views are remarkable. With Paul Mountain towering overhead, the pretty ribbon of Eightmile Creek lies in the bottom of the deep valley spread out at your feet.

39 Lookout Mountain

Rating: More difficult
Round trip: 8.5 miles
Hiking time: 5 hours
Elevation gain: 2100 feet
High point: 5500 feet
Best season: December through early March
Map: Green Trails: Twisp No. 84
Who to contact: Okanogan–Wenatchee National Forest,
    Methow Valley Ranger District
Permits/fees: No parking pass required

The Lookout Mountain route combines a modest warm-up hike up a narrow access road with a long cross-country climb along the open steppes of a windswept flank of Lookout Mountain. The route provides plenty of local scenery to admire and enjoy, but the real thrill is found on the upper slopes, where sweeping views encompass most of the Okanogan–Wenatchee National Forest.

Directions: From Twisp drive south on State Route 153 to Carlton and continue another mile before turning right (west) onto Libby Creek Road (Forest Road 1049). Stay right at the first road junction at 2.5 miles, and at 3.6 miles turn left onto FR 1046. Drive 0.5 mile on this road, and park at the small unofficial sno-park area at the base of FR 200 on the left.

Route: This is one of the classic snow routes in an area famous for nonmotorized winter recreation. The Methow Valley has long been recognized as a mecca for cross-country fanatics, but snowshoers will find the hills and valleys

Rock and ice mark the route up Lookout Mountain

of this thinly forested mountain region just as much fun.

The first 1.5 miles follow FR 200 as it climbs the west side of Elderberry Canyon toward the summit of Lookout Mountain. The ascent along this section is gradual, gaining just over 1000 feet in that distance. As the road crosses the creek and starts to climb the opposite valley wall, the going gets tougher. For the easiest approach, stick to the road as it loops south 0.5 mile before switching back and climbing north to reach the ridge top.

Because the trees are thin from here on out, if you are feeling adventurous, leave the road to the skiers and put your snowshoe cleats to the test by angling up the valley wall at a steeper angle, crossing the road somewhere after it has started back from the long loop south. This will

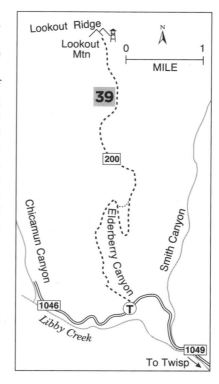

shave about a mile off the hiking distance, but it will put a burn in your thighs. Take a breather after you rejoin the road and enjoy the increasingly spectacular views. To the south, the Sawtooths are rising into view and to the north, straight up the ridgeline, the small elevated wooden cabin at the summit of Lookout Mountain beckons.

Take a visual bearing off the lookout cabin, and lay in a course to intercept it. The upper ridge is open meadow and generally easy going. Nearly 1.5 miles separate the upper end of the road and the lookout structure, but the slope is only moderately steep and the snow is generally well packed by the breezes that continually caress this peak.

The lookout tower is boarded up for winter—no need to watch for fires when the forests are wrapped in a protective cocoon of snow—but you can enjoy a well-deserved snack on the leeward side of the building while soaking in the world-famous winter scenery of the sprawling Methow Valley. Gaze out over the ragged crest of the Sawtooth Range to the south, admire the expansive Twisp River and Methow River valleys to the north and east, and stare in awe at the shimmering white peaks of the Cascade Crest to the west.

40 Eagle Creek

Rating: Backcountry
Round trip: 5 to 16.6 miles
Hiking time: 4 hours to 2 days
Elevation gain: Up to 4900 feet
High point: 7300 feet
Best season: January through early March
Map: Green Trails: Buttermilk Butte No. 83
Who to contact: Okanogan–Wenatchee National Forest,
    Methow Valley Ranger District
Permits/fees: No parking pass required

Snowshoe up the steadily climbing Eagle Creek valley for 3 or 4 miles for pretty views of Duckbill Mountain and out across the Twisp River valley to Canyon Creek Ridge. The trail pierces sun-dappled old-growth pine forests and climbs alongside a sparkling mountain stream.

Directions: From Twisp drive 14 miles west on the Twisp River Road (Forest Road 44) to War Creek Campground. Continue 0.25 mile past the campground, and turn left onto a small road leading across a bridge spanning the Twisp River. After crossing the river, turn left onto FR 4420 and drive 1 mile to the base of a small spur road, FR 080, on the right. Park here. At times, the end of the plowed road will be at the bridge above War Creek. If that is the case, park in the wide plowed-out parking area at the end of the road and walk the mile to FR 080.

Route: This route is virtually ignored when blanketed in snow, so snowshoers are almost assured of solitude in this winter paradise. Although the route is recommended as a day hike, snowshoers with advanced skills and winter savvy may use this trail as the launching pad for adventures of several days in the wild, wonderful Lake Chelan–Sawtooth Wilderness Area. The Eagle Creek Trail rolls around the flanks of Duckbill Mountain and beyond to Eagle Pass in the shadow of Battle Mountain on the crest of the Sawtooth Range.

However far you plan to go, start by snowshoeing up FR 080, pausing at times to turn and look back at the wide Twisp River valley and the towering wall of Canyon Creek Ridge above it. The road angles west, and then switches back to the east to end at the Eagle Creek trailhead after just 1 mile. The trail then climbs alongside Eagle Creek, almost immediately weaving through a minicourse of switchbacks

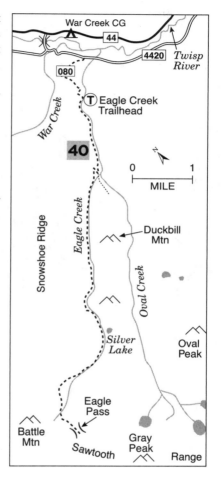

before entering a long, climbing run up the valley. The trail is generally easy to spot, even in heavy snow, as it boasts a wide corridor through the thin old forest. Watch for wildlife along the creek—birds and small mammals frequently scurry around the trail.

At 2.5 miles (3800 feet), the trail forks. This is an excellent place to pause for lunch, enjoy a leisurely exploration of the local flora, and then turn back for a shorter outing.

If you want to put a few more miles under your snowshoes, you must make a decision. The left fork climbs a steep series of switchbacks to gain a high bench on the flank of Duckbill Mountain. It then traverses east to follow Oval Creek upstream into the Lake Chelan–Sawtooth Wilderness. The right fork is

A windswept ridge above Eagle Creek

the preferred route. It loops through a single switchback, and then continues upstream along Eagle Creek.

After another 4 miles, near mile 6.5, the trail hooks right and climbs steeply toward the ridge at the head of the wall. At 8.3 miles, the trail crests the ridge at Eagle Pass (7300 feet). Getting to this point requires winter mountaineering skills and advanced avalanche-recognition skills.

Opposite: Snow-loving Sophie blasting through the windswept snow near Eightmile Creek

STEVENS PASS

41 Surprise Lake

Rating: Backcountry
Round trip: 8 miles
Hiking time: 6 hours
Elevation gain: 2300 feet
High point: 4500 feet
Best season: December through early April
Map: Green Trails: Stevens Pass No. 176
Who to contact: Mount Baker–Snoqualmie National Forest,
     Skykomish Ranger District
Permits/fees: Northwest Forest Pass required

This trail climbs a narrow side valley above the Skykomish River, offering pretty views, sparkling waterfalls, and deep forest environments to explore and experience.

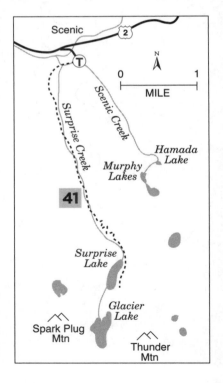

Directions: From Everett drive east on US Highway 2 to the town of Skykomish and continue east another 10 miles. Turn right (south) into the small community of Scenic just before the railroad underpass on the highway. Cross the river, and turn right again onto a small spur road signed as the Surprise Creek/Surprise Lake trailhead.

Route: The Surprise Creek Trail is popular with snowshoers, but don't expect to encounter many skiers here. The trail is far too narrow and the forest is way too close for most skiers' comfort.

All but the first 0.5 mile of trail is within the Alpine Lakes Wilderness, so the forest is ancient, undisturbed old growth. That provides healthy habitat for an array of wildlife, and even in winter a lot of scurrying and flittering occurs along the trail.

Snowshoers can look for, and frequently see, animals such as martens, hares, and deer. They can also find tracks of cougars, bobcats, coyotes, and foxes, though these animals seldom allow themselves to be seen by humans. Birds in the area include the always-present whiskey jacks, ptarmigans, owls, ravens, falcons, and woodpeckers. Delicate waterfalls and deep blue pools are found along the plunging creek, and views of the rocky summits of Spark Plug and Thunder Mountains are spectacular along the upper end of the trail.

The snowshoe hike begins with a short walk up an old, narrow dirt road. Cross Surprise Creek about 0.5 mile up, pass under the powerlines, and start up the Surprise Creek valley proper. Just above the powerlines, the road gives way to a narrow hiking trail, at 2200 feet, and begins to climb steadily. For 0.5 mile, the trail stays well above the creek, but it then tapers down the valley wall and, at 1 mile, comes abreast of the creek and stays there most of the way to the lake. Several small side creeks are crossed, and near the 1.8-mile mark, the trail crosses to the west side of Surprise Creek.

A snow-frosted tree stands watch over Surprise Lake.

Several small, unnamed waterfalls and miniature sets of rapids accent the little stream. These features are beautiful any time of year, but when the stream banks are cloaked in snow and the river rocks rimmed with ice, the tumbling waters are like sparkling jewels, glinting in the cold, winter sunshine.

At 3 miles, the trail leaves the creekside to climb east through a series of steep, tight switchbacks before banking south a bit and rolling the final 0.25 mile on fairly gentle slopes to the lakeshore. From the banks of the big lake, enjoy views of Spark Plug Mountain (6311 feet) to the west, Thunder Mountain (6556 feet) to the south, and the deep Skykomish River valley due north.

42 Lake Susan Jane

Rating: More difficult
Round trip: 7 miles
Hiking time: 3.5 hours
Elevation gain: 1200 feet
High point: 5200 feet
Best season: December through early April
Map: Green Trails: Stevens Pass No. 176
Who to contact: Mount Baker–Snoqualmie National Forest,
    Skykomish Ranger District
Permits/fees: No parking pass required

Few sections of the Pacific Crest Trail (PCT) can be enjoyed in midwinter, but this is one of them. The trail leads from a crowded ski area to a tiny wilderness lake amid a snow-blanketed forest.

Directions: From Everett drive east on US Highway 2 to the summit of Stevens Pass. Park in the ski area parking lots on the south side of the highway.

Route: Snowshoers can amuse themselves watching the out-of-control antics of downhill skiers and snowboarders on the first mile of the hike, then put those crowds behind them and enjoy a quiet day amid wildlife of a different sort—whiskey jacks, snowshoe hares, snowy white ptarmigans (large, ground-roosting birds), martens, and even an occasional fox may be seen darting through the drifts.

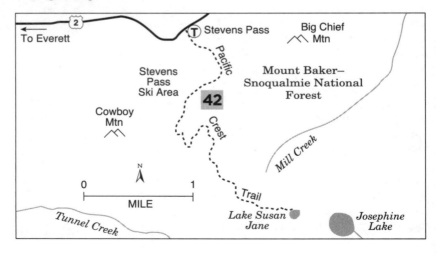

Wind-sculpted snowdrift

Before strapping on the snowshoes, walk up the slope past the ski lodge and angle off to the left to get clear of the downhill ski runs. The Pacific Crest Trail (PCT) actually slices diagonally across the ski area, but snowshoeing on groomed ski runs is frowned upon. So stay on the outside edge of the ski runs on the left, and climb up along the border of the ski area.

As the ski runs taper south to merge at the top of the Tye Chairlift, veer southwest, still skirting the downhill runs, to traverse along a wide bench at the base of a steep hillside. Continue to climb, slanting off to the right, until the top of the ridge is reached in about 1.5 miles (5200 feet).

Turning south, drop off the back side of the ridge to skirt around the headwall of the Mill Creek valley, and pass under the high-tension powerlines that carry electricity from the upper Columbia River dams across Stevens Pass to the Puget Sound area.

The PCT drops steeply downslope, looping through a few switchbacks. Most winter recreationists find it easier to just angle down and across the slope. Continue almost due south, staying above the 4500-foot level on the eastern flank of the ridge that is the Cascade Crest. An old road is passed at about 2.5 miles, and Lake Susan Jane—a small pond set in a quiet forest glade—is reached at 3.5 miles.

43 Skyline Lake

Rating: More difficult
Round trip: 3 miles
Hiking time: 2 hours
Elevation gain: 1100 feet
High point: 5100 feet
Best season: December through early April
Maps: Green Trails: Benchmark Mountain No. 144,
   Stevens Pass No. 176
Who to contact: Mount Baker–Snoqualmie National Forest,
   Skykomish Ranger District
Permits/fees: No parking pass required

A short but strenuous climb to a high alpine lake, buried deep in snow, is what awaits here. The length of the trail and the steepness with which it climbs are secondary considerations, however, for snowshoers will find a remarkable amount of natural beauty and winter wilderness on this route.

Directions: From Everett drive east on US Highway 2 to the summit of Stevens Pass. Park in the ski area parking lots on the north side of the highway.

Route: The idyllic basin around Skyline Lake is situated in such a way that snowshoers who pause here for lunch may enjoy unmatched views of the whole of the Alpine Lakes Wilderness—from Mount Daniel to Mount Stuart—as well as the Glacier Peak Wilderness Area to the north, the Lake Chelan–Sawtooth Wilderness Area to the east, and the beautiful Skykomish Valley to the west.

From the parking area, climb north along a groomed road leading past a number of small skier cabins on the edge of the forest above the highway. The groomed snow-cat track angles north away from the highway and ends abruptly near a power shack about 0.25 mile up the slope. Dig your snowshoe cleats into the hillside and continue straight up the hill. Stay near the trees on the west side of the open slope to minimize avalanche danger and collisions with telemark skiers whooshing down the slope. After nearly a mile of climbing, at the 5000-foot level, the slope tapers off a bit and the climbing becomes easier.

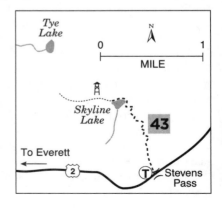

Pause here to catch your breath and soak in the views.

Turn and look south. At what seems just an arm's length away, the Stevens Pass Ski Area sprawls out across the slopes on the opposite side of the highway. Above and beyond those groomed runs (long, white scars on the dark green forest) stand the summits of the Alpine Lakes peaks. Mount Stuart, like a massive granite wall, looms in the southeast. Mounts Daniel and Hinman, the glaciated peaks in the center of the wilderness, rise like twin towers to the southwest. Nearer in, Thunder Mountain rises on the Cascade Crest just south of the ski area, and Bulls Tooth sits on the southern horizon.

From this 5000-foot resting point, veer left as the roadway turns right. Following the roadway leads to a cell phone tower with limited views (other than of the communications tower). Staying left puts you on the route up to the ridgetop lake.

After a well-deserved rest, continue climbing the now mod-

A meteorology tower near Skyline Lake

erate slope, and in just 0.5 mile, trudge through a young stand of fir to come upon the shores of Skyline Lake. At 5100 feet, this lake is generally high enough that the ice cap on it freezes solid enough to support skiers and snowshoers; indeed, the broad flat surface of the lake is almost always crisscrossed with ski and snowshoe tracks. It's always safer to skirt the lake's shore rather than risk the ice, however; sometimes the surface ice on lakes in the Cascade Range gets melted by unseen warm springs underneath.

A long, relaxed lunch along the shores of the lake allows ample time to marvel at views to the south as well as the now-revealed vistas to the north, which include views of Glacier Peak and Lichtenberg Mountain. To extend the outing, amble west along the crest of Skyline Ridge for up to 2 more miles before returning to your car.

44 Lake Valhalla

Rating: More difficult
Round trip: 7.5 miles
Hiking time: 5.5 hours
Elevation gain: 1700 feet
High point: 4800 feet
Best season: December through early March
Map: Green Trails: Benchmark Mountain No. 144
Who to contact: Okanogan–Wenatchee National Forest,
    Wenatchee River Ranger District
Permits/fees: No parking pass required

According to Norse mythology, Valhalla is the beautiful home of heroes slain in battle. Fortunately for snowshoers, this Valhalla is no myth, and visiting it doesn't require mortal combat. Lake Valhalla is a wondrous basin nestled alongside the Pacific Crest Trail (PCT) just north of Stevens Pass. Tucked between Mount McCausland and Lichtenberg Mountain, the lake appears remote and isolated.

Directions: Drive east on US Highway 2 to the summit of Stevens Pass and continue another 6 miles east to the Mill Creek exit. Make a U-turn at Mill Creek to get into the westbound lanes of the divided highway, and drive west 1.2 miles to a narrow parking strip on the right (north) side of the highway. This is the nearest parking area to the Smith Brook trailhead, which is another 0.1 mile to the west.

Route: Although summer hikers can access Lake Valhalla by way of the PCT, snowshoers will find it easier, and safer, to make use of the narrow road leading up the Smith Brook valley to the east, and then to traverse cross-country

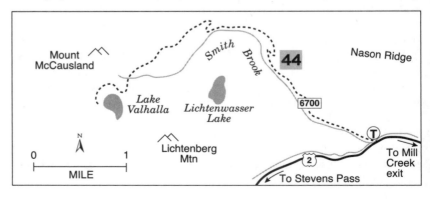

Setting up camp on the ridge top

through the head of that valley to the lake basin. This path provides good footing, safety from avalanche danger, and stunning views along its route.

With snowshoes in hand, follow the shoulder of the highway west to the start of Forest Road 6700 (Smith Brook Road). The plows will have left a high, vertical wall of snow between the road surface and the top of the untracked snow, so a climb is generally required. In heavy snow years, this embankment has been known to be as much as 18 feet high, but generally it is less than 10 feet. An ice ax can be handy here, not only for added traction in climbing but to chop out steps. If you don't want to chop your own, bear in mind that by midmorning Saturday on most winter weekends someone will have dug a rough staircase into the bank.

The trail follows the narrow Smith Brook Road through a thin stand of forest along a near-level bench for the first 0.25 mile before beginning a gentle climb up the creek valley. The lower section of the valley has been logged, so the second-growth forest is dotted with clearcut sections for the first 1.5 miles of the hike. Look for birds and small animals where the forests and meadows meet: generally, camp-robber jays (a.k.a. whiskey jacks) flit through the area, and snowshoe hares leave tracks by the edges of the meadows.

At nearly 2 miles, the road switches back twice to gain elevation above the creek bed. Here, in the midst of a sloping clearcut meadow, some nice views open up west toward Mount McCausland and north to Union and Jove Peaks. The route then follows the creek as it banks toward the west.

Just over 2.5 miles up, at 4000 feet, the road again loops through a switch-back turn. This is the end of the road, but not the trail. Leave the road at the apex of that switchback, and traverse the open hillside above Smith Brook. Climb slightly while snowshoeing across the valley wall to get near the 4600-foot level in the next mile. There, at 3.5 miles from the trailhead, catch the snow-obscured PCT, cross the head of the Smith Brook valley, and hike another 0.25 mile southwest to the Lake Valhalla basin at 4800 feet. Enjoy a rest at the lake while soaking in the views of Lichtenberg Mountain, Nason Ridge, Union and Jove Peaks, Mount McCausland, Valhalla Mountain, and Skyline Ridge.

45 Lanham Lake

Rating: More difficult
Round trip: 3.2 miles
Hiking time: 3 hours
Elevation gain: 1100 feet
High point: 4100 feet
Best season: December through early March
Map: Green Trails: Benchmark Mountain No. 144
Who to contact: Okanogan–Wenatchee National Forest,
    Wenatchee River Ranger District
Permits/fees: Stevens Pass Nordic Center charges $12 per day
    for snowshoers

This narrow forest trail climbs gently alongside a gurgling ice-rimmed creek and leads to a picturesque alpine lake. The trail is often attempted by cross-country skiers, but the narrow path and thick forest often send them packing before they complete the first mile, so a high degree of quiet solitude can be found at this lake, despite the shortness of the access trail.

Directions: Drive east on US Highway 2 to the summit of Stevens Pass and continue another 6 miles east to the Mill Creek exit. Turn right onto Mill Creek Road, and drive a few hundred feet to park in the Mill Creek Sno-Park (the lower lot). The lot nearest the buildings is provided for the commercial Nordic ski facilities run by the Stevens Pass Ski Area. To avoid conflicts, avoid snowshoeing on the groomed trails wherever possible.

Route: Lanham Lake is ringed with snow-laden trees, but some nice views of the jagged top of Jim Hill Mountain appear to the south. The lake is also an ideal destination for novice winter campers—not too far to snowshoe but far enough to get into a true wilderness setting. The thick old growth around the lake provides plenty of shelter for a snug winter camp.

Snowshoers climbing to the Lanham Lake basin

The route starts about 10 yards up Mill Creek Road—one of the ski area's groomed trails, so snowshoe along the uphill edge of this groomed track to avoid incurring the wrath of skiers on your way to the trailhead. Bear left into the trees at the well-marked start of the Lanham Lake Trail.

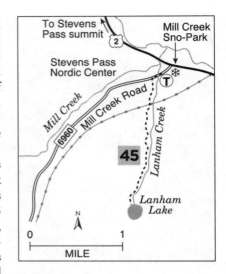

This narrow hikers' trail follows the west bank of Lanham Creek as it climbs the gentle valley to its headwaters in the lake. About 0.25 mile up, the trail crosses a clearing, passes under high-tension power-lines—these carry the juice that keeps Puget Sounders out of the dark—and crosses a groomed ski trail (part of the commercial operation).

Try to ignore the buzzing electrical lines and the unnaturally flat track left by the groomer. The trail leaves both behind quickly as it continues the steady climb up the creek valley. About a mile up the trail, the valley narrows considerably. The trail is now close to the creek, and footing is sometimes slick where the trail enters a brief, steep pitch for a couple hundred yards.

The last 0.5 mile is only moderately steep as the valley widens again and finally opens into a deep bowl cradling the lake. If you are the adventurous type, trek up the slope on the far (south) side of the lake to explore the flanks of Jim Hill Mountain, but if avalanche danger is moderate or higher, skip this added adventure and stick to the lake basin for any extra exploration.

46 Wenatchee Ridge

Rating: Easiest to more difficult
Round trip: Up to 11 miles
Hiking time: 7 hours
Elevation gain: 2000 feet
High point: 4000 feet
Best season: January through late February
Map: Green Trails: Wenatchee Lake No. 145
Who to contact: Okanogan–Wenatchee National Forest, Wenatchee River Ranger District
Permits/fees: No parking pass required

This trail combines the serene beauty of the Little Wenatchee River valley with the thrilling vistas found on the high benches of Wenatchee Ridge. Stick to the lower half of the route and enjoy a quiet day in a picturesque mountain valley, or trek the entire route, climbing to panoramic views of peaks and ridges of the eastern Cascades.

Directions: From Leavenworth drive north on US Highway 2 to Coles Corner and turn right (north) onto State Route 207. Continue north on SR 207 for 11 miles, passing Lake Wenatchee, and turn left (west) onto the Little Wenatchee River Road (Forest Road 65). Drive 1.5 miles to an unofficial sno-park area at the end of the plowed road.

Churned snow marks the place where a coyote caught and fed on a snowshoe hare.

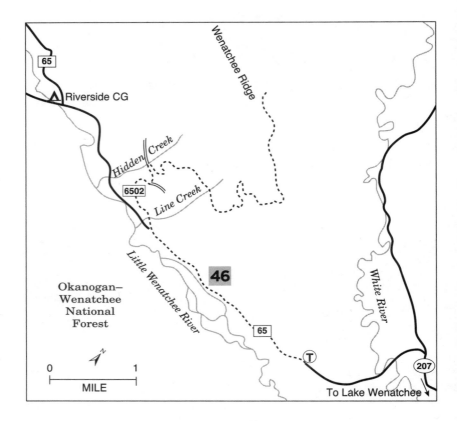

Route: Kids will love the flat, snowy track along the Little Wenatchee River, and families can make a day of it by hiking along the valley bottom, reveling in the musical sounds of the river splashing over the icy rocks of its bed. Nice views up to the jagged crest of Wenatchee Ridge to the north and the high, snowy crowns of Mounts Mastiff and Howard to the south round out this part of the trail.

To start, hike FR 65 as it heads upstream alongside Little Wenatchee River. Actually, the road is several hundred feet from the river, with some broad meadows and thin groves of alder and pine between, but a mile up the valley, the road and river come together to provide some waterside entertainment. Look for the quick movements of water ouzels—small birds dipping in and out of the frigid waters—and small flotillas of ducks in the pools of the stream.

At 2 miles, a side road (FR 6502) angles off to the right. This is the route up the ridge. Snowshoe up it as it traverses for 0.5 mile before climbing more steeply through a wide series of switchbacks. FR 6502 passes three side roads in its first mile—stay left at the first main intersection and right at the next two.

At mile 3, the track begins a long, curving traverse east around the snout of the ridge. There are some nice views through openings in the forest cover. To the south, over the Little Wenatchee Valley, Nason Ridge is in view—anchored on the west by Mount Mastiff and on the east by Round Mountain.

At mile 4, the route turns sharply to the left to climb around a small knob at 3300 feet. The road continues to climb gradually for the last 1.5 miles, rolling around to the north side of the ridge before ending at 4000 feet before the jagged crest of the ridge. Adventurers will love the moderate climb up the snout of Wenatchee Ridge.

47 Chiwaukum Creek

Rating: More difficult
Round trip: 10.4 miles
Hiking time: 6 hours to 2 days
Elevation gain: 1200 feet
High point: 3200 feet
Best season: December through early March
Map: Green Trails: Chiwaukum Mountains No. 177
Who to contact: Okanogan–Wenatchee National Forest,
   Wenatchee River Ranger District
Permits/fees: No parking pass required

This narrow wilderness trail follows Chiwaukum Creek upstream to a junction with several other trails, providing opportunities for unbounded rambling in the winter wonderlands of the Alpine Lakes Wilderness. Most snowshoers, though, will find plenty of beautiful country, awesome views, and outstanding snowshoeing along the first 5 miles of the trail.

Directions: From Leavenworth drive north on US Highway 2 about 9 miles to Tumwater Campground. Continue north another mile and turn left onto Chiwaukum Creek Road (Forest Road 7908). Drive 2 miles to the end of the road at 2200 feet, or to the snow line if it is lower than that. The summer trailhead is at the road end.

Route: The Chiwaukum Creek Trail pierces pine and fir forests, nicely blanketed in pristine white snow. Along the way, snowshoers can gawk in wonder at the towering ramparts of Big Jim and Snowgrass Mountains. They can enjoy the musical stylings of Chiwaukum Creek as it bounds over ice-crusted boulders and snow-laden logs. And, unfortunately, they can skip the whole thing if the avalanche danger is moderate or higher. The last mile of the road to the summer trailhead and the first mile of trail are at the base of a steep,

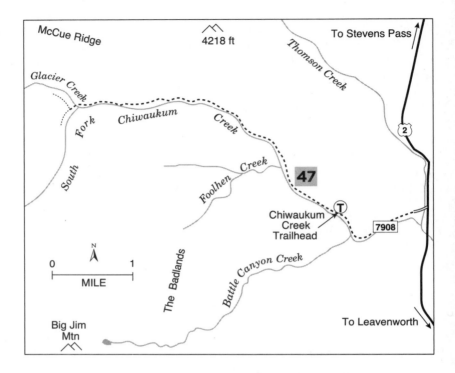

slide-prone slope and should only be crossed when the risk of avalanche is low or nonexistent. But if the conditions are right, this trail is not to be missed.

Chiwaukum Creek cuts through a narrow valley along its lower reaches. It is nearly flat, gaining just 1200 feet in more than 5 miles, and it pierces some of the most beautiful old forests of pine and fir in the region. The ponderosa pine is particularly pretty in this setting, with its bright-orange bark scales offsetting the brilliant white of the snow and the sparkling blue of the creek.

The trail rolls upstream, curving gently to the west and opening up views of McCue Ridge towering above the upper Chiwaukum Creek valley and Big Jim Mountain to the south. Numerous wide areas in the sheltering forests offer excellent sites in which to pitch a camp, and the possibilities of making an extended snowshoeing adventure out of this trip are endless.

At 5.2 miles the trail splits. This is where most of you will turn back, but if you are a hearty winter fanatic, consider pushing on into the deeper regions of the Alpine Lakes Wilderness. Do this only if you are adequately prepared for extended winter exposure.

At the trail fork, the path on the right climbs steeply to the Chiwaukum Lake and Larch Lake basins. This trail crosses several avalanche slopes and is best left for summer explorations. The left trail, though, follows the South

Snow frosts the rocks of Chiwaukum Creek.

Fork Chiwaukum Creek for 3 miles, passing several other trails along the way. Good campsites are found at Timothy Meadows, about 2 miles upstream from the original trail split.

48 Eightmile Creek

Rating: Backcountry
Round trip: 12.4 miles
Hiking time: 1 to 2 days
Elevation gain: 2600 feet
High point: 4600 feet
Best season: December through early March
Map: Green Trails: Chiwaukum Mountains No. 177
Who to contact: Okanogan–Wenatchee National Forest,
   Wenatchee River Ranger District
Permits/fees: No parking pass required

In addition to peaceful solitude, this trail offers unmatched wilderness beauty. High alpine lakes appear in table-flat meadows covered by blankets of billowing white fluff. Crystalline creeks rush through icy channels alongside the trail. Above it all towers the monarch of the central Cascades—Mount Stuart. Joining that great bulk on the horizon are Cannon, Eightmile, and Cashmere Mountains.

Directions: From Leavenworth drive north on US Highway 2 and, at the northern edge of town, turn left (west) onto Icicle Creek Road. Continue west 8.5 miles to Bridge Creek Campground. Turn left onto Forest Road 7601, and park near the bridge over Icicle Creek. In heavy snow years, it may be necessary to park farther down the valley and snowshoe a few miles up Icicle Creek Road to Bridge Creek Campground (2000 feet). In light snow years, it is sometimes

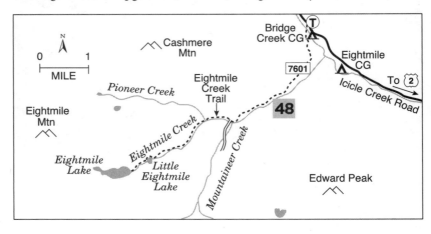

Snowshoers climbing up to Eightmile Lake

possible to drive another mile or so up FR 7601 before being stopped at the snow line. Mileage figures for the hike are measured from Bridge Creek Campground.

Route: One of the most heavily visited trails in summer, the Eightmile Trail is virtually ignored by winter recreationists. Cross-country skiers find the narrow trail and occasional steep pitches difficult to navigate while wearing their long boards, but today's snowshoes are tailor-made for tromping in and around tightly spaced trees and up steep slopes.

This trail can be more tiring than one might think, but don't fret if you are forced to turn back before reaching the upper end of the trail. There is plenty to see and enjoy on the lower half of this route to make even an abbreviated snowshoe trek here worthwhile.

Bear in mind that this trail is at the bottom of a narrow valley in steep mountain country, so avalanche hazards are extreme. Knowledge of how to recognize and avoid avalanche dangers is essential for visitors on this trail.

The snowshoeing begins on the wide, moderately pitched FR 7601. This road contours along the hillside above Mountaineer Creek, gaining just

1300 feet in the 3 miles to the junction with Eightmile Creek. The lower valley is wide and scenic, providing plenty of pretty views south to Cannon Mountain and east to Icicle Ridge. At 3 miles, the road crosses Eightmile Creek. Instead of crossing the creek with the road, turn right and start up the narrow Eightmile Creek Trail, which weaves through the tight forest of pine and fir on the lower flanks of Cashmere Mountain.

The trail climbs gently for nearly a mile until, at 4 miles out, the route steepens as the valley narrows. At times, the trail is obscured completely, and routefinding skills are tested. But getting lost isn't much of a threat because the trail parallels the creek, so routefinding is merely an exercise in finding the most efficient path up the steep slopes. Fortunately, the steepest pitch is only a few hundred feet long. Then the trail returns to its moderate pitch. In fact, there is a mere 1100-foot gain from the point where the trail leaves the road to Little Eightmile Lake, encountered at 5.7 miles. Some potential campsites are found around this little pond, but much better sites can be found 0.5 mile farther up the valley—and another 200 feet higher in elevation—at Eightmile Lake.

This sprawling plain of ice and snow is in the shadow of Eightmile Mountain, which looms to the north, and you will find that a camp here is blessed with magnificent sunrises. Watching the morning sky brighten and seeing the icy face of Eightmile Mountain glow with dawn's orange light is an experience of a lifetime.

Opposite: Looking up onto the sheer face of Rampart Ridge from Gold Creek

SNOQUALMIE
PASS

49 Mount Teneriffe

Rating: Most difficult
Round trip: 13 miles
Hiking time: 8 hours
Elevation gain: 3800 feet
High point: 4788 feet
Best season: December through February
Maps: Green Trails: Mount Si No. 174, Bandera No. 206
Who to contact: Department of Natural Resources, South Puget Sound Region, Mount Si Natural Resources Conservation Area
Permits/fees: Washington State Discover Pass required

Regardless of the air temperature, be prepared to sweat. Although the route is broad and easy to follow, it climbs steeply and seemingly endlessly. The route may be light on snow at the start, but the trail gains elevation quickly and, as it climbs, the snow deepens. Still, this route is best enjoyed during cold spells when snows have inched down into the lowlands.

Sophie the Lab hikes the Teneriffe Trail.

Directions: From Seattle drive east on Interstate 90 to exit 32 (436th Avenue SE). Turn left (north) over the freeway and drive 0.5 mile to North Bend Way. Turn left (west), and in 0.25 mile turn right (north) on Mount Si Road. Follow the road 2.5 miles to the Mount Si parking area and continue about 1 mile beyond to a wide turnaround area. Park here, well clear of the road, and do not block any gates or driveways.

Route: Start your trek at the gated road, commonly called the Mount Teneriffe Trail, on the left of the parking area. If the snow on this old logging road is thin, you might want to carry your snowshoes for a couple of miles as the route ascends gradually—gaining just 500 feet in 2 miles—through old grown-over clearcuts.

At the 2-mile mark, the roadbed turns steeper, and generally the snow gets deeper. The route switchbacks up through forest for another 2 miles to

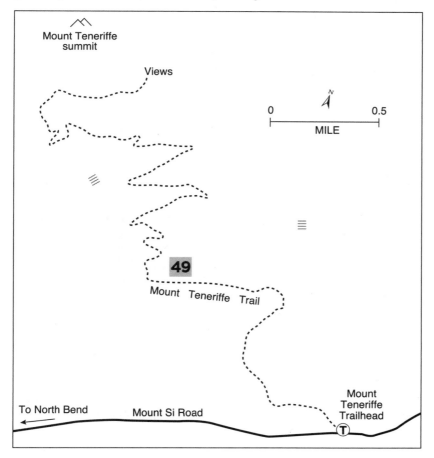

the 3200-foot level at 4 miles from the trailhead. This can be a great stopping point for tired hikers as it offers glorious views from a broad clearcut hillside. To the south lies the Cedar River watershed, Rattlesnake Ledge, and the long spine of Rattlesnake Ridge. To the east is Mailbox Peak and the summits of the Middle Fork Snoqualmie Valley.

Summit-seeking snowshoers should push onward and upward, gaining another 1000 feet of elevation in the next 2.5 miles as the road finally gains the summit ridge. Slightly more than 6.5 miles from the trailhead, at 4200-feet elevation, you'll find a broad ridgetop saddle with grand views. Another 0.5 mile of trekking will put you on the true summit, but this ridgeline perch offers all the views you'll find above, without the hazards and efforts of scrambling up the narrow, slick summit trail. Play it smart and stop here.

50 Taylor River

Rating: More difficult
Round trip: 10 miles
Hiking time: 6 hours
Elevation gain: 650 feet
High point: 1750 feet
Best season: December through February
Maps: Green Trails: Green Trails Mount Si No. 174 and Skykomish No. 175
Who to contact: Mount Baker–Snoqualmie National Forest, Snoqualmie Ranger District, North Bend office
Permits/fees: Northwest Forest Pass required

When snow conditions are favorable, the Taylor River Trail to Big Creek Falls offers some of the most enjoyable snowshoeing in the state. Wandering up the lush moss-laden forest valley to a sparkling ice-rimmed waterfall is magical.

Directions: From Seattle, drive east on Interstate 90 to exit 34 (Edgewick Road). Turn left (north) onto 468th Street and follow it to the junction with the Middle Fork Snoqualmie Road (Forest Road 56). Turn right and continue up the Middle Fork Snoqualmie Road for 12.5 miles to the Taylor River Road (just past the Middle Fork trailhead parking area). Turn left onto the Taylor River Road and drive to a wide parking area at its end, in about 0.5 mile. If snow conditions don't allow access to the Taylor River trailhead, make use of the Middle Fork trailhead and simply walk the extra 0.5 mile to the start of this route.

Ice balls dangle above the Taylor River.

Route: Because this route is relatively low elevation, the window of snow-shoeing opportunity is slim. The peak season seems to be from Christmas to Valentine's Day, when the chance for snow in the Puget Sound foothills is highest. When the forecast calls for snow in the 1000-foot elevation range, make tracks for Taylor!

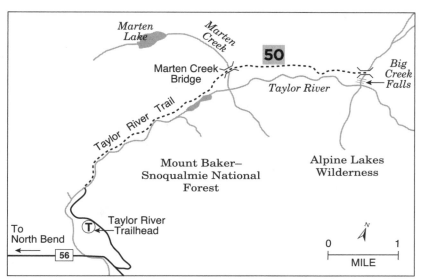

Start up the Taylor River Trail as it rolls east through moss-laden second-growth forest. At 0.4 mile, when the road forks, stay right to continue to weave your way up the valley. The track crosses Marten Creek at 3 miles—be very careful here as the bridge deck can be precarious if the snow is deep.

Beyond the bridge, the route rolls gently up the valley for another 2 miles to a broad concrete bridge over Big Creek. This structure appears to be out of place here. The wide concrete bridge belongs on a highway—somewhere other than a backcountry trail—but it's a remnant of the old road and a developer's dream, a dream that fortunately died. The wide road that was planned to the headwaters of the Taylor River valley never progressed much beyond a logging road, and even that has largely disappeared, leaving this primitive trail.

The Big Creek Bridge may be the first thing to grab your attention when you reach the creek, but it fades into the background as soon as you step onto its deck. Big Creek Falls tumbles off a hillside near the bridge, over a series of granite steps and down smooth granite faces to create a sparkling tapestry of frozen gems on the rocks around the falls. Turn around here.

51 Talapus Lake

Rating: Most difficult
Round trip: 8.5 miles
Hiking time: 7 hours
Elevation gain: 1600 feet
High point: 3280 feet
Best season: January through early March
Map: Green Trails: Bandera No. 206
Who to contact: Mount Baker–Snoqualmie National Forest, Snoqualmie Ranger District, North Bend Office
Permits/fees: Northwest Forest Pass required

The trail ascends through open fir and hemlock forests, dips low and rolls alongside a pretty mountain stream a time or two, and finally deposits dedicated snowshoers on the shores of a wide, pretty alpine lake nestled below a steep, avalanche-ravaged ridge. The views from the lake basin include looks up to Bandera Mountain and Pratt Mountain, and east to Granite Mountain.

Directions: From North Bend drive east on Interstate 90 for 15 miles to exit 45. After exiting the interstate, turn left, cross under the freeway, and follow Forest Road 9030 west 1 mile to its junction with FR 9031 on the left. Park here, or if the road isn't plowed, park at the end of the plowed area, well clear of the freeway exits, and snowshoe the mile to the junction.

Route: Overcrowded in summer months, this trail is too often overlooked in the winter. Sure, the route requires a modest hike up a snowy road before getting to the trailhead, but that's the perfect way for snowshoers to warm up and swing into stride.

FR 9030 is easy to find, although it can be a bit difficult to follow if the snow is crusty and slick. Be sure to have good cleats on both heel and toe to ensure a solid "bite" on the crusty snow that is often the curse of this trail.

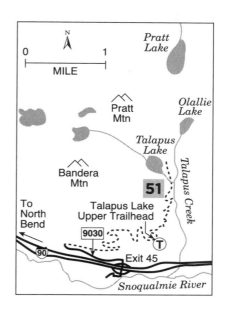

A snowshoer stops for a drink on the way to Talapus Lake.

Start up FR 9030, signed as the access to the Talapus Lake trailhead, as it rolls up through a series of small switchbacks. The road offers good views upslope toward the summit of Bandera Mountain thanks to several open clearcut areas that flank the road. The 2.5 miles of the road hike goes fast. At the end of the road, in the wide parking area of the Talapus Lake upper trailhead, enjoy stunning views of Granite Mountain before starting up the narrow trail.

Usually you will have the trail to yourself from this point on. Skiers often kick their way up the road as far as the trailhead, but few of those folks care to struggle with their long skis on the winding, forest trail. With snowshoes, you will have no problems with the twisting, turning trail as it rolls around trees and rocks. At 3.5 miles, after a mile of snowshoeing on the narrow trail, the path dips into a valley to follow close alongside Talapus Creek the last 0.75 mile to the lake.

The lake basin is the most likely place to find snowslides, so be aware of avalanche potential as you approach the lake. If the avalanche hazard was reported as moderate or higher for this part of the Cascades, it's best to skip the trail component of this outing. The roadway makes a nice, gentle outing on snowshoes without the danger of being swept away.

52 Ira Spring Approach

Rating: Easiest
Round trip: Up to 8 miles
Hiking time: 5 hours
Elevation gain: 100 feet
High point: 2900 feet
Best season: January through early March
Map: Green Trails: Snoqualmie Pass No. 207
Who to contact: Mount Baker–Snoqualmie National Forest, Snoqualmie Ranger District, North Bend Office
Permits/fees: Northwest Forest Pass required

This road and lower section of trail explore pretty forest with periodic views of the broad South Fork Snoqualmie valley. The relatively flat roadway makes for easy travel for a casual day or winter adventure.

Directions: From Seattle drive east on Interstate 90 to exit 45 (Forest Road 9030). Turn left under the freeway, and then make a left on FR 9030. Park here if the road is gated or if snow blocks access, but make sure the roadway is left clear and unobstructed by your vehicle. At all times—at all freeway exits—always park well clear of any freeway interchange and off- and on-ramp area.

Snowshoers pulling a sled toward Mason Lake

If FR 9030 is not gated and isn't blocked by snow, continue up it as far as it is safe to travel given the snowpack before parking.

Route: The "trail" here is actually the road accessing the Ira Spring Trail. While trekking up this track, give a thought to the trail's namesake: Ira Spring was a tireless advocate for trails, working both behind the scenes and as one of the most recognizable trails spokesmen in the country. He lobbied Congress, influenced local land-management decisions, and introduced several generations of hikers to the wonders of Washington's trail network through the hiking guide series he created with Mountaineers Books.

From your parking location, hike west along FR 9030 as it angles slightly uphill through lush moss-laden forest. If you parked near the freeway, you'll find a fork at 0.8 mile from the freeway off-ramp. Going right would take you toward Talapus Lake on FR 9030, which is Route 51. Stay straight on the left-hand fork to ramble gradually upward on FR 9031 through the second-growth forest of young Douglas fir and hemlock. In another 3 miles you'll reach the broad open parking area of the Ira Spring Trail. If you continue up the trail, you'll find nearly 2 miles of broad trail along an old roadbed before it turns steeper and narrower as it approaches Mason Lake.

The Ira Spring trailhead parking area makes a great turnaround point for a casual day or winter exploration.

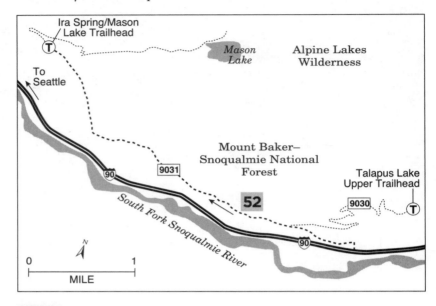

53 Denny Creek Campground

Rating: Easiest
Round trip: Up to 4 miles
Hiking time: 3 hours
Elevation gain: 100 feet
High point: 2900 feet
Best season: January through early March
Map: Green Trails: Snoqualmie Pass No. 207
Who to contact: Mount Baker–Snoqualmie National Forest,
    Snoqualmie Ranger District, North Bend Office
Permits/fees: Northwest Forest Pass required

Nestled between the spread arms of Interstate 90, the forested valley of the South Fork Snoqualmie River offers some wonderful snowy landscapes to explore with little effort. Novices can trek through the campground loops, while more adventurous souls can venture forth toward the cascades of Franklin Falls.

The view up to the peaks around Snoqualmie Pass

Directions: From Seattle drive east on Interstate 90 to exit 47 (Asahel Curtis/Denny Creek). Turn left over the overpass and proceed to a T. Turn right and travel 0.25 mile to Denny Creek Road (Forest Road 58). If FR 58 is not plowed, park here. At all times—at all freeway exits—always park well clear of any freeway interchange and off- and on-ramp area. If FR 58 is plowed, continue up it 3 miles to the campground entrance—or to the end of the plowed section if before that—and park well clear of the roadway.

Route: After hiking along the road as needed, you'll find the campground loop a great place of wintry marvel to explore. The campground hugs the

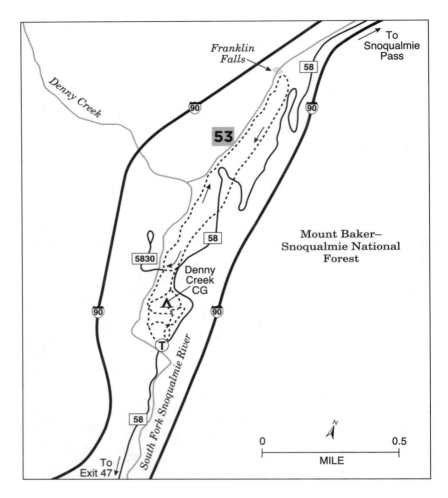

South Fork Snoqualmie River, providing some incredible opportunities to view natural ice sculptures, while the forests around the camp provide great terrain to scramble through and over, providing good lessons in snowshoe travel on unbroken snow. The loop and campground exploration can cover up to a mile of trekking.

For additional adventure, push on past the campground entrance and hike up FR 58 for a few hundred yards before taking a left at the junction with FR 5830. Hike up this snow-laden road as it turns into a wide trail, leading in 1 mile to a view of Franklin Falls. Avoid getting too near the falls as rocks and broken ice frequently come crashing down—the footing (especially in snowshoes) is tricky over the last 100 yards anyway, so you'll do well to avoid that section.

54 Snow Lake

Rating: Backcountry
Round trip: Up to 10 miles
Hiking time: 7 hours or 2 days
Elevation gain: 2000 feet
High point: 5100 feet
Best season: January through early March
Map: Green Trails: Snoqualmie Pass No. 207
Who to contact: Mount Baker–Snoqualmie National Forest,
    Snoqualmie Ranger District, North Bend Office
Permits/fees: Northwest Forest Pass required

The route begins by heading to Source Lake but pushes on past that easy-to-reach day-hiking destination and climbs steeply to crest the saddle separating Snow Lake from the South Fork Snoqualmie River drainage. This makes for a rigorous outing but one well worth the effort—especially for those seeking a winter camping destination.

Directions: From Seattle drive east on Interstate 90 to exit 52 (Snoqualmie Pass, West Summit) and turn north, crossing under the freeway. Continue north on FR 9040, the Alpental Access Road, to the Alpental Ski Area parking lot.

Dogs and snowshoers enjoy a late-season snow camp near Snow Lake.

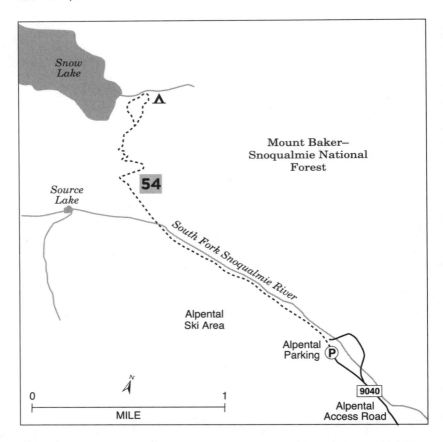

Route: Snow Lake may be the most popular wilderness trail in the Pacific Northwest. From June through September, it gets thousands—maybe tens of thousands—of hiker visits. But come winter, only a few hardy folks make the long slog through deep snow to the glorious lake basin. Part of the reason for this is that the route crosses some pretty substantial avalanche chutes, creating a danger for unwary snow travelers. But those who take the time to check avalanche snow conditions and closely monitor avalanche dangers can find a safe time to trek this route.

From Alpental, follow the route to Source Lake, staying on the west side of the Snoqualmie river basin. About 0.3 mile before you would reach Source Lake, as the valley wall curves west, swing north and start climbing the increasingly steep slope below Chair Peak, angling north and east up the slope. At about 3 miles, you will find the slope tapers off and you enter a broad, tree-dotted meadow atop a broad saddle between Chair Peak and Snoqualmie Mountain. Stop and catch your breath here as you peer out at the surrounding glory. Denny

Peak lies to the south, flanked by The Tooth, Bryant Peak, and Chair Peak to the west. To the north, a high ridge links Chair Peak to Snoqualmie Mountain on the northeast, which is in turn flanked by Lundin Peak, Red Mountain, and finally Guye Peak to the southeast.

Due north, just a few hundred feet below you, lies the long, flat oval of Snow Lake. You can descend to the lakeshore to make camp, or find a comfortable place to pitch your tent on the ridgeline, where the views are far better. Just find a nice flat in the lee of a stand of trees, and you'll be warm and comfy. To continue your outing and to gain a panoramic view of the basin, head east from the lake and climb to the low ridge above the lake, exploring to your heart's content.

55 Commonwealth Basin

Rating: Backcountry
Round trip: Up to 10 miles
Hiking time: 7 hours
Elevation gain: 2300 feet
High point: 5300 feet
Best season: January through early March
Map: Green Trails: Snoqualmie Pass No. 207
Who to contact: Mount Baker–Snoqualmie National Forest,
    Snoqualmie Ranger District, North Bend Office
Permits/fees: No parking pass required

Commonwealth Basin affords excellent views of the iron-rich flanks of Red Mountain, although snowshoers will be at a loss to explore the source for the mountain's name since it is covered in a deep quilt of white snow all winter. There are also excellent views up to Kendall Peak and Snoqualmie Mountain from the basin.

Directions: From Seattle drive east on Interstate 90 to exit 52 (Snoqualmie Pass, West Summit). Stay right and park in the open ski area lots closest to the freeway. Carefully paying attention to traffic, walk through the underpass to reach the trailhead on the north side of I-90. **Note:** Do not park within the freeway interchange zone (anywhere under or around the freeway underpass between the on- and off-ramps) as the Washington Department of Transportation will tow vehicles parked there.

Route: The section of the Pacific Crest Trail (PCT) north of Snoqualmie Pass is overrun with hikers every summer weekend, but put a few feet of snow on the trail and the crowds ignore it. That's great news for snowshoers,

When the snow is deep enough, the Commonwealth Basin area is a good place for igloo-building practice.

because the trail is easy to get to and enjoyable for snowshoeing. The route to Commonwealth Basin follows the PCT for more than 2 miles through shadowy old-growth forest—with an occasional break in the trees for views of the surrounding peaks—before setting off on a smaller path into the wide, rocky basin at the base of Red Mountain.

Just north of the freeway underpass, a small snow-covered road climbs off to the right. Snowshoe up this road into a wide summer parking area at the PCT trailhead. The trail leads off from the east end of the parking lot, rolling

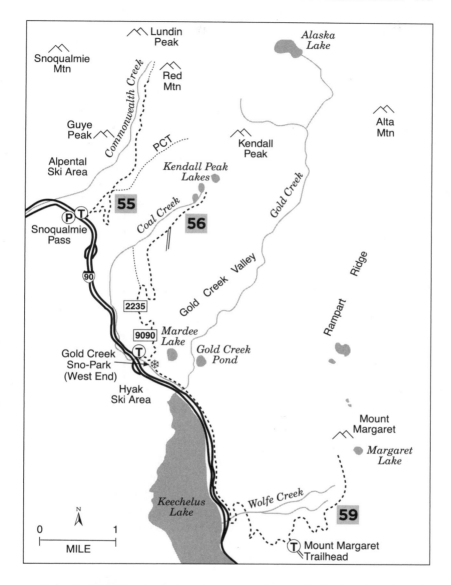

up through thick forest on a long traverse to the east before looping through a switchback corner near 0.7 mile and climbing northwest. After looping through a couple more short switchbacks, the trail rolls north to a junction at 2.5 miles (4000 feet).

Though steeper, some trekkers prefer an alternate route when snow is very deep. This option heads up the narrow valley directly above the PCT parking area. Stay left and climb through the trees, keeping the small creek basin on your left until reaching the broad mouth of Commonwealth Basin.

The primary PCT route to this point is easy to follow because the trail corridor is wide and obvious in the heavy forest. The trail stays under the forest canopy nearly all of the first 2.5 miles, although it does cross the base of a large avalanche slope and then recross the slope higher up after climbing through a switchback. Cross this slope with care, and if the avalanche danger is higher than moderate, avoid the area. The point where the trail crosses the slope is on the runout section of the chute rather than the trigger area, so it is unlikely that you will trigger a slide here, but caution is still required.

At the trail junction, stay left—the PCT climbs steadily to the right—and follow the Commonwealth Creek valley up into the basin. The trail is a long, straight ascent up the valley, climbing gradually as it enters the basin. The forest thins and finally falls away at 4 miles, leaving you on open slopes at the base of Red Mountain. Potential for avalanches exists here beyond timber line, so care and common sense must be used in heavy doses. If the snow is stable and safe, it's possible to scramble up to the 5300-foot level (about 5 miles from the trailhead) at a low saddle on the ridge between Red Mountain and Lundin Peak. The last 0.5 mile of climbing is steep and should be attempted only by those with experience in snowshoe mountaineering.

56 Kendall Peak Lakes

Rating: More difficult
Round trip: 9 miles
Hiking time: 7 hours
Elevation gain: 1700 feet
High point: 4400 feet
Best season: January through early March
Map: Green Trails: Snoqualmie Pass No. 207
Who to contact: Mount Baker–Snoqualmie National Forest, Snoqualmie Ranger District, North Bend Office
Permits/fees: Washington State Sno-Park Pass required. You may also need a Washington State Discover Pass; check www.parks.wa.gov/130/Winter-Recreation.

The roar of the highway is unmistakable when starting up this track, but soon the beauty of the winter wilderness surrounding the trail makes everything else fade into the background. The dark green firs and hemlocks lining the ridge, the open, quilted meadows of snow, and the wide avenue of the trail make this a perfect destination for snowshoers.

Midway up the Kendall Peak route

Directions: From Seattle drive east on Interstate 90 over Snoqualmie Pass to exit 54, 2 miles east of the pass's summit. Exit I-90, turn left, and cross under the freeway to reach the Gold Creek Sno-Park just a few hundred feet north of the highway interchange.

Route: This trail leads to a pair of small alpine ponds nestled in a deep cirque on the flank of towering Kendall Peak (5675 feet). The mountain dominates the skyline from the lake's basin, as well as along the last mile of the trail leading into the basin. But Kendall isn't the only peak on the horizon. To the east is Alta Mountain and the long line of Rampart Ridge. To the south is the peak used as the Snoqualmie Summit Ski Area—a low broad peak lined with the wide white slashes of alpine ski runs. Below the lakes, the broad meadows along the bottom of the Gold Creek valley glimmer a brilliant white in the afternoon sun.

Although the trail ascends nearly 2000 feet, the climbing is gradual and the trail is easy to follow. Because of that, first-time 'shoers and young kids will enjoy this outing as much as experienced snowshoe enthusiasts. Of course, all of those features coupled with the trail's close proximity to the Seattle metropolitan area means a lot of snowshoers and skiers on any winter weekend. Strap on the snowshoes midweek, though, and the trail will be virtually deserted.

From the Sno-Park, snowshoe up Lake Mardee Road, staying close to the left (west) side of the valley, and in a few hundred yards find an old logging road (Forest Road 9090) climbing left into the trees and up the valley wall. This road is steep for 0.25 mile, and then the ascent moderates considerably.

The road, now FR 2235, enters an old clearcut just past the 0.5-mile mark and twists and turns its way up the slope. You can either stay with the moderate pitch of the road or take a steeper, more direct, northerly approach straight up the slope, cutting off the switchback corners. Pause often to rest. Use the excuse of stopping to admire the increasingly pretty views south over the Gold Creek basin, Hyak Ski Area, and Mount Catherine if you are the competitive sort who doesn't like to admit to fatigue!

At 1.7 miles, the route hooks through a sharp hairpin turn to the right. A wide spur road heads off to the left, leading to a nice overlook of the lower Coal Creek basin and the ski areas at Snoqualmie Pass. Stay right if you are bound for the lakes. The road traverses east toward the snout of a narrow ridge and, at that leading edge of the ridge, turns north and climbs steeply through forest and meadow. The track stays on the west side of the ridge crest, banking right at 2.6 miles, and at 3.5 miles hooking sharply south in a switchback turn.

Stay north, snowshoeing off the road near the apex of the hairpin corner, climbing through mostly open slopes to the ridge crest leading to Kendall Peak Lakes. The trail nears Coal Creek at 4.2 miles and follows it the remainder of the way to the lakes' basin, rolling over two small knolls before reaching the lower of the twin Kendall Peak Lakes. Avoid the upper lake because the tight, avalanche-prone walls of the cirque are not a safe way to approach it.

57 Gold Creek Pond Loop

Rating: Easiest
Round trip: 2 miles
Hiking time: 2 hours
Elevation gain: 100 feet
High point: 3000 feet
Best season: December through February
Map: Green Trails: Snoqualmie Pass No. 207
Who to contact: Mount Baker–Snoqualmie National Forest, Snoqualmie Ranger District, North Bend Office
Permits/fees: Washington State Sno-Park Pass required. You may also need a Washington State Discover Pass; check www.parks.wa.gov/130/Winter-Recreation.

Gold Creek Pond, cradled in the lower Gold Creek valley, is a wonderful destination for kids and novice snowshoers. By mid-December, the snow is usually deep enough for the outing to be enjoyable, making this a great destination for families who gave each other snowshoes for Christmas.

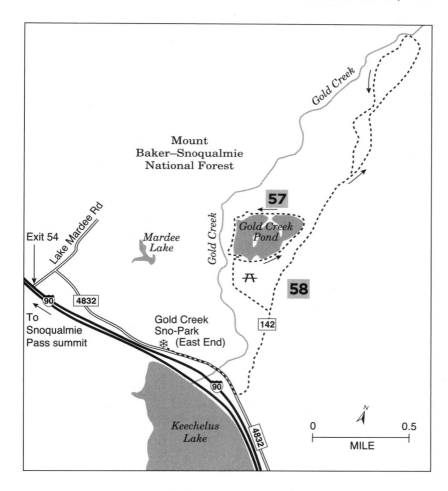

Directions: From Seattle drive east on Interstate 90 over Snoqualmie Pass to exit 54, 2 miles east of the pass's summit. Exit I-90, turn left, cross under the freeway, and just a few hundred feet north of the highway interchange turn right onto a narrow paved road, FR 4832, and drive east parallel to the freeway for 1 mile. Cars generally line both sides of this road, as the shoulder is the primary parking area for the long Gold Creek Sno-Park. Park toward the east end of the plowed road.

Route: This trek features little elevation change, with grand views for virtually the entire outing. Kendall Peak looms to the north and Rampart Ridge towers over the eastern side of the valley.

Start the hike by continuing east along the frontage road to its junction with Forest Road 142, signed for Gold Creek Pond. Turn left (north) onto this

A silver-frosted fir marks the start of the Gold Creek Pond Loop.

road and follow it 0.5 mile through a woodland area before breaking out into an open clearing. Veer left at the first road junction, signed for Gold Creek Pond parking. From that parking area, head west onto the route of the summer trail that loops around the pond basin. Snowshoeing counterclockwise ensures the best views are in front of you for most of the trek.

The route wanders alongside a willow-lined creek before stepping up onto a boardwalk section—this may not be noticeable in heavy snowpacks, so simply continue west-northwest—that leads to a crossing of the marshy area at the north end of the pond. The views open up here as you look across the pond to the south. The broad expanse of the flat pond surface beacons snowshoers, but you must resist that call—ice doesn't form thick enough in most Cascade lakes to be safe for human weight.

Continue your mile-long circuit around the pond back to the summertime trailhead/parking area, and then head back down the access road to your vehicle.

58 Upper Gold Creek Valley

Rating: Easiest
Round trip: 6 miles
Hiking time: 5 hours
Elevation gain: 1200 feet
High point: 4200 feet
Best season: January through March
Map: Green Trails: Snoqualmie Pass No. 207
Who to contact: Mount Baker–Snoqualmie National Forest, Snoqualmie Ranger District, North Bend Office
Permits/fees: Washington State Sno-Park Pass required. You may also need a Washington State Discover Pass; check www.parks.wa.gov/130/Winter-Recreation.

This wedge-shaped valley slices due north from the hustle and bustle of the interstate and crowded ski areas to enter the quiet country of the Alpine Lakes Wilderness.

Directions: From Seattle drive east on Interstate 90 over Snoqualmie Pass to exit 54, 2 miles east of the pass's summit. Exit I-90, turn left, cross under the freeway, and just a few hundred feet north of the highway interchange turn right onto a narrow paved road, FR 4832, and drive east parallel to the freeway for 1 mile. Cars generally line both sides of this road, as the shoulder is the primary parking area for the long Gold Creek Sno-Park. Park toward the east end of the plowed road.

Looking north up the Gold Creek basin

Route: The deep cut of the Gold Creek valley begins as a broad swath of meadows but quickly tapers into a narrow canyon between the craggy ridgelines of Rampart Ridge and Kendall Peak. Winter explorers can enjoy many miles of relatively easy snowshoe travel, but they must be aware of the avalanche conditions as the upper valley is prone to bombardment from avalanches off the steep slopes above the valley floor.

Start the hike by continuing east along the frontage road to its junction with Forest Road 142, signed for Gold Creek Ponds. Turn left (north) onto this road and follow it 0.5 mile through a woodland area before breaking out into an open clearing. Instead of turning left toward Gold Creek Ponds (Route 57), continue due north, heading deeper into the Gold Creek valley. As you hike up the valley, the view of Kendall Peak gets better and better, while on your right, Rampart Ridge rolls majestically along. As the valley narrows, the meadows give way to wide stands of trees and small forest clearings. The walls close in tighter and tighter on the valley floor, and the views become more dramatic. At about 2.5 miles in, stop and enjoy the scenery and the feeling of power that this winter wilderness emits.

At the northern end of Rampart Ridge is the bulky summit of Alta Mountain; directly opposite is the vertical face of Kendall Peak. The steep walls of these mountains seem to rise from the ground at your feet. Continue to press on up the valley, but only if you know how to evaluate avalanche dangers. Even on the valley floor, hikers are susceptible to avalanches. The mammoth slides can come barreling off the valley walls with enough momentum that they sweep well out onto the basin's floor.

Stroll to your heart's content along the valley floor, and then weave your way through the trees back to the starting point for a gentle day on the snow.

59 Mount Margaret

Rating: Easiest to more difficult
Round trip: 9 miles
Hiking time: 6 hours
Elevation gain: 2800 feet
High point: 5200 feet
Best season: Late December through late February
Map: Green Trails: Snoqualmie Pass No. 207
Who to contact: Okanogan–Wenatchee National Forest, Cle Elum Ranger District
Permits/fees: Washington State Sno-Park Pass required. You may also need a Washington State Discover Pass; check www.parks.wa.gov/130/Winter-Recreation. *See map for Route 59 on page 168.*

Views of the entire eastern half of the Snoqualmie Pass area, including the sprawling blue waters of Keechelus Lake and the snow-covered summits of Mount Catherine and Tinkham Peak to the south, can be had from the upper reaches of this route. The lower section, unremarkable though it is, does serve as a good warm-up for the long climb ahead.

Directions: From Seattle drive east on Interstate 90 over Snoqualmie Pass to exit 54, 2 miles east of the pass's summit. Exit I-90, turn left, cross under the freeway, and just a few hundred feet north of the highway interchange turn right onto a narrow paved road, FR 4832, and drive east parallel to the freeway for 1 mile. Cars generally line both sides of this road as the shoulder is the primary parking area for the long Gold Creek Sno-Park. Park at the end of the plowed road, near the small bridge over the stream connecting Mardee Lake to Keechelus Lake.

Approaching the summit of Mount Margaret

Route: Because this area is close to the metropolitan centers, a lot of skiers and snowshoers share the trail. That, combined with the closeness of the busy freeway, means the chances of seeing wildlife are pretty slim. Still, where people play in the woods, camp-robber jays look for handouts. This valley is also patrolled by many red-tailed hawks and ravens, so watch the skies for raptors and corvids, and look for the tiny tracks of their prey (mice, hares, and grouse) in the meadows.

The first 1.5 miles of the snowshoe hike follow the road southeast from the parking area, parallel to I-90. This leg of the journey is frequently used by cross-country skiers who are just learning their craft, and it makes a nice place to familiarize yourself with your snowshoes. The road curves around the base of Rampart Ridge, with just a few modest views west toward Mount Catherine and Roaring Ridge above the waters of Keechelus Lake.

After crossing Wolfe Creek, the road climbs gradually, switches back to recross the creek, and just a few hundred yards beyond the second crossing, switches back once more to start a long, traversing climb through intermittent forest and clearcuts to mile 2.5. Two more switchbacks are encountered in the next 0.5 mile, and at 3.2 miles, the road splits. The left fork continues to climb while the right stays at a level traverse before dropping toward the I-90 valley. Staying left, climb for another 0.5 mile to 3600 feet and a gate marking the Mount Margaret trailhead.

The trail is wide for a hiking path—it's actually an old jeep road—so it is very easy to follow even when deep in snow. The path zigzags steeply up the side of a ridge, through broad clearcut meadows. Save some travel time by angling east, still climbing steeply, to the eastern edge of a large meadow. Pause here to soak in the views of the Snoqualmie Pass area, Keechelus Lake, and the sprawling clearcut-pocked mountains of the South Cascades. On clear days, Mount Rainier and sometimes even Mount Adams are visible to the south.

Continue uphill toward the ridge crest (now heading north), following the road through a small forested area, another meadow, and finally a solid, respectable stand of trees. The last 0.5 mile is along a true hiking trail in deep forest. It climbs, weaving around trees, along the crest of the ridge to a high promontory below the craggy summit of Mount Margaret. Below, on the eastern side of the ridge, is tiny Margaret Lake. Reaching its shores, though, requires a steep descent along an avalanche-prone slope, so stay on the ridge and enjoy the wonderful views.

60   Keechelus Ridge

Rating: More difficult
Round trip: 6.4 miles
Hiking time: 5 hours
Elevation gain: 2100 feet
High point: 4900 feet
Best season: Late January through late February
Map: Green Trails: Snoqualmie Pass No. 207
Who to contact: Okanogan–Wenatchee National Forest, Cle Elum Ranger District
Permits/fees: Washington State Sno-Park Pass required. You may also need a Washington State Discover Pass; check www.parks.wa.gov/130/Winter-Recreation.

Snowshoers who like to climb will love this route. Although the trail is broad and easy to follow all the way to the ridge crest, ample opportunities exist for those who want to show off their climbing abilities by heading straight up the open slopes. Views from the route are incredible, and the higher snowshoers go, the better the panoramic scenery. The jumbled peaks of the South Cascades spread away to the southern horizon with Mount Rainier dominating the skyline.

Directions: From Seattle drive east on Interstate 90 over Snoqualmie Pass to exit 62, signed Kachess Lake, about 10 miles east of the summit. Exit I-90, turn left, cross over the freeway, and turn left onto the freeway on-ramp and drive westbound on I-90 for 1.5 miles to the Price Creek Westbound Sno-Park. (Although another Sno-Park is located on the other side of the freeway, there is no way to cross the interstate to reach it.)

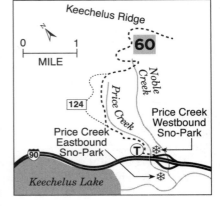

Route: Plenty of rewards await the dedicated athletes who point their snowshoes toward the top of this ridge, but even those who cut their trips short of the top will find the journey pays off tremendously.

A small trail leads northwest from the Sno-Park for a 0.25 mile to Forest Road 4832. Turn left and hike west a couple hundred feet to leave the multi-use crowds behind. (Snowmobilers, skiers, skijorers—skiers pulled by one or more dogs—and even dogsledders use this trail.) Climb to the right onto a small side road, FR 124. This road climbs steeply up the flank of Keechelus Ridge alongside Price Creek for 0.5 mile before angling west away from the creek in a long, looping route that isn't too steep but does cover several miles. You can stick with the road, but a faster, more enjoyable route is to head cross-country up the slope, slicing across old clearcuts and thin stands of forest.

The best cross-country "trail" is found about 1.3 miles out from the Sno-Park. As the road rolls farther west away from Price Creek, snowshoe up the slope away from the track, staying right while the road goes left. Parallel Price Creek uphill, but stay on the bench above the stream rather than descending into the brambles alongside it. The slope rolls upward over several small benches and false summits, crossing clearcuts old and new. In light snow years, take care to avoid hooking a snowshoe on some of the brush protruding in the older, grown-over cuts.

The climb covers about 1 mile of distance before crossing another heavily used road, FR 4934, just below the ridge crest (4300 feet). Emerge onto that road at about the same place as FR 124, which finally loops back from its long journey around the ridge flank.

Rather than joining FR 4934—a popular snowmobile route that creates a long loop when coupled with several other roads in the area—merely snowshoe across it, and head toward the ridge crest. This last 0.5 mile of climbing

Snowshoe hare tracks mark a delicate snow bridge.

is also cross-country travel, although you can follow the road (FR 124) here too, if you are nervous about routefinding on the open ridge. The top is easily identifiable on the approach by tall radio relay towers. Once there, put the towers behind you (thus keeping them out of sight) and enjoy the panoramic vistas of the eastern Cascades.

61 Amabilis Mountain

Rating: Most difficult
Round trip: 8 miles
Hiking time: 6 hours
Elevation gain: 2100 feet
High point: 4554 feet
Best season: Late January through late February
Map: Green Trails: Snoqualmie Pass No. 207
Who to contact: Okanogan–Wenatchee National Forest, Cle Elum Ranger District
Permits/fees: Washington State Sno-Park Pass required. You may also need a Washington State Discover Pass; check www.parks.wa.gov/130/Winter-Recreation.

Sometimes it's nice to cut a switchback or two, to go where skiers and snowmobilers can't, to work up a sweat on a cold day while enjoying spectacular local scenery and distant views. This trail offers all that. There is enough open country on the side of the mountain that snowshoers can just point their shoes uphill and go, jumping onto the road when necessary to avoid particularly steep pitches or brambly clearcuts.

Directions: From Seattle drive east on Interstate 90 over Snoqualmie Pass to exit 63, signed Cabin Creek. Turn right after exiting the interstate, and enter the Cabin Creek Sno-Park on the right.

Route: This route is steep and has a high danger of avalanche at times, so avoid the mountain when forecasters report moderate or higher avalanche danger.

All the open country on the way up Amabilis Mountain makes prime hunting habitat for raptors—red-tailed hawks and falcons—and ravens. Owls prowl the forest fringes, and bald eagles soar through between fishing trips up the Yakima River. Those birds are here for a reason, and that reason is rabbits, or more accurately, hares—snowshoe hares, which bound through the meadows and burrow in the snow to eat the grasses underneath. Even if the white rabbits aren't seen, their tracks frequently are.

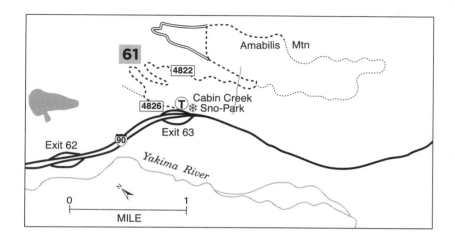

Before strapping on the snowshoes, walk north across the freeway overpass and find the start of Forest Road 4826 on the left. Snowshoe north on this wide, flat road. Note that the road is usually groomed, with tracks frequently set for skiers (twin, parallel grooves carved into the snow by a grooming machine), so steer your snowshoes well clear of the tracks. A quarter mile up the road, turn onto FR 4822 and start to climb toward the summit of Amabilis. This trail switches back and forth a few times before slanting off to the south on a long traverse of the middle section of the mountain.

Snowdrifts along the crest of Amabilis Mountain

Cross a small creek, and at about 2 miles the road forks. A hard hairpin turn to the left leads you on a long looping route to the mountaintop. Snowshoeing straight off on the right-hand road leads to an even longer loop to the same point at the summit (which, incidentally, is almost directly upslope from this intersection).

Either road will get you to the top, but if you are looking to avoid the roads, start off along the left fork, and in 0.5 mile leave the road by climbing on a more direct route up the slope while still slanting slightly to the left. The views are now spectacular. Looking south and west, the Yakima River and Keechelus Lake valley spread out at your feet, and beyond the rolling hills (with their many square scars of open clearcuts) the South Cascades sprawl to the horizon.

A half mile farther on, near the 3-mile mark, cross the road, which has flipped through a switchback turn and is now climbing south, and head straight upslope to the ridge crest. Turn right and follow the crest another mile to the 4554-foot summit. A thin stand of trees lines the summit crest, providing a degree of protection from the wind while you enjoy a scenic lunch before heading down the steep slopes.

62 Twin Lakes

Rating: Easiest
Round trip: 4 miles
Hiking time: 5 hours
Elevation gain: 400 feet
High point: 3100 feet
Best season: December through late February
Map: Green Trails: Snoqualmie Pass No. 207
Who to contact: Okanogan–Wenatchee National Forest,
   Cle Elum Ranger District
Permits/fees: Washington State Sno-Park Pass required.
   You may also need a Washington State Discover Pass;
   check www.parks.wa.gov/130/Winter-Recreation.

This is a pleasant forest walk, offering a fairly easy outing for the family. The route holds to a broad, easy-to-follow road for the first 1.5 miles before dropping into the woods to ramble along a narrow hiking path. At the end of the route, you'll find a small lake set deep in the woods.

Directions: From Seattle drive east on Interstate 90 over Snoqualmie Pass to exit 54, signed Hyak. Turn left and drive about 1.5 miles south on Forest Road 2219 to the Hyak Sno-Park.

Wind-driven snow paints the trunks of trees near Twin Lakes.

Route: Despite its proximity to the popular ski areas of Snoqualmie Pass and the busy roadway of I-90, this is a wonderful place to find wildlife in the winter. Deer frequent this valley, as they find forage in the deep forests, but it is

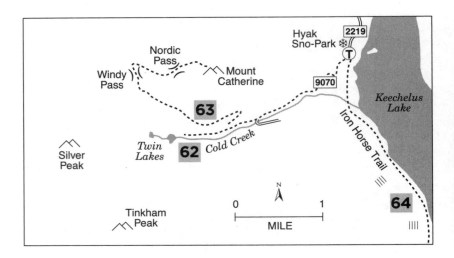

far more likely you'll see tracks and trails of snowshoe hares, martens, weasels, and—hot on the trail of those three—bobcats and cougars. You'll find grouse perched in the trees and gray jays flitting through the branches. The only thing missing is expansive views, but sometimes it's nice to focus on beauty close at hand, and this route offers that aplenty.

From the Sno-Park, trek about 0.75 mile east along the Iron Horse Trail before finding blue blazes to the south, marking your turn onto FR 9070. Frequently during the winter, both the Iron Horse Trail and FR 9070 are groomed by the Summit Nordic Center of The Pass Ski Resort. Be sure to stick to the outside edges of the trail if it is groomed, and if not groomed, avoid any well-laid ski tracks whenever possible.

FR 9070 climbs the Cold Creek valley, heading west around the southern flank of Mount Catherine. The going is easy as the road climbs just 400 feet in nearly 1.5 miles. Watch the edges of the road, and peer under the eaves of the forest along the road for signs of wildlife.

At 1.5 miles and 3000 feet, the road rounds a sharp hairpin turn. Leave the road, dropping off the left side of the road just before the apex of the turn, and continue trekking west (the road begins to climb north-northwest to Route 63, Windy Pass/Mount Catherine). There is a narrow hiking trail here, but with a blanket of snow the trail is nearly impossible to find. No need to worry, though. Just pick a route that carries you west at a fairly level pace—a slight ascent is what you're actually going for, but not much. At just 0.5 mile past the point where you left the road, you'll find a small lake nestled in the deep second-growth forest. (The "twin" of this Twin Lake is farther up the valley and is too small and insubstantial to bother with.) Stay off the lake ice—the forest and the relatively low elevation prevent thick ice from forming.

63 Windy Pass & Mount Catherine

Rating: Most difficult
Round trip: 7.5 miles
Hiking time: 7 hours
Elevation gain: 2300 feet
High point: 5052 feet
Best season: December through late February
Map: Green Trails: Snoqualmie Pass No. 207
Who to contact: Okanogan–Wenatchee National Forest,
    Cle Elum Ranger District
Permits/fees: Washington State Sno-Park Pass required.
    You may also need a Washington State Discover Pass;
    check www.parks.wa.gov/130/Winter-Recreation.

As you approach Snoqualmie Pass while driving east on Interstate 90, you notice a large forested mountain straight ahead. The road swings north in a large loop through the pass and then heads back south before turning east again. The big, forested mountain that forced the highway to make that northern jag is Mount Catherine, and snowshoers can explore its flanks and summit by trekking up the eastern side. Along the way, you will enjoy ample opportunities to experience wildlife and some glorious views of the Snoqualmie Pass peaks.

Directions: From Seattle drive east on I-90 over Snoqualmie Pass to exit 54, signed Hyak. Turn left and drive about 1.5 miles south on Forest Road 2219 to the Hyak Sno-Park.

Route: From the Sno-Park, trek about 0.75 mile east along the Iron Horse Trail before finding blue blazes to the south, marking your turn onto FR 9070 (as on Route 62, Twin Lakes). Frequently during the winter, both the Iron Horse Trail and FR 9070 are groomed by the Summit Nordic Center of The Pass Ski Resort. Be sure to stick to the outside edges of the road if it is groomed, and if not groomed, avoid any well-laid ski tracks whenever possible.

At 1.5 miles, the road rounds a sharp, switchbacking turn to the right (Route 62 to Twin Lakes continues straight ahead). Continue up the road and soon it swings back to the west, now climbing a bit more steeply, gaining 800 feet in the next 1.5 miles. The route cuts across the southern flank of Mount Catherine to reach Windy Pass (3800 feet) at 3 miles. Windy Pass provides wonderful views west into the South Fork Snoqualmie River valley (home to I-90) and across to Granite Mountain. To the south, Silver Peak looms tall, while to the northeast Mount Catherine awaits.

Snowshoe hare tracks along the ridge at Windy Pass

Turn around here, or if you want to push on for an extended outing, veer north from Windy Gap to climb north about 1.5 miles along the timbered slope of Mount Catherine, weaving upward to the summit of the forested peak.

64 Keechelus Lake & John Wayne Trail

Rating: Easiest
Round trip: 4 miles
Hiking time: 3 hours
Elevation gain: 200 feet
High point: 2700 feet
Best season: December through late February
Map: Green Trails: Snoqualmie Pass No. 207
Who to contact: Okanogan–Wenatchee National Forest,
    Cle Elum Ranger District
Permits/fees: Washington State Sno-Park Pass required.
    You may also need a Washington State Discover Pass;
    check www.parks.wa.gov/130/Winter-Recreation.

Well, pardner, if you're looking for a gentle but rustic outing, John Wayne can help you out. The old railroad right-of-way that runs across the state is known as the John Wayne State Park, while the actual physical trail (the old railbed) is the Iron Horse Trail. But whether you call it the John Wayne Trail, the Iron Horse Trail, or the Keechelus Lake Trail, you'll find the flat, well-graded trail is perfect for kids of all ages.

Directions: From Seattle drive east on Interstate 90 over Snoqualmie Pass to exit 54, signed Hyak. Turn left and drive about 1.5 miles south on Forest Road 2219 to the Hyak Sno-Park.

Route: Climbing slightly west from the trailhead to get on the trail, turn left (southeast) and stroll along the trail as it hugs the slope above the waters

Dogs are banned from this section of the Iron Horse Trail along Keechelus Lake.

of Keechelus Lake. The trail (like the old train route before it) pushes east to Idaho, but there's no need to think so far out. The trail is often groomed, and when it is, snowshoers should stick to the outside edges of the path—don't tread on established ski tracks if it can be avoided.

From the trail, you can look across the lake at the rushing traffic on I-90, and above that ribbon of frenetic activity, you'll see the jagged crown of Rampart Ridge and the high summit of Mount Margaret at the northern end of Keechelus Ridge.

At about 2 miles from the trailhead, you'll find the base of some steep avalanche chutes. Until the late 1990s, huge old wooden structures covered the route here. They were snow sheds—basically, roofs over the railroad tracks to divert avalanche snows from covering the train route. This is a great place to turn around—move much farther east and you risk running out of snow as the trail continues to drop in elevation.

65 Kachess Campground Loops

Rating: Easiest
Round trip: 5 miles
Hiking time: 3 hours
Elevation gain: 400 feet
High point: 2550 feet
Best season: December through late February
Map: Green Trails: Snoqualmie Pass No. 207
Who to contact: Okanogan–Wenatchee National Forest, Cle Elum Ranger District
Permits/fees: Washington State Sno-Park Pass required. You may also need a Washington State Discover Pass; check www.parks.wa.gov/130/Winter-Recreation.

This flat route offers a chance to explore the snow-laden lakeshore without excessive effort. You might share part of the route with snowmobiles, but you can get away from them by dropping off the roadway and walking the lakeshore itself, and once in the campground you have a plethora of routes to explore and enjoy.

Directions: From Seattle take Interstate 90 east to exit 62, signed Kachess Lake. Turn left from the exit ramp and drive northeast on Kachess Lake Road (Forest Road 49) to the Kachess Sno-Park at the end of the county road, about 4 miles from I-90.

Flocked trees along the slope above Kachess Lake

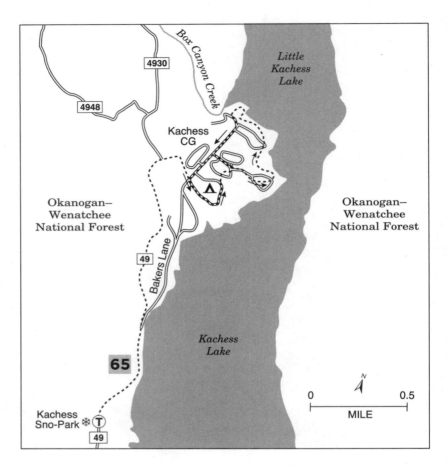

Route: From the Sno-Park, head north along the Kachess Lake Road as it follows the western shoreline of Kachess Lake. For the first mile, the road runs very near the lake and snowshoers can find plenty of opportunities to cut through the trees to drop to the lakeshore. When the lake levels are low, you can wander along the shoreline rather than following the road. Sticking to the road, though, puts you at the entrance to the campground in just 2 miles with ample views to enjoy along the way of the lake and the surrounding peaks.

At about the 2-mile mark, turn right onto the campground road and descend into the campground. The best adventures are found on the northern campground loop as it swings up near the mouth of Box Canyon Creek. Ramble through the camps and shorelines, enjoying the sights—deer are frequently seen here as are an array of birds—before heading back down the road to the trailhead.

66 Hibox Approach

Rating: More difficult
Round trip: 12 miles
Hiking time: 8 hours
Elevation gain: 600 feet
High point: 2750 feet
Best season: December through late February
Map: Green Trails: Snoqualmie Pass No. 207
Who to contact: Okanogan–Wenatchee National Forest,
   Cle Elum Ranger District
Permits/fees: Washington State Sno-Park Pass required.
   You may also need a Washington State Discover Pass;
   check www.parks.wa.gov/130/Winter-Recreation.

The Rachel Lake Trail is one of the most popular summer hiking routes in the eastern Cascades, but come winter, it's the road to the trailhead rather than the hiking trail itself that offers grand adventures. This route follows the Forest Service road that endures tens of thousands of automobile trips each summer, but a blanket of snow creates an incredible transformation. Snowshoers will share the route with a few snowmobilers, but more often than not, the route is quiet, serene, and highly scenic.

Directions: From Seattle take Interstate 90 east to exit 62, signed Kachess Lake. Turn left from the exit ramp and drive northeast on Kachess Lake Road (Forest Road 49) to the Kachess Sno-Park at the end of the county road, about 4 miles from I-90.

Route: Leave the trailhead and hike north along Kachess Lake Road (FR 49) to its junction with the Kachess Campground access road. While Route 65, Kachess Campground Loops, turns right into the campground, this route goes left, onto FR 4930, and climbs away from Little Kachess Lake into the lower reaches of Box Canyon. As you climb along this road, views to the northwest open up and soon you'll be enjoying the sight of Hibox Mountain looming large above you.

*A snowshoer taking a break
on the road below Hibox*

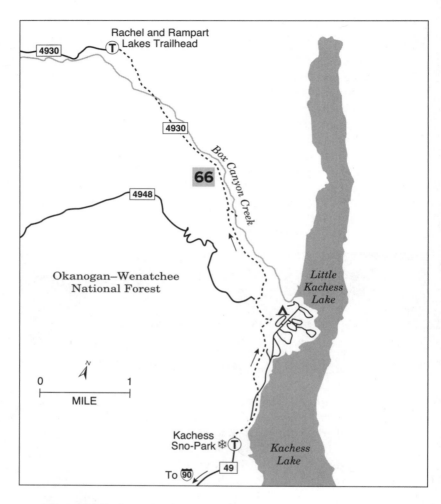

The road rolls through a few switchbacks after leaving the lakeside but soon levels out into a long, rolling ascent of Box Canyon. Frequently the creek can be seen (and heard) to your left. You can explore along the creek as you like, and around the 4-mile mark you'll find some nice openings that offer good views of both the creek and the ridgelines above. Stop here for a rest (or a turnaround for a shorter outing). Continuing on leads to the summer trailhead for Rachel and Rampart Lakes at 6 miles out from the Sno-Park. This is the ideal turn-around point for a long leg-stretcher of a snowshoe adventure.

Opposite: Daytime snowmelt creates new ice sculptures each night as the runoff refreezes.

EAST & CENTRAL CASCADES

67 Hex Mountain

Rating: More difficult
Round trip: 7 miles
Hiking time: 6 hours
Elevation gain: 2600 feet
High point: 5034 feet
Best season: Late December through March
Map: Green Trails: Kachess Lake No. 208
Who to contact: Okanogan–Wenatchee National Forest,
       Cle Elum Ranger District
Permits/fees: No parking pass required

This trail represents the epitome of snowshoeing in the Cascades: a long, steady, often-steep climb through lush old forests ending at a high ridge with panoramic views of unmatched beauty. After soaking in the scenic splendor at the summit, snowshoers then reverse direction and follow their tracks back down the slope.

Directions: From Seattle drive east on Interstate 90 over Snoqualmie Pass to exit 80, signed Roslyn. Turn north onto the Bullfrog Cutoff Road, and drive to its end at a junction with State Route 903. Turn left and continue north 9 miles, passing through the towns of Roslyn and Ronald, to reach the junction of Forest Road 116 on the right. If a turnout is plowed out here, park in it; otherwise, go back down SR 903 about 300 feet to a plowed area on the west side of the highway near where it crosses Newport Creek.

Route: What sets this trail apart from others is that the slopes are well forested and sheltered, so avalanche hazards are minimal and snowshoeing, though steep at times, is relatively easy. Starting from Salmon la Sac Road (SR

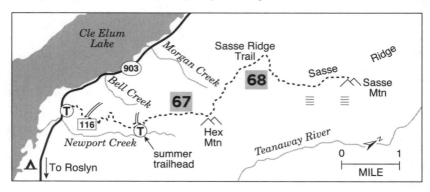

Approaching the top of Hex Mountain

903), the snowshoe hike begins with a climb on an old, winding logging road through mixed forest and small clearcuts. Some nice views are found on the way up the trail, but the best are left until snowshoers top the ridge and turn around to see the breathtaking vistas to the west. Cle Elum Lake sprawls directly underfoot, and just beyond that is Mount Baldy, Thomas Mountain, West Peak, and Thorp Mountain along the crest of Kachess Ridge.

If you park at Newport Creek, walk up the highway to FR 116 before strapping on your snowshoes and starting the climb. FR 116 leads northeast, always climbing, past several spur roads and side trails. Most of these are easily discernible as secondary roads, but at times the forks and junctions can be confusing. Unfortunately, trying to map all the junctions and byways is difficult, so you will have to use your best judgment and occasionally backtrack if you make a wrong turn. (Fortunately, the side roads are generally short, so you'll quickly realize your errors. For example, if the road dips or heads too far off the northeast bearing that is required, it's the wrong road.)

After the first mile of the road, the options decrease and the main road is the only one to follow until, at 1.2 miles, the road traverses above a small creek valley and, at 1.7 miles, ends at the summer trailhead parking area. Here is where the fun really begins. Snowshoeing up the narrow forest trail as it climbs the ridge crest toward Hex Mountain is a wonderful experience. With snowshoes you can easily climb, weave around trees, and generally enjoy the day as you soak in the beauty of the forest environment. This area is home to red foxes and an assortment of birds and small animals. Of course, whiskey jacks pester every human who enters the forest, thus living up to their alias, camp-robber jays, and great horned owls silently patrol the woods in search of mice, voles, martens, and hares.

The trail climbs for more than 1.5 miles, with only occasional glimpses of the world beyond the trees. At 3.3 miles from the start of the hike, the trail tops out on the south end of Sasse Ridge, just below the summit of Hex Mountain (Route 68, Sasse Ridge, continues along Sasse Ridge). Turn right onto the Sasse Ridge Trail, and hike 0.25 mile to the summit for striking views of the eastern Cascades.

68 Sasse Ridge

Rating: Backcountry
Round trip: 15 miles
Hiking time: 2 days
Elevation gain: 2700 feet
High point: 5400 feet
Best season: Late December through March
Map: Green Trails: Kachess Lake No. 208
Who to contact: Okanogan–Wenatchee National Forest,
    Cle Elum Ranger District
Permits/fees: No parking pass required

After a modest climb to the ridge crest, this route lets snowshoers stay high and enjoy an endless bounty of beautiful views and remarkable scenery. The trail rolls south to north and opens up on views of the Alpine Lakes Wilderness peaks, Cle Elum Lake, and the entire eastern Cascade Mountains.

Directions: From Seattle drive east on Interstate 90 over Snoqualmie Pass to exit 80, signed Roslyn. Turn north onto the Bullfrog Cutoff Road, and drive to its end at a junction with State Route 903. Turn left and continue north 9 miles, passing through the towns of Roslyn and Ronald, to reach the junction of Forest Road 116 on the right. If a turnout is plowed out here, park in it; otherwise, go back down SR 903 about 300 yards to a plowed area on the west side of the highway near where it crosses Newport Creek.

Route: Few folks visit the north end of this trail in winter, so those snowshoers who do venture out along the route will find it empty of human company. Still, they won't be alone. A host of wintering animals thrive here, including a few who perform chameleon acts by changing into snowy white coats each winter. Snowshoe hares, ptarmigans, and weasels are seen as flashes of white against the white snow only when they move. But even their winter

Traversing the slope heading up Sasse Ridge

camouflage can't save them from the predators who prowl this area. Coyotes, bobcats, cougars, red-tailed hawks, golden eagles, falcons, and great horned owls all compete for the few small animals that scamper about the snowy forests and meadows of Sasse Ridge.

Start up FR 116 as described in Route 67, Hex Mountain. At the top of the trail, at 3.3 miles, instead of turning right for a short scramble to the summit of Hex, turn left onto the Sasse Ridge Trail and start the long, scenic snowshoe north. The trail follows the crest of the ridge for more than 7 miles, but you can find plenty of fine, protected campsites all along the route, so tailor the length of the snowshoe trek to your own preferences.

From the 4900-foot junction with the Hex Mountain Trail, the Sasse Ridge Trail heads north, dropping gradually through thin forests in the first mile before climbing once more until, at 5.3 miles, the trail rolls under the crown of a high, unnamed peak (5159 feet). The trail then banks right, drops slightly into a high saddle, and climbs again to 5400 feet at 5.8 miles. Wind exposure and potential avalanche dangers are possible on this stretch of the trail. If conditions are unstable, head back and make camp in the first sheltered site, either near the saddle or on the south side of the unnamed peak.

The trail curves north again at 5.9 miles and at 7.5 miles passes just under the summit of Sasse Mountain. The scramble to the summit is easy because the peak is open and round. Enjoy unmatched views from the top of Sasse, and either find a suitable campsite in the thin forests on the mountain's protected southern flank or head back down the trail to find a sheltered camp.

North of Sasse Mountain, the trail crosses a steep, open ridge section that is a dangerous avalanche area. The windswept ridge is seldom stable or secure, so only highly experienced winter mountaineers should even consider going farther, and they should do so only when avalanche dangers are low.

69 Salmon la Sac Creek

Rating: Most difficult
Round trip: 6.4 miles
Hiking time: 5 hours
Elevation gain: 1300 feet
High point: 4700 feet
Best season: Late December through March
Map: Green Trails: Kachess Lake No. 208
Who to contact: Okanogan–Wenatchee National Forest,
    Cle Elum Ranger District
Permits/fees: Washington State Sno-Park Pass required.
    You may also need a Washington State Discover Pass;
    check www.parks.wa.gov/130/Winter-Recreation.

A number of good trails lead out of the Salmon la Sac area, but this is one of the few that is almost completely ignored by snowmobilers and skiers, leaving it for snowshoers to explore in quiet solitude. The trail rolls east, climbing gradually through pretty ponderosa pine and larch forest.

Directions: From Seattle drive east on Interstate 90 over Snoqualmie Pass to exit 80, signed Roslyn. Turn north onto the Bullfrog Cutoff Road, and drive to its end at a junction with State Route 903. Turn left, and continue north a little more than 17 miles, passing through the towns of Roslyn and Ronald, to the end of the plowed road at the Salmon la Sac Picnic Area and Sno-Park.

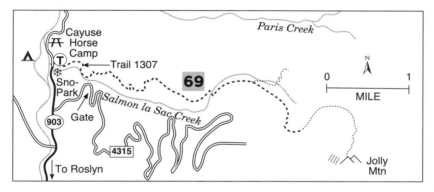

Route: Forest shelters this trail for most of its length, but there are enough openings in the canopy to provide some nice views of the Cle Elum River basin and the mountains beyond. Between those panoramic peeks, the sparkling little creek and snow-swaddled forest offer all the scenic diversion any snowshoer could want.

The trail leaves the Salmon la Sac area from behind the Cayuse Horse Camp facilities. Follow the signs for Trail 1307. The path weaves through the trees, climbing gradually for the first 0.5 mile before finally traversing south to the Salmon la Sac Creek basin. The creek is a tiny rivulet that sparkles and splashes along its ice-laden banks, providing a pretty picture for winter recreationists.

The trail becomes steep, and for the next mile it climbs ruthlessly through a long series of switchbacks, staying high above the creek. At 1.6 miles, the trail levels somewhat and begins a long, climbing traverse into the creek basin, crossing the creek at 2.7 miles (4300 feet) and following it another 0.5 mile to a trail junction at 4700 feet. This is a good turnaround point. If you have plenty of energy and daylight left, follow the right fork for another mile to a bench below the summit of Jolly Mountain.

A snowshoe hare den in the forest

This trail climbs steeply toward its end, but a few avalanche chutes should keep you away any time the avalanche danger is moderate or higher. The left fork at the junction is steep and slide-prone much of the time, so avoid it at all times.

70 Cooper River

Rating: More difficult
Round trip: 8 miles
Hiking time: 6 hours
Elevation gain: 400 feet
High point: 2900 feet
Best season: Late December through March
Map: Green Trails: Kachess Lake No. 208
Who to contact: Okanogan–Wenatchee National Forest,
    Cle Elum Ranger District
Permits/fees: Washington State Sno-Park Pass required.
    You may also need a Washington State Discover Pass;
    check www.parks.wa.gov/130/Winter-Recreation.

Thank goodness the Salmon la Sac area has plenty of roads, because they keep the snowmobilers off quiet trails like this one that parallels Cooper River upstream to Cooper Lake. Cross-country skiers occasionally use this trail, but more often than not, snowshoers will find they have the wide, pretty trail all to themselves.

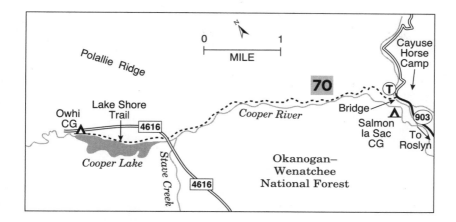

Directions: From Seattle drive east on Interstate 90 over Snoqualmie Pass to exit 80, signed Roslyn. Turn north onto the Bullfrog Cutoff Road, and drive to its end at a junction with State Route 903. Turn left and continue north a little more than 17 miles, passing through the towns of Roslyn and Ronald, to the end of the plowed road at the Salmon la Sac Picnic Area and Sno-Park.

Route: The trail is relatively flat, and finding the route is not difficult, even in heavy snow years, because the trail corridor is wide and nearly straight. Snowshoers can enjoy their surroundings here as they stroll up the path, gazing in wonder at the beautiful snow-shrouded landscape. The forest is a mixed bag of old pine and fir, so it is generally open and light. Sun streaks in through the thin canopy to keep the valley bright and sunny. Deer are frequently seen in this valley, even in winter, and many small birds and animals can be seen along the trail as well. Kids and adults alike will enjoy studying and trying to identify the many animal tracks left in the snow beside the trail and along the riverbanks.

Snowshoe up the road past the ranger station, and cross the river toward the Salmon la Sac Campground. The trail is well signed and easy to find. Stay right, and snowshoe up a small service road. The trailhead is located on this road, about 200 feet past the gated entrance to the campground. The trail stays alongside, but not too near, the Cooper River for its entire length. If you have difficulty finding the trail—especially in the first 0.5 mile—just head northwest, keeping the river off to your left, but no more than 50 or 60 yards away.

The first 0.5 mile is in fairly open, airy forest, so the snow piles deep and obscures landmarks and trail tread. Beyond this section, the route is easy to find. The wide corridor skirts the bottom edge of the Polallie Ridge wall where it meets the Cooper River valley bottom. The views, while not amazing, are quite picturesque. In addition to the scenic river views, you can catch occasional glimpses up the valley of Polallie Ridge on the right and Chikamin Ridge straight ahead.

Crystal structures dangling above the Cooper River

The valley narrows considerably after the first 0.5 mile, and at 1 mile, the trail is squeezed tight into a narrow gorge. The river quickens, and the trail climbs until, at 2 miles, it levels out and the valley opens up again. The walls stay close, but not nearly as confining as the section just passed. The last 1.5 miles of trail ramble gently and serenely to a junction with Forest Road 4616 along the banks of Cooper Lake. To see the lake, and enjoy a lunch spot with pretty views of the lake and the high ridges around it, turn right onto the road and hike up a few yards to catch the Lake Shore Trail on the left. Drop down along this trail, and skirt the lake to any one of a dozen good viewpoints and picnic areas. Owhi Campground is just 0.5 mile up the lakeshore if a larger lunch spot is needed.

71 Indian Creek

Rating: Easiest to more difficult
Round trip: Up to 14 miles
Hiking time: 2 to 10 hours
Elevation gain: 1300 feet
High point: 3600 feet
Best season: Late December through March
Map: Green Trails: Mount Stuart No. 209
Who to contact: Okanogan–Wenatchee National Forest,
  Cle Elum Ranger District
Permits/fees: Washington State Sno-Park Pass required.
  You may also need a Washington State Discover Pass;
  check www.parks.wa.gov/130/Winter-Recreation.

Many individual mountains in Washington are extremely beautiful, but no range of peaks is more spectacular than the long, jagged line of the Stuart Range. Along this route, snowshoers will amble up the wide Teanaway Valley and gaze in awe at the impressive summits. The pretty Wenatchee Mountains, a lower, less spectacular range, provide a picturesque foreground for the more massive Stuarts.

Directions: From Seattle drive east on Interstate 90 over Snoqualmie Pass to exit 85 and turn north onto State Route 970. Drive 5 miles before turning left (northwest) onto Teanaway Road (Forest Road 9737). About 7 miles up the valley, when the road (and river) splits, stay right on the North Fork Teanaway Road and continue 2 miles to the end of the plowed road at the wide Lick Creek Sno-Park.

Route: Because of the wonderful views, not to mention the beautiful forest and river environments of the Teanaway Valley itself, this area gets a lot of winter visitors. Snowshoers will find the road well-traveled by skiers and snowmobilers, as well as other snowshoers. The route described here lets snowshoers enjoy the views, while tolerating the crowds, before climbing a side valley that is much quieter and less visited. Indian Creek Road climbs the deep basin of the creek, but the road ends before the valley does. That, and the fact that the Stuart Range isn't visible from the valley, keeps most snowmobilers out of the basin, and skiers prefer the more scenic valleys farther up the Teanaway. Snowshoers might consider these other routes, too, but since skiers can travel faster on the flat Teanaway Road, they beat the 'shoers to the viewpoints. So Indian Creek valley is the snowshoers' best bet for a Teanaway trek.

Snowshoers along Indian Creek

Start up North Fork Teanaway Road as it curves northeast alongside the pretty Teanaway River. Stop to enjoy the meadows along the river bottom by stepping off the road now and again and ambling out across the open snow for close-up looks at the river. Or head off into the stands of trees that separate the many meadows, keeping a close eye out for small birds and animals that thrive in these protected woods.

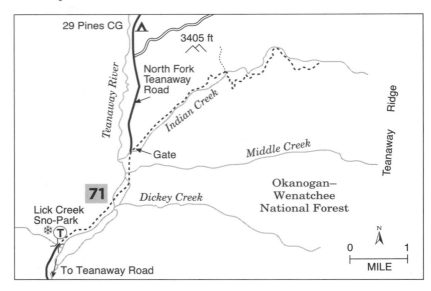

The valley slowly hooks north, gradually revealing more and more of the snowcapped rocks of the high Stuart Range. The road crosses the river at about 1.5 miles, and at about the 2-mile mark, the road and the valley it climbs in are pointed due north. This is where Mount Stuart bursts onto the horizon. The western end of the staggeringly beautiful Stuart Range is anchored by this mountain—a high, near-vertical wall of rock and ice. In front of the great range lies the lesser but also beautiful Wenatchee Mountains. The peaks along this front are less dramatic—no vertical walls of granite here—but they are high enough, and craggy enough, to provide an outstanding foreground to the towering Stuarts in the background. Together, the two ranges create a perfect picture, so make sure to bring along a smartphone or camera.

At 3 miles, just after crossing Indian Creek, find Indian Creek Road angling off to the right. A gate across the bottom of the road—and the fact that the road dead-ends in a few miles—keeps snowmobilers out. Stay right and hike up the little-used road, crossing meadows, clearcuts, and deep forests for up to 4 more miles before turning back. A half mile up the valley, all views of the Stuarts are cut off, but Indian Creek is a pretty little stream, and the snowbound valley is a fun playground. Enjoy this route for its own sake rather than for rewards at its end, because on this route the rewards are found as you go.

72 Swauk Forest Discovery Trail

Rating: Easiest
Round trip: 2 to 5 miles
Hiking time: 2 to 5 hours
Elevation gain: 450 feet
High point: 4552 feet
Best season: December through late March
Map: Green Trails: Liberty No. 210
Who to contact: Okanogan–Wenatchee National Forest, Cle Elum Ranger District
Permits/fees: Washington State Sno-Park Pass required. You may also need a Washington State Discover Pass; check www.parks.wa.gov/130/Winter-Recreation.

The Blewett Pass area may be one of the finest snow recreation spots in the state, with trails set aside for motorized and nonmotorized recreation. The Sno-Parks are used by all, but snowshoers and skiers can find quiet solitude even in this popular winter playground. What's more, you can find richly rewarding routes to explore whether you have just a few hours to roam or a few days.

Exploring Swauk Meadow

Directions: From Seattle, drive east on Interstate 90 to Cle Elum. Take the second (eastern-most) exit, and continue northeast on State Route 970 about 12 miles to a junction with US Highway 97. Continue north on US 97 (following signs to Wenatchee). At the crest of Blewett Pass, about 27 miles from I-90, turn right (south) into the Blewett Pass Sno-Park.

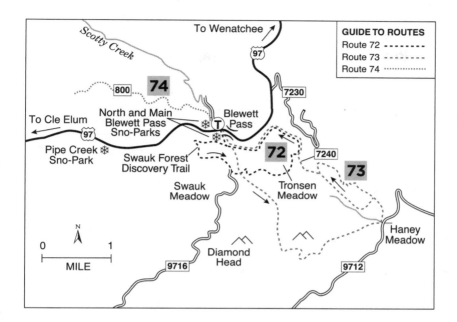

Route: The Swauk Forest Discovery Trail—popular in summer as a won-derful place to learn a little about our woodland ecosystems—provides a great easy day outing for snowshoers. The actual summer trail meanders for about 2 miles through the woods and meadows near the Blewett Pass summit, but snowshoers can take advantage of the heavy cushion of snow to cut corners and shorten the route or push beyond the trail's limits and extend their travels out into the adjacent Tronsen Meadow. Whether you slog a mile or 5 miles through the snow you'll find great winter wonderlands opening at your feet. A huge colony of snowshoe hares reside here, and where there are hares, there are also foxes, coyotes, and bobcats. Keep your eyes open for the cautious crit-ters—if you don't see the beasts themselves, you're sure to spot their tracks.

Strap on your snowshoes and start up the well-traveled snow track on the south side of the parking lot (this frequently groomed road is used by snow-mobilers, skiers, and snowshoers). A short way up the road, veer right along a break in the trees and leave the groomed track behind. You'll climb gently now, heading almost due west away through the forest, picking a path of least resistance. If you stay on a nearly level contour along the slope—or better yet, maintain a slightly ascending route—in less than 0.5 mile from the groomed track you'll find yourself veering south once more as the hillside banks that way. Keep climbing, and you'll top a small knoll at 4552 feet. Modest views are found from this little hillock, including peeks south to the rocky monolith of Diamond Head.

Bear left now, heading east and in 0.5 mile or so you'll encounter the groomed road once more. Turn left on the road and descend (northbound). If you want to keep your outing short (2 miles), just trek on back to the trailhead along the road. If you want to push on a little farther, leave the road within a few hundred yards. Simply look for an opening on the right that looks promising and step off into the untracked snow. Heading east now, you'll find yourself slanting through stands of trees interspersed with broad meadows. Skiers and snowshoers frequent these meadows—the upper reaches of the Tronsen Meadow area—but snowmobiles are prohibited from leaving the main road routes.

Moving north, downhill, you'll penetrate deeper into the interconnected series of meadows, while traversing east will extend your trip and keep you up in the trees a little longer. While exploring the forested sections of the route, stay quiet and move slowly and you might see wildlife. At the very least, you'll likely see the endless tracks of snowshoe hares left as they scurry in search of forage in these snowy timberlands.

When tired or out of time, cut northwest and you'll close your loop. If you head too much to the north, you'll come out on US 97—no problem, just head back up the hill a little ways, and then turn and parallel the highway back to the trailhead.

73 Haney Meadow Loop

Rating: More difficult
Round trip: 7 to 12 miles
Hiking time: 8 hours to 2 days
Elevation gain: 1600 feet
High point: 5700 feet
Best season: December through late March
Map: Green Trails: Liberty No. 210
Who to contact: Okanogan–Wenatchee National Forest, Cle Elum Ranger District
Permits/fees: Washington State Sno-Park Pass required. You may also need a Washington State Discover Pass; check www.parks.wa.gov/130/Winter-Recreation.

When you want solitude and serenity without a lot of uphill effort, the Haney Meadow Loop is a great option. The route doesn't soar up onto high, windswept viewpoints, but it does roll through a plethora of open meadows, dark forests, and a few low ridges that sport modest views. What's more, you'll find a great diversity of plants and animals to examine and enjoy along the way, and you'll likely have all or part of the route to yourself.

Forest below Haney Meadow

Directions: From Seattle, drive east on Interstate 90 to Cle Elum. Take the second (eastern-most) exit, and continue northeast on State Route 970 about 12 miles to a junction with US Highway 97. Continue north on US 97 (following signs to Wenatchee). At the crest of Blewett Pass, about 27 miles from I-90, turn right (south) into the Blewett Pass Sno-Park.

Route: Walk up Forest Road 9716 as it leads south into the trees and about 0.25 mile out, climb left off the road to find a poorly marked but generally well-traveled trail paralleling the road for the next mile. At the 4400-foot level, veer left and angle southeast, climbing across the northern flank of Diamond Head to catch another poorly marked (look for white or orange reflective blazes nailed onto trees) skier trail at 4800 feet. If you miss the trail, just keep angling upward as you slide around to the east flank of Diamond, being sure to stay well up on the wall above the creek that runs in a broad valley on the east side of the peak.

At about 2 miles, you'll emerge on the crest of a low saddle (5500 feet) between Diamond Head and an unnamed peak to the east. Here, turn east and skirt the unnamed hillock on its southern flank. As you move east, you'll slowly gain elevation, climbing a whopping 200 feet in the next mile before descending just as slowly back to 5500 feet at the edge of Haney Meadow. FR 9712 passes the meadow and snowmobilers occasionally venture out along this road (but not too often, since it's a dead end for them).

You can find wonderful campsites around the broad meadow. Rolling drifts create a pillowy texture on the expansive field of snow, and watching the golden rays of twilight dance on the shimmering white hills is a great way to end a day.

Whether you camp or not, when you leave the meadow you'll turn northwest and descend along the walls of a small creek valley. You can choose your own path, east or west. A summer hiking trail drops along the eastern wall, but the western side is less steep. In just over a mile, you'll find FR 7240 on the upper edge of Tronsen Meadow. Stick to a course that moves northwest along the edge of the hillside meadows before turning and angling west, parallel to US 97, to close the loop at the Sno-Park.

74 Wenatchee Crest

Rating: Easiest
Round trip: 6 miles
Hiking time: 5 hours
Elevation gain: 400 feet
High point: 4500 feet
Best season: December through late March
Map: Green Trails: Liberty No. 210
Who to contact: Okanogan–Wenatchee National Forest,
    Cle Elum Ranger District

Permits/fees: Washington State Sno-Park Pass required. You may also need a Washington State Discover Pass; check www.parks.wa.gov/130/Winter-Recreation.

If you don't mind company but prefer to have an easy-to-follow, modestly graded route to explore, this is it. It's perfect for families or for first-timers who just want to get a feel for their new snowshoes. The trail sticks to an old dirt road—groomed on a semi-regular basis—that follows the crest of the Wenatchee Mountains from Blewett Pass Sno-Park to a point directly above the Pipe Creek Sno-Park.

Directions: From Seattle, drive east on Interstate 90 to Cle Elum. Take the second (eastern-most) exit, and continue northeast on State Route 970 about 12 miles to a junction with US Highway 97. Continue north on US 97 (following signs to Wenatchee). At the crest of Blewett Pass, about 27 miles from I-90, turn left (north) into the North Blewett Pass Sno-Park. If this small parking area is full, cross the highway to the main Blewett Pass Sno-Park.

View from Wenatchee Crest

Route: From the trailhead, find the start of Forest Road 800 on the north end of the parking lot and start walking. The trail sticks to this road for the next 3 miles to the road end. The road rolls up and down modestly, providing plenty of opportunity for novices to practice different snowshoeing techniques and build their skills. About 0.5 mile out, the road splits. Stay left (west) to follow the ridgeline. The right-hand road drops steeply into Scotty Creek basin. This is another area you can explore, but remember that every foot you drop down has to be regained in the long slog back up.

FR 800 hugs the crest of the ridge separating Scotty Creek basin from the Swauk Creek basin (home to US 97). You'll encounter occasional clearings with stellar views north and south. Looking north, you'll see Tronsen Ridge stretch before you, while to the south Diamond Head and Table Mountain rise above Blewett Pass.

The road ends at an open clearing about 3 miles from the trailhead. Enjoy the views here while having a picnic lunch, and then return the way you came to close out the day.

Opposite: Peering south from Panorama Point toward Mount Adams

MOUNT RAINIER
& SR 410

75 Sun Top

Rating: More difficult
Round trip: 10 miles
Hiking time: 7.5 hours
Elevation gain: 3000 feet
High point: 5280 feet
Best season: Early January through late February
Map: Green Trails: Greenwater No. 238
Who to contact: Mount Baker–Snoqualmie National Forest,
    Snoqualmie Ranger District, Enumclaw Office
Permits/fees: Washington State Sno-Park Pass required.
    You may also need a Washington State Discover Pass;
    check www.parks.wa.gov/130/Winter-Recreation.

The route to the top of Sun Top is often groomed for cross-country skiers, but snowshoers will still enjoy this trek. After all, the views are just as spectacular, and the winter landscape just as pretty, even when the trail has been leveled for skiers. Just stick to the edges of the road to avoid tromping on skiers' tracks, and take advantage of any opportunity to climb off the road and cross open meadows for maximum snowshoeing fun.

Directions: From Enumclaw drive east on State Route 410 for 24 miles and turn right (south) onto Forest Road 73 (Huckleberry Creek Road). Drive south 1.5 miles to the Sun Top Sno-Park.

Route: Attaining the summit of Sun Top requires considerable energy, but the workout is well rewarded with unmatched views of the country northwest of Mount Rainier. The White River valley stretches below the mountain, and Mount Rainier towers above. The lower section of the route is sometimes visited by the White River elk herd, so keep an eye out for the big beasts. This is also prime cougar country (due, in large part, to the presence of the elk). Seeing one

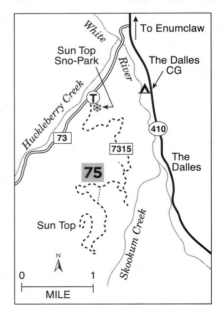

of the big cats is a pleasure. Cougars pose little threat to adult humans, although kids shouldn't be allowed to run ahead. The odds of seeing a mountain lion are extremely low, but a couple of lucky snowshoers have excitedly reported seeing the tawny cats streaking away from the road when the elk are nearby.

The route to the summit follows FR 7315. Snowshoe up the only road leaving the Sno-Park, pass the gate, and in a couple hundred feet, turn left up FR 7315. The road climbs steadily to the summit, and because of the frequent clearcuts encountered along the hike there are ample opportunities to stop, rest, and savor the scenery spread out before you. As the trail climbs the ridgeline, look down into the wide White River valley and the narrower, darker Huckleberry Creek basin. The best place to find elk is along the lower clearcuts, although from the higher clearcuts it's possible to look down into the open meadows along the rivers. Using a good pair of binoculars, scan the river meadows for the large herds that live in the White River drainage.

Hoar frost coats brush at the summit of Sun Top.

A few spur roads are found along the way, and these make nice diversions from the well-traveled main road. Snowshoe out along them for a new view, and then angle up through the trees and meadows to rejoin the main trail. By climbing straight through the larger clearcuts rather than following the looping road, you can save nearly a mile and enjoy some untracked snow.

Following the road all the way, it is 5 miles to a high bench below the summit of Sun Top. The summit approach requires crossing some serious avalanche slopes, so attempt the top only when conditions are stable and avalanche dangers are reported as low. For the best views south to Rainier, angle southwest around the bench about 400 yards to an open view of Mount Rainier and all the lesser peaks between.

76 Bullion Basin

Rating: Backcountry
Round trip: 4.5 miles
Hiking time: 4 hours
Elevation gain: 1500 feet
High point: 5800 feet
Best season: Early December through early March
Map: Green Trails: Bumping Lake No. 271
Who to contact: Mount Baker–Snoqualmie National Forest,
   Snoqualmie Ranger District, Enumclaw Office
Permits/fees: No parking pass required

This trail has high, subalpine meadows blanketed in deep snow, wonderful views of the surrounding craggy peaks, and an array of destination options to assure solitude for those who want it. The trail climbs steeply, and there are some serious avalanche slopes around the area, so snowshoers here need to be ready for a workout and must know how to recognize and avoid avalanche dangers. But when the conditions are stable, this is a wonderful winter world to explore and experience.

Directions: From Enumclaw drive east on State Route 410 to the end of the plowed highway and turn left onto Crystal Mountain Road (Forest Road 7190). Continue up this winding road to the Crystal Mountain Ski Area. Park in the upper parking lot if space is available. The ski area asks that backcountry travelers sign in with the ski patrol so they can account for any cars left in the lot after the lifts close down.

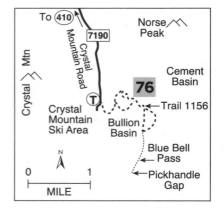

Route: Snowshoers flock to this trail on winter weekends, but there is something unusual about a lot of the snowshoers here. Many of them have long planks strapped to their backs as they ascend the steep trail. These are cross-over 'shoers. They use their shoes to get them to the top of steep, deep slopes and then trade their snowshoes for snowboards and swoosh down the smooth slopes. Even nonboarding snowshoers will appreciate the artistry these backcountry snowboarders exhibit on their downhill runs.

Looking into the Crystal Mountain basin

The route follows Trail 1156 east toward Blue Bell Pass. The trailhead is found to the east (left, as you face the ski slopes) side of the ski area parking lot behind the condominiums and buildings on the hillside. From the upper end of the parking lot, angle left up the steep slope, skirting the beginners' ski slope at the base of the valley wall. Snowshoeing along the tree line, find an old roadway and more skier cabins. A small ski lift on the right ends near the road—stay well to the left of it to the first switchback on the narrow road. The trail sign should be visible at this switchback in all but the heaviest snow years.

Trail 1156 climbs left along a traverse across the slope to 5000 feet, and then switches back a few times before settling in for a long climb up the small Bullion Creek draw. If the trail is drifted over and difficult to find, simply pick a route along the north side of the creek and, in just over 1.5 miles, traverse right to cross the creek (near 5600 feet). Hike through a thin stand of forest, climbing straight up the slope above to reach the open meadows of Bullion Basin at 5800 feet.

Plenty of variations are available on the approach route, but generally, evaluate the slopes and find a path as near to the actual route of the summer hiking trail as possible while steering clear of the steep slide-prone slopes. A lot of open country is found along the way, so views are spectacular all the way up. From Bullion Basin enjoy views of the ski area as well as of the snowboarders playing nearby. If you are the adventurous sort, choose to scramble another mile (gaining some 600 feet) up steep slopes to the ridge crest at Blue Bell Pass. However, Bullion Basin is so pretty and scenic, there is really no need to go any higher in your explorations. Scramble around the basin to find a nice, quiet picnic spot, enjoy a leisurely meal, and then head back down.

77 | White River

Rating: Easiest
Round trip: 2 to 4 miles
Hiking time: 3 hours
Elevation gain: 400 feet
High point: 3200 feet
Best season: Early December through February
Map: Green Trails: Bumping Lake No. 271
Who to contact: Mount Baker–Snoqualmie National Forest, Snoqualmie Ranger District, Enumclaw Office
Permits/fees: Washington State Sno-Park Pass required. You may also need a Washington State Discover Pass; check www.parks.wa.gov/130/Winter-Recreation.

Bring the kids, even if the kids are too young to snowshoe themselves. On this easy route, you can pull them in a sled or carry them on your shoulders. This is a route perfect for novices who want to practice walking on snowshoes for the first time, or for anyone seeking a gentle, relaxing day in the snow without a lot of exertion or fuss.

Directions: From Enumclaw drive east on State Route 410 to the end of the plowed highway and turn left onto Crystal Mountain Road (Forest Road 7190). Immediately (about 20 yards) after turning onto Crystal Mountain Road, turn right into the Silver Springs Sno-Park. If the Sno-Park has not been plowed, turn around and return to the highway. Park well off the highway on the edge of the chain-up area adjacent to the highway.

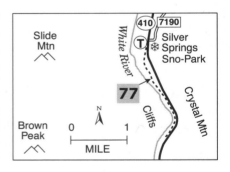

Route: From the Sno-Park, angle south through the trees and hop on the snow-covered expanse of State Route 410. You can follow the highway south into Mount Rainier National Park as far as you'd like, but you can also drop off the road and stomp through the snow along the rocky shores of the White River for a mile or so. Be sure you and your kids stay well clear of the river itself and be careful around side channels and creeks, since running water can hollow out holes under the snow—you don't want to crash through and land in an icy bath.

White River ice sculptures

I recommend strolling south at least a mile to enjoy views across the river to a high wall of cliffs on the far bank. In summer, this is just another damp wall of rock, but come winter, it's a mosaic of rock and ice as the water oozing out of the rock freezes in long beards of ice. At about a mile, the river forces hikers back onto the road, making this a nice place to turn around—if you have slogged up the river bed, you can relax and return on the road. Or vice versa. If you want to continue, follow the road south another mile or so before turning back. Beyond that point, the scenery doesn't change much, but the road gets steeper.

78 Copper Creek Hut

Rating: More difficult
Round trip: 8.8 miles
Hiking time: 5 hours or 2 days
Elevation gain: 1000 feet
High point: 4200 feet
Best season: December through early April
Map: USGS: Mount Wow
Who to contact: Mount Tahoma Trails Association
Permits/fees: Washington State Sno-Park Pass required.
You may also need a Washington State Discover Pass;
check www.parks.wa.gov/130/Winter-Recreation.

The Copper Creek Hut lacks the expansive views of some of the other huts in the Mount Tahoma Trails Association system, but it is an ideal destination for families and novice snowshoers looking for a comfortable winter camping experience.

Directions: Drive east from Tacoma on State Route 7 to Elbe and turn left onto SR 706—the Road to Paradise—and continue east toward Ashford. Just past milepost 6, turn left (north) onto Forest Road 92. Drive up to 6 miles, passing a white Mount Rainier Lions building in the first 0.5 mile, to the lower or upper 92 Road Sno-Park—depending on the snow level—at the road's end. This route is described from the upper Sno-Park.

Route: The Mount Tahoma Trails Association system comprises a series of huts and yurts set in the well-roaded foothills just outside Mount Rainier National Park. In the summer months, these hills are a marred world of clearcuts and densely packed tree farms. But come winter, the heavy blankets of snow turn the clearcuts into expansive meadows and the roads into meandering trails.

The Copper Creek Hut in the north district of the trail system is one of the easiest to reach and most scenic huts in the network. The hut sleeps twelve and offers a gas-fired kitchen and a large common room for lazing away the long dark evenings. Reservations are required.

From the upper 92 Road Sno-Park, the road climbs steeply for the first 50 feet but then tapers off for a long, moderate ascent through the rich second-growth forests of the area. The trail slices through meadows and forests and, at

A cornice sculpted by the winds along the ridge above Copper Creek Hut

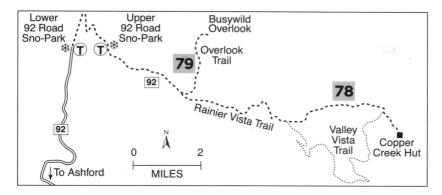

3.9 miles, turns right at a well-signed junction. Follow the signs for the Rainier Vista Trail. The next 0.5 mile slants upward, with the final 0.1 mile ascending ruthlessly to the hut. From the hut, you can look down on the Nisqually River valley and east to Mount Rainier.

Snowshoers seeking more adventure, and a lot more exercise, have the option of returning to the trailhead by way of the Valley Vista Trail, found at the junction a half-mile before the hut. This alternative route adds nearly 3.5 miles and few scenic rewards.

79 Busywild Overlook

Rating: Easiest
Round trip: 6.5 miles
Hiking time: 4 hours
Elevation gain: 900 feet
High point: 3500 feet
Best season: December through early March
Map: USGS: Mount Wow
Who to contact: Mount Tahoma Trails Association
Permits/fees: Washington State Sno-Park Pass required.
You may also need a Washington State Discover Pass; check www.parks.wa.gov/130/Winter-Recreation.

This trail climbs steadily but gradually, piercing rich second-growth forests full of wildlife and winter wonders. At the trail's end, you'll find views down into the green-gray valley of Busywild Creek. Beyond the creek stretch the long gray hills of the Rainier Timber Company's tree farms, and to the east lie the old-growth stands of the Glacier View Wilderness abutting Mount Rainier National Park.

Tracks of a small marten near Busywild

Directions: Drive east from Tacoma on State Route 7 to Elbe and turn left onto SR 706—the Road to Paradise—and continue east toward Ashford. Just past milepost 6, turn left (north) onto Forest Road 92. Drive up to 6 miles, passing a white Mount Rainier Lions building in the first 0.5 mile, to the lower or upper 92 Road Sno-Park—depending on the snow level—at the road's end. This route is described from the lower Sno-Park.

Route: This is a perfect route when the snows have been falling heavy and low down on the hills. In those situations, you'll be using the lower 92 Road Sno-Park, giving you an extra mile of snow to enjoy. And enjoy it you will. This route provides an easy alternative for snowshoers who'd rather avoid the popular path to the Copper Creek Hut (Route 78).

From the lower 92 Road Sno-Park, head north along FR 92. After 0.5 mile or so, the road curves sharply to the south and climbs a bit more steeply over the next mile. As you trek up the road, scan the undisturbed snow under the eaves of the forest adjacent to your path. Chances are good you'll be able to pick up the tracks of snowshoe hares, and maybe even the wily critters that hunt them—bobcats, red (and gray) foxes, and coyotes.

At about 3300 feet, the road grade levels out somewhat, still climbing but far more gently. A bit over 2.5 miles from the lower Sno-Park, the road forks. Straight ahead on the main path is the route to Copper Creek Hut. Turn left onto the faint trail climbing north. This road, the Overlook Trail, rolls nearly due north for about 0.75 mile to a broad open area above Busywild Creek. This is your turnaround point. But before heading back, stop and enjoy the views down into Busywild and north to Puyallup Ridge and beyond.

80 Snow Bowl Hut

Rating: More difficult
Round trip: 8.4 miles
Hiking time: 7 hours or 2 days
Elevation gain: 2000 feet
High point: 4400 feet
Best season: December through early April
Map: Green Trails: Randle No. 301
Who to contact: Mount Tahoma Trails Association
Permits/fees: Washington State Sno-Park Pass required.
    You may also need a Washington State Discover Pass;
    check www.parks.wa.gov/130/Winter-Recreation.

The south district of the Mount Tahoma Trails Association (MTTA) network offers spectacular snow recreation, even though you're seldom above 4500 feet. Although this route is relatively low, you'll generally find good snow, and great views of impressive mountains and craggy peaks are to be had. From the ridge above Snow Bowl, you can stare north to Mount Rainier, while closer at hand, the dark wall of High Rock stands like a black monolith to the east.

Directions: Drive east from Tacoma on State Route 7 to Elbe and turn left onto SR 706—the Road to Paradise—and continue east to Ashford. At the edge of town, watch for the brown South District Access Road sign, and take the next right onto 1 Road. At the T intersection (2.8 miles from the highway), turn left at the brown sign pointing toward 1 Road. At mile 4, veer left at the fork. The first, lower 1 Road Sno-Park is located at mile 6.4. If the snow line is higher, continue to the second, upper 1 Road Sno-Park, staying left at 6.7 miles (following the signs to the Outer Loop Trail). The second Sno-Park is at mile 7.5.

Route: Snow Bowl Hut sleeps eight and sports a wide, view-rich deck complete with barbecue pit. Make the effort to pack a few extra provisions if you're planning to stay to take advantage of the hut's amenities. Reservations are required.

From the lower 1 Road Sno-Park, trek up the road to the second. From there, you'll continue on the road, climbing at a brisk pace. The road is wide

View from the crest of Snow Bowl

and frequently groomed by MTTA volunteers, but it isn't easy. The road climbs a touch over 2000 feet in 3 miles. Take your time, and enjoy frequent breaks. Even if you aren't tired, stop for a break now and then if only to admire the increasingly nice views east toward High Rock.

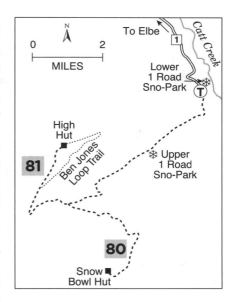

At about 2.5 miles, the road forks. To the right is the High Hut ridge (Route 81, High Hut). Stay left and start climbing south. The road now pushes on to a more moderate final mile. You're now largely above tree level. Or rather, you are now in broad ridgetop meadows broken by periodic stands of forest. As a result, the winds are more active here and the road is often swept with deep drifts. Take your time crossing this final mile, since this is where the hard work of the lower 2.5 miles really pays off. As you near the Snow Bowl Hut, you'll find clear views north to Mount Rainier and south across the expanse of the Gifford Pinchot National Forest.

If there are skiers in your party, or sharing the hut with you, you can enjoy watching them carve up the pristine snow in the perfect slope of the snow bowl behind the hut. The skiers can shred 600 vertical feet of Cascade snow here, but snowshoers can get in on the act, too—just remember to bring a lightweight sled, and note that if you slide down, you'll have to hike back up.

81 High Hut

Rating: More difficult
Round trip: 7.8 miles
Hiking time: 7 hours or 2 days
Elevation gain: 2400 feet
High point: 4800 feet
Best season: December through early April
Map: Green Trails: Randle No. 301
Who to contact: Mount Tahoma Trails Association
Permits/fees: Washington State Sno-Park Pass required.
You may also need a Washington State Discover Pass;
check www.parks.wa.gov/130/Winter-Recreation.

High Hut is situated on a windswept ridge with unmatched views of Mount Rainier, High Rock, Griffin Mountain, and all of the Gifford Pinchot National Forest, offering a glorious retreat from the hectic business of modern life. Whether you are out just for the day or are overnighting, the hut is worth the considerable effort required to make the visit.

Directions: Drive east from Tacoma on State Route 7 to Elbe and turn left onto SR 706—the Road to Paradise—and continue east to Ashford. At the edge of town, watch for the brown South District Access Road sign, and take the next right onto 1 Road. At the T intersection (2.8 miles from the highway), turn left at the brown sign pointing toward 1 Road. At mile 4, veer left at the fork. The first, lower 1 Road Sno-Park is located at mile 6.4. If the snow line is higher, continue to the second, upper Sno-Park, staying left at 6.7 miles (following the signs to the Outer Loop Trail). The second Sno-Park is at mile 7.5.

Route: High Hut is the jewel in the crown of the Mount Tahoma Trails Association. This ridgetop lodge offers an incredible winter getaway for snowshoers and skiers. With gas-powered lights and cooking stove, and a wonderful wood-fired heating stove, this hut is comfortable and cozy.

From the lower Sno-Park, continue up the road, sharing the first 2.5 miles with the route to Snow Bowl Hut (Route 80). But as the road climbs out of the broad valley and attains the ridge saddle (4000 feet) at 2.5 miles, bear right instead of left. This leads you northeast on a long slant to the ridge crest. The

The roof of High Hut overshadowed by Mount Rainier

last 0.9 mile climbs 800 feet, leaving you winded and tired when you finally push over the last of the wind-scoured ridge to stomp onto the hut's broad deck.

If you have the energy after reaching the hut, explore the ridgeline on the Ben Jones Loop Trail before it drops steeply off the ridge to the northeast. The full Ben Jones Loop is best left to skiers, who actively welcome the pull of gravity. An alternative is to tromp west through the wind drifts and small stands of trees along the ridge behind the hut.

82 Kautz Creek

Rating: More difficult
Round trip: Up to 11 miles
Hiking time: 7 hours
Elevation gain: 2800 feet
High point: 5300 feet
Best season: January through early March
Maps: Green Trails: Mount Rainier West No. 269, Randle No. 301
Who to contact: Mount Rainier National Park
Permits/fees: National park entry fee required

Although the Kautz Creek valley has historically been the scene of geologic destruction, the area is awash in beauty. This route follows the tumultuous creek, then climbs through ancient forests, and finally rolls through wide, open meadows with spectacular views.

Directions: Drive east from Tacoma on State Route 7 and bear left onto SR 706 at the town of Elbe. Continue east through the Nisqually entrance of Mount Rainier National Park, and proceed 3 miles farther to the parking area on the right just beyond the Kautz Creek Bridge. The trail begins on the north side of the road.

Route: Kautz Creek offers not only an excellent snowshoe excursion but also a chance to experience the geologic history of Mount Rainier. The trail climbs along the route followed by mudflows, lahars, and floods that date back tens of thousands of years. Lest one think that is all ancient history, bear in mind that the last massive mudflow in this valley occurred in 1947 when some 50 million cubic yards of mud, water, and debris flashed through the valley, burying the Road to Paradise and killing most of the trees in the lower valley bottom. A forest of silver snags is what remains today.

The Kautz Creek Trail is wide and easy to follow. The early section may be thinly covered in snow some years, so you might have to begin the outing with your snowshoes attached to your pack instead of your feet. However, the trail

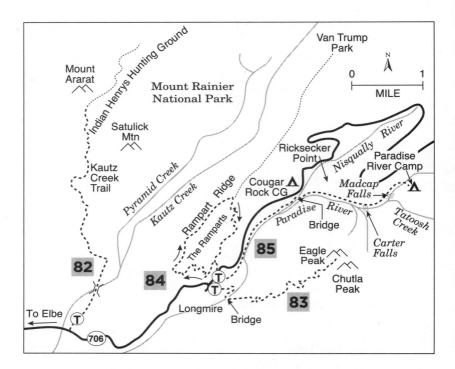

climbs steadily, and the snow is generally deep enough to require snowshoes well before the footbridge is reached at the 1-mile mark. Check with a ranger before heading out in early spring to make sure this bridge is intact: spring floods sometimes wash it away. Exercise caution when crossing the bridge. The snow accumulated on it tends to pile up at an angle, so the first person across should take his or her time and kick out good, solid footpads for those following. It may be necessary to remove your snowshoes to increase your stability when crossing.

Once over the creek, the trail begins to climb the valley wall, angling up through the forest between Tumtum Peak and Satulick Mountain. You can catch occasional peeks at these summits as you climb. The climb begins as a gradual straight-on pitch and then turns into steep switchbacks. Around the 4000-foot level, the trail swings into a long hillside traverse around the head of a small creek valley (a tributary of Pyramid Creek), followed by another series of switchbacks.

At 4 miles from your car, the route enters the first long, broad meadow. Views south to the Kautz Valley and north to the glacier-covered flank of Mount Rainier are found here. This makes an excellent place to have lunch and turn around. If you prefer an extended adventure, carefully climb through the

Natural winter art along Kautz Creek

meadow and a tricky traverse through another clearing in the next mile before finding a long 0.5-mile traverse around the flank of Mount Ararat to reach the beginning of Indian Henrys Hunting Ground.

83 Eagle and Chutla Peaks Trail

Rating: Most difficult
Round trip: 7 miles
Hiking time: 6 hours
Elevation gain: 2900 feet
High point: 5600 feet
Best season: January through early March
Maps: Green Trails: Mount Rainier West No. 269, Randle No. 301
Who to contact: Mount Rainier National Park
Permits/fees: National park entry fee required

Climbing through mossy old-growth forest, this trail ascends the western flank of the Tatoosh Range. The trail is quiet and often overlooked by snowshoers—it is often overlooked by summer hikers as well—but it offers a chance to interact with an array of wildlife.

Directions: Drive east from Tacoma on State Route 7 and bear left onto SR 706 at the town of Elbe. Continue east through the Nisqually entrance of Mount Rainier National Park, and proceed to the Longmire Ranger Station and Lodge. Park in the plowed area behind the lodge.

Route: Some of the wild animals you might see along this trail include the ever-present camp-robber jays (a.k.a. gray jays or whiskey jacks), red foxes, bobcats, and blacktail deer. A flash of white movement seen in the snowy forest could be a ptarmigan, a weasel, or a snowshoe hare, all of which trade in their brown summer coverings for white winter coats.

The route begins with a hike up the service road behind the ranger station, passing the employee housing area and crossing the Nisqually River via a narrow one-lane bridge. Continue up the road 100 yards to the trailhead on the left. In low-snow years, you may not need your snowshoes for the first 0.5 mile or so, but even when the snow is relatively shallow, snowshoes and their sure-grip cleats and crampons can be helpful on the trail.

Along the route heading up to Eagle Peak

The route climbs through a couple of moderate switchbacks, each followed by long traverses across the hillside, before entering a series of increasingly short switchbacks in the shady forest. The trail is always climbing, but never too steeply. At 2 miles, the trail crosses a tiny creek—the stream it has followed up the hillside for the previous mile.

The forest around the trail is thick, and the trail rolls through an endless series of tree wells and snow mounds. These features form when a large opening in the forest canopy allows more snow to reach the ground, piling it deeper than that accumulated under the trees. The walking isn't overly difficult, but the constant up-and-down motion does make the going slow. But this is a trail to be savored and enjoyed, not rushed through. The broad canopy and forest of ancient trees is worth experiencing. Stop and listen to the birds. Smell the wet cedars. Feel the sun as it streams through openings in the canopy, and taste the water as it drips off the fir limbs and onto your face.

Near the 3.25-mile mark, the trail enters a sidehill meadow. This clearing provides good views of Eagle and Chutla Peaks ahead. If snow conditions allow it, continue up through this meadow to reach Eagle Saddle—between Eagle and Chutla Peaks—for vistas that sweep over Mount Rainier, Tumtum Peak, and Eagle and Chutla Peaks, as well as the rest of the Tatoosh Range. On very clear days, the top of Mount Adams may be seen peeking up on the southeastern horizon.

84 Rampart Ridge

Rating: More difficult
Round trip: 4.5 miles
Hiking time: 5 hours
Elevation gain: 1200 feet
High point: 4050 feet
Best season: January through early March
Map: Green Trails: Mount Rainier West No. 269
Who to contact: Mount Rainier National Park
Permits/fees: National park entry fee required

This is a forest trek through ancient cedars and firs, with panoramic views of the wide Nisqually Valley and nearby peaks. There are also occasional glimpses of the snowy face of Mount Rainier, but the real beauty of this route is the wonderful local scenery. The deep old-growth forest is home to an assortment of birds and animals, including ravens, red foxes, and snowshoe hares.

A camp-robber jay swoops in to steal some snacks.

Directions: Drive east from Tacoma on State Route 7 and bear left onto SR 706 at the town of Elbe. Continue east through the Nisqually Entrance of Mount Rainier National Park, and proceed to Longmire Ranger Station and Lodge. Park in the plowed area behind the lodge, and find the start of the trail in the meadows across the road.

Route: Because it is on the lower flanks of the mountain, this trail gets its snow later than the routes near Paradise. But once the big winter storms of January and February hit, Rampart Ridge is an excellent option, especially on those days when the Road to Paradise stays gated at Longmire well into late morning. The route is a loop trip that is best when hiked clockwise from Longmire Lodge, as there are gentler slopes to climb this way.

The snowshoe hike begins on the well-marked Trail of the Shadows nature walk. Go left on this small loop trail, and in just a few hundred yards, bear left again, leaving the meadow and starting up a wide, well-signed trail (Rampart Ridge Trail) into the trees. Even under deep snow, the trail is easy to follow through the woods. Continue upward, weaving between the mammoth old trees as the trail goes from one wide switchback to another.

In 2 miles, you'll reach the crest of the ridge and open views to the west of Nisqually Valley and the cone-shaped Tumtum Peak. A short bit beyond, you'll pass the high point of the route and look down over th the ridge its name—The Ramparts. From here it's a relatively i hiking, with occasional meadows and views of Rainier, before junction with the Wonderland Trail.

If you want a bit more adventure, and a few more clear looks at the mountain, go straight to continue along the upper reaches of Rampart Ridge. The trail leads another 2.5 miles to Van Trump Park, gaining another 1500 feet along the way. This extension would increase your round-trip mileage to nearly 10 miles.

To close the loop, go right at the junction with the Wonderland Trail and descend through a long series of switchbacks, slicing through thick forest along the way. The final 0.5 mile of the trail is pretty much a gentle straight shot back to the road, just above Longmire. Hike the last 100 yards west along the shoulder of the Road to Paradise to reach the Longmire Lodge area.

85 | Wonderland Trail

Rating: Easiest
Round trip: Up to 7.6 miles
Hiking time: 5 hours
Elevation gain: 1300 feet
High point: 4100 feet
Best season: December through early April
Map: Green Trails: Mount Rainier West No. 269
Who to contact: Mount Rainier National Park
Permits/fees: National park entry fee required

Snowshoe through some of the oldest, most beautiful ancient forest left in Washington's Cascades while enjoying views of the rolling, crashing waters of the milky Nisqually River. Families will appreciate the nearly flat, easy trek through the trees along the first half of the route, while those with an appetite for more adventure will enjoy the last half of the hike as it skirts the base of a steep slope, climbs steadily along the rushing river, and passes a pair of pretty waterfalls on its way to Paradise River Camp.

Directions: Drive east from Tacoma on State Route 7 and bear left onto SR 706 at the town of Elbe. Continue east through the Nisqually Entrance of Mount Rainier National Park, and proceed to Longmire Ranger Station and Lodge. Park in the plowed area behind the lodge.

Route: From the ranger station, hike east along the Wonderland Trail. (Find the trailhead to the left of the ranger station.) The trail is nestled alongside the Road to Paradise for the first 0.5 mile, and then is pinched tight between

Exploring a section of the Wonderland Trail near Longmire

the road and the Nisqually River for a few hundred feet before the road angles left away from the river and trail. The forest around the trail is Douglas fir and cedar. An assortment of wildlife thrives in this rich forest environment, and the most visible member of the forest community is the fearless gray jay, a.k.a. camp-robber jay, a.k.a. whiskey jack. These birds act as if they are all starving as they flit from limb to limb in the trees around the trail whenever hikers are near. The brazen beggars will even go so far as to land on a raised arm, a shoulder, or a head if there is a chance of a quick bit of bread or granola. The chittering, flittering chaps are harmless, and if you can resist their piteous begging, they will leave you alone.

At 0.75 mile, the trail skirts the line between forest and riparian environments, with the Nisqually River just a stone's throw away to the right. The trail stays fairly level alongside the river to the 2-mile mark, where it passes the picnic area of Cougar Rock Campground. This is the last time the trail approaches the road—the trail crosses the wide Nisqually on a stout bridge and climbs up the Paradise River valley while the road sticks to the Nisqually River valley.

Paradise River is a smaller, more scenic stream, and the trail sticks close to its banks, skirting the base of the steep slope of a narrow gorge for 0.5 mile. There is a danger of snow slides here, so avoid this trail section in times of high or moderate avalanche conditions. The gorge slowly opens up and, at 3.3 miles, passes Carter Falls and, at 3.6 miles, Madcap Falls. Both cascades are pretty plunges of the Paradise and are worthy of a photo and leisurely contemplation. Just above Madcap Falls is Paradise River Camp (a small backcountry campsite). Turn around here for a modest day's outing.

86 Reflection Lakes

Rating: More difficult
Round trip: 3 miles
Hiking time: 3 hours
Elevation gain: 560 feet
High point: 5100 feet
Best season: December through early May
Maps: Green Trails: Mount Rainier East No. 270, Paradise No. 270S
Who to contact: Mount Rainier National Park
Permits/fees: National park entry fee required

This trail stays right along the edge of timber line, making it one of the most spectacular routes for snowshoers (and cross-country skiers) in Mount Rainier National Park. The trail provides a wonderful experience in a winter forest, the chance to visit frozen alpine lakes, and subalpine meadows in which to play and soak up the scenery.

Directions: Drive east from Tacoma on State Route 7 and bear left onto SR 706—the Road to Paradise—at the town of Elbe. Continue east through the Nisqually Entrance of the park, and proceed to the Narada Falls View Area parking lot, which is kept plowed each winter.

Route: From the upper end of the parking area, go right along a plowed driveway, passing a warming hut and restrooms, as well as a long maintenance shed, to find the trail. If the snow is stable and not too deep, climb the steep, open slope directly ahead to reach the main trail. If conditions are icy, or the climb looks too steep, follow the orange blazes to the left through the trees as the trail parallels the bottom of the hill. Soon you'll begin angling uphill and quickly top out on a wide, level trail—it is actually the Paradise–Stevens Canyon Road.

Looking down on Reflection Lake

Turn right, and snowshoe along this road as it loops out around the flank of Inspiration Point. The road quickly bears to the left and enters a long corridor in the forest. The way has little elevation gain, but it can't be called level because the snow rolls through tree wells and snowdrifts.

This trail through the trees brings you right to the edge of Reflection Lakes at 1.5 miles—although don't count on seeing your reflection because the lakes stay frozen over until June. That doesn't mean, however, that the ice is safe. This is an active volcano, and all that geothermal power keeps warm springs bubbling around and in most of the lakes in the area. That, in turn, keeps the ice on the lake surface thin and dangerous. But do take some time and expend a little energy exploring this lake basin and enjoying the stunning views of Mount Rainier, as well as the jagged line of peaks in the Tatoosh Range to the south.

87 Pinnacle Saddle

Rating: Most difficult
Round trip: 6 miles
Hiking time: 5 hours
Elevation gain: 1400 feet
High point: 6100 feet
Best season: December through early May
Maps: Green Trails: Mount Rainier East No. 270, Paradise No. 270S
Who to contact: Mount Rainier National Park
Permits/fees: National park entry fee required

Imagine a view that encompasses the three great volcanoes of southern Washington, with Oregon's Mount Hood and Mount Jefferson tossed in for good measure, and the jagged line of the Goat Rocks peaks capping off the panoramic splendor. That's exactly what's found at the end of this scenic, if somewhat strenuous, trek up the flank of the Tatoosh Range to a wide saddle between Pinnacle Peak and The Castle.

Directions: Drive east from Tacoma on State Route 7 and bear left onto SR 706—the Road to Paradise—at the town of Elbe. Continue east through the Nisqually Entrance of Mount Rainier National Park and proceed to the Narada Falls View Area parking lot, which is kept plowed each winter.

Route: Proceed up the trail to Reflection Lakes (Route 86) at 1.5 miles, and from the southern shore of the larger lake, start a slow, steady climb up the steep meadows to the south. The route heads up a wide, open bowl near the lake's eastern end, providing the most gradual ascent and the least danger of avalanche. Near the top of the snowy meadow, the trail bears right near the tree line and traverses out around a small ridge crest. The snowshoe route lies roughly along the path of the Pinnacle Peak Trail from this point on.

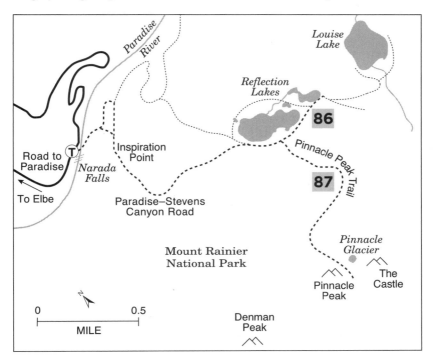

Pinnacle Saddle

At the end of the small ridge, bear left with the trail and climb along the crest of the ridge as it angles due south toward Pinnacle Peak. The ridge is thinning forest, so the snowshoeing is easy. Pick the path of least resistance through the pretty snow-laden trees, and keep climbing the moderately sloped ridge crest. Just 1 mile past Reflection Lakes, the route steepens significantly. To avoid the steep climb, angle left into an open snowfield. Although still pitched at an angle, this bowl is less steep than the route straight up Pinnacle Peak. Follow the open snowfield up to a high saddle with Pinnacle Peak on the right and The Castle to the left. **Note:** This last section is steep and frequently icy, requiring advanced skills to negotiate up it.

Though the summits of the two peaks seem to beckon, bear in mind that well-honed winter climbing skills, and the necessary hardware, are required to make either summit (and the narrow summits are typically crowned with dangerous cornices). The views from this saddle are comparable to what's found at the top of either peak anyway.

Speaking of views, as soon as you reach the saddle, turn around and soak in the awesome sight of Mount Rainier looming to the north. The saddle looks out across the valley to easily seen Paradise and, higher on the mountain, Camp Muir. Walk to the southern edge of the saddle, and look out across the Gifford Pinchot National Forest to Mount Adams, the Goat Rocks, Mount St. Helens, Mount Hood, and on really clear days, Mount Jefferson on the far southern horizon.

88 Glacier Vista

Rating: Easiest
Round trip: 3 miles
Hiking time: 3 hours
Elevation gain: 700 feet
High point: 6300 feet
Best season: December through early May
Maps: Green Trails: Mount Rainier East No. 270, Paradise No. 270S
Who to contact: Mount Rainier National Park
Permits/fees: National park entry fee required

Paradise. Close your eyes, and whisper the name. The image that pops into the minds of most folks will be white sand beaches and warm blue waters. But for some of us, Paradise is best served cold. Rather than white sand, we see undulating drifts of white snow. Rather than warm blue waters, we see deep sapphire ice. Palm trees are replaced with dark green alpine firs. Paradise, to us, is the alpine landscape of Mount Rainier. Snowshoers can experience this wintry wonderland at the aptly named Paradise meadows of Mount Rainier National Park.

Snowshoers dig a massive snow cave along the Glacier View route.

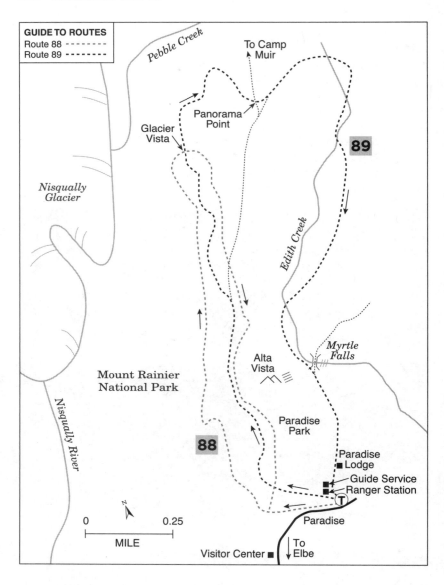

Directions: Drive east from Tacoma on State Route 7 and bear left onto SR 706 at the town of Elbe. Continue east through the Nisqually Entrance of the park, and proceed up the plowed road to the Paradise Lodge parking area.

Route: If you want an easy, family-friendly introduction to snowshoeing, there is no better route than the gentle climb through the sprawling meadows above Nisqually Glacier.

From the west end of the parking area, near the climbers hut, climb the groomed trail up through the tall snowbank surrounding the parking lot (depending on the snowfall, the snowbank can be upwards of 25 feet high). The trail passes the guide service building and leads to the groomed sledding run the Park Service maintains in the lower meadows. Stay to the left of these runs and slowly work your way uphill while drifting west. When you come to the tree line, turn north and follow the edge of the meadow uphill, working around the various drifts and dips that form when the wind whips the snow.

Continuing up the slope about 1 mile, you'll find frequent breaks in the trees on your left. These provide clear views down on the jagged, rock-strewn expanse of the Nisqually Glacier that fills the valley below. At a little more than 1 mile from the parking lot, you'll be in a broad open area known as Glacier Vista, with wonderful views of the whole Nisqually Valley, as well as up to the towering hulk of Mount Rainier. Behind you, the Tatoosh peaks line the southern horizon.

You can return the same way you came, but to vary things a bit, turn right and cross the upper meadow back down to Alta Vista. From the north end of this knoll, look east down into the Edith Creek basin. Then descend along the west side of the hill (the east side of Alta Vista is too steep and slide-prone to be safely traversed) to return to the sledding runs and the parking lot.

89 Panorama Point

Rating: Most difficult
Round trip: 5 miles
Hiking time: 4 hours
Elevation gain: 1300 feet
High point: 6800 feet
Best season: December through early May
Maps: Green Trails: Mount Rainier East No. 270, Paradise No. 270S
Who to contact: Mount Rainier National Park
Permits/fees: National park entry fee required

The open snowfields, bowls, and meadows above Paradise draw snow lovers of all kinds, from skiers to snowboarders, but snowshoers have the edge on them all on the way up. Climbing the sometimes steep slopes is best done on a stout pair of snowshoes, and while the skiers and boarders may zip down faster than snowshoers, they blast past the awesome views that snowshoers can admire at their leisure as they slowly descend the mountain's flank.

A snowshoers' camp below Panorama Point

Directions: Drive east from Tacoma on State Route 7 and bear left onto SR 706 at the town of Elbe. Continue east through the Nisqually Entrance of Mount Rainier National Park, and proceed up the plowed road to the Paradise Lodge parking area.

Route: Countless opportunities for snowshoeing can be found in the open areas of Paradise, but heading up toward Panorama Point is the best of the bunch. From the west edge of the parking lot, snowshoe up the steep meadow behind the guide service building, skirt around the left side of the groomed-snow play area, and hike north along the west side of the tree-covered crown of Alta Vista peak. The route rolls uphill through meadows and thin tree cover, with excellent views of the mountain when the weather is clear.

From the small saddle on the north side of Alta Vista, climb along the prominent ridge crest as it leads straight toward Mount Rainier. The route parallels the massive finger of Nisqually Glacier, and at 1.5 miles, crosses a flat bench aptly named Glacier Vista. This is the best place to find a panoramic view of the sprawling glacier as it stretches from high on the flank of the mountain nearly to the Road to Paradise. If you are tired from the relentless climbing, turn back here knowing you have experienced some of the best views of the route; or catch your breath while soaking in the scenery, and then continue up to Panorama Point.

From Glacier Vista, the route climbs steeply northeast through open hillside meadows (with a few thin stands of wind-savaged alpine trees) to another broad bench nearly 1 mile farther up the mountain. (The distance varies from 0.6 to 1 mile, depending on how steeply you climb.)

Panorama Point lives up to its name, with grand views of the mighty mountain, its lower flanks, and the serrated ridgeline of the Tatoosh Range to the south. On clear, cold days, the rocky spires of the Goat Rocks Wilderness Area as well as the perfect cone of Mount Adams are visible to the southeast.

To return to Paradise, head east across the bench of Panorama Point and descend the wide open slopes of the upper Edith Creek basin. The basin is wide and you can pick your own path once you enter it, but use caution when making the first drop into the basin. For the safest route, hike southeast no less than 0.5 mile from Panorama Point to skirt out and around the steepest slopes, which are always heavily corniced. Once past the obvious cornices and steep drops, head down the slope along Edith Creek and past Myrtle Falls. Follow the creek all the way down to Paradise, passing under Alta Vista and entering the upper Paradise Valley to approach the Paradise Lodge and parking area from the east.

90 Mazama Ridge

Rating: More difficult
Round trip: 6 miles
Hiking time: 5 hours
Elevation gain: 900 feet
High point: 5700 feet
Best season: December through early April
Maps: Green Trails: Mount Rainier East No. 270, Paradise No. 270S
Who to contact: Mount Rainier National Park
Permits/fees: National park entry fee required

This is a wonderful trail for snowshoers of all tastes. Like to 'shoe where there are great panoramic vistas of mountain peaks? No problem. Like trails with pretty scenery? This one has some of the finest subalpine meadows and forests in the country, all blanketed in the deepest snow found in Washington. Want to watch other recreationists play? Snow boarders and telemark skiers love this trail, with its many open slopes on which they can practice their turns. Looking for a chance to see wildlife? Besides the wide variety of avian life, snowshoe hares, red foxes, and a variety of small, scurrying beasts inhabit the forest fringes.

Directions: Drive east from Tacoma on State Route 7 and bear left onto SR 706 at the town of Elbe. Continue east through the Nisqually Entrance of Mount Rainier National Park, and proceed up the plowed road to the Paradise Lodge parking area.

Route: Snowshoers will find that they are not bound by a specific trail on this route. Hiking up Mazama Ridge, they can amble off in any direction and pick their own paths through the deep snow of the meadows along the ridge crest. There is no finer place for snowshoers to enjoy the total freedom of movement that their 'shoes afford them.

From near the guide service and ranger station buildings, climb the slope above the parking area and head off to the right, staying above Paradise Lodge, to enter the broad open meadows of the upper Paradise Valley. Staying above the roadway, cross Edith Creek on a wide footbridge, just above ice-cloaked

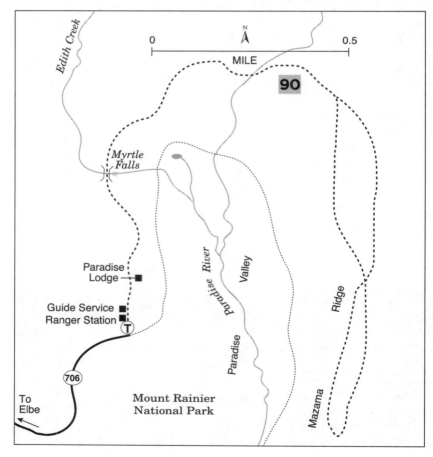

Snowshoers pause to enjoy the views on the way up Mazama Ridge.

Myrtle Falls. From the bridge, head due east, traversing around the head of Paradise Valley to approach the steep wall of Mazama Ridge at about 0.7 mile.

Start up the ridge, angling right (south) while climbing steeply for 0.5 mile to attain the ridge crest at 5700 feet. Cross to the eastern side of the crest for great views in that direction. Then turn right and follow the ridge south through thin stands of dwarf trees (their growth stunted by the howling winds that frequently scour this open ridge) and wide open meadows. Looking south, the multiple peaks of the Tatoosh Range—Pinnacle Peak, The Castle, Unicorn, Boundary Peak, and the rest—are visible as a jagged line against the sky. At the southern end of Mazama Ridge, near the 2.5-mile mark, look down onto Reflection and Louise Lakes and east along the deep cut of Stevens Canyon. To the north, Mount Rainier towers over it all.

To return, go north along the western edge of the ridge to meet the tracks you made along the eastern edge on your way in. Turn and follow those tracks back to Paradise.

91 Camp Muir

Rating: Most difficult
Round trip: 10 miles
Hiking time: 9 hours or 2 days
Elevation gain: 4400 feet
High point: 10,000 feet
Best season: February through early May
Maps: Green Trails: Mount Rainier East No. 270, Paradise No. 270S
Who to contact: Mount Rainier National Park
Permits/fees: National park entry fee required

The route to Camp Muir is long, strenuous, and very susceptible to poor weather, but it can also be incredibly beautiful, with views that can't be found anywhere else.

Directions: Drive east from Tacoma on State Route 7 and bear left onto SR 706 at the town of Elbe. Continue east through the Nisqually Entrance of Mount Rainier National Park, and proceed up the plowed road to the Paradise Lodge parking area. Because Camp Muir is a difficult outing, it is recommended that anyone, even day trippers, heading up there should register their trip with the rangers at Longmire.

Route: Camp Muir, named for the legendary naturalist John Muir, is the gate to the summit of Mount Rainier. Virtually every climbing party that heads up from Paradise passes through Camp Muir. But you don't have to be summit-bound to enjoy a trip to the camp—and you don't have to camp to visit the camp. When the skies are clear and the snow is firm, snowshoers can slog up the long, steep slopes, pausing whenever they need a breather, and enjoy endless views south. Mount Adams can be seen beyond the Goat Rocks peaks. Mount St. Helens can be seen on the far side of the Tatoosh Range. Far to the south, Mount Hood stands, and beyond it, far down in central Oregon, Mount Jefferson can sometimes be seen on the hazy horizon.

This long climb is best done late in the winter or better yet, in the spring, when the days are longer so you'll have extra daylight hours to make the long plodding climb. The route should also be reserved for days when the weather forecast calls for clear, stable weather. The long, barren slopes all clad in white can be extremely confusing and dangerous when the clouds blow in. The trek here should be considered an alpine mountaineering experience rather than just a stroll in the snow.

Opposite: A line of snowshoers head up to Camp Muir.

From the western side of the parking area, start up through the meadows, following the route to Panorama Point (Route 89). Snowshoe up past the groomed sliding areas populated by families with inner tubes, and continue around the west side of Alta Vista, plodding up the long slope to Panorama Point. Here, you're nearly halfway to the camp. Before heading onward and upward, stop and enjoy the views—look south to The Castle, Pinnacle Peak, and Denman Peak in the heart of the Tatoosh Range. You can also see the long, craggy line of the Goat Rocks peaks leading south to Mount Adams. To the southeast, look for the abbreviated top of Mount St. Helens.

From Panorama Point, your route continues north, climbing through the Pebble Creek valley (7200 feet) a bit more than 1 mile from the point. In the valley, you'll find some big drifts that need to be crossed. Be careful with these drifts—some can be 20 or more feet tall and corniced at the top.

Beyond Pebble Creek, you enter the Muir Snowfield and the long, straight shot over the final miles and the last 2800 feet of elevation. You'll see the knob of McClure Rock on your right just after crossing Pebble Creek, and as you approach 9000 feet, you'll see the iron-hard frame of Anvil Rock. The last 0.5 mile, covering nearly 900 feet of elevation, makes you work for that final goal of reaching Camp Muir.

At the camp, though, you can rest and relax. If you're staying, you can relax for as long as you like. (Check with the ranger before heading up the mountain if you want to stay at Camp Muir. You'll need an overnight permit.) If you're day tripping, don't relax too long—you have a long slog back down the slope before nightfall.

92 Silver Falls & Grove of the Patriarchs

Rating: More difficult
Round trip: 3 miles/5 miles
Hiking time: 2 hours/3.5 hours
Elevation gain: 200 feet/400 feet
High point: 2500 feet
Best season: January through early March
Maps: Green Trails: Mount Rainier East No. 270, Packwood No. 302
Who to contact: Mount Rainier National Park
Permits/fees: National park entry fee required

This is an excellent route for snowshoers looking for a quiet forest outing, without the need to struggle with a lot of climbing and routefinding. The route follows the gorgeous Ohanapecosh River upstream from Ohanapecosh Campground, slicing through lush old forests and passing the beautiful Silver Falls—made even more beautiful by the silver shards of ice that line the rocks around the cascade. The trail continues up the valley to a haunting stand of massive trees on a broad island in the middle of the Ohanapecosh River.

Directions: From Packwood drive east on US Highway 12 to its junction with State Route 123 and turn left (north). Drive to the Ohanapecosh Campground on the left. (At times, this is the end of the plowed road, although usually the road is plowed another 1.5 miles to the Stevens Canyon entrance of Mount Rainier National Park.) Park in the plowed lot at the campground.

Route: The trail is generally flat and wide, and it is low enough so that the snow doesn't obscure the trail. It's so easy to follow that snowshoers can spend their time enjoying the views around them rather than looking for the path through the trees.

Snowshoe down the road leading into the campground, and just before the road crosses the Ohanapecosh River, turn into the northern loop of campsites. The trail begins at the northernmost end of this loop, just before the loop turns east away from the river.

A gray jay (a.k.a. camp-robber jay) patrols the trail.

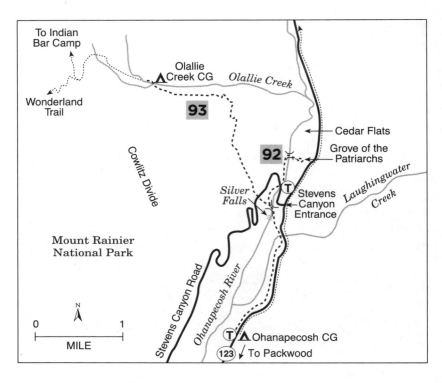

To Indian Bar Camp

Olallie Creek CG

Olallie Creek

93

Wonderland Trail

Cowlitz Divide

Cedar Flats

Grove of the Patriarchs

92

Laughingwater Creek

Silver Falls

Stevens Canyon Entrance

Mount Rainier National Park

Stevens Canyon Road

Ohanapecosh River

N

0 ——— 1
MILE

Ohanapecosh CG

123 To Packwood

Start up the trail as it climbs gradually to a bench above the river and rolls north through thin forests between the river and the road. The trail is wide and offers plenty of views of the river while staying well clear of the roadway (which is frequently used by skiers and occasionally by snowmobilers). This trail is generally unused except by other snowshoers, so there is plenty of solitude and quiet time along the way.

The trail crosses the river at 1.5 miles on a wide, rustic bridge with pretty views up the river to the crashing waters of Silver Falls. The bridge is usually slick, but with handrails on both sides, the crossing is easy and the wide deck is spacious enough for you to pause and enjoy the views.

For a closer look at the falls, continue across the bridge and turn right on the trail on the far bank to climb upstream alongside the falls. After snapping a few pictures and admiring the cascade, either turn back and return to Ohana-pecosh Campground or continue upstream for another 0.5 mile to Stevens Canyon Road. (Stay right at the junction a few hundred yards above the falls; the left fork leads to Route 93, Olallie Creek.)

Cross the wide road near the tollbooths, and head up the wide, well-signed trail to the Grove of the Patriarchs. The trail skirts along the west bank of the river and, in 0.5 mile (mile 2.5), crosses the river on a narrow suspension bridge.

This bridge is usually very slick, so cross with extreme care, making full use of both handrails. The Grove of the Patriarchs is a beautiful cathedral in summer months, but when the forest floor is blanketed with a white quilt of snow, the enormous trees of the grove seem even larger than they are. The stark contrast of the brilliant white snow and the dark, scaly tree trunks makes the immensity of the cedars, hemlocks, and firs almost incomprehensible.

After enjoying the scenic splendor of the forest, return the way you came, or follow the Stevens Canyon Road and SR 123 south to Ohanapecosh Campground for a quicker return.

93 Olallie Creek

Rating: Most difficult
Round trip: 6.8 miles
Hiking time: 7 hours or 2 days
Elevation gain: 1800 feet
High point: 3800 feet
Best season: January through early March
Maps: Green Trails: Mount Rainier East No. 270, Packwood No. 302
Who to contact: Mount Rainier National Park
Permits/fees: National park entry fee required

Often overlooked, this trail is overflowing with opportunities for snowshoers looking for solitude along a quiet forest path. The huge, old trees, abundant wildlife, and remarkable sylvan environment of this area, coupled with a general dearth of winter visitors, means this trail is an ideal retreat from the busy schedules of modern life.

Directions: From Packwood drive east on US Highway 12 to its junction with State Route 123 and turn left (north). Drive to the end of the plowed road at the junction with the Stevens Canyon entrance to Mount Rainier National Park. Occasionally, the road is plowed only as far as the Ohanapecosh Campground. If that is the case, park in the lot at the campground and snowshoe 1.5 miles along the roadway to the entrance.

Route: This trail boasts no sweeping panoramas, no drop-dead gorgeous views of peaks, valleys, or rivers. Instead, there are endless small graces along the route—snow-draped ferns, ice-adorned lichens, cathedral-like stands of cedar and fir, tracks of birds and animals to identify, and usually plenty of the birds and animals who laid the tracks. The trail can be enjoyed as a simple, unhurried day hike or as a multiday snowshoe trek, with many options for an ultimate destination, including a high ridge route that does offer incredible

Splashing water forms icicles above Olallie Creek.

views and picturesque panoramas. But the real beauty of this trail is the quiet forest, and that can be enjoyed by hiking as little as the first mile of the route.

Just west of the tollbooths at the Stevens Canyon Entrance, turn left and enter the forest on a wide trail, signed Silver Falls Trail, and hike southwest 0.25 mile to a junction with a trail on the right. Turn right onto this path, signed Olallie Creek, and hike through the forest a few hundred yards, cross the wide Stevens Canyon Road, and reenter the forest on the north side of the road. The trail climbs steadily but not too steeply for the next 2.5 miles, traversing a lush old-growth forest as it ascends the slopes. At 1.7 miles, the trail crosses a small creek and, at 2 miles, climbs a short series of switchbacks before turning west and traversing the slope above Olallie Creek.

The trail levels out near mile 3 and tapers toward the creek in the valley bottom. Near mile 3.4, the trail crosses the stream at Olallie Creek Campground. Enjoy a quiet lunch in this serene forest camp, and then retrace your steps. If you are looking for more adventure, continue up the trail as it ascends the Olallie Creek valley and ends at a junction with the Wonderland Trail at the crest of the Cowlitz Divide. Head north on the Wonderland and climb a steep ridge to Indian Bar Camp (9.7 miles from the trailhead), with its stunning views of the mountain and all the peaks to the south.

Opposite: Exploring the frozen shores of June Lake

SOUTH CASCADES

94 Packwood Lake

Rating: Most difficult
Round trip: 9 miles
Hiking time: 7 hours or 2 days
Elevation gain: 500 feet
High point: 3200 feet
Best season: Late January through early March
Map: Green Trails: Packwood No. 302
Who to contact: Gifford Pinchot National Forest, Cowlitz Valley
    Ranger District
Permits/fees: Northwest Forest Pass required

This lake is a popular summer destination for family campers, and it is even more impressive when visited in winter. The large lake is just outside the border of the Goat Rocks Wilderness Area, and an old service road slices through the forest alongside a water pipeline all the way to the dam at the lower end of the lake. The hike from the road end to the lake weaves through thick, old forest, and views are limited, but the local scenery makes up for the lack of distant sights.

Directions: From Seattle drive south on Interstate 5 to US Highway 12. Continue east on US 12 to Packwood. Turn right at the Packwood Ranger Station, and continue 6 miles on Packwood Lake Road to the trailhead. If you can't get to the official trailhead, park at the snow line and start walking from there. In periods of unusually heavy snow, the 4.5 miles of trail may be stretched by an additional 2 or 3 miles of road walking. But that extra mileage just makes for a more rewarding payoff at camp at day's end.

Route: Packwood Lake Road provides easy early-winter access to skiers and snowmobilers. After a few snowstorms, the road is made impassable by avalanches, and snowshoers will find the trail through the young forest silent and seemingly made with them in mind. The trail, though, is in avalanche

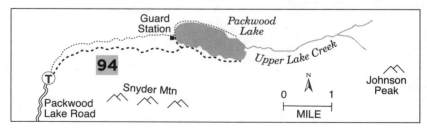

Looking up the unbroken trail to Packwood Lake

country too, so snowshoers must know the current avalanche conditions and should avoid this trail when the danger is any higher than moderate.

Whether you walk or drive to the official trailhead, you'll want to spend a few minutes there. The view is remarkable because a big, open window in the trees perfectly frames that big snow cone to the north, Mount Rainier.

Upon leaving the trailhead, the trail is fairly wide and easy to follow. It dips immediately into the sparse old forest and enters a shadowy world of green, gray, and white. The trail meanders up and down, gradually gaining elevation over the first 4 miles only to drop more than 200 feet in the last 0.5 mile before rolling out along the lakeshore.

The snow underfoot is bright against the dull gray fir and cedar tree trunks, while overhead, waxy green boughs and droopy beards of green lichen provide color to this cold sylvan world. But the best of the scenery is not the stationary stuff around you; it's the small gray streaks that flit from tree to tree. These feathery bundles of energy go by many names—whiskey jacks, gray jays, or camprobbers—but regardless of what you call them, you will enjoy their company.

The south shore of the lake is the safest haven for camp because it is gently graded and well forested, which minimizes the threat of snowslides. It also offers the best views. Plenty of sheltered areas for camps are scattered along the length of the lake, but smart campers will pitch their tents at the far end of the lake so they can enjoy the fiery sunsets that illuminate Mount Rainier to the north. If weather clouds the horizon, though, the views to the south are nearly as stunning: 7487-foot Johnson Peak looms large at the head of the Packwood Creek valley.

A word of warning: amidst all this beauty, danger lurks close by. The snowy mantle covering the lake looks stable and strong, but this is a big body of water at the relatively low elevation of 2900 feet, so the ice is always too thin to bear the weight of heavy bodies tramping across it. Stay off the lake. If you don't, you'll likely end up in the lake, and in winter that means hypothermia.

95 Sand Lake

Rating: More difficult
Round trip: 6.6 miles
Hiking time: 5 hours or 2 days
Elevation gain: 900 feet
High point: 5300 feet
Best season: Late December through early March
Map: Green Trails: White Pass No. 303
Who to contact: Gifford Pinchot National Forest, Cowlitz Valley
    Ranger District
Permits/fees: No parking pass required

Skirting beautiful high alpine meadows, the Pacific Crest Trail (PCT) rolls north from White Pass on a gentle climb, providing snowshoers with a wonderful opportunity to enjoy the high country of the Cascades in winter without a long slog up a wide logging road.

Directions: From Packwood drive east on US Highway 12 to the summit of White Pass. Park on the north (left) side of the highway in the large overnight parking area near the White Pass Ski Area (just west of the large hotel).

Route: This route dips into thick old stands of forest, but it is the open meadows, long ridges, and high peaks that make it a special section of the PCT. Pass by large circular plains of snow (frozen lakes) and rolling dunes of drifted snow. Immerse yourself in the dreamlands of mountain country in winter. Snowshoers of all abilities will find enjoyment here, as the terrain is open and gentle. They can hike as much, or as little, as they desire.

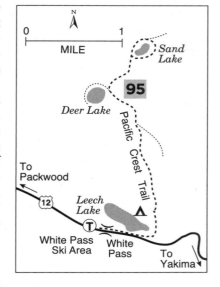

The PCT actually crosses US 12 to the east of the ski area, but you can catch it by skirting Leech Lake—which abuts the parking area—on its south shore, staying well to the side of the groomed ski tracks. Follow the curve of the lakeshore to the north for 0.5 mile, and just like that, jump on the PCT.

The trail climbs gently through a thick stand of fir and then open meadow for 1.4 miles to a small creek basin. Stay left here (a trail also leads off to the right, cruising down the creek valley through open forest to Dog Lake in 1.5 miles), and traverse a large meadow at the head of the creek valley, passing the nearly round Deer Lake basin at 2.7 miles. At the lake, the trail turns north once more and rolls gently uphill through meadows broken occasionally by thin stands of wind-gnarled trees. The trail is obliterated by snow in this open country, but the route stays along the broad crest of a shallow ridge as it leads due north.

At 3.3 miles, find Sand Lake on the right (east) side of the ridge. The lake is often obscured because the gentle slope of the banks and the surrounding open country allow the snow to drift in and cover it. So look for an oblong flat surface just below the ridgeline at 5300 feet. This is the place to turn around, unless you plan on pitching camp out in the winter wilderness. For extended

Partially frozen Sand Lake illustrates why snowshoers shouldn't venture out onto "frozen" lakes.

exploring, hike on up the trail as it rolls north, pushing through more meadows, forests, and past small alpine lakes.

The Sand Lake basin and the small ridge above it offer nice views of the surrounding peaks, including Cramer Mountain to the north, Spiral Butte to the east, and Round Mountain to the southeast. It's sometimes possible to see the summit of Mount Adams protruding on the southern horizon, too.

96 Cramer Lake

Rating: Most difficult
Round trip: 9 miles
Hiking time: 7 hours
Elevation gain: 800 feet
High point: 5000 feet
Best season: Late December through early March
Map: Green Trails: White Pass No. 303
Who to contact: Okanogan–Wenatchee National Forest, Naches Ranger District
Permits/fees: No parking pass required

Starting at the shore of a wide lake basin, this route has views of pretty peaks, meandering creeks—sometimes in old-growth forest settings, sometimes weaving gracefully through open meadows—and long, panoramic views of the South Cascade summits and deep canyons of the eastern foothills.

Directions: From Packwood drive east on US Highway 12 to the summit of White Pass. Continue east 1.5 miles to Dog Lake Campground. Generally a wide pullout is cleared at both the west end of the lake (near the campground) and at the east end (near the highway bridge over the lake's outlet stream). Park in whichever area is available.

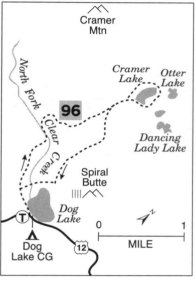

Route: This route offers terrain and scenery similar to that found along the Pacific Crest Trail to Sand Lake on Route 95. But far fewer people visit the Cramer Lake Trail, so snowshoers can add solitude to the list of wonders they'll encounter along the route.

Although this is a backcountry trail, the route is generally easy to follow with some moderate climbing, so most snowshoers with a solid hiking background will enjoy the workout and the rewards found here.

From the highway, snowshoe west along the southern edge of the lake and pick up the trail at the north side of Dog Lake Campground. The trail traverses the slope away from the lake, staying above the small feeder stream that pours in from the north. A mile up the trail, cross the creek in a thin stand of trees and begin a moderately steep climb northeast along the slope.

The forest gives way frequently to large, open meadows, and the round top of Spiral Butte dominates the view to the east. At 4800 feet, about 2 miles from the trailhead, the trail turns left and heads straight north across open meadows and thin forest. The trail here is fairly flat and straight, leading to the shores of Cramer Lake at 4.5 miles.

For a variation on the return, start back on the same trail, but just 1 mile south of the lake, veer southeast toward Spiral Butte. Cross a small creek basin, and traverse the flank of the butte at about 4900 feet. A long line of open meadows, separated by thin strands of forest, cover the side of the mountain,

Climbing above Cramer Lake

and you can work your way down to the 4300-foot level as you continue south around the mountain.

When the Dog Lake basin is in view, drop down into the thin forest at the north end of the lake and cross the flat meadow to get back to the western side of the lake for the final 0.25-mile snowshoe back to the trailhead. Avoid the eastern shore of the lake unless snow conditions are very stable because the lake butts up against a steep avalanche chute.

97 Tieton River Meadows

Rating: Easiest
Round trip: Up to 10 miles
Hiking time: 8 hours
Elevation gain: 350 feet
High point: 3500 feet
Best season: Late December through early March
Map: Green Trails: White Pass No. 303
Who to contact: Okanogan–Wenatchee National Forest, Naches Ranger District
Permits/fees: Washington State Sno-Park Pass required. You may also need a Washington State Discover Pass; check www.parks.wa.gov/130/Winter-Recreation.

Is there anything more serene than snow-flocked pine trees? This route ambles gently up the wide Tieton River valley, rolling through broad meadows and through sun-streaked forests. Elk can often be found browsing amongst the trees, and even if the majestic big beasts are absent, you'll likely encounter lesser critters. Pine martens scurry through the snow, as do weasels, snowshoe hares, bobcats, cougars, coyotes, foxes, and an array of birds.

Directions: From Packwood drive east on US Highway 12 to the summit of White Pass. Continue east 7.5 miles to Clear Lake Road (Forest Road 1200). Turn right and drive 3 miles to the Tieton River Sno-Park at the junction with FR 1207.

Route: Hike up FR 1207 as it slides gradually up the Tieton River valley. On either side of you are towering valley walls that at times show vertical rock faces, while at other times they are lined with lush pine forests. The route crosses Hell Creek at about 1 mile, and moves along the base of the north valley wall. Here, the boundary of the Goat Rocks Wilderness is just a snowball's throw away to the right. As you continue up the road, you can enjoy wonderful views of Old Snowy Mountain, which stands like a sentinel at the head of the valley.

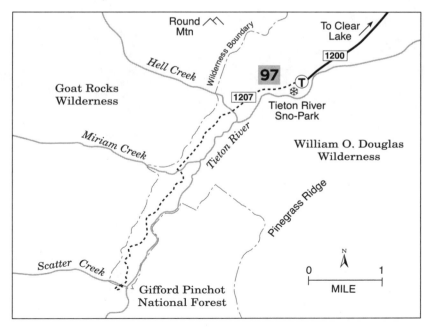

An athletic dog catches tossed snowballs during a break on a trip through the Tieton River meadows.

At 2.8 miles, the road crosses Miriam Creek and edges back toward the middle of the valley for the final run to the road's end at 5 miles, at the edge of the wilderness. (The road corridor is a 5-mile-long peninsula of unprotected land jutting into the wilderness.)

Beyond the road's end, summer hiking trails continue up the valley, one eventually leading to the very summit of Old Snowy Mountain. But this trail is steep and difficult to follow come winter. Leave that for warm summer days. Instead, stick to the valley road, and if you need further adventures, bust out into the various meadows and clearings along the way to explore those wildlife refuges.

98 American Ridge

Rating: Backcountry
Round trip: 5.6 miles
Hiking time: 5 hours
Elevation gain: 2600 feet
High point: 5900 feet
Best season: Late December through early March
Map: Green Trails: Bumping Lake No. 271
Who to contact: Okanogan–Wenatchee National Forest, Naches Ranger District
Permits/fees: Washington State Sno-Park Pass required. You may also need a Washington State Discover Pass; check www.parks.wa.gov/130/Winter-Recreation.

This is a winter scramble up a ruthlessly steep trail, but the views and the scenery along the way are unmatched.

Directions: From Yakima drive west on US Highway 12 to its junction with State Route 410. Turn right (northwest) onto SR 410 and drive 34 miles to the Hells Crossing Sno-Park on the left (south), just opposite the Hells Crossing Campground (closed).

Route: The route climbs quickly up a steep ridgeline on a narrow hiking trail, and snowshoers won't find much to look for in the first mile as they struggle up the slope. Although the trail may be demanding, it is a route used only by snowshoers. Many of the other trails in this area are so dominated by cross-country skiers and snowmobilers that snowshoers will welcome the workout, knowing that they don't have to share the trail with noisy speedsters.

Snowshoers who enjoy wildlife may want to stroll around the meadows in the valley bottom near the Sno-Park before starting up the trail. A large herd of elk roams this valley, and there is always the possibility that they will be browsing near the Hells Crossing area, so give a look for them before starting the climb.

Checking avalanche conditions near American Ridge

The trail climbs south from the Sno-Park, heading up the east side of a small draw. The route isn't too steep for the first 0.5 mile, and after that it makes a long traverse east around the flank of the hill to the ridge crest. At 1 mile, the trail turns vertical as it ascends the steep ridge crest, heading south toward the towering summit of Goat Peak. The route is exposed at times, and there are some tricky pitches, especially near 1.2 miles and again at 1.8 to 2 miles. Treeless sections are occasionally scoured by wind.

The trail dips down onto the eastern side of the ridge at 2.5 miles, and the last 0.25 mile is a gentle traverse to the top of American Ridge just before the Goat Peak summit. It is possible to climb to the top of the peak, but the approach on the American Ridge Trail is exposed and heavily corniced at times. It is better to just enjoy the stunning views from the ridge crest at the top of the trail and leave the summiting for a summertime outing.

From the top of American Ridge, the views are outstanding. To the east is the long, open country of the eastern foothills of the Cascades. To the north is Fifes Ridge and 6375-foot Fife Peak. To the south is the expansive William O. Douglas Wilderness and, beyond, the perfect cone of Mount Adams.

99 Mount St. Helens Summit

Rating: Backcountry
Round trip: 8 miles
Hiking time: 9 hours
Elevation gain: 5700 feet
High point: 8365 feet
Best season: Late December through early February
Map: Green Trails: Mount St. Helens Northwest No. 364S
Who to contact: Mount St. Helens National Volcanic Monument
Permits/fees: Washington State Sno-Park Pass required.
You may also need a Washington State Discover Pass; check www.parks.wa.gov/130/Winter-Recreation.

On this climb up Mount St. Helens, snowshoers can simply walk straight up the deep snow piled on the flank of the big volcano, taking a direct approach to the rim of the massive crater. Along the way, they can enjoy sweeping views out over the southern reaches of Washington's Cascades.

Directions: From Woodland drive east on State Route 503 to the community of Cougar and continue east another 7 miles to a junction with Forest Road 83. Turn left (north) onto FR 83, and drive 5.8 miles to the Marble Mountain Sno-Park at the end of the plowed road.

Route: Snowshoers have an advantage over summer climbers in that permits are not needed for midwinter ascents. From May 15 to October 31 every year, anyone attempting the summit must have one of the limited number of climbing permits (only forty are issued each day). But after the first of November, the mountain is open to anyone who wants to climb its snow-blanketed slopes.

From the Sno-Park, snowshoe north on Swift Creek Trail No. 244 as it follows the east bank of the creek toward the mountain. The trail climbs gradually, allowing you to loosen up and get into a good swing for the long, steady climb ahead. At 2.2 miles, the trail passes a well-marked side trail on the right leading down to June Lake (also reached via another trail described in Route 100, June Lake). Stay left and climb northwest, moving above timberline to cross Swift Creek at 2.5 miles.

Once past Swift Creek, continue to traverse to the left (northwest) for another 0.25 mile, and then turn straight up the slope and start the long slog to the top. The idea is to follow the path of least resistance, flowing with the contours of the mountain. If the slope becomes too steep directly above, contour to the left or right until the pitch of the slope lessens somewhat or a more attractive avenue of ascent is found. By maintaining a bearing of nearly due north, with just a bit of correction to the west, you can top out on the ridge near the upper end of Monitor Ridge—the long, high spine to the west of Swift Creek.

Monitor Ridge is the route used by summer climbers and leads to the best viewing site on the crater rim, although the true summit is found around to the northwest from the top of Monitor Ridge. Once at the summit, snowshoers can peer cautiously over the edge of the crater rim to see the steaming lava dome building in the crater and look out over the miles of destruction wrought by the May 18, 1980, blast.

Snowshoeing through the forest on the lower slopes of Mount St. Helens

Because the upper slopes of Mount St. Helens are open and treeless, a great deal of wind scours the snowpack up there. This can result in deep drifts of soft snow or sheets of hard-packed snow and ice, depending on the conditions during the storms. Come prepared with snowshoes featuring aggressive mountaineering cleats on both heel and toe, and carry—and know how to use—an ice ax for self-arresting in the event of a fall. This is a mountain climb and winter mountaineering skills are required.

100 June Lake

Rating: More difficult
Round trip: 5 miles
Hiking time: 3 hours
Elevation gain: 500 feet
High point: 3100 feet
Best season: Late December through early March
Map: Green Trails: Mount St. Helens Northwest No. 364S
Who to contact: Mount St. Helens National Volcanic Monument
Permits/fees: Washington State Sno-Park Pass required. You may also need a Washington State Discover Pass; check www.parks.wa.gov/130/Winter-Recreation.

Exploring the June Lake Trail on snowshoes, with the deep old forest, wide lake basin, and crashing waterfall all swaddled in a blanket of white, is the only way to enjoy the truly wild nature of the area. The trail is a gentle path through the woods, and snowshoers of all ages and abilities will appreciate and enjoy the remarkable beauty of the route.

Directions: From Woodland drive east on State Route 503 to the community of Cougar and continue east another 7 miles to a junction with Forest Road 83. Turn left (north) onto FR 83, and drive 5.8 miles to the Marble Mountain Sno-Park at the end of the plowed road. Small maps of the local winter trails are generally available in the kiosk inside the warming hut at the Sno-Park.

Route: Located on the south side of the big volcano, this trail doesn't delve into the blast zone, nor does the scenery make snowshoers think about the volcanic nature of the area. Indeed, if the eruption of 1980 comes to mind, it's usually in the context of "I can't believe an area this beautiful survived such a big eruption." The Mount St. Helens summit is visible along the trail to the lake, but looking up at the south flank of the mountain, with its snowy mantle of winter, it looks like just another big, beautiful peak. And June Lake is such

Climbing into the June Lake basin

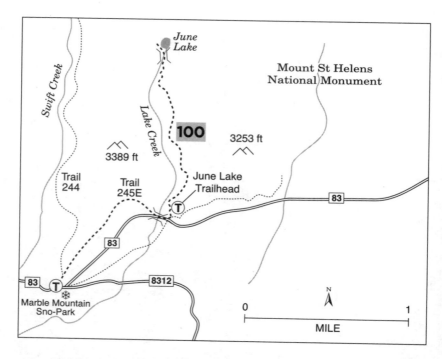

a remarkable setting that it doesn't need the powerful imagery of the eruption to make it a wonderful snowshoeing destination.

From the Sno-Park, snowshoe north from the upper parking lot on the well-signed Pine Marten Trail No. 245E. This trail, which is often groomed for skiers, parallels the road, but it is off-limits to snowmobiles. (You can also hike up the road to the June Lake trailhead, but it is often crowded with speeding snowmobiles.) The trail heads north for 0.75 mile, and then hooks right (east) and dips down to join the road at 1 mile. After using the road bridge to cross the wide Lake Creek, turn left and snowshoe into the large parking area of the well-marked June Lake trailhead.

The trail leaves the north end of the broad lot and crosses a large meadow in full view of Mount St. Helens. The open, treeless slopes are painted stark white by the drifting snow, and most weekends when the weather is clear, snowshoers on the June Lake Trail can watch snowshoers and skiers climbing the Monitor Ridge route (see Route 99, Mount St. Helens Summit) to the summit of the volcano.

The trail stays well above Lake Creek as it climbs gradually through a few stands of second-growth forest and open clearcuts before finally crossing into the protected national monument at 2.4 miles. The last few hundred yards of trail dip steeply down to cross the creek on a wide bridge before rolling north to the shore of June Lake. Across the lake, on the right, is a waterfall cascading down through a curtain of interlaced icicles. The wide bench at the lakeshore makes a wonderful picnic spot with its spectacular views.

Forests take on new dimensions and beauty come winter.

RESOURCES &
LAND MANAGERS

WEATHER
Northwest Avalanche Center (NWAC)
7600 Sandpoint Way NE
Seattle, WA 98115
(206) 526-6677
www.nwac.us

PERMITS & FEES
Methow Valley Trails Pass
www.methowtrails.org/winter-trails/passes/

National Park Service America the Beautiful Pass
www.discovernw.org/store_recreation-passes_1PASS/

Northwest Forest Pass
www.fs.usda.gov/detail/r6/passes-permits/recreation/?cid
=fsbdev2_027010

Stevens Pass Nordic Center
www.stevenspass.com/site/mountain/nordic/nordic-tickets

Washington State Discover Pass
www.parks.wa.gov/167/Discover-Pass-Fees

Washington State Sno-Park Pass
www.parks.wa.gov/130/Winter-Recreation

LAND MANAGERS
Nonprofits
Mount Tahoma Trails Association
PO Box 206
Ashford, WA 98304
www.skimtta.com

Washington State Parks
www.parks.wa.gov

Mount Pilchuck State Park
c/o Washington State Parks Northwest Region
220 N Walnut Street, Box 487
Burlington, WA 98233
(360) 755-9231

National Park Service
Mount Rainier National Park
Headquarters
Tahoma Woods, Star Route
Ashford, WA 98104
(360) 569-2211
www.nps.gov/mora

Mount St. Helens National Volcanic Monument Headquarters
42218 NE Yale Bridge Road
Amboy, WA 98601
(360) 449-7800
www.fs.usda.gov/mountsthelens

Olympic National Park
Visitor Center and Wilderness Information Center
600 E Park Avenue
Port Angeles, WA 98362
(360) 565-3130 and (360) 565-3100
www.nps.gov/olym

Gifford Pinchot National Forest
www.fs.usda.gov/giffordpinchot

Cowlitz Valley Ranger District
10024 US Highway 12
Randle, WA 98377-9105
(360) 497-1100

Mount Baker-Snoqualmie National Forest
www.fs.usda.gov/mbs

Darrington Ranger District
1405 Emens Street
Darrington, WA 98241
(360) 436-1155

Mount Baker Ranger District
810 State Route 20
Sedro-Woolley, WA 98284
(360) 856-5700

Skykomish Ranger District
74920 NE Stevens Pass Highway
Skykomish, WA 98288
(360) 677-2414

Snoqualmie Ranger District—Enumclaw Office
450 Roosevelt Avenue E
Enumclaw, WA 98022
(360) 825-6585

Snoqualmie Ranger District—North Bend Office
902 SE North Bend Way, Building 1
North Bend, WA 98045
(425) 888-1421

Okanogan-Wenatchee National Forest
www.fs.fed.us/r6/okawen

Cle Elum Ranger District
803 W Second Street
Cle Elum, WA 98922
(509) 852-1100

Methow Valley Ranger District
24 W Chewuch Road
Winthrop, WA 98862
(509) 996-4003

Naches Ranger District
10237 US Highway 12
Naches, WA 98937
(509) 653-1401

Wenatchee River Ranger District
600 Sherbourne Street
Leavenworth, WA 98826
(509) 548-2550

Olympic National Forest
www.fs.usda.gov/olympic

Hood Canal Ranger District—Quilcene Office
295142 US Highway 101 S
Quilcene, WA 98376
(360) 765-2200

Washington State Department of Natural Resources
South Puget Sound Region
950 Farman Avenue N
Enumclaw, WA 98022-9282
(360) 825-1631
www.dnr.wa.gov/RecreationEducation/Topics/OpenClosureNotices
/Pages/amr_south_puget_sound_region_rec.aspx

Looking out over Gold Creek Pond during a low-snow year

INDEX

ABOUT THE AUTHOR

Dan Nelson grew up hunting, fishing, and hiking the wild country around the Snake River canyons and Blue Mountains of southeastern Washington. After leaving college in 1989 with a BA in history, he put in a short stint as a general news beat reporter for some daily newspapers before becoming executive editor of *Washington Trails* magazine. While there, he continued writing for the *Seattle Times* Outdoors section, providing features and a regular gear review column. He also started working with several national outdoor magazines, including *Men's Journal, Backpacker,* and *Outside.* He has authored nearly a dozen guidebooks and launched a number of popular series with Mountaineers Books, including *Snowshoe Routes* and *Best Hikes with Dogs.* He also currently serves as editor of GearInstitute.com.

THE IMPACT AND IMPROVEMENT OF
SCHOOL TESTING PROGRAMS

Officers of the Society
1962-63
(Term of office expires March 1 of the year indicated.)

WALTER W. COOK

(1965)

University of Minnesota, Minneapolis, Minnesota

EDGAR DALE

(1964)

Ohio State University, Columbus, Ohio

LAURENCE D. HASKEW

(1963)

University of Texas, Austin, Texas

ROBERT J. HAVIGHURST

(1963)

University of Chicago, Chicago, Illinois

HERMAN G. RICHEY

(1965) (Ex-officio)

University of Chicago, Chicago, Illinois

STEPHEN M. COREY

(1964)

Teachers College, Columbia University, New York, New York

RALPH W. TYLER

(1965)

Center for Advanced Study in Behavioral Sciences, Stanford, California

Secretary-Treasurer

HERMAN G. RICHEY

5835 Kimbark Avenue, Chicago 37, Illinois

THE IMPACT AND IMPROVEMENT
OF SCHOOL TESTING PROGRAMS

*The Sixty-second Yearbook of the
National Society for the Study of Education*

PART II

By

THE YEARBOOK COMMITTEE

and

ASSOCIATED CONTRIBUTORS

Edited by

WARREN G. FINDLEY

Editors for the Society

NELSON B. HENRY and HERMAN G. RICHEY

19 NSSE 63

Distributed by THE UNIVERSITY OF CHICAGO PRESS • CHICAGO, ILLINOIS

The responsibilities of the Board of Directors of the National Society for the Study of Education in the case of yearbooks prepared by the Society's committees are (1) to select the subjects to be investigated, (2) to appoint committees calculated in their personnel to insure consideration of all significant points of view, (3) to provide appropriate subsidies for necessary expenses, (4) to publish and distribute the committees' reports, and (5) to arrange for their discussion at the annual meeting.

The responsibility of the Society's editors is to prepare the submitted manuscripts for publication in accordance with the principles and regulations approved by the Board of Directors.

Neither the Board of Directors, nor the Society's editors, nor the Society is responsible for the conclusions reached or the opinions expressed by the Society's yearbook committees.

Published 1963 by

THE NATIONAL SOCIETY FOR THE STUDY OF EDUCATION

5835 Kimbark Avenue, Chicago 37, Illinois

Copyright, 1963, by HERMAN G. RICHEY, *Secretary of the Society*

First printing, 10,000 Copies

Printed in the United States of America

The Society's Committee on the Impact and Improvement of School Testing Programs

RALPH F. BERDIE

Professor of Psychology and Director of the
Student Counseling Bureau
University of Minnesota
Minneapolis, Minnesota

WARREN G. FINDLEY

(Chairman)
Professor of Education and Co-ordinator of Educational Research
University of Georgia
Athens, Georgia

LAURENCE D. HASKEW

Vice-Chancellor, University of Texas
Austin, Texas

MERLE M. OHLSEN

Professor of Educational Psychology
University of Illinois
Urbana, Illinois

ARTHUR E. TRAXLER

Executive Director, Educational Records Bureau
New York, New York

J. WAYNE WRIGHTSTONE

Assistant Superintendent
Board of Education of the City of New York
New York, New York

Associated Contributors

JOHN M. BECK
Professor of Education and Assistant Dean
Chicago Teachers College, South
Chicago, Illinois

PAUL I. CLIFFORD
Professor of Education
Atlanta University
Atlanta, Georgia

THEODORE CLYMER
Professor of Education
University of Minnesota
Minneapolis, Minnesota

WALTER W. COOK
Dean, College of Education
University of Minnesota
Minneapolis, Minnesota

ROBERT L. EBEL
Vice President for General Programs
Educational Testing Service
Princeton, New Jersey

MAX D. ENGELHART
Director, Division of Student Examinations
Chicago City Junior College
Chicago, Illinois

JOSHUA A. FISHMAN
Dean, Graduate School of Education
Yeshiva University
New York, New York

ELIZABETH HAGEN
Associate Professor of Education
Teachers College, Columbia University
New York, New York

LUCILE LINDBERG
Professor, Queens College
City University of New York
Flushing, New York

CLARENCE A. MAHLER
Professor of Psychology
Chico State College
Chico, California

ROBERT D. NORTH
Associate Director, Educational Records Bureau
New York, New York

HARRY W. SMALLENBURG
Director, Division of Research and Guidance
Los Angeles County Schools
Los Angeles, California

RALPH W. TYLER
Director, Center for Advanced Study in the Behavioral Sciences
Stanford, California

Editor's Preface

At the June, 1959, meeting of the Board of Directors, it was noted that, although the National Society for the Study of Education had published several important yearbooks on the development and use of scales, standardized tests, and other forms of measurement and had published a larger number of yearbooks in which aspects of measurement were treated in the context of a variety of subjects, many years had elapsed since the Society had brought out a volume which focused on the best thought and most useful practices in any broad area of the field of testing.

Beginning with its earlier yearbooks on the subject, e.g., *The Measurement of Educational Products* (1918) and *Intelligence Tests and Their Uses* (1922) and extending to its more recent publications, the Society has been fortunate in being able to number among its contributors such leaders in the field as Thorndike, Courtis, Trabue, Starch, Whipple, Terman, Pintner, Thurstone, Gates, and many others of like stature.

It was decided that the Society would seek to have the successors of these men formulate and present the best in current theory and evaluate the impact of testing programs upon the schools. To plan the volume and to advise in assembling the talent needed to prepare it, the Society turned to Warren G. Findley, Assistant Superintendent for Pupil Personnel Services of the Atlanta Schools and more recently, Professor of Education at the University of Georgia.

Mr. Findley and the members of his committee decided, so far as it proved practicable, to present the materials in the form of a series of recommendations with supporting arguments based upon a rigorous evaluation of research and practice.

The committee and its collaborating authors have succeeded in making many issues and problems in testing understandable to teachers and laymen, have made clear that there is no causal relation between the growth in testing during the last decade or more and the increasing acuteness of educational and social problems during the same period, and have produced what Dilworth or

Fenning, famous authors of early eighteenth-century textbooks, would have called *A Sure Guide to the Use of Tests*.

NELSON B. HENRY
HERMAN G. RICHEY
Editors for the Society

Table of Contents

CHAPTER I

Purposes of School Testing Programs and Their Efficient Development

WARREN G. FINDLEY

The use of professionally standardized tests in the schools and colleges is growing apace. Their use is not new, rather it represents a revival. Standardized testing in the schools bloomed suddenly in the 1920's as a result of experiences of World War I, during which group measures of "intelligence" proved invaluable in the rapid classification of recruits. Achievement tests based upon test-construction techniques similar to those employed in the development of group intelligence tests seemed to promise to some persons the solution of the vexing problems of "quality control"; to others, a whole new "science of education." Because such test construction demanded a statistical competence not widely available, the test development of those days became too largely the province of statisticians who often lacked experience in instruction below university level and understanding of the larger functions of schools. School people bowed to technical requirements with some misgivings, amply justified in the 1930's when the earlier tests were rejected for their failure to promote and measure a balanced set of educational objectives, including ability to use or apply knowledge as opposed to mere encyclopedic mastery of more or less important facts.

World War II and the events which followed it gave a new kind of test a chance to prove itself. During the period of disenchantment with old tests, that is, during the 1930's, some new tests of basic skills and reasoning processes were developed. Power tests superseded speeded tests. Testing with newer types of tests proved itself helpful in a more modest, supplementary fashion in evaluating reading readiness, in establishing intraindividual as well as interindividual differences in mastery of skills and understandings to guide classroom instruction and sectioning, and in predicting both generally and differentially advanced educational and vocational success. Testing was already on the increase when the NDEA, in 1958, gave it a special place in the guidance programs supported by the Act. Today, testing, in the schools and elsewhere, is very much with us and appropriately is subject to searching examination by the society that is increasingly using it.

In these days of bigness, a certain impersonal quality has invaded much that used to involve rich personal experience. We flock to huge urban complexes to live. We travel in crowded public vehicles or in private ones that become crowded among great numbers of other private vehicles. We eat mass-produced and frozen foods; we dress in well-styled, comfortable, durable clothes made available to us at prices we can afford because they are mass-produced and mass-consumed. We choose these comforts and conveniences, but often strike out at or respond emotionally to the frustrations arising from crowding and impersonal servicing. Purple prose and extravagant criticisms of "mechanization" provide outlets for our frustrations over personal isolation and rootlessness amid more and more impersonal bounty.

Education does not escape these effects, many of which spill over from the world outside the school. Children fail to realize, as they always have, their parents' ambitions for them. But now this happens in a world and in a school fraught with frustrations emanating from forces at considerable social distance. The board of education is remote from the parent, just as is the president of the corporation for which the father works. Just as he feels unable to penetrate the intervening echelons to work out his job dissatisfactions with the top, he often feels unable to reach the top of the school system with his complaint—if indeed he is sure of just what he should complain. In this situation of school-coping frustrations piled upon job- and family-coping frustrations, it is only natural to look for a symbol of the impersonal forces in education—tests, their statistics, and the data-processing machinery associated with their efficient use—as the villains of the piece. Even some schoolmen, nostalgic for the days of Mark Hopkins and the log but forgetful that few in those days worried about those who fell off the log, are drawn into the popular pastime of hissing the villain.

To offer this interpretation as rebuttal of the criticisms of standardized tests and their use in the schools would be to beg the question. Rather, let us propose it as justification for picking our way carefully among the constructive uses and the abuses of tests, among the charges and countercharges of their effects. As a basis for such effort, let us begin with an effort to define a school testing program:

A school testing program consists of the systematic use, at more than one level and in more than one area, of one or more tests where the selection, administration, recording, and interpretation of the tests are all planned and conducted in close accord with the major objectives of the educational program.

This rather elaborate definition is necessary to do justice to the school testing programs that characterize major city school systems, most suburban schools, and increasing numbers of county and local systems. A structure of uniform testing of some sort is assumed, but a school testing program is not limited to uniform testing of all students at particular points in their educational careers. It is quite common to give a readiness test to all comers at the beginning of first grade, batteries of subject-matter achievement tests to all students every one, two, or three years through elementary and junior high school grades, group tests of mental ability every two or three years from fourth grade to some point in high school at which multiple aptitude tests may be used. The uniform program may also include interest inventories, personality questionnaires, general achievement measures, and special subject tests in high school. In addition, standardized group tests are commonly available for optional use by individual schools and teachers, or may be prescribed for all students presenting needs for special diagnosis or evaluation—poor readers, those suspected of mental retardation, those showing specific disability in any subject, those seeking educational or vocational guidance, or those thought to be in need of special opportunity to develop superior abilities. College selection testing programs are designed for students belonging in this latter category. (For fuller discussion of their impact, see chaps. v and ix.) Also, there ordinarily will be provision for individual testing of students at the extremes of achievement, ability, or adjustment by professionally trained specialists. In sum, the school testing program is a program of testing designed to assist the school in accomplishing its primary educational objectives.

RECOMMENDATION 1. *Testing is an essential supplementary tool in the operation of schools but should never be a dominant one.*

To the great body of professionally minded test specialists, who subscribe to what has already been stated in this and subsequent chapters of this yearbook, it will seem unnecessary to include the final qualifying clause. How can anyone believe the school testing program should play a dominant part, or even an autonomous part, in the operation of schools, they ask. It is true that few, if any, believe that testing should play such a prominent part, but it is often allowed to do so through the failure on the part of those responsible to devote the time and attention required to involve all concerned school personnel in the planning and operation processes. The program may be too casually assigned to a centralized staff borne down with other responsibilities, or may be introduced too hastily in an effort to "catch up" or to be doing something in an area that has suddenly commanded attention locally. In some communities so much is made of average achievement scores in a school, or differences in average scores between schools are so highly publicized, that test results are often accepted without qualification as evidence of the worth and effectiveness of the total program. (See especially chaps. vi, x, and xi for expansion and elucidation of these points.)

Rather, the supplementary role of a testing program needs to be clarified to all so that they may understand the many ways it supplements teacher judgment in planning instruction (see especially chaps. ii and iii), counselor judgment in advising students (see especially chaps. vii and xii), and administrators' judgment in evaluating the general effectiveness of the educational program, including special administrative arrangements.

RECOMMENDATION 2. *A school testing program should take full advantage of the great variety of appraisal devices available.*

If the school testing program is to play a supplementary role in the school's instructional program, if it is to help teachers help children learn, it must have a design or plan, a set of purposes, to be served in each instance by selection and use of appropriate testing instruments, devices, and procedures. It is the task of those charged with the responsibility of making the choices to select the instruments and techniques that are most relevant, most meaningful, most objective, and most administrable, with due regard for all these factors, but with concern for them generally in the order stated.

In making their choices, there is now available for use a wide array of techniques, instruments, and devices. As long ago as 1938, Wrightstone[1] described the variety then available. Current textbooks on educational measurement and evaluation list and describe them. In addition to standardized tests of achievement and scholastic aptitude, there are standardized interest inventories; questionnaires[2] and check lists to obtain self-reports from students of their attitudes, purposes and self-concepts; anecdotal and observational procedures for describing student behavior in day-to-day ongoing activities. If an evaluation program lacks balanced emphasis on the school's educational objectives, it may be the result of failure to utilize the variety of instruments available or of failure to make adequate use of instruments and procedures other than standardized tests needed to assist in school operations. (See chap. iii for further elaboration of this view.)

Within the field of achievement testing, a special problem has arisen recently. In the introductory remarks it was noted that the trend in testing is away from emphasis on encyclopedic knowledge of detailed factual information and toward ability to use knowledge to interpret materials, evaluate alternatives, or solve problems new to the student. In some cases it appears that this trend has gone so far that exercises proposed as evidence of achievement mastery depend largely on reasoning ability without regard to a systematic accumulation of relevant knowledge. "Useful knowledge on tap in

---

1. J. Wayne Wrightstone, *Appraisal of Newer Elementary School Practices.* New York: Bureau of Publications, Teachers College, Columbia University, 1938.

2. For discussion of peer choice techniques as a guide to classroom management read *Sociometry in Group Relations: A Work Guide for Teachers.* Edited by Helen H. Jennings. Washington: American Council on Education, 1948.

form ready to apply" may be said to strike the ideal balance between the extremes.[3]

RECOMMENDATION 3. *It should be recognized that standardized tests have been developed and refined and have proved to be the most promising and helpful instruments to meet the demand for measurement of continuous growth and of variability in intellectual-personal-social development.*

The standardized test is a product of scientific and highly technical procedures designed to help meet the very real and difficult problem of appraising intellectual growth. Few would question the central position of promoting intellectual growth among the objectives of any school program. Appraisal of such growth is of equal importance. It is important to know how much has been attained by each individual and class if instruction is to be built on knowledge of strengths and weaknesses, if guidance is to be offered with confidence, and if evaluation of the process is to be fed back into improving further learning by the students and better adaptation of teaching techniques in future teaching of the same knowledge and concepts. (See chap. iii for further discussion.)

The absence of any ready reference scale based on reliable absolute units presents a problem with which the test-maker must cope. There is no zero-point in the measurement of learning from which to start. Nor can we say that one student knows twice as much as another or that the difference between what John knows and what Harry knows is the same as the difference between what Harry knows and what George knows. In the absence of such absolute measures, we must turn to certain observed stabilities. One of these stabilities is how much a large representative group of students will learn under typical learning conditions, both the average they will attain and the extent to which they will vary from that average. To describe the attainment of any student, we must relate it to the levels of attainment of appropriate peer groups. Mental ages, grade

3. For further elaboration, see chap. viii in this yearbook, and also *The Measurement of Understanding,* chap. iv. (Forty-fifth Yearbook of the National Society for the Study of Education, Part I. Chicago: Distributed by University of Chicago Press, 1946.)

scores, and percentile equivalents are different types of comparative measures.

A process of comparison is thus forced upon us in interpreting the individual student's attainment. A current witticism presents one educational psychologist asking another, "How's your wife?" The second answers, "Compared to what?" The problem of describing educational achievement in comparative terms is, however, a serious one. It invites comparison in many situations where only description is wanted. Perhaps the most useful device for keeping this comparative emphasis within constructive bounds is the graphic profile of individual achievement. The student, the parent, or whoever else consults a profile notes first the individual student's high and low points, his strengths and weaknesses compared to his own average attainment. Thereafter, only to the extent that external comparisons are helpful need they be made. Such graphic profiles are essential features of all test offerings, and refinements in their structure and use are increasingly being made. (See chap. viii.)

One of these refinements is related to profile interpretation. The concept of a standardized test as a miniature representative sample of the infinite set of questions that might have been asked in an area has provided a basis for understanding measurement by such tests as having a sampling error of measurement that can be described and controlled. Thus, each test that is used gives a somewhat imperfect estimate of the hypothesized true achievement that would be measured by the infinite set of questions if they could be asked and answered. Graphic profiles on certain tests—the *Cooperative STEP* and *SCAT* series and the *Differential Aptitude Tests*—now provide for showing graphically the width of the error of measurement and, hence, the degree of difference between performances on two measures that is necessary to reflect dependable difference in "true" ability.

These graphic devices represent but a part of the assistance now provided in the test manuals and accessory materials. Today such manuals are a far cry from the technical reports of statistical evidence that once accompanied tests and correspond much more to the teacher-aids that accompany the better textbooks. (Again, see chap. viii for a full account.)

Another important feature of modern standardized tests is the continuity of measurement they afford. At the beginning of the testing movement, achievement tests were available only for the elementary grades, running through Grade VIII as befitted the almost universal school pattern of that day. In 1930, the Cooperative Test Service was created with foundation support to prepare tests for secondary schools, and these were primarily subject tests in the subject areas of high-school instruction. Today, each publisher has responded in his own way to the pressure of school people for measures of growth in the major areas of instruction from elementary school through Grade XII, or even junior college. Tests in the separate high-school subjects are still available, but teachers are now able to measure and discuss development of basic skills and knowledge over the full school career. In particular, articulation between levels of schooling housed in separate structures has been facilitated.

A feature of development of standardized tests that is often not fully appreciated is the extent to which most test publishers place reliance on panels of subject-matter specialists in constructing achievement tests. The details of their procedures vary from publisher to publisher and from test to test, but certain basic characteristics are quite common. First, the test specifications as to content and processes to be measured are prepared and reviewed by persons directly engaged in teaching the subject matter at the grade levels at which the test is to be used. Usually, these persons have been selected on nomination by teaching groups and are representative of the country geographically as well as of schools of thought in the subject area. Second, one or more persons—usually more—who are similarly qualified as subject-matter specialists prepare the test questions. Often they are the same persons who prepared the outline of specifications. Third, these same individuals or others similarly qualified review and revise the test questions by correspondence or in committee. These subject specialists, therefore, establish the integrity of the test materials. The publishers and their specialists then pretest the questions on student samples and build and standardize final forms. This latter part is done with technical competence, but the basic strength of each standardized test is in the carrying out of the planning and question production by qualified subject-matter specialists.

The foregoing paragraphs summarize briefly the salient features of test production that have evolved since its earlier development as described in the introduction to this chapter. They indicate and describe practices and devices developed to produce the quality of tests and test-use demanded by the schooling of today. The remaining chapters of this volume constitute the full account of the response to that demand.

RECOMMENDATION 4. *In planning or evaluating school testing programs, it is important to recognize that the purposes they serve in the operation of schools may be classified broadly as (a) instructional, (b) administrative, and (c) guidance.*

The distinction among the instructional, administrative, and guidance purposes served by tests in the school program is helpful in many ways. From first to last, schools have always been concerned with instructional outcomes, particularly as they portend readiness for further instruction. This justifies supplementing teacher judgment by use of readiness tests at the point where formal schooling in reading and number concepts begins, currently for most children, at the beginning of first grade. Parenthetically, one could wish the concept of readiness had antedated that of intelligence, for our group intelligence tests are some of our best readiness measures and could be recommended for such use if they did not offer the possibility of computing and recording a dangerously unreliable I.Q. at an early age.

After formal schooling begins, continuity in learning makes the use of continuous measures of appraisal important and also suggests the desirability of testing at the beginning of the school year when pupils are new to the teacher and up-to-date information can be obtained for all members of the class. Testing late in the year, on the other hand, misses transfers into the school, requires transmittal of less timely information from one teacher to another, and has the less wholesome effect of encouraging direct teaching and learning for the test. Autumn testing has the effect of obtaining the integrity of a candid camera shot as contrasted with a posed photograph. The obvious implication of the timing is to secure information useful in the planning of teaching and learning in the year ahead.

The administrator has been concerned with maintaining a

"quality control" check on progress in his school(s). This suggests annual measurement, at the same time each year, with related instruments that permit reliable evidence of growth as well as of present status.

The point at which the measurement of each skill and substantive area of knowledge is worked into the annual fall testing of achievement is clearly indicated in many test batteries. There is a logic, however, that should guide those selecting the battery and subtests to be used. Reading comprehension (word, sentence, paragraph) is significant and measurable from the start. Testing of other skills, like spelling and computation, may well be postponed beyond the primary level because, even though they can be tested at that level, such testing puts a premium on the mechanics of the subjects at the expense of other important learning outcomes. (If standardized testing of arithmetic reasoning is introduced too early, student success is apt to depend as much on reading ability as anything else.)

All of which brings us naturally to the point of discussing the testing of listening comprehension. This is done most often in remedial reading programs, where the individual's level of listening comprehension is used to set an expectation of the level of reading comprehension he may be expected to attain with successful remedial instruction. Listening comprehension is coming to be recognized as an important skill in its own right, a proper objective of direct instruction. Moreover, it possesses in considerable measure the predictive powers of the group intelligence test without yielding a dubious I.Q. estimate. The future of standardized testing in the primary grades belongs to oral and pictorial testing of learning outcomes outside of reading comprehension.

In the intermediate grades, it becomes appropriate to test not only reading comprehension and listening comprehension but also arithmetic computation, arithmetic reasoning, language usage, social studies, science, and study skills, as is possible in most batteries. Interpretation of results by the use of a profile in the ways previously discussed becomes the order of the day. And the testing in these major areas extends upward into high school as far and at as frequent intervals as the total school program demands.

The guidance function is a supplement to instruction which attempts by counseling and placement to fit the curriculum experience more effectively to each student. This type of adaptation evolves from the adaptations managed by the primary-grade teacher in her self-contained classroom and continued by other classroom teachers through whatever grade this pattern of school organization provides. The guidance emphasis appears first in the school testing program at the point where group tests of mental ability are introduced to guide evaluation of achievement relative to potential, usually in the upper elementary grades. Guidance use of tests emerges into full view at that point in the school career where departmentalization or course choice is first encountered. The tests used depend on the extent to which general mental ability tests and/or achievement tests are used to predict general and differential success in the academic programs of high school and college. Much that is of concern in this connection is discussed elsewhere in this chapter in the treatment of individual needs-readiness. Suffice it to note at this point that two or three determinations of general mental ability in Grades V through IX justify themselves in terms of improved decisions with regard to sectioning in junior high grades when they are used to supplement teacher evaluations and achievement test results.

At the point in an instructional program at which the opportunity to choose a vocational curriculum is first presented, a multiple-aptitude battery, like the *Differential Aptitude Tests,* and an interest inventory are useful instruments by which evidence may be obtained to combine with other considerations in giving positive guidance. A full discussion of these uses and of the merits of various batteries and inventories for the purpose is given in chapter viii. However, the author of this chapter wants to note that such tests and inventories might profitably be used as a screening device in many school systems where the comfortable rationalization prevails that those not meeting the curriculum and behavioral standards of the academic high school are likely to do better in a vocational school or (*sotto voce*), at least, in such a school they won't keep the serious-minded academic students from having a full opportunity to learn. After screening those who show greater promise in vocational than in academic programs, the school system may be asked to face separately and solve in the way most appropriate to that system the problem of instructing those who show little promise of success in either the academic or vocational programs offered students generally.

The total program of testing might well include one other systematic element. Today more than ever, high schools find they are teaching students with varied backgrounds deriving from their varied school experiences in science and social studies. It would seem to be in the interests of efficiency to precede instruction in any high-school course in these fields with a pretest of knowledge already mastered. Standardized achievement tests in the several subjects provide a natural check since they tend to cover what has typically been the content of the advanced courses. Having students exchange papers and taking a show of hands on the number right on each question will give the more detailed information needed for instructional planning. The initial student scores may be used to provide a benchmark against which to measure what is learned during the course if an alternate form of the test is administered near the end of instruction.

Finally, a staff of qualified psychological examiners should be charged with the responsibility of testing individual students requiring more extensive diagnostic study and remedial help than the time and competence of the classroom teacher and/or counselor permit. Close liaison between teacher and specialists can result in rehabilitation—sometimes rapid—of students with serious emotional and/or learning difficulties; or in determining that special help and placement are required.

RECOMMENDATION 5. *A multipurpose testing program offers efficiencies over piecemeal testing for separate purposes.*

This is a corollary of the preceding generalization. Annual fall testing with achievement tests of the same series provides information immediately valuable to teachers at the beginning of instruction in each grade. The same data may be summarized later by school and subdistrict as well as system-wide for purposes of administrative appraisal or "quality control." Further, the data on individual students will provide the basis for immediate and long-range guidance of their choices of courses, colleges, and careers.

As an example, consider the use of an arithmetic achievement test in eighth grade. It first serves the teacher as a semidiagnostic indicator of strengths and weaknesses of the class and its individual members in the arithmetic to be taught in that grade. Second, it serves a guidance function in helping to identify those strong enough to be admitted to algebra at the earliest opportunity and thereby to be prepared for advanced placement in mathematics in college, perhaps in engineering. Later, the results of this same arithmetic test can be tabulated to serve as part of the summary of eighth-grade achievement in the school or school system for review by the administrator. This is simply one illustration of the three-way usefulness of achievement test data. It could be repeated for reading, language usage, science, and social studies. (For further discussion of these uses, see chap. vii.)

An important point to observe is that the test should be chosen with instructional use first in mind. The results of a test long enough to give dependable evidence for instructional purposes may be condensed for guidance and administrative uses. On the other hand, somewhat briefer tests appropriate for general appraisal or guidance may provide too little detail for instructional use.

Certain external testing programs, of which the *Preliminary Scholastic Aptitude Test (PSAT)* of the College Entrance Examination Board is a good example, serve efficiently a different purpose. Until the test became available to Juniors in the fall of 1958, many students and their parents were advised by counselors that the *Scholastic Aptitude Test* should be taken at the spring administration in the Junior year for the experience and guidance value provided for taking the test in the Senior year for college admission. This was advisable in many ways, but the *PSAT*, which parallels the *Scholastic Aptitude Test,* can now be given less formally by the school at a much reduced fee, and results returned by December of the Junior year are in time for guidance and scheduling for the second semester of the Junior year in high school.

RECOMMENDATION 6. *The usefulness of test data obtained on an every-pupil basis warrants systematic testing without separate justification in terms of immediate usefulness to every pupil tested.*

It is fair to ask the examining authority to have a purpose and a use for any testing done in the school testing program, but the purpose and use may be the obtaining of information for group evaluation, the compilation of local norms, the study of relationships between test scores and other data, or the identification of individuals not initially suspected of particular capabilities or defects, rather than usefulness to each individual tested. The converse of this proposition would be that the total testing program should consist largely of testing directly useful to the examinee in his school career.

RECOMMENDATION 7. *It should be recognized that, at any given moment, an individual's instructional needs and his readiness for a program of instruction are opposite faces of the same coin.*

Programs of instruction in the schools are designed, through group arrangements, to meet the needs of individual children as they grow and mature toward adult responsibility. The definition of these needs involves assumptions regarding the nature of adult responsibility in our society—in the home and in community affairs as well as in productive labor—and regarding the developmental tasks that face all individuals as they progress through school. In these important respects we are more alike than different. At the same time, it is recognized that individuals progress at different rates and along different paths toward different positions of adult responsibility. Assessment of each individual's readiness for particular steps in the instructional program is a recognition of these differences as they affect the suitability of instructional arrangements. It is in furtherance of this function that tests, and particularly a school testing program, systematically contribute useful data. Particular note should be taken of the complex nature of the readiness discussed in this paragraph. Readiness implies capability to achieve. It, therefore, implies assessment of current achievement as basic to further achievement and as indicative of the point of departure for developing that achievement. As long ago as 1937 Bingham[4] in his classic work on aptitudes and aptitude testing pointed out that the best aptitude test in the sense of predicting future achievement is a measure of present achievement. Today this conclusion is accepted widely, and the earlier easy distinction between aptitude

4. Walter V. Bingham, *Aptitudes and Aptitude Testing*. New York: Harper & Bros., 1937.

and achievement tests on the basis of capacity to learn versus what has been learned has been qualified, if not supplanted, by a distinction based on the purpose—predictive or evaluative—for which particular tests are used. However, we now also recognize that different types of advanced achievement depend in varying degree on different levels and kinds of past achievement—from very general skills for coping with the environment (seen most clearly in tasks posed in individual tests of intelligence) through basic skills of reading and arithmetic to specific mastery of particular concepts and knowledge on which more advanced concepts and organized knowledge may be built. Two examples spring to mind. The skill of comprehending the spoken word is a skill basic to the mastery of reading just as truly as reading is basic to mastery of substantive knowledge presented in books. Second, the power of a test, like the College Board's *Scholastic Aptitude Test*, to improve prediction of college achievement over what can be predicted on the basis of high-school grades or achievement tests indicates that, for most college work, a high level of basic skill in reading and arithmetic is quite as important as mastery of previous specific subject-matter learning. In both instances, the concept of readiness must be broadened to include a variety of evidences of readiness which can be measured by tests, and these sources of readiness are established by a combination of correlational research and analytical insight into the learning process. The task of the teacher, aided by the test specialist through the school testing program, is to be continually alert and sensitive not merely to current achievement but to all evidences of readiness which, in combination, indicate readiness or promise for learning.

RECOMMENDATION 8. *Because an individual's instructional needs-readiness is a product of his cumulative experience to date, maintenance of individual cumulative record folders is a corollary requirement of any school testing program.*

This corollary requirement is offered on the basis of the preceding discussion. There is justification for maintenance of cumulative records for individual children apart from a school testing program. The child-study emphasis in many schools and teacher-education programs warrants the keeping of such records. But it must be clear that any instructional program which uses a school testing program to help teachers help children learn through sensitiveness to all evidences of readiness is an extension of the child-study emphasis and hence, for each child, will need to take account of a rich cumulative record of such materials as information on home background, health history, and mobility data, as well as earlier test results and subject marks. Knowledge obtained from such records of unusual factors that have affected a child's development add to the meaning of current information. A systematic school testing program in a school maintaining such individual records assures that generally useful measures of readiness are available for each child, not only for immediate assessment but cumulatively for evidence of growth trends. A child doing better this year than last, however poorly he may yet be achieving, merits positive commendation for what, for him, may be outstanding progress. An implication of this approach for the school testing program is that the tests used in successive grades should be related to each other in some intrinsic way that provides comparable scores. Such comparability may result from the use of a series developed by the same publisher and/or from the use of locally developed norms. This point is more fully developed in the discussion of Recommendation 5 on the merits of a multipurpose testing program.

RECOMMENDATION 9. *Instructional programs should take fuller account of the fact that the range of intellectual differences among children of the same chronological age (or school grade) in a subject area is far greater than the differences between averages for individuals one year apart in chronological age (or grade placement).*

The extent of individual differences has been discussed and recognized for a long time. The range and scope of these individual differences are described in the foregoing recommendation in terms that relate to the present grade structure of our schools. Any acceptable plan for organizing a school must be a scheme for the best instruction of individuals who differ to the extent described in the statement.

This proposition is treated thoroughly in chapter iv, so only a few further statistics will be presented in this chapter. The writer, in a survey[5] conducted by him, found that both the local distribution for white pupils in Atlanta and the distribution characteristic of the national sample on which the current edition of the *Stanford Achievement Test* was standardized showed at Grade VI a spread from below Grade II to above Grade XI in reading level, with appreciable numbers of children (over 2 per cent of each population) at the grade extremes indicated. And despite the fact that median reading-grade levels varied from 8.5 to 3.8 in schools in the socioeconomically favored areas and the slums, respectively, the range of reading levels in sixth grade was only a grade or two narrower in the individual schools than in the city-wide and national distributions. Note that throughout this discussion the data for Atlanta simply reflected the national situation presented by the test norms.

RECOMMENDATION 10. *Account needs to be taken of the less commonly stressed fact that individuals differ, often substantially, in their intellectual competence in different areas of instruction.*

While it is certainly true that children who do outstanding work in, say, reading are more likely than not to be above the average of their peers in arithmetic, nevertheless a profile of individual strengths and weaknesses will commonly show greater achievement in one field than in another. The differences in the competencies of the individual are covered more fully in chapter iv.

Table I is designed to illustrate differences of individual competence by presenting data on reading and arithmetic achievement for a school with three classes in the seventh grade (N = 103). The data, tabulated by half-grade intervals provide the basis for showing the situation that would exist in classes that might be formed by grouping for instruction on the basis of reading level, the skill basic to success in the greater part of the academic curriculum.

The differences among the means of the arithmetic scores of the members of such classes do not provide an adequate guide for instruction. Another way of summarizing the data is to count

5. *Learning and Teaching in the Atlanta Public Schools, 1955-56.* Princeton, N.J.: Educational Testing Service, 1957.

the individuals who stand in the same third of the group in both subjects. There are 21 in the upper third (approximate) in both subjects, 16 in the middle third on both, and 18 in the lower third on both. This means that 55, or barely half, of the 103 children would be classified the same in both subjects. Significantly, there are 6 who stand in the top third in one subject and the bottom third in the other. These include the boy with the highest score in arithmetic (9.6) who is reading below grade (6.5).

TABLE 1

SCATTER-DIAGRAM OF ACHIEVEMENT SCORES IN READING AND ARITHMETIC, STANFORD ACHIEVEMENT TEST, ADVANCED, FORM J, FOR 103 PUPILS IN GRADE VII IN A SCHOOL WITH AVERAGE ACHIEVEMENT

Average Arithmetic

Average Reading	4.5–4.9	5.0–5.4	5.5–5.9	6.0–6.4	6.5–6.9	7.0–7.4	7.5–7.9	8.0–8.4	8.5–8.9	9.0–9.4	9.5–9.9	
11.0–11.4								2	1			
10.5–10.9							2					
10.0–10.4					1		3	1	1	1		
9.5–9.9							1	2				36
9.0–9.4						1	1	2	3	1	1	
8.5–8.9			1			4	1	1	3	2		
8.0–8.4				1	2	3		1		1		
7.5–7.9			2		2	3	3	2	2	1		35
7.0–7.4					3	2	5	2				
6.5–6.9			1	2	1	2	2				1	
6.0–6.4	1		1	2	3		1	2	1			
5.5–5.9				2	1	4	1					
5.0–5.4												32
4.5–4.9		1	1									
4.0–4.4			1									
3.5–3.9					1							
			30				39			34		

At high-school levels, this type of discrepancy is one significant clue in educational and vocational guidance. Those markedly stronger in mathematics are advised of the greater probabilities of success in natural or social science, or engineering, while those much stronger linguistically are advised of more favorable probabilities in the arts, literature, journalism, or the law. We are uncertain of the causal factors in these intraindividual differences, but their existence is real from early in school life. Kelley[6] found evidence of significant differences in facility with numbers and facility with words as early as Grade III.

These findings call into question the concept of the "straight A" student when sufficiently challenging tasks are presented in different subject areas. They justify homogeneous grouping, subject by subject, in high school as recommended by Conant.[7] Solutions for the elementary school are not so clear. (See chap. iv.) The Advanced Placement Program[8] of the College Entrance Examination Board supported by elaborate procedures for guiding college-level study in high school and appraising the college equivalence of achievement by tests, is a promising approach.

A special note should be inserted here, pending fuller discussion in chapter xii. Profiles of ability or achievement are based on relation to a standardization group. Wherever there is an unstable situation, as in science education today, where society is shifting its value judgments and curriculum experimentation of all sorts is shifting the grade placement of subject matter to lower grade levels and introducing new advanced materials at higher levels, excellence relative to an outdated norm becomes treacherous to interpret. In view of the spread of curriculum revision from field to field in the schools today, it is of great importance that interpretation, even of relatively stable measures of basic skills, be done with caution.

6. T. L. Kelley, *Crossroads in the Mind of Man*. Stanford, California: Stanford University Press, 1928.

7. James B. Conant, *The American High School Today*. New York: McGraw-Hill Book Co., 1959.

8. Edward T. Wilcox, "Seven Years of Advanced Placement," *College Board Review*, XLVIII (Fall, 1962), 29-34.

RECOMMENDATION 11. *Testing should be adapted to the level of competence of every student, so far as possible.*

In view of the tremendous magnitude of individual differences already discussed, if the school testing program is to provide information most useful to the classroom teacher and others concerned with the individual student's learning, the testing must be related to the individual student. More useful information concerning a student's present achievement and readiness for further achievement can be obtained from a test that challenges him than from one that either overwhelms him or presents no challenge to him. It does little good to test a child in the sixth grade with an achievement battery adapted to the reading level of the average sixth-grader if he reads at third-grade level and his test scores primarily reflect his poor reading ability rather than his relative mastery of the several subject areas covered. Conversely, superior students are sometimes prevented from showing their true excellence by the low "ceiling" of the test. On such tests the top scores often go to less outstanding students who answer with almost complete accuracy the less challenging test material presented. It is time to start "testing the child where he is," as we have been attempting for some time to "teach the child where he is." This is being done in some places by grouping students at their reading levels when giving achievement tests.[9] In a recent paper,[10] the writer reported the effects of testing with lower level tests on records of group achievement. As had been expected, the median achievement measures matched those of previous years and only the lower quartiles were reduced by measuring at low levels students who had previously obtained spuriously high scores because the lower limits of the scale for the higher level test did not go low enough to measure the low level of mastery of some students in various parts of

9. Warren G. Findley, "Use and Interpretation of Achievement Tests in Relation to Validity," *Eighteenth Yearbook of the National Council on Measurement in Education*, p. 24. Ames, Iowa: Department of Psychology, State University of Iowa, 1961.

10. Warren G. Findley, "The Effect of Adapting Standardized Tests to Reading Level in Grades IV-VII on Interpretation." Paper presented before American Educational Research Association, Atlantic City, February, 1962.

the test. The teachers and principals were overwhelmingly in favor of the adaptation.

The foregoing study was made with a test that was not designed for adaptation. Students had to be tested in special groups—in this case, the grouping was by reading level, groups already set up for instructional purposes—and some of the lower level tests lacked subsections present in higher level tests. The more recently standardized *Cooperative Sequential Tests of Educational Progress (STEP)* and *School and College Ability Tests (SCAT)* are constructed so that the tests at successive levels in reading, social studies, science, and the like, have the same instructions, time limits, and numbers of questions. This feature makes it possible to give simultaneously these tests at different levels in the same classroom, obviating the need for special testing arrangements.

RECOMMENDATION 12. *In interpreting and using test results, account must be taken of the fact that the individual's response to a test may have been influenced by factors other than his competence in the area covered by the test.*

Much has already been said about the influence of reading ability on achievement. This influence is seen most clearly when students are so poor in reading as to be unable to read questions that most of their peers can read readily. In classroom testing in science in third grade, where students master many terms and concepts when presented orally and visually over TV but cannot read or write about them, much could be done by reading questions and short answers aloud to them while they follow a printed test sheet and indicate choices by underlining. But reading comprehension enters in more subtle fashion into test results. A feeling for the precise meanings of words helps in discriminating between a "best" answer and others. Because of the necessity to present questions and answers in written form, the level of reading comprehension required by a test is a factor to be considered in choosing between competing test series, even at high-school and college levels. (See chap. viii for fuller discussion of the reading factor in tests.)

Factors of socioeconomic deprivation or advantage affect individuals' achievement, aptitude, and attitude scores in individual ways as well as in ways predictable from their group membership.

Students who have had success with tests face new tests with confidence; those who have had little success in the past fear the worst. Students may be said to "accept" or "reject" tests, too, in proportion to the degree that they seem sensible or relevant to their personal purposes. Test specialists have often noted that under-privileged children and adults do even worse, relatively, on certain non-verbal tests than on tests requiring reading or school learning. In an effort to be fair to poor readers, test exercises requiring no reading are used. But these usually involve abstract figures. Persons from favored homes will have been accustomed to puzzles or brain-teasers of this sort as parlor games; to those from under-privileged areas, however, such exercises may seem basically mean-ingless. The latter may be poor readers or poor achievers generally, but they accept reading and school achievement tests as presenting proper requirements, while abstract materials are just that.[11]

In responding to attitude, interest, and personality inventories, individuals may give false reports of their positions, intentionally or unintentionally. We all like to appear at our best. "Desirable" responses may be given to please the teacher or, in competitive situations, to make favorable treatment more likely. In some cases this is done unconsciously.

Test specialists are alert to these problems and make every attempt known to them to prevent misinterpretations. In particular, it is constantly stressed that measures involving self-report can be interpreted at face value only in counseling situations where the examinee has been enlisted in his own interest to answer faithfully. The elaborate precautions taken by major test publishers in develop-ing their tests to insure accuracy, unambiguous statement of in-structions and of individual test questions and to secure more representative and more varied norms samples and the preparation of manuals to guide teacher use of tests are a source of professional pride to those engaged in test development. (See chap. viii for fuller discussion.)

11. A fuller discussion of this point is presented in Warren G. Findley, "Factors That Affect Test Results," *National Elementary Principal*, XLI (November, 1961), 6-10.

RECOMMENDATION 13. *The appraisal of the extent to which individuals and groups achieve up to their capacity is a complex activity requiring a strong background of technical competence as well as understanding of the learning process.*

For years, we have known that the appraisal of "capacity" or "potential" is complicated, but it is still too common to find studies based upon scores on a group test of general mental ability employed as handy statistical measures of capacity. This is true despite evidence that (*a*) there is so great overlap in the measures of capacity and achievement that the measurement errors loom large in interpreting the individual's performance, (*b*) corrections must be made for the "regression effect" of errors of measurement if one is to avoid systematic errors of interpretation favorable to those of low capacity and unfavorable to those of high capacity, and (*c*) the unitary nature of mental ability is questioned by the great majority of psychological research specialists, thus making dubious the evaluation of achievement in specific areas on the basis of a general measure of capacity.

Earlier discussion in this chapter has pointed to the undependability of group measures of mental ability at early grade levels. Even when conditions of distractibility are controlled by testing in small groups, young children will differ in their response to formal testing. Moreover, each skill learned is dependent on precursory skills. In reading, these include at least (*a*) listening comprehension, (*b*) visual discrimination, (*c*) breadth of reality experience. Measurement and observation of these competencies are more relevant to determining potential for learning reading than a global measure of a hypothesized general ability on a group test. (Individual tests are not used because of their prohibitive cost per pupil.) Much the same could be said of learning arithmetic, although this area has not received the thorough attention that has been accorded to reading.

At higher levels of instruction it is evident to both teachers and research specialists that reading is precursory to learning from the printed page and that competences in arithmetic computation and arithmetic reasoning are precursory to handling the learning in certain advanced work, especially in the physical sciences, where quantitative relationships are involved. If we add study habits and organized relevant knowledge as factors in advanced study, the influence of a global general mental ability as it relates to specific learning at the high-school and college level is best viewed as a possibly relevant contributor, but one to be considered as supplementary to other more direct factors. If general mental ability does indeed influence later achievement, in part directly and in part through facilitating the mastery of basic skills directly involved in the advanced learning, since the group test of mental ability tends to involve reading and arithmetic particularly, one may well ponder whether this complication does not render causal interpretation virtually impossible. Certainly there is little comfort in noting that at the college-entrance level the College Entrance Examination Board's *Scholastic Aptitude Test* depends almost entirely on reading comprehension and arithmetic reasoning and yields scores for those skill components separately, without regard to a concept of general mental ability. The factor studies of Thurstone and, more recently, of Guilford make it seem probable that a multiple factor view of intelligence makes for the most logical explanation. To return to our earlier statement, however, the best use of measures obtained from a group test of general mental ability is to supplement measures of basic skills and other factors in specific advanced achievement in setting an expectation against which to compare the level of advanced learning achieved.

Interpretation of achievement relative to expectation involves two other points that should be noted in way of a warning. The first is the tendency for most of those who rank low on aptitude measures to rank somewhat higher in achievement and, conversely, for many of those ranking high in aptitude to rank somewhat lower in actual achievement. It is obvious in the extreme cases that the one who ranks highest in aptitude cannot possibly rank higher than that in achievement and that the one ranking lowest in aptitude cannot do worse than that in achievement. It is also true that those predicted low will include more whose aptitude scores involve more unfavorable than favorable errors of measurement on the predictor measures (see discussion under Recommendation 3), while the reverse will be true in the case of those predicted high. The use of regression equations to make predictions will correct for this tendency and is common in research studies, but the warning is necessary because less sophisticated studies are frequently made and reported.

The second point to be made has to do with what Shaw[12] calls the hidden underachiever. Some underachievers not only do poorly on achievement tests and make low school grades but also do poorly on the measures used to estimate their capacity to learn. In other words, their poor achievement is equally reflected in both types of measures, and relatively poor achievement appears simply what might be expected of relatively modest ability. Here a teacher's judgment, based on observations of what the student can do at his best, when he temporarily puts forth more than his typically inadequate effort, is crucial. A special case of this hidden underachiever is the truly outstanding student who does superior work compared to that of his peers, yet does not extend himself intellectually. Teacher judgment must again be used to detect the existence of such a situation. In such instances we are often at a loss for comparative standards for lack of other students of comparable ability. It seems only reasonable to point out that this argues for bringing together able students, subject by subject, to stimulate one another. Many of them will respond to the increased intellectual challenge of their classmates. (For fuller discussions that differ somewhat from that given in this chapter and from each other, see chaps. vii and xii.)

RECOMMENDATION 14. *There need be no essential opposition between the serving of the examinee's needs and purposes and those of the society in which he lives and grows.*

This recommendation presents a very broad philosophical issue, but has a specific application to school testing programs and their use. Individuality is inescapably imbedded in the group culture. The individual is not merely unable to withdraw from society but attains full self-realization through interaction with his fellows. He, therefore, has an individual interest in social goals which are fur-

12. Merville C. Shaw, II, "Definition and Identification of Academic Underachievers" in *Guidance for the Underachiever with Superior Ability*, chap. ii. Office of Education Bulletin 1961, No. 25. Washington: Office of Education, U.S. Department of Health, Education, and Welfare, 1961.

thered by developing socially useful talents to the full—as measured and monitored in a school testing program—and in being guided by tests toward developing his varied talents in ways that are socially most useful.

The foregoing statement, however, cannot stand by itself because, narrowly interpreted, it could be used as a rationalization for regimentation. It is intended as a positive assertion of the democratic values of group membership and participation; it also rejects assertion of individuality at the expense of others' individuality. As to school testing programs, it implies that programmed testing is justified as undergirding the instructional and administrative operations of schools.

With regard to guidance, the use of tests must be within a framework in which social usefulness is broadly defined to include an appreciable quota of poets, philosophers, religious leaders, novelists, performing artists, and the like, so that students may properly be guided to choose such careers despite any feeling of compulsion about other socially necessary vocations. In any event, effective use of test results in guidance and instruction must stop far short of coercion. Able students may and doubtless should be counseled to take challenging subjects, but they and their parents make the final decision as to what subjects and how many in the light of all evidence, including tests.

Summary

This chapter is necessarily broad in its coverage, being introductory to the remainder of the volume. In this discussion of the purpose and efficiency of school testing programs, the writer has made evident that he believes that such programs may be highly useful to schools. He regards the unfavorable criticisms of such programs, referred to in his introductory remarks, as a welcome sign of interest in the purposes and uses of testing programs. He welcomes an impartial investigation (advocated by some critics) of these programs and is confident that they would benefit rather than suffer from an independent audit of their influence. It is suggested, however, that such an investigation should consider (a) how matters would be handled better without the testing programs or with better programs, and (b) what better use might be made of the results and findings of school testing programs already in operation.

In closing, it seems appropriate to offer a specific suggestion. Any school testing program will be more effective if those primarily engaged in the instructional program, the teachers, can acquire a background of general understanding of testing that is appropriate to them as teachers rather than as potential administrators, counselors, or test specialists. There are many excellent books to which teachers may turn, e.g., a recent one by Thomas, which is especially suitable for elementary-school teachers.[13] Others among current books, notably those by Torgerson and Adams,[14] have been addressed to teachers at elementary- and secondary-school levels, respectively. Many new paperbacks are being devoted to specific points of test interpretation, test construction, and the like. The future of readable material in this field is promising. Relatedly, the future of testing programs depends, in part, upon the knowledge and understanding of them possessed by laymen, by teachers, and by other school personnel.

13. R. Murray Thomas, *Judging Student Progress*. New York: Longmans, Green & Co., 1960 (second edition) [Distributed by David McKay, Co., Inc., 119 West 40th St., New York.] The writer introduces each chapter by depicting a natural school situation: a student-teacher discussing objectives with his supervisory teacher, a teacher discussing with a mother her child's low achievement on a test, a teacher discussing the meaning of standardized test results with his principal. Similar treatments for other levels will no doubt be made available.

14. Theodore L. Torgerson and Georgia Sachs Adams, *Measurement and Evaluation for the Elementary-school teacher*. (New York: Dryden Press, 1954. Distributed by Holt, Rinehart & Winston, Inc.); Georgia Sachs Adams and Theodore L. Torgerson, *Measurement and Evaluation for the Secondary-school Teacher* (New York: Dryden Press, 1956. Distributed by Holt, Rinehart & Winston, Inc.).

CHAPTER II

The Relation of Testing Programs to Educational Goals

ROBERT L. EBEL

Any activity which takes the time of students and teachers can be justified only if it contributes to the attainment of educational goals. Indeed, most educators would probably say that not only tests but every aspect and arrangement of the educational enterprise, such as facilities, staff, materials, organization, administration, curriculum, instruction, guidance, evaluation, and the like, should be selected and operated to contribute to attainment of the goals of education. But, since test results are often used as one indication of the success of the school program, as well as the successes of individual pupils, the importance of relating tests directly to educational objectives deserves particular emphasis and leads to several recommendations.

RECOMMENDATION 1. *Choose tests and plan the school testing program so as to measure as directly as possible as many as possible of the school's educational objectives.*

Like many other reasonably obvious recommendations, this one is easier to state than to follow. The first problem is to determine what the school's educational objectives ought to be. A second, closely related problem is to state these objectives clearly enough to provide unequivocal guides to test selection and use.

The literature on educational objectives is extensive. It extends back into history at least as far as Plato, and probably beyond.[1] Even the contemporary references on this topic are numerous and varied. Volume xii of *The Education Index*, covering the period

1. Bernard Bosanquet, *The Education of the Young in the Republic of Plato.* Cambridge: Cambridge University Press, 1917.

from July, 1959, to June, 1961, lists approximately 140 articles under the heading, "Education—Aims and Objectives." Such diverse titles were included as the following: "Academic Excellence and Cosmic Vision," "Citizenship Responsibility in Education," "Man, Values, and the Machine," "Social Purposes of Education," and "Triumph of Achievement over Inquiry in Education." Clearly, the goals of education are conceived to be numerous, various, and complex.

Logically minded educators find this situation quite unsatisfactory. Over thirty years ago John Dewey described the problem as he saw it then and suggested a possible solution.

The sum of the matter is that at the present time education has no great directive aim. It grows, but it grows from specific pressure exerted here and there, not because of any large and inspiring social policy. It expands by piecemeal additions, not by the movement of a vital force within. The schools, like the nations, are in need of a central purpose which will create a new enthusiasm and devotion, and which will unify and guide all intellectual plans.[2]

Interestingly enough, the most recent work containing an authoritative consensus relating to educational goals is entitled *The Central Purpose of American Education*,[3] as if in answer to Dewey's plea.

Many other writers have attempted to give direction to the educational enterprise by formulating a statement of its single basic purpose or general goal. For example, Spencer said, "Education has for its object the formation of character."[4] Huxley elaborated the point in these words, "Perhaps the most valuable result of all education is the ability to make yourself do the thing you have to do, when it ought to be done, whether you like it or not."[5] Whitehead said this: "Education is the acquisition of the art of the utiliza-

2. John Dewey, "Some Aspects of Modern Education," *School and Society*, XXXIV (October, 1931), 583-84.

3. *The Central Purpose of American Education*. Washington: Educational Policies Commission of the National Education Association, 1961.

4. Herbert Spencer, *Social Statics*, Part II, chap. xvii. New York: Robert Schalkenback Foundation (50 East 69th St.), 1954. (Originally published in 1851.)

5. Thomas Henry Huxley, *Science and Culture, and Other Essays*. London: Macmillan Co., 1882.

tion of knowledge." [6] More recently, Conant expressed the view that, "Our purpose is to cultivate in the largest possible number of our future citizens an appreciation of both the responsibilities and the benefits which come to them because they are Americans and are free." [7]

While many educators would challenge the views of one or another of these writers, most would applaud their intentions. That is, they would regard a valid statement of basic educational objectives as the foundation of the whole educational enterprise. Given a carefully prepared statement of objectives, they imply one should be able to deduce the proper characteristics for all other aspects of the enterprise, and so know how to conduct it properly. If asked where authorization can be found for such a statement of ultimate educational goals, they might reply, as Aristotle, Aquinas, Rousseau, Hutchins, Maritain, and Sheen have replied, that the appropriate ends of education can all be deduced from the true nature of man.

But there are others who find this conception of the source and function of educational objectives quite unrealistic. The educational enterprise, as they view it, is far from a tight, logical, hypothetic-deductive system. They are skeptical of "true" and complete statements of educational goals based on the "true" nature of man. They doubt that what goes on in Mrs. Everett's fourth-grade classroom at 9:30 A.M. on Tuesday, January 9, 1962, has been, or conceivably could be, deduced in all particulars from any verbal statement of single or multiple educational goals. They would argue that the educational activities in that room are determined largely by what the school, and Mrs. Everett, and her pupils now are, as products of their past history. They might claim that any statements of educational objectives which the school or Mrs. Everett may express or endorse are more truly results than causes of the total educational process.

Grieder has recently expressed skepticism concerning the meaningfulness, validity, and necessity of some recent formal statements of educational goals:

6. Albert N. Whitehead, *The Aims of Education*, p. 16. New York: New American Library (Mentor Book), 1949.

7. James B. Conant, *Annual Report to the Board of Overseers, Harvard University*. Cambridge, Massachusetts: Harvard University Press, 1943.

Are not the goals of a society largely unformulated, like the unwritten British Constitution? They develop slowly and through a continuous process of interaction among various segments and levels of a
society, and among societies.[8]

Most educational activities are clearly purposeful activities, but
it does not follow that all of these purposes can be explicitly stated.
Nor does it follow that all of them can be derived by logical analysis from a very few statements of general goals. The foundation
on which the structure of education has been erected is the nature
and the needs of man and of the society in which he lives. No abstract statement of educational goals can specify or imply all of
the details of these natures and needs. The best they can do is to
highlight certain aspects which may have been overlooked in the
past or made important by contemporary developments.

RECOMMENDATION 2. *Use statements of educational objectives
to focus special attention on limited, clearly defined, particularly
important aspects of the school's total educational program.*

A statement of educational goals is composed of abstract generalizations, derived from observed processes of education but
modified to express the authors' ideas of how those processes could
be improved. They do not precede the educational endeavor, as the
architect's drawings precede the erection of a building. Rather
they report certain salient features of the educational endeavor, including proposed changes, as a road-builder's map reports the salient features of an existing territory. Like both blueprints and
maps, these statements of educational goals omit many details which
the builder, or the traveler, must supply from his own experience.

Statements of educational goals serve a useful purpose if they
are clear expressions of realistic choices among attractive alternatives; if they express realistic expectations instead of fond hopes;
if they establish priorities which honestly recognize that, to achieve
certain desired goals, other desirable goals will have to receive less
attention or no attention at all. Such a statement of educational
goals would be more than mere window dressing for the sake of

8. Calvin Grieder, "Is It Possible to Word Educational Goals?" *Nation's
Schools*, LXVIII (October, 1961), 10 ff.

public relations. It would provide working specifications for change —and, hopefully, improvement—in the school program.

Unfortunately, many current statements of educational goals are designed only to be read with approval, not to serve as tools for the building of educational progress. In such statements, ambiguity is more useful than explicitness, and inclusiveness more acceptable than selectivity. But even a tough-minded, realistic, directive set of educational goals is not a sufficient basis for developing the school's testing program. It is a factor to be considered, but only one of the factors. What the school is and what it does day by day must be given full consideration, along with the statement of its goals, in planning its testing program.

RECOMMENDATION 3. *In planning the school testing program, consider not only the educational objectives made explicit in a formal statement of goals but also those which are implicit in every purposeful activity which constitutes the school's educational program.*

Each of the multitude of activities which occupy the hours in school of a teacher and her pupils implies an educational goal. Few of these activities could be derived by rigorous, logical deduction from any statement of ultimate educational goals. Probably all of them could be defended as plausibly relevant to one or more of such ultimate goals. But so, also, could a host of other activities which this particular class has not undertaken. In deciding whether this or that specific activity should be undertaken by a class, a teacher may find it helpful to refer to a statement of general goals of education. But seldom will a wise decision be possible on this basis alone. She must consider also her own capabilities, the unique needs of her pupils and their capabilities, the facilities of the school, the wishes of the community, and the like.

The tasks of the school—even the tasks of teaching a particular subject in a particular grade—are too numerous and diverse to be fully expressed or even implied by any manageably concise statement of goals. To build an effective school testing program one must consider much more about the school and its program than can be conveyed by a verbal expression of the school's educational goals. No school should develop its testing program solely on the basis of a formal statement of objectives or without regard for the detailed actualities of its educational program.

RECOMMENDATION 4. *Whenever it is feasible, use descriptions of enlightened, effective behavior to clarify the meaning of verbal statements of educational objectives.*

The tendency for many statements of educational objectives to be abstract, general, and ambiguous has already been noted critically. One solution for this problem is to define the goals in terms of the overt behavior which indicates achievement of the objective. This helps to make the statements concrete, specific, and definite. The use of job analysis in developing tests of vocational competence, no doubt, suggested this approach for tests of educational achievement. Perhaps the broad appeal of behavioristic psychology also had something to do with it. Whatever the reason, it has become the generally recommended technique, at least among specialists in educational measurement, for defining educational goals in meaningful, useful terms.

Ralph W. Tyler was one of the early advocates of the definition of educational goals in behavioral terms. In a book published in 1936 he wrote:

In order to make a list of major objectives usable in building examinations, each objective must be defined in terms which clarify the kind of behavior that the course should help to develop among the students. That is to say, a statement is needed which explains the meaning of the objective by describing the behavior we can expect of persons who have attained it.[9]

Many other writers, particularly those concerned with educational measurement, have expressed similar views. There have been three major efforts, culminating in the publication of three separate volumes, to define educational goals in behavioral terms at the levels

9. Herbert E. Hawkes, E. F. Lindquist, and C. R. Mann, *The Construction and Use of Achievement Examinations*, pp. 9-10. Boston: Houghton Mifflin Co., 1936.

of (a) the elementary school,[10] (b) the secondary school,[11] and (c) the college.[12] At present, most specialists in educational testing recommend or approve the definition of educational goals in terms of the observable behavior of the student.

But in spite of their virtues, behaviorally defined objectives have not proved to be entirely satisfactory. The virtue of specificity involves the burden of multiplicity. Behavioral definitions tend to be books, not paragraphs, sections, or even chapters. Even in the books, the definitions cannot be completely specific, for it is obviously impossible to specify fully and exactly *all* the particular behaviors that are desired. The virtue of concreteness involves the burden of complexity. Appropriate behavior in any concrete situation is always the resultant of awareness of all relevant factors and their interactions and of balanced judgment concerning the weight to be accorded to each factor. Abstractions, for all their faults, do have the virtue of relative simplicity. The virtue of definiteness involves a danger of overemphasis on conformity. For, if the goals of education are defined in terms of narrowly specific behavior desired by the curriculum-makers and the teachers, what need is there for critical judgment by the student; what freedom is there for creative innovation; what provision is there for adaptive behavior as the cultural world changes?

RECOMMENDATION 5. *Give high priority, among the behavioral goals of education, to independence of decision and action on the basis of broad knowledge, thorough understanding, and reflective thought.*

The point we are concerned with here has been expressed by Jane Loevinger in these words:

In regard to education at the nursery-school and kindergarten level, no doubt specific behaviors can be used to measure the success of the educational endeavor. The aim of university education is emphatically

10. Nolan C. Kearney, *Elementary School Objectives.* New York: Russell Sage Foundation, 1953.

11. Will French and Associates, *Behavioral Goals of General Education in High School.* New York: Russell Sage Foundation, 1957.

12. Benjamin S. Bloom, *Taxonomy of Educational Objectives.* New York: Longmans, Green & Co., 1956.

not to inculcate such stereotyped behavior patterns, but to free the graduate from conformity to cultural and behavioral stereotypes.[13]

This suggests that the goals of education (at least for the upper levels of education) should be defined, not only in terms of patterns of desired behavior—the *end products of* effective living—but also in terms of tested potential for inventing appropriate behavior—that is, the *means to* effective living.

This view has been emphasized in a recent publication of the Educational Policies Commission, in which the need for rational independence is described by its authors in these words:

> To be free, a man must be capable of basing his choices and actions on understandings which he himself achieves and on values which he examines for himself. . . . He must understand the values by which he lives, the assumptions on which they rest, and the consequences to which they lead. . . . He must be capable of analyzing the situation in which he finds himself and of developing solutions to the problems before him. . . . The free man, in short, has a rational grasp of himself, his surroundings, and the relation between them.[14]

The goals of education as these men would see them, and as we see them, are concerned with developing processes as well as products; with adaptability as well as with adaptations. To regard the development of specific desired behaviors as the sole goal of education is to treat the rising generation as servants of our past rather than as masters of their future.

RECOMMENDATION 6. *Recognize and make use of the behavioral definitions of educational objectives which are implied by the tests in the school testing program.*

What a student is asked to do to demonstrate his competence provides a matter-of-fact definition, in behavioral terms, of what the goals of instruction really are. Students recognize this and tend to study most carefully the matters on which they expect to be examined. If the tests which a school uses are poor or seriously

13. Jane Loevinger, "A Theory of Test Response," *Proceedings, 1958 Invitational Conference on Testing Problems.* Princeton, New Jersey: Educational Testing Service, 1959.

14. *The Central Purpose of American Education.* Washington: Educational Policies Commission of the National Education Association, 1961.

incomplete measures of the school's educational objectives, two unfortunate results are likely to follow. Not only are the measures obtained from the test likely to be inaccurate indications of the school's real achievements but also the efforts of the teachers and students are likely to be diverted from the goals they are supposed to be pursuing.

Reference was made earlier in the chapter to the unfortunate tendency of many statements of educational objectives to be generously comprehensive, boldly optimistic, and conveniently vague. Whatsoever things are of good report are sometimes included among the school's claimed objectives, in the hope that the school can find a way of teaching these things and measuring student achievement of them. Examination of the tests a school actually uses, and the other means it employs for evaluating student achievement, can help to curb the more extravagant of these flights of fancy.

Tests can be valuable tools for motivating and directing student achievement *if* they are good tests and if the students and teachers know of their general nature at the beginning of a course of instruction. Of course this does not mean that teachers or students should seek advance knowledge of and engage in special practice for particular questions which occur in the tests. What they do need to know is the kind of abilities they are expected to develop and the tasks by which their achievement will be judged.

The intimate relation between tests and educational objectives, namely, test selection guided by educational objectives and tests helping to define the objectives, has two extremely valuable consequences. Consideration of the limitations of tests and other techniques of evaluation helps to keep our statements of objectives more realistic. Consideration of the definitions of desired achievement provided by the test helps to make teaching and learning more purposeful and effective.

RECOMMENDATION 7. *When any outcome of education is claimed to be important but unmeasurable, inquire concerning the clarity with which it has been defined. If an operational definition is possible, the outcome can be measured. If not, its claim to importance cannot be verified.*

Education is a complex process which results in complex, and often subtle, outcomes. It is not surprising, therefore, that writers sometimes mention the existence and importance of intangible outcomes of education. Such writers are likely to suggest that the intangible outcomes of education are difficult to measure and may be entirely unmeasurable.

An alternate view is based on two propositions. (*a*) A human trait is measurable, in at least an elementary sense, if the assertion that one person possesses more of it than another can be independently verified by two or more observers. This means that, if having more or less of a trait makes any observable difference, that trait is measurable. (*b*) In order to be important, an outcome of education must make an observable difference in the behavior of persons who have attained different degrees of it. If attaining an alleged goal of education does not change the overt behavior of the person who attains it in any way, on what basis can it be said to be important?

To say that all important outcomes of education are potentially measurable is not to say that all can be measured easily. But it is to say that any distinction between the tangible and the intangible outcomes of education, between the measurable and the nonmeasurable, is spurious.

Why is this point so often misunderstood? Two possible reasons can be suggested. The first is that we use vague, undefined, general terms in talking about the goals of education—terms like character, citizenship, open-mindedness, creativity, excellence, and adjustment. Now there is nothing wrong in the use of general terms to express general ideas. On the contrary, it would be impossible to do otherwise. And statements invoking general terms do serve a useful purpose at some levels of discourse. But we err if we assume that there exist somewhere real, clearly definable, important, human characteristics corresponding to each of the many names we use in describing human behavior. We err further if we think that our main task is that of discovering the true natures of these characteristics rather than that of defining what we mean when we use these trait names. We err most grievously if we attribute difficulty in measuring these named characteristics to limitations in our techniques of testing instead of attributing it to vagueness or lack of agreement as to what the name signifies.

Any unambiguous definition of a quantitative attribute clearly implies a method of measuring it. Conversely, any test or other means of quantifying an attribute implies a definition of it. If we know how to specify the method for determining which member of any pair of persons possesses the greater amount of the attribute in question, we know both what the attribute means and how to measure it. But if the method remains to be developed, we not only lack measurements of the attribute but also a clear idea of what the attribute means.

A second reason why some outcomes of education are held to be unmeasurable may be that the measurement is thought to refer properly only to processes which meet all the requirements for fundamental physical measurement. Some writers, like B. Othanel Smith,[15] have concluded that mental testing leads to numbers which are not measurements at all. Others, like Lorge [16] and Comrey,[17] recognize the value in quantitative processes which do not involve equality of units or an absolute zero. Bergmann and Spence [18] have pointed out that *fundamental* measurement of some attributes of great interest to us is unattainable in principle. But if this were taken to mean that these attributes are unmeasurable, we should have to find some other term for our successful and useful processes of dealing with them in quantitative terms.

A third reason for denial of the measurability of some important educational outcomes may be the opportunity it provides for committed antiscientists to re-emphasize the limitations of scientific methods. Further, the measurement of human traits opens the door to evaluations and judgments, which, since they might be unfavorable, are sometimes feared. Thus, there may be some elements

15. B. Othanel Smith, *Logical Aspects of Educational Measurement*. New York: Columbia University Press, 1938.

16. Irving Lorge, "The Fundamental Nature of Measurement," in *Educational Measurement*. Edited by E. F. Lindquist. Wahington: American Council on Education, 1951.

17. Andrew Comrey, "Mental Testing and the Logic of Measurement," *Educational and Psychological Measurement*, XI (Autumn, 1951), 323-34.

18. Gustav Bergmann and Kenneth W. Spence, "The Logic of Psychophysical Measurement," *Psychological Review*, LI (January, 1944), 1-24.

of defensiveness in the opposition to probings of the human mind
—some comforting shelter to be found in attributing impenetrable
mysteries to the human spirit—which encourage belief in narrow
limitations to the scope of educational measurements.

The practical limitations of effective educational measurement
are real and many, as anyone who has labored to improve educational measurements can testify. But they are not fixed eternally
by the nature of man, nor is it useless to try to overcome them.
The possibility of measuring the degree of attainment of all important outcomes of education does exist.

RECOMMENDATION 8. *Include in the school testing program tests
for all the educational outcomes which the school is actually working to achieve.*

If a school includes tests of such things as attitudes, interests, and
values in its testing program, it implies a concern for these things as
educational goals. The tests may have limitations, and the school's
efforts to educate toward these educational goals may be somewhat
uncertain, but the fact that students are tested on them implies that
the school regards them as important. Hence, a testing program
can recognize nonintellectual goals. In so far as the school program purposefully pursues such goals, and in so far as available
evaluation techniques permit, it *should* include measures of nonintellectual educational outcomes in its testing program.

What do we mean when we speak of nonintellectual goals?
Plato [19] suggested *emotional* and *volitional* goals, for he identified
affection (emotion) and conation (will), in addition to cognition
(intellect), as three aspects of the human soul. Spencer [20] discussed
moral and *physical*, along with *intellectual* goals, as aspects of education. The authors of the NSSE Yearbook on *Learning and Instruction* [21] included chapters on motor learning, interests, motives

19. Rupert C. Lodge, *Plato's Theory of Education*. London: Kegan Paul,
Trench, Trubner & Co., 1947.

20. Herbert Spencer, *Education: Intellectual, Moral and Physical*. New
York: A. L. Burt Co., 1861.

21. G. Lester Anderson and Others, *Learning and Instruction*. Forty-ninth
Yearbook of the National Society for the Study of Education, Part I. Chicago:
Distributed by the University of Chicago Press, 1950.

and attitudes, aesthetic responses, and personal and social adjustment, as well as on the more conventionally intellectual aspects—
information, concepts, generalizations, and problem-solving.

It seems clear that none of these goals of education is purely
nonintellectual or wholly devoid of intellectual content. But it
seems equally clear that the emphasis placed on intellectual goals
has varied from age to age, usually in response to social pressures.
In recent years there has been a sharp increase of emphasis on personal and social adjustment. Even so, there has been more concern
for excellence than for adjustment. One can applaud or deplore
the current emphasis on intellectual achievement as an objective
of education. From the point of view of this chapter, it is a desirable emphasis which deserves continuing support.

RECOMMENDATION 9. *Let the school testing program emphasize
the cognitive outcomes of education, in recognition of the school's
central, fundamental, all-pervasive goal of intellectual development.*

It may be appropriate to mention here that any paper-and-pencil
test is essentially an intellectual task. Whatever the name of the
test, whatever it purports to measure—attitudes, interests, values,
character, personality, adjustment—the examinee who seeks to perform well on such a test will respond to it as thoughtfully and as
wisely as he can. He will report what he knows or thinks about his
attitudes, interests, values, and the like, or what he believes he ought
to report. Such a test is, for him, a test of self-knowledge and
self-understanding. It may or may not indicate how these attributes
affect his behavior in daily life.

Reference has already been made to the intellectual component
of most educational goals. While one cannot maintain physical
health and vigor or develop motor skills solely by thinking about
them, it does help to have and to be able to use the knowledge
relevant to the attainment of such goals. This point is stressed per-
suasively in the recent publication of the Educational Policies Commission already quoted:

> The purpose which runs through and strengthens all other educa-
> tional purposes—the common thread of education—is the development
> of the ability to think. This is the central purpose to which the school
> must be oriented if it is to accomplish either its traditional tasks or those

newly accentuated by recent changes in the world. To say that it is central is not to say that it is the sole purpose or in all circumstances the most important purpose, but that it must be a pervasive concern in the work of the school. Many agencies contribute to achieving educational objectives, but this particular objective will not be generally attained unless the school focuses on it. In this context, therefore, the development of every student's rational powers must be recognized as centrally important.[22]

The Educational Policies Commission, in a section on "Developing Rational Powers," notes the importance of the "inquiring spirit." This is a gentler term than *skepticism* or *critical thinking* but involves the same approach to education. Unfortunately, it is not the approach favored by some among those who stress the nonintellectual goals of citizenship, character, attitudes, values, interests, appreciations, or personal and social adjustment. Nor is it the approach of those who would define educational goals in terms of an extensive catalog of desired responses to particular situations.

Those who warn against overemphasis of intellectual goals sometimes are reflecting concern, not over the neglect of other goals, but over pressure on students who find it difficult to achieve goals of any kind. Education should be enjoyable, they argue, not stressful. The child's happiness is as important as his intellectual development, perhaps more so, they say. Surely the emphasis on intellectual excellence can be overdone. To some extent such overemphasis is self-defeating and, hence, self-correcting. But overemphasis on moment-to-moment happiness is equally dangerous.

The remaining two recommendations deal with the effect of external testing programs on a school's educational freedom and initiative. What evidence there is suggests that the possibly harmful effects tend to be exaggerated and can be neutralized quite simply. Preoccupation with supposed dangers may distract attention from positive values. These considerations lead to the following recommendations.

RECOMMENDATION 10. *Participate actively in wide-scale testing programs as one effective means of stimulating and directing efforts to achieve common educational goals.*

22. *The Central Purpose of American Education, op. cit.,* p. 12.

RECOMMENDATION 11. *Balance external tests with appropriate internal tests of purely local goals, or of common goals which may be neglected in the wide-scale testing programs.*

It seems beyond question that testing affects teaching and learning. Students tend to study the things on which they expect to be tested and to neglect the other things. If the teachers know that their students will be judged on the basis of some outside test, they tend to teach most thoroughly the things likely to appear in the test. Indeed, advance notice and description of tests is used by many teachers to motivate and direct student learning. Similarly, educational organizations sometimes introduce new tests in their programs not so much to measure achievement as to stimulate educational effort in the area of the test.

Recognition of the influence of tests on teaching has led to expressions of fear that the "test-makers" may determine the goals of education and control the curriculum. Such fears are easily exaggerated. Most tests are prepared with the co-operation of teachers who are experts in the subject matter of the test.[23] They are deeply concerned with the fairness of their tests to all students who have had good instruction in that subject. If their tests do not reflect the best judgments of other experts with respect to appropriate content and outcomes, either the tests will not be accepted or widely used or the test-makers will be subject to sharp and determined criticism. In the relation of testing to teaching, the influence of teaching on the tests is far stronger and more directly effective than the influence of the tests on teaching.

But there is another aspect of this relation which deserves attention. Even though tests do reflect a consensus of the best teachers, it is a consensus, not a diversity. Is there educational harm in shaping all teaching of a subject to a single pattern, however good that pattern may be? No doubt there could be, though it may well be that education in the United States has suffered more from the diversity of local educational programs, particularly with respect to the quality of those programs, than it has from any pressures to conform.

23. *ETS Builds a Test.* Princeton, New Jersey: Educational Testing Service, 1959.

The Regents Examinations in New York State are frequently cited by advocates of educational freedom and initiative on the part of the local school, as examples of the repressive and stultifying effects of external examinations. No doubt a few teachers in New York, who could be creative and stimulating teachers, have assumed wrongly that the Regents Examinations required them to act as robot drillmasters. No doubt some teachers have used these examinations as an excuse for the drab performances which represented about the limit of their capabilities in any case. But many more have seen these examinations as an opportunity to show how good they really are. They have perceived that imaginative, skilful teaching was more likely to be recognized in an educational system which tries to assess the quality of its output than in one which takes the quality for granted or ignores it.

It is interesting to observe that when nation-wide testing permits comparisons of educational achievements among the states, New York State tends to rank at or near the top. To assert that evidence of this kind *proves* the value of state-wide achievement-testing would be to go beyond the evidence, but this evidence does no harm to such an hypothesis.

No one has seriously urged that an absolutely uniform educational program should be imposed on all school children in this country. No one has seriously urged that a local school or an individual teacher should have unlimited freedom in planning and operating an educational program. Some uniformity is essential. Some freedom is essential. The problem is to find the most effective balance between the two.

Wide-scale testing programs are appropriate for measuring the attainment of uniform regional or national objectives. If this kind of testing is all that a school does, the uniform, externally accepted objectives may come to receive disproportionate emphasis. If a school does have special local goals for which it is teaching purposefully, then it ought to have a local testing program to assess progress toward those goals. Under these conditions the use of external testing programs will not limit a school's educational freedom and initiative.

Not all readers are likely to agree with the soundness of all these recommendations. Some of them imply a certain skepticism regarding some oft-repeated assertions and some common practices. These points have been selected for emphasis because they deal with matters on which change and improvement seem possible and urgently necessary.

Education in the United States is remarkably effective, considering the magnitude of its problems. But it could be and needs to be much more effective. One of the ways of making it so is to abolish our double standards of talk and action. What we *say* about education ought to agree much more closely than it often does with what we *do* about education. Idealists say we must improve our performances without lowering our sights. Realists argue that we ought to do two things: (*a*) identify our targets a little more clearly and check to see whether they are actually within range, and (*b*) improve our marksmanship and gunnery. Education is a powerful tool, but there are limits to its accomplishments. Realistic, clearly perceived goals can help us maximize those accomplishments.

CHAPTER III

The Relation of Testing Programs to Teaching and Learning

J. WAYNE WRIGHTSTONE

Teaching and learning are affected both directly and indirectly by school testing programs. The quality of the tests themselves set limits to what can be accomplished through their use, while the way tests are used in a school testing program determines their impact on the teaching and learning that goes on in the school.

RECOMMENDATION 1. *School testing programs may profitably take advantage of the expanded range, nature, and scope of objectives measured by modern tests.*

In recent decades, the range, variety, and nature of tests and techniques for appraisal of pupil growth and development have expanded to meet new educational needs. Modern tests are a far cry from early objective tests. Schools have increasingly emphasized not only concepts, skills, and information but also understanding, interpretation, and appreciations. This trend has required the development of tests of basic study skills, tests of interpretation of data and application of principles as well as measures of appreciations, interests, and attitudes. This trend toward comprehensive evaluation was illustrated in early studies by Smith, Tyler, and others[1] and by Wrightstone.[2]

During these decades, tests of differential aptitudes and primary mental abilities, based on factor analysis studies, appeared. Tests of

1. Eugene R. Smith, Ralph W. Tyler, and Associates, *Appraising and Recording Student Progress*. New York: Harper & Bros., 1942.

2. J. Wayne Wrightstone, *Appraisal of Newer Elementary-school Practices*. New York: Bureau of Publications, Teachers College, Columbia University, 1938.

general educational development were devised. These tests were designed to measure the ability of the individual to understand and interpret information and concepts. In general, they permit a differential diagnosis of fundamental abilities and skills. The design of newer tests encourages the teacher and the learner to concentrate not only upon mastering factual information but also upon abilities, skills, attitudes, and interests of more lasting value. Moreover, there will always be a need for assessing educational objectives by methods other than tests—observational techniques, checklists, rating scales, projective techniques, and sociometric methods.

RECOMMENDATION 2. *Tests should be used to clarify and refine the objectives of the educational program. There should be a continuous interaction among instruction, learning, and testing based upon the changes in definition, clarification, and refinement of objectives.*

The philosophy of education in any school will be important in determining the values or objectives. For some schools the objectives will be comprehensive; for others they will be more limited. For all schools, however, the objectives include a common core of abilities—for example, reading comprehension, mathematical abilities, selected study skills, and understandings in general education. The interaction may be described by starting at any point in the cycle. For example, the test specialist recognizes the need for objectives defined in terms of changes in behavior which can be objectively measured by test exercises. School personnel realize that an effective way of emphasizing an educational objective is to measure progress toward it by means of informal and formal tests. For both, the teacher and the pupil, the clearly defined objective becomes a goal that may be realized in day-by-day teaching and learning. The test exercises, properly constructed, help to clarify and to refine the objectives for teacher and pupil. This interaction of instruction, learning, and testing is desirable. It should be continuous. Testing can contribute to the organization and nature of instructional and learning experiences. These, in turn, may indicate desirable changes in the organization and content of tests.

RECOMMENDATION 3. *Tests must be considered fundamental tools*

in research involving evaluation of modern educational and psycho-
logical theories of teaching and learning.

Education in the United States has been characterized by a willingness of many schools or school systems to experiment with different ways and means of education. The schools constitute a huge
social laboratory in which thousands of experiments are in progress.
In many of these experiments, tests play an important role in arriv-
ing at judgments about their worth.

In 1897, Joseph M. Rice[3] published his study entitled, "The
Futility of the Spelling Grind." Rice compared the achievement of
pupils who spent a considerable amount of time on spelling drill
with that of others who spent less time. To obtain a measure of
achievement, he devised a spelling test which may be considered
the first modern, formal type of test.

Since 1897, thousands of studies have used tests as the main
source of evidence to arrive at conclusions about teaching and learning in the areas of reading, arithmetic, science, and social studies.
One need only consult published yearbooks of the National Society
for the Study of Education for indisputable proof of this generalization. Currently, tests are used in evaluation of such diverse educational and psychological teaching and learning methods as programmed learning, team teaching, individualized reading, and
teaching by television, to mention but a few.

RECOMMENDATION 4. *Tests are rightly used as an important aid*
to the teacher and supervisor for identifying and meeting the range
of individual differences among pupils in their abilities, achieve-
ment, interests, attitudes, and needs. They provide guidance for
individualized as well as group instruction.

The teacher frequently does not realize the diversity of ability
and achievement among pupils in a classroom. In the average classroom, there are wide ranges of pupil achievement. This range of
ability and achievement increases from grade level to grade level.
Studies show that increasingly wide ranges of achievement are
characteristic of reading comprehension, vocabulary, mechanics of

3. Joseph M. Rice, "The Futility of the Spelling Grind," *Forum*, XXIII
(April and June, 1897), 163-72, 409-19.

English composition, and mathematics as one proceeds through the grades and on into high school.[4] For extensive documentation of this point, the reader is referred to chapter iv of this yearbook.

In addition to the differences in achievement, the teacher and supervisor will discover individual differencs in aptitudes, interests, motivations, and attitudes. Tests will help the teacher and supervisor identify and make intelligent provision for individual differences and needs of pupils through individualized instruction, intraclass grouping, and differentiated and supplementary assignments. But, basically, tests, observations, and interviews help the teacher and supervisor know each child better as an individual and guide him more wisely.

RECOMMENDATION 5. *Tests should be used to facilitate the diagnosis and treatment of learning difficulties. They help the teacher and learner to discover strengths and weaknesses in learning.*

Since most learning difficulties are complex and involve not only intellectual abilities but also physical, social, and emotional concomitants, all these should be evaluated by available tests and other techniques. Frequently, however, some symptoms of learning difficulties may be detected in discrepancies among measures of abilities and achievement. For mild cases of learning difficulty, remedial action may, after brief diagnosis, be initiated by the teacher.

More complex learning difficulties in reading or mathematics, for example, may require specialized tests and testing not only of academic skills and abilities but also of physical and emotional characteristics. The treatment may likewise require the counsel or more extensive services of one or more specialists—the school counselor, psychologist, social worker, psychiatrist, and others. During the treatment phase, tests are usually administered periodically to estimate the progress of the learner.

RECOMMENDATION 6. *Tests should and do play an important role in motivating students toward educational and vocational goals.*

4. Walter W. Cook, *Grouping and Promotion in the Elementary School.* College of Education Series on Individualization of Instruction, No. 2. Minneapolis: University of Minnesota Press, 1941.

The test results, interpreted by the guidance counselor, permit the student to decide on tentative educational and vocational goals.

As the individual matures, he reaches an age of decision, as it were, about his educational and vocational goals. Some pupils may be able to enlist the aid of a guidance counselor. Others will have only their teachers as guides. In conference with a teacher, adviser, or counselor, results from an interest inventory, achievement test, aptitude battery, and other test data may be available to the student. This permits him to gain a deeper insight into his abilities, interests, and attitudes. He may set tentative educational and vocational goals, in part, as a result of the impact of testing programs in his school career. Dressel and Matteson [5] conducted a study to measure the effects of the use of test data in counseling. The evidence suggested that students who participated in the interpretation of their test scores gained more in self-understanding and became more secure in their vocational choices than the students who did not so participate. Gustad [6] reached similar conclusions in his studies and his reviews of other studies of test information as it related to counseling.

RECOMMENDATION 7. *Account should be taken of the way motivational factors affect test performance. Tests may affect motivation for achieving learning goals.*

Motivational factors may play a prominent role in test performance with certain types of children. Most middle-class American school children and college students today are not only testwise but they are also generally motivated to succeed in academic work and in test situations. In such groups, rapport can be obtained with little difficulty. Special motivational problems are encountered, however, in testing certain groups, such as emotionally maladjusted individuals, young children, ethnic minority groups,

---

5. Paul L. Dressel and Ross W. Matteson, "Effect of Client Participation in Test Interpretation," *Educational and Psychological Measurement*, X (Autumn, 1950), 693-706.

6. John W. Gustad, "Test Information and Learning in the Counseling Process," *Educational and Psychological Measurement*, XI (Winter, 1951), 788-95.

and children from low socioeconomic homes. Emotionally disturbed persons or juvenile delinquents, especially when tested in an institutional setting, are likely to manifest a number of unfavorable attitudes, such as suspicion, insecurity, fear, or cynical indifference. Specific abnormal factors in the past experience of such persons are also likely to influence their test performance adversely, according to Sears.[7] Such individuals may, for example, have developed feelings of hostility and inferiority toward any academic material, as a result of early failures and frustrations in school.

Observation of the performance of lower-class children on speeded tests leads one to suspect that such children often work very rapidly through a test, making responses more or less at random. Apparently they are convinced in advance that they cannot do well on the test, and they find that by getting through the test rapidly they can shorten the period of discomfort which it produces. It is interesting to note that almost the identical reaction was observed among Puerto Rican school children tested in New York City, as reported by Anastasi and Cordova.[8]

Group testing in the primary grades must be done with due regard for the fact that young children are often distractible. In a recent summary, Findley[9] points out the unreliability of measures of general mental ability at the primary level and has noted that many school systems, aware of this unreliability, defer group testing of pupils (to determine their I.Q.'s) until they reach the intermediate grades. He also notes that instructions for many standardized measures at these levels prescribe that testing shall be done in small groups of five to ten children to insure dependable effort. He makes much of children's "acceptance" of testing as a general concept to cover a variety of motivational effects.

Some persons have assumed that more frequent tests will increase the motivation and effort of the student to achieve immedi-

7. Robert R. Sears, "Motivational Factors in Aptitude Testing," *American Journal of Orthopsychiatry*, XIII (May, 1943), 468-93.

8. Anne Anastasi and F. A. Cordova, "Some Effects of Bilingualism upon the Intelligence Test Performance of Puerto Rican Children in New York City," *Journal of Educational Psychology*, XLIV (January, 1953), 1-19.

9. Warren G. Findley, "Factors That Affect Test Results," *National Elementary Principal*, LII (November, 1961), 6-10.

ate educational goals. Carried to a ridiculous conclusion, this might mean one test per teaching period. When tests are administered too frequently, their motivational value is reduced. In a variety of fields at the college level, studies [10] show that when weekly tests are given, discussed, and corrected, the lower-ability students achieve more on a final examination of similar questions than with less frequent examinations. The more-able students may be retarded because of too frequent testing. The less able profit mainly from direction of their learning to specifics and to practice in selecting the correct responses. The more-able students are not aided by frequent—weekly or daily—tests.

In an early and carefully controlled experiment, Panlasigui [11] administered a short weekly test in mixed fundamentals in arithmetic to matched pairs of fourth-grade pupils. In the experimental classes, the amount of progress was stressed, recorded on a chart, and discussed. Knowledge of progress was related to the amount of success from week to week. The more-able pupils profited most. The less-able pupils were not stimulated to greater effort. However, Ross [12] found that knowledge of progress was not so important a factor in classroom learning as in laboratory learning. Certainly, informing students of their progress is effective only on the assumption that they are willing to learn in the first place. In the absence of all other motives, information about progress is of little consequence.

10. James E. Kirkpatrick, "The Motivating Effect of a Specific Type of Testing Program," *University of Iowa Studies in Education*, IX (June 15, 1948), 41-68; C. C. Ross and Lyle K. Henry, "The Relation between Frequency of Testing and Learning in Psychology," *Journal of Educational Psychology*, XXX (November, 1939), 604-11; Noel Keys, "The Influence on Learning and Retention of Weekly Tests as Opposed to Monthly Tests," *Journal of Educational Psychology*, XXV (September, 1934), 427-36.

11. Isidoro Panlasigui, "The Effect of Awareness of Success on Skill in Arithmetic." Unpublished Doctor's dissertation, State University of Iowa, 1928. (Experiment reported by Isidoro Panlasigui and F. B. Knight in *Report of Society's Committee on Arithmetic*, pp. 611-19. Twenty-ninth Yearbook of the National Society for the Study of Education. Chicago: Distributed by University of Chicago Press, 1930.)

12. Clay C. Ross, "The Influence of Achievement upon Knowledge of Progress," *Journal of Educational Psychology*, XXIV (November, 1933), 609-11.

Written examinations or tests have commonly been used as the chief evaluation device. Early investigations [13] showed that students who were tested periodically—daily or at the end of each unit of study—made slightly higher scores on final examinations and on delayed-recall tests than those students who were not tested prior to the final examination.

The way in which the results of any test or examination are treated may also influence learning. Curtis and Woods [14] in an early study, and Curtis [15] later, found that high-school students who scored their own examination papers and discussed the correct answers made higher scores on subsequent tests than did students whose papers were checked by the teacher. Such findings are useful, but hardly surprising, since in most cases the discussion of the examination serves as an additional review of the material covered, as well as provides insight into the kind of responses desired by the teacher. This latter kind of "test wisdom" can have a significant effect on subsequent performance.

RECOMMENDATION 8. *Notice should be taken of the impact of specific types of questions and examinations on study techniques.*

Early studies indicated that objective tests predisposed students to memorize concepts and details, while essay examinations led them to identify major topics and to prepare to write about them. Newer types of test exercises can be expected to stress study for broader goals of understanding.

13. Sister Felicita Gable, *The Effect of Two Contrasting Forms of Testing upon Learning* (Baltimore, Maryland: Johns Hopkins University, 1936); Oscar E. Hertzberg and Others, "The Value of Objective Tests as Teaching Devices in Educational Psychology Classes," *Journal of Educational Psychology*, XXIII (May, 1932), 371-80; Harold E. Jones, "Experimental Studies of College Teaching: The Effect of Examination on Permanence of Learning," *Archives of Psychology*, No. 68 (New York: Columbia University Press, 1923); George Forlano, *School Learning with Various Methods of Practice and Rewards* (New York: Bureau of Publications, Teachers College, Columbia University, 1936).

14. Francis D. Curtis and G. G. Woods, "A Study of the Relative Teaching Value of Four Common Practices in Correcting Examination Papers," *School Review*, XXXVII (October, 1929), 615-23.

15. Francis D. Curtis, "Testing as a Means of Improving Instruction," *Science Education*, XXVIII (February, 1944), 29-31.

With the advent of the "new-type" test following World War I, questions began to be raised about the effects of short-answer forms of tests in contrast to essay tests upon the motivation and study practices of pupils. A number of investigators sought through interviews and questionnaires addressed to high-school and college students to find out whether the form of test used made any difference in their study practices. The results of these investigations, as typified by the reports of Douglass and Tallmadge [16] in 1934 and George Meyer [17] in 1935, showed that a considerable majority of the students reporting, both in high school and in college, followed clearly different study procedures when they anticipated being given a "new-type" test from those followed when they expected an essay examination.

According to Findley,[18] the task set by the essay question is artificial. It is practically the only writing situation in life in which the individual writes to prove to someone who already knows the answer that the writer also knows the answer. It is the judgment of Findley that the writing of answers to essay questions runs counter to the formation of the writing abilities needed in more natural and creative situations in school and life experiences.

Newer types of objective-test exercises emphasize interpretation of data and making inferences from the information presented to the student. These test exercises have changed methods of preparation for newer types of tests. The new emphasis minimizes the use of memory to recall specific concepts or specific details. It involves the ability of the student to derive and express from data or information broader concepts and generalizations or to identify these concepts and generalizations in a multiple-choice test situation.

For the earlier versions of "new-type" objective tests, the majority of students reported that they went over and over assigned

16. Harl R. Douglass and Margaret Tallmadge, "How University Students Prepare for New Types of Examinations," *School and Society*, XXXIX (March 10, 1934), 318-20.

17. George Meyer, "Experimental Study of Old and New Types of Examination," *Journal of Educational Psychology*, XXV (December, 1934), 641-61; XXVI (January, 1935), 30-40.

18. Warren G. Findley, "The Ultimate Goals of Education." *School Review*, LXIV (January, 1956), 10-17.

material, seeking to memorize concepts, including specific details. For an essay test, the majority of students gave much less attention to specific details in the assignment and more attention to identifying a few major points around which they could write brief descriptive or expository paragraphs. The studies made it clear that students were strongly influenced in preparing for tests by their perceptions of what the tests measured, that is, what behavior they would need to exhibit and with what content. Newer types of test exercises emphasize understandings, generalizations, inferences, and applications of principles to specific situations. Preparation for such test exercises stresses the ability to think critically.

The Regents' Inquiry into the Character and Cost of Public Education in New York State, in 1936-37, provided objective evidence regarding the influence of testing on teachers as well as students. "An intensive study was made of sixty-one school districts within the state, examining their curriculum guides and testing their high-school students for several of the objectives specified in the curriculum guides. It was found that the achievement of the students paralleled more closely the objectives tested by the Regents' examinations than the objectives given major emphasis in the local curricula. Interviews with a sample of teachers in these communities revealed the fact that most of them were conscious of the objectives being tested in the Regents' examinations and sought to emphasize these kinds of learning in their classes rather than to follow the objectives recommended in the local curriculum guides."[19] At times, the examinations updated available guides.

RECOMMENDATION 9. *The scope and nature of the testing program should reflect the major objectives of the school and should be flexible so that it will not freeze or standardize the curriculum.*

Since tests have a powerful directive influence on teaching and on the learning of pupils, the school must seek to establish a testing program which faithfully reflects the objectives sought by the school. Only in this way can the influence of testing operate to

19. Ralph W. Tyler, "What Testing Does to Teachers and Students." *The 1959 Invitational Conference on Testing Problems*, p. 11. Princeton, N.J.: Educational Testing Service, 1960.

reinforce the other efforts of teaching. In order to reflect faithfully the school's educational objectives, the total testing program
must include some appraisal of student achievement of all of the
major objectives. This, of course, places a joint responsibility both
upon the school and upon the producers of tests. The school in
its selection of tests and in making clear its needs creates a demand
for tests which appraise important educational objectives, while
the thought, ingenuity, and effort of test producers are required
to develop and distribute the kind of testing instruments that are
needed.

There is more to this policy than may be apparent at first glance.
For a test or other form of evaluative instrument to be appropriate
for a given educational objective, it must evoke from the student
the kind of behavior which is implied by the objective, and it must
also deal with the content which the objective implies. Thus, if
one of the objectives of a social-studies course is to develop an
understanding of the concepts useful in analyzing the social structure of an American community, an appropriate test will require
the student to show the extent of his understanding. He will not
be called upon merely to give or recognize a memorized statement
of the concepts but to state them in his own words, to recognize
examples, to give illustrations of the concepts, and to compare and
contrast related concepts. These kinds of behavior are commonly
considered to be involved in understanding something. Furthermore, an appropriate test will deal specifically with those concepts
useful in analyzing the structure of an American community. A test
of this type will focus the attention of the student and teacher upon
objectives actually sought in the course rather than directing his
efforts at some more general achievement that is really irrelevant
to it.

If the tests measure important study skills and problem-solving
abilities, emphasize generalizations and their application to new
situations, clarify important and neglected objectives, and focus
attention on the ultimate objectives of education, they will have
the general effect of providing flexibility for the curriculum of the
schools and of stimulating the development of more acceptable
teaching methods, objectives, materials, and learning procedures.

RECOMMENDATION 10. *A serious student should not spend money or time on special coaching for scholastic aptitude tests. He will probably gain as much from a systematic review of his courses, especially in mathematics, and in reading a few good books.*

Another indication of the influence of testing on students and teachers is the prevalence of coaching for tests. Some schools turn "the junior and senior classes in the college-preparatory curriculums" into "coaching sessions several weeks before external tests are to be given. Some schools do not modify the teaching in the regular classes but arrange for special coaching for students planning to take these tests. In some communities, where no provisions for coaching are made in schools, some parents arrange for special coaching classes or for tutoring, in the belief that this will aid their children to perform better on the tests. A quick examination of bookstores and of advertisements also provides an indication of demand for coaching. Books and pamphlets purporting to help students pass important tests are widely sold." [20]

A number of studies [21] reveal that coaching for general ability tests is generally unproductive. The effects on basic ability and on achievement are slight.

A series of studies has been carried out by the College Entrance Examination Board in each of which students coached for their *Scholastic Aptitude Test* were compared by analysis of covariance methods with students who received no special training for the test. In each study, forms of the *SAT* given prior to coaching were used to control differences in ability. And in each instance, differences in the amount of gain from first test to final test, which would not be accounted for by differences in initial ability, were attributed

20. See *ibid*. The College Entrance Examination Board publishes pamphlets with many sample questions similar to the questions in the tests. One is entitled *A Description of the College Board Scholastic Aptitude Test;* another is *A Description of the College Board Achievement Tests.*

21. John W. French and Robert E. Dear, "Effects of Coaching on an Aptitude Test," *Educational and Psychological Measurement,* XIX (Autumn, 1959), 319-30; John W. French, "The Coachability of the *SAT* in Public Schools," *Research Bulletin,* Vol. LV, No. 26 (Princeton, New Jersey: Educational Testing Service, December, 1955, multilithed report); Edward Frankel, "Effects of Growth, Practice, and Coaching on *Scholastic Aptitude Test* Scores," *Personnel and Guidance Journal,* XXXVIII (May, 1960), 713-19.

to practice on special timed tests and exercises containing items similar to those of the *SAT*. In a study comparing individually coached groups at ten schools with uncoached control groups, some significant differences were found, but these amounted at most to 20 points on *SAT-V* and 30 points on *SAT-M*, on the scale which extends from 200 to 800. These differences are less than the standard errors of the tests. For *SAT-V*, the difference in average gains is smaller than the average gain in a year of normal growth (35 points). For *SAT-M*, the differences in gains are similar except for paired individuals not studying any Senior subject involving calculations. In such cases the coaching performs a review function. A side study showed that even when items identical to those on the test were imbedded in the practice exercises, no substantial gain was likely to occur on the final test unless a large percentage of the items could be duplicated. What is known about commercial coaching schools suggests that coaching by them would be less effective than the results of systematic study of the regular courses in high school.

RECOMMENDATION 11. *Since tests supply only a small part of the evidence needed by the administrator to rate teacher competency, many other criteria and types of evidence should be used.*

Evaluation results may sometimes be misused. If the design of the appraisal program is narrow and limited, the testing program may tend to produce emphasis upon certain specific objectives of the curriculum to the detriment of others and to the detriment of desirable trends in pupil growth. Sometimes, test results of a very partial nature are used to estimate or to rate the teacher's teaching ability. While such evidence may properly serve as a part of the data to be considered in rating teachers, few educators would defend a rating made solely upon this basis. Some administrators, however, misuse test results by employing them in this manner. Reliable and valid instruments of measurement are, by their very nature, restricted to an appraisal of limited aspects of pupil behavior or growth. It is impossible to measure the whole result of an educative experience by any one test or battery of tests and measures. The fact remains, however, that, by systematically evaluating many important and vital aspects of experiences, appraisals may be obtained of the relative merits of diverse educational practices employed by different teachers.

RECOMMENDATION 12. *The use of tests of general educational development and of aptitudes has influenced teaching and learning in desirable directions. Tests should be consciously employed to achieve these ends. Other test developments which have constructively influenced instruction and learning are* (a) *factor analysis of mental abilities, and* (b) *measurement of individual and group dynamics.*

The modern teacher and the supervisor are concerned with important functional learning outcomes, many of which are less tangible and less easily measured than the concepts, skills, and abilities represented in subject-matter tests of the past several decades. The concern for the total development of the child—physical, emotional, social, and intellectual—has resulted in an emphasis upon a sound understanding of child growth and development and of individual and group differences, as well as upon the personal and social adjustment of the pupils. This represents an emphasis upon Gestalt, or organismic, psychology, which recognizes the interrelationships of the multiple aspects of growth in an individual.

An increasing emphasis on the measurement of understanding [22] and interpretation, rather than upon isolated information, skills, and abilities is particularly observable in present-day tests of general educational development. These are represented by such test batteries as the *United States Armed Forces Institute Tests of General Educational Development* and the *Iowa Tests of Educational Development*. A similar trend is evident in the tests recently constructed by the College Entrance Examination Board and such other tests devised by the Educational Testing Service as the *Sequential Tests of Educational Progress*, the *National Teacher Examinations*, and the *Graduate Record Examinations*.

Tests of general educational development usually present in-

---

22. *The Measurement of Understanding.* Forty-fifth Yearbook of the National Society for the Study of Education, Part I. Chicago: Distributed by the University of Chicago Press, 1946.

formation in verbal, graphic, or other form, with the test exercises devised to measure the ability of the individual to comprehend and interpret the material presented. This contrasts with the isolated test item which emphasizes the recall or recognition of items of information. General educational development tests usually cover such areas as language arts (including literature), social studies, science, and mathematics.

The increased use of informal or teacher-made test exercises to supplement formal or standardized tests in many recent evaluative programs is to be commended. Some surveys show that the average classroom teacher uses five or six teacher-made tests for each standardized test employed. Informal tests are valuable in the day-by-day appraisal and guidance of pupils in specific units of classroom study.

Factor analysis of mental abilities, a development in which L. L. Thurstone[23] led and in which Carl C. Brigham[24] made pioneering application on the College Entrance Examination Board *Scholastic Aptitude Test*, represents another important approach. By statistical analysis of many mental ability tests, Thurstone isolated seven primary mental abilities. These include: a verbal factor, which involves vocabulary and reading comprehension; a number factor, which involves speed and accuracy in computation; a space factor, which involves visualization of space relationships; a rote memory factor; a perceptual factor, which involves discrimination of likenesses and differences; a word-fluency factor, which involves naming isolated words at a rapid rate; and a reasoning factor, which involves finding a rule or principle governing a series of numbers, letters, or words. The mental-ability tests incorporating the results of this analysis, called *Tests of Primary Mental Abilities*, are published in batteries for various age levels by the Science Research Associates of Chicago. Constructed along somewhat similar lines, although not based so explicitly on factor analysis, are the *Differential Aptitude Tests*, published by the Psychological Cor-

23. L. L. Thurstone, *The Vectors of Mind*. Chicago: University of Chicago Press, 1935; also by same author, *Primary Mental Abilities*. Psychometric Monograph, No. 1. Chicago: University of Chicago Press, 1938.

24. Carl C. Brigham, *A Study of Error*. New York: College Entrance Examination Board, 1932.

poration. The *Differential Aptitude Tests* measure similar abilities and are especially useful for guidance work and counseling of high-school students, for both educational and vocational guidance purposes.

One study by Davis [25] concerning the measurement of reading achievement analyzed the factors involved in reading comprehension and served as the basis for the development of the *Cooperative Reading Comprehension Tests*. In this analysis, Davis identified two general factors and six specific factors in reading comprehension. The general factors are (*a*) word meaning and (*b*) reasoning in reading, which requires the ability to weave together several ideas and to show their relationships as well as the ability to draw correct inferences from written statements. The specific factors isolated are (*a*) ability to determine the writer's purpose, intent, or point of view; (*b*) ability to understand the writer's explicit statements or to get the literal meaning;(*c*) ability to follow the organization of a passage; (*d*) ability to select the main thought or idea of a paragraph or passage; (*e*) ability to determine from context the meaning of an unfamiliar word; and (*f*) ability to determine the tone and mood implicit or explicit in a passage. The impact of testing for these factors may have a direct effect on reading instruction.

Another development in recent evaluation studies is measurement of the role of the individual, as well as of small groups, in studies of group dynamics. This trend has shown itself in several ways. One is the measurement of the social status of groups and individuals. Warner [26] and Hollingshead [27] are particularly noted for this type of work. A second manifestation is the work on group dynamics that has been carried on by various organizations, especially the Research Center for Group Dynamics at the University of Michigan. Another manifestation is the various sociometric analyses that have been made in the studies of intergroup educa-

25. Frederick B. Davis, "What Do Reading Tests Really Measure?" *English Journal*, XXXIII (April, 1944), 180-87.

26. W. Lloyd Warner, Marcia Meeker, and Kenneth W. Eells, *Social Class in America: A Manual of Procedure for the Measurement of Social Status*. Chicago: Science Research Associates, 1949.

27. August de B. Hollingshead, *Elmtown's Youth: The Impact of Social Classes on Adolescents*. New York: John Wiley & Sons, 1949.

tion. The dynamics of individual and group behavior are directly related to the effectiveness of instruction.[28] Teaching and learning operate in a social situation—not in a vacuum. The measurement of the climate of the classroom is important in assessing the learning processes.

Finally, we are just beginning to note an impact of research on creativity. We are indebted especially to J. P. Guilford for his organizing concept of "divergent" as distinguished from "convergent" thinking. The creative person thinks divergently in being able to summon up and express a rich variety of relevant associations when confronted with words, quantitative data, configural patterns, or practical problem situations. The findings of recent research by Getzels and Jackson, Torrance, and others indicate the possibility of a new dimension in testing.

28. Helen H. Jennings, "Sociometric Grouping in Relation to Child Development," in *Fostering Mental Health in Our Schools.* 1950 Yearbook of the Association for Supervision and Curriculum Development. Washington: National Education Association, 1950.

CHAPTER IV

The Impact of Testing on School Organization

WALTER W. COOK and THEODORE CLYMER

When a new instrument becomes available in any field, its usefulness is estimated in terms of its power to facilitate the achievement of currently accepted objectives within the prevailing form of organization and procedures. The fact that the results of the new instrument constantly point to the need for revising objectives and for changing procedures and organization usually goes unheeded for some time. The influence of standardized tests in and on the schools has followed this pattern.

Objective tests were first used simply as examinations had always been used: to determine achievement as a basis of promotion, acceleration, or assignment to sections and to evaluate the effectiveness of a teacher or the quality of a school system. In more recent years, measurement has played a much more fundamental role in the education process—for the results of testing provided the data for a re-examination of the basic assumptions of prevailing school organizational patterns, objectives, and procedures.

Historically, school reform has invariably proceeded from attempts to make the students fit the system. When all else fails, the system is sometimes adjusted to the characteristics of the children. Our concern is that many school organizational procedures have sustained themselves long after their lack of worth was clearly demonstrated. School reform should be directed at how to meet the needs of individual pupils in heterogeneous groups, not toward the goal of providing homogeneous groups. Studies of trait differences indicate that even the individual child is not "homogeneous."

Soon after their introduction, standardized tests began to challenge many tenets of the concept of school organization by grades. Recommendations which relate to organization and which are supported by the results of testing and other evidence are presented in this chapter.

RECOMMENDATION 1. *In their organization and operation, schools should reflect the implications of wide differences in achievement among pupils found in a single grade. Grade levels do not signify definite standards of achievement.*

A consistently observed and yet seemingly disregarded characteristic of test results is variability of achievement. This variability of achievement exists whether the test instrument measures personality factors, academic knowledge, or intellectual characteristics and whether the test is administered to students beginning or nearing the end of their education. This variability exists whether the group under study is labeled "homogeneous" or "heterogeneous."

In spite of this virtually universal finding of educational measurement, instructional programs from the elementary level through the graduate level are often planned with only a partial understanding of the extent and nature of these differences. Goodlad [1] reports that parents consistently underestimate pupil variability at the elementary-grade levels. Indeed, the extent of variability and the overlapping ranges of ability from grade to grade are often neglected or minimized even by scholars in dealing with curriculum practices. Anderson,[2] for example, in a recent yearbook of this Society presented hypothetical distributions of achievement for second- and third-grade children in which he appeared to suggest that, in a three-track grouping system, the top achievement in a second grade would be equivalent to the average or median achievement of the third grade. An examination of actual, not hypothetical, data reveals that such an approach greatly minimizes the extent of variability and the degree of overlap between grades. Clymer [3] pointed

1. John I. Goodlad, "Individual Differences and Vertical Organization of the School," in *Individualizing Instruction*, p. 217. Sixty-first Yearbook of the National Society for the Study of Education, Part I. Chicago: Distributed by the University of Chicago Press, 1962.

2. Robert H. Anderson, "Organizing Groups for Instruction," in *Individualizing Instruction, op. cit.*, p. 258.

3. Theodore Clymer, "Criteria for Grouping for Reading Instruction," in *Reading Instruction in Various Patterns of Grouping*, p. 45. Supplementary Educational Monograph, No. 89. Edited by Helen M. Robinson. Chicago: University of Chicago Press, 1959.

out in 1959 that the spread of abilities in the usual heterogeneously grouped classroom is two-thirds of the chronological age of the typical pupil of the grade under consideration. Findley [4] has presented clear evidence of variability in academic achievement at the elementary-grade levels in terms of national norms and those for the Atlanta public schools. Figure 1 presents the range of grade-score differences between upper and lower quartiles at the beginning of the school year for Grades III through VII on national norms of the *Stanford Achievement Tests* for the "Paragraph Meaning" subtests.

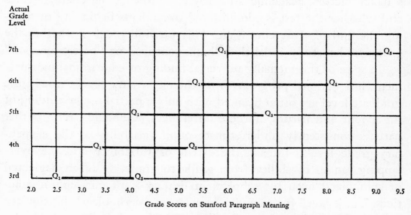

Actual
Grade
Level

Grade Scores on Stanford Paragraph Meaning

FIG. 1.—Grade score equivalents of quartile differences for beginning of Grades III-VII, National norms for Stanford Achievement Paragraph Meaning Subtest. (Adapted from Findley)

Keeping in mind that this figure represents *only the middle 50 per cent* of the students at each of the grade levels portrayed, several significant facts about grade levels and academic variability are evident. First of all, a great deal of overlap exists between succeeding grades. There are, for example, many students in third grade who perform at levels equal to or higher than students in the fourth grade, and some who equal or surpass medians for fifth, sixth, and higher grades. The higher the grade level examined, the greater the amount of overlap from one grade to another.

4. Warren G. Findley, "Use and Interpretation of Achievement Tests in Relation to Validity," Eighteenth Yearbook of the National Council on Measurements Used in Education, pp. 23-24. Ames, Iowa: The Council, 1961.

Along with an increasing overlap in achievement of students in successive grades, there is a gradual increase in the spread from Q_1 to Q_3 within grade levels. At Grade III, this difference is 1.3 grades. This spread of achievement of the middle 50 per cent increases from 2.3 to 3.2 from Grade IV to Grade VII. This gradually widening spread continues through the educational grade hierarchy until dropouts or curricular segregation eliminates the lower range of the distribution.

Learned and Wood [5] have presented one of the most thorough analyses of variability at the secondary and college levels. Their examination of college and secondary-school distributions revealed that neither variability in achievement nor intellect had disappeared by the time the upper levels were reached. Overlap from grade level to grade level was surprisingly great. For measures of intellect, for example, the median for college Seniors was only one-half of a standard deviation above the median for college Sophomores. When tests of educational achievement were considered, one high-school Senior in ten exceeded the average college Senior performance. One college was selected for intensive study of educational characteristics. An analysis of the results of a series of educational achievement tests revealed that, if the graduating class had been selected from the total student body on the basis of test scores made instead of from the Senior class on the basis of credits collected, the graduating class would have been composed of 28 per cent of the Seniors, 21 per cent of the Juniors, 19 per cent of the Sophomores, and 15 per cent of the Freshmen!

The evidence presented in this section should be a strong antidote for viewing grade levels as representing uniform standards of achievement. At all levels, in all types of measures, variability is the key word. There is no escape from this finding. Successful school programs will not ignore this fact; instead, curricular offerings will be adjusted to the diversity of skills and knowledge that the students possess.

5. William S. Learned and Ben D. Wood, *The Student and His Knowledge*. Carnegie Foundation for the Advancement of Teaching, Bulletin No. 29. New York: Carnegie Foundation for Advancement of Teaching, 1938.

RECOMMENDATION 2. *Schools should be so organized and operated as to take account of the differences in achievement that individual pupils show in different subject areas. Pupils tend not to be equally proficient in all areas of the curriculum.*

The first recommendation, which deals with individual differences, or interindividual differences, must be considered in conjunction with the research findings in trait or intraindividual differences. The curriculum organization must take into account variability among individuals of the same age or grade groups. In addition, the findings of trait differences must play an important role in shaping the curriculum.[6] The variability of the pupil in achievement in the different basic skills has been found to be 80 per cent as great as the variability of his grade group in these skills.[7]

Assigning pupils to an A, B, or C section (in the 1920's we called them X, Y, and Z) can be done with a great deal of assurance if pupils are rather consistent in their performances in various achievement areas. If students are relatively inconsistent or variable in their performance from one area to another, students grouped on the basis of one criterion will not be similar when the group is examined on another basis. What does the research reveal about this dissimilarity?

Tyler[8] has presented some recent data on trait variability. While his research was restricted to seventh-grade pupils, the results approximate the findings of other studies. Using Stanford Achievement subtests as criterion measures, Tyler investigated the spread of achievement for students who scored in narrow ranges on average reading and average arithmetic reasoning. Some typical results of his investigation providing clear evidence of wide trait (intraindividual) differences are presented in Table 1. For example, students who score from 8.0 to 8.4 in average reading ability

6. Marvin G. Burr, *A Study of Homogeneous Grouping.* Contributions to Education, No. 457. New York: Teachers College, Columbia University, 1931.

7. T. L. Purdom, *An Evaluation of the Use of Certain Mental Measurements for the Purposes of Classification.* Contributions to Education, No. 302. New York: Teachers College, Columbia University, 1928.

8. Fred T. Tyler, "Intraindividual Variability," in *Individualizing Instruction, op. cit.,* chap. x.

varied at least four years in arithmetic reasoning, word meaning, and paragraph meaning, and as much as six years in arithmetic computation.

TABLE 1

DISTRIBUTION OF SCORES ON VARIOUS TESTS FOR SEVENTH-GRADE PUPILS HAVING AVERAGE READING AND AVERAGE ARITHMETIC REASONING GRADE EQUIVALENTS OF 8.0-8.4

GRADE EQUIVALENT	PUPILS WITH AVERAGE READING GRADE OF 8.0-8.4				PUPILS WITH AVERAGE ARITHMETIC REASONING GRADE OF 8.0-8.4		
	PM	WM	R	C	C	I.Q.	
10.5-10.9...	......	......	......	......	2	......	......
10.0-10.4...	1	3	2	3	4	140-149...	1
9.5- 9.9...	1	6	7	......	......	130-139...	8
9.0- 9.4...	2	......	5	5	6	120-129...	32
8.5- 8.9...	10	8	14	9	22	110-119...	26
8.0- 8.4...	6	18	2	8	17	100-109...	20
7.5- 7.9...	14	7	12	9	19	90- 99...	2
7.0- 7.4...	8	4	4	5	18	......	......
6.5- 6.9...	3	1	1	1	7	......	......
6.0- 6.4...	2	1	1	5	3	......	......
5.5- 5.9...	1	......	......	1	......	......	......
5.0- 5.4...	......	......	......	1	......	......	......
4.5- 4.9...	......	......	......	1	......	......	......

Tyler's analysis shows clearly that the creation of instructional groups on the basis of a single criterion or even multiple criteria will not produce a group of homogeneous students who can be treated uniformly.

Data from an unpublished study by Clymer provide similar conclusions for sixth-grade children. Clymer investigated the range of ability in vocabulary, spelling, map-reading, use of reference material, arithmetic computation, and problem-solving, as measured by the *Iowa Tests of Basic Skills* for students who scored between 6.0 and 6.4 on the reading-comprehension section of the same battery. These data, which are presented in Table 2, closely parallel the findings of Tyler.

The research is clear in supporting the generalization that grouping on one basis will not produce homogeneous groups when another characteristic is considered. Students assigned to a classroom or a class section on one basis, e.g., reading ability, may be somewhat homogeneous in reading ability, but no safe statement can be made about the group being homogeneous with regard to spelling ability or problem-solving. A group formed on the basis of one criterion is almost certain to have a wide range of ability when another characteristic is considered.

TABLE 2

DISTRIBUTION OF SCORES ON VARIOUS TESTS FOR SIXTH-GRADE PUPILS HAVING READING COMPREHENSION GRADE EQUIVALENTS OF 6.0 TO 6.4

GRADE SCORES	VOCABULARY	SPELLING	MAP READING	REFERENCE MATERIALS	ARITHMETIC COMPUTATION	PROBLEM-SOLVING
10.5–10.9	.....	.....	.....	.....	.....	.....
10.0–10.4	.....	.....	.....	.....	.....	.....
9.5– 9.9	.....	.....	.....	.....	.....	.....
9.0– 9.4	.....	.....	.....	.....	.....	.....
8.5– 8.9	.....	1	.....	1	.....	.....
8.0– 8.4	1	.....	.....	2	2	2
7.5– 7.9	5	2	3	1	.....	1
7.0– 7.4	1	1	8	4	10	6
6.5– 6.9	4	5	9	12	12	7
6.0– 6.4	3	10	4	7	4	6
5.5– 5.9	9	8	3	3	2	7
5.0– 5.4	6	3	2	2	2	3
4.5– 4.9	3	2	1	.....	.....	.....
4.0– 4.4	.....	.....	1	.....	.....	.....
3.5– 3.9	.....	.....	1	.....	.....	.....
Totals	32	32	32	32	32	32

RECOMMENDATION 3. *School promotion policies should reflect the findings that strict standards for promotion (a) do not produce high achievement of pupils (b) nor do they reduce the range of ability in the upper grades.*

Two research approaches have been used in studying the effects of promotional policies on average achievement. One has been to compare achievement levels in school systems which are similar except for their promotional policies. The second is to compare the changes in achievement level in a school system when a change occurs in promotional policy.

The most comprehensive application of the first approach has been made by Cook and is reported in *Grouping and Promotion in the Elementary School.*[9] Cook compared groups which were identical except for their promotional policies: one group of schools practicing nonpromotion to a great extent, the other group of schools utilizing nonpromotion rarely. The results of extensive comparisons indicated that average achievement was greater in those schools with liberal promotion policies. Table 3 presents data for a group of seventh-grade pupils from each of the types of school systems. The results clearly favor liberal promotion policies.

TABLE 3

COMPARISON OF MEAN CHRONOLOGICAL, MENTAL, AND ACHIEVEMENT AGES OF SEVENTH-GRADE PUPILS IN SCHOOLS WITH HIGH AND LOW RATIOS OF OVERAGENESS*

ITEM	MEAN†			STANDARD ERROR OF DIFFERENCE	DIFF. S.E. diff.
	High-Ratio Schools (280 Cases)	Low-Ratio Schools (280 Cases)	Difference		
Chronological age........	13.13	12.56	0.57	0.08	7.13
Mental age.............	12.12	13.34	−1.22	0.10	12.20
Intelligence quotient.....	101.58	106.82	−5.24	1.13	4.64
American history........	12.20	13.00	−0.80	0.17	4.71
Arithmetic fundamental.. operations............	13.01	13.00	0.01	0.15	0.07
Arithmetic problems.....	12.91	12.97	−0.06	0.16	0.38
Elementary science......	12.81	13.11	−0.30	0.18	1.67
English capitalization....	12.64	13.65	−1.01	0.18	5.61
Literature..............	12.36	12.70	−0.34	0.20	1.70
English punctuation.....	12.13	12.82	−0.69	0.22	3.14
English usage..........	12.66	13.08	−0.42	0.18	2.33
Geography.............	13.13	13.70	−0.57	0.18	3.17
Reading...............	11.66	12.59	−0.93	0.20	4.65
Spelling...............	12.68	12.97	−0.29	0.16	1.81

*From Walter W. Cook, *Grouping and Promotion in the Elementary School,* p. 38. Minneapolis: University of Minnesota Press, 1941.

†Means are given in years except in the case of intelligence quotient.

An illustration of the second research approach—a comparison of achievement levels when a change in promotional policy occurs in a school system—is provided by Hall and Demarest. Comparing the average achievement of fourth- and sixth-grade pupils over a ten-year period, they found no significant change in achievement when the Phoenix school system changed from a rigorous to a lib-

9. Walter W. Cook, *Grouping and Promotion in the Elementary School.* Series on Individualization of Instruction, No. 2. Minneapolis: University of Minnesota, 1941.

eral promotion policy. They concluded that "this study . . . supports other recent research in indicating that regular promotion of children, that is, keeping children with their own age group, does not result in a lowering of academic achievement." [10]

Since strict policies of promotion tend to collect large numbers of slow-learning and disabled readers in the upper grades, it is not surprising that the research results favor liberal promotional policies. "Hoarding the dull and disabled" is no way to elevate school standards.

The classroom teacher may be relatively unimpressed with problems of "general achievement" of a class. The fact that the average reading achievement of a class is two or three months or perhaps even eight months higher or lower may not be as significant

TABLE 4

DIFFERENCES IN VARIABILITY OF CHRONOLOGICAL, MENTAL, AND ACHIEVEMENT
AGES FOR SEVENTH-GRADE PUPILS IN SCHOOLS WITH
HIGH AND LOW RATIOS OF OVERAGENESS*

ITEM	STANDARD DEVIATION†			STANDARD ERROR OF DIFFERENCE	DIFF. S.E. diff.
	High-Ratio Schools (280 Cases)	Low-Ratio Schools (280 Cases)	Difference		
Chronological age........	1.16	0.80	0.36	0.06	6.00
Mental age.............	1.14	1.27	−0.13	.07	1.86
Intelligence quotient.....	14.00	12.73	1.27	.80	1.59
American history........	1.88	2.12	−0.24	.12	2.00
Arithmetic fundamental operations...........	1.76	1.73	0.03	.10	0.30
Arithmetic problems.....	1.87	1.93	−0.06	.11	0.55
Elementary science......	2.10	2.18	−0.08	.13	0.62
English capitalization....	2.21	2.17	0.04	.13	0.31
Literature..............	2.24	2.50	−0.26	.14	1.86
English punctuation.....	2.45	2.82	−0.37	.16	2.31
English usage...........	1.96	2.19	−0.23	.12	1.92
Geography..............	2.07	2.15	−0.08	.13	0.62
Reading................	2.22	2.58	−0.36	.14	2.57
Spelling................	1.75	1.84	−0.09	0.11	0.82

*From Walter W. Cook, *Grouping and Promotion in the Elementary Schools*, p. 39. Minneapolis: University of Minnesota Press, 1941.

†Standard deviations are given in years exeept in the case of the intelligence quotient.

10. William F. Hall and Ruth Demarest, "Effect on Achievement Scores of a Change in Promotional Policy," *Elementary School Journal*, LVIII (January, 1958), 204-7.

to the teacher as the spread or range that must be dealt with within a classroom. The study by Cook also investigated the range of ability in schools with liberal and with strict promotional policies. As shown in Table 4, a comparison of the ranges of ability indicated that high standards of promotion had not reduced the range of talent which must be met at the upper grades.

RECOMMENDATION 4. *Schools should welcome and embrace variability in achievement among pupils at all grade levels as the expected result of good teaching.*

If education is viewed as a process of "name," "list," "define," and "recite," some progress can be made in reducing variability at the upper-grade and high-school levels. If, for example, our goal is to be able to recite the presidents in order, differences in the group can be reduced by the dint of zealous drill and repetition. However, if the goal is to help pupils assess the influence of each president's background and point of view on the actions he took as president, differences will increase.

The differences in these two illustrations are mainly those of the scope of the goals of the curriculum. If goals are limited—name, list, and the like—variability can be reduced. If our goals are less limited and involve reading comprehension, problem-solving, the application of principles in novel situations, that is, if they involve the higher mental processes, then differences will be increased rather than reduced by excellent teaching. Under superior teaching, the slow move ahead substantially but never enough to catch their fast-moving classmates. If the goals of the curriculum are broad in scope, the only way to keep pupils alike is to teach them nothing, for the moment we begin to teach, some students learn a little and others learn a lot. The net result of good teaching is growth for all but greater growth for the capable and, hence, greater spread.

RECOMMENDATION 5. *Organizational plans for reducing the variability in classroom groups should be studied open-mindedly but critically.*

The history of the American public schools during the present century could be written in terms of our attempts to meet the wide range of differences among students. Pupil variability, repeatedly demonstrated through test surveys and research programs, has served as the spur for countless innovations in the school organizational program. Studies of trait (or intraindividual differences) have been almost completely ignored. In order to understand these organizational "solutions" it is helpful to identify three types of adjustment which have been commonly made in response to problems of individual differences. The three types of adjustment are:

1. Grouping of students
2. Revision of the curriculum
3. Combination of grouping and curricular revisions

As Shane [11] has indicated, the greatest number of organizational plans have been various types of groupings of students. Most often the same curriculum is administered to the students, but the time is varied, the amount of material is varied, or expectations are altered to meet the level of student maturity. The XYZ Plan, the development of "college," "business," "general," and "vocational" curriculums at the secondary level, the Winnetka Plan, "cultural imperatives," and the creation of ungraded or nongraded elementary schools are all illustrations of one or another of these three approaches to adjustment to individual differences.

In evaluating the suitability and feasibility of any grouping plan, a number of specific questions should be kept in mind. Among the many which could be considered, the following eight questions centered in five areas, as posed by Clymer,[12] seem important:

The criteria
1. Is the criterion of major importance in educational progress?
2. Can the criterion be accurately measured?
3. Is the criterion stable and constant enough to be useful?

The learner
4. Do the groups formed on the basis of the criterion learn more efficiently?

The teacher
5. Do the groups formed on the basis of the criterion increase the teacher's effectiveness?

11. Harold G. Shane, "Grouping in the Elementary School," *Phi Delta Kappan*, XLI (April, 1960), 313-19.

12. Clymer, *op. cit.*, p. 45.

6. Does the method of grouping accept individual differences among teachers?

The administrator

7. Is the method of grouping administratively possible?

The public

8. Is the method of grouping socially acceptable?

For any of the systems or methods of grouping, the answers to the foregoing questions will seldom be a definite "yes" or "no." More often the response will be a measure of the extent or degree to which the answer is "yes" or "no."

Question 7 deserves attention both in terms of grouping and curricular revision. Many of the currently offered solutions are simply not administratively possible in many schools of America. While the merits of differentiated curriculums for the high school cannot be denied, it must be noted that the typical (median) high school in the United States enrols less than 200 pupils. This is a good deal below the figure many educators consider as adequate for a comprehensive high school.

At the present time, increasing attention is being given by school administrators and teachers at both elementary and second-ary levels to "new" forms and plans of school organization. Questions are being asked about the self-contained classroom: Should it give way to departmentalization, even into the primary grades? Special part-time ability groupings are being tried: Is the Joplin Plan the answer to instructional problems of individual differences in reading, arithmetic, spelling, and other skill areas? Even the concept of grades and grade levels are being challenged: Will the "ungraded" or "nongraded" school provide for greater pupil growth toward the academic and social-personal goals of the school? The answer to these—and many other questions about school organizational patterns—are not available and will not be available for some time. In the absence of definite research findings, we can, at present, rely upon only a logical and reasoned analysis of the proposed organizational pattern and add to this any information available from research.

Donald D. Durrell, in an address before the general assembly of the 1962 Conference of the International Reading Association, proposed a plan for evaluating organizational procedures. He suggested that each plan or technique be evaluated in terms of its ability (*a*) to adjust to individual differences and (*b*) to enrich learning. Under each of these two main headings he listed several points which he considered vital in an effective organizational pattern or teaching technique. His set of criteria is as follows:

In adjusting to individual differences, does the approach provide for:

1. Levels of ability
2. Differing rates of progress
3. Sub-skill needs
4. Intensive practice

In enrichment, does the approach provide for:

1. Understanding
2. Thinking and application
3. Initiative and self-direction
4. Personal-social objectives

The application of these criteria to proposed plans of organization demonstrate that no one plan or technique, including the conventional plans generally found in elementary and secondary schools today, meets all the criteria. This does not mean that the plan or technique must be discarded. It only indicates that the new approach is not a passport to utopia but simply a partial solution to a vexing problem. Part of our difficulty may lie in seeking a general solution to the problem. Perhaps different solutions fit different school situations, as reflected in different school populations or in different patterns of academic competence among school faculties.

With this brief background as a starting point, let us examine several of the current "new" patterns or plans for reorganizing the elementary school. The "ungraded" or "nongraded" primary or elementary school has been proposed by Goodlad and Anderson[13] as a promising solution to problems of individual differences in the elementary school. The school is "ungraded" by elimination of grade labels. Children are grouped primarily by age, but to some

---

13. John I. Goodlad and Robert H. Anderson, *The Nongraded Elementary School*, p. 248. New York: Harcourt, Brace & Co., 1959.

extent by reading ability. Instead of being as concerned about passing grades or mastering certain amounts of subject matter, the teachers adopt a philosophy of bringing each child along at a rate commensurate with his ability. Presumably, little pressure exists to master, for example, certain levels of reading by a stated time. The plan provides for children to complete the old primary division of the elementary school in two, three, or four years, depending upon the rate of growth.

To a critical observer, the plan does not depart to any great extent from the procedures followed (or at least recommended) in a good graded elementary school. However, by removing grade labels and by centering attention on variable rates of progress, the plan may relieve teachers of pressures to bring all or nearly all children up to certain standards by the end of the year. In so far as differential rates of promotion are employed, this is accomplished without the self-negating effects of being "left back" for a whole year at the end of third grade or the sharp pressure for adjustment occasioned by "skipping" a whole grade.

It seems that the major aspect of the nongraded elementary school is the philosophy behind the changes rather than the changes themselves. To effect the changes may be, in a sense, a declaration of faith—although some once-nonbelievers or partial-believers have joined the cause, as Anderson and Goodlad point out in a recent article.[14]

Few research data are available on the merits of the nongraded program. Carbone[15] reported that nongraded schools (or at least those labeled "nongraded") were generally less successful than the traditional or graded schools. In a survey of opinions and practices by Anderson and Goodlad,[16] few schools were found that permitted pupils to leave the primary division before they had completed three years' work.

14. Robert H. Anderson and John I. Goodlad, "Self-Appraisal in Nongraded Schools: A Survey of Findings and Perceptions," *Elementary School Journal*, LXIII (February, 1962), 261-69.

15. Robert F. Carbone, "Achievement, Mental Health, and Instruction in Graded and Nongraded Elementary Schools." Unpublished Ph.D. dissertation, Department of Education, University of Chicago, 1961.

16. Anderson and Goodlad, *op. cit.*, p. 265.

The "teacher-team" approach is another organizational plan for the elementary school. While the following description greatly oversimplifies the program, it appears to be essentially a three-track (Detroit X, Y, Z) plan with complete departmentalization through Grade I. In addition, certain "master teachers" have special responsibilities to co-ordinate the instruction. Flexible size of instructional groups is another feature claimed for the program, but this evidently occurs less frequently in practice than the descriptions indicate.

While the plan provides for teachers to specialize in arithmetic, or science, or some other subject-matter area, a number of questions arise. To what extent do pupils, especially those in the primary grades, have difficulty adjusting to the many teachers with whom they come in contact? Are subject-matter specialists really needed in the early grades? To what degree can elementary-school teachers know and adjust to individual differences when great numbers of students are met each day?

These are stated as questions, but this plan seems to present insurmountable obstacles to adjustment to individual differences. With brief contact and multitudes of students to be met, the teacher must find it almost impossible to make any effective adjustment to differences within a class. Teaching under this plan converts the elementary teacher into a subject-matter specialist, as in high school. The basic question is how far and to what benefit is departmentalization to be introduced into the elementary school.

The major strength of this plan is that it provides an opportunity for flexible planning and the use of special talents and interests of teachers. Rather than organize the entire school day by the teacher-team approach, perhaps a better plan might be the informal exchange, in which teachers follow a "You teach my music; I'll teach your art" approach. Here, teacher strengths can be utilized without the loss of the valuable teacher-pupil knowledge and relationship.

The Dual Progress Plan, as advocated by Stoddard,[17] is another organizational plan being given some attention at the present time.

17. George D. Stoddard, *The Dual Progress Plan*, p. 225. New York: Harper & Bros., 1962.

According to its originator, this plan is a downward extension through Grade I of a modified form of the junior high school organization. The school day is divided into halves; the halves are designated as Segment A, consisting of the "cultural imperatives," and Segment B, the "cultural electives." (Some readers may be surprised to learn that science and mathematics are cultural electives.) Segment A is described as "graded," and Segment B as "ungraded."

Under this plan, the homeroom teacher provides the instruction in all of the cultural imperatives—English (including reading, spelling, literature, and writing) and the social studies (including geography, history, and government). The organization of Segment A resembles a junior high school core plan. The remainder of the courses, the cultural electives, are taught by specialists on a subject-matter basis. To a great extent, this part of the program is like many junior and senior high schools.

The Dual Progress Plan appears to have some advantages over an organization such as the teacher-team. Under the Dual Progress Plan, the contact of a teacher and a group of pupils through half of the school day (Segment A) to some extent permits the teacher to know the pupils and also provides the time necessary to make adjustment to individual differences. Continuation with each class for two years, dropping and acquiring only one group a year, works in this same direction. At the present time, no reliable data concerning the value of the plan are available.

The Joplin Plan is another form of organization which has had some use in the elementary school. This plan is essentially a departmentalization of the reading program with pupils assigned to instructional groups on the basis of their reading ability (not necessarily on their rate of progress). However, all teachers teach reading. At a designated time, pupils leave their "regular" classrooms and move to rooms where instruction is given which is at their level of reading ability. Thus, during the reading period, selected pupils from the fourth, fifth, and sixth grades might be placed together for reading instruction at the sixth-grade level.

This plan may produce disregard for trait differences: Not all pupils who read at the same grade level, say fifth grade, have the same sub-skill needs in word recognition, comprehension, or rate.

In addition, as the plan is often practiced, the instruction given is uniform, on the assumption that all pupils assigned to a class for reading are alike in reading ability. Another problem of this plan —and all other plans which involve multiple teachers for elementary children—is the need to provide information about reading skills, problems, and interests to the other teachers working with a particular pupil. The research on the Joplin Plan [18, 19, 20, 21] does not indicate that consistent superiority in reading growth results from this type of organization.

This discussion of various organizational plans for the elementary school has touched on only a few of the programs being used and promoted in various places throughout the country. Our purpose is not to present a complete catalog of such plans or of their merits. We have presented these plans as illustrations of what programs are being considered and how the traditional patterns of organization are being re-evaluated. This interest and serious appraisal of current school patterns is a healthy one. But a number of cautions need to be observed. First, we must acknowledge that most of the "new" plans are only modifications or variations of practices of twenty, forty, or even fifty years ago. A principal in a school still using the platoon plan states the situation clearly: "If I can just hold on for a few more years, I'll be out in front again."

In spite of the fact that most of the plans for reorganization have been used in some form or another in the past, we should give these ideas a careful and impartial hearing. Some of the plans can be rejected on the basis of what we know about the characteristics of pupils and how they learn. Some plans will require a care-

18. Cecil Floyd, "Meeting Children's Reading Needs in the Middle Grades," *Elementary School Journal*, LV (October, 1954), 99-103.

19. Elmer F. Morgan, Jr., and Gerald R. Stucker, "The Joplin Plan of Reading *vs.* a Traditional Method," *Journal of Educational Psychology*, LI (April, 1960), 69-73.

20. David H. Russell, "Inter-class Grouping for Reading Instruction in the Intermediate Grades," *Journal of Educational Research*, XXXIX (February, 1946), 462-70.

21. D. R. Green and Hazel M. Riley, "Inter-class Grouping for Reading Instruction in the Middle Grades," *Journal of Educational Research* (accepted for publication).

ful and thoughtful evaluation in limited school settings. In all cases in which tryouts are made, systematic plans must be provided for a critical evaluation of the results of the new organizational plan. Such tryouts are not easily made, but our claims to professional status rest on our ability to demonstrate the value of what we do.

A second and sobering consideration in looking at school organization concerns the research literature on the relation of school organization to pupil achievement. A thoughtful reader of this literature is led to a disquieting conclusion: Organizational patterns seemingly have little to do with pupil achievement when viewed in relation to the quality of the instructional program.

In our zeal to improve the schools, we must not lose sight of the fact that what we do in teaching pupils is far more important than how we assign pupils to a classroom. The quickest, surest, but certainly not the most dramatic way to improve the schools is simply to improve the quality of what we do in our present organizational framework.

RECOMMENDATION 6. *Regardless of the organizational pattern under which schools are administered, the administrative and curriculum policies should have four major goals:*

A. To provide a program in which the teacher has an opportunity to know his pupils well; their strengths, limitations, interests, social qualities, health problems, and family background.
B. To provide a program in which students are held to requirements which match their abilities, interests, cultural backgrounds, and future vocational goals.
C. To free the teacher from prescribed subject matter and rigid procedures so that he can adjust his program to pupil needs.
D. To provide instructional materials and make provision for techniques with a range of difficulty equal to the range of abilities of the students.

In achieving these four major goals, the following characteristics of instruction deserve special attention.[22]

---

22. For a more detailed consideration of the following items, see *Educational Measurement,* chap i. Edited by E. F. Lindquist. Washington: American Council on Education, 1951.

1. Class size must be held to reasonable limits. This may vary with circumstances, but classes of twenty-five pupils in the primary grades and thirty pupils in the intermediate grades have been recommended as ideal. At the secondary level with academic specialists, the problem of knowing students becomes greater because of the complexity of the subject matter and the large number of pupils customarily met in a day's instruction. The provision of longer blocks of time at this level can serve two major purposes. First, it enables a teacher to know better the students he meets; in addition, the longer periods of time permit research projects and activities which would be impossible in the traditional period.

2. Provision should be made for the use of the results of a systematic testing program which reveals status and growth of each pupil at least once a year in the basic skill areas and content subjects. The measures should center in the application of skills and intellectual understandings rather than in the specific content of a subject area.

3. A record folder should be kept for each pupil. This folder should be kept up to date and should contain, in addition to current test results, the pupil's health record, samples of his classwork, as well as special notations of strengths and weaknesses in personal and academic areas. Such a collection of material can be a valuable source of information in evaluating a pupil's growth.

4. Pupils should be assigned to basic class groups at the elementary level largely on the basis of physical and social development—which are probably best indicated by chronological age. A child should live and work in groups he regards as his equals. The group must accept him, and he must accept the group.

5. There must be grouping within any classroom on the basis of skills and needs in specific content and skill areas. The size and nature of these groups will vary with the specific classroom and the skill area being considered. The groups will change in size and with respect to objectives as needs dictate.

6. At the elementary level a competent teacher should be encouraged to remain with a group of pupils for more than one year. There are certain problems of personality conflict and special

strengths (or weaknesses) of the teacher which must be considered if the plan is to be carried out.

At the high-school level, superior teachers should be encouraged to teach the same pupils for two or more years in areas in which there is a sequence of more than one year, such as English, mathematics, science, social studies, and language.

7. At the high-school level there should be special classes for students who demonstrate special ability and interest in mathematics, language, science, and humanities. These classes may take the form of informal seminars in the small high school.

8. The school day should not be considered as consisting of a fixed number of inflexible periods. The schedule at both the elementary and secondary level must be flexible within the limits imposed by an effective administrative organization.

9. A broad range of instructional material must be provided. A single textbook cannot meet the needs of any class in terms of reading ability, background, or interest in a topic. Classroom collections should include extensive reference materials suitable to the abilities of the students. In content fields, special reference materials should be available. In all classrooms, encyclopedias, yearbooks, almanacs, atlases, and dictionaries should be readily available. It is not sufficient that these books be available from the central school library. The classroom collection, excepting the reference materials, should be returned to the central school library and replaced with fresh material of current interest when a new topic is begun.

CHAPTER V

The Impact of Testing Programs on College Preparation and Attendance

PAUL I. CLIFFORD and JOSHUA A. FISHMAN

Introduction

In considering the impact of college-selection testing programs on college preparation and attendance, it is necessary, first, to make explicit four notions which are relevant to the discussion which follows, but which might be overlooked if they were not specifically identified. The first of these is that college-selection testing programs are means which may contribute to the attainment of either desirable or undesirable ends, depending on whether they are used properly or improperly. The discussion which follows presumes that those who use data derived from college-selection testing programs seek to use them for relevant and proper purposes. To put it another way, it is assumed that users of data derived from college-selection testing programs employ test results to facilitate the emergence of potentially worthwhile intellectual outcomes and to eliminate or reduce any potentially deleterious effects.

Secondly, college-selection testing programs generally assay only those aspects of behavior which are most responsive to objective measurement and quantification. These are the domains of academic aptitude or, more precisely, of developed mental ability or academic achievement. The restrictions which are placed upon college-selection testing programs by limitation to these domains must be borne in mind in the discussion which follows.

The third point is that the data which are yielded by college-selection testing programs constitute only one kind of evidence concerning the degree to which a given applicant is likely to succeed in a given institution of higher education. Data yielded by college-selection testing programs must supplement and be supplemented by a variety of other kinds of valid information in the selection process.

Finally, academic success in institutions of higher education is not restricted to those individuals who obtain relatively high scores on admissions tests. Conversely, the attainment of high scores provides no guarantee that success in a given institution is inevitable. Test data, along with other evidence, enable us to reduce the gross errors in college admission policies to a point where we can take a calculated risk in terms of probabilities. Testing programs do not yield data that enable us to deal in absolutes. Even the most sophisticated use of test results permits us only to formulate tentative hypotheses concerning the behavior or behaviors which a test is used to evaluate or predict.

Generalizations

Several facets of the impact of testing programs on college preparation and attendance are examined in this chapter. They may be expressed as a series of questions, with answers given in the form of a series of broad generalizations.

1. Do college-selection testing programs promote or restrict equality of opportunity for higher education? Subsumed under this general question are the following specific questions: Are college-selection testing programs biased against various subcultural groups? against nonconformers? against women? against individuals who lack test sophistication? or against intelligent applicants whose preparatory school achievement was substandard?
2. Do college-selection testing programs adversely affect secondary-school programs?
3. Do college-selection testing programs contribute to the production of undesirably homogeneous student bodies?
4. Do college-selection testing programs lend themselves to the stratification of colleges on an invidious prestige scale?

GENERALIZATION 1. *In the main, college-selection testing programs promote rather than restrict equality of opportunity for higher education.*

Equality of opportunity to attend institutions for higher education does not presently exist in the United States. There are instances where admission to a given institution is, in effect, denied a particular candidate because of sex, color, religion, social class, socioeconomic status, family background, geographic location of residence, and other comparable barriers.

However, in the contemporary American social order, several variables interact in such a way as to produce increasing pressures upon our colleges and universities to promote greater degrees of equality of opportunity for higher education. The college-age population is increasing in numbers. The number of young people reaching eighteen each year, ready to enter the labor force or to go to college, will increase from 2.6 million in 1960 to 3.8 million in 1965. This is a rise of nearly 50 per cent.[1] A greater proportion of college-age youth is desirous of acquiring a college education, while the general public is placing greater value upon the attainment of a college degree. The leadership of American higher education in all sections of the country is espousing increased equality of educational opportunity, not only for the good of the individual but also for the welfare of the nation. These pressures are resulting in an increasingly determined effort to eradicate the artificial barriers which have restricted opportunities for higher education for certain segments of the population. These forces are at the same time creating many problems, which further complicate the already difficult tasks that confront those responsible for college admissions.

Gardner[2] predicts that in the decade ahead, even more than today, the college population will manifest a wide range of abilities and motivations. Great differences will doubtless characterize the educational needs of the students of the next decade, who will have to be educated in diverse institutions of higher education with varying programs and curricula.

No single institution of higher education can meet effectively the educational needs of all the applicants who desire to gain admission to it. It follows that one alternative to sheer trial and error in college admissions is for a given college or university to attempt clearly and precisely to identify the level of academic performance it will expect its students to attain. There are those who say that an institution of higher education has no need to define

1. *Manpower Challenge of the 1960's,* p. 4. United States Department of Labor Pamphlet. Washington: Government Printing Office, 1959.
2. John W. Gardner, "National Goals in Education," in *Goals for Americans,* p. 90. New York: American Assembly, Columbia University, 1960.

such expectancy levels, and there are others who hold that such definition is impossible. Both groups point to the fact that some good colleges and universities accept students whose potentials for achievement show wide variability. In reply to these arguments, it must be admitted that clear and precise identification and definition of expected levels of student attainment is a difficult and involved process, but efforts in this direction are necessary if college admission procedures are to become more rational and impartial. Once a college or university has established by self-study its level of expected student attainment, it is in position to identify with some precision and validity those applicants who show promise of reaching this level. An effective admission policy increases the probability that those applicants who can profit maximally from the kinds of educational experiences which they will undergo at a given institution will be admitted, and that those who show little likelihood of attaining the expected level of attainment will be less likely to gain admission.

College-selection testing programs yield data which can provide an institution of higher education with one kind of evidence which is relevant to deciding, on grounds of academic promise rather than on academically irrelevant grounds, who should and who should not be admitted. Since college-selection testing programs can provide such data, their proper use promotes equality of opportunity for higher education. College-selection testing programs have identified many young people with the potentialities for success in some college or family of colleges who otherwise might have gone unnoticed.

In the National Merit Scholarship Program, the number of participating secondary schools had increased from 10,338 in 1955 to 15,461 in 1961. In 1961, 135 sponsors were offering a total of more than 525 sponsored Merit Scholarships at an estimated cost of $2.5 million. From 1955 to 1961, sponsors paid or pledged $10.8 million to support Merit Scholarships. Nearly 600,000 students, or about one-third of all high-school Juniors, participated in the National Merit Program during the year 1961.[3] The director of this program reports that, in selecting scholarship winners, no consideration is given to the student's family background or social or economic status. Merit, it is indicated, is the only criterion for selection.[4] In the process of determining the relatively small number of winners, so many other able students are identified that it has become a recognized function of the competition to award 25,000 certificates of merit each year to the most outstanding nonwinners, thereby calling them to the attention of colleges and other sources of scholarship aid. In turn, those thereby aided from external scholarship sources leave available institutional funds to other needy applicants in an ever-widening circle.

Since 1952, over 60,000 Negro applicants for admission to the thirty-odd members of the United Negro College Fund have participated in the Cooperative Intercollegiate Examination Program. Their numbers increase yearly.

The College Entrance Examination Board, which is composed of 504 colleges, 165 secondary schools, and 41 educational associations, continues each year to provide for an increased demand from secondary-school students throughout the nation for participation in its testing program. The American College Testing Program and all the other mass testing programs demonstrate the same trend. One inevitable salutary result of the increased magnitude of college-selection testing programs is the likelihood of identifying more and more secondary-school students who, for a variety of reasons, might otherwise escape attention and therefore would not have the opportunity to profit from a college education.

Some severe critics[5,6] of tests contend that college-selection testing programs generally identify a much greater proportion of individuals from within the upper-income, professional segments of the population than from the lower-income, laboring classes as having the kinds of abilities sought after by colleges. However, it is a well known fact in differential psychology that scores on

4. *Ibid.*, p. 60.

5. Russell Allen, "Class Bias in Education," *I.U.D. Digest*, VI, No. 4 (Winter, 1961), 71-80.

6. John Kord Lagemann, "Let's Look Again at Those I.Q. Tests" (Condensed from the *PTA Magazine*), *Reader's Digest*, LXXIX (December, 1961), 91-95.

aptitude and achievement tests are positively correlated with socio-economic status and occupational level. It should be understood that one of these variables (test scores) is not directly caused by the other (parental income). It is likely that both phenomena are the results of a multiplicity of other causal factors. To disparage testing programs for revealing the inequities which still exist in the social, the economic, the educational, and the cultural domains of American life is as erroneous as it would be for residents of Bismarck, North Dakota, to condemn the use of thermometers as biased, when, as this is being written, the temperature in Bismarck is −11° F. and in Miami, Florida, it is 83° F. Test data reveal symptoms of psychological damage resulting from inequalities in our social order, just as the thermometer indicates broad deviations in temperature.

The manner in which college-selection testing programs increase equality of educational opportunity is illustrated by the admissions and financial-aid policies of the College of the University of Chicago. The 1961 entering Freshman class at Chicago was drawn from 1,911 completed applications. Of the number who completed application, 1,071, or 56 per cent, were admitted, while 573 (54 per cent of the admitted students) matriculated. The mean *SAT Verbal* score for the entire class was 646; for the men in the class, 640; and for the women, 657. The mean *SAT* Mathematical score for the entire class was 645; for the men, 665; and for the women, 611. It might be thought that *SAT* scores attained by Chicago applicants would preclude the admission of a boy or girl from the lower socioeconomic classes. This is not the case at all. The major barrier to attending the University of Chicago is financial. Tuition, effective with the autumn quarter of 1962, was $1,410.00 for the academic year. This makes the cost of attending Chicago without some outside assistance beyond the reach of the children of the great majority of American families, since, according to O'Connell, only 5 per cent of the country's families had annual incomes of $15,000 or more in 1959. [7]

O'Connell writes, "There is a tradition at Chicago of a broad-gauge student body, intellectually tough and alert, as free of

7. Charles D. O'Connell, "Admissions 1962: The Year of the Cat," *University of Chicago Magazine*, LIV (December, 1961), 19-23.

snobbery as it is of foppery, drawn from every economic and social level, selected only for its qualities of excellence."[8] In fulfilling this tradition, Chicago's financial-aid program seeks to assure that no able student who is admitted and who remains in good standing will be deprived of a Chicago education because of financial need. The identification of the poor, but able, student who not only gains admission to Chicago but also gets needed financial assistance is accomplished in part via his *SAT* scores. It is likely that the Chicago policy is followed in some form or other in the majority of our major institutions of higher education.

Data yielded by college-selection testing programs may be used to identify applicants who show little or no probability of success in a given college, thereby making it possible for the openings in that college to be filled by more promising candidates. A possible corollary of rejection of unpromising candidates would be the rejection of candidates whose capabilities far exceed the present expectation of the college. A mediocre college that accepts excellent students does so at the risk of not being able to develop to the maximum the potentialities of such students. Many colleges would look with a jaundiced eye upon such a self-negating policy, but this kind of realistic appraisal is indicated by the great variability in quality which characterizes the institutions of higher education in this nation.

GENERALIZATION 2. *Programs which sample degrees of college preparation are not inherently biased against various subcultural groups.*

An individual who seeks admission to an institution of higher education is, in effect, asking for the privilege of becoming socialized in the core values of a particular kind of subculture, that is, the college culture. The primary values of the college culture are centered in academic achievement, intellectual accomplishment, and social and emotional development. Regardless of an applicant's perceived racial identity, religion, socioeconomic status, social class antecedents, or ethnic background, he should provide evidence that his past experiences have enabled him to develop his abilities and

3. John M. Stalnaker, "The Nation's Greatest Talent Hunt," *Saturday*
8. *Ibid.*, p. 23.

to fulfil his capacities to a degree which adequately prepares him for successful interaction within the college subculture. Testing programs, which sample an applicant's preparation for college, should involve measurements of the kinds of behavior which he will be expected to manifest and develop in a specific institution of higher education. If an individual's experience has been of such a quality that the probability of his succeeding in a given college is relatively low, both he and the college should become aware of that fact. Data derived from college-selection testing programs can provide a culturally disadvantaged applicant with many nuances of this needed awareness.

College-selection testing programs, which sample degrees of college preparation, provide various subcultural groups with at least two kinds of polar information. The first kind of information enables an individual who belongs to a culturally disadvantaged group to ascertain with some degree of validity whether, in spite of cultural deprivation or environmental handicap, he has developed his abilities to the degree that he can look forward to success in a given institution of higher education. Indeed, his past success under difficulties more often than not indicates greater promise of future achievement than can be projected for his heretofore more advantaged peer. On the other hand, an applicant may become aware, through his performances on tests of college ability, that his cultural disadvantages have limited the development of his intellectual competence to such a degree that success in a given college would be highly unlikely. If the individual gains such insight early enough, through a school testing program or otherwise, he may, if he possesses relatively high levels of "underdeveloped ability" and if he is highly motivated toward academic achievement, be able to repair those deficiencies which the test data have indicated.

Unfortunately, there are some colleges and universities which base student selection, in part, upon unofficial or unwritten racial or religious quotas. In such cases, the utilization of college-selection test data to lend academic respectability to these practices is an improper use of these data. In every instance where data from college-selection testing programs are used as part of the college-admission process, acceptance or rejection of applicants should be considered on an individual, not a group, basis. No college-selection testing program can be used legitimately to either eliminate all the members of one group or include all the members of another group. On college-admissions tests, individual members of all subcultural groups can conceivably be found at any point in the total spectrum of scores. This means that although a particular subcultural group, when viewed in terms of central tendencies of performance, may score significantly lower than another group, individual members of the culturally disadvantaged group may reach or exceed the average obtained by the more advantaged group. For those applicants from culturally deprived populations who can demonstrate a readiness for college work in this manner, college-selection testing programs must be considered culturally neutral for purposes of academic selection insofar as they are concerned. Acceptable performance on such instruments can also be viewed as a vehicle for generating necessary degrees of psychological security.

Every college must, of course, be permitted to set its own admissions standards in terms of criteria that are effective in terms of the institution's program and legitimate functions and purposes. To go beyond this requires a decision of the larger society which supports higher education. To argue that college-selection testing programs are generally fair and do serve to uncover talent that might otherwise go unnoticed is not to argue that such testing programs are equally effective in identifying educational potential in all population groups in American society. One solution of this difficulty is to make college admission virtually unrestricted and to let selection be accomplished by attrition. Another is to retain selectivity at college entrance, but to promote a prior program of early identification and special opportunity. Still another approach is to greatly increase the total effort in elementary and secondary schools by providing the necessary support and to depend upon this generally increased availability of opportunity to render present selective procedures appropriate to the total youth group. No matter which one of these policy decisions is made, it should be recognized that it is the decision, rather than the use of testing programs to implement the decision, that is chiefly responsible for the character of the selection program. Tests are available to implement decisions of many types.

GENERALIZATION 3. *College-selection testing programs do not unduly penalize the bright nonconformer.*

Testing programs which are utilized to yield data relevant to college admissions sample a wide spectral band of behavior. So-called "brightness" is one aspect of mental functioning which is assessed in such programs, but "brightness" alone does not guarantee success in college. The kind of psychological climate which pervades the campuses of our best colleges and universities is characterized by certain degrees of academic rigor, disciplined thinking, and even obsessive-compulsive precision. Nonconformity in the intellectual domain, if it is anchored in the reality of the academic demands of the college, is part of the psychodynamic undergirding of creativity, but nonconformity, in and of itself, even when coupled with relatively superior mental abilities, may be a serious obstacle to success in college.

Certain kinds of behavior sampled by college-admissions testing programs pertain precisely to those aspects of functioning which provide evidence relevant to the amount of reality testing in which an individual characteristically engages. In view of the realities of the demands of academic life, testing programs do not penalize the bright nonconformer who is seeking admission to college. What such programs do for a bright nonconforming applicant is not to penalize him but to identify certain aspects of his intellectual functioning which need to be subjected to an academic regimen which, up to the time he has applied for college admission, has been lacking. It could also be said that some bright nonconformers may not be "college bright" but, instead, are only "beatnik bright." To expect a college or university to provide an avenue to fame (or oblivion) for such nonconformers is to ask what is logically impossible, since the college is necessarily somewhat conventional and disciplined, while these nonconformers are essentially unconventional and undisciplined. Most colleges are not and cannot be organized to deal with more than a measure of nonconformity. Admission policies and procedures must take into account the purposes and resources of the college as well as the nature of the students admitted to it.

GENERALIZATION 4. *College-admissions testing programs do not normally involve biases for or against women.*

College-admissions testing programs are designed to be utilized with both men and women applicants. Those psychological domains in which sex differences exist, and which are relevant to college-admissions policies, are balanced against one another so that potential biases toward either sex are inconsequential. Sex differences are also taken into account in the building of norms so that bias due to such differences does not vitiate the interpretation of the test data. Female superiority in verbal or linguistic ability, especially verbal fluency, and male superiority in quantitative reasoning ability and spatial relationships represent the most important sex differences in psychological functioning which appear in the results of college-admissions testing programs.

If the sex differences which appear in responses to college-aptitude test items are relevant for the performance one wishes to predict, then items showing differences should remain in the test. However, if the differences are not relevant, the items which show differences should be removed or controlled through proper weighting.[9] Since the differences in abilities that have been identified above are relevant to predicting certain facets of college success, items which show such differences properly appear in college-admissions testing programs. Differentials in the normative data for men and for women facilitate clear interpretations.

GENERALIZATION 5. *Test-wise individuals are not unduly favored by college-admissions testing programs.*

Familiarity with the demands of test-taking reduces the likelihood that an applicant for college admission will perceive test-taking as a novel situation. Test-wise individuals bring to the testing session a set which is salutary in terms of adequate performance. The taking of tests is an increasingly important facet of the total school culture, therefore test sophistication is a desirable kind of behavior for students to acquire and to exhibit. Test sophistication does not place an applicant for college admission in a position to spuriously raise his scores on college-admissions tests. It does, however, in-

9. William E. Coffman, "Sex Differences in Responses to Items in Aptitude Tests," in the *Eighteenth Yearbook of the National Council on Measurements in Education*, pp. 117-24. Edited by Edith M. Huddleston. Ames, Iowa: National Council on Measurements in Education, 1961.

crease the probability that the scores obtained by a test-wise individual more adequately reflect the totality of competencies which he brings to the testing situation.

Vernon,[10] reporting on the effects of coaching and practice on intelligence-test performance, writes that coaching plus practice results in improvement, but that it is also true that "intelligence" cannot be "taught" at all in the same sense as are school subjects. The total increase in performance is limited and there is no continued improvement with continued training. According to Vernon, the results tend to be specific to the domain in which the coaching and practice occur. Even the general sophistication effect merely means familiarity with the kinds of items and the methods of work appropriate to most psychological tests. Similar findings for the College Board's *Scholastic Aptitude Test* have been reported repeatedly. (See chap. ix for further discussion.)

It is generally agreed that school instruction or out-of-school coaching, which aims at improved test scores as its major objective, is to be both deplored and discouraged. Except as such coaching amounts to refresher study of a basic skill that has suffered disuse, it has no intrinsic educational value.

GENERALIZATION 6. *College-admissions programs properly reward preparatory-school achievement over sheer tested "intelligence."*

Only a relatively small minority of those students of high mental ability who do poorly in preparatory school is likely to do well in college. What institutions of higher education attempt through their admissions programs is to identify not only those applicants who possess relatively high mental abilities per se, but to select those individuals who have developed a strong undergirding for academic success in a given institution through the growth and development of their mental abilities under the stimulation of preparatory-school educational experiences. The applicant for admission to a college who possesses a high level of untutored mental ability, but who has not developed basic skills and knowledge

10. P. E. Vernon, *Intelligence and Attainment Tests*, p. 135. New York: Philosophical Library, 1960.

structure and whose high-school performance is consequently weak, is not likely to achieve great success in most colleges. College-admissions testing programs sample the extent to which a given applicant has developed his mental capacities through prior learning and education. This is proper, since institutions of higher education are concerned with elaborating and deepening the individual's mental development which was initiated in the elementary school and continued in the secondary school. College-admissions testing programs, then, reward the student of relatively high mental abilities who has developed those abilities through sound preparation and achievement in elementary and secondary school.

GENERALIZATION 7. *Tests for college admission have potentiality for affecting secondary-school programs.*

It is well known that testing programs have considerable influence upon instructional programs. Testing programs inevitably affect both teachers and learners. If the test behavior sampled by college-admissions testing programs differs in either quality or quantity from the behavior which is implied in the statement of objectives of secondary education, a considerable number of teachers and students in secondary schools will show greater concern for acquiring the kinds of behavior measured by the testing program than in achieving the stated objectives of the schools, since superior test performance vitally affects a student's probability of admission to the college of his choice. Thus, college-selection testing programs have the potentiality of motivating teachers and learners to jettison the secondary school's objectives and to substitute for them behavioral acquisitions which may be less desirable in terms of the instructional program of the school. Testing programs which are not relevant to the school's program increase the temptation to coach for tests, despite evidence already cited that coaching is generally ineffectual.

College-admissions testing programs provide data which can be misused in a variety of ways. Unwarranted comparisons or contrasts among secondary schools and teachers, as well as misinterpretation of the meaning of test data in relation to secondary-school curricula and instruction represent some of the major means by which college-admissions testing programs might adversely affect the secondary school. One way to obviate the potentially deleterious effects of college-admissions testing programs upon the secondary school would be to have colleges and secondary schools co-operate with the test producers in constantly revising college-selection testing programs so that they sample in more adequate ways the degree to which a student has acquired the kinds of behavior which are implied in statements of school objectives. If the behavior sampled in the college-selection testing programs were in congruence with the behavior implied in the statements of schools' objectives, the college-admissions testing program and the secondary schools' instructional programs would be mutually reinforcing. It would still be necessary to educate teachers, administrators, and the public at large not to employ college-selection test results for comparisons and evaluations for which the tests were not intended.

GENERALIZATION 8. *The use of college-admissions testing programs should not, and need not, result in undesirably homogeneous student bodies.*

A desirable admissions policy permits an institution of higher education to indicate clearly and validly which applicants it ought to admit and which it ought to reject, without risking the non-fulfilment of the academic promise of the applicant or compromising the academic standards of the institution.

An institution of higher education must clearly identify and define its educational objectives and clearly delineate the image of the kind of student in which it desires its objectives to come to full fruition. After these two processes have been completed, the institution is in a position to select the kinds of student, from among all its applicants, that it ought to admit. Testing programs provide one source of data which facilitates the process of selecting these students.

The choosing of a college by a student and the selection of an applicant by the college do not involve simply the matching of the college and the student. As Boroff[11] writes, such an unexciting matching can result in a "dull, gray, compatible marriage" without

11. David Boroff, *Campus U.S.A.: Portraits of American Colleges in Action*, p. xiii. New York: Harper & Bros., 1961.

the desirable and meaningful conflict, polarity, and opposition which characterize genuine intellectual stimulation.

Conflict, polarity, and opposition, if carried too far, however, eventuate in chaos. The best interest of both the applicant and the institution is served only when the college selects its student body in terms of the interrelationship of the objectives of the college and the characteristics of the students. If this kind of procedure is followed, the student body which is selected will show similarities in those aspects of their behavior which are relevant to the objectives of the institution. It is necessary that a degree of this kind of homogeneity of behavior characterize the student body of a given institution in order to increase the probability that the objectives of the college will be realized in the behavior of its students. This kind of homogeneity is not undesirable; in fact, it is necessary. Variability within the individual and variation among individuals will combine to produce desirable degrees of heterogeneity within a student body, no matter upon what aspects of behavior attempts are made to secure homogeneity in certain delimited areas of behavior. Testing programs can contribute to an institution's effort to secure the kind of student body which can profit maximally from attending that institution without at the same time producing undesirable homogeneity.

On the other hand, it is quite possible for the admissions policy of a college, and the image prospective students hold of it, to result in an undesirably homogeneous student body. It is also possible to identify certain institutions which currently illustrate this danger. For this reason, it is necessary for college-admission officers to be constantly alert to this danger and to take every precaution that data yielded by college-selection testing programs are not misused for this purpose. Thus, the recently published *Manual of Freshman Class Profiles*,[12] giving as it does Freshman class characteristics for several score American colleges and universities, may serve to "homogenize" these institutions by attracting to them more students like those already there. On the other hand, the *Manual* also enables colleges to state in what ways they hope that their future entering classes will be different from the current one—thus inviting hetero-

12. *Manual of Freshman Class Profiles*. Princeton, New Jersey: College Entrance Examination Board, 1962.

geneity wherever that is deemed desirable. However, in either case, test data are only a small part of the total institutional characterization reported, although, as is usual, such data lend themselves to somewhat sharper presentation. The cure for self-homogenizing images and reputations would seem to be the wider dissemination of such institutional data, for there is infinitely more to fear from uninformed, traditional images than from precise score distributions —actual and desired.

What might be termed the "comprehensive college" will probably occupy the intermediate position between the polar institutions described by Gardner.[13] He writes that in the decade ahead some institutions of higher education will specialize in training those students whose educational plans or potentialities are least ambitious, while at the other extreme some colleges and universities will limit their student bodies almost exclusively to those who intend to go on to professional or graduate schools. At the center of the spectrum will be the majority of colleges and universities, especially state universities, which will accept students representing a wide range of abilities and enrol them in different curricula and programs. Such institutions, according to Gardner, will accept high-school graduates with minimal qualifications and provide them with work comparable to that offered in the junior college. At the same time this "comprehensive college" will operate honors programs comparable in difficulty to any in the country.

In spite of the desirability which Gardner sees in heterogeneity as a characteristic of institutions of higher education, he demands homogeneity in one domain:

. . . we must insist that every college student be stimulated and challenged in terms of his own potentialities. A college education should be a reasonably arduous experience.

In the great variety of institutions and programs that make up American higher education there will continue to be both liberal arts and vocational programs. Each has its place. But *no* institution should be without a strong liberal arts component.[14]

It is precisely in relation to this *sine qua non* of higher education

13. Gardner, *op. cit.*, pp. 90-91.

14. *Ibid.*, p. 91.

that college-selection testing programs can make their greatest contributions.

GENERALIZATION 9. *College-admissions testing programs should not, and actually cannot, be used to stratify colleges on an invidious prestige scale.*

There are well over fifteen hundred institutions of higher education in the United States. These colleges and universities vary in numberless ways. From the standpoint of this discussion, the more important dimensions of variation are:

1. The history and tradition of the institution.
2. The distinction, prestige, and visibility of the institution's faculty within the total academic world.
3. The accomplishments of the graduates of the institution.
4. The research and publications of the faculty.
5. The amount and nature of the institution's financial support.
6. The selectivity of the institution's admissions criteria.
7. The institution's policies of academic retention.
8. The qualitative and quantitative requirements for graduation.
9. The institution's general aims and specific educational objectives and the degree to which these are being attained in the behavior of students.
10. The institution's criteria for assigning grades of varying quality.
11. The kinds of behavior required of students while enrolled in the institution.
12. The instructional program.
13. The values and other cultural concomitants which characterize and pervade the institution's community of scholars and learners.
14. The facilities, equipment, and plant.

These sources of variation among institutions of higher education, together with the interactions among them, are the major contributors to the differences in prestige and academic excellence of American colleges and universities. From the preceding discussion it is apparent that an attempt to stratify colleges on some kind of prestige scale poses a problem which cannot be completely resolved by the use of data derived from college-admissions testing programs. Test data could identify some of the variance associated with the many dimensions and degrees of difference among the nation's institutions of higher education, but any such attempt would, of necessity, have to warn loudly of the shortcomings and the dangers inherent in such procedures. A general academic quality scale upon which all institutions could be placed with some degree of objectivity might conceivably be devised. This would entail the identification and definition of those criteria by which academic quality might be judged. In addition, valid means of measuring the degree to which a given institution meets each criterion would have to be devised. It could then be hypothesized that the correlation between valid measures of institutional quality and mean student academic accomplishment would differ significantly from zero. If such an hypothesis were confirmed and the obtained correlations were of sufficient magnitude, further study in this area would be indicated. Careful research in this area might result in the development of a valid scale, but its use would require many safeguards.

To return from what might be to what is, the admonitions of Bloom and Peters[15] with respect to their academic prediction scales have relevance to the problem of stratifying colleges and universities on a prestige scale. Academic prediction scales and other devices for improving the prediction of college grades from previous kinds of behavior make use of data on a quantitative scale. It is improper to interpret a quantitative scale as a qualitative scale of the merits of a particular educational program. This point is clearly made in the following statement quoted from Bloom and Peters:

It is quite likely that the efficiency of the scales for prediction will frequently be misinterpreted as evidence that a scale is an index of the relative educational merits of different schools and colleges or of different educational curricula. We find it quite conceivable that a school that places low on the *Academic Prediction Scale* may be doing a more effective educational job than many schools that place higher on the scale. The qualitative characteristics of educational programs should be evaluated by determining how effectively they achieve their educational objectives. A school with one group of students may need to do a quite different educational task than a school with a very different group of students. A school or college operating within one community or educational setting may need to offer a very different set of learning experiences than a school within

15. Benjamin S. Bloom and Frank R. Peters, *The Use of Academic Prediction Scales for Counseling and Selecting College Entrants*, pp. 113-14. New York: Free Press of Glencoe, Inc., 1961.

a different context. Thus, there may be many different types of educational programs that have important and meaningful qualitative differences; such differences are not reflected in a simple quantitative scale designed to maximize the predictability of academic achievement as measured by grades.[16]

Hills, Franz, and Emory,[17] in discussing what should and should not be attempted with their prediction formulas, support the quoted statement from Bloom and Peters.

Conant,[18] with characteristic candor, reminds us that the mere holding of a bachelor's degree from an American university or college means next to nothing because our more than 1,500 institutions of higher education are so diverse in both standards of admission and requirements for graduation. Conant writes:

. . . no one would publish a rank list of institutions or even be willing to be quoted publicly to the effect that a straight A record in one college has about the same meaning as a C record in another. In the United States we have a hierarchy of institutions granting the first degree and a tight conspiracy of silence as to the existence of such a hierarchy. This is a consequence of the American doctrine of equality of status, and I do not decry it. It does render ridiculous, however, any serious contemplation of raising college or university entrance requirements the country over in order to improve the work of the high schools.[19]

Conant's unwillingness to decry the "conspiracy of silence" in American education concerning the qualitative ranking of our institutions of higher education is probably not shared by several groups, including authorities in the testing field. These specialists realize, however, that college-selection test data, which are quantitative in nature, do not properly lend themselves simply or directly to the making of qualitative judgments about the kinds of complex phenomena which would have to be considered in the development

---

16. *Ibid.*

17. John R. Hills, Gretchen Franz, and Linda B. Emory, *Counselor's Guide to Georgia Colleges*, p. 4. Atlanta, Georgia: Office of Testing and Guidance, Regents, University System of Georgia (244 Washington St., S.W.), 1959.

18. James Bryant Conant, *Slums and Suburbs: A Commentary on Schools in Metropolitan Areas*, p. 93. New York: McGraw-Hill Book Co., Inc., 1961.

19. *Ibid.*, pp. 93-94.

of any hierarchical arrangement of American colleges and universities.

Recommendations

The generalizations presented in this chapter could have been, in most instances, reformulated as recommendations. Together with the discussion and supporting statements, they lead to more specific recommendations. These recommendations are directed to those individuals who are immediately concerned with the use and interpretation of data derived from college-selection testing programs.

RECOMMENDATION 1. *Data yielded by college-selection testing programs should be treated as professional information.*

Those persons who use and interpret data from college-selection testing programs should take every precaution to utilize the information in an expert, objective, professional manner for relevant, legitimate, and proper purposes within the nexus of the goals of the American social order and the objectives of American higher education. Misuse for any purpose should not be tolerated.

RECOMMENDATION 2. *There should be continuous evaluation of college-selection testing.*

Personnel in institutions of higher education and in secondary schools, in concert with the test-makers, should, through research, continually determine the degree of effectiveness which characterizes the psychometric instruments which are developed and used to select college students. Those whose concern with college-selection tests is most immediate should be the most critical appraisers of the assumptions, hypotheses, and conclusions which give validity to their work.

RECOMMENDATION 3. *Communication among test-makers, test-users, examinees, and the public demands continuing high priority.*

Professional personnel who construct and who use college-selection testing programs should pursue with vigor the objective of adequate and effective communication about their work, not only with those candidates who sit for such tests but also with the lay public. Professional people in education who are not experts in measurement should be included in the effort to increase understanding of what is involved in the building, use, and interpretation of college-selection testing programs. The kind of communication envisioned here will contribute to the acquisition of an objective attitude toward tests on the part of all who are concerned with college-selection testing programs. In the absence of an objective attitude toward testing, much of the good which is inherent in psychological measurement is both dissipated and distorted.

Concluding Statement

This chapter has presented evidence that mass college-selection programs are exercising salutary influence upon college attendance and preparation. The authors would not argue that the instruments of selection have been perfected, that they are never misused, or that their potential is always fully realized. The authors do assert, however, that much of the criticism directed toward such programs would be better directed toward policy decisions which are antecedent to their use.

CHAPTER VI

Effects of Testing Programs on the Attitudes of Students, Teachers, Parents, and the Community

CLARENCE MAHLER and HARRY SMALLENBURG

Introduction

One authority[1] on testing estimated in 1954 that each year more than 75 million standardized tests were being taken by 25 million persons in the United States. This was an average of about three tests for the persons tested, most of whom were pupils in elementary and secondary schools. More recent estimates of the number of testees and tests given are somewhat higher. A number of questions arise: What is the effect of tests upon the attitudes of the pupils? Do testing programs encourage excessive competition? Do they encourage dishonesty? Do they create undue anxiety? Do they interfere with genuine student-teacher co-operation? Do they help or harm community relations? Are popular protests against personality testing as an invasion of privacy warranted? How do tests affect a student's values and self-perceptions? Does confidentiality affect attitudes? How do attitudes toward testing affect the validity of test scores?

Considering the vital importance of these questions, relatively little attention has been given to them. In this chapter consideration will be given to effects of testing programs upon the attitudes of (a) children and youth, (b) teachers and administrators, (c) parents, and (d) the community. Recommendations for improvement will be submitted under each topic.

1. J. Wayne Wrightstone, *What Tests Can Tell Us About Children*, p. 2. Chicago: Science Research Associates, 1954.

Effects of Testing Programs upon Students

Seymour B. Sarason[2] and his colleagues have made the most comprehensive study to date of anxiety in school children. After an extensive review of the literature on this topic, Sarason comments: "Despite the significances which are attributed to anxiety in the development of the child, systematic research on anxiety is practically nonexistent."

In a series of experiments extending over a period of six years, Sarason studied the effect of the testing program upon the attitudes of children. One major conclusion which emerged was that a child's perception of himself in relation to the testing situation affects his test performance and that, for many children, a degree of anxiety is aroused which interferes with maximum use of their potential.

In another rather extensive review of the literature, French points out that "much attention has been given to the correlation between scores on an anxiety scale and level of intelligence."[3] He summarized as follows:

In most cases a low negative correlation has been found. (Sarason and Mandler 1952, Sarason 1957, Spielberger 1959, Matarazzo et al. 1954, Hastings 1944, Sarnoff et al. 1959, Kerrick 1955, Purcell et al. 1952, Calvin et al. 1955, Zweibelson 1956, Dreger and Aiken 1957.) The first two listed above were using the College Board Scholastic Aptitude Test (SAT). Sarason and Mandler (1952) also note a low positive correlation between anxiety and the Henmon-Nelson intelligence test, and Sarason (1957) a low positive correlation between general anxiety and grade-point-average. Some correlations around zero were also found by a few of the workers mentioned above and a number of others. (Spielberger 1959, Dreger and Aiken 1957, Sarason 1956, LaMonaca and Berkun 1959, Schulz and Calvin 1955, Klugh and Bendig 1955, Matarazzo et al. 1954.) Alpert and Haber (1960) found "general" anxiety scales to be less related to the SAT than specific "test" anxiety scales. The test anxiety scales were found to be useful in contributing to the prediction of academic achievement already provided by the SAT. Among

2. Seymour B. Sarason, Kenneth S. Davidson, Frederick F. Lighthall, Richard R. Waite, Britton K. Ruebush, *Anxiety in Elementary School Children*, p. 81. New York: John Wiley & Sons, Inc., 1960.

3. John W. French, *A Study of Emotional States Aroused during Examinations*. Research and Development Reports, *Research Bulletin*, RB-61-6, March, 1961. Princeton, New Jersey: Educational Testing Service.

the test anxiety scales, a scale devised to measure facilitating anxiety and another for debilitating anxiety had expected negative correlations with each other. Even though these workers have studied an important aspect of anxiety, its relation to intelligence, this does not answer the question at issue in the present experiment. Evidence that anxiety is usually found to accompany low test scores proves nothing about the part that anxiety plays in bringing about the low scores."[4]

French conducted a study to learn about emotional states aroused in students during college-entrance testing and to "obtain estimates of the effects of these states on the test scores and on the validity of the test." He asked: "Are there some groups of candidates who cannot perform at their best levels when working under the conditions of pressure that prevail during a College Board examination? Does excessive anxiety of the candidates reduce the validity of the test?"[5] He endeavored "to answer these questions by administering a 'relaxed' test to some candidates a few days before and to others a few days after the January 1960 SAT [Scholastic Aptitude Test]." In each instance an alternate form of the relaxed test was administered concurrently with the SAT. Following the tests a questionnaire was used to obtain information regarding the "students' background, academic ambitions, feeling of anxiety, and reasons for feeling anxious. Two scales measuring generalized anxiety were included. Teachers' grades in four different high-school subjects were collected."[6] The examination of these data showed that the effects of anxiety were small:

A comparison of scores on the relaxed tests with alternate test forms taken with the SAT indicates no effect of anxiety for boys, while anxiety seems to be associated with a slight but significant improvement of girls' mathematical scores relative to their verbal scores. Since the relaxed test, the "anxious" test taken with the SAT, and the SAT itself were all found to have substantially the same concurrent validities, it is also unlikely that anxiety has had any effect on predictive validity. Responses to the questionnaire brought out expected statements about anxious feelings, and a small, possibly significant, tendency for "academically minded" boys to do relatively poorly on an anxious test as com-

---

4. *Ibid.*, p. 4. The references cited by French in the quotation are listed in his study, pp. 54-57.

5. *Ibid.*, p. i.

6. *Ibid.*

pared to a relaxed test, while academically minded girls show the opposite tendency. These effects are all well below the standard errors of measurement of the test.[7]

Reese[8] reported a study of fourth- and sixth-grade children who were given the *Children's Manifest Anxiety Scale* and an arithmetic achievement test, consisting of 40 addition problems, administered under a time limit. It was found that measures of manifest anxiety were inversely and monotonically related to the scores on the achievement test. Partialing out I.Q. had little effect on the correlations between manifest anxiety and achievement, but predictions of achievement were not appreciably improved by the combination of manifest anxiety with I.Q. Irvin Sarason summarized his study of text anxiety and the intellectual performance of college students as follows:

The present findings demonstrate that for both men and women there are significant negative relationships between anxiety reported by subjects as being experienced in testing situations (TA) and a variety of measures of intellectual performance. These results also confirm the findings of a previous study (Sarason, 1959) which showed (a) TA to be negatively related to many of the same intellectual variables with which the present study was concerned and (b) other personality measures to be unrelated to intellectual performance. In the present research none of the personality scales, except TA, related significantly to performance in any consistent manner for both male and female college students. Thus, support was given for the hypothesis that the more specific the measure of personality (in this case, anxiety) is to the situation being studied, the more consistently will the personality measure relate to performance (Sarason, 1960). It was hypothesized also that TA scores would be more negatively related to aptitude test measures than to the six high school grade point averages. The present study suggests that this well may be the case. The Need for Achievement Scale might have been expected to relate negatively to intellectual performance since its items appear to reflect strong need and anxiety to achieve. There was an indication that this might be true for male students but not for female students.

Two problems then seem to be posed by the present findings of consistent negative relationships between TA and 13 intellectual measures and also of greater strength of those negative relationships involving

7. *Ibid.*, p. i-ii.

8. Hayne W. Reese, "Manifest Anxiety and Achievement Test Performance," *Journal of Educational Psychology,* LII, No. 3 (June, 1961), 132-35.

aptitude tests as compared with high school grade point averages. First, what factors contribute to the negative relationships obtained? Second, why is test anxiety less of a detrimental factor for course grades than for aptitude tests?

With respect to the first question, it would seem prudent at present to interpret the present results as simply indications of poorer intellectual performance for high than for low test anxious students. If this is due to intellectual differences among subjects differing in TA scores, then it may be the case that high test anxiety scores simply reflect realistic concern over intellectual ability. If, however, students differing in test anxiety do not differ in intellectual ability then it would be worthwhile to determine which psychological aspects of testing and academic situations arouse anxiety responses in high TA scorers and whether or not the conditions of either the testing situation or of anxious students can be modified in such a way as to raise anxious students' performance level. Results of experimental studies indicate that under neutral or reassuring conditions high and low anxious subjects do not differ in their performance levels but that under stress they do differ in the same direction as obtained in the present research (Sarason, 1958a; Sarason & Palola, 1960).

In view of this evidence it seems possible that the answer to the second question posed, that of the explanation of the stronger correlations with TA of aptitude test scores than of grade point averages, may be in the opportunity of the student in class to be reassured and to reassure himself. In the course of a quarter or a semester the anxious student can come to know his instructors and peers, as well as to increase his familiarity with and to overlearn the material to be learned. These possibilities are largely absent in group aptitude testing. Greater emphasis in future research on the interpersonal aspects of learning and performance situations should make clearer the implications of these findings.[9]

Another way to study the impact of testing programs on students is to check their reactions to opportunity of reviewing test results with a trained counselor. Pustell[10] used a Freshman class in college that had taken the *Minnesota Multiphasic Personality Inventory* (*MMPI*) as a part of the entrance battery to check the hypothesis that opportunity for limited self-referral to a psychological coun-

9. Irwin G. Sarason, "Test Anxiety and the Intellectual Performance of College Students," *Journal of Educational Psychology*, LII, No. 4 (August, 1961), 204-5.

10. Thomas E. Pustell, "A Note on Use of the MMPI in College Counseling," *Journal of Counseling Psychology*, V (Spring, 1958), 69-70.

selor for test interpretation would be more attractive to the poorly adjusted students. Five hundred and fifty students were read a notice in Freshmen orientation class that all students could see the counselors to discuss the implications of the personality inventory. Pustell found that the level of adjustment of those who reported for counseling did not differ from those who did not report.

Twenty-three per cent of the females as compared with 11 per cent of the males responded to the invitation to discuss the implications of the inventory. On the basis of the author's criterion, 17 per cent of the males and 9 per cent of the females were classified as atypical. These percentages are in agreement with the experience of many counseling centers and mental hygiene clinics that have found that men tend to be more reluctant to seek out professional personnel than do women. If further research confirms the existence of significant sex differences in willingness to secure professional help in self-understanding, such differences should be taken into account in the planning of test programs.

Published reports on students' reactions to their test results are few in number. Bell[11] secured the reactions of 151 college Freshmen and Sophomores to their test interpretation interviews. All the interviews were conducted by one counselor. The average length of the test interview was forty-five minutes. In addition to high-school records, the testing program consisted of the *ACE Psychological Examination;* the *Cooperative Achievement Tests in Social Science, Natural Science, Mathematics,* and *English;* the *Whipple Silent Reading Test;* the *Bell Adjustment Inventory;* the *Bell Preference Inventory;* and the *Allport-Vernon Study of Values.* Two or three weeks after each interview a brief questionnaire was sent to each student asking for the student's reaction to his conference at which the personnel tests had been interpreted. Seventy-three per cent of the students completed the questionnaire.

The two major reasons students gave for requesting an interview were: "(1) taking the tests made me want to learn about my test

11. H. M. Bell, "Students Reactions to Learning Their Scores on a Battery of Personnel Tests," *Report of the Seventh Annual Workshop in Counseling and Guidance, Summer, 1955,* pp. 39-51. Chico, California: Chico State College, 1955.

results; and (2) another student told me about his experience with the test interview." At the time of the study (1947-48) tests were under strong criticism by Rogers and others. Bell attempted to assess the validity of the criticisms of Rogers by getting the perceptions of the testing interview from the students. Of the ten evaluative statements following Rogers' points, the two which stood out above the other statements were: (*a*) Made me feel the counselor explaining the test results had very superior knowledge about me; and (*b*) the more I listened to the counselor explain my scores, the more I came to feel that I should ask him to make my decision for me since he had such superior knowledge. In an over-all reaction to the value of the interview, 97 per cent of the students indicated that the interview experience had been helpful. Bell concluded that, while Rogers' criticisms of the use of test results had some justification, for the most part students made good use of test results and very few were disturbed by the test results. It was found that particular care must be given to interpreting test results to students whose grades and test scores are widely disparate. While the results of this study are positive as to the value to the students of receiving test results, it is obvious that much more research is needed on the way to help students utilize the test results in building or rebuilding their own self-perceptions.

Experimental studies of the effect of test interpretation upon the behavior of students are very few in number. There are, however, some partly related studies which may provide some understanding. Klingelhofer[12] conducted an experimental study of counseling probationary college students through a "directive" inventory-oriented approach with the variation in approaches being one interview of one hour *vs.* a series of four one-hour interviews. The first hour for all counselees centered on the results of the *College Inventory of Academic Adjustment* and the permanent record. The counselor summarized the interview and indicated positive steps the individual might take to improve his scholastic performance. The three additional conferences held during the semester dealt

12. Edwin L. Klingelhofer, "The Relationship of Academic Advisement to the Scholastic Performance of Failing College Students," *Journal of Counseling Psychology*, I (Fall, 1954), 125-31.

with the progress of the student in his courses. By use of analysis of variance procedures, a significant difference was found between the grade-point results of all counselled students and their counseling grade-point averages. No differences were attributable to the method or time (one hour *vs.* four hours of counseling employed).

The implications for interpretation of test results are clear. Students who are clearly motivated (i.e., readmitted students on probation) may be much more receptive to utilizing test results in helping to change their school work habits. Further studies using additional variations in length of counseling time and control groups receiving no test interpretation or help would aid our attempts to establish the validity of our counseling efforts when test results are part of the process. It would be very helpful to school counselors who deal with a great many students experiencing scholastic difficulties to have more definite information as to the use of test results and the amount of counseling time that will yield the best returns.

In a study by Froehlich and Moser[13] ninth-grade pupils drew their own percentile-rank profiles on eight subtests of the *Differential Aptitude Tests* and approximately fifteen months later redrew the profiles from memory. Correlations between obtained and reported percentile ranks were from +.41 to +.57. There was a tendency to remember scores as being somewhat higher than they really were. A large proportion of students remembered their highest tested aptitude, but relative scores on other aptitudes were less accurately reported from memory. The study is limited in design since even good memory for test results is not shown to relate closely to self-concept.

From the aforementioned and other studies, it may be concluded that tests have marked effects upon many pupils. These effects may be positive in that the knowledge that tests are to be given serves as a strong stimulation to study, and the report of pupils' test performance provides a strong re-enforcement of success or failure which helps to maintain the motivation for learning; or the effects may be negative in that they create anxiety in pupils who worry about failure or fear that they will achieve inadequately in relation to their goals. This anxiety may interfere with the pupil's

13. C. P. Froehlich and W. E. Moser, "Do Counselees Remember Test Scores?" *Journal of Counseling Psychology,* I (Fall, 1954), 149-52.

achievement on the test and help to produce feelings of inadequacy and lack of self-confidence.

RECOMMENDATIONS BASED ON AN EXAMINATION OF THE EFFECTS
OF TESTING UPON STUDENTS

Since research indicates that testing programs do have some influence on attitudes of many pupils and perhaps a strong effect on the attitudes of some pupils, the following recommendations are made in the interests of enhancing the positive values of testing and testing programs:

1. Develop an evaluation program which adequately reflects the objectives sought by the school. This would mean that the testing program should provide for the assessment of student accomplishment of all of the major objectives of education.

2. Involve pupils as well as teachers and parents in the formulation and discussion of educational objectives so that pupils will perceive a testing program as one of the means of appraising progress toward these objectives.

3. Help pupils to understand that a variety of devices, e.g., standardized tests, teacher-made tests, self-ratings, samples of class work, and the like, are involved in the total evaluation process and that their school status does not depend upon the results of a single test.

4. Make the testing situation as natural as possible so that the test is regarded as a regular part of the instructional and guidance program.

5. Present clearly the reasons for the testing program, the objectives which the program is planned to achieve, and the manner in which each aspect of the program contributes to the attainment of the objectives.

6. Provide practice sessions to help pupils obtain a clear understanding of the types of items to be included in the tests and the way such items should be attacked.

7. Choose tests on the basis of well-established criteria—validity, reliability, appropriateness of difficulty level, adequacy of norms, and considerations relating to their administration.

8. Furnish the instructional staff with necessary guidance in the use of test data, pointing out the techniques whereby the teachers can derive the most benefit from the results. Develop a systematic

follow-up program which will reveal the extent to which the testing actually achieved the purposes for which it was undertaken and the reasons for any failure to attain these goals.

Attitudes of Teachers and Administrators toward Testing Programs

Dramatic evidence of the attitude of some administrators toward testing programs may be found in the booklet, *Testing, Testing, Testing*,[14] referred to in chapter ix. Although directed chiefly against external standardized tests—those originating outside the school system—the report also levels criticisms at testing in general. "To teach without testing is unthinkable," the Joint Committee commented, but it warned that testing can be considered out of hand when some college-bound students take five tests during the eleventh and twelfth grades, any one of which "would tell as much about their scholarship as any other."[15]

The most serious objections to external testing reported in the booklet were: (*a*) finality is, too often, attached to test scores; (*b*) cost is high in money and in time; (*c*) evaluation of the pupil is limited; (*d*) too many pupils are overlooked; (*e*) control of the curriculum can result; (*f*) external pressure is put on teachers and pupils; (*g*) prestige is often conferred with wrong effect; (*h*) testing programs may interfere with basic functions of high schools. (See chapter ix for a fuller discussion of external testing programs with particular reference to this survey. See, also, forthcoming reports from "Project Talent.")

The Regent's Inquiry into the Character and Cost of Public Education in New York State,[16] begun in 1936, presented evidence regarding the influence of testing on teachers as well as students. An intensive study was made of 61 school districts within the state. Their curriculum guides were examined and their high-school stu-

---

14. *Testing, Testing, Testing.* Prepared by a Joint Committee of the American Association of School Administrators, Council of Chief State School Officers, and National Association of Secondary School Principals. Washington: National Education Association, 1962.

15. *Ibid.*

16. *The Regents' Inquiry into the Character and Cost of Public Education in the State of New York.* New York: McGraw-Hill Book Co., Inc., 1938.

dents were tested for several of the objectives specified in the curriculum guides. It was reported in this investigation that students' achievement was more influenced by the Regents' examination than by tests on local objectives and that teachers sought to emphasize the learnings tested by the Regents' examination (see chapter iii).

Tyler's experience in the Eight-Year Study (see chap. ix)[17] clearly supports the conclusion that external tests have been an influence in shaping curriculum practices and the teachers' decisions relating to what should be taught, and his statement concerning the prevalence of coaching classes is also relevant to any discussion of the influence of external testing on the behavior of students, teachers, and parents.

While it has been very difficult to obtain evidence of the effect of test results upon teachers' attitudes, it is possible to find studies which have used psychological testing as one of the main means of collecting data. Some of these may have relevance for this chapter. Revie[18] studied the effect of psychological casework on the teacher's concept of the student. By the use of the Q (sorting) technique, and using social and personal characteristics of students, the congruence of the perceptions of the psychologist and teacher was obtained for each case. Three sorts were made—one at the time of referral; the second, at the time the findings were presented to the teacher; and third, when the written case report was sent to the teacher. The findings indicated that the teacher is more likely to describe the child from her point of view of classroom control and the psychologist from the child's point of view. In the process of case discussion, the perceptions of the teacher and the psychologist tended to move toward each other's first position.

While there has been steady improvement in testing programs in recent years, there are still very few school systems that have developed a systematic plan of providing teachers and individual

17. Ralph W. Tyler, "What Testing Does to Teachers and Students," *Proceedings*, 1959 Invitational Conference on Testing Problems. Princeton, New Jersey: Educational Testing Service, 1959.

18. Virgil A. Revie, "The Effect of Psychological Case Work on the Teacher's Concept of the Pupil," *Journal of Counseling Psychology*, III, No. 2 (Summer, 1956), 125-29.

schools with the results of testing programs in such form that curriculum improvements can be based upon identified weaknesses. An outstanding example of a well-developed and continuing program is that of Denver (Colorado). For the last nine years a triennial survey of its school children has been conducted. A confidential report is prepared for each school. The principal sets up faculty meetings to discuss the test results. These results may be compared with those for the entire system, but even more important is the opportunity to compare the results with those obtained in the same school three years earlier. The significance of the Denver program resides in the careful planning given to the use of test results and the provision for periodic checking of accomplishments. There is a regular testing program that is carried out each year, but the triennial survey is designed specifically for providing teachers and the community with an indication of how the schools are doing.

A serious limiting factor in the use of test results by teachers has been the unavailability of test results on a student. Usually the test results are recorded in a cumulative file and often in a fashion that makes comparison of test results difficult. Solutions for making test results available to teachers without the necessity of always going to the counseling office are very much needed. A recent project,[19] (supported by the National Defense Education Act funds) by the San Diego City Schools explored the use of punch cards to summarize test data for more effective use by teachers. The stanine system—dividing scores from 1 to 9 on a standardized basis—was employed. In addition to providing a summary of the results of achievement tests, such as the *Stanford Achievement Test*, the card provided a green band, three stanines in width, indicating the range of the tested mental ability of the student.

It was possible to provide all teachers with a card that not only gave the achievement test results for each of his students but an indication of the extent to which each student was making use of his ability. Each teacher received a punched card for each student in his classes. This necessitated nine identical cards being provided for each student in high school. While the mechanics of the card

19. *IBM Profile of Test Performance Card Questionnaire Evaluation.* San Diego City Schools Research Department Report, No. 31, June 24, 1960. San Diego, California: San Diego City Schools, 1960.

distribution was a bit complicated, the plan goes far to make needed test results readily available to teachers. There is need for good in-service training in the use of test results, and this should be provided regardless of methods of reporting results. San Diego personnel explored the use of the profile card with parents and found use for it in conferences with parents. There was strong agreement that such profile cards should not be sent home, but should be used only when parents are conferring with school personnel.

The strong trend toward sharing test results with teachers, parents, and youth must be accompanied by study to determine the most effective means of communicating test results to all of these groups. Some large city systems have the staff to develop comprehensive test utilization plans, but most small school districts have not had the time nor the professional staff to develop adequate programs. Our national pupil personnel and psychological associations should devote more time and study to the effective utilization of test results.

In summarizing the attitudes of teachers and administrators toward testing, it may be stated that they recognize that testing is an essential part of an effective instructional and guidance program but that they are not aware of the limitations of testing or of the dangers attending it.

RECOMMENDATIONS BASED ON AN EXAMINATION OF THE ATTITUDES
OF TEACHERS AND ADMINISTRATORS ON TESTING

The recommendations growing out of the examination of the attitudes of students toward testing are supported by the review of teachers' and administrators' attitudes toward testing and testing programs. In addition, the following recommendations are made:

1. Involve teachers and administrators appropriately in each step of evaluation: formulation of objectives; definition of objectives in terms of pupil behaviors; development of formal as well as informal procedures for evaluation; collection of data related to objectives of education; and summarization and interpretation of data.

2. Provide for in-service meetings on procedures for using test results in instruction and guidance.

3. Seek to limit the number of "external" tests used in the school district or taken by any student to those relevant to his purposes, recognizing the advantage of having competing programs and services.

Effects of Testing Programs on Attitudes of Parents

The interest of parents in the results of tests taken by their children is shown vividly in reactions by parents to a series of articles on school tests in the *PTA Magazine*. Reader reactions were most intense to an article by Lagemann entitled "Let's Abolish I.Q. Tests."[20] The February, 1962, issue of the *PTA Magazine* contained the following statement by the editor of the section "Opinions by Post":

Nobody could call our readers unresponsive. Letters for and against and in the middle have been pouring into the office—and not only letters but whole articles, offers of articles, suggestions about people who should be asked to write articles, point-by-point refutations, point-by-point affirmations, and hearty approbation for starting such an important and interesting ball rolling.[21]

Reproduction of ten of the first group of responses published, described as being "snippings" from the editor's correspondence, reflect a range of attitudes toward testing.

By all means, let's! I rejoice over this article's creative consideration of the too-long-accepted I.Q. test as the chief means of determining a child's capabilities. For years I have been wondering how testing could acknowledge (1) the unique spiritual, emotional, social, and physical forces that cause a child to be what he is; (2) will and emotion as well as intellect; (3) basic civilizing character traits: good will, self-control, self-discipline, responsibility, respect, reverence. Moreover, any good teacher or parent can identify the children who are not responding or not working to capacity.

. . . .

Abolish I.Q. tests? Please do not. Just train teachers in using them as one of the many yardsticks in handling pupils. No I.Q. test can ever re-

20. John Kord Lagemann, "Let's Abolish I.Q. Tests," *PTA Magazine*, LVI (December, 1961), 7-10.

21. "Opinions by Post," *PTA Magazine*, LVI (February, 1962), 33-34.

place a dedicated teacher, but no teacher, alone, can accomplish what an I.Q. test does. I am for more and better I.Q. tests. I am for better trained teachers, who, realizing their limitations, enlist the aid of parents, I.Q. tests, and all other teaching aids in order to inspire themselves and their students. Please don't take away the friend who has stuck with me through thick and thin, the I.Q. test.

. . . .

Just had to write a few lines of praise of Mr. Lagemann's article. He has expressed, in writing, exactly the feelings of many people in regard to these so-called I.Q. tests.

. . . .

The I.Q. is indeed one, but only one, of the "major factors" that the school considers in guiding a pupil. Typically, an individual's scores based upon group tests vary from only a point or two to perhaps ten points during the interval between six and seventeen years of age. When scores are very erratic, it is not necessarily the fault of the test; it is more likely to be due to the pupil being tested. A standard I.Q. test, which is known to yield fair to good correlations with academic success, is better than no test at all.

The unfortunate thing about the article is that although it is a curious mixture of truths, half-truths, misinterpretations, and unwarranted assumptions, it will be read and accepted by thousands of parents.

. . . .

I agree with the article. While in some cases I think the tests serve a useful function, the danger involved in overemphasizing them is so present and so great that I concur with the title.

. . . .

I will be the first to agree that tests may be worthless or even harmful when they are misused. However, tests can be of considerable value when administered by trained and competent individuals. As a professionally trained counselor, I have always made an effort to use tests with discretion and caution, and I am firmly convinced of their value in many instances as students are attempting to find themselves. To say that we should abolish tests or to say that all test results are infallible is to express a very extreme opinion indeed. The true merit of a test in the educational program lies somewhere in between.

. . . .

As an educational psychologist who has worked closely with the P.T.A. and as a former high school teacher, I am shocked by this sensational journalism, written by a man who seems to have stepped right out of 1920, when a few of his strictures might have been appropriate. You have done a great disservice to highly competent test constructors, testers, and counselors by confusing the parents and teachers whom they serve. This article seems meant to set legitimate testers and counselors back forty years in their public relations. One does not have to sacrifice human judgment in order to use test scores (not I.Q.'s, in most situations, but standard scores instead) as one kind of evidence among many kinds. . . .

Lagemann's solution is the familiar throwing out the baby along with the dirty bath water. Because a few persons misuse scholastic aptitude tests even today, he disregards clear evidence of the appreciable —but of course not perfect—validity of these tests, which date back to 1905.

. . . .

One vote for John Kord Lagemann *and* Dr. Benjamin Bloom. If there be divine predestination, let's not confuse it with predetermination of a child's destiny, whether it be social, physical, or mental, whether by parent, psychologist, or educator.

. . . .

I certainly want to register a protest against the article. The author takes the exceptional case and makes it sound like an everyday happening. His alternative is so absurd that it should give any careful reader a clue as to the validity of the whole argument. Don't let's throw away our spear until we get a bow and arrow.

Mr. Lagemann says that an I.Q. score won't tell you anything that you can't find out by observation in the classroom and on the playground. This I do not believe, after eleven years of watching children in the classroom and on the playground, and I do not want Mr. Lagemann assessing my children's ability that way. These tests, used in conjunction with the judgment of teacher, counselor, and parent, are a most valuable tool in any school organization.

. . . .

I was absolutely astonished to read that anybody still takes the results of I.Q. tests seriously.

I would never have gone to college if an I.Q. of 120 had been needed. If I had not gone, I would have been poorer in both experience and learning. I am a little talented in a lot of things, but the I.Q. does not measure these because it measures mainly intellect.

From the foregoing comments, two conclusions seem obvious. Parents are greatly interested in the testing programs conducted by the schools and especially in the tests taken by their children. There is considerable misunderstanding on the part of parents about the purposes of tests, the types of tests given, the meaning of a pupil's scores, and the like.

RECOMMENDATIONS BASED ON AN EXAMINATION OF THE EFFECTS
OF TESTING PROGRAMS ON THE ATTITUDES OF PARENTS

The reactions of parents to testing and the importance of a better understanding of testing, on their part, makes it appear that to the recommendations already made (pp. 111-12 and 115-16), the following should be added:

1. A systematic plan of presenting the strengths, limitations, procedures, and practices of the testing program should be developed for use with parents and community groups.

2. Consideration should be given to the organization of an advisory council of parents, administrators, and teachers to consider ways of improving the testing program.

3. Consideration should be given to setting up a plan for parent-teacher or parent-teacher-pupil conferences so that test data as well as other information about pupils can be communicated in face-to-face situations.

4. The school district should give consideration to preparing a layman's guide to the testing program, and to organizing a series of meetings or workshops on testing and evaluation.

ISSUES REGARDING CONFIDENTIALITY OF PUPILS' TEST SCORES

Implicit in the responsibility of the counselor, teacher, and administrator is to summarize and interpret test data to pupils and parents and the need for them to treat test data as entirely confidential material. Ethical behavior on the part of counselor, teacher, or administrator in the handling of test data is essential, but even the proper use of test materials may lead to accusations of libel and slander. For the staff member handling confidential information to be legally guilty of either libel or slander it must be proved that, in writing or in speech, the accused damaged the reputation of the student, accused him of crime or moral turpitude, or brought him into the contempt, hatred, or ridicule of his peers.[22]

The real test of the privilege of the staff member in the

22. Based upon speech by Dr. Elmer Wagner, Assistant Dean, School of Education, University of Southern California, to Los Angeles County Guidance Group at a special meeting sponsored by the Los Angeles County Superintendent of Schools Office and the Los Angeles County Guidance Directors Group, January 11, 1962.

performance of his responsibilities will depend upon (*a*) whether or not his action was a part of his assigned duty; (*b*) the legal right of the recipient to have the information imparted; and (*c*) the legal responsibility of the parties involved to discuss the information about the child.

In addition to behaving ethically, in general, and specifically observing the basic principles that govern privileged communication, persons who handle test data should take the precaution (*a*) of writing down the essential data regarding a conference because recall of past observations may be full of defects and inaccuracies; (*b*) of making certain that confidential information about pupils cannot be overheard by a third party whose presence is not necessary for the purpose of the communication or consultation; and (*c*) of eliminating from any publication in which reference is made to the child any statement that could possibly lead to his identification.

RECOMMENDATIONS FOR CONDUCT OF PARENT-TEACHER CONFERENCES

1. Report to the parent in terms of the child's achievement in relation to his capacity—how he is developing in relation to his strengths and limitations.

2. Report on the child's attainments in any learning situation in relation to the others in his group.

3. Report also on the child's aptitudes and achievements in relation to the larger numbers of children beyond his particular school and community—by reference to published norms.

4. Make certain that parents and teachers share observations about the child. The teacher should listen rather than lecture.

5. Differences in points of view are to be expected and respected.

6. Avoid comparison of the student with individual classmates.

7. End conference on a constructive note of confidence in the child and his development. Consider all aspects of the child's growth—not just intellectual.

Effects of Testing Programs on the Attitudes of the Community

General attitudes toward testing, on the part of the community are made evident by studies by regional or state-wide educational committees. An example of such a study is the recently completed report of the Joint Interim Committee on the Public Education System of the State of California. The main study was made by a 77-member citizens' advisory commission. Over a two-year period the Citizens Advisory Commission held more than fifty public hearings. From these extensive hearings specific recommendations were presented. The recommendations relating to testing are as follows:

EDUCATIONAL PROGRAM—STATE TESTING

As a matter of principle, the Commission approves of mandatory state-wide testing of public schools. The Commission believes that in order to properly and effectively evaluate the education program of the public school system in California a level of instruction must be set by the legislature through the State Board of Education.

The Commission recommends to the Legislature that: Mandatory state-wide examinations be utilized to establish this standard.

They will provide the local school district a yardstick by which it may reassure itself that its pupils are not being deprived of the educational opportunities that they deserve, as well as providing a strong supervisory instrument for stimulating high academic achievement.

Purposes of the Tests:

1. Schools can be evaluated in the light of their total educational program.

2. These tests will set a minimum level of instruction beyond which the teacher should be encouraged to develop the most comprehensive, meaningful, and challenging program of instruction.

3. They are to stimulate high academic achievement.

4. They will provide an excellent prognostic index for measuring the standards in the various schools throughout the State.

5. They are a means to an end, rather than an end in themselves, and follow the curriculum rather than determine it.[23]

Before assessing the implications of the commission's position on testing, comment should be made about the very vitriolic report of a minority group of three members. Two of their recommendations relate to the use of testing instruments:

Recommendation No. 3

That the Legislature withhold ADA funds from any district found administering behavior, personality, attitude, life adjustment or similar

23. *Report of the Joint Interim Committee on the Public Education System of the State of California.* Sacramento, California: Senate of the State of California, 1961.

tests to elementary, high school, or junior college students. These vicious tests should be barred from use in this State by anyone, including the State Department of Education.[24]

Recommendation No. 11

That all records of a child must be readily available to his parents and guardians. The child is not the property of the public schools, but belongs to his parents; therefore, to deny any information regarding the child is an infringement on the parents' rights and should not be tolerated. Much of the present criticisms of education would have been averted if schools had considered the education of the child as a shared responsibility. . . . Also, these cumulative records can contain results from attitude, behavior and personality tests. This damaging information would follow the child throughout his school career and become permanent records.[25]

It is clear that the perception of the California commission on testing programs is very restricted when compared with the widely different purposes advocated in this book. Furthermore, the strong desire to have a testing program which would permit comparison of one school district with another indicates considerable misunderstanding of the broad function of testing programs. There has been concern among professional educators for many years that state-wide testing programs for elementary and secondary schools would result in a pressure toward curriculum conformity. It is now apparent that the test specialists and local test-users have not done as much as might have been done to help the community understand how tests can be used as an aid in maintaining the quality level of an educational program without dominating it. Running through the entire report, and particularly through the minority report, is the demand on the part of community members for more understanding of the standings of their own local schools compared with other districts throughout the state and nation.

The same concern for parents' rights to test results that is so strongly voiced in California is heard in many states. In New York State the right of a parent to inspect test results and other information in the student's cumulative record folder was upheld by the

24. *Ibid.*, p. 69.

25. *Ibid.*, p. 73.

State's Supreme Court. The final conclusion of the Court was that in the absence of "constitutional, legislative, or administrative permission or prohibition, a parent is entitled to inspect the records of his child maintained by the school authorities as required by law.[26]

There is no argument with the proposition that parents have a right to know the school records of their child. The confusion that has arisen stems from the lack of clarity as to what legally constitutes the school record. The Commissioner of Education for New York, James E. Allen, appointed an Advisory Committee on Pupil Records to make a study of pupil records and to prepare recommendations. This committee has made two main recommendations:

1. That appropriate communications be issued upon the commissioner's authority to distinguish more clearly (*a*) school records, (*b*) background data which teachers and other staff members use to prepare records, and (*c*) communications which co-operating agencies furnish to inform and advise the school staff.
2. The preparation of a manual on school records for the guidance of all school districts.[27]

Some school districts have developed comprehensive plans for the use of test results to help the community understand the efforts of the schools to improve their performance. One of these school districts is Denver, Colorado. Superintendent Oberholtzer instituted a testing program of the pupils in the Denver Public Schools with tests given in Grades III, VI, IX, and XII, later changed to Grades III, V, IX, and XI. System-wide testing surveys were made in 1950, 1953, 1956, 1959, and 1962. The testing instruments used in the 1962 survey were alternate forms of the same tests used in previous surveys.[28] These included the *Stanford Elementary Battery*, the *Mental Health Analysis* (Elementary, Intermediate, Secondary Forms), and the *Iowa Tests of Educational Development*.

The testing itself is not the unique aspect of the program. The main value of the project resides in the comprehensive plan for the

26. Case of Van Allen *vs.* McCleary, New York Supreme Court, 1961.

27. "Report of the Advisory Committee on Pupil Records to the Commissioner of Education, New York State, August 4, 1961" (mimeographed).

28. "The Denver Public Schools Look at Themselves, Highlights from the 1962 Evaluation Study," *Report from Denver Public Schools*, 1962.

use of the test results. An understandable report, *The Denver Public Schools Look at Themselves,* was prepared for the community. This report represents an outstanding example of a school district providing the community, in a meaningful manner, with the results of tests given to the children. While most schools have regular testing programs, few schools have designed a plan that regularly informs teachers and parents how the youth of their school are doing. Denver has been able to compare results from previous surveys and thus take a longer look at program improvement than that which is provided by the hurried testing that often follows a flare-up of negative reaction toward the schools.

More study needs to be given to the factors that are responsible for the rising demand for the release of data on students to parents. While a few parents are guided by a deep distrust of the schools, it is clear that many parents wish to be better informed about their children. Much progress has been made in increasing the number and improving the quality of parent and parent-student conferences with school personnel in recent years. This has been evident in the large number of NDEA projects which have been related to parent counseling. Our attention should be directed to exploring and developing the most effective means of communicating a student's progress to both parent and student. Regardless of the kind and type of information given to parents, the basic issue remains, i.e., how can school records (and test results) best be used to further the education of each youth. Evaluation studies comparing excellent record systems with poor record systems and studies of the utilization of records and of test results need to be made.

Newly devised and developed test interpretation systems suitable for teachers, parents, and youth must be shared by many. One new system that is similar to that of San Diego involves the use of a band rather than a single score, to report the test results for each student on the new STEP series developed by the Educational Testing Service.

Summary Recommendations

1. Training of those responsible for school testing programs must shift from a major concern with understanding of measurement to focus on testing as understanding people.

2. In order to avoid the misuse of test results and to make the results of tests more meaningful to all concerned, more adequate systems of test interpretation must be developed. Along with the development of new systems of test interpretation, more adequate education must be provided in the interpretation of use of all kinds of guidance data.

3. Test results must be integrated into an understandable pattern with the other kinds of data available in the cumulative record.

4. Persons responsible for testing programs must be more concerned to give the programs continuity and to make them more meaningful to pupils, parents, and teachers.

5. Research on the methods of providing understanding of test results must be greatly enlarged and improved.

CHAPTER VII

Testing Programs and Counseling in the Schools

RALPH F. BERDIE

Testing programs have much relevance for counseling, just as they have for other processes in education. Testing is not counseling (and counseling is more than testing), but, just as testing is essential in instruction and administration, so is it necessary in counseling. Much of what the counselor does depends on his work with tests, and the effectiveness of his counseling is a function of his sophisticated and informed use of tests.

The counselor's use of tests in the school is unique, but it will be found that every chapter in this volume discusses aspects of testing which concern the counselor. The goals of education determine the tests used in the schools, and, as has been shown in earlier chapters, tests also influence the choice of the school's objectives. The counselor works with students who are striving toward these objectives, and the way he uses tests influences the student's choice of objectives and the effects of the objectives on the student. The student being counseled is participating in the school's curriculum, and in so far as the curriculum and the instructional program are influenced by tests and, in turn, determine the tests to be used, the counselor must be sensitive to these interactions.

Counselors increasingly have direct relationships with parents, particularly as the parents and their children become concerned with post-high-school plans, and the impact of testing programs on parents, schools, and the community in general are of direct concern to the counselor.

The counselor does research with tests and attempts to develop new methods of using them and new ways of testing abilities, achievements, personality, and interests. He constantly is faced with the problem of understanding the meaning of test scores and communicating this meaning to others. The interpretation of tests is one of the counselor's important assignments. Obviously, the counselor's interest in testing is not a narrow or specialized one; most of the problems that are discussed by the authors of preceding and following chapters are important to all counselors.

The Role of the Counselor

Counseling consists of an informed conversation between a professionally trained counselor and a pupil, and the topic of that conversation encompasses characteristics of the pupil which make him unique from or similar to other persons. In this conversation the counselor and the pupil explore the implications of these individual characteristics and attempt to integrate the student's growing knowledge about himself into his plans and action.

The counselor is aware that learning about one's self, just as acquiring any other knowledge, is not only a function of the student's higher thought processes but also involves his perceptions and his emotions. This awareness of the nonintellectual processes which influence learning naturally forces the counselor to realize that students can increase their self-understanding only to a limited extent through the objective examination of information about themselves. Counseling is teaching, but the subject matter is the pupil. Some of the methods used in teaching pupils about mathematics may be effective in teaching them about themselves, but additional teaching procedures also are necessary.

The purposes of counseling ultimately are the purposes of education. The counselor, just as the teacher, hopes that as a result of his education the pupil eventually will function as a productive and happy member in society and improve and transmit his culture. More uniquely, however, the purpose of counseling is to increase the pupil's understanding of himself and of his relationships with others, with the expectation that his behavior will be influenced by this understanding. No research evidence at present supports the assumption that the more a person knows about himself, the better his self-understanding; the more accurate his perception of himself, the happier and more productive he will be. This assumption, however, has been accepted by the greatest minds in history for the past two thousand years, and man's entire purpose in life is divided between seeking understanding of his universe and of himself. The two modern geniuses that exemplify these strivings are Einstein and Freud. Einstein sought to teach men the nature of the universe, just as teachers seek to teach students of the world about them. Freud sought to teach men about the nature of man, just as counselors attempt to teach students about themselves. Understanding the universe benefits no man who does not understand himself, and no man can understand himself who does not comprehend the universe of which he is a part. Thus, the teacher and the counselor must strive hand in hand as they aid their pupils to learn and to achieve fulfilment.

Increasing a person's knowledge about himself is a means to a further objective, consisting of observable behavioral change. The extent to which a person's self-knowledge has increased can be determined only through observations of behavior change, and increased self-knowledge is a sterile end unless it is accompanied by such change. Some examples of behavior changes in students sought by counselors and made possible by increases in self-knowledge on the part of the student are: (a) increased consistency between educational and vocational goals and their aptitudes, abilities, and interests; (b) expressions of satisfaction with progress in school, relationships with family and friends, and general feeling tone; (c) increased productivity in school and on the job as shown by changes in learning and output; (d) satisfactory relationships with others and with society, as shown by the number and kinds of associations, constructive co-operative efforts, and decreasing conflicts with others.

The dictionary defines counseling as "advising or recommending." Although counseling as defined by professional psychologists and educators encompasses advising and recommending, it includes more.[1] Counseling, using the dictionary definition, has been done by a variety of persons and about a variety of topics. Counselors, accepting this use of the term, have consisted, among others,

1. J. W. Gustad, "The Definition of Counseling," *Roles and Relationships in Counseling.* Edited by R. F. Berdie. Minneapolis: University of Minnesota Press, 1953.

of parents, attorneys, ministers, friends, employers, fellow workers, insurance salesmen, and travel agents. On the other hand, professional counseling, as the concept is used in this chapter, is performed by persons having professional training and titles of
counselors. This counseling is also performed by teachers (including principals and other school personnel) who have been trained
as counselors. Sometimes these persons are called "teacher-coun-
selors." Teachers with no special training as counselors are properly
called "advisers," or perhaps "interested teachers."

Society needs counselors trained at different levels. Counseling
is different from a specialty such as neurosurgery. No patient
wishes to have surgery performed by a surgeon who has only limited surgical skill. An expert is demanded. However, counselors
who have limited counseling skill usually are able to restrict their
practice to persons, problems, and situations demanding only the
skills they possess. Even professional counselors may possess a
variety of backgrounds of training and of competencies. Some
counselors have only a year of graduate training in psychology
and related fields beyond their baccalaureate. Other counselors
have several years of post-doctoral training and supervised experience in counseling. Some counselors limit themselves to relatively
specific tasks, such as helping students improve their reading or
study skills. Other counselors help students make educational and
vocational decisions, work with students as they attempt to resolve
family problems, and help them better understand their own values
and emotional experiences.[2]

RECOMMENDATION 1. *In the light of the foregoing discussion
of the counseling process, every professional counselor, just as every
teacher, must be acquainted with the basic principles of educational
and psychological measurements. Every counselor should be acquainted with the principles underlying the measurement of abilities and aptitude, academic achievement, vocational interests, and
personality.*

2. "Standards for the Preparation of School Counselors," *Personnel and
Guidance Journal*, XL (1961), 402-7.

Knowledge about and competency to use tests vary among counselors.[3] The extent of the counselor's knowledge of specific tests and his skill in using them depend on the counseling he undertakes and, in turn, set limits to the types of counseling he can do successfully. An attempt has been made in this chapter to include information about testing programs with which all persons in education having responsibility for counseling should be familiar.

Counselors do not agree on the importance of tests in counseling. Rogers, who writes about counseling as if it were psychotherapy, assigns a small role to testing in what he calls "client-centered therapy," or nondirective counseling.[4] Only a few systematic attempts have been made to isolate the contribution made by testing to counseling. A study made in England [5] compared the occupational adjustment, two and four years after counseling, of school-leaving children counseled with and without the use of tests. The counselors who used tests were more successful as shown by the better adjustment of their counselees. A few other studies summarized by Tyler [6] show similar results.

The Use of Test Results and Other Information in Counseling

To understand how test information is used in counseling, one must understand the use and communication of all information in counseling. The uses made of information in counseling are chiefly two: First, counselors use information to construct hypotheses or "little theories," which eventually may lead to a better understanding of the pupil's behavior.[7] The second use of information gained

---

3. T. J. Hastings *et al.*, *The Use of Test Results.* Co-operative Research Project No. 509. Urbana, Illinois: University of Illinois Bureau of Educational Research, 1960 (mimeographed).

4. C. Rogers, *Client-centered Therapy.* New York: Houghton Mifflin Co., 1951.

5. E. P. Hunt, "The Birmingham Experiments in Vocational Selection and Guidance," *Occupational Psychology* (London), XVII (1943), 53-63. See also, E. P. Hunt and P. Smith, "Vocational Psychology and Choice of Employment," *Occupational Psychology* (London), XIX (1945), 109-16.

6. L. Tyler, *The Work of the Counselor.* New York: Appleton-Century-Crofts, Inc., 1961 (second edition).

7. H. B. Pepinsky and Pauline N. Pepinsky, *Counseling Theory and Practice.* New York: Ronald Press, 1954.

through making observations and weighing them is to aid the counselor as he evaluates the validity of previously formed hypotheses about pupil behavior.[8] As the counselor attempts to understand the pupil so that he can, in turn, help the pupil better understand himself, he conceptualizes the pupil's behavior as a scientist conceptualizes any natural phenomenon which he is attempting to explain or understand. The information a counselor obtains from interview observations, cumulative records, ratings of teachers, reports from parents, or psychological or educational tests corresponds to the information a scientist obtains from observations through a microscope, readings of an electrical meter, statistics of a sociological survey, or results of a psychophysical experiment. In seeking understanding, a counselor acts as a scientist. In using this understanding, however, his procedure is not necessarily scientific, and his improvisations and applications may more resemble those of a violinist or dramatist than those of a scientist.

Information from tests, or test scores, is one special kind of information, but the use made of test scores corresponds to the broad uses that are described in this chapter. Frequently, counselors at first have little understanding of a pupil's needs, personality, and problems. Much of the initial phase of counseling is spent by the counselor in developing theories, hypotheses, or models that help explain the pupil. This hypothesizing, however, is not limited to the initial phase of counseling, for it proceeds during the entire process. Usually it is most frequent in the early part of counseling, and, consequently, counselors use tests more often early in counseling than they do later.

RECOMMENDATION 2. *Tests should be used as an essential tool in constructing theories to explain student behavior—as a first step in understanding such behavior.*

Some examples will illustrate this *theory-making* use of tests. John Jensen discussed his poor grades with his counselor, and the counselor examined John's records and observed percentile scores ranging from 5 to 15 on the *School and College Ability Tests.*

8. L. J. Cronbach and G. C. Gleser, *Psychological Tests and Personnel Decisions.* Urbana, Illinois: University of Illinois Press, 1957.

From this, he derived the hypothesis that John's academic difficulty was a result of or markedly influenced by his limited intellectual ability. This was a hypothesis suggested by the test scores, and the counselor's acceptance or rejection of the hypothesis then depended on his evaluation of additional evidence.

Nancy Kaye was a high-school Junior who, until the beginning of her Junior year, had been a happy and academically successful girl. During her Junior year her scholastic work deteriorated, and her teachers observed that she was becoming increasingly depressed and anxious. Nancy Kaye visited her counselor, and they discussed, among other things, Nancy's social life, her family, her health, and her out-of-school activities. Nothing that Nancy said provided the counselor with any clues regarding possible sources of the difficulty. The counselor then had Nancy take the *Minnesota Counseling Inventory* and immediately noticed that, on the Family Relation Scale, Nancy's standard score was 81. All of the other scores were in the normal range. This profile of scores suggested to the counselor that the origin of Nancy's difficulty lay in her relationship with her family, and in the next interview Nancy and the counselor devoted much time to further discussion of the family.

Midway in the interview, Nancy started to describe how her parents increasingly had been placing more and more pressure on her to maintain the level of work she had done in the past. Inasmuch as Nancy's academic ability was somewhat limited, the increasingly difficult competition she faced as she progressed in school made it more difficult for her to earn A's and B's. The evidence that Nancy provided and later interviews with her parents led the counselor to conclude that the initial hypothesis based on the *MCI* profile was reasonable, and this, in turn, led to remedial steps.

From these examples, the second use of test scores now becomes obvious.

RECOMMENDATION 3. *Test scores are to be used as evidence to aid in the evaluation of the validity of hypotheses about pupil behavior; they provide not only a source of hypotheses but also a standard for examining hypotheses.*

As an example, Katherine was doing poorly in English and mathematics and well in home economics and music. The counselor noted this discrepancy and hypothesized that her difficulty in English and mathematics was due to a deficiency in verbal and quantitative abilities. The scores on the *School and College Ability Tests* confirmed this hypothesis.

James was a college Freshman in engineering when he reported to his counselor that he found none of his courses interesting. The counselor observed the record of James' hobbies and activities and hypothesized that what James had interpreted as an interest in engineering really was an interest in mechanical work. The scores on the *Strong Vocational Interest Blank* showed that James' vocational interests resembled interests of men in engineering occupations, not the interests of men in mechanical trades, and consequently the counselor rejected this hypothesis and searched for others that would explain James' reactions.[9]

Kim was a high-school Sophomore who had trouble with much of his school work. He told the counselor he did not like to read, and the counselor hypothesized that he was handicapped by a reading deficiency. The scores on the *Cooperative Reading Test* confirmed this hypothesis and revealed that Kim was a slow reader who found reading an uncomfortable activity.

Some hypotheses that are evaluated on the basis of test scores have been derived from other test scores. For example, a counselor observed that a student had an extremely high score on the College Entrance Examination Board's *Scholastic Apitude Test*. On the basis of this information, he constructed the hypothesis that the student would succeed in college curricula requiring high-level verbal and numerical ability. However, he was unwilling to accept this hypothesis, which was based on a test he knew well and for which he had respect, without further evidence. To check the hypothesis, he had the student take the *College Qualification Test*, and the student's high score on this test supported the counselor's hypothesis.

9. W. L. Layton, *Counseling Use of the Strong Vocational Interest Blank.* Minneapolis: University of Minnesota Press, 1958.

Hypotheses in counseling, like hypotheses in science, are never proved. The counselor, just as the scientist, always is thinking in terms of probability, and the evidence that is collected about any hypothesis serves to establish the probability that the counselor attaches to that hypothesis. A girl who had much trouble in English was considering taking stenography. On the basis of her low English grades, the counselor thought that the probability was extremely small that the girl could succeed in the subject. He had her take a shorthand aptitude test, and on this test her score was somewhat above average. The counselor still considered that the probability was great that the girl would not succeed in a short-hand course, but the score on the test caused him to revise his estimate of the probability of her success.

Many hypotheses derived by counselors are not based on information about the student in question but, rather, on the knowledge the counselor has of the species of student. The counselor's experience with high-school and college students provides him with the knowledge that a large proportion of students who do eminently well in high-school mathematics succeed in college-mathematics courses. His experience informs him that a large proportion of students who do poorly in academic courses have inadequate abilities. His experience teaches him that many hostile and arrogant boys in the eleventh grade are at odds with their parents. He has information about the culture from which his students come; he has established for himself normative information that is useful in considering the specific case; he understands base rates regarding the frequency of occurrence of different behaviors within the population with which he works.[10] The uses of tests that have been discussed have been largely in terms of the counselor's own thought processes. They represent the ways in which test scores can be incorporated into the problem-solving and reasoning processes of the counselor.[11] More observable and overt uses are made of test scores by counselors.

10. P. E. Meehl and A. Rosen, "Antecedent Probability and Efficiency of Psychometric Signs, Patterns, or Cutting Scores," *Psychological Bulletin,* LII (1955), 194-216.

11. C. A. Parker, "As a Clinician Thinks," *Journal of Counseling Psychology,* V (1958), 253-61.

Tests contribute to counseling by providing information about the counselee to the counselor, but the ultimate purpose is to help the pupil learn about himself. Students can use test scores to learn about their intellectual potential, variations in their intellectual abilities, such as differences in numerical and verbal aptitude, academic achievements, special aptitudes—particularly mechanical and clerical aptitudes—vocational interests, and other personality characteristics. Many of the questions students have about themselves can be answered by providing them with carefully interpreted test scores: (a) Do I have enough ability to do college work? (b) Do I have enough ability to do the work involving mechanical, clerical, musical, or artistic ability? (c) Would I like a given occupation if I entered it, providing I had the ability? (d) Should I stay in school? (e) Are my study habits adequate? (f) Do I have a good enough academic background to go into this particular field? [12]

RECOMMENDATION 4. *Counseling should take full advantage of the proven predictive power of particular tests.*

Another view is obtained of the use of tests in counseling when they are regarded as predictors. Psychological testing from this viewpoint consists of a sampling of present behavior to provide a basis for inference regarding future behavior. The teacher primarily is concerned with future classroom behavior or academic learning and tries to predict how pupils will react and how they will learn if placed in certain learning situations containing special content of a specified difficulty. The counselor is more concerned with predicting behavior seen in larger segments. He wishes to make inferences about the probability of the student's success in high school, or in a curriculum, or in a designated college. He wishes to know the probability of a student's success and satisfaction in a variety of occupations. He is concerned with predictions of educational and occupational success and satisfaction.

Much information other than test information is used for predicting. The counselor may predict, on the basis of his experience with a medical school, that a girl who applies for admission to that

12. R. F. Berdie, "An Aid to Student Counselors," *Educational and Psychological Measurement*, II (1942), 281-90.

school will have less chance of being admitted than a boy of equal ability. In helping the girl understand the probability of achieving her vocational goal of being a physician, the counselor makes use of this non-test information. Non-test information about family, financial status, health, and interests are used to predict behavior.

The rigor with which counselors use test scores to make predictions varies. A counselor may glance at one or several test scores and quickly arrive at an inference, with little apparent reasoning, and make a prediction. Or he may use test scores to enter a carefully derived statistical formula or table and, after considerable contemplation, make a prediction.

The counselor's role in making predictions from test scores has been argued repeatedly.[13] A prediction based on previous experience tables and statistics and reflecting the probabilities derived from these experiences completely apart from the subjective considerations of the counselor is called an actuarial or statistical prediction. A prediction influenced by the subjective or intuitive judgment of the counselor is called a clinical prediction. In making clinical predictions, counselors consider a variety of information, and some of this information can be test scores or even actuarial predictions.

When a counselor talks with a student who is considering attending a given college, he can attempt to predict the student's success in a number of ways. If he wishes to make an actuarial prediction, he will use regression equations or prediction and expectancy tables showing how students with certain test scores fared in that college. In one college, the following regression equations predict students' grade-point averages in English, social studies, mathematics, natural science, and their over-all grade-point averages. The variables used for predicting are the four scores on the *American College Testing Program Test* (English, mathematics, social studies, and science). The equations derived by Lindquist[14] follow:

13. P. E. Meehl, *Clinical versus Statistical Prediction*. Minneapolis: University of Minnesota Press, 1954.

14. E. F. Lindquist, *Interpreting the 1961 ACT Research Reports*. Chicago: Science Research Associates, 1961.

English grade-point
average $= .0667(1) + .0014(2) + .0328(3) + .0031(4) - .0883$

Mathematics grade-
point average $= .0347(1) + .0352(2) + .0197(3) - .0012(4) + .2696$

Social studies grade-
point average $= .0256(1) + .0305(2) + .0352(3) + .0157(4) - .2601$

Natural science grade-
point average $= .0276(1) + .0090(2) + .0460(3) + .0244(4) - .3117$

Over-all grade-
point average $= .0471(1) + .0180(2) + .0364(3) + .0050(4) - .2052$

Where (1) = English test standard score
(2) = Mathematics test standard score
(3) = Social studies test standard score
(4) = Natural science test standard score
Multiple R's $= .51, .40, .43, .49, .55$
Standard errors of estimate $= .65, .82, .82, .77, .60$

The counselor can insert the student's test scores into the regression equations, perform the necessary computation, and report to the student his predicted grade-point averages. At the same time, he will wish to explain the standard error of estimate to the student to make clear to him the significance of the predictions. Scores obtained through national and regional testing programs can be of much use to counselors if research services make available the information counselors need.

The counselor can use another actuarial aid. Table 1, an expectancy table, shows how four test scores and four high-school

TABLE 1

EXPECTANCY TABLE: SPECIAL COMPOSITE OF SCORES AND GRADES VERSUS OVER-ALL GRADE-POINT AVERAGE

PREDICTED GRADE-POINT AVERAGE	NUMBER OF STUDENTS	PER CENT OF STUDENTS IN EACH PREDICTOR INTERVAL WHOSE COLLEGE GRADE-POINT AVERAGE EQUALED OR EXCEEDED A GIVEN GRADE*			
		"D" and Above	"C" and Above	"B" and Above	"A"
3.8 "A"	0	0	0	0	0
3.3 --- 3.7......	0	0	0	0	0
2.8 "B" 3.2......	126	100	96	66	0
2.3 --- 2.7......	493	98	81	19	0
1.8 "C" 2.2......	415	93	43	2	0
1.3 --- 1.7......	77	81	10	0	0
.8 "D" 1.2......	0	0	0	0	0
Lower............	0	0	0	0	0

*Total number of students in this table, 1111.

grades can be combined to achieve a predicted index that allows inferences to be made concerning the probability of any student obtaining any given grade average in the college for which the table was formulated. Thus, a student with a predicted grade-point average of from 1.8 to 2.2 has 43 chances in 100 of earning an average of at least C; two chances in 100 of earning an average of at least B; and practically no chance of earning an A average.

The expectancy table, presented in the *Counselor's Guide to Georgia Colleges* [15] probably represents the most usable form of regression information. The state testing agency uses the complete multiple correlation analysis to arrive at a predictive equation for each college situation, but then simplifies the process of its use and interpretation by converting the equation to one with integers for coefficients. The counselor is then offered a table showing the probabilities that high-school students with given predictive composites from the simplified equation will make grade averages as Freshmen of C or better, B or better, or A, as in the preceding illustration.

An adaptation of the prediction or expectancy table has been presented by Eells.[16] He developed a flow chart that shows for a given group of students the percentage that attained certain levels and achieved certain proficiencies. A separate chart is provided for each group of students, classified on the basis of test scores or other information. With these charts students can quickly learn what has happened to students who have the same characterstics as they possess. The information and analysis needed to provide counselors with such aids usually can be obtained only through large testing programs. Only recently, however, have these programs begun to provide these aids to counselors.[17]

15. J. R. Hills, G. Franz, and L. B. Emory, *Counselor's Guide to Georgia Colleges*. Atlanta: Office of Testing and Guidance, Regents, University System of Georgia, 1959.

16. K. Eells, "A Vivid Method of Presenting Chances of Academic Success," *Journal of Counseling Psychology*, VIII (1961), 344-50.

17. Hills, Franz, and Emory, *op. cit.*; Lindquist, *op. cit.*; and E. O. Swanson, J. C. Merwin, and R. F. Berdie, *Expectancy Tables for Freshmen Entering Minnesota Colleges*. [Research Bulletin of the Office of the Dean of Students, University of Minnesota, Vol. III, No. 2, March 30, 1961 (multilithed)].

The foregoing are examples of actuarial predictions. Now let us assume that the counselor has additional information about the student. He knows what the student's scores and high-school grades are, but he also knows that the student will have to commute one and three-quarters hours each day and that he will have to spend approximately twenty-five hours a week working. The counselor has no regression equation or prediction tables that take these variables into account in making predictions of grades, but his experience suggests to him that the more time this student has to study and the less time he must spend on outside work, the greater the probability is that he will obtain high grades. Consequently, the counselor incorporates this "knowledge" into his prediction. If the prediction table, based on tests and grades alone, indicates that the student has 70 chances out of 100 of being a "C" student, the counselor might adjust this and conclude that the probability that the student will do "C" work is not much greater than 50 in 100. The counselor has clinically adjusted the actuarial prediction. He can go through the same process without the statistical prediction and, on the basis of his interview impressions, test scores, and the student's grade record, arrive at a clinical judgment concerning the student's probability of success.

RECOMMENDATION 5. *Counselors should generally pay most attention to statistical predictions when they are available, and correspondingly restrain tendencies to correct the predictions in the light of other information.*

The evidence available suggests that most counselors and clinicians are not able to improve significantly on the actuarial prediction.[18] In some instances, counselors can use supplementary information and improve the accuracy of actuarial predictions, but the mass of evidence suggests that most counselors make better predictions if they stick closely to the statistical prediction.

The great need is not to improve the ability of counselors to make intuitive or clinical judgments but, rather, to make available to all counselors an increasing amount of information leading to

18. E. L. Kelly and D. W. Fiske, *The Prediction of Performance in Clinical Psychology.* Ann Arbor, Michigan: University of Michigan Press, 1951. See also, Meehl and Rosen, *op. cit.*

accurate statistical prediction. If we suspect that students' academic success is influenced by the number of hours they do outside work, the area in which they live, or the education of their parents, these variables should be included in the prediction equation tables. No extensive testing programs in operation in 1962 included "non-test" variables, other than high-school grades.

RECOMMENDATION 6. *Review predictive procedures at regular intervals to be sure underlying circumstances have not changed so markedly as to affect their predictive accuracy.*

The counselor who wishes to use his actuarial predictions is faced with a dilemma. Actually, this dilemma is present as he uses clinical predictions, but usually it is ignored. The dilemma evolves from changes that occur during the passing of time. In order to accumulate information that can be summarized in prediction tables or regression equations, a given generation of students must be measured, observed, and analyzed. The experience data for this generation are then applied to the next generation, but generations change one from the other and, consequently, the counselor never knows whether the prediction tables based on yesterday's students are appropriate for those of today. In general, correlational analyses show that relationships between test scores and school grades do not change much from one year to the next, but some experiences have suggested that such changes can occur. For example, at the University of Minnesota, the correlations between college aptitude test scores and college grades fluctuated wildly from 1946 through 1948, a period during which many returning veterans were in attendance. The prediction equations that were appropriate for students before and after this era were inappropriate for returning veterans, and prediction equations based on one group of returning veterans were not appropriate for a group the following year.

All test data used for predictive purposes, just as all clinical data, have to be reviewed carefully and frequently, and when multiple regression weights or expectancy-table probabilities are used by counselors, the counselor must maintain a proper skepticism concerning them and not be unduly influenced by their mathematical magic. Every testing program must be subjected to continuing review, and counselors cannot assume test validity, when once established, remains unchanged.

RECOMMENDATION 7. *Test results should be used to stimulate the counselee.*

Tests serve an additional use in counseling in so far as they provide information to counselees that stimulates the counseling process. Students frequently are led to consider new educational alternatives or new occupational possibilities as a result of test scores. When a counselor discusses with a student his scores on ability tests, he discusses the abilities and aptitudes of the student. When he discusses scores on educational achievement tests, he discusses a history of educational experiences extending over many years. Test scores help counselors and counselees understand many aspects of student abilities, interests, motivation, and opportunity.

Personality Dimensions Relevant for Counseling

The question often arises as to what and how many personality dimensions can be accurately evaluated and effectively used in counseling. The writer recommends the broad view.

RECOMMENDATION 8. *All personality characteristics which merit measurement for educational purposes are relevant for counseling.*

Every aspect of the pupil which is of interest to the teacher or administrator also concerns the counselor. The "whole pupil" is a phrase that, during the past decades, has become trite and misused until a stigma has become attached to the term. Nevertheless, the the counselor works with every pupil behavior. He is not necessarily concerned with the same dimension of behavior with every pupil, but the behaviors of the total counseling case load approach the repertoire of behaviors demonstrated by all adolescents. All measurable dimensions of behavior and many dimensions that today defy accurate measurement are the counselor's business.

Abilities.—The counselor, in order to be effective, must have a continuing and inclusive picture of the pupil's aptitudes and abilities. This can be obtained best through a carefully developed testing program. Abilities and aptitudes develop in time. In some children, verbal proficiency appears at an early stage, and, in others, much later. Some children show unusual mechanical skills at an early age; others do not show these skills until later. Some children appear only average in intelligence or, perhaps, even intellectually retarded until puberty, and then they may show unusual academic talent. Some children show seemingly precocious development, only to develop into mediocre or below-average adults. In order to understand the child's abilities and aptitudes and in order to make inferences concerning his future behaviors, a counselor must know the history of the development of these aptitudes. This requires continuing and repeated ability tests.

Theories used by the counselor to explain the organization of mental abilities influence his choice of aptitude and ability tests, and tests included in testing programs reflect, often without explicit recognition, the theoretical biases of those responsible for the programs. If the counselor subscribes to a theory which places emphasis on a general or central kind of intelligence, he will use tests similar to the *Stanford-Binet* or *Wechsler Intelligence Test* or group tests conceptually derived from them. From scores on such tests, he will make inferences concerning the general intellectual ability of the pupil and base predictions of future behavior on these inferences. On the other hand, if the counselor subscribes to a theory of mental organization that emphasizes special or specific abilities, he is more likely to use multiple aptitude or factor tests. He will be concerned not only with the general intellectual level of the pupil but also with the pupil's numerical ability, verbal ability, ability to perceive spatial relations, mechanical comprehension ability, and various kinds of language aptitude.[19]

Achievement.—In order to better understand the pupil and to aid him to better understand himself, the counselor must have a longitudinal picture of the pupil's achievements, a picture that reveals the information and skills possessed by the pupil. The counselor is well aware that educational aptitude and educational achievement are not the same phenomena, but that the behaviors

19. C. Burt, *The Factors of the Mind.* New York: Macmillan Co., 1941. See also, G. H. Thomson, *The Factorial Analysis of Human Ability.* New York: Houghton Mifflin Co., 1939.

observed to make inferences concerning them are not independent. Most aptitude tests are achievement tests, to some extent, and, similarly, most achievement tests are aptitude tests. *The Minnesota Clerical Aptitude Test* usually is used as an aptitude test, but, in order to take the test, the pupil must know how to read and something about numbers. This aptitude test requires academic achievement of a relatively high order. Many vocabulary tests serve as aptitude tests and, yet, vocabulary is learned and is an educational achievement. Achievement tests are prognostic of future behavior, often of behavior not directly related on the surface to the educational content included in the test. Counselors long have known that one of the best predictors of how well a student will do is how well he has done. Achievement tests, considered along with academic records, provide a sound basis for predicting future behavior. Included among achievement tests are tests of special skills, such as reading tests and study skills tests.

Interests.—Frequently students being counseled are making decisions and choices which are heavily influenced by the students' systems of values and interests, and counselors must have information about values and interests if they are to help students understand their own needs and motives sufficiently to make wise and rational choices. Information about values and interests is obtained through observing the choices the student has made in the past, the decisions he makes concerning how he will spend time, energy, and money, his hobbies, and his expressions of liking and disliking. Soon after the development of group intelligence tests, psychologists began to develop tests to help counselors assess students' interests and values,[20] and increasingly these tests have demonstrated their validity for counseling.[21] Up to 1963, no national

20. D. Fryer, *The Measurement of Interests.* New York: Henry Holt & Co., 1931.

21. See R. F. Berdie, *"Strong Vocational Interest Blank* Scores of High-School Seniors and Their Later Occupational Entry," *Journal of Applied Psychology,* XL (1960), 161-65; C. C. McArthur, "Long-Term Validity of the *Strong Vocational Interest Test* in Two Sub-Cultures," *Journal of Applied Psychology,* XXXVIII (1954), 346-533; and E. K. Strong, Jr., *Vocational Interests Eighteen Years after College* (Minneapolis: University of Minnesota Press, 1955).

testing programs included tests or other systematic indexes of interests, but several city or state testing programs included interest tests.

Other personality dimensions.—Another dimension of personality of concern to the counselor has been subdivided into social relationships, emotional stability, motivational level, and character. Social relationships consist of pupil behaviors which directly influence the reactions of other persons to him and which reflect his reactions to others. Emotional stability concerns the affective life of the student, his emotions, feelings, and moods, and in a most general way, his mental health. The student's level of motivation is related closely to his interests and values and is suggested by the extent to which he "uses" his ability. His character consists of behaviors that have been labeled reliability, dependability, delinquency, and loyalty. These behaviors directly touch values that society has incorporated into its legal and moral systems. Few testing programs include tests of these characteristics, although increasing experience with personality inventories in testing programs suggests they have much to contribute to counseling.

RECOMMENDATION 9. *The counselor should combine all relevant evidence in predicting student success. In particular, he should combine data from school records and tested aptitude, rather than use either alone.*

The counselor is concerned with these dimensions of pupil personality: abilities and aptitudes, achievement and skills, interests and values, and social relations, emotional stability, motivation, and character. Counselors learn about these dimensions in many ways. They make inferences about pupils on the basis of direct observation, reports and records, student self-descriptions, and psychological and educational tests. Regardless of its source, each bit of information must be evaluated as to its reliability and validity. In selecting means for collecting information about pupils, the counselor also must be concerned with the relative cost and efficiency of the method used. Always the counselor must have more than isolated bits of information if accurate inferences are to be made, and, if possible, the counselor should have information from a variety of sources. An inference about a student's academic future should not be based only on aptitude tests or only on school records but, rather, on a combination of these data. Inferences concerning a student's values and interests should not be based only on a vocational interest test or only on a student's description of his recreational habits, but, rather, the student and the counselor must review interest tests, the student's report of his own behavior, and reports of others. The acquisition of such information requires carefully planned and programmed testing.

Characteristics of Tests To Be Considered by Counselors

RECOMMENDATION 10. *Counselors must know and make allowance for the relative reliabilities of the measures they use and the validity of each measure for specific uses.*

Counselors are concerned with the relevance of measurement; that is, with test validity, and with the consistency of measurement, or reliability. The validities and the reliabilities of tests vary according to the dimensions being assessed.[22] Tests of academic achievement are slightly more reliable than tests of academic aptitude, and academic aptitude and achievement tests tend to be more reliable than interest inventories, which in turn are more reliable than personality inventories. Little is known about the relative validities of these tests, but, obviously, any generalizations derived from comparisons of tests must vary with the criteria used and with the method of validation. Much is known about the predictive validities of academic ability tests, particularly when these tests are used to predict first-year college grades. College aptitude tests and educational achievement tests are about equally valid for this purpose, and validity coefficients tend to range from .40 to .60.[23]

22. B. Baxter and D. G. Paterson, "A New Ratio for Clinical Counselors," *Journal of Consulting Psychology*, V (1941), 123-26.

23. See Lindquist, *op. cit.*; and E. O. Swanson and R. F. Berdie, *The Relation of the Minnesota State-wide Program Test Scores to First-Year Grade-Point Averages in Minnesota Colleges and a Survey of Scholastic Aptitude in Minnesota Colleges*. Research Bulletin, Vol. III. Minneapolis: University of Minnesota Office of the Dean of Students, 1961.

The work of Thorndike and Hagen [24] indicates that some vocational aptitude tests and educational and trade achievement tests have little validity when used to predict success in a given occupation but that they have more validity when used to differentiate persons who enter various occupations. Results obtained at the University of Minnesota by Berdie [25] suggest that predictions of academic success are made best with academic aptitude and achievement tests but that groups graduating from various curricula can be differentiated best by vocational interest tests.

Although counselors can use academic achievement and aptitude tests to predict average college grades, particularly in the early college years, they cannot use these tests for predicting differential college achievement beyond the broad areas sometimes referred to as the "reading" courses and the technical courses. Tests of verbal comprehension and quantitative reasoning often differentiate to a significant degree between those who readily master extensive reading courses and courses heavily dependent on mathematics, respectively. It is difficult to identify students who will do well in mathematics and poorly in physics, or well in English and poorly in history. [26]

Few tests that predict occupational success are available for counseling purposes, but vocational interest tests and, to some extent, multiple aptitude tests will predict group membership. On the basis of test scores, the counselor can indicate that a student resembles men or women who have entered and persisted in one occupation to a greater extent than he resembles persons who have entered other occupations.

RECOMMENDATION 11. *Validity is crucial to the use of any measure or group of measures in counseling individuals.*

24. R. L. Thorndike and E. Hagen, *10,000 Careers*. New York: John Wiley & Sons, Inc., 1959.

25. R. F. Berdie, "Aptitude, Achievement, Interest, and Personality Tests: A Longitudinal Comparison," *Journal of Applied Psychology*, XXXIX (1955), 103-14.

26. R. F. Berdie, P. Dressel, and P. Kelso, "Relative Validity of the Q and L Scores of the ACE Psychological Examination," *Educational and Psychological Measurement*, XI (1951), 803-12.

Four kinds of test validity have been distinguished: predictive validity, content validity, concurrent validity, and construct validity. Counselors will generally be more concerned with the concepts of predictive and construct validity than with those of content or concurrent validity. In so far as the counselor makes inferences concerning the student's future behavior and develops explanatory hypotheses or theories to explain student behavior, the predictive validity of measures and the hypothetical construct validity of the counselor's behavior theories as applied in individual cases will be of most help to him. With these two validities, the counselor can help the student understand how he is likely to behave in the future and why he will behave that way.[27]

Ideally a counselor helps a student make differential classifications and predictions. For example, Sam Flinders came to a counselor at the end of his Freshman year in college and said he had been unable to decide between dentistry and medicine. He had been about a B+ or A— student in a superior high school, and his Freshman grades in college had consisted of about three B's to each C. His B's had been in mathematics and science, with his C's in English and social studies. His academic ability scores placed him in the upper one-third of college Freshmen in his state university. The life of a physician as he saw it appealed to him, but he was afraid of the many years and the money required for a medical education. He said that in order to practice the kind of medicine he wanted to practice, he would have to spend several years of work in graduate study and as a resident. He had two good friends who were dentists, and the work these men did appealed to him, and he liked the lives these men lived. He felt, however, that physicians had higher status in the community than dentists and greater opportunity to make larger incomes.

The counselor compared his pattern of aptitude, achievement, and interest test scores with the patterns of students tested as Freshmen who later graduated from either dentistry or medicine. On all of the aptitude and achievement tests, Sam's scores were higher than the average scores of Freshmen who later became dentists.

27. For further discussion of the concepts of validity raised here, see chap. x.

His scores on English, social science, and biological science tests were considerably higher than the average Freshman scores of physicians, but his scores on the physical sciences and on mathematics placed him in the lower 20 per cent of students who later graduated from medical school. His vocational interest scores indicated that his interests were significantly more similar to the interests of dentists than they were to the interests of physicians, although his score on the physician scale of the *Strong Vocational Interest Blank* was a B, suggesting that his interests were not incompatible with those of physicians.

The counselor discussed this information with Sam and said that it looked as if he had enough ability to succeed in either dentistry or medicine. There was some question on the basis of Sam's grades as to whether he would be admitted to a medical school, whereas there was very little question that he would be admitted to the local school of dentistry. The counselor suggested that he might be at least an average or above-average student in dentistry, whereas, although there was much reason to expect he could succeed in medical school, the chances were that he would be a below-average student. The discussion quickly turned to the question of whether the student wanted to enter a curriculum where he would be one of the superior students or if he wanted to enter a course where he might look forward to being no better than mediocre. He finally decided that if he had a reasonably good chance of succeeding in medicine, he would rather be a physician than a dentist. He planned to learn more about medical education and practice before making a final decision.

In this case the counselor had validity information that helped the student compare himself to persons in various groups and at the same time make predictions of differential success in different curricula.

RECOMMENDATION 12. *Counselors must understand the difference between the reliability of a test and the stability of a trait the test measures.*

Reliability is another concept that must be understood by the counselor, and here he must carefully distinguish between test reliability and trait consistency. For example, the emotional stability scale of the *Minnesota Counseling Inventory*, when used with eleventh- and twelfth-grade boys, has a reliability of .81 based on scores on independent halves of a test given at one administration, and yet the correlation of test scores with scores obtained on re-testing one year later was .35. The test-retest reliability for this scale was .77 after a period of one month, so we conclude that the trait consistency is low over a longer period of time. A test with high immediate or short-term reliability may be useful for inferring hypotheses that help explain a student's present behavior, whereas, if this test has low test-retest reliability over a period of time, it will not be of much use for predicting persistence of that trait or of others dependent on it.

RECOMMENDATION 13. *In considering reliability and validity, the counselor must be concerned with the reliability and validity of the test he is reviewing as compared to the reliability and validity of information obtained from other sources.*

Sometimes coefficients of test reliability and validity appear low, but they often look better when they are compared to similar figures describing information derived from other sources. Personality inventories do not have high reliabilities, but usually these reliabilities are higher than those of judgments made by trained interviewers.[28]

RECOMMENDATION 14. *Counselors will find multiple norms useful when they use tests.*

When a student is considering two colleges, separate norms for each college allow the counselor to help the student compare himself to each group, as was done in the case of Sam Flinders. In one state, a college aptitude test was given to all high-school Juniors, and at first norms were available only for those who later became college Freshmen. When a counselor spoke with a student, he could help the student compare himself to college Freshmen, and many students were depressed when they learned that their scores placed them in the lower one-third of college Freshmen. Later, counselors were given norms based on all high-school Juniors, and thus many

28. Kelly and Fiske, *op. cit.*

students who had been depressed to learn that they were below average when compared to college Freshmen were somewhat heartened to realize that, compared to high-school Juniors, their scores appeared considerably better.

For many years, different norms have been available for the *Minnesota Clerical Aptitude Test,* so that the scores of students can be compared to the scores of persons in different grades and with a variety of occupational experiences. A student can be shown that his scores on the clerical aptitude test are considerably above average when they are compared to scores of persons who have not been employed as clerical workers, but somewhat below average when compared to scores of experienced clerical workers. In this way, the student learns that the meaning of the test scores is not fixed and that test scores and other information must be considered relatively.

In working with parents, counselors can use aptitude and achievement test norms based on national groups, on state groups, on local system groups, and even on local school groups to help parents understand their childrens' potentials as well as to learn more about the community in which they live. Adequate test norms usually can be obtained more easily through systematic testing programs than through more casual testing.

RECOMMENDATION 15. *Norms based on the same population are essential to comparability.*

Not only is the counselor helped by having a number of norms for each test but he also benefits from having a group of tests for which common norms are available. Frequently, counselors must help students make decisions concerning the relative strengths of their aptitudes, abilities, achievements, and interests, and this can be done well only if interpretative data from a common reference or norm group are available. Usually common norms are found in multiple aptitude batteries, and tests, such as the *Differential Aptitude Tests* and the *Flanagan Aptitude Classification Tests,* provide norms derived from the same groups so that counselors can indicate to students that, when compared to a specified group, some scores are above average and others below.

The Integration of Counseling Information

Test scores seldom are used in isolation from other information. The counselor, just as every other test-user, must decide what his purposes are for using information, must know how his own values and attitudes influence how he uses information, and must combine and communicate information to achieve his purposes. Seldom will the counselor use test scores without combining them with other information. Already we have seen that a statistical combination is more likely to be accurate than an intuitive combination, but the counselor nevertheless must face the question as to the most accurate and most efficient method of combining and communicating information.

RECOMMENDATION 16. *The counselor should seek to attain an understanding of the basic statistical methods used in prediction.*

Correlational analyses leading through multiple correlations to the development of regression and prediction equations provide effective means of combining counseling data for predictive purposes. Most sophisticated prediction studies, regardless of other methods used, have used correlation and regression analyses.[29] These prediction equations, placed in the hands of competent counselors, provide a means whereby information about a student can be translated into probability figures.

The advantages of the regression-equation approach are apparent. Most statisticians know how to perform such analyses, and many counselors know how to interpret the results. The process is strictly mathematical and objective, and no subjective judgments are necessary once the analysis begins. Many kinds of information can be combined, and the only requirement is that the predicting and predicted variables be quantified. A convenient means is available in the standard error of estimate to gauge the accuracy of the prediction. A minimum number of assumptions are made in the process.

29. See Hills and Franz, *op. cit.*; D. B. Stuit, G. S. Dickson, T. F. Jordan, and L. Schloerb, *Predicting Success in Professional Schools* (Washington: American Council on Education, 1949); and Swanson and Berdie, *op. cit.*

The disadvantages of the regression method are not so obvious. First, the results of this procedure are rather difficult for most counselors to present or describe to students. Some counselors find it difficult to understand the procedure and its results. Multiple correlational analyses sometimes have been used without adequate investigation as to the shape of the correlational surfaces. The assumption frequently is made that relationships are rectilinear, whereas analysis might prove them to be markedly curvilinear. Many analyses have demonstrated that predictions of failure can be made more accurately than predictions of success, and the traditional regression-equation approach does not provide a means for taking this into account.

Regression equations can be made more accurate by tailoring them to specific subpopulations.[30] The correlations used in predicting academic success sometimes are different for boys and girls, and more accurate predictions can be made if separate equations are used for the two sexes.[31] Similarly, differences sometimes can be found among children coming from different socioeconomic levels and different geographical areas and among children with different personality structures and different attitudes.

Discriminant function analyses and multiple discriminant analyses provide another multivariant statistical technique for combining information.[32] This method has the advantage of not requiring the criterion variable to be quantified, and membership in a variety of classes can serve as the predicted variable. The results of the analysis can be presented in terms of probabilities and in some instances are easier to interpret to students than is information obtained from regression equations. The statistical procedures are complex and cumbersome, and the estimate of error is not as precise as that for the multiple correlational analysis.

30. R. F. Berdie, "Intra-Individual Variability and Predictability," *Educational and Psychological Measurement*, XXI (1961), 663-76.

31. H. Seashore, "Women Are More Predictable Than Men," *Journal of Counseling Psychology* (in press).

32. D. V. Tiedeman and J. G. Bryan, "Predictions of College Field of Concentration," *Harvard Education Review*, XXIV (1958), 122-39.

Essentially, these two methods of combining data have different purposes. The multiple correlational method is used to predict degree of success, whereas the multiple discriminant analysis primarily is used to predict group membership.[33]

Possible combinations of these methods are potentially valuable to counselors. *The Strong Vocational Interest Profile* essentially is a method of multiple discriminant analysis whereby the response on each item of the interest blank constitutes one of the predicting variables, and the criterion groups are the occupational groups to which membership is being predicted. The counselor attempts to help the student study the probabilities of joining and remaining in a variety of occupations, taking into consideration information about the student's interests and interests of persons successful in those occupations.

At the same time that the counselor uses the vocational interest profile, he may use a series of aptitude tests combined in such a way as to provide predictive indexes of success in a variety of university or school curriculums. The counselor may combine the results from *Differential Aptitude Tests* into regression equations and derive predicted grades in engineering, industrial training, agriculture, and law. On the basis of the first analysis, the student can study the degree to which he resembles persons in a variety of occupations and, on the basis of the second analysis, learn more about his probabilities of success in the occupations of which he is potentially a member.

Neither of these two analyses is easily explained to students, although profile analyses of certain kinds that have been used with the *Strong Vocational Interest Blank* can be presented meaningfully by a counselor sophisticated in the use of that instrument.[34]

RECOMMENDATION 17. *The counselor must face the paradox of defeating his predictions—when they are unfavorable—through counseling.*

33. J. W. French, "The Logic of and Assumptions Underlying Differential Testing," in *Proceedings of Invitational Conference on Testing Problems, October 29, 1955*, pp. 40-48. Princeton, New Jersey: Educational Testing Service, 1956.

34. Layton, *op. cit.*

The counselor's use of test scores for predictive purposes already has been mentioned, but parenthetically we should note that when the counselor accepts the responsibility for making a prediction, he does not accept the obligation to see his prediction fulfilled. Frequently, the counselor's obligation is just the opposite; that is, he must overthrow his own prediction. For example, a counselor used available prediction equations and expectancy tables to describe to a student his probabilities of succeeding in a college being considered. The statistical prediction was failure, and the probabilities were small that the student would succeed in that college. Let us suppose that the student, after reviewing and considering all of the information, decided that he was willing to risk the chance of failure. The rewards he anticipated following success in that college were great enough to warrant his accepting a small probability of success. He was a gambler. Once he decided to enter the college of his choice, provided he was admitted, the counselor's responsibility was to see that the student had every possible chance of succeeding in his choice. The counselor would help the student diagnose his own deficiencies and provide counseling that would help him remedy his disabilities. He would help the student learn what must be done if the probability of success in college were to be maximized. If the student was successful, and if the counselor was successful in helping the student, then the counselor's prediction of failure was ruined. The possibilities here of a completely successful counseling program confounding the predictions of a similarly successful admissions program are intriguing.

RECOMMENDATION 18. *Because of the many purposes besides counseling that are served by the school testing program, co-operative planning of the program by all concerned is essential.*

If the only purpose of testing in the schools were to provide information for counseling, planning and conducting a testing program would be relatively simple. In light of the many uses made of tests, however, planning a testing program that will serve counseling needs and at the same time serve other purposes is difficult. A school cannot justify having several testing programs, and the program it adopts must serve the administrator, the teacher, and the counselor and must provide information useful in curriculum organization and revision, classroom teaching, and counseling.[35]

If a testing program is to meet the needs of these persons, then all of them must co-operate in planning and managing the program. In many schools the counselor is the person best trained in psychological and educational measurement. In some schools he may be the only person who has had even a single course in tests and measurements. Because of the special training and competence of the counselor, he sometimes is assigned or takes sole responsibility for testing and determines which tests are to be used and when and how they are to be used. A wisely planned testing program must result from co-operative discussion, and although the counselor may assume some leadership—and certainly he will make available his special information about tests—the testing program must not be a "counseling testing program" but, rather, a "school testing program."

An effective school testing program will provide continuing and comparable information about pupils so that a longitudinal picture of the individual will be obtained. The continuity of the testing program is particularly relevant for the counselor, who must know the history of the student's development if he is to understand the pupil as he is today and as he is likely to be tomorrow in order to assist the student to gain in self-understanding.

RECOMMENDATION 19. *The school's counseling program ideally conceived is a comprehensive and continuous one.*

Ideally the counselor wishes for a testing program that includes tests of relevant personality dimensions, abilities and aptitudes, academic achievement and skills, educational and vocational interests, and character and personality. These tests would be introduced into the school program when the pupils' ages allow reasonably accurate and reliable measurement. Appropriate tests for these dimensions would be available at different age levels and the frequency of repeating tests would depend on the counselor's need for informa-

35. W. G. Findley, "Where Testing Is Part of Instruction," *Professional Growth Guide for Administrators*, pp. 3-4. New London, Connecticut: Arthur C. Croft Publications, February, 1958.

tion. For example, a school testing program might well begin in the first grade with a test of reading readiness and perhaps a test of general intelligence. Repetitions of the reading readiness tests presumably would not be needed in the systematic testing program, although provisions would be made for using these tests later with individual pupils. The intelligence test or a test of academic aptitude might well be given in the third grade, in the sixth grade, and repeated in Grades IX and XI. A test of this kind would be used when the student entered college and, perhaps, also later. Academic achievement tests would be introduced early in the student's elementary-school career and would be repeated annually. A test battery, such as *The Iowa Tests of Basic Skills* or *The Sequential Tests of Educational Progress* might be given every year to provide a picture of the student's educational development.

The measurement of differential aptitudes is limited, of course, by the age at which these aptitudes appear and become relevant to instructional and guidance programs. Little evidence warrants using multiple aptitude tests before Grades VII or VIII. A counselor might wish to have included in the school testing program a test such as the *Differential Aptitude Test* at Grade IX and be satisfied that, for most pupils, this single differential aptitude test was enough, reserving retesting for selected individuals.

The counselor might wish to use interest inventories early in the student's career, but, unfortunately, such psychological instruments useful for elementary and younger high-school children have not been developed. *The Strong Vocational Interest Blank* and *The Minnesota Vocational Interest Inventory* provide useful and frequently necessary information relevant to students about to make both broad and specific educational and vocational decisions. Unfortunately, these inventories must be used with extreme care with students below the Senior year in high school. Needless to say, all tests must be used with extreme care with all pupils, but the use of vocational interest inventories with younger high-school students is particularly precarious. Even other interest inventories with norms for lower grades must be used and interpreted judiciously because they depend on reading ability and on familiarity with the great variety of activities offered for choice or approval.

Many counselors also wish to include personality inventories in the school testing program. Scores on these inventories serve a variety of purposes. They help the counselor to quickly identify students in need of special counseling attention. Whereas it might take counselors and teachers several months, if not longer, to learn of students who have particularly distressing family or emotional conflicts, scores on personality inventories can call to the attention of the counselors many of the students who merit more attention than can be given to all students. Scores on personality inventories also help counselors evaluate the condition of students being counseled. A student may come to a counselor expressing a particular personal problem, and a personality inventory may substantiate the counselor's impression that a problem exists. If the counselor is able to compare the student's score at the time of counseling with a similar personality inventory score taken a year or so earlier, he can learn something about the history and development of the pupil's problem. Frequently, a problem of long standing is handled quite differently from a problem resembling it very much on the surface but which has appeared only recently.

Counselors sometimes are warned to use personality inventories only if they are particularly well trained in personality theory, measurement, and counseling. This warning might be extended to apply to all counselors using information about students' personalities regardless of the observational method through which it was derived.

An important part of the school testing program provides for the use of tests in special cases, when they are necessary. For example, reading tests used in the elementary grades will help identify pupils who have difficulty in reading. To pupils with extremely low scores, diagnostic reading tests may be administered, and still further tests may be given to students selected on the basis of these latter scores. Provisions must be made for teachers to use diagnostic tests within entire classes in order to learn more about their own teaching and in order to understand the progress made by pupils. The counselor will derive cues and suggestions about individual students from scores on tests administered to all pupils in the school. In order to learn more about these cues, the counselor frequently will wish to give other tests to these individuals. Thus, a counselor may be working with a girl considering stenographic work and may note that the girl's score on the clerical speed and accuracy test of *The Differential Aptitude Test* was low. Being unwilling to place too much weight on a single test score, the counselor may give the girl *The Minnesota Clerical Aptitude Test*. Another counselor might be counseling a boy who is considering attending a trade school after high-school graduation. The boy's scores on *The Differential Aptitude Test* might be low, and the counselor may gather additional information by referring the boy to the State Employment Office, where he can take *The General Aptitude Test Battery*. The school may not include a musical aptitude test in its systematic testing program, but the counselor occasionally may wish to give *The Seashore Musical Aptitude Test* to students considering professional careers in music.

The school testing program thus provides for systematic testing of designated groups of pupils at specified times and at the same time provides for other tests to be administered to individual pupils or groups of pupils as the needs arise.

RECOMMENDATION 20. *External testing programs should be incorporated into the school's testing program.*

Increasingly important in school testing programs are "external tests." Womer[36] characterized external tests as those the results of which are used by some institution or organization other than the school and concerning which the school has or feels it has no real choice as to whether they are taken by the students. The oldest external testing program is that of the College Entrance Examination Board. Newer programs include the American College Testing Program, the National Merit Scholarship Program, the Betty Crocker Program, and other scholarship and contest testing programs.

Programs such as the Guidance Testing Program of the Educational Testing Service, the Iowa Test of Educational Development Program of the Science Research Associates, and the Minnesota and Iowa high school state-wide testing programs are not external programs because the scores are used only by the schools, who are

36. F. B. Womer, "Pros and Cons of External Testing Programs," *North Central Association Quarterly*, XXXVI (1961), 201-10.

under no duress from outside agencies to participate.

Regardless of the primary purpose of tests used in external programs, the scores usually have great usefulness for counselors, and their availability influences the planning of the school testing program. When only some of the students in a school take tests included in an external program, considerable overlapping of tests may be inevitable. If external tests are given to a large proportion of the students, they will influence the choice of tests given by the school.

External testing agencies, for the most part, accept responsibility for making scores available to the school for counseling, and usually these scores assume increasing importance as counselors gain experience with them.

RECOMMENDATION 21. *Provision should be made in the school testing program for some tests that are primarily, or almost solely, for counseling use.*

Although counselors at times find useful information from almost all educational and psychological tests, certain tests which are particularly useful in the high-school testing program are worthy of note.[37]

Among general ability or academic aptitude tests are included *The School and College Ability Tests, The College Qualification Test, The Scholastic Aptitude Test* of the College Entrance Examination Board, *The Lorge-Thorndike Intelligence Test, The California Test of Mental Maturity* (and the short form of that test), *The Henmon-Nelson Test of Mental Ability, The Kuhlmann-Anderson Intelligence Test, The Kuhlmann-Finch Intelligence Test, The Ohio State University Psychological Test, The Otis Quick-Scoring Mental Ability Test,* and *The Terman-McNemar Test of Mental Ability.* These tests provide one or occasionally a few scores that indicate the general intellectual level of the student. They are all authored by reputable persons, published and distributed by established organizations, and meet what are

37. Evaluative analyses of most of the tests listed here can be found in *The Fifth Mental Measurements Yearbook* (Edited by O. K. Buros. Highland Park, New Jersey: Gryphon Press, 1959) and in D. E. Super and J. O. Crites, *Appraising Vocational Fitness* (New York: Harper & Row, 1962).

generally considered at least minimum psychometric standards. The information provided by these tests allows the counselor, the student, and his family to make estimates of how far the student will be able to go in school, the general occupational level to which he can aspire, and the grades in school which he is capable of earning.

Multiple ability tests provide more differentiated information. Some examples of these tests are *The Differential Aptitude Tests, The Flanagan Aptitude Classification Test, The General Aptitude Test Battery, The Guilford-Zimmerman Aptitude Survey, The Holzinger-Crowder Uni-Factor Test,* and *The Multiple Aptitude Tests.* These tests all provide several scores for each pupil, and each score reflects an ability relatively independent of other abilities measured by the tests. On the basis of these tests, a counselor should be able to make inferences regarding which of a pupil's abilities are strong and which are weak. This allows the counselor to attempt differential predictions so that students will understand that their chances for success are greater in one endeavor than in another. Unfortunately, although the evidence suggests that these tests do so differentiate to a small extent, the degree to which such differentiation is now possible is not great. Nevertheless, many counselors will find these tests useful.

Some persons contend that all or most of the information obtained from aptitude tests can be obtained as efficiently from educational achievement tests. Regardless of whether the counselor wishes to use ability tests, certainly he will find it necessary to obtain information about the student's educational background. Educational achievement tests, available for counseling as well as for other uses, include *The Iowa Tests of Educational Development, The California Achievement Test, The Co-operative Achievement Tests, The Sequential Tests of Educational Progress, The Essential High School Content Battery, The Iowa Tests of Basic Skills, The SRA Achievement Tests, The Metropolitan Achievement Test,* and *The Stanford Achievement Test.* These tests all provide opportunities for the counselor to learn about the student's information and skill as it is related to such subjects as language, mathematics, science, and social studies. Again, these tests are all by reputable authors and published by established organizations. The tests have varying emphases, and some tests, appropriate for one school, may be less appropriate for another. Counselors will find useful almost all achievement batteries that serve other purposes in their schools.

Vocational interest inventories are particularly useful for high-school counselors working with students about to graduate. *The Strong Vocational Interest Inventory* provides the pupil an opportunity to compare his interests and personality characteristics with the interests and characteristics of men successful in and satisfied with a variety of occupations. Perhaps more research has been done on *The Strong Vocational Interest Blank* than on any other single test used by counselors. The Strong blank has been useful mainly for students considering occupations relatively high in the occupational hierarchy. In 1961 a vocational interest inventory was described by Clark[38] that is useful for students considering skilled trades. Clark's inventory, *The Minnesota Vocational Interest Inventory*, is somewhat similar to the Strong blank and provides the student with an opportunity to compare his interests with the interests of men successful in a number of skilled trades. This inventory promises to be of great value to counselors.

Personality inventories will be used by many counselors as part of the systematic school testing program and by most counselors, at least, for testing individual students. The number of personality inventories available for school use is small. *The Minnesota Counseling Inventory* provides information to counselors concerning several variables: (*a*) the relationships existing between a student and his family; (*b*) the relationship existing between him and his peers; (*c*) his emotional stability; (*d*) his tendency toward delinquency; (*e*) his mood; (*f*) his approach to or retreat from reality; and (*g*) his leadership attitudes. In addition, a validity score provides information concerning the student's attitude toward taking the inventory. *The Mooney Problem Check List* is not a psychometric instrument, but, nevertheless, it is a type of personality test used by counselors to acquire information concerning the personal adjustment of their pupils. This list consists primarily

38. K. E. Clark, *The Vocational Interests of Nonprofessional Men.* Minneapolis: University of Minnesota Press, 1961.

of statements of problems encountered by pupils, which the pupil is asked to read and then mark those problems troubling him. *The Minnesota Multiphasic Personality Inventory* was developed primarily for use in medical and psychiatric studies, but many counselors are able to acquire valuable information about pupils with this inventory. Some impressive research [39] suggests the usefulness of this inventory in work with predelinquents.

Conclusion

An effort has been made in this chapter to demonstrate that counselors use test information somewhat differently from the way it is used by others in the school but that most of the test information used by the counselors is also useful to others. It has been emphasized that counseling is more than testing and that, if a school is to have a counseling program, it must have a testing program, but that having a testing program does not indicate that a school has a counseling program. The usefulness of test data in counseling depends largely on the relationship between the counselor and the pupil, and the role of the counselor frequently is to help the pupil interpret for himself the meaning of tests he has taken so that he increasingly and continually will learn more about those aspects that make him different from and similar to other persons.

39. S. R. Hathaway and E. D. Monachesi, *Analyzing and Predicting Juvenile Delinquency with the MMPI.* Minneapolis: University of Minnesota Press, 1953.

CHAPTER VIII

The Improvement of Tests

MAX D. ENGELHART and JOHN M. BECK

Introduction

In the local situation, occasions occur in which it is necessary to compare tests, test batteries, or other measuring instruments in order to decide which ones are relatively most suitable for local use. Local test experts may give consideration to technical aspects, local curriculum specialists or classroom teachers may evaluate test content in relation to local instructional objectives, and school administrators may consider the tests with reference to the kinds of data they regard as most helpful in solution of school problems. Similarly, school psychologists and guidance counselors may evaluate tests with reference to local problems of adjustment and guidance. Editions of the *Mental Measurements Yearbook*, the *Technical Standards*, issues of the *Review of Educational Research* on "Educational and Psychological Testing," bulletins of test publishers, and leading texts on measurement and evaluation are of value in helping such persons make valid judgments. It is also very helpful for teachers and counselors to take the test themselves and to try it out on a sample of pupils prior to city-wide use. These are matters, however, more properly discussed in Chapter x on the selection and use of tests in a school testing program. In this chapter we are also concerned with evaluation of the quality of tests but in relation to such questions as "How have tests improved over the years?" "How can better tests be constructed?" and "In what directions should test development be promoted?" In answer to these questions a number of generalizations and recommendations are listed. It is altogether possible that other authors would list somewhat different generalizations and present different evidence or make somewhat different recommendations. In another context and to an audience of specialists the questions could be answered much more technically and in much greater detail. The authors of this chapter hope that in dealing with such aspects of test quality as validity, reliability, norms, and other means of interpreting scores, the reader will obtain at least a helpful introduction to the ways in which tests have and can be improved. While much has been accomplished, much remains to be done.

How Have Tests Improved Over the Years?

GENERALIZATION 1. *There has been improvement in the validity of achievement tests and achievement test batteries with reference to instructional objectives ranging from knowledge through intellectual abilities and skills.*

Among the tests which best reflect this improvement are the newer and more widely used standardized achievement tests and batteries, certain of the achievement tests included in national testing programs for college admissions and college scholarships, and achievement or proficiency tests produced by college or university examiners working with teachers in higher institutions having programs of general education. The construction of these tests and batteries has been characterized by increased efforts to formulate lists of generally acceptable instructional objectives, sometimes operationally defined. The writing of the test questions or items has been guided by the objectives and, in the manuals of the better published tests, the objectives and their sources are summarized and, in some cases, the distributions of test items relevant to each major objective are indicated.

This is exemplified by such test batteries as the *California Achievement Tests* (1957), the *Cooperative General Achievement Tests* (1956), the *Area Tests of the Graduate Record Examinations* (1954), the *Iowa Tests of Basic Skills* (1955-56), the *SRA Achievement Series*, (1954-57), the *Sequential Tests of Educational Progress* (1956-58), and the *Metropolitan Achievement Tests* (1959). Consider in this connection the following paragraph quoted from Virgil E. Herrick's review of the *Iowa Tests of Basic Skills:*

A major strength of this new battery is its curricular validation. Besides the usual widespread administration of sample test items and the establishment of discrimination and difficulty indexes, extremely careful identification and definition of the skill processes being tested was done before test items were devised. This aspect of test development is not usually undertaken with such care, and the authors are to be commended for the way the curricular validation of their test items was done. School staffs attempting to improve their curriculum in the skill areas could use with profit the definitions of the skill objectives developed by the Iowa staff. These curricular analyses are found in the Teacher's Manual and form a basis for helping teachers plan remedial or corrective instruction following evaluation. Here each basic skill is analyzed, the test items related to it identified, and corresponding teaching suggestions made.[1]

Analysis of the reviews in successive editions of the *Mental Measurements Yearbook* tends to support the generalization concerning improvement, as qualified in preceding paragraphs, of the validity of tests. For example, *all* of the achievement batteries reviewed in the *Nineteen Forty Mental Measurements Yearbook* are criticized with reference to content validity. While some of the achievement batteries reviewed in the *Fifth Yearbook* are criticized regarding curricular validation, the favorable comments relevant to most of the batteries reviewed are in striking contrast to the critical comments found in earlier reviews. Similar evidence could be presented concerning leading standardized achievement tests not included in achievement batteries. Study of achievement tests or "comprehensive" examinations prepared under the direction of college boards of examiners also reveals improvements in validity with reference to a range of curricular objectives.

A number of tests and batteries, seemingly valid with respect to objectives generally accepted as desirable, are uneven in this quality. Several of the newer batteries have been criticized for too great emphasis on evaluation of intellectual skills to the neglect of evaluation of basic concepts or knowledge of a field. An example of such criticism occurs in Robert W. B. Jackson's review of the *STEP* tests. Although he states that this series "is undoubtedly one of the best available," he contends that many test-users will not consider its use appropriate "since for many school people the acquirement of

1. *The Fifth Mental Measurements Yearbook*, p. 32. Edited by Oscar Buros. Highland Park, New Jersey: Gryphon Press, 1959.

knowledge of subject matter is still deemed to be a primary and even laudable aim of education."[2]

More than one achievement test or battery has been found wanting in evaluation of English skills. It is contended that knowledge of grammatical terms and rules receives more attention in test items than functional skills relevant to standard usage. Furthermore, items often require, for "correct" responses, knowledge of usage no longer considered the one accepted usage by authorities on English expression.

Tests are not equally valid in all situations. Validity of tests for local purposes presents certain peculiar issues. A given test or battery may be judged valid with respect to the instructional objectives which directed its production, and these objectives may be deemed to be in harmony with generally accepted aims of education, but, even so, the test or battery may not be satisfactorily valid with reference to local instructional objectives. In the local situation, the actual objectives of instruction may be restricted in scope to acquisition of information or knowledge to the neglect of intellectual skills and abilities. The information or knowledge evaluated by the test or battery may not be compatible with the knowledge taught. There may be numerous exercises relating to concepts and skills that pupils have not had opportunities to learn. Since validity is fundamentally related to the purposes of testing, it is essential to select achievement tests in terms of local purposes and local objectives of instruction. However, it should be recognized that, apart from improvement of standardized tests of achievement in valid measurement of comprehensive ranges of desirable objectives, much can be done to improve validity through reconstruction of local objectives. Study of the best of contemporary standardized achievement tests and their manuals can do much to promote local recognition of worthwhile objectives hitherto neglected. "Teaching for the test" should, of course, be avoided.

While there has been considerable improvement of the validity of achievement tests where validity is estimated in terms of relevance of the items to behaviors defined as objectives of instruction, there is little evidence that pupils or students will behave in other than

2. *Ibid.*, p. 67.

the test situation as predicted by their scores. Relevance of test items to objectives operationally defined in behavioral terms is evidence of content validity. Correlations between scores on achievement tests given at much the same time are indicators of concurrent validity. Predictive and construct validity are also important in achievement testing.[3] Achievement test scores and marks based on them are of use in the making of decisions as to subsequent instruction and in guidance with reference to future educational and vocational careers. Hence, there should be more concern for the predictive validity of achievement tests. Too little is known concerning the mental processes underlying test scores. Effort to determine validity of this kind or "construct" validation has received some but not much attention. More adequate understanding of the extent to which various mental processes are effectively measured by achievement exercises or tests of different kinds would do much to advance our knowledge of instructional methods. For example, test items requiring interpretation of controversial selections may comprise a test of critical-thinking skills in social studies. The techniques of construct validation must be applied before we can know how such skills can best be taught and measured. More will be said about these matters in presenting the recommendations listed in the next section of this chapter.

GENERALIZATION 2. *There has been definite improvement in the validity of tests of general and of special aptitudes.*

Application of the techniques of factor analysis, multiple-correlation and regression, and other types of correlation analysis have greatly contributed to improvement in the construction of aptitude tests and to the technology of their use. The problems of prediction are better understood. Actually, to state that the validity of aptitude tests has increased can only mean that better instruments are now available and can be used effectively where the purposes of prediction have been defined and the inadequacies of even the best instruments have been recognized.

The Stanford-Binet Scale, the *Wechsler Adult Intelligence Scale,* and the *Wechsler Intelligence Scale for Children* are, of course,

---

3. For a fuller definition and interpretation of these concepts, see chap. x.

the dominant individual intelligence tests. No brief categorical comment concerning their validity seems justified. Reviews of revisions of these instruments in successive volumes of the *Mental Measurements Yearbook* testify both to definite improvements and to persistent limitations. Although there is a wealth of literature concerning these scales, most reviewers ask for more data on validity. While these scales are magnificent contributions to psychometric and clinical measurement, it is probably fair to say that far more than other tests, their validity depends upon the skill with which they are administered and interpreted.[4]

Widely used and generally superior group tests of intelligence or of general scholastic aptitude include the *California Test of Mental Maturity*, the College Entrance Examination Board's *Scholastic Aptitude Test*, the *Cooperative School and College Ability Tests*, the *Henmon-Nelson Tests of Mental Ability*, the *Kuhlmann-Anderson Intelligence Tests*, the *Lorge-Thorndike Intelligence Tests*, the *Otis Quick-Scoring Mental Ability Tests*, and the *Pintner General Ability Tests*. Most of these tests named above exemplify the prevailing interest in separate verbal and quantitative or verbal and non-verbal scores. Such tests reflect the influence of factor analysis as do the multiple aptitude tests discussed in later paragraphs. The trend in group testing of intelligence or general ability is away from the traditional provision of a single global measure. The *Cooperative School and College Ability Tests* (*SCAT*) differ most from the others with reference to the measurement of "school-learned abilities," although the *Scholastic Aptitude Test* (*SAT*) also puts considerable dependence on reading comprehension and arithmetic problems. Certainly, they differ from the ways in which intelligence or general scholastic aptitude is measured by the tests they supersede, the *American Council on Education Psychological Examinations* (*ACE*). The *Lorge-Thorndike Tests* are especially commended by

---

4. For excellent discussions of these scales consult such leading texts on measurement as: Anne Anastasi, *Psychological Testing*, pp. 175-204 and 306-27 (New York: Macmillan Co., 1954); Lee J. Cronbach, *Essentials of Psychological Testing*, pp. 157-213 (New York: Harper & Bros. 1960); and Robert L. Thorndike and Elizabeth Hagen, *Measurement and Evaluation in Psychology and Education*, pp. 226-31. (New York: John Wiley & Sons, 1961 [second edition]).

Frank S. Freeman for the authors' efforts to obtain content and construct validity, although he claims there is a "lack of adequate predictive and concurrent validity." [5]

While for many of the leading individual and group tests of mental ability much data are reported concerning concurrent validity and considerable data are reported with reference to predictive validity in the test manuals and other published sources, much more data are needed with respect to the latter. Especially needed in local situations are predictive validity studies that take into account local purposes or types of decisions which are based on data locally obtained. While construct validity has received much attention in factor-analysis studies, and in others as well, more needs to be known concerning the mental processes underlying group test scores. Finally, high correlations between scores on group tests of intelligence and school achievement tests, while testifying to the predictive validity of the former with reference to school achievement, do raise questions concerning their validity as measures of "native capacity." [6] Although serious efforts have been made (as exemplified by the *Davis-Eells Games* and the *IPAT Culture Free Intelligence Test*) to produce tests that are at least culture fair, opinion and evidence provided by research are divided with reference to the success of these efforts.

Among the leading multiple-aptitude tests are the *Differential Aptitude Tests (DAT)*, the *Flanagan Aptitude Classification Tests (FACT)*, the *General Aptitude Test Battery (GATB)*, the *Guilford-Zimmerman Aptitude Survey*, the *Holzinger-Crowder Uni-Factor Tests*, the *Multiple Aptitude Tests*, and the *SRA Primary Mental Abilities*. Both John Carroll and Norman Frederiksen comment on the wealth of validity studies reported with reference to the DAT.[7] Both are enthusiastic concerning the technical excellence of the tests, the manual, and the booklet, *Counseling From Profiles: A Casebook for the Differential Aptitude Tests*. Both are critical

5. *Fifth Mental Measurements Yearbook, op. cit.,* pp. 380-81.

6. William Coleman and Edward E. Cureton, "Intelligence and Achievement: The 'Jangle' Fallacy Again," *Educational and Psychological Measurement,* XIV (Summer, 1954), 347-51.

7. *Fifth Mental Measurements Yearbook, op. cit.,* pp. 669-76.

of the differential validity of the tests, but Carroll stresses the difficulty of attaining high differential validity:

> Of course, any multifactor battery like the DAT tends to be handicapped by the fact that even if truly independent aptitudes exist, the differences between them are obscured by common educational experiences and by degrees of motivation for school learning and for test taking which more or less uniformly make for a high, medium, or low level of performance on a series of tests. There is not much chance that *any* set of differential tests designed chiefly for general educational guidance, as DAT is, would not be substantially affected by these influences.[8]

It should be noted that the simple rule specified by the authors of the *DAT* that no difference between two scores is to be considered significant unless portrayed by one inch or more of vertical difference in the student's profile encourages cautious interpretation by counselors. It seems justified to conclude that the *Differential Aptitude Tests* are without peer among tests of this kind.

Closely second to the DAT in quality is the *General Aptitude Test Battery* developed for use in the counseling program of the United States Employment Service and also used by State Employment Services which collaborate in validating this battery in local work situations. A vast amount of validity data are available, but Andrew L. Comrey, Clifford Froehlich, and Lloyd Humphreys, though largely favorable in their reviews, stress need for more validity studies.[9] In his excellent comparison of the DAT and the GATB, Lee Cronbach comments with respect to the latter that "one cannot expect to measure with the precision of the DAT, using subtests only one-fourth as long."[10] It should be pointed out in conclusion, however, that all of the critics seem to believe that this battery is serving effectively in the role for which it was developed.

While the reviews of Harold Bechtoldt, Ralph Berdie, and John Carroll are appreciative of the effort and experience involved in the development of the *Flanagan Aptitude Classification Tests,* all three are critical of the paucity of empirical validity data.[11] Bechtoldt

---

8. *Ibid.,* p. 673.

9. *Ibid.* pp. 695-700.

10. Cronbach, *op. cit.,* p. 274.

11. *Fifth Mental Measurements Yearbook, op. cit.,* pp. 684-92.

and Carroll are especially unenthusiastic about Flanagan's emphasis on a "critical-job-element" approach to the neglect of the use of factor analysis and the collection of adequate predictive validity data. All three hope that its defects may be remedied and that the battery will develop "into a useful counseling tool." Though definitely based on factor analysis research the *Guilford-Zimmerman Aptitude Survey*, considered "promising," needs more normative and empirical validation data.[12] The *Holzinger-Crowder Uni-Factor Tests* are praised by Anne Anastasi for their technical merits, but criticized for lack of differential validity. She notes that the general scholastic aptitude score obtainable through use of a multiple-regression equation yields "somewhat higher validities than generally found with intelligence tests."[13] The *Multiple Aptitude Tests*, also based on factor analysis, are criticized for lack of independence of scores, praised in a number of respects, and also regarded as "promising." [14] The *SRA Primary Mental Abilities* and its predecessor, the *PMA*, have been severely criticized in successive volumes of the *Mental Measurements Yearbook*. In his review, Albert Kurtz summarizes the criticisms and concludes:

> The theoretical rationale underlying the test is sound. It may well be that an excellent test can be developed upon this foundation. Until the reliabilities are improved and satisfactory validity data are available, the potential user should investigate other possibilities also.[15]

The preceding paragraphs have discussed some, but not all, of the leading multiple-aptitude test batteries. It is evident that progress has been made toward valid measurement of various basic and important abilities, that adequate independence of scores is difficult to obtain, and that differential predictions can be made only with caution. Especially needed are validation studies by those using the tests in local situations that are not entirely representative of the population for which the test was constructed.

12. See the reviews of Anne Anastasi, Harold Bechtoldt, John Carroll, and Philip Vernon in *The Fourth Mental Measurements Yearbook*, pp. 693-98. Edited by Oscar Buros. Highland Park, N.J.: Gryphon Press, 1953.

13. *Fifth Mental Measurements Yearbook, op. cit.*, p. 701.

14. See the reviews of Ralph Berdie and Benjamin Fruchter in *Fifth Mental Measurements Yearbook, op. cit.*, pp. 604-14.

15. *Ibid.*, p. 717.

Most of what has been said about multiple-aptitude tests also applies to tests of special aptitudes. Some of the best of such tests are included in the aptitude batteries, for example, the *Mechanical Reasoning* and *Clerical Speed and Accuracy* tests of the *DAT*. Again, the major problem is the devising of tests which will measure skills whose functioning requires unique rather than general abilities or aptitudes. Otherwise, prediction may be more effective when based on measurement of general aptitude and evaluation of actual proficiency in the special field.

GENERALIZATION 3. *There has been some improvement in the validity of tests and inventories produced for the measurement of interests, attitudes, values, temperament, and other aspects of personality.*

It seems quite well established that such interest inventories as the *Strong Vocational Interest Blank* and the *Kuder Preference Record* yield measures of interests that are reasonably stable if obtained beyond the early high-school years. Interest scores discriminate fairly well between men in various occupations and between men satisfied or dissatisfied with their occupations. It has been shown that interest scores obtained from college students on the Strong Blank were quite effective in predicting actual occupational area almost 20 years later. Interest inventories have shown, however, small predictive value for occupational success, for success in vocational training, or for academic grades, and the fact that interest can be "faked" makes the prospect unfavorable for the usefulness of interest measures in competitive selection situations. From uncertain evidence it appears that the use of such measures can be made to enhance the prediction of academic or vocational success, though this remains to be proved. Factor analysis of the Strong blank and the development of inventories based on factor analysis such as the *Kuder Preference Record* and the *Guilford-Schneideman-Zimmerman Interest Survey* have promoted progress in the growth of a theory of interests. The *Kuder* and the *Guilford* inventories exemplify efforts to obtain scores relevant to areas of interests such as "outdoor," "mechanical," "linguistic," and so on, rather than for specific vocational fields. Interest inventories show promise as means of assessing certain other aspects of personality, but much research is needed before such use can be made with assurance.

In the school situation, interest inventories are especially useful in counseling students, not for the purpose of identifying some specific vocation for which the student should prepare, but as a means of helping the student better to understand himself. (See chap. vii.)

A reading of reviews of self-report personality inventories in successive volumes of the *Mental Measurements Yearbook* offers only very limited support for the generalization that there has been "some" success in increasing the validity of such instruments. Even in the *Fifth Yearbook* (1959) such comments as "the total impression is that adequate validity has not been demonstrated," "no evidence of predictive validity is presented," and "the reviewer at this time can see no good reason why a test user should want to obtain the scores" occur with distressing frequency. Also distressingly frequent are adverse criticisms of the techniques used in obtaining validity data and condemnations of exaggerated claims for validity—some such claims approaching sheer dishonesty.[16] A number of reviewers are laudatory in their comments on the efforts made to develop self-report inventories on the basis of factor-analysis studies and in terms of personality theories, but Cronbach's comment in this connection is apt:

"There is at present no consensus among factor analysts as to the number of factors that have been reliably identified, the best organization of them, or their most appropriate names."[17]

In the development of self-report personality inventories there has been no lack of formulation of constructs pertaining to personality traits, but there has been a paucity of well-designed efforts toward construct validation. Even factor-analysis studies do not contribute much in cases in which factors derived from one study cannot be identified as the same factors in another study. Concurrent validation resulting in numerous correlations between scores obtained from various inventories contributes little or nothing if

16. *Fifth Mental Measurements Yearbook, op. cit.,* pp. 86-212.

17. Cronbach, *op. cit.,* p. 467.

the validity of none of the instruments has been satisfactorily established. Badly needed are defensible studies of predictive validity since the ultimate justification of such instruments is their effectiveness in predicting behavior.

The authors of this chapter agree with Cronbach that, in the hands of a competent counselor who is aware of the limitations of self-report inventories, such inventories as the following may be used to screen pupils in need of adjustment: The *Allport-Vernon-Lindzey Study of Values*, the *Billet-Starr Youth Problems Inventory*, the *Kuder Preference Record—Personal*, the *Mooney Problem Check Lists*, and the *SRA Youth Inventory*. More evidence on validity is needed with respect to the *California Personality Inventory*, the *California Test of Personality*, the *Edwards Personal Preference Schedule*, the *Gordon Personal Profile*, the *Gordon Personal Inventory*, the *Guilford-Zimmerman Temperament Survey*, and the *Minnesota Counseling Inventory* to justify their use even by well-trained counselors except in study of individual cases and in the collection of research data.[18] Certainly, the *Minnesota Multiphasic Personality Inventory* should be used only by those who have adequate training and experience in clinical psychology and who have thoroughly studied the conflicting evidence regarding its validity.

What has been said with reference to such nonprojective personality instruments as the *Minnesota Multiphasic* applies with possibly greater force to such projective techniques as the *Rorschach*, the *Thematic Apperception Test*, the *Bender-Gestalt Test*, and other such instruments. Study of reviews in recent volumes of the *Mental Measurements Yearbook*, the texts by Anastasi, Cronbach and Thorndike and Hagen referred to earlier, and other sources support the view that in general the validity of such instruments remains to be established.[19] Their use should definitely

18. *Ibid.*, pp. 495-99.

19. See reviews in recent volumes of the *Annual Review of Psychology* on such topics as "Assessment of Individual Differences," "Theory and Techniques of Assessment," and "Personality," or pertinent reviews in recent issues of the *Review of Educational Research* on "Educational and Psychological Testing." The reviews in these sources and the sources earlier cited, especially the *Mental Measurements Yearbook*, include extensive bibliographies.

be restricted to clinical psychologists and psychiatrists aware of their limitations and to research psychologists.

GENERALIZATION 4. *Aptitude and achievement tests have improved in reliability; advances have been made in methods of administering, scoring, and reporting of scores; norm data have become more adequate; and increasingly useful means have been supplied to facilitate interpretation of scores.*

Much more is known than formerly regarding the nature of test reliability, the factors contributing to reliability, and the techniques for estimating it.[20] The factors contributing to improved test reliability and, through improved reliability, to improved test validity include increased skill in exercise writing and editing prior to first use, systematic elimination or revision of items on the basis of item-analysis data, greater recognition of the fact that the reliability of a test increases with its length, more general acceptance of the necessity for three or four plausible distractors in each objective exercise, and greater realization that representative sampling of the universe of possible test items contributes both to reliability and validity. There is also more widespread understanding of the advantages and limitations of various types of reliability estimates, for example, test-retest with the same test form, test-retest with parallel or equivalent forms, and Kuder-Richardson or split-half Spearman-Brown techniques. Also better understood are the effect of speededness of tests and of heterogeneity of the group tested on the magnitude of reliability coefficients. Test-users should be especially suspicious of standardized tests whose manuals do not define the populations used in determining reliability coefficients nor specify the methods used in determining them.

There has been much improvement in the standardization of the more widely used aptitude and achievement tests and batteries.

---

20. For an introduction to the extensive literature on test reliability see: Anastasi, *op. cit.*, pp. 94-119; Lee J. Cronbach, "Test 'Reliability': Its Meaning and Determination," *Psychometrika*, XII (March, 1947), 1-16; Harold Gulliksen, *Theory of Mental Tests* (New York: John Wiley & Sons, 1950); Robert L. Thorndike "Reliability," in *Educational Measurement*, pp. 560-620 (Edited by E. F. Lindquist. Washington: American Council on Education, 1951); Thorndike and Hagen, *op. cit.*, pp. 174-94; and Robert C. Tryon, "Reliability and Behavior Domain Validity: Reformulation and Historical Critique," *Psychological Bulletin*, LIV (May, 1957), 229-49.

Modern techniques of stratified or cluster sampling are more often used than formerly in the establishment of norms. It is more generally recognized that the practice of obtaining norms on the basis of data voluntarily supplied by test-users is unacceptable. Examples of instruments that have utilized modern methods of establishing norms include the new *California Achievement Tests*, the new *Metropolitan Achievement Tests*, the *Sequential Tests of Educational Progress*, and the *School and College Ability Tests*. Also to be mentioned in this connection are the desirable trends toward increased utilization of deviation quotients, modal-grade norms, percentile ranks, stanines, and other types of derived scores in replacement of, or in addition to, the more usual grade-score norms. These trends have led to better interpretation of scores. More defensible interpretation is also being promoted by the increased emphasis on percentile bands in the case of single scores, and on profile distances equivalent to two standard errors of measurement in the case of differences between scores. Also helpful are the increasing efforts to include in test manuals explanations of score interpretation more easily understood by school administrators, teachers, and counselors.[21] In the norming of tests there should be fewer attempts to establish norms by equating new forms of tests with supposedly equivalent or parallel forms that were standardized a decade or more previously. Also needed are more widespread efforts to supplement national norms with local norms and the determination of the comparability of norms of the several tests and batteries that are used to measure much the same aptitudes or achievements.[22]

Photoelectric scoring of special answer sheets and the use of electronic computers now make possible extremely rapid and accurate scoring of objective tests and analysis of the scores as well as reporting of the data obtained in large scale testing programs. Such scoring and analysis is done at the Measurement Research Center at the State University of Iowa, the Educational Testing

21. There should be more booklets comparable to George K. Bennett and Others, *Counseling from Profiles*. New York: Psychological Corporation, 1951.

22. For an excellent discussion of matters briefly described above, see: John C. Flanagan, "Units, Scores, and Norms," in *Educational Measurement*, pp. 695-763 (Edited by E. F. Lindquist. Washington: American Council on Education, 1951); and Charles I. Mosier, "Batteries and Profiles," *op. cit.*, pp. 764-808.

Service in Princeton, and the Psychological Corporation in New York City. Similarly, the development by the International Business Machines Corporation of answer cards for use by pupils or students should expedite rapid and accurate scoring and analysis of tests or test data in local school systems and in higher institutions. Such scoring and analysis may gradually replace work now done by the older IBM scoring machines and should promote more widespread use and analysis of locally constructed objective achievement tests.[23] Unfortunately, in spite of extensive research conducted at the Educational Testing Service and elsewhere, not a great deal of progress has been made in achieving reliable scoring of essay examinations. Two investigators have published articles on the essay examination that should be read by all persons interested in this type of testing.[24] On the problem of reliable scoring of such tests, Findley has recently written that average ratings based on brief reading and global grading on a scale of 3 to 7 points by several readers may provide a breakthrough long awaited.

In concluding this discussion of ways in which tests have been improved, it seems appropriate to summarize the contributions made by such publications as *Technical Recommendations for Psychological Tests and Diagnostic Techniques* and *Technical Recommendations for Achievement Tests* and test reviews in editions of the *Mental Measurements Yearbook* and in other sources. In spite of occasional complaints by reviewers that defects mentioned in earlier reviews have not been remedied, the leading test publishers take very seriously the recommendations and critical comments presented in the aforementioned and other publications. It is evident that these publishers appreciate *competent* and *responsible* reviewing by authors who are informed about the tests and are objective

23. For a comprehensive discussion of the scoring of objective tests, including the more typical IBM machine scoring, see: Arthur E. Traxler, "Administering and Scoring the Objective Test," in *Educational Measurement*, pp. 329-416. Edited by E. F. Lindquist. Washington: American Council on Education, 1951.

24. Verner Martin Sims, "The Essay Examination Is a Projective Technique," *Educational and Psychological Measurement*, VIII (Spring, 1948), 15-31; and John M. Stalnaker, "The Essay Type of Examination," in *Educational Measurement*, pp. 495-530. Edited by E. F. Lindquist. Washington: American Council on Education, 1951.

in their evaluations. While valid criticisms are taken most seriously by test authors, test editors, and other specialists, consideration is also given to unfair criticism. The leading publishers try to make changes in the light of valid adverse criticism as soon as it is practicable to do so. Leading test publishers testify to the generally helpful impact of *Technical Recommendations* and test reviews on their practices in producing and in revising tests.[25]

How Can Better Tests Be Constructed?

RECOMMENDATION 1. *Achievement tests should be constructed in the light of carefully formulated operational definitions of instructional objectives.*

As mentioned earlier in this chapter, implementation of this recommendation is exemplified by the better achievement tests and achievement batteries. The evidence may be obtained by study of the tests in relation to information concerning objectives reported in their manuals.

The basic requirement in the construction of a good test is a definition of what is to be measured. This important step in test development has been discussed by numerous test experts. Probably the earliest comprehensive discussion and illustration of this step is to be found in an early work by Ralph Tyler.[26] His rationale, based on curriculum analysis, emphasizes the formulation of instructional objectives which are defined explicitly in terms of behavioral outcomes.

Other distinctive patterns of identifying and defining curricular objectives for purposes of measurement may be cited. Brownell

---

25. The above paragraph was written after careful reading of long and thoughtful letters received from B. E. Bergesen, Jr., of *Personnel Press*; Willis W. Clark of *California Test Bureau*; Robert Ebel of *Educational Testing Service*; Roger T. Lennon of *Harcourt Brace and World*; Harold T. Miller of *Houghton Mifflin Co.*; Harold Seashore of *Psychological Corporation*; and Lyle M. Spencer and Robert L. French of *Science Research Associates*.

26. Ralph W. Tyler, *Constructing Achievement Tests*, p. 110 (Columbus, Ohio: Ohio State University, 1934). For a critical discussion of operational definitions of instructional objectives in relation to the validity of achievement tests, see: Max D. Engelhart, "Operationally Defined Instructional Objectives in Relation to Validity," *Eighteenth Yearbook of the National Council on Measurement in Education*, pp. 15-21. (Ames, Iowa: Department of Psychology, Iowa State University, 1961).

and his yearbook committee described the measurement of understanding in twelve curriculum areas.[27] Kearney presented objectives in nine areas and at three levels as a basis for construction of achievement tests for the elementary school.[28] Another co-operative effort by a committee of college and university examiners, headed by Bloom, set forth six types of objectives in the "cognitive domain" with numerous examples of types of test exercises for the measurement of each objective.[29] Achievement exercises evaluating a wide range of instructional objectives in the natural sciences on the high-school and college levels are to be found in *Questions and Problems in Science*, a folio of over 13,000 items published by Educational Testing Service. There should be more such folios.

This approach to achievement-test construction requires considerably more thought and effort than the traditional plan involving a chapter-by-chapter analysis of a textbook until enough test items are written. Moreover, the results attending the first approach are readily observable in the better achievement tests—tests which emphasize the evaluation of understanding and intellectual skills, rather than recall of isolated facts.

A two-dimensional chart of content and behavioral objectives can profitably be used in the construction of achievement tests. In such a two-way grid, the subject or content aspects of the objectives are listed along one axis and the behavioral aspects of the objectives along the other. Such a technique is valuable to professional test-makers as well as to classroom teachers in developing test items and exercises designed to measure the defined outcomes of instruction. This procedure should be more widely and systematically used.

RECOMMENDATION 2. *There should be greater emphasis on measurement of understanding and other higher mental processes in achievement tests.*

27. *The Measurement of Understanding.* Forty-fifth Yearbook of the National Society for the Study of Education, Part I. Chicago: University of Chicago Press, 1946.

28. Nolan C. Kearney, *Elementary School Objectives.* New York: Russell Sage Foundation, 1953.

29. Benjamin S. Bloom and Others, *Taxonomy of Educational Objectives: Handbook I, Cognitive Domain.* New York: Longmans, Green & Co., 1956.

This recommendation can be implemented by writing tests according to specifications derived from formulations of instructional objectives which range from important elements of knowledge in a subject field through the intellectual skills and abilities to be developed by instruction in that field. It can also be promoted by developing wider teacher recognition of such ranges of objectives. Teachers should be trained to realize that intellectual skills cannot be evaluated unless exercises present novel problems. They should not react to such exercises with the comment, "We did not teach it that way." On the other hand, the background knowledge expected to contribute to the solution of such exercises should not be esoteric.

Until recently, most standardized achievement tests have emphasized rather strongly the purely informational goals of instruction. However, more and more tests now require the student to perform various mental tasks rather than only to recall learned facts. More frequent attempts are being made to measure achievement in previously unmeasured instructional objectives relating to nonrational behavior, artistic abilities, values, and attitudes; more tests are attempting to measure the general outcomes of instruction rather than content recall or specific skills narrowly defined. This approach to measurement, based upon a sound understanding of pupil growth and development, the nature of learning, and individual and group differences, calls for more widespread utilization of the requisite testing techniques. Progress toward attainment of this goal should be promoted by appropriate modifications in the training of teachers and other constructors of achievement tests.

Several theoretical models can be used to categorize the higher mental processes. The *Taxonomy of Educational Objectives*, mentioned earlier, provides a hierarchical classification of measurable educational objectives in the cognitive area. The six major categories are arranged in levels of varying complexity, ranging from the lowest category of knowledge to the higher levels of comprehension, application, analysis, synthesis, and evaluation. Each category, in turn, is divided into sub-categories on the basis of differences in student behavior. Illustrative test items are provided for each category. Another guide, demonstrating specific applications in the subject fields, may be found in the previously cited Forty-fifth

Yearbook of the National Society for the Study of Education, *The Measurement of Understanding.*

More research should be conducted on other than objective types of tests, particularly on the essay test, generally assumed by teachers to measure more desirable outcomes of education than objective tests. As Stalnaker has pointed out, the essay question is said to be especially suited to obtaining samples of the higher-order mental processes of the student—his ability to organize, to show critical judgment, to synthesize, and so on.[30] However, the values claimed for the essay test have not been definitely established. Since its potential values are great and since it continues to be used widely by the classroom teacher, further development and research should be undertaken to determine what unique contributions the essay test may be able to make to the measurement of instructional objectives.

RECOMMENDATION 3. *There should be more studies seeking a better understanding of the relationships between achievement test scores and the mental processes functioning in the attainment of the scores.*

Among the several kinds of studies which should receive greater emphasis should be those employing factor analysis in which achievement tests are given to students in conjunction with tests of various primary abilities. Another approach was developed by Bloom and Broder in their exploratory investigation of the problem-solving processes of college students. They demonstrated a means by which analysis can be made of mental processes rather than of mental products. These investigators are convinced that such studies of problem-solving processes are basic to the understanding of individual differences.[31] Similar studies should be conducted on all educational levels and in a variety of fields. Finally, relevant to this recommendation, there should be many more studies of the construct validity of achievement tests through experimentation involving instruction directed at varying instructional goals—the nomological net type of

30. Stalnaker, in *Educational Measurement, op. cit.,* pp. 510-15.

31. Benjamin S. Bloom and Lois J. Broder, *Problem-solving Processes of College Students.* Chicago: University of Chicago Press, 1950.

construct validation.[32] Construct validation should be especially useful in determining what variables account for scores on tests and for estimating the relative importance of these variables. Its contribution can be most valuable in studying the validity of measurement of such intangible outcomes of instruction as artistic judgment, reasoning abilities, personality and character traits, and personal-social adjustment.

RECOMMENDATION 4. *There should be more extensive use of established rules and principles of exercise writing.*

Many practical rules for the preparation of objective test exercises have been established on the basis of past experience and test experimentation. Discussions of the writing of test exercises are available in a number of texts on the use of tests in education. One of the best sources on the general requirements for writing test exercises is Ebel's chapter in *Educational Measurement*.[33] Also of considerable value to test-makers is the volume by Gerberich which includes a detailed classification of items according to types of learning outcomes to be measured.[34]

Another excellent discussion on the art of exercise writing in the college fields of humanities, natural sciences, and the social sciences is reported in the *1957 Invitational Conference on Testing Problems*, published by the Educational Testing Service.[35]

Discussions of exercise writing have been directed primarily toward the writing of achievement test items. While many of the

32. Clark presents an extensive resumé, drawn from 130 publications between 1946 and 1958, tracing developments and applications in the area of construct validity. See: Cherry Ann Clark, "Developments and Applications in the Area of Construct Validity," *Review of Educational Research*, XXIX (February, 1959), 84-100.

33. Robert L. Ebel, "Writing the Test Item," in *Educational Measurement*, pp. 185-249. Edited by E. F. Lindquist. Washington: American Council on Education, 1951. See also: Max D. Engelhart, "Suggestions for Writing Achievement Exercises To Be Used in Tests Scored on the Electric Scoring Machine," *Educational and Psychological Measurement*, VII (Autumn, 1947), 357-74.

34. J. Raymond Gerberich, *Specimen Objective Test Items*. New York: Longmans, Green & Co., 1956.

35. "Improving Measurement through Better Exercise Writing," *Proceedings of the 1957 Invitational Conference on Testing Problems*, pp. 35-69. Princeton, N. J.: Educational Testing Service, 1958.

suggestions and precautions enumerated also have application to the writing of items for aptitude and personality tests, there is little or nothing comparable specifically directed toward the writing of such items. It would indeed be a valuable contribution if examples of various types of aptitude items were classified in a manner comparable to the classification of items in the *Taxonomy* and were accompanied by discussions of the art of writing them. A similar recommendation could be made with reference to personality measurement.

RECOMMENDATION 5. *Tests should be built through exercise-selection from pools of exercises for which item analysis data are available.*

Nearly all literature on item analysis indicates its value as a means of improving tests. Item-analysis data make possible revisions of exercises, selection in terms of difficulty, and estimation of total score parameters. Such data may also be useful in providing a basis for defining levels of competence on a test and in improving the curriculum and instruction.

Various procedures have been devised for making item analyses. Despite the tendency toward the use of highly specialized statistical techniques, simplified methods have been developed to reduce the tallying and computational tasks and to make the procedure more comprehensible to the generally less technically prepared classroom teacher. For example, Findley has presented an easily obtained and readily understood discrimination index D. [36]

Even in the case of involved mathematical analysis, the long computation problem has been minimized by such devices as the Flanagan table and the Davis item analysis chart.[37] The graphic item counter of the IBM electric scoring machine has made item analysis

36. Warren G. Findley, "A Rationale for Evaluation of Item Discrimination Statistics," *Educational and Psychological Measurement*, XVI (Summer, 1956), 175-80.

37. John C. Flanagan, "General Considerations in the Selection of Test Items and a Short Method of Estimating the Product-Moment from the Data at the Tails of the Distribution," *Journal of Educational Psychology*, XXX (December, 1939) 674-80. See also: Frederick B. Davis, "Item-analysis Data: Their Computation, Interpretation, and Use in Test Construction," *Harvard Education Papers*, No. 2. Cambridge: Graduate School of Education, Harvard University, 1946.

much more easily performed where such equipment is available. With such equipment one can also readily obtain analyses for each distractor in objective exercises which have been shown to be non-discriminating in a prior analysis restricted to percentages of students in upper and lower groups giving correct responses.

The general use of factorial methods for item analysis should become the rule now that the further development of electronic computers has rendered them capable of extracting factors from large matrices of intercorrelations with a substantial saving in time.

RECOMMENDATION 6. *There should be more research on readability formulas to provide a suitable index of reading ease for different standardized tests.*

Thus far, little has been done to determine the reading level essential to understand the content of standardized testing material. The available findings indicate that many tests are being administered to pupils who do not comprehend them because the readability of the tests is too difficult. Researchers in this area contend that since test scores may differ due to varying reading abilities of students, knowledge of the readability level of the test is necessary to insure reasonably accurate test selection and interpretation.

The results of limited research in the measurement of test readability seem to justify further investigation. In one study of test readability, using the Flesch formula, the over-all readability of commonly used tests ranged from a grade level of 5.5 to 15.0. The selected tests varied in the relative reading difficulty of the test content and also in the directions given for taking the test. For example, the *Bell Adjustment Inventory* had a grade level of 7.0 in content and a grade level of 9.5 for test directions. In contrast, the *Strong Vocational Interest Blank* was placed at a grade level of 15.0 in content readability, while the directions for the test were rated at a grade level of 7.5.[38] However, to make the measurement of test readability feasible, research is needed to develop a reliable readability formula for tests which will yield an index of reading ease without being excessively time consuming.

38. Ralph H. Johnson and Guy L. Bond, "Reading Ease of Commonly Used Tests," *Journal of Applied Psychology,* XXXIV (October, 1950), 319-24.

RECOMMENDATION 7. *There should be concerted efforts in the development of better measures in the areas of aptitude and personality, especially for the prediction of success in a variety of fields.*

Essential technical recommendations, previously referred to, indicate that more efforts in test research and development should be directed to studies of predictive validity, construct validity, and cross-validation. In this connection, Michael cited a pressing need for improving communication links between psychologists and test specialists, and key personnel in schools, professions, civil services, business, industry, and organized labor. The constant exchange of ideas could lead to modifications in testing practices and result in a more meaningful evaluation of success in positions as well as basic changes in curricula and in specialized in-service training programs in industry and business.[39]

One study has demonstrated the possibility of improving the use of tests by discovering subgroups of individuals for which a particular test is especially effective. The findings indicated that such a method may not only permit more accurate predictions for members of the subgroups, but may reduce for other individuals of the group errors in prediction which are due to the use of a less-valid predictor. Although not regarded as entirely conclusive, the results do suggest possible advantages to be gained from this method of analysis.[40]

To provide counselors with specific information about the relation between test scores and success in various educational programs, Frederiksen recommended more local validity studies, provision in each local study for identification of the group and sufficient data to permit actual predictions, the development of expectancy tables, and the collection and publication of computing diagrams for translating predictor measures into predicted criterion scores in a wide variety of educational and vocational situations.[41]

39. William B. Michael, "Differential Testing of High-level Personnel," *Educational and Psychological Measurement*, XVII (Winter, 1957), 475-90.
40. Norman Frederiksen and S. Donald Melville, "Differential Predictability in the Use of Test Scores," *Educational and Psychological Measurement*, XIV (Winter, 1954), 647-56.
41. Norman O. Frederiksen, "Making Test Scores More Useful for Prediction," *Educational and Psychological Measurement*, XI (Winter, 1951), 783-87. See also chap. vii.

In the area of personality appraisal, the vast array of available instruments, projective and nonprojective, does not include a generally acceptable instrument. The search for adequate criterion data for establishing validity has been generally unsuccessful. Consequently, the acknowledged deficiencies have resulted in restricted application of personality tests. With few exceptions, inventory scores have failed generally to predict the future success of the individual either in school or on the job, or in his personal living. According to Krugman, the trend is away from attempts at omnibus or global measurement of personality and toward a specific examination of a limited sample of behavior in a specific situation. Meanwhile, recommendations are made for the utilization of the best available instruments as tools, to supplement case studies and observational techniques, rather than as goals.[42]

RECOMMENDATION 8. *There should be more research aimed at the development of a meaningful and effective rationale governing the imposition of time limits on test performance.*

There is no clear consensus of the extent to which test scores should be influenced by time limits or speed. In practice, the setting of time limits is too often a matter of administrative convenience determined by the length of class periods. The time-limit test has the advantage of serving to discourage idleness and time-wasting on the part of faster students, but speed is a legitimate element in achievement tests *only* when speed is an objective of the course.[43] Speeded tests have lowered validity for measuring the knowledge or intellectual skills of individual students since many able students are slow workers.

The trend in educational achievement testing is to minimize the speed factor. This is to be welcomed in the measurement of complex activities, such as those involving problem-solving or productive

42. Morris Krugman, "Changing Methods of Appraising Personality," *1956 Invitational Conference on Testing Problems,* pp. 48-57. Princeton, N.J.: Educational Testing Service.

43. Lee J. Cronbach, *Essentials of Psychological Testing,* pp. 221-23. New York: Harper & Bros., 1960. See also: "Symposium: The Effects of Time Limits on Test Scores," *Educational and Psychological Measurement,* XX (Summer, 1960), 221-74.

thinking. There should be research, however, to discover how best to measure those traits for which speed is a necessary aspect of ability. In certain areas, such as reading, arithmetic, and typewriting, the ability to work rapidly is a worthwhile objective.

Test-makers have a need for research to establish the amount of time to be set for different types of test material. There is an almost virgin field for research on the optimum rates of test administration in many subject fields and at different educational levels.

RECOMMENDATION 9. *There should be much greater effort to promote comparability of norms of "standardized" aptitude and achievement tests and to promote meaningful interpretations of test scores.*

There is increasing and widespread recognition of the necessity for determinations of the comparability of norms of tests presumably designed to measure the same aptitudes or achievements. Professional educational organizations such as the American Association of School Administrators and the North Central Association, deeply concerned with the multiplicity and overlapping of testing programs, urge comparability determinations as a means of reducing the amount of testing to which students are subjected. Within large school systems there is growing recognition that comparison of derived scores from one test to another or even from one subtest to another in an achievement battery are hazardous.[44]

A major step toward providing a basis for comparison of norms of different tests is "Project Talent." The research involved in this project is resulting in the development of "anchor" tests in most areas of aptitude and achievement which can be administered with other tests in the same areas in order that norms can be corrected for whatever differences are shown by the anchor tests.[45] Of course, it should be remembered that comparisons must take into account

44. Warren G. Findley, "Use and Interpretation of Achievement Tests in Relation to Validity," *Eighteenth Yearbook of the National Council on Measurement in Education, op. cit.,* pp. 23-34.

45. *Ibid.,* p. 28. For a brief description of "Project Talent," see: John C. Flanagan, "Project Talent: The First National Census of Aptitudes and Abilities," *Seventeenth Yearbook of the National Council on Measurement in Education,* pp. 37-44. Ames, Iowa: Department of Psychology, Iowa State University, 1960.

the probability that two tests designed to measure the same aptitude or ability may be measuring significantly different aptitudes or abilities.

Apart from the need for more effort to promote comparability of derived scores, there is need for greater effort to promote meaningful interpretation of scores, not only in terms of comparison of aptitudes or achievements of individual students or groups of students with national or local norms but also in terms of what the scores signify with reference to behavior or mental processes evaluated by tests presumed to measure the same functions. All too little is known concerning the relationships between behavior operating in the test situation and behavior in other than the test situation. For example, how well do arithmetic reasoning scores obtained from an objective test relate to pupil ability to solve the same kind of problems in other than the testing situation? If 63 per cent of the pupils in an eighth-grade class answer a multiple-choice exercise on compound interest correctly, what per cent of the same class could help their fathers determine the total cost of buying a car after borrowing the money to do so?

As has been indicated earlier, much has been accomplished in aiding teachers and counselors to interpret scores through the development of stanines, percentile bands, and rules for interpretation of score differences as exemplified by rules relating to the *DAT* profiles. These developments should be promoted. Also needed is more dissemination of information to teachers and counselors on how to interpret growth in achievement where students are tested at intervals with equivalent or higher forms of the same tests or test batteries. The measurement of growth is a much more difficult problem than many test-users realize.[46] More should be written about this problem for the less sophisticated reader.

In What Directions Should Test Development Be Promoted?

The foregoing recommendations represent the major areas to be considered in further improvement of tests, dealing primarily with

46. Fredric M. Lord, "The Measurement of Growth," *Educational and Psychological Measurement*, XVI (Winter, 1956), 421-37. See also: Quinn McNemar, "On Growth Measurement," *Educational and Psychological Measurement*, XVIII (Spring, 1958), 47-55.

such aspects of test quality as validity, reliability, norms, and other means of interpreting scores. But there are also external problems which must be solved in order to insure the development of more effective tests and testing programs. These problems are crucial in the present "boom" period of standardized testing in a test-conscious nation. They are, to a large extent, found in the area of test utilization—a serious weakness of current testing.

To some extent the problems of test utilization are related to limited test selection in both the qualitative and quantitative sense. In view of evaluative concepts based on an increasingly comprehensive appraisal of the individual, more standardized achievement tests should be produced in the important elementary, high-school, and college fields. In particular, there is a dearth of acceptable tests in the subject fields of art, music, health education, and physical education, which constitute a substantial part of the curriculum in Grades I to XII. Perhaps even more apparent is the greater inadequacy of methods and techniques used in the measurement of nonintellectual factors. Much more experimentation should be devoted to the creation of dependable instruments for the measurement of interests, attitudes, values, and temperament. Improving the quality and scope of measurement in these areas would make the task of test selection much less hazardous.

Aside from proposed developments in testing programs, test utility in general would stand to benefit from a co-operative plan to develop competence in the use and interpretation of test data by teachers, guidance counselors, and administrative personnel. The extensive advances in psychometric theory and test construction have widened the prevailing communication gap between test specialists and test-users. Studies have demonstrated that counselors, principals, and teachers have encountered considerable difficulty in understanding test manuals, in selecting appropriate tests, and in interpreting test performance.[47]

For the most part the problem of communication reflects the lack of agreement among test specialists concerning answers to practical questions raised by school personnel. It would be desirable

47. Roger B. Allison, Jr. and Gerald C. Helmstadter, "Communicating Test Information in a Test Manual," *Journal of Counseling Psychology*, XXXVII (June, 1953), 185-90.

for test experts to devise more comprehensible manuals in addition
to simplifying and standardizing basic information for test consumers. But the unsophisticated user of tests presents still other
problems in communication. There is, for example, the naïve belief
among many teachers that the very publication of a test is its badge of
excellence with respect to construction, validation, and standardization. Too many teachers also share the view that the absolute value
of a test score is far more significant than its relation to scores of
other pupils. Probably the most serious misconception is the one
that has led teachers to believe that tests are not only unnecessary
but detrimental to education. By and large, the misuses of and mis-
conceptions in testing, whatever their source, may be traced to a
lack of formal preparation in educational measurement. Surveys
of teacher-training institutions reveal that only a small percentage
require a measurements course of all undergraduates preparing to
teach. An equally small percentage of the states specify any required course in educational measurement for certification.[48]

The APA, AERA, and NCME committees on test standards have
recognized the importance of co-operative efforts to expand and
improve courses in measurement and to develop professional leadership among school staffs. With this in mind, Durost proposed the
appointment of a committee on the training of test-users. Such a
committee would undertake to (a) consider content and method in
undergraduate and graduate courses in measurement; (b) consider
means to be used to persuade state educational bodies to include
courses in measurement as prerequisites for teacher certification;
(c) consider ways to publicize information on superior practices in
testing currently in use; (d) consider minimum programs of instruction for specialists in test utilization as contrasted to test construction
and statistical method; and (e) consider projects to outline and
produce "how to do" materials that will make in-service education
more effective.[49]

48. Victor H. Noll, "Requirements in Educational Measurement for Prospective Teachers," *School and Society*, LXXXII (September 17, 1955), 88-90.

49. Walter N. Durost, "Present Progress and Needed Improvements in
School Evaluation Programs," *Educational and Psychological Measurement*,
XIV (Summer, 1954), 247-54.

Changes implied by the foregoing list of suggestions are essential to the improvement of test utilization. It is urgent that professional organizations initiate programs and provide the leadership for promotion and organization of in-service education as a pivotal point in developing the required competences in the use of tests. National organizations, such at the APA, AERA, and NCME, could make the goal attainable by establishing local associations, at least in urban centers, to render service through sponsoring discussions and participating in the in-service programs, workshops, and institutes.

Apart from what they can accomplish through in-service training programs, test specialists can be instrumental in the improvement of testing by directing greater efforts to the critical appraisal of the construction, validation, and use of published tests. As yet these appraisals do not provide sufficiently trustworthy information on many of the growing number of tests on the market. Since 1938, succeeding editions of *Mental Measurements Yearbook* (Buros) have been a dependable source of expert opinion to guide consumers in the selection of tests. However, the compilation of critical test reviews has certain shortcomings. Critical reviews are often restricted to the judgment of one or two persons. They are written by persons of varying training and experience. The reviewer may be biased with respect to the type of testing—for example, an exponent of projective tests of personality may be asked to review a nonprojective one. Some reviewers denounce various details of a test, but conclude in favor of the test as a whole. A review may not solve the problem of selecting a test for some specific purpose inherent in a local situation. Many reviews are fragmentary and do not cover all of the important aspects which should be discussed. Other reviews are too technical for all but the test specialist. Of course, some of the weaknesses, e.g., fragmentary reviews and reviews that are too technical, can be corrected. On the whole, it would appear that most of the serious weaknesses would be extremely difficult to eliminate even in a co-operative test-reviewing project. What is needed, and has been advocated by test specialists and test-users, including Buros, is an independent fact-finding and test-evaluation agency which would be able to weed out inferior tests and act in an advisory and selective capacity. It is difficult to justify current publication of tests by publishers who do not strive to satisfy the standards set forth in *Technical Standards*. A test bureau or organization, perhaps co-operatively sponsored by professional groups in measurement, could make a rigorous application of the adopted standards and assure the consumer that the approved instrument has the essential qualities for a designated purpose.

In conclusion, it may be said that much has been accomplished to improve the quality of tests and their application, but much remains to be done. The more urgent problems which require attention are problems dealing with such basic aspects of test quality as validity, reliability, norms, and other means of interpreting test scores. Of major concern, too, are the problems related to test usage, test evaluation, and teacher preparation in educational measurement. In these respects, the immediate years appear most promising. The widespread emphasis on testing and guidance should lead to new developments in test theory and to greater efficiency of measurement. A hopeful sign of progress is evident in the increasing multiplicity of testing programs that are accompanied by efforts to educate test-users in the better understanding of the purposes, characteristics, and interpretation of tests.

CHAPTER IX

The Impact of External Testing Programs

RALPH W. TYLER

American school administrators are currently interested and concerned with the effects upon the high schools of the great increase in pupil participation in external testing programs. Indicative of this interest and concern was the establishment in 1959 of the Joint Committee on Testing of the American Association of School Administrators, the Council of Chief State School Officers, and the National Association of Secondary School Principals. Furthermore, at its annual meeting in 1960, the North Central Association of Colleges and Secondary Schools directed its Committee on Articulation of High Schools and Colleges to make a study of current practices and problems in testing required of students in NCA high schools by external agencies and institutions. It has prepared two reports on external testing and is continuing its study. This is at present a subject of serious discussion at numerous professional meetings.

Defining an External Testing Program

The Joint Committee on Testing [1] defines external tests "as those tests which are initiated by, or sponsored by, one or more agencies or organizations outside the local school district." This definition makes most published tests "external" since most tests are initiated by authors or publishers outside the local school district. If this definition were applied to other school materials, then textbooks, laboratory equipment, and most teaching aids would be external. A further perusal of the Joint Committee's report indi-

---

1. *Testing, Testing, Testing*, p. 8. Report of the Joint Committee on Testing, National Education Association. Washington: National Education Association, 1962.

cates that this sweeping definition is not the one actually used in focusing most of its discussion.

The North Central Association's Committee on Articulation [2] defines external tests as "those which are used primarily by some institution or organization other than the high school, and those over which the local school has or feels it has no real choice as to whether its students take these tests." This definition is a much more meaningful one than that formulated by the Joint Committee on Testing. The North Central Association's Committee definition sets up two criteria for tests to be external—their primary use and their control. Tests which are used primarily by other institutions and organizations and thought to be controlled by others are the tests about which high schools are particularly concerned. These include the tests of the College Entrance Examination Board, the battery of the American College Testing Program, the *National Merit Scholarship Qualifying Examinations*, the tests used in state-wide testing programs, and most of those used in connection with college admissions and the award of college scholarships.

Problems of External Testing as Seen by School Administrators

Since 1950, external testing programs have increased tremendously both in magnitude and scope. Several of the national programs test more than 300,000 pupils and, taken together, are including a majority of American high schools. As an example of widening scope, the College Entrance Examination Board, originally an organization of a few colleges, mostly on the eastern seaboard, is now testing some students in all of the states. This rapid growth has been largely due to four factors: the great increase in college enrolments, which has required many colleges to select the number of students it can take from a larger number of applicants; an increase in the incomes of many families, which has made it possible for them to support the education of their children in colleges at some distance away where the local high schools are not

2. *North Central Association Today*, p. 1. Chicago: North Central Association of Colleges and Secondary Schools, August, 1961.

well-known to the college; a considerable increase in scholarship funds, providing opportunities for high-school students throughout the nation to apply; and the invention and utilization of electronic methods of scoring and reporting, which have greatly reduced the cost of centralized testing programs. Although each of these developments is a good thing, many schools were unprepared for them, and the resulting effects upon the schools have, in many cases, created problems.

PRESSURE TO PARTICIPATE

The problem which was first recognized by high-school administrators was that they were put, or thought they were put, under pressure to participate in some of the external programs before they had studied them or developed relevant policies regarding them. For example, a high school in Pennsylvania, from which only one or two graduates per year had previously gone away to college, was surprised in 1956 to have 32 students wanting to take college-entrance examinations. Later, leading parents in the community urged the principal to arrange for giving the *National Merit Scholarship Qualifying Examination*. In the questionnaire given by the Joint Committee on Testing to a probability sample of high-school administrators, 12 per cent replied that they felt under pressure from the community to participate in one or more national or state testing programs.

USE OF RESULTS FOR INVIDIOUS COMPARISONS

Another problem which is particularly irritating to the high schools arises from the use by others of results from a testing program to make unfavorable comparisons and to draw unfair conclusions about the quality of the schools. Some schools give publicity to scholarship winners as they do to athletic winners. For example, at a high-school commencement in a California city recently, the principal announced that his school this year had more winners of college scholarships and more students who "qualified" for college admission than any other high school in that area. This was picked up by the state newspapers to the great discomfort of other principals in the area.

It is common practice for an individual school or school system to give tests in order to compare the performance of its students on these tests with the performance of students from other schools. More than half of the school administrators responding to the Joint Committee's questionnaire said that they used external test results to compare their schools with other schools, and a similar number reported that they used the results of external tests to interpret their schools to the public. It is helpful to gain some perspective of student performance in one's own school by comparing it with the performance in other schools. It becomes offensive to other schools when publicity is given to the lower performance of other schools in comparison to the school making the report. It is misleading if the school making the study selects other schools for comparison that are not essentially comparable or when the test results used do not reflect student performance on goals to which the schools involved have been justifiably giving serious attention.

INFLUENCE ON THE SECONDARY SCHOOL

A third problem voiced by school people is indicated by their fear that external tests will exert an undue influence on the secondary school, particularly on the curriculum and the instructional program. Thirteen per cent of the school administrators who returned the questionnaire to the Joint Committee on Testing reported that they believed that the external testing programs in which they participated were having an undesirable influence on what was being taught in their schools and on how it was being taught. Some said that their teachers were coaching students on test materials rather than following the curriculum. On the other hand, a great majority of the administrators responding to the questionnaire said that this was no problem. They chose tests and participated in testing programs to serve their own educational purposes.

Another type of influence on the secondary school mentioned by some school principals is the greater emphasis most test programs give to college admission and to the college-bound student, with a resulting neglect of appropriate tests for appraising and guiding the progress of students not planning on going to college.

The extent to which this influence is felt by school administrators was not determined in the study of the Joint Committee.

EFFECTS ON THE EMOTIONAL STABILITY OF PUPILS

A fourth problem is mentioned by the Joint Committee but not in the North Central reports. The report, *Testing, Testing, Testing*,[3] raises the question: "Is the emphasis on test results having harmful effects on the emotional stability and mental health of pupils?" The questionnaire did not provide information on this point, so that the extent to which this is seen as a problem by school administrators is not known. This would be relevant to the influence of external testing programs in so far as participation in such programs gave greater emphasis to test results than resulted from the local school's testing program.

TIME DEVOTED TO TESTING

A fifth problem is that of the time devoted to external testing. In the replies to the Joint Committee's questionnaire, only 7 per cent of the school administrators considered this to be a problem. Most of them reported that external tests were given on Saturday or at off-hours. The NCA Committee comments as follows:

It is true that high-school students now spend much more time taking tests than they did a few years ago. However, the actual amount of school time used for external tests is relatively small as compared with the time used for other out-of-class activities by the average student during a school year. Such testing, of course, also makes heavy demands on school administrators and counselors. However, it appears that at least part of the current stress is caused by the adding of external test programs without any reduction of the school's internal test programs.[4]

DUPLICATION OF TESTING

A sixth problem is one of duplication of testing. According to the report of the Joint Committee: "College-bound pupils in one state take five tests during the eleventh and twelfth grades, and

3. *Testing, Testing, Testing, op. cit.*, p. 6.

4. *North Central Association Today, op. cit.*, p. 2.

any one of them would tell as much about their scholarship as any other one." [5] However, only 9 per cent of the school administrators responding to the Committee's questionnaire reported duplication of testing as a serious problem. The NCA Committee reports: "It is generally agreed that the recent mushrooming of external testing has resulted in considerable duplication of testing." [6] The most common type of duplication grows out of the desire of the student (or that of his parents for him) to qualify for admission in several colleges and universities, not all of which are using the same admission testing program. Some colleges have their own unique admission tests, but the number is rapidly diminishing as colleges continue to join a state, regional, or national program. Some states have their own unique testing programs for college admission, but these too are disappearing as the states become affiliated with regional or national programs. Of the latter, there are two major programs, that of the College Entrance Examination Board and the American College Testing Program.

The second most common type of duplication grows out of the student's desire to qualify for scholarship aid on two or more programs. Scholarship tests unique to an individual college are largely disappearing as the colleges have learned to use the results of national, regional, or state testing programs. The unique state programs are also disappearing as states join in national programs. The special scholarship tests selected and administered by commercial and industrial donors are also being eliminated as these donors join programs like that of the National Merit Scholarship Corporation. At the present time there are three major testing programs for scholarship purposes which operate nationally. It is possible for the same high-school student to take three national scholarship tests and two national admission tests, although this occurs infrequently. It is this possibility which makes the problem of duplication loom large in the minds of some school administrators.

5. *Testing, Testing, Testing, op. cit.*, p. 14.
6. *North Central Association Today, op. cit.*, p. 2.

COST OF TESTING

A seventh problem is one of cost. According to the Joint Committee on Testing:

Taking tests costs money. This is one more item that adds weight to the observation that public education is not as free to the pupil and parent as many persons assume it to be. In some cases the cost of testing alone adds an appreciable financial burden to families of low or modest means, and testing represents no small investment for some school districts.[7]

In spite of this view of the Committee, only 2 per cent of the school administrators responding to the Committee's questionnaire considered the cost a serious problem. Perhaps most school administrators took the view expressed by Womer, of the University of Michigan, who wrote:

Another practical objection that is sometimes raised to external testing is that it costs too much money. NMSQT costs $1.00; PSAT costs $1.00; CEEB costs $5.00 for SAT and $8.00 for the Achievement Tests, and ACT costs $3.00. This is a total of $18.00 if all four tests are taken. This is a fair amount of money, it is true. But consider for a moment how many school pictures, name cards, and graduation announcements one can buy for $18.00. Or consider what portion of the cost of a class ring could be covered for that amount of money. How much money is "too much" is a relative decision.[8]

The North Central Committee defined the problem of cost in a broader context in its second report. It stated:

Additional testing will inevitably increase the costs of education to the student, the school, and the college. The costs of providing a better education for students through measuring the individual differences more exactly and selecting their educational experiences more efficiently can be justified. Costs that accrue through excessive or unwise participation in external testing are indefensible.[9]

CONTROL OF TESTING PROGRAMS

The eighth problem, and the last in this list, is one that is rarely stated directly. This is the problem of the control of external test-

7. *Testing, Testing, Testing, op. cit.*, p. 15.
8. Frank B. Womer, "Pros and Cons of External Testing Programs," *North Central Association Quarterly*, XXXVI, (Fall, 1961), 204.
9. *North Central Association Today, op. cit.*, p. 2.

ing programs. It is implied by the report of the Joint Committee which states:

In the United States considerable responsibility for administering the schools is assumed by the local community. This insures that the school will meet local, as well as national, needs; it provides the people of a community with the continuous challenge of taking part in the education of their children and youth. . . . Nowhere in the world have democracy and education been so closely identified. Large-scale external testing programs may detrimentally impinge upon this relationship. There is evidence that this is occurring.[10]

The NCA Committee expresses this problem in the following words:

Many school people feel strongly that the colleges in general have failed to consult the high schools when making plans for external testing and that such precipitous actions have great impact on the schools. They also feel that many colleges are requiring tests before they are prepared to make effective use of the test results, or even to use constructively the test scores which schools already furnish.[11]

Whatever may be the wording used in published reports, some school administrators express their views orally that there should be no program of any sort involving the schools in which school representatives are not included in the direction, planning, and administration. Since all of the current major external testing programs have school representatives on advisory bodies, it seems clear that the problem is one of control. Some administrators believe that all external testing programs should be under their control, either wholly or partially.

Resolving These Problems

The eight problems outlined above are not equally important, nor are they equally real. In one sense, if a person believes that a situation presents a problem to him, it is a real problem to him even though an objective analysis of the situation would show that what he believed did not actually exist. However, from the standpoint of improving the constructive use of external testing in the

10. *Testing, Testing, Testing, op. cit.,* p. 28.

11. *North Central Association Today, op. cit.,* p. 2.

schools, it makes a great difference whether attention should be focused on the external situation or on personal attitudes and beliefs, or on both.

HANDLING PRESSURES TO PARTICIPATE

In the case of the first problem listed above, the pressure on the high-school principal to participate in external testing programs, there is no doubt that an increasing number of high-school students and their parents are asking for the opportunity to take college admission tests and to compete for scholarship funds. Reluctance on the part of the high-school principal to become involved in these testing programs may lead to pressure from some students and parents to participate. On the other hand, a principal who wants to encourage greater interest in higher education on the part of students and parents may stimulate their desire to take part and will be pleased to see larger numbers involved. Whether this is a problem depends on the administrator's attitude. This may explain the report of the North Central Committee that many school people feel under considerable pressure whereas others do not feel undue pressure and make their own decisions about student participation in external testing. This does not appear to be a major problem requiring action at the national or state level. As the NCA Committee suggests: "Clearly each high school must formulate and apply a set of criteria and policies which will keep such participation in external testing at an appropriate and desirable level." [12]

ELIMINATING INVIDIOUS COMPARISONS

In the case of the second problem, a sufficient number of incidents in which unfavorable comparisons were made have been reported to justify the identification of this as a real problem. However, in the cases examined, it was not the external test organization which made the comparisons, but, rather, certain schools which published the information to put them in a favorable light in comparison with other schools. This is a problem which can be dealt with by state, regional, or national organizations of school adminis-

12. *North Central Association Today, op. cit.*, p. 2.

trators. These organizations need to set up guiding principles and procedures for reporting test scores and scholarship awards which will reduce invalid and invidious comparisons to a minimum.

USING TESTING TIME CONSTRUCTIVELY

Before considering the third and fourth problems at greater length, the fifth, sixth, and seventh problems can be discussed more briefly. In the case of the fifth problem, the use of time for external tests, both the responses to the Joint Committee questionnaire and the results of the North Central inquiry indicate that most of the student time is on Saturdays or on off-hours. Student time devoted to the tests is small compared to the hours devoted to extracurricular activities, social affairs, TV and radio listening. The staff time used is a more significant matter, particularly if the results are studied and then interpreted and discussed with students. This will be viewed as a serious problem in schools for which the information provided by the tests is not employed as part of the guidance process, or as an aid to the further education of students. The solution to the problem is the development of a comprehensive program of guidance and testing which is appropriate to the purposes and conditions of the local school. Such a program will include participation only in external testing which contributes to the local program. Time used in such external testing is time used to further the school's own purposes.

REDUCING DUPLICATION OF TESTING

In the sixth problem, the desirable solution is the elimination of unnecessary duplication. This is not likely to mean that a school will be involved in only one testing program for college admissions and scholarships. Colleges do differ in the effectiveness with which they can serve students with different characteristics. For example, the information about students most helpful in estimating how well Princeton would serve them is different in some respects from the information most helpful in estimating how well the State University of Iowa would serve them. At present, the admission tests used in these two universities are different and, to a certain extent, these differences reflect the different kinds of information needed. As research continues, these admission tests will probably become more different. This will reflect further knowledge about the differences in the educational processes at different institutions; further knowledge about the characteristics of students, which are significant in their responses to different kinds of educational situations; and further development of testing technology.

A second reason for believing in the desirability of at least two programs in any area is the efficiency stimulated by competition. Since the establishment of a second national program of testing for college admission, the prices have been reduced, and the services provided have been markedly increased.

After recognizing the desirability of two or more programs, we must not lose sight of the need to eliminate unnecessary duplication. A good deal of this has already taken place as individual colleges have substituted state, regional, or national tests for their own unique ones, and as state programs have joined in regional or national ones. The same trend is obvious in scholarship programs. The development of so-called equivalency tables for translating scores of one test into scores of another will be of some use in reducing duplication, but in so far as the tests focus on different characteristics and are standardized on different types of populations the translation of scores has little meaning.

The state and regional organizations, which include both schools and colleges, are serving as effective agents for the study of the problems of duplication and the working out of arrangements to eliminate unnecessary overlapping of external testing. The NCA Committee on Articulation is an excellent example of a constructive approach to this and to other types of problems which involve the relationship of schools and colleges.

COVERING THE COST OF TESTING

In the case of the seventh problem, the number of school administrators who view the cost of external testing as a serious situation is very small. With the development of electronic methods and large-scale programs, schools and colleges are now able to get a large amount of information very rapidly at a small fraction of the cost required a few years ago. For example, the scoring, analysis, and reporting of the battery of tests used in the Eight-Year Study of the 1930's cost about $27 per pupil. Similar tasks can now be done on a large scale at a cost of less than $7 per pupil. Testing programs today are relatively less expensive than ever before.

Those who see a serious cost-problem in external testing may be posing the issue in terms of who should pay the cost of testing for college admissions or for scholarships. Some may argue that all testing is part of instruction and guidance; therefore, the school should cover this cost, as it does other costs of instruction and administration. Others may argue that the colleges or the scholarship donors should pay these costs. In these days when schools and colleges are having difficulty in obtaining adequate financial resources, it is unlikely that they will choose to cover costs which can be borne by the students or the parents. However, schools in poorer areas would face a real problem in that participation in desirable testing programs would be seriously reduced if parents in these areas were required to meet the cost of such a program. Some have found that special funds can be raised by civic organizations to defray the costs of testing, and, in some cases, the school district has provided the needed money.

The problem of cost of testing for scholarship donors is a part of the problem of keeping the cost of administration of scholarship programs as low as is compatible with doing a good job so that scholarship recipients will receive the largest possible share of the resources available. Many scholarship donors seek to open the competition for scholarship aid to as wide a group as possible. But, each additional thousand students permitted to compete adds to the cost of testing an amount which is nearly equivalent to the cost of a full-expense scholarship. Hence, the decision is commonly made to ask each of those who wishes to compete to pay a few dollars rather than to reduce the number of scholarships which can be provided those who qualify on the basis of ability and need. Certain schools, in which the economic level of the homes makes it impossible for some promising scholarship candidates to pay the cost of participation in scholarship testing, are following the same practice in obtaining funds for scholarship testing as they are for college admission and guidance testing.

THE INFLUENCE OF TESTING ON THE SCHOOL

Returning to the third problem, the possibility that external tests will exert an undue influence on the secondary school, particularly on the curriculum and instructional program, there are only a few studies which provide data on the impact of external testing programs separate from the impact of tests, whether they be external or conducted by the school. The use of testing to influence students is a long-established practice. Teachers have often been classified by their pupils as "tough" or "soft" in terms of the frequency and searching character of their examinations. Well-motivated students have commonly put extra time and effort into their study when they thought they were soon to be tested. Quite probably, too, pupils having great difficulty in their school work felt even more incompetent when confronted with a test and, because it seemed too difficult, were not stimulated thereby to study more effectively. These differential effects of testing on students, whether external or internal, have been mentioned in the literature of teaching since the earliest years of publication.

As early as the 1930's, an investigation [13] provided evidence that student achievement is likely to parallel more closely the objectives of external tests than those of the local school, and that teachers, aware of the objectives of external tests, are most likely to emphasize learnings related to the objectives of such tests rather than to those related to local objectives. Interviews with a sample of teachers in sixty-one communities revealed the fact that most of them were conscious of the objectives being tested in the *Regents' Examinations* and sought to emphasize these kinds of learning in their classes rather than to follow the objectives recommended in the local curriculum guides.

My own experience in the Eight-Year Study corroborated these findings. When new ideas regarding the secondary-school curriculum were advanced, we always found teachers raising the question of the relationship of these new proposals to the achievements which were being appraised by the College Entrance Examination

13. See Wrightstone's comment in chap. iii (p. 54) on the *Regents' Inquiry into the Character and Cost of Public Education in New York State.*

Board tests. Only through the arrangement worked out with colleges which permitted high-school graduates to be considered for admission on the basis of scholastic aptitude tests and test data submitted by the schools in the Eight-Year Study were we able to get thoughtful consideration by the teachers of new curriculum proposals. Many were then able to shift from their previous practice of planning their teaching to correspond with their view of what would be required of their students on college-entrance tests to planning based on judgments of the educational values of various kinds of learning.

Fortunately, since the Eight-Year Study and, perhaps, as a result of it, the major external testing programs for college admission and for scholarship purposes do not include tests which emphasize specific objectives widely different from the objectives approved by the leaders of secondary education. The student performance measured in these tests largely includes vocabulary, reading, interpretation, and analysis of situations and problems presented in the tests, and mathematical exercises. There is no longer an emphasis upon the recall of specific items of information characteristic of the college-entrance tests and the *Regents' Examinations* of thirty years ago. Hence, if the school staff members were very familiar with the major external tests, they would not find it necessary to deflect their teaching in undesirable directions in order to teach what the tests measure.

But in spite of the great changes in the nature of these tests, coaching for tests is still prevalent in some schools. Coaching is most likely to be found in schools enrolling children whose parents greatly value admission to certain highly selective colleges, and who have not themselves attended these colleges.

It is hardly necessary to point out here that research evidence clearly indicates that coaching for scholastic aptitude tests and tests of general educational development quickly reaches a point of diminishing return; coaching in contrast to long-term instruction in the abilities measured by these tests produces only small improvements in test scores. However, the belief in the efficacy of coaching produces the undesirable practices, even though this belief is invalid.

REDUCING TEST ANXIETY

Before discussing steps which may help to deal with the impact of external tests on the school, attention might be given to the fourth problem, which is closely related to the third. It is sometimes claimed that testing creates undue anxiety on the part of pupils, who anticipate difficulties or inadequacies of test performance at the level to which they aspire. This emotional tension, it is charged, not only interferes with successful performance on the test but also increases the pupil's preoccupation with self-criticism and distracts his attention from schoolwork generally, thus lowering the effectiveness of his learning. A related criticism is that test scores are often seen by parents and children as ends in themselves in the competition to do better than their neighbors and to rise in the scale of social esteem. This obsession with getting high test scores attaches motivation to an external criterion rather than aiding the student to find satisfactions in learning and to become motivated to continue study and inquiry under his own steam. The extent to which these criticisms are valid has not been established by comprehensive empirical studies, but there is enough case material to justify the conclusion that, for some undetermined number of children, the anticipation of taking a test sets off an anxiety mechanism and that some parents use the results of tests as a basis for rewarding or punishing children beyond the limits of common practice of teachers. It also seems clear from available cases that, for many pupils and teachers, test performance is viewed as the major end of school instruction rather than being a useful but not infallible indicator of student achievement.

These effects of testing apply to all tests which are thought by pupils, teachers, and parents to be important, whether or not they are external tests. The procedure used to diminish undesirable emotional reactions to other tests apply to external tests. One helpful practice is to use similar tests throughout the instructional program and to review with the students their performance on each test. This reduces markedly the likelihood that the novelty of the test will affect the pupil's performance on it. This practice also diminishes the emotional tension surrounding testing. Testing becomes a natural part of the total learning process rather than an infrequent and traumatic experience. Tests, properly selected so that pupils who take them are able to demonstrate what abilities they have and what they have learned as well as what they have still to master, can help build confidence in taking tests rather than arouse anxiety.

POLICIES TO INCREASE VALUES IN TESTING

Because all testing, internal and external, has potentialities for both good and bad, general testing policies are needed that are likely to achieve the maximum good potential and to minimize or eliminate the bad. The problem cannot be met by advising schools to eliminate or to cut down sharply on their testing. The need, by the schools themselves as well as by colleges and scholarship donors, for more objective appraisals of pupil abilities and achievements is increasingly being recognized, and the use of tests is increasing sharply. External testing programs will continue, and the problem to be faced is how to improve them and derive the greatest benefit from them.

For the local school, the solution to the problem is to develop its own comprehensive testing program which serves the local school purposes, including the provision of opportunities for high-school pupils to participate in those external testing programs which aid the students in continuing their own education, or aid the pupils and their parents in making intelligent decisions about further education, or aid the school in gaining information relevant to its purposes. The school administrators who reported in the Joint Committee's questionnaire that they had developed a comprehensive school testing program also indicated that they had no serious problems with external testing programs. The next chapter discusses in some detail the procedures helpful in planning, developing, and administering a school testing program.

The colleges and scholarship donors can contribute to the solution of the problem by giving careful consideration to the impact on the schools of the external testing programs in which they are involved. Sometimes, they have planned programs solely in terms of their own interests and convenience. By taking into account, first, the educational interests of students and, then, the impact on the schools, the plans developed in these external testing programs are likely to be most helpful to the schools and most easily integrated into each school's own testing program. It is not easy to recognize all the ways in which the educational interests of students are affected by an external testing program, nor is it easy to assess its total impact on the schools. Advisory bodies, which include school representatives, can help to sensitize those who operate external testing programs to possible influences. But, in addition, periodic evaluations of the impacts of these programs after they have been operating for a time are needed to provide information to guide their improvement.

CONTROLLING EXTERNAL TESTING

In a monolithic educational system there are no problems of controlling external testing because all testing is under national control along with all other educational activities. In the United States there is no single educational authority. With thousands of public school districts, thousands of private schools, and many hundreds of colleges and universities, each unit has a considerable degree of autonomy. This decentralization of control depends for its effectiveness upon each administrative unit taking the initiative and the responsibility to discharge its functions. Public schools are not given control over private schools nor private schools over public schools. Colleges are not given control over high schools nor high schools over colleges. The American policy is to give responsibility for each unit to carry on its work, to plan, to assemble resources, and to conduct the educational program for which it has been established.

Although there are problems in decentralization of education, the system works and is likely to continue. Hence, it is against this background that the problems of control of external testing must be considered. The school's own testing program, developed for its own purposes to meet its own needs, will be under its control, for it is one of the resources the school uses to meet its educational responsibilities. Correspondingly, college testing programs will be under control of the college. Testing for admission is part of the college testing program, for the college has the responsibility of selecting students likely to benefit from the educational program provided by the college.

With testing programs controlled by different institutions or groups, how can conflicts be eliminated and co-ordination be effected? The previous discussion has suggested policies and procedures which serve these ends. The external testing program must have something positive to offer schools or they will not participate. Furthermore, the way in which the school takes part in an external testing program and uses the results eliminates conflict with school purposes and helps to co-ordinate local and external testing. Conscious consideration by the colleges of the interests of students and the effects upon the schools provides another means of co-ordination. As a further and final instrument of co-ordination, the regional accrediting associations and the school and college organizations furnish channels of communication and opportunities to establish articulation committees under which conflicts and misunderstandings may be adjudicated. With a voluntary structure of this sort, the impact of external testing programs can be made constructive and dynamic. The state programs, like the New York *Regents' Examinations*, which have legal authority to establish and require particular tests generally slow down or inhibit new and competing ideas in testing. The kind of control largely characteristic of this country promotes initiative, encourages constructive inventions, and provides an important context for the improvement of testing.

CHAPTER X

The Selection and Use of Tests in a School Testing Program

ARTHUR E. TRAXLER and ROBERT D. NORTH

Several thousand objective tests have been published, and some hundreds of these are on the active lists of the various test publishers. *The Fifth Mental Measurements Yearbook* lists a total of 957 titles.[1] In almost every field where appraisal may be made by means of objective procedures, several promising tests are available. The care with which selections are made from among the available tests and the understanding and skill with which the results are used will determine in large measure the nature and success of a school's testing program.

The selection and administration of tests are among the more neglected aspects in the planning of a testing program because they often seem, at first thought, to be routine procedures that almost any teacher can handle with little or no preparation. On the contrary, wise choice of the specific tests to be used and careful administration of the tests to all pupils are critically important phases of a school testing program which call for a considerable amount of understanding and experience in educational measurement. As noted by the New York State Education Department, "Experience indicates that most educators have little difficulty in deciding the areas to be tested. The chief problem is choosing the specific tests to use."[2]

---

1. Oscar K. Buros (Editor), *The Fifth Mental Measurements Yearbook.* Highland Park, New Jersey: Gryphon Press, 1959. See also Oscar K. Buros, *Tests in Print: A Comprehensive Bibliography of Tests Used in Education, Industry, and Psychology.* Highland Park, New Jersey: Gryphon Press, 1961.

2. New York State Education Department, *The School Testing Program: A Guide to the Selection and Use of Standardized Tests,* p. 23. Bulletin No. 1415. Albany, New York: University of the State of New York, 1953 (revised).

The program should be planned and carried on with meticulous attention to detail. In discharging these duties and in making provisions for the use of the test results, the school staff responsible for the testing program may find it helpful to observe the following recommendations.

RECOMMENDATION 1. *In selecting tests, keep in mind that there are some tests which every pupil should take and other tests which will be of use only for special needs.*

Some tests belong in the school-wide testing program, while others should be placed in the supplementary program for individual pupils. A group test of mental ability, for instance, should be taken by all pupils, whereas a test of aptitude for art may well be reserved for pupils who show an interest in this field.

The school-wide testing program is preferably administered to all pupils every year. Where this is not possible because of time, expense, or other considerations, the tests should be administered at the points where they will be the most useful, as, for example, where a pupil transfers from elementary school to junior high school. The school-wide tests may be given in the fall, at mid-year, or in the spring, or during each of these periods, depending in part on the seasonal applicability of the norms. Other considerations are discussed in chapter i. The supplementary tests will be given to individuals as needs arise because of learning difficulties, personal and social problems, and the like, or in some instances because there may be doubt concerning the accuracy of certain test scores obtained in the regular school-wide program.

RECOMMENDATION 2. *The school-wide testing program should be comprehensive and co-ordinated.*

The testing program should cover all grade levels in the school and should include as a minimum, tests of both scholastic aptitude and achievement. This does not mean that any one test should cover all grades. As a rule, only one to four grades will be included in any one booklet, but it is advisable to have a series of co-ordinated booklets for different grade levels. For example, the

Metropolitan Achievement Tests[3] include a Primary I battery for Grade I, a Primary II battery for Grade II, an Elementary battery for Grades III and IV, an Intermediate battery for Grades V and VI, and an Advanced battery for Grades VII, VIII, and IX. A particular grade score yielded by this test is intended to mean the same thing, regardless of the level from which it is derived.

Nevertheless, the pupils should be tested with the level that is most appropriate to their abilities, even if this necessitates sectioning in a heterogeneous class for testing. When pupils take a test that is too difficult for them, they may become discouraged or they may indulge in excessive guessing, thereby reducing the reliability of the scores. If a test is too easy for the pupils, they may attain perfect scores without showing their maximum abilities.

The achievement tests selected should cover all major academic fields of study. There should be tests in mechanics and effectiveness of expression, mathematics (with emphasis on newer developments), Latin, French, Spanish, German, and possibly Russian and Oriental languages, physical and biological sciences, and social studies. The *Cooperative Achievement Tests*[4] include, among others, tests of English, mathematics, foreign languages, science, and social studies.

Some elementary-school achievement batteries fail to include tests in science or social studies, and some of the batteries offered for secondary-school use do not reflect the content of specific subjects, such as Latin, geometry, or ancient history. The selective inclusion of some major subjects in the standardized achievement test battery and the omission of others may lead pupils to develop a distorted conception of the relative importance of the various subjects they are studying.

Achievement tests that measure mastery of basic skills and specific subject content may be supplemented or supplanted by achievement tests that are designed to appraise the development of general comprehension and reasoning abilities in the major subject areas. Examples of tests of this nature are the *Sequential Tests*

3. Published by Harcourt, Brace, & World, Inc., Tarrytown, New York.
4. Published by Educational Testing Service, Princeton, New Jersey.

of Educational Progress [5] and the *Iowa Tests of Educational Development.* [6] When such tests are used to the exclusion of standardized tests of the more traditional type, the brunt of measurement of specific attainment must be borne by informal teacher-made tests. The latter type of test should, however, be considered an integral part of the school's achievement testing program, regardless of the type of standardized tests used.

Measures of interests, such as the *Kuder Preference Record* [7] or the *Strong Vocational Interest Blanks,* [8] may also be used profitably in the school-wide testing program, although not, as a rule, below the secondary-school level. The Kuder record, which covers interests in broad fields, may be used throughout Grades IX-XII; the Strong blanks stress interests corresponding to those of men and of women in specific occupations and are preferably confined to the upper high-school years and the college and adult levels.

RECOMMENDATION 3. *The tests chosen for supplementary use should meet needs not served, or only partially served, by the tests in the school-wide program.*

Tests for supplementary use should include diagnostic tests, as, for instance, the separate vocabulary, comprehension, and rate booklets of the *Diagnostic Reading Tests.* [9] They should also include tests of aptitude for special fields, such as art and music, and personality inventories. Alternate forms of achievement tests that are in the regular all-school program should also be available to check the results of an occasional pupil whose scores seem much out of line with other information about him. Diagnostic tests, tests of specific aptitudes, and personality inventories are not ordinarily included in the school-wide testing program because they are time-consuming and because not all pupils need them. Ordinarily, the supplementary tests are more likely to serve clinical uses than do the tests in the school-wide program.

5. Published by Educational Testing Service.
6. Published by Science Research Associates, Chicago, Illinois.
7. Published by Science Research Associates.
8. Published by Consulting Psychologists Press, Palo Alto, California.
9. Published by Committee on Diagnostic Reading Tests, Inc., Mountain Home, North Carolina.

RECOMMENDATION 4. *The tests should be chosen by a committee representing administrators, classroom teachers, counselors, and the testing department.*

It is important to have the instruments in the testing program represent the consensus of the entire faculty so that the tests will be closely related to school needs and generally accepted by all. Since it would be impracticable except in small schools [10] for all teachers to have a direct voice in choosing the tests, the test-selection committee needs to keep open avenues of communication with the faculty so that the committee may have the benefit of the experience and advice of faculty members concerning the tests to be used.[11]

The size of the test-selection committee will, of course, be determined to some extent by the size of the school system being served or by the number and kind of different schools involved. For the testing program of the Educational Records Bureau, in which several hundred independent schools co-operate, the tests are chosen by a committee of six, and this number has for years worked out well in practice for this particular program. A committee of this size could, likewise, serve the needs of a city school system, but it may be advisable to use a larger committee so that each school unit will feel that it is adequately represented. Hence, in a large city, the committee charged with responsibility for choosing the tests to be used throughout the system may reach a size of twenty or more members; but the committee will be well advised to leave most of the work to a smaller group, which will bring recommendations before the larger body for consideration.

While it is, as a rule, highly desirable to have a common testing program throughout a school system, there may be circumstances under which the choice of tests should be left to individual schools within the system. The decision here depends on whether the range of pupil ability in the different schools is similar and

10. J. A. Kelley, "Use of Tests in the Counseling Program of the Small Secondary School," *High School Journal*, XL (May, 1957), 289-96.

11. C. C. Ross and Julian C. Stanley, *Measurement in Today's Schools*, p. 215. New York: Prentice Hall, Inc., 1954 (third edition).

whether there is a common set of objectives which are adhered to by the various schools in the system.

RECOMMENDATION 5. *One of the two main guides in the selection of tests, particularly achievement tests, is the school's objectives.*[12]

Emphasis should be placed on objectives which are clearly and definitely stated and which may influence the school's day-to-day work. The broad, general objectives to which the school subscribes should be broken down into specific objectives in order to serve as guides for both instruction and measurement. Not every educational objective can be measured with existing tests, but a concerted effort should be made to locate and select the best measures and other evaluative procedures for as many of the school's objectives as possible.

In areas such as citizenship, creative thinking, and moral values, suitable standardized tests are not likely to be found. For most academic achievement areas, however, tests that have a substantial degree of communality with the school's instructional objectives can probably be obtained from one publisher or another. The areas covered by measurement are constantly being expanded. For instance, in the field of creative ability and creative thinking, which until recently was regarded as a highly intangible area, is gradually yielding to research through which we may expect that objective instruments for measurement will soon be available.[13]

In choosing tests for supplementary use in connection with the counseling of individual pupils, the objectives of the counselee should also be kept in mind. For this reason, as well as for other reasons, it may be advisable, as suggested in chapter xii,[14] to allow a pupil who is being counseled to participate in the choice of the tests to be taken by him.

It is well to remember that a testing program ought to be designed so that it will function as a part of the total program of

12. See also chaps. ii and iii.

13. E. P. Torrance, "Explorations in Creative Thinking," *Education,* LXXXI (December, 1960), 216-20.

14. See chap. xii.

evaluation which should cover the entire range of the school's objectives.[15]

RECOMMENDATION 6. *The other main guide to the selection of tests is the quality of the test itself. Certain characteristics of the tests being considered should be examined carefully by the committee.*

Two publications which appeared in the mid-1950's are generally regarded as standard guides to the preparation and selection of tests. These are the *Technical Recommendations for Psychological Tests and Diagnostic Techniques*, prepared in 1954 by a joint committee of the American Psychological Association, the American Educational Research Association, and the National Council on Measurements Used in Education and published by the American Psychological Association,[16] and the *Technical Recommendations for Achievement Tests*, prepared over a period of a year or more by a joint committee of the American Educational Research Association and the National Council on Measurements Used in Education and published by the AERA in 1955.[17] Each of these manuals states a series of recommendations and indicates for each recommendation whether it is regarded as essential, very desirable, or desirable. The use of the first of these manuals is well illustrated by Rothney, Danielson, and Heimann,[18] through application of each recommendation to the examiner's manual for the *School and College Ability Tests*.[19]

It is scarcely practicable for a test-selection committee to study each test under consideration in such detail nor is this necessary,

15. V. Cord and J. Epstein, "Team Approach to Testing," *National Education Association Journal*, XLVIII (November, 1959), 23-24.

16. American Psychological Association, *Technical Recommendations for Psychological Tests and Diagnostic Techniques*. Supplement to *Psychological Bulletin*, LI (March, 1954), 1-38.

17. Committee on Test Standards of American Educational Research Association and National Council on Measurements Used in Education, *Technical Recommendations for Achievement Tests*. Washington: American Educational Research Association, 1955.

18. John W. M. Rothney, Paul J. Danielson, and Robert A. Heimann, *Measurement for Guidance*. New York: Harper & Bros., 1959.

19. Published by Educational Testing Service, Princeton, New Jersey, 1957.

for factors other than purely technical ones are likely to weigh
heavily in the decision as to which one of several tests to use in a
certain field. For instance, the Test Selection Committee of the
Educational Records Bureau has continued to regard the *American
Council Psychological Examination* as more suitable for independent school use than the *School and College Ability Tests*, even
though the technical information provided in the manual for
the latter test is far superior to that given for the former one.
Nevertheless, a committee charged with the responsibility of
choosing tests should be aware of the existence of *Technical
Recommendations* and should avoid tests which repeatedly violate
its recommendations.

Other things being equal, preference should be given in test
selection to tests for which favorable data on validity and reliability
are available.

In the practical task of choosing tests for a school testing program, a first question is whether the test does well the job it is designed to do. If several tests in the same field are under consideration, the test-selection committee will wish to know which test
performs the function best. These are questions of validity, and
they are always, or nearly always, specific to the circumstances in
which the test is to be used in the local school.

Sometimes schools find it desirable, however, to subvert purely
local considerations in favor of participation in a common program
along with other schools, such as a state-wide program or a program for schools of a particular type, e.g., an independent school
testing program or a testing program for suburban schools with
certain defined characteristics. Through this kind of participation,
special norms can be established that are often more useful for the
participating schools and schools like them than are national norms.

Regardless of whether the program is a strictly local one or a
common one, tests must be chosen and someone has to do the
choosing. As already indicated, validity is a prime consideration.
There are several ways of assessing validity,[20] and the suitability
of these depends to some extent on conditions. If the test to be
chosen is one of scholastic aptitude, it is well to examine the nature

20. *Technical Recommendations, op. cit.*

and content of the different parts in order to infer whether each one is likely to contribute to scholastic aptitude or to some other quality, such as achievement, interest, or personality.

Content validity usually is given special weight where various achievement tests are being considered for a particular course. Each test is likely to be studied carefully to determine whether its content bears a good deal of similarity to the content of the course. If it does not, its use with the pupils who have been studying the course could hardly be justified, but it may still be a good test. The possibility that it is the course that needs changing should be taken into consideration.

Evidence of concurrent validity, or correlation with some accepted criterion of scholastic aptitude, such as the individual *Stanford-Binet Scale*, is also helpful in evaluating different tests of scholastic aptitude. High correlation of a group test with this well-regarded individual test would be evidence favorable to the use of the group test. The individual test requires so much time in administration and scoring as to be generally impractical for use in the school-wide program.

Of considerable importance in most situations is the predictive validity of the test—how well scores on it correlate with some criterion of future success. For example, a test-selection committee may wish to know the correlation between scores on a test proposed for use in the tenth grade and college Freshman grades. Predictive validity is the prime consideration in choosing an aptitude test.

Needless to say, where several tests are involved, the one having the highest correlation with criteria is not necessarily to be regarded as the best unless it can be shown that the conditions under which the correlations were obtained were similar. This means that the conditions of obtaining concurrent, predictive, and other validity correlations reported in test manuals should be described precisely and in detail.

Sometimes, the validity of a completely new and different test cannot be appraised in any of the ways thus far discussed. For example, when the *Strong Vocational Interest Blank* for men and for women first made its appearance some thirty years ago, it was offered to the public with a thorough explanation of the underlying theory on which it was constructed, namely, that if a person possessed interests similar to those possessed by persons successfully engaged in an occupation, his chances of success in that occupation were enhanced.[21] With the recent attempts at construction of new and ingenious tests for such areas as motivation and creativity, construct validity is growing in importance and often needs to be considered in choosing tests for a well-rounded testing program.

Another important criterion of the worth of a test is its reliability—the consistency with which it measures whatever it does measure. Coefficients of reliability are easily computed and are reported profusely in many test manuals. It is not easy, however, for the prospective test-user to compare reliabilities reported for different tests. The reliability of the same test may vary greatly according to the method of computation used and the range of talent included.

The split-half method is the most commonly used way of determining the reliability of a test. This procedure involves a single administration of a test to a group of pupils at one grade level, the obtaining of scores on half the test (usually the odd-numbered items) and scores on the other half (usually the even-numbered items), the computing of a correlation between the two sets of scores, and the prediction of the reliability of the entire test through the use of the Spearman-Brown formula. This method usually results in high coefficients of reliability because fluctuations in the performance of the students themselves are virtually eliminated. If scores on the tests are determined in part by speed of work on items that are relatively homogeneous in difficulty, the split-half method would indicate spuriously high reliability and should not be used.

The Kuder-Richardson method of estimating reliability from a single administration of a test, likewise, fails to take into consideration changes in the performance of the individual himself. It tends to yield reliabilities that are minimum estimates of those obtained with the split-half method.

21. E. K. Strong, Jr. *Vocational Interests of Men and Women.* Stanford, California: Stanford University Press, 1943.

The test-retest method is used where only one form of a test is available, but two administrations are desired. The shorter the time between the two administrations of the test, the higher the obtained reliability is likely to be, since memory usually will operate to make the scores of each individual similar on the two administrations, but since some fluctuation is allowed in individual performance, reliabilities will run lower than with the split-half method.

The administration of alternate forms of the same test and the correlation of the scores is a third method of finding reliability. The forms are preferably given with a time interval of a week or two between administrations. The items in the two forms should be equivalent in number, type, and difficulty. Equivalence can usually be assumed if the two forms were constructed at the same time from a common pool of items. The equivalent-forms method of reporting reliability is to be preferred to the other methods. It allows fluctuations in the behavior of each individual to influence his performance on the test and provides a more thorough check on performance, since two samples of the area measured instead of one are involved. The reliability coefficients resulting from this method may be expected to be lower than those obtained with the other methods, as may be inferred from Table 1.

Reliability coefficients—and validity coefficients, as well—are markedly influenced by the range of talent in the group used. The wider the range, the higher the coefficients will tend to be. The test manual should indicate, as a minimum, the number, age, sex, and educational levels of the subjects whose scores were used in computing the correlations.[22] It would also be desirable to indicate the socioeconomic level of the communities from which the subjects were drawn, since the combining of subjects from widely different socioeconomic levels into one group could greatly extend the range and raise the correlation.

The size of the reliability coefficients is also affected by other factors, such as the number of items in the test. The subtest scores of many tests are so unreliable as to be worthless for use with individuals. Tests that yield more than one score, but not so many scores

22. *Technical Recommendations for Psychological Tests and Diagnostic Techniques, op. cit.,* p. 32.

TABLE 1

Alternate-form Reliabilities Compared with Spearman-Brown Split-half Reliability Coefficients on Verbal and Reasoning Parts of Holzinger-Crowder Uni-Factor Tests*

Factor	Grade	N	Alternate-Form r	Mean AM	Mean BM	S.D. AM	S.D. BM	N	Alternate-Form r	Mean BM	Mean AM	S.D. BM	S.D. AM	N	Split-Half r	Mean	S.D.
Verbal	7	112	.851	23.2	24.8	9.3	10.5	101	.832	25.6	30.0	10.0	10.8	152	.883	22.1	9.1
	9	67	.799	41.0	47.0	11.4	13.9	61	.898	41.5	39.8	12.4	11.8	134	.925	37.8	11.9
	11	41	.889	49.8	52.6	14.8	17.5	81	.934	55.1	52.2	16.9	15.1	101	.938	50.9	13.7
Reasoning	7	40	.758	26.2	29.7	13.3	13.6	91	.837	35.1	39.8	17.0	17.7	152	.930	39.0	13.6
	9	67	.813	50.3	54.9	15.8	18.6	67	.813	45.2	55.2	14.9	17.0	134	.953	55.6	15.3
	11	60	.901	61.2	68.7	18.4	19.7	51	.810	54.7	64.7	17.2	17.7	101	.955	62.0	15.6

*Appreciation is expressed to Harcourt, Brace, & World, Inc., for permission to use this table as adapted from Holzinger-Crowder Uni-Factor Tests Manual.

that their reliability and usefulness are lost, are to be preferred. A good rule for most tests is to consider scores based on a testing time of less than 20 minutes as too unreliable for interpreting individual performance. In fact, 30 minutes might be better, generally. The chief exceptions to these rules would be vocabulary tests and others where many responses can be obtained in a short time.

Also to be preferred are tests that are accompanied by norms appropriate for the local pupils; tests that are in a co-ordinated series going through a succession of grades and across several areas; tests that are simple in design, clearly printed, easy to administer, and not too difficult to score. Also give preference to tests whose items pass critical inspection by teachers (one approach to content validity), but do not eliminate a test from consideration simply because fault can be found with one or two items out of perhaps a hundred or more. Subjective judgment, even when authoritative, is not always infallible, and, even where criticism is completely justified, a single questionable item will not invalidate the score of an otherwise meritorious test.

If a test is published in both a consumable booklet edition and in a separate answer sheet edition, consideration should be given to the fact that responses marked in a booklet are an aid to the teacher in making an informal diagnosis of the pupils' test performance, whereas responses marked on a separate answer sheet cannot so readily be used in this manner; however, separate answer sheets can be scored more quickly and more economically.

RECOMMENDATION 7. *Give full consideration to the desirability of participating in a regularly planned state or national testing program that may be available to the school.*

A list of tests will usually be recommended through some central agency for common use in the program. These will probably include scholastic aptitude and achievement tests, and perhaps interest measures, as well. These tests should be considered in the light of the school's objectives and curriculum and the range of pupil ability in the school.[23] If it is found that their content agrees reason-

---

23. C. E. Bish, "Implications of National and State Testing Programs," *Bulletin of the National Association of Secondary-School Principals*, LXIII (April, 1959), 312-14.

ably well with the school's stated purposes and that they provide for adequate measurement of the entire range of ability of the pupils in the local school, it will ordinarily be advantageous to use the recommended tests, since they will have been carefully selected by a group of experts in curriculum, guidance, and measurement, and since dependable norms for schools comparable to the local school will probably be available. The tests offered in the common program will often need to be supplemented with tests chosen by a local committee.

RECOMMENDATION 8. *Place the testing activities in the hands of a director or co-ordinator of testing and give him full autonomy in administering the program.*

This does not mean that a testing director should have full power of decision concerning the school's testing program. Policy decisions and the choice of tests are the responsibility of the entire faculty and should be made by them or their appointed representatives. But the giving and scoring of tests and the recording and reporting of test results should be put under the direction of one faculty member who has special aptitude and training for this work. This individual should have taken courses in measurement and statistics and, preferably, guidance as well, and he should be acquainted with the better current tests. The remaining recommendations in this chapter are intended, first of all, for this functionary, although all faculty members ought to be familiar with them.

RECOMMENDATION 9. *If the school has not previously had a testing program, it is advisable to introduce the new program gradually.*

An elaborate testing program introduced all at once would be in danger of overwhelming the faculty with a mass of unintelligible data, thus leading to confusion and an unfavorable attitude toward measurement. Testing in a teacher's own subject before he is ready to interpret and make constructive use of the results is very likely to make him feel defensive toward his teaching. It is advisable to begin with tests in which there is the greatest interest and value and which will not place any particular group of teachers too much on the defensive. Tests of reading ability, preferably in conjunction with tests of scholastic aptitude, are usually desirable tests for introducing the program. The results of these tests should be used to educate the faculty to the meaning and use of test scores, after which the program may gradually be expanded to include all subject areas when the teachers are ready for active and intelligent participation.

RECOMMENDATION 10. *Plan in detail for the administration of the tests.*

Examiners and proctors should be carefully selected and briefed on procedures for administering tests to groups. The examination schedule should be duplicated and a copy distributed to every faculty member. All pupils should be informed as to when and where the tests are to be given and that they are to be taken as a part of the regular school work. Allow pupils who have never taken an objective test an opportunity to take a practice test before the regular testing begins. Do not overemphasize the importance of the tests with the pupils, but give them some feeling for their purpose. Advise that all tests be taken without special preparation. Give written instructions to each examiner and proctor, listing his duties during the examination and the material he will need. Instruct the examiners to adhere to the exact wording of the printed directions in the manual for each test and to time the examination with great care. Where tests are given with separate answer sheets, make sure that the desk space is adequate for all pupils.[24] Where the same booklets are used with successive groups, arrange to have the booklets inspected after each use. Marked booklets should be discarded or all notes and other writing should be thoroughly erased. Provide for absentees to take the tests later and *see that they do*. This is a bothersome step, but it is the only way to assure that test records for each pupil are complete.

RECOMMENDATION 11. *See that all tests are scored promptly and accurately.*

24. Arthur E. Traxler and Robert N. Hilkert, "Effect of Type of Desk on the Results of Machine-scored Tests," *School and Society*, LVI (September 26, 1942), 227-29.

Where financially feasible, careful consideration should be given to the possibility of using outside services for scoring. Rapid and expert services of this kind are available in many states and from certain national organizations. Whenever possible, teachers should be spared the clerical task of scoring objective tests and making statistical tabulations of the results. If the scoring must be done by teachers or clerks, run a training session in advance. Have the teachers work in groups, with each one responsible only for certain operations. In assigning teachers to different jobs in the scoring process, try to take advantage of the different kinds of experience they may have had. Carefully check each individual's work until it is free, or practically free, from error. Occasionally a teacher, even a very capable one, will be found who seems constitutionally unable to learn to score tests accurately. If, after further trial, this seems to be the case with a teacher, it is better to excuse him from scoring duties than to have the morale of the other teachers impaired and the whole process slowed down by the constant need for rescoring his work.[25]

RECOMMENDATION 12. *Report the test results to the faculty promptly in a form they can understand and use (such as percentiles) and furnish faculty members with an explanation of the meaning and legitimate uses of the results.*

Even percentiles are often misunderstood by teachers and need to be clarified by explanation and illustration. Giving test results to teachers in a form which they can understand and will use is one of the most important steps of all, and it should be handled with great care. Summary statistics, such as medians, quartiles, and ranges of scores for the class, grade group, and school should be provided to give the teacher background data for interpreting an individual's scores. Graphic presentation of results on profile forms supplied by the testing agency is particularly helpful.

RECOMMENDATION 13. *Provide a basis for evaluating achievement test scores in relation to the academic aptitude test scores.*

25. Victor H. Noll, *Introduction to Educational Measurement,* pp. 337-39. Boston: Houghton Mifflin Co., 1957.

This basis may be percentile norms derived from essentially the same population for the two tests, expectancy tables, or charts. Relationships based on national, regional, or state-wide data may be supplemented by those derived from local data. It is well known, of course, that achievement is not clearly differentiated from aptitude. Both are based on the combined effects of native ability and learning, which cannot be separated in measurement.

Still, for diagnosing learning difficulties, useful information can be obtained through a comparison of scores from achievement tests which sample the results of formal instruction and from tests of academic aptitude which measure abilities that are not as heavily dependent upon instruction or the school curriculum for their development. For example, an English achievement test may sample a pupil's knowledge of the rules of grammar and other aspects of his knowledge of English, while a verbal aptitude test may call upon a pupil's ability to deal with word relations and verbal concepts. Dependable information concerning the pupil's verbal aptitude, as indicated by the latter kind of test, may be vital to interpretation of what he has learned in the field of English, as measured by the former kind of test.

RECOMMENDATION 14. *Have the test results entered on individual cumulative record forms and make these forms available to counselors and teachers.*

When done manually, this is an extremely detailed, tedious, and often frustrating procedure, which calls for great care and constant checking of entries. But it is a necessary step, for test scores should be interpreted against the background of a cumulative record if they are to achieve their fullest meaning and usefulness. Encourage teachers to review the cumulative records of their pupils at the beginning of each school year and to make regular use of the records during the school year.

In 1962, the Educational Testing Service announced the availability of an electronic system for preparing and maintaining cumulative records of test scores, school grades, and other data. This very rapid and efficient system had been introduced in one state

(Georgia) and was being tried out experimentally in several other states.[26]

RECOMMENDATION 15. *Provide opportunities for the faculty to participate in an in-service training program in the use of test results for the improvement of pupil instruction and counseling.*

In-service training should go on continuously through group meetings and conferences with individual faculty members. Well-selected, up-to-date books and other references on testing and on the use of test results should be available in the faculty reading-room. Seminars and workshops with specialists from outside the school are frequently useful, but enough trained leadership should be developed within the school to keep the in-service training going constantly.[27]

Undertake to familiarize the administrators and faculty members with all legitimate uses of tests, but also call attention to pitfalls and unwise uses that are sometimes made of test data. Among the desirable uses are the following:

1. Use tests, along with other information, for purposes of classification of pupils into grade levels and for instructional grouping.
2. Employ tests in diagnosis of pupil strengths and weaknesses, as a starting point for remedial work and for checking on pupil progress as the remedial work goes forward.
3. Constantly take account of test results in counseling and guidance, and give the counselee an opportunity to familiarize himself with and to use his own test scores, if his interest warrants this procedure, first making sure that the scores are sufficiently reliable and valid to be used in individual counseling.
4. Where the content validity is high, tests may be used as one basis of assigning marks to pupils.
5. Use tests of appropriate difficulty in the identification and study of gifted children and in awarding scholarships.
6. Refer to test results in conferring with parents about the progress of their children; at the same time, carefully explain the meaning of the scores in terms as nearly nontechnical as circumstances will

26. Wesley W. Walton, "The Electronic Age Comes to the Schoolhouse," *Systems for Educators* (January-February, 1962). New York: Remington-Rand Co.

27. W. Coleman, "Assisting Teachers in Using Test Results," *Personnel and Guidance Journal*, XXXVI (September, 1957), 38-40.

permit. Again, graphic presentation in profile form will be helpful.

7. A use of test results that may at times be purposeful and may at other times be a by-product of other uses is in the motivation of under-achievers to better achievement.

8. Tests may be used in public relations and in interpreting the scores to the community, but there are pitfalls in this procedure, and it should be undertaken only with great care and caution to make sure that all variables have been taken into consideration.

9. Use tests in educational research broadly conceived and in "action" research directed toward improvement of methods and curriculum of specific courses.

A use of test results that is sometimes made but is unwarranted in most situations is their employment in the evaluation of teacher effectiveness. Unless all variables, such as pupil ability and suit-ability of the tests for the curriculum and methods of the course, are carefully controlled, this kind of use can be very unfair and misleading.

RECOMMENDATION 16. *If the all-school or supplementary pro-gram includes multi-aptitude tests, tests of special aptitude, interest inventories, or personality inventories, special care should be taken to assure judicious and adequate use of the results.*

Scores derived from some of these instruments are often limited in reliability and validity, and they should be interpreted to the students by a staff member who has had some training in tests and measurements and who is aware of the pitfalls involved in making comparisons among scores in different areas and on different tests.[28]

RECOMMENDATION 17. *The school's policy regarding the release of test results to pupils, parents, P.T.A.'s, and other organizations should be clearly formulated.*

Even among test specialists, some rather sharp differences of opinion exist concerning the advisability of releasing test results to parents and other laymen. In some states, access by parents to school records of test data is required by law. The school should clarify for the public the extent to which test records are open for inspection and present reasons for its practice with respect to this

28. Rothney, Danielson, Heimann, *op. cit.*, pp. 282-319.

question. A view supported by many specialists in the measurement and guidance field is that, in the absence of a state requirement, test results may be interpreted to parents provided this is done in conference where questions may be raised and answered. Whether or not the actual scores should be given to parents is a moot question. The answer depends largely on circumstances and on the background and understanding of educational measurement on the part of the parents themselves.

In a school in a college town or suburban community where the majority of the parents are college-trained, it may be desirable for the school, after a period of indoctrination, to release the scores themselves to the parents; in other types of communities, the school's policy is necessarily more guarded, and the period of indoctrination is longer and more intensive. The ultimate aim is to have the test results used as fully as they can be used understandably.

ADDITIONAL REFERENCES

1. BERDIE, RALPH F., and Others. *Counseling and the Use of Tests: A Manual for the State-wide Testing Programs of Minnesota.* Minneapolis: Student Counseling Bureau, University of Minnesota, 1959.

2. BOLDEN, W. S. "When Is a School Ready for a Testing Program?" *Elementary School Journal,* LIX (January, 1959), 225-27.

3. CHRISTIE, S. C., and BLACK, K. "What Is a Desirable Testing Program To Meet Current Needs of Students?" *Bulletin of the National Association of Secondary-School Principals,* XLIII (April, 1959), 210-14.

4. CLARK, P. I. "Teacher's Use and Understanding of Tests," *Journal of Education,* CXXXIX (April, 1957), 23-38.

5. CRONBACH, LEE J., and MEEHL, PAUL E. "Construct Validity in Psychological Tests," *Psychological Bulletin,* LII (July, 1955), 281-302.

6. DOWNIE, NORVILLE M. *Fundamentals of Measurement: Techniques and Practices.* New York: Oxford University Press, 1958.

7. EBEL, ROBERT L. "Eight Critical Questions about the Use of Tests," *Education,* LXXXI (October, 1960), 67-68.

8. FINDLEY, WARREN G. "Appraisal of Evidence," *Seventeenth Yearbook of the National Council on Measurements Used in Education,* pp. 45-47. Ames, Iowa: Department of Psychology, Iowa State University, 1960.

9. FLANAGAN, JOHN C. "Testing Programs: Their Function in Education," *California Journal of Secondary Education,* XXXV (January, 1960), 41-45.

10. FULLMER, D. W. "Testing Program: What Constitutes Minimum?" *Bulletin of the National Association of Secondary-School Principals,* XLII (May, 1958), 80-87.

11. GARRETT, HENRY E. *Testing for Teachers.* New York: American Book Co., 1959.

12. HOLT, C. C. "External Testing Programs." *Bulletin of the National Association of Secondary-School Principals,* XLV (April, 1961), 402-7.

13. JORDAN, ARTHUR M. *Measurement in Education: An Introduction.* New York: McGraw-Hill Book Co., 1953.

14. LORGE, IRVING. "The Fundamental Nature of Measurement," in *Educational Measurement,* pp. 533-59. Edited by E. F. Lindquist. Washington: American Council on Education, 1951.

15. MAYO, S. T. "Testing and the Use of Test Results," *Review of Educational Research,* XXIX (Fall, 1959), 5-14.

16. MERRITT, C. B. "Use of Tests in Secondary Schools," *High School Journal,* XLI (December, 1957), 66-70.

17. MILLER, C. H. "Guidance and Programs of Testing," *School Life,* XLII (Spring, 1959), 18-20.

18. ORAHOOD, E. "Making the Testing Program Effective," *School and Community,* XLVI (January, 1960), 23.

19. REMMERS, H. H., and GAGE, N. L. *Educational Measurement and Evaluation.* New York: Harper & Bros., 1955 (revised).

20. SAPER, B. "Interpretation of Tests in Counseling Students," *Educational Record,* XLII (April, 1961), 117-20.

21. SEASHORE, H., and DOBBIN, J. E. "How Can the Results of a Testing Program Be Used Most Effectively?" *Bulletin of the National Association of Secondary-School Principals,* XLII (April, 1958), 64-68.

22. SUPER, DONALD E. "The Use of Multifactor Test Batteries in Guidance," *Personnel and Guidance Journal,* XXXV (September, 1956), 9-15, and the following issues through May, 1957.

23. THOMAS ROBERT MURRAY. *Judging Student Progress.* New York: Longmans, Green, & Co., 1960 (second edition).

24. THORNDIKE, ROBERT L. "Reliability," in *Educational Measurement,* pp. 560-620. Edited by E. F. Lindquist. Washington: American Council on Education, 1951.

25. THORNDIKE, ROBERT L., and HAGEN, ELIZABETH. *Measurement and Evaluation in Psychology and Education.* New York: John Wiley & Sons, Inc., 1961 (second edition).

26. WEITZ, H. "Minimum Essentials for a Testing Program," *American School Board Journal,* CXXXV (Spring, 1957), 41-43.

27. WOOD, BEN D. *Measurement in Higher Education.* Yonkers, New York: World Book Co., 1923.

28. WRIGHTSTONE, J. WAYNE. "Do Students Benefit from Testing?" *High School Journal,* XLI (December, 1957), 75-78.

29. WRIGHTSTONE, J. WAYNE; JUSTMAN, JOSEPH; and ROBBINS, IRVING. *Evaluation in Modern Education.* New York: American Book Co., 1956.

CHAPTER XI

Staff Competence in Testing

ELIZABETH HAGEN and LUCILE LINDBERG

Basic to a successful school testing program is the acceptance by the staff and students of the idea that the testing program is an integral part of the educational process. If this idea is to become functional, then each person in the school must be aware of his role in the total program and must have the competence to discharge that role effectively.

The role of each member of the staff is not a distinct and isolated entity but a part of the total mosaic of the educational program. The role of each staff member in the school testing program interacts with and supplements the role of every other member of the staff. If one staff member fails to discharge his role effectively, then the total program will be weakened. Not only is there an interaction of roles in the testing program among staff members but there is also an interaction of each staff member's role in the testing program and his role in the total educational program.

What are these roles that need to be played in a testing program? Some light can be thrown on this question by considering the tasks that must be accomplished in order to have a successful school testing program. First, decisions must be made about the purposes or functions that the school testing program is to serve. Second, decisions have to be made concerning which students or grades are to be tested and when they are to be tested. Third, tests must be selected to achieve the purposes of the testing program. Fourth, the tests must be ordered, scheduled, and distributed to the appropriate places at the appropriate times. Fifth, the students must be prepared for taking the tests and the tests must be administered. Sixth, the tests must be scored and the test results analyzed in preparation for use. Seventh, the test results must be communicated to all interested parties. Eighth, action must be taken to use the results in the ways indicated by the purposes of the testing program. The tasks involved in setting up and carrying out the school testing program indicate that the roles involved are those of a philosopher, a test technician, a co-ordinator, an administrator, a statistician, an interpreter, and an implementer.

Who fulfils these roles? This question is not a simple one because the answer is determined, to a large extent, by situational factors. For example, in a small school or school system, particularly if funds are limited, the number and kinds of personnel available are also likely to be limited. In this situation, an already overburdened classroom teacher, principal, counselor, or supervisor may be called upon to fulfil all or several of the roles. On the other hand, in larger schools or school systems or in schools supported at a high level, a greater number and variety of personnel are usually available or can be employed.[1] In such a situation, specialists in testing can be employed to fulfil certain roles, or highly qualified personnel already employed in the school system can be assigned certain duties. However, it should be pointed out that, although experts outside of the school system can provide valuable assistance in a school testing program, no school testing program can be successful unless the permanent staff of the school understands the basic principles of testing and can interpret and use test results competently. A person unfamiliar with a school and its needs will not be able to set up an effective testing program for that school no matter how expert he is in the field of testing. A consultant from outside the system cannot be constantly available to interpret test results and to see that the results are used properly; the permanent staff must be competent in these areas. The point being made is that certain competencies in testing must be developed and maintained among the permanent staff in order to have an effective testing program. These competencies and the methods by which they are developed are the subject of the present chapter.

1. Certain problems related to testing personnel and programs are, in some ways, less pressing in large school systems, e.g., New York, Detroit, etc., in which leadership and assistance in testing is provided by a bureau or similar agency which is staffed by a corps of specialists of various kinds and grades.

RECOMMENDATION 1. *The competencies in testing possessed by staff members should be analyzed carefully before a testing program is launched in a school or school system.*

No person involved in administering the curriculum of a school would think of scheduling a class in Russian or atomic physics unless there was someone available who was competent to teach the class. Yet elaborate testing programs are set up in many schools and school systems without consideration of the fact that staff members have only a vague impression of what a standardized test is and how test results should be interpreted. In most schools there is a realization that it is inadvisable to administer individual intelligence tests or projective tests to students unless someone on the staff is qualified to administer and interpret them. However, in these same schools, there is often a feeling that no special competence is needed to administer, interpret, and use group tests. The notion exists in some schools that anyone who can read is able to administer group tests. Anyone who has had experience with school testing programs has seen the unfortunate results that have stemmed from such assumptions.

It is impractical to expect administrative officers in a school to make a systematic investigation of the skills and competencies in testing possessed by all staff members. It is desirable, however, that they make an attempt to locate staff members who have had formal academic work in testing or previous experience in working with testing programs. It would then be desirable to investigate more carefully the skills in testing that these people possess.

The attempt of administrators to determine the competencies in testing possessed by the staff is sometimes hindered by the fact that many administrators have limited knowledge of testing; therefore, they have little basis for judging how competent a staff member is in testing. In such a situation, an outside consultant who is expert in testing could help, but such a consultant is not always available. In instances in which there is a testing program already in operation, there are indications of weaknesses or deficiencies in the testing program that an alert administrator can look for and recognize.

RECOMMENDATION 2. *If the classroom teachers are hostile or indifferent to the testing program and view it as an unnecessary burden that takes valuable time away from their teaching, the program should be examined to determine whether it has been inadequately set up or administered.*

The causes of teacher hostility must be identified before steps can be taken to remedy the defects in the organization and administration responsible for that hostility. Possible causes are numerous. Many classroom teachers have had little or no formal training or in-service training in testing. They do not see the relationship between the standardized tests that are administered to their students and the teaching-learning experiences that they provide for the students. This situation usually results either from failure to identify the purposes of the testing program before it is set up or the failure to include teachers in the initial planning of a testing program, or both. A testing program that is imposed from above without co-operative planning of all who are to be concerned with the use of the test results is unlikely to be well received or to be effective. Such an imposition is also indicative of a lack of understanding of testing.

Marked hostility of teachers toward the testing program commonly has its roots either in the misuse of test results or in the withholding from teachers of the results of tests. In too many schools teachers are required to bring the class results of testing to the principal and to explain why certain students "did not come up to the norm." Such a practice is a clear indication that there is no understanding of what a norm is. One local test specialist has quipped that he can always get a headline by reporting that half the children in his city's system are below the average. Administrative officers frequently convey the feeling that outstanding test results are to be achieved at any cost—an indication that there is little or no understanding of what a standardized test is, what it is measuring, or what its limitations are. In the same category are those schools in which the effectiveness of the teacher is judged solely on the basis of results of achievement tests. As indicated above, the hostility of teachers to the school testing program may also stem from the failure to make results available to them. The with-holding of intelligence test scores occurs most frequently. The basis for such action is the conviction of the persons responsible for the school testing program that teachers do not know how to interpret intelligence test results. This conclusion is a valid one in the case of many teachers, but the proper solution is not withhold-ing test results or in making them accessible only at times and under conditions that discourage their examination by teachers. Teacher hostility toward tests can be reduced or eliminated, and teacher effectiveness can be increased through in-service education in the interpretation and use of test results.

RECOMMENDATION 3. *The classroom teachers must have a key role in a successful school testing program.*

No matter how highly organized a testing program may be on paper, it is the teachers who will make the program a success or a failure. No testing program is good unless it is used effectively, and it is the classroom teachers who will make primary use of it.

Nothing is gained if test scores are filed when received, never to be discussed or referred to again, while teachers proceed with plans entirely uninfluenced by the test results. Even when meet-ings are called and there is much discussion of the scores, their meaning, and the implications of the results for working with students, there is no assurance that, when teachers next work with students, the ideas developed through the discussion will be considered. We do not imply that teachers as a rule deliberately ignore test results but, rather, that it is difficult for them to accept that which they do not understand.

If testing is to play a part in determining classroom activities, the teachers must really see a relationship between it and what they are doing. To accomplish this, they must participate directly or in-directly in every aspect of the testing program.

The goals of a good testing program should be formulated to conform with and to support the over-all goals of the educational program. It is, therefore, essential that the teachers be involved in planning and administering the testing program if the goals sought through it are to be achieved.

The classroom teachers in elementary schools should meet both in grade groupings and in groupings which cut across grade lines, in order that they may perceive the problems both horizontally and vertically. Since every teacher needs to use the results of tests, every teacher must be included in the planning. It is not enough to choose a representative from each grade or from each building. Resistance can be just as great to the ideas passed along by a fellow teacher as to those coming from an administrator, sometimes greater. In high schools, departmental meetings will serve most vertical purposes; faculty meetings and counselor co-ordination will accomplish the rest.

After the goals are determined, teachers should participate in examining available tests so that those chosen will be effective in guiding instruction. Planning with the test co-ordinator can assure that only the most suitable tests will be studied in detail. Much is learned in the process of examining these tests.

If a teacher is deeply concerned with evaluation and participates eagerly in examining and improving his work, his pupils are also likely to participate eagerly in every aspect of the evaluation, including the testing. When tests are administered to such pupils, they are accepted as one more device which will be a help to the pupils as well as their teacher.

Test scores are important to the children in a classroom and can be used so that each pupil may assess and enjoy the progress he is making. When children are in the habit of self-assessment, they come to see that test scores are only one piece of data available, and they become interested in improving the total evaluative procedure.

Parents are interested in the progress their children are making. The teachers of their children are key figures in determining the type of attitudes parents will have toward tests and the demands they make concerning them. Where teachers have tried consistently to help parents see the whole picture of a child's progress, and where parents are aware of many criteria for assessing growth, there is less likelihood that the parents will demand to know test scores or to look upon them as a means of comparing children. When parents have been helped to understand the over-all goals that the teachers feel are appropriate for their respective children, they relate their inquiries to these goals, and the teachers can speak about the test results in a general way without arousing anxiety.

Each teacher has an obligation to make notes of the ways in which he uses the tests in the testing program. Other teachers may find this valuable, and administrators and test co-ordinators may get new insights into aspects of specific tests or of the total program which they did not have before. Then, too, teachers often complain about the ways in which tests have been administered or scored but fail to make their concerns known to the appropriate persons. Passing on such concerns is an obligation of each teacher. From many sources teachers and administrators may acquire the information and background that will enable them to play their respective roles in the testing program. Since, as previously stated, their roles are in many respects different, so will their qualifications differ.

RECOMMENDATION 4. *The administrators in a school system need to have a general understanding of the proper uses and limitations of standardized tests and norms.*

It is important that those who work directly in the testing program be the ones with the more specialized knowledge, but unless administrators have a general understanding of the kinds of tests available and of their uses and limitations, they are likely to expect a testing program to achieve results which are not in keeping with reality. Unless they have some knowledge about interpretation of statistical results in testing, they are likely to make claims for test scores which should not be made, and they may miss the implications which these scores have in evaluating the total educational program.

Unless an administrator has a general knowledge of testing programs, he will not be able to use test results intelligently as he talks with groups and writes his reports. Very often it is the administrators who have the most widespread contact with both public and professional groups. If they do not use test results, the testing program will not realize its full potential; if they misuse test results, they may spread confusion in a community.

As already noted, if administrators do not understand tests, they are likely to regard them as a means of checking on teacher performance or perhaps to view test results as the goals of instruction rather than to use them as tools in the development of a continuous program of evaluation. Such conceptions of goals of testing on the part of the administrator makes it unlikely that the testing program in his school will be effective.

The primary role of the administrative staff in the testing program requires competence in administration, in the development of personnel, and in interpersonal relations. Most of these skills can or should be developed during the formal educational program pursued in preparing for administrative positions. Specific competency in general aspects of testing and evaluation can probably best be developed in workshops and institutes staffed by various kinds of experts, including one in testing and evaluation. A most useful resource in helping administrators understand testing and problems associated with it are the articles that appear from time to time in various professional journals intended primarily for administrators.

As previously inferred, no part of the administrative personnel is without a role or roles in the testing program.

RECOMMENDATION 5. *School principals, their assistants, supervisors, and other administrative personnel should play the role of facilitators in administering a testing program and using the results.*

It is the business of these administrators to see that each person understands what his specific responsibilities are. It is the chief administrator who makes certain that someone is co-ordinating the planning, that there is a clear understanding concerning who will administer and score the tests.

While the administrators may not have specific assignments in the administration of the testing program, their participation in planning all aspects of it is important. This is true because evaluation and development go hand in hand. It is also important that they know what is going on so that they do not interfere unwittingly with schedules by interposing other activities. The facilitating of testing programs by administrators involves the establishment of conditions under which such programs can develop.

RECOMMENDATION 6. *The administrators in a school system must assume responsibility for developing an atmosphere conducive to the development of a good testing program and the constructive use of results.*

It is the administrator who will suggest the kinds of meetings or other arrangements which will make possible the continuous study of the school testing program. It is they who set the tone which makes all concerned aware of the close relationship of planning and evaluation.

Not only do they see that there is a qualified person to coordinate the testing program but also that this person has time in which to carry out his functions. It is a temptation to assign so many other tasks to a person who does not have a specific classroom assignment that he is unable to give his best efforts to carrying out his functions in the testing program.

It is the administrators in a school system who should be alert to the need for specialized help from outside and make such help available. It is they who see that the necessary planning is done for the use of such help, that workshops or institutes are made available.

RECOMMENDATION 7. *Because teachers need such help, each school system must take responsibility for providing orientation and in-service training in testing.*

It is unrealistic to assume that teachers can learn all that they need to know about testing during their preservice courses. What they do learn does not seem real when they get into their own classrooms. Unless some provisions are made for continuing their study of tests, testing is likely to remain on the periphery and even be considered a nuisance inflicted upon them by the administrators.

In general courses in educational psychology, the undergraduates should get some basic information about tests. In their student teaching they frequently become familiar with the way in which a teacher uses tests.

There are many things which can be done in a school to facilitate continued learning in this area, as will be pointed out in this chapter in discussing the role of the test co-ordinator. Prior to the administration of tests, orientation sessions are needed. These should provide more than directives concerning mechanical procedures. Much is gained if those participating are familiar with the way each test has been developed, have noted the goals of the authors, and have discussed the values which can be gained by relating the test results to other data that are being collected on the students.

In many systems, in-service courses are given from time to time. A varying number of sessions is held according to the other demands being made on teachers. Sometimes such courses are conducted by the test co-ordinator, other times by a consultant from a near-by university. They are more vital if based on the testing program in the district so that case material from that program can be used.

Handbooks which are developed by a local committee are helpful. Some commercial publishers have some such materials which are free for the asking. These need to be checked with the test co-ordinator to make certain that the principles developed in them are in keeping with those accepted in the school system.

Most school systems have a library of professional books. Among these should be carefully selected books on evaluation and testing. If quotations from some of these books are distributed or if brief and stimulating reviews are given, teachers may be motivated to study them.

Often curriculum committees meet together to study test data. Ideas are shared and experts may be called upon to explain the meanings of the scores in relation to the curriculum and curriculum problems. After several teachers have read a good book or article on testing, they may come together to discuss it.

Some school systems have held very successful workshop sessions in which the whole testing program was examined. In these, it is possible to have demonstrations of how test results can be used, often by a special consultant.

RECOMMENDATION 8. *An effective testing program requires detailed planning, precise scheduling, and careful administration.*

Anyone who has seen many school testing programs in operation has seen evidence of lack of planning at all levels. Just from examining some school testing programs on paper, one can see evidence of lack of initial planning. Most school testing programs do not seem to have been developed but to have grown by accretion. It is not unusual to see a school testing program that uses three or four different intelligence tests between Grades I and XII and at least that many different achievement tests in the same grades. Such a practice indicates a lack of understanding of the need for continuity and correlation in the school testing program and usually a lack of understanding of the meaning of test scores.

In some schools, elaborate testing programs are found which require a large amount of testing time and which yield very little information about the students. For example, one can find school testing programs that schedule for an eighth grade a general intelligence test, such as the *Otis Quick-Scoring Mental Ability Test,* and a multi-factor battery, such as the *Differential Aptitude Test,* plus an achievement battery, such as the *Iowa Test of Basic Skills,* and, in addition, a separate test of reading comprehension and vocabulary. In such a program, duplicate information about the students is acquired, and testing time is not spent efficiently. Generally, in schools in which this situation prevails, there is no central responsibility for planning the testing program, and tests are added generally because one or two individuals on the staff want the tests. In such schools, most individuals on the staff do not really know what the tests they are giving measure nor how to use the results constructively. In too many instances there seems to be a lack of understanding among school personnel that tests are not given just for the sake of testing or just to keep up with Community X, but that tests are given to be used for the eventual improvement of the teaching-learning situation for an individual student or for all the students.

Although in most schools or school systems, some one person is usually designated as having primary responsibility for the testing program, the specific responsibilities of this person are not clear. For example, no one is told that he is responsible for making a detailed schedule for administering the tests, and as a result vague instructions are given to administer the tests "sometime this fall." Such instructions may result in some students being tested in October and some in December, so that comparable data are not obtained on all students. Then, there are situations where tests are scheduled for a regular class period without checking to see if that period is long enough for distributing materials, giving instructions to students, and for taking the test. For example, a test requiring fifty minutes of student working time may be scheduled for a fifty-minute period but, by the time the materials are distributed and the directions read, only forty minutes of working time may remain; so the students are stopped and the next day are given ten additional minutes of working time. Such a procedure violates the "standardized" conditions designated to make test results comparable and indicates little understanding of the concept of testing.

Two additional weaknesses in school testing programs frequently are perceived. The first of these is the failure to provide for adequate motivation of the students who are to take the tests, and the second is the failure to provide for adequate administration of the tests. It seems odd that in a situation where the students are the crucial factor in obtaining data so little attention is paid to establishing a setting where the student is more likely to put forth his best efforts. In many schools, students receive no feedback of their test results; therefore, they cannot see any point in taking the tests. In some schools, students may be told that tomorrow they will be given some tests but are not told why the tests are being given nor how the test results will benefit them. In other schools, students are told about the tests but, in a misdirected effort to avoid an anxiety-producing situation, the students are given the impression that neither the tests nor the results of the tests are very important, thus contributing to the development of a carefree or lackadaisical attitude toward the tests that is unlikely to produce useful and meaningful results. In a few schools, particularly those in which the effectiveness of the teachers is being judged solely on the basis of results of standardized tests, the teachers may present the testing situation in such a way that the students feel threatened by it. Many teachers are given no help in preparing students adequately for the tests and do not know how much they can or should tell students about the tests.

The second deficiency in school testing programs mentioned at the beginning of the previous paragraph, i.e., inefficient administration of the tests, usually occurs either because the classroom teachers are used as the administrators, without being given adequate instructions, or because the classroom teachers are eliminated from the testing process.

In certain schools it is recognized that, although group tests are not difficult to administer, their administration does require a measure of skill that few classroom teachers have acquired. However, in too many instances, instead of providing an orientation period to train the teachers, devious methods are used to bypass them. One such method is to administer the tests through the intercommunication system of the school. Someone sits in the central office at the controls and reads the directions while the classroom teachers and the students listen in the classroom. One admires the attempt to obtain uniformity of administration, but one wonders what happens when a fire engine roars by outside and drowns out the voice on the loudspeaker, when the precise timing necessary to follow the directions over the loudspeaker is upset by the accidental dropping of materials, by slowness in passing out the materials, or by a broken pencil point. What do the classroom teachers do under this method of administration when the students have not understood the directions?

Another method that has been used is to assign the task of administering the tests to one or two people in the school who have special competence in testing, such as a counselor or special teacher; to herd several hundred students into an overcrowded, poorly lighted cafeteria or auditorium, where there is not enough room to handle the test materials and where getting help from a neighbor is easy; and to have one or two selected testers administer the tests to all the assembled students. This procedure may get the testing done in a hurry, but it is not conducive to eliciting good, honest effort on the part of students. A third method is to send one or two people who are competent to administer tests to the individual classrooms to administer the tests. If the school is not large, this procedure may work satisfactorily, but a strange person—particularly at the lower grade levels—can be very distracting to the pupils. Then, too, the stranger does not know the pupils as well as the classroom teachers and therefore cannot anticipate the difficulties that the pupils are likely to encounter in taking the test. How much simpler it would be to provide an orientation program for the classroom teachers that would include a discussion of the purposes of the testing program—such as that described under Recommendation 9. Every person in the school should have a role in the school testing program, and he must either have or develop the competency to discharge this role if the testing program is to be effective.

It has already been noted that the roles involved in a successful school testing program are those of a philosopher, a test technician, a co-ordinator, an administrator, a statistician, an interpreter, and an implementer. Any or all staff members at different times may play all of these roles; however, we are now concerned with who should have specific responsibility for either discharging the role or seeing that the role is discharged.

RECOMMENDATION 9. *In each school system, one person designated as test co-ordinator should be appointed with the major responsibility for co-ordinating, managing, and developing the school testing program. Within each school, one person should be designated as test co-ordinator for that school to assist the test co-ordinator for the school system.*

The primary function of the test co-ordinator is to insure the smooth operation of the school testing program. He should be responsible for the mechanical and administrative details of the testing program, such as ordering test materials, maintaining current inventories of test materials, planning the master schedule for administering the tests, distributing test materials to the places where they are needed, maintaining the security of tests and testing materials, and arranging for scoring of the tests. If the testing program involves the use of reusable test booklets, he has the responsibility to see that the booklets are examined before each use to make sure that they have not been marked in any way. Although the test co-ordinator may delegate some of these tasks to clerical personnel, he himself must have the authority to carry through the operations.

Also, the test co-ordinator should arrange for the administration of the tests and for orientation sessions for teachers. If the classroom teachers are to be used as the administrators of the tests, the test co-ordinator must arrange for training sessions to prepare the teachers for the discharge of this responsibility. Initially, the orientation program should include an introduction to the purposes of the testing program; familiarization with the tests used in the program; practice in administration of the tests, preferably involving role-playing that will indicate the kinds of student questions that can and cannot be answered; and some instruction in the interpretation and use of test results. The detailed orientation program need not be attended by all teachers every year. For teachers who have been in the school or school system and have had the complete orientation program, a short refresher session at the time the testing schedule is presented will be sufficient. In some instances, a carefully worded memorandum stressing crucial points will suffice. However, care should be taken to see that teachers new to the system are thoroughly oriented to the school testing program.

The test co-ordinator should also be responsible for the preparation of statistical summaries of test data. He may prepare them or he may, in consultation with other persons in the school, specify the kinds of analyses to be made and delegate the actual preparation to outside test-scoring agencies or to other personnel within the school. He should take the leadership in establishing local norms [2] for the tests and in developing statistical aids such as expectancy charts that facilitate the interpretation and use of test results by all persons in the system.

The test co-ordinator should also assume leadership in the continuous evaluation of the school testing program, preferably working with an advisory committee made up of representatives of all personnel concerned with the testing program. The test co-ordinator should keep abreast of new tests and developments in the field of testing. He should maintain a file of specimen tests and should evaluate them. He and his advisory committee should seek

---

2. The procedures for preparing local norms for tests are described fully in the manuals for interpreting each of the *Sequential Tests of Educational Progress* published by Educational Testing Service (Princeton, N.J.). Manuals for other tests and textbooks on educational measurement may also be consulted. See also chap. xii of this yearbook.

suggestions and opinions about the testing program from other school personnel. On the basis of this continuous evaluation, he and his advisory committee should recommend changes in the testing program if and when need for such changes becomes apparent.

The test co-ordinator, working with the administrative and teaching staff, should also have responsibility for preparing reports of test results to be released to the public or interested lay groups.

The test co-ordinator should also be available as a resource person to individual teachers or groups of teachers to help them interpret and use test results constructively.

Last, the test co-ordinator, to the extent that his time permits, should take the leadership in preparing accessory materials. For example, a helpful handbook on the testing program to be given to all teachers or forms for reporting test results to students and parents can be prepared.

If a person is to fulfil the role of test co-ordinator adequately and to discharge all of the functions mentioned, it is clear that he must possess a high level of competence in testing.

RECOMMENDATION 10. *The test co-ordinator must have a sound background in testing and testing theory and the ability to apply his knowledge in a practical situation.*

The test co-ordinator must understand the concepts of reliability, validity, norms, and test construction. Minimally he should know descriptive statistics, including simple correlation, and ideally he should be competent in inferential statistics. He must be able to read and evaluate technical test manuals and published research on tests and testing. He should know the sources of tests and test information. Ideally he should be able to plan and carry out simple studies involving the use of test data.

Since the test co-ordinator must work with all other people in the school or school system, he should also be able to plan, administer, and delegate. He should be highly skilled in communicating technical information to people with limited technical backgrounds. The communication skill is vitally essential to his role of interpreter to the classroom teachers and the public and as helper of the latter.

Lastly, since the person is working in a school setting, he should have a thorough understanding of the goals and objectives of the school, of the nature of the school population and community, and of the total school program.

RECOMMENDATION 11. *Formal academic training in testing is basic to the development of the competencies needed by the test co-ordinator. This training should be supplemented by internships or field work or institutes.*

Although it is possible for an exceptional person to become competent in testing without any formal academic training, it is unlikely that most people can obtain a thorough background in the basic core of testing without at least one good formal course that systematically covers and emphasizes the concepts of reliability and validity, the nature and meaning of test scores and norms, the basic principles of good item-writing, the nature, advantages, and limitations of the methods available for measuring human attributes, and the uses and misuses of test results.

A course such as the one described can provide the intellectual foundation for competency in testing, but it needs to be supplemented by realistic, preferably supervised, experience in the field from which the ability to apply this knowledge may be acquired or improved.

Visiting schools which are known to have sound testing programs and studying those programs can contribute greatly to the preparation of a person for the job as test co-ordinator. If possible, opportunity should be provided for the person to work over an extended period of time in such a school. After the person has had experience in schools where the testing program is known to be effective, he can also profit from the experience of working in schools that are known to have only moderately effective or completely ineffective school testing programs. Such work experience, if it is combined with a properly designed and administered seminar can be extremely effective in preparing a person to discharge his responsibilities as a test co-ordinator.

For continued professional development, the test co-ordinator should be encouraged to attend special institutes or workshops on testing.

RECOMMENDATION 12. *In order to discharge their functions in the testing program effectively, the classroom teachers must have a basic understanding of the evaluative process and the place of the testing program in the total evaluation of the students and the educational program.*

This understanding must be based upon a knowledge of both philosophical and technical aspects of testing and evaluation. The concepts which are held of the role of the school and of how children learn are important determinants of the type of evaluative procedures which are appropriate.

An understanding of the basic concepts of reliability, standard error of measurement, and validity is essential. They must be able to read a test manual and to interpret and use the information provided in it. They should be able to follow the directions given.

RECOMMENDATION 13. *Classroom teachers should know the general types of tests available and be aware of their uses, strengths, and limitations.*

Although classroom teachers cannot be expected to be experts in testing, there are certain basic types of tests they should know. They certainly should know well all of the tests used in their school's testing program. If they have some idea of how these tests were developed, it will help them to see the tests in perspective and to use them wisely.

RECOMMENDATION 14. *Classroom teachers should be able to combine available test data with other records and to interpret them as they relate to individual children in their classes.*

It is through such a process that teachers are able to determine the probable progress and needs of students. The ability to interpret simple statistical data such as means, percentiles, and standard scores is required. Also required is skill in conferring with students and with parents. Misuse of data often results in misunderstandings and can throw a whole testing program into disrepute. Competence in use of data should give a teacher a sense of security, which makes it unnecessary to be dogmatic in interpreting tests and in discussing progress. In general, conferences should be focused on the individual student and his needs rather than on the test scores.

RECOMMENDATION 15. *The qualified counselor, who may be the test co-ordinator within a school, should be the "expert" resource in testing in the school.*

The very nature of the job of a counselor requires that he have a thorough knowledge of tests, understands the proper use of test results, and possess the ability to integrate test and nontest data in the counseling process. The qualified counselor is a specialist, and full use should be made of his talents. We are writing now about a person who is qualified for his job and not about an inadequately prepared person who has been dubbed "counselor" by the administration.

Good counselors are particularly skilled in the use of test results. They generally have or should have extensive knowledge of the kinds of prediction that can be made from test scores. They use test results (together with other data) for counseling individual students and parents. They can be equally effective in helping classroom teachers improve their competency in interpreting and using test results, particularly in cases in which the teacher is concerned with an individual student. More particularly, a good counselor can serve as a force against overenthusiastic interpretations of test results or of their misapplication. In other words, he can serve as the "devil's advocate" as far as the testing program is concerned. The counselor may, in some situations, assume leadership for follow-up studies and the evaluation of the testing program.

In order to fulfil these functions, the counselor must have a thorough background in testing and, in addition, he must be a master of the counseling process. He needs to be well grounded in the research literature and must be able to read and evaluate research. He must be able to make full use of descriptive statistics and have some understanding of inferential statistics. He should also know and be able to explain the different kinds of available tests, their uses, limitations, and advantages. Above all, he must be able to establish rapport with teachers, students, administrators, and parents.

The basic skills and competencies of the counselor should probably be developed initially in formal educational programs. Maintenance of his competency should be achieved through attendance at professional meetings, special institutes, and conferences. Finally, no counselor can really maintain a desired level of competency unless he systematically reads the professional journals and literature for counselors and for testers.

RECOMMENDATION 16. *Schools should take advantage of the many available resources, some free, that provide help in developing and maintaining the competencies of staff members in testing.*

First, most schools can afford to have some kind of professional library for their staffs. Every school using tests should try to have available Buros' *Fourth* and *Fifth Mental Measurements Yearbooks.*[3] These yearbooks are valuable not only in selecting tests for use in a school testing program but also in helping to educate the reader about the technical aspects of tests and the importance of these technical aspects to the use of the tests. One or two good textbooks in measurement and evaluation should be available in the school library. A good textbook in testing not only helps the reader understand the technical aspects of testing but also helps him understand better how to use and interpret test results. If money for a library is limited, reviews of the available books that appear in competent journals should be consulted before a choice is made.

There are a number of sources of free materials that should be a part of the school library. The Psychological Corporation, Educational Testing Service, Harcourt Brace and World Testing Department, California Test Bureau, Houghton Mifflin Company Test Division, Science Research Associates, and the Bobbs-Merrill Company Test Division, all publish free test bulletins that are available on request. Some of these bulletins emphasize general aspects of testing and testing programs. They are written for people who are not experts in testing and, on the whole are quite useful. However, some of the bulletins are written for the express purpose of promot-

---

3. Oscar K. Buros (Editor), *Fourth Mental Measurements Yearbook* (1953). *Fifth Mental Measurements Yearbook* (1959). Highland Park, New Jersey: Gryphon Press.

ing the publisher's tests and are biased. It would be helpful if a school could get impartial evaluation of these materials, perhaps from a university or a state department.

A second source of help on testing may be tapped through correspondence with the test publishers. Most of the major test publishers maintain some sort of advisory service. Sometimes the service is free, particularly to the users of the publisher's tests, and sometimes there is a fee for the service. One of the outstanding advisory services available from a test publisher is the Evaluation and Advisory Service of Educational Testing Service. In addition to publishing helpful booklets on testing that are free, the Advisory Service also answers queries about testing problems. Information on the kinds of service available can be obtained by writing to the Educational Testing Service, Princeton, New Jersey. Some test publishers maintain consultants or representatives in different geographical regions who are made available to schools for various purposes upon request. However, one should be cautious in the use of some of these representatives because too many of them have not been trained in testing; their primary job is distributing the publisher's tests.

A third source of help in testing is the department of education in the state in which the school is located. Many state departments, from time to time, publish materials on testing that are quite informative and also offer free consultant services to the schools in their states. Since the National Defense Education Act has been in operation, many state departments can provide consultant help to the schools. A person concerned with testing in a school should write to his state department of education to determine precisely what kinds of help are available from that source.

Schools or school systems that are located near colleges or universities can usually obtain consultant help from them. Many state universities have research and service units devoted to public education and provide help to public schools free of charge. The services available in the different state universities vary so much that only by writing to the university of his state can one determine what services, if any, are available either free of charge or for a nominal fee.

Many professional organizations from time to time publish materials on tests or testing. The yearbooks of the National Council on Measurement in Education contain many articles on the use of tests. Every third year, dating back from February, 1962, the *Review of Educational Research* has featured an issue on educational and psychological testing of the preceding triennium. The National Education Association has published a series of articles designed for lay audiences on intelligence testing and other testing problems. It has also made available a color filmstrip on the meaning of intelligence test results. The National Education Association, in conjunction with the International Film Bureau, Inc., has issued three movies on testing (*Who Is Pete?* and *The Standardized Test: An Educational Tool*, which emphasize the use of group test results, and *Introduction to the Stanford-Binet Test of Intelligence*, which demonstrates the administration, interpretation, and use of the individual intelligence test). All of these movies can be rented, and all are particularly useful in in-service programs on testing.

Above all, every staff member should bring the articles or materials about testing that are published in the professional journals that he reads to the attention of the members of the staff.

CHAPTER XII

Interpretation of Test Scores

MERLE M. OHLSEN

As the title indicates, this chapter is concerned with the interpretation of test scores for students and their parents. Increased self-understanding on the part of students is the obvious reason for interpreting tests, but it is not the only reason for testing. The other major reasons for testing were presented in the earlier chapters.

This chapter begins with a number of recommendations, which are followed by a review of the research literature, a discussion of the meaning of test scores, suggestions for interpreting tests commonly used by counselors and teachers, and a discussion of ethics of testing.

Recommendations Relating to the Interpretation of Test Scores

1. Orientation for acceptance and use of test results should precede testing.

2. Until someone is qualified to use and interpret a test, that test should not be given.

3. Tests and test scores should be released to only those persons who are qualified to use and interpret the tests.

4. Test scores should be interpreted to only appropriate individuals, e.g., students and their parents or legal guardians. In all instances, the pupils' scores should be interpreted within a setting in which unauthorized persons cannot listen in on the interpretation or see the results.

5. Inasmuch as test scores are often misinterpreted by laymen, scores should be interpreted for pupils and parents, not merely distributed to them. Furthermore, scores should be interpreted when pupils or their parents request information. Unless there is

a genuine felt need for information, the odds are against an increase in self-understanding on the part of the pupil or understanding on the part of the parent or even against the acceptance by the parent of information about his child.

6. Before interpreting a test, a teacher or counselor should familiarize himself with the non-test data available on the student. During the test interpretation he also should encourage the pupil to supplement the test results with non-test data.

7. A test-interpreter should encourage student participation in interpreting test scores. To help a student recall what a test, or a part of a battery, was like, the teacher or counselor can describe it in nontechnical language, and he will usually find that it is helpful to show the student sample items from the test, before encouraging the student to estimate how well he did on it. If the counselor is to do this successfully, it is obvious that he must know the student and be thoroughly familiar with the tests in order to communicate accurate information to the student.

8. The test-interpreter must be very sensitive to cues which suggest that the student does not comprehend the information which is being given him.

9. The student should be encouraged to react to the test results —to raise questions or to comment on how he feels about the way the test or tests describe him. When he feels that interpreted remarks are appropriate, he will often respond to data quite spontaneously—telling how pleased he is with some scores or how he does not like or cannot accept others. For the test-interpreter it is important that he detect these feelings and that he be able to respond to them. Helping a student examine these feelings increases the chances for helping him understand and accept himself as he is.

10. There is no justification for arguing with a student about his test scores. Moreover, little can be accomplished by either defending a test or criticizing it. What test-interpreters should do is explain how the results may be used by the student to understand himself and to make certain predictions, and with what certainty.

Even when students seek information about themselves, they often fail to learn from the conference what the teacher or counselor tried to communicate. A staff member can try to understand how a student reacts to the information given him and can encourage him to discuss it, and the student still may distort or reject that part of the information which is not congruent with his present self-image. The chances for helping a student accept and use any information are even poorer when someone tries to provide him with information which is not solicited by him. Where test data are involved, he usually does not understand why the tests were given and the relevance of the results to him. Sometimes he resents being given information about himself—either because he sees no need for such information or because he is afraid that he will discover that he lacks the abilities or aptitudes to achieve some goal which is very important to him or to someone whose love and respect he needs.

These ten recommendations can as well be applied in interpreting tests to parents. Like pupils, parents do not always learn from a conference what the teacher or counselor tried to communicate. Prior to seeking information about their child, most parents have some preconceived notions about him. Along with this image, they usually have developed some aspirations for him. Sometimes the image is not accurate, but the parents are so committed to the goals that they cannot accept test data which suggest that these goals are unrealistic for their child. There also are occasions when parents cannot accept higher test scores than they anticipated. If, for example, poorly educated parents feel that having a bright child means that they should send him to college, they may not be able to accept a high scholastic aptitude test score because, either consciously or unconsciously, they may believe that educating him may cause him to reject them. Use of technical terms may interfere with the communication of test information to parents, too. Consequently, those who interpret tests for parents must take cognizance of many of the same human needs that they consider in interpreting tests to children.

Research on Test Interpretations

The fact is that, all too often, conscientious workers interpret test scores but fail to improve students' understanding of themselves. Though there are studies which clearly indicate that careful interpretation of test scores to students by qualified personnel does improve the students' self-knowledge, there are more studies which indicate the failure of test interpretation to produce increased self-understanding. Those studies which used high-school students as subjects will be reviewed first, followed by those which used college students as subjects. Except for some studies which are in progress, there is nothing to report on the extent to which interpreting test scores improves accuracy of self-image for elementary-school children.

Adamek[1] compared changes in perceptions of interests, mental abilities, and problem areas for three groups—two experimental and one control—of ninth-graders who participated in a testing program which included the *Kuder Preference Record–Vocational*, the *Chicago Primary Mental Abilities Test*, and the *SRA Youth Inventory*. For experimental Group A, the tests were interpreted by a well-qualified counselor in an individual interview in which emphasis was placed upon communicating information—no effort was made to deal with effect. For experimental Group B, the same counselor used the publisher's suggested technique for self-interpretation in small groups. Neither method of test interpretation improved significantly the congruency between test-estimates and self-estimates.

Froehlich and Moser[2] also used ninth-graders as subjects. They administered the *Differential Aptitude Tests,* had pupils draw their own test profiles during the test interpretation, and permitted them to keep their profiles. Pupils also were encouraged to request further assistance. In a fifteen-month follow-up the pupils were asked to re-draw their profiles. Most did not report their scores accurately in the follow-up. Although this does not prove that the self-image was not changed, it certainly raises questions about the use of this approach in increasing self-understanding.

Lallas[3] used eleventh-grade students to compare three methods

1. Edward G. Adamek, "The Effects of Testing and Test Interpretation on Selected Self Perceptions." Unpublished doctoral dissertation, University of Illinois, 1961.

2. C. P. Froehlich and W. E. Moser, "Do Counselees Remember Test Scores?" *Journal of Counseling Psychology*, I (Fall, 1954), 149-52.

3. John E. Lallas, "A Comparison of Three Methods of Interpretation of Results of Achievement Tests to Pupils." Doctor's thesis, Stanford University, 1956. [*Dissertation Abstracts*, XVI, No. 10 (1956), Item 1842.]

of test interpretation: individual interview, group interpretation, and group interpretation plus individual interview. He found that after test interpretation all three experimental groups were superior to the control group in ability to estimate their ability and to identify areas of greatest and least ability. He concluded that all three procedures improved a student's ability to make self-estimates.

Belovsky, McMasters, Shorr, and Singer[4] used twelfth-graders as subjects. Though they labeled what they did as counseling, their treatment consisted primarily of testing accompanied by individual interpretations of tests for one group and of testing accompanied by group interpretation of tests for the other. Using realism of vocational choice as a criterion, they found that chance could account for the slight differences noted between the two groups (58 per cent *vs.* 57 per cent made a realistic choice). Obviously it could be argued whether the findings of this study represent the effects of the treatment or reflect the inadequacy of the criterion.

Lane[5] compared the effectiveness of "traditional" and "permissive" techniques for interpreting test results to eleventh- and twelfth-grade clients. He interpreted the tests for both groups himself. After one week he administered a multiple-choice check list and an essay question, both designed to measure memory of test scores. Three weeks later the tests were re-administered and a correlation of .76 between the scores of the two testings was obtained. He also checked to determine whether he actually played different roles in the two experimental treatments and found that he did. Since he found almost identical scores for the two groups, he concluded that there were no differences in the effectiveness of the methods.

In a study of the interests of high-school students, Singer and Stefflre[6] obtained self-estimates of interests prior to testing and counseling and again three months following test interpretations.

4. David Belovsky, William McMasters, Joseph Shorr, and S. L. Singer, "Individual and Group Counseling," *Personnel and Guidance Journal*, XXXI (1953), 363-65.

5. David Lane, "A Comparison of Two Techniques of Interpreting Test Results to Clients in Vocational Counseling." Doctoral dissertation, Columbia University, 1952 [*Dissertation Abstracts*, XII (1952), 591-92.]

6. Stanley L. Singer and Buford Stefflre, "Analysis of the Self-Estimate in the Evaluation of Counseling," *Journal of Counseling Psychology*, I (1954) 252-55.

They found some significant differences between both means and standard deviations, which suggested increased congruency between test-estimates and self-estimates. They concluded that use of correlational approaches and tests of significance of differences between means in these and similar studies were not adequate. They suggested that investigators who use self-rating techniques should examine the direction of discrepancies between test-estimates and self-estimates as well as the mere size of these discrepancies.

Arsenian[7] investigated the extent to which taking tests increased college Freshmen's estimates of their scholastic aptitude, achievement, adjustment, and interests. He also compared overestimators and underestimators. Post-testing ratings agreed better with test scores than pretesting ratings. However, the variability in estimates continued to be large. Those who grossly overestimated and underestimated their abilities, knowledge, and adjustment were somewhat less intelligent and less well-adjusted than the rest of the group.

Biersdorf[8] recruited from introductory psychology and speech courses male college students who were interested in receiving assistance with vocational plans. Using random methods, the students were divided into three groups for (a) limited group treatment, (b) extended group treatment, and (c) purposes of control. The first group received group interpretation of the vocationally relevant tests which they had taken. The second group received, in addition to the test interpretation, a discussion of factors relevant for making vocational plans. She concluded that neither the limited group treatment nor the extended group treatment was more effective than no treatment.

From discussions with their counseling staff, Dressel and Matteson[9] concluded that there were wide variations in procedures used by their counselors in interpreting tests. These procedures differed

7. Seth Arsenian, "Own Estimates and Objective Measurement," *Journal of Educational Psychology*, XXXIII (1942), 291-302.

8. Kathryn R. Biersdorf, "The Effectiveness of Two Group Vocational Guidance Treatments." Doctor's thesis, University of Maryland, 1958. [*Dissertation Abstracts*, XIX, No. 1 (1958), 162-64.]

9. Paul L. Dressel and Ross W. Matteson, "The Effects of Client Participation in Test Interpretation," *Educational and Psychological Measurement*, X, No. 4 (1950), 693-706.

largely in the amount of client participation involved. For the purposes of their study they developed a test of self-understanding in order to determine the actual increase in the client's self-knowledge of characteristics tested, and they also constructed a reliable rating scale which was used by judges to assess the degree of client participation in test interpretation. They found that counselors varied greatly among themselves in the amount of participation elicited from clients (university Freshmen) and that the mean gains in self-understanding made by clients appeared to be closely related to the mean client-participation index. These findings suggest that counselors who encourage a high degree of client-participation were more successful in stimulating client growth than were the other counselors.

Gustad and Tuma[10] investigated the effects of three methods of test introduction (with varying degrees of responsibility assumed by the counselor for introducing the idea of testing) and four methods of test interpretation (with varying degrees of responsibility assumed by counselor for pointing out discrepancies between students' self-estimates and test-estimates). Neither the methods of introducing tests nor the methods of interpreting tests showed any differential effects on client learning. Client learning was positively related to initial accuracy of self-ratings, but not to scholastic aptitude. In another paper, they[11] also reported the effects of client and counselor personality on client learning. Counselors who used essentially the same method with similar clients produced different effects. The investigators concluded that there was a positive relationship between amount of client learning and amount of client-counselor similarity.

Holmes[12] compared the effectiveness of four methods (varying

10. John W. Gustad and A. H. Tuma, "The Effects of Different Methods of Test Introduction and Interpretation on Client Learning in Counseling," *Journal of Counseling Psychology*, IV, No. 4 (1957), 313-17.

11. A. H. Tuma and John W. Gustad, "The Effects of Client and Counselor Personality on Client Learning," *Journal of Counseling Psychology*, IV, No. 2 (Summer, 1957), 136-43.

12. June E. Holmes, "The Comparison of Four Techniques Used in Presenting Test Information to Freshmen Students." Doctor's thesis, Boston University, 1959. [*Dissertation Abstracts*, XXI (1961), 11, Item 3379.]

in amount of student participation encouraged) of presenting test
information to Freshmen students in teacher education. The students were matched for age, sex, and residence. She concluded that
all four methods tended to help these students understand themselves. Furthermore, the extent to which student participation was
encouraged did not seem to influence students' attitudes toward
their counselor.

Johnson[13] used volunteer male clients to study effects of vocational counseling on increased accuracy and certainty of self knowledge. He concluded that significant growth was achieved in both.
A follow-up a month later indicated that these gains were maintained. Gains in self-understanding were greatest with respect to
intelligence, followed by interests and personality, respectively.

Kamm and Wrenn[14] appraised clients' acceptance of self-in-
formation based on forty educational-vocational planning interviews with General College Freshmen at the University of Minnesota. They reported that a client was most apt to accept information
when both the client and the counselor were relaxed, when the
client was expressing positive attitudes, when the information which
was given was directly related to the client's immediate problem,
and when the information was not in opposition to the client's
self-concept. Moreover, information which made the client appear
to be like others was better accepted than information which made
him appear to be different from others. They concluded that a
counselor would do well to pay less attention to the content of
what the client says and to devote more attention to how the client
seems to feel about what he is learning about himself.

Rogers[15] compared two kinds of test interpretation: (a) a test-
centered method in which there was little client involvement, and
(b) a self-evaluation method in which there was much emphasis on

---

13. Davis G. Johnson, "The Effects of Vocational Counseling on Self-
Knowledge," *Educational and Psychological Measurement*, XIII, No. 2 (Summer, 1953), 330-38.

14. Robert B. Kamm and C. Gilbert Wrenn, "Client Acceptance of Self-
Information in Counseling," *Educational and Psychological Measurement*, X,
No. 1 (Spring, 1950), 32-42.

15. L. B. Rogers, "A Comparison of Two Kinds of Test Interpretation
Interview," *Journal of Counseling Psychology*, I, No. 4 (Winter, 1954), 224-31.

self-study and use of non-test as well as test data. Both methods seemed to contribute to improved self-understanding of college students with respect to abilities and interests. No statistically significant differences in the effectiveness of the two methods were noted.

Torrance[16] used college Freshmen as subjects for his study. Like Arsenian, he found that there was little relationship between self-estimates and test-estimates. For example, in the original estimate over 65 per cent of the total group placed themselves in the upper fourth in scholastic ability, and 95 per cent placed themselves in the upper half of their class. When given a chance to re-evaluate themselves after conferences with counselors and academic advisers, there was a general revision downward in the direction of more realistic self-evaluation. Women evaluated themselves much more accurately than did men, and also more frequently underevaluated themselves. Follow-up clinical studies suggested that those who made the greatest errors in describing themselves were plagued by a sense of vulnerability.

Wright[17] compared the effects of two methods of interpreting tests. He used two experimental groups and one control group. Both experimental groups were invited by letter to have their Freshman guidance tests interpreted. Students assigned to Group I had their tests interpreted in individual interviews, whereas those assigned to Group II had their tests interpreted in groups of from five to ten. For both groups, self-estimates became significantly more congruent with test-estimates of aptitude and achievement profiles, but for only Group I were self-ratings on interest tests improved. While very few differences were obtained between the two counseled groups, both improved significantly more than the control group.

From these studies it appears that maturity of clients may be a factor in determining the extent to which students profit from

16. E. Paul Torrance, "Some Practical Uses of a Knowledge of Self-Concepts in Counseling and Guidance," *Educational and Psychological Measurement,* XIV (1954), 120-27.

17. E. Wayne Wright, "A Comparison of Individual and Multiple Counseling for Test Interpretation Interviews." Unpublished dissertation, University of California, Berkeley, 1957.

test interpretation. At least, best results were consistently obtained with more mature students. O'Hara and Tiedeman[18] presented support for the hypothesis that maturity is a factor. They investigated ninth- and twelfth-grade boys' estimates of their present status with reference to aptitudes, interests, social class, general values, and social values. Except for the area of social class, self-estimates of twelfth-graders were more congruent with test estimates than were self-estimates of ninth-graders. At Grade IX, self-estimates correlated with test-estimates as follows: interest, .70; work values, .69; general values, .56; and aptitudes, .44. However, at Grade XII the correlations were: interest, .83; work values, .84; general values, .63; and aptitudes, .69. The authors concluded that self-concepts are clarified as boys pass through Grades IX to XII.

Schulman[19] hypothesized that a high-school education would increase accuracy of self-image between Grades IX and XII. To test his hypothesis he matched a sample of ninth- and twelfth-graders. Following group discussions led by experienced school counselors to provide them with an understanding of the required task, the students rated themselves on the eight subjects of the *Differential Aptitude Tests,* then took the tests. Like O'Hara and Tiedeman, he also concluded that Seniors have a more realistic picture of their abilities than do ninth-graders.

In many of the studies that have been cited, a self-rating device was used to appraise effectiveness of test interpretations. Berdie,[20] although stating that these devices are useful for such purposes, stressed the distinction between learning and accepting; he indicated that learning refers to ability to reproduce verbally, while accepting refers to changes in the total pattern of behavior. His point is a good one. Until these changes in self-images which clients reproduce verbally are integrated and translated into improved behavior,

---

18. R. P. O'Hara and D. V. Tiedeman, "The Vocational Self-Concept in Adolescents," *Journal of Counseling Psychology,* VI, No. 4 (Winter, 1959), 292-301.

19. Jacob Schulman, "A Comparison between Ninth- and Twelfth-Grade Students on Self-Estimates of Abilities and Objective Scores on the Differential Aptitude Tests," *Dissertation Abstracts,* XVI (1956), 285-86.

20. Ralph F. Berdie, "Changes in Self-Ratings as a Method of Evaluating Counseling," *Journal of Counseling Psychology,* I, No. I (Winter, 1954), 49-54.

little has been accomplished by improving congruency between self-estimates and test-estimates. It is likely, however, that more accurate self-ratings precede improved behavior.

The extent of student participation also seems to be a factor in increasing congruence between self-estimates and test-estimates. This may have relevance for Berdie's notion of acceptance. For some time Rogers has attacked the idea of a counselor using tests to evaluate a client. He has argued that if real growth is to be achieved, the locus of evaluation must remain within the client. He sums up his case as follows:

> In sum, it is my concern that this major trend in clinical work leads gradually and subtly to some loss of confidence in the ability of the self to evaluate, to a basic dependence growing out of loss of self-confidence, to a lesser degree of personhood, to a subtle and sincerely well-meaning control of persons by a group which, without realizing it, has selected itself to exercise that control.[21]

Torrance[22] concluded that the use of self-evaluation procedures contributed to college Freshmen's understanding of themselves:

> The self-evaluation procedures built into the testing program itself contributes to the development of more realistic self-concepts. The initial estimates produce a set for self-evaluation. Having this set, the freshmen may be expected to view the test-taking from the standpoint of self-evaluations.[23]

He also went on to show how this point of view encouraged students to continue self-evaluations by discussions with peers and by conferences with counselors and academic advisers.

The concern about readiness for testing is not new. For many years clinical psychologists have been concerned about those extraneous factors which influence test scores and about developing rapport with pupils in individual testing in order to obtain accurate test scores. What is relatively new is the idea of preparing students for group testing and for interpretation of test scores. In 1946

21. Carl R. Rogers, "Divergent Trends in Methods of Improving Adjustment," *Harvard Educational Review*, XVIII (October, 1948), 209-19.

22. *Op. cit.*

23. *Ibid.*

Bordin and Bixler[24] suggested that counselors encourage client participation in selecting appropriate tests for vocational counseling. From their experience they concluded that client participation in selection of tests made the testing experience itself more meaningful to the client and altered his attitudes toward himself. Seeman[25] appraised Bordin and Bixler's technique. His results indicated that clients selected, from tests available, the appropriate ones for prediction in 93.2 per cent of the possible cases. Seeman also concluded that the manner in which an individual approaches vocational choice is a function of total prevailing level of adjustment. Ambivalence and conflict in selecting tests offer the same opportunities for counseling as any other problem. This writer[26] hypothesized that many of the advantages cited for client-participation in test selection can be achieved by careful orientation of students for group testing. His own experience also suggests that these experiences increase students' readiness for test interpretation.

Goldman said that when a client participates in reaching conclusions about himself from test results, as well as other data, it is very likely that he:

. . . (1) is more accepting and less defensive about the interpretations, since they are in part his; (2) learns about himself more effectively and will remember better and longer what he has learned, because he was an active participant in the learning process; (3) brings in more new relevant data about himself and family, his experiences, and so on, so that the interpretations finally arrived at are more valid than would be true otherwise.[27]

As Goldman sees it, taking the client's frame of reference involves more than trying to understand the client. One who attempts interpretation of test scores also must try to sense the client's per-

24. Edward S. Bordin and Roy H. Bixler, "Test Selection: A Process of Counseling," *Educational and Psychological Measurement*, VI (1946), 361-73.

25. Julius Seeman, "A Study of Client Self-Selection of Tests in Vocational Counseling," *Educational and Psychological Measurement*, VIII, No. 3 (Winter, 1948), 327-46.

26. Merle M. Ohlsen, "Effects of Orientation to Testing on Motivation for and Outcome of Test Interpretation," Appendix A for Project No. 1344, Cooperative Research Program. Washington: U.S. Office of Education, 1961.

27. Leo Goldman, *Using Tests in Counseling*, pp. 381-95. New York: Appleton-Century-Crofts, Inc., 1961.

ception of his abilities, e.g., what it means to him to have average college aptitude.

Although, in the following statement, Cronbach is discussing the use of tests in vocational planning and takes more of an external frame of reference than any of the authors quoted in the preceding paragraphs, he also stresses the importance of helping the client accept as well as understand test results:

> One reason is that vocational choice is not a single final throw of the dice. As a person goes through school and into his first jobs, he has many occasions to narrow his field of concentration or even to transfer to a new area. High-school courses and introductory college courses provide opportunities for him to explore and develop aptitudes and interests. In an expanding economy, workers change positions or change responsibilities within the same establishment. The engineer in the technical firm, for example, may become a manager, a salesman, a creative designer, or an expert on detailed specifications. Wise choice requires self-understanding; no 'prescription' filled out by a tenth-grade or freshman-year counselor can anticipate these subsequent decisions. Test interpretation is only one step in a long process of self-discovery.
>
> Secondly, the client is more likely to accept recommendations which he understands. The counselor may be convinced that a freshman should get out of engineering and into advertising. Even though advertising is consistent with the boy's talents and interests, he may resist or ignore the recommendation. If he has been visualizing himself as an engineer for years, such a change of program requires him to alter his entire self-concept and may seem like an admission of defeat. To accept the new goal requires that he understand the facts the counselor considers significant. Acquiring a new self-image requires both factual and emotional learning.[28]

Knowing the Test

It is essential that test-users have a thorough knowledge of a test before attempting to interpret it. Those responsible for test use must know how the results can be used to help students achieve self-understanding, how the results can be made available to the staff to increase understanding of students needed for planning learning experiences, what the author of the test was attempting to measure, what the test actually measures and/or predicts, with

28. Lee J. Cronbach, *Essentials of Psychological Testing*, pp. 284-85. New York: Harper & Bros., 1960.

whom one compares his students when he uses the test norms, how accurate and stable the scores are, and the conditions under which the tests were administered. If the recommendations made in chapter x are followed, the person(s) in charge of the testing program will know the test thoroughly before selecting it and will make every reasonable effort to insure that those who use the test know it thoroughly before they attempt to interpret it. Chapter vii explains how tests may be used by a counselor to help students understand themselves and use test data in making important decisions. Finally, chapter xi presents a program for developing staff competencies for using tests. Two points will be repeated here for emphasis: (*a*) the test manual should be studied with care, and (*b*) the person who is in charge of the in-service education program should know the major research studies on the test and review them for the staff. At least he should be thoroughly familiar with the reviews of the test presented in such standard works as *The Fifth Mental Measurements Yearbook*[29] and the earlier volumes of the series.

ACCURACY OF TEST SCORES

From careful study of a test and from other activities enumerated in the preceding paragraph, those who use tests should get some notions concerning how accurate its scores are. In part, however, the degree to which a given score describes a student accurately is a function of the way he responded to taking the test and the conditions under which the test was administered. Errors in measurement also account for inaccuracy in test scores. The standard error of measurement is the most common device for taking account of measurement errors in test interpretation. The standard error of measurement (σ_M) is the product of the standard deviation (σ_N) of the scores of the group on which the coefficient of reliability (r) was computed, and the square root of the difference between 1 and the coefficient of reliability ($\sigma_M = \sigma_N \sqrt{1\text{-}r}$). If the test manual does not provide both σ_N and r, these data, needed for the computation of the standard error of measurement, can be obtained from the

29. *The Fifth Mental Measurements Yearbook.* Edited by Oscar K. Buros. Highland Park, New Jersey: Gryphon Press, 1959.

publisher. Regarding the constant (σ_M), the test-user can say that for approximately two-thirds of the persons tested, their observed scores should fall within $1\sigma_M$ of their true scores (or, if they want to be more certain, that 95 per cent of the observed scores should fall within $2\sigma_M$ of the true scores). Recently test publishers [30] have used this fact to help teachers and counselors take cognizance of measurement errors in testing. Since the test-interpreter does not know the true score, he needs an estimated true score in order to define limits within which he is reasonably certain the true score falls. Though he is not completely justified in doing so, he usually is encouraged to use the observed score as the estimated true score to define limits within which he would expect the true score to fall. If, for example, he found that $\sigma_M = 6$, he would assume that for an observed score of 64, the most likely true score is 64 and two-thirds of observed scores of 64 would reflect true scores falling between 58 and 70.

Test publishers [31] have also used the standard error of measurement to define test bands for graphic devices which take account of measurement errors in test interpretations. This technique has the obvious advantage of giving a visual image of the relationship among test scores. It also enables those who interpret the test to estimate the extent to which chance can account for the differences noted between any pair of scores.

Almost a quarter century ago Garrett [32] and Guilford [33] presented arguments for and against the use of the standard error of measurement as a method for taking cognizance of measurement errors. Periodically the issue has been argued since Garrett and

30. "How Accurate Is a Test Score?" *Test Service Bulletin* (Psychological Corporation), No. 50 (1956), 1-3.

31. John E. Dobbin, "The Scores on *SCAT* and *STEP*." Princeton, New Jersey: Cooperative Test Division, Educational Testing Service, 1958 (mimeographed).

32. H. E. Garrett, "An Interpretation of the Standard Error of Measurement," *American Journal of Psychology*, XLIX, No. 4 (October, 1937), 679-80. See also, "A Rejoinder," *American Journal of Psychology*, XLIX, No. 4 (October, 1937), 683-85.

33. J. P. Guilford, *Psychometric Methods*. (New York: McGraw-Hill Book Co., 1936), and "More concerning the Interpretation of the Standard Error of Measurement," *American Journal of Psychology*, XLIX (1937), 680-83.

Guilford presented their views. Those who have a basic knowledge of statistics could profit from Patterson's[34] careful review of the literature on this issue. He said:

While the observed score is an estimate of the true score, it is not the true score, nor is it necessarily the best estimate of the true score. It would appear that this type of interpretation is therefore questionable. Statements concerning the true scores of individuals with a given observed score should be based on the regressed score and its standard error of estimate. While the effort involved in this procedure of estimating true scores may not be justified, statements concerning the true scores associated with observed scores should be limited to such regressed scores. Rigorous logic would indicate, therefore, that statements should be of the type given by Guilford and Lindquist. Nevertheless, use of the observed score as the estimate of the true score is commonly accepted, and appropriate statements concerning the true scores of individuals with a given observed score taken as evidence of the true score are given.[35]

STABILITY OF TEST SCORES

Anyone who has examined intelligence test scores of school children is aware of the wide variations one finds in the scores of certain individuals. Even scores on individual intelligence tests vary considerably from testing to testing, especially scores obtained for individual preschool and primary-school-age children. With reference to this point Cronbach wrote as follows:

Scores of emotionally disturbed or uncooperative children are especially unstable. If maladjustment is continuous, the child's test score and his general performance may be constant, at an impaired level. But, if the causes of emotional disturbance are remedial, drastic changes in I.Q. occur. Long-range planning on the basis of the I.Q. is justified so long as two precautions are observed: Interpretation must consider the elements in the child's background which tend to raise or lower scores, and all judgments must be made tentatively, leaving the way open for a change of plans when change in development appears. . . . Test scores are unstable when behavior patterns are being acquired, and we would expect a pencil-and-paper test score to be unstable in the earliest school years. . . . Despite this stability [at age 17], the tester

34. C. H. Patterson, "The Interpretation of the Standard Error of Measurement," *Journal of Experimental Education*, XXIII, No. 3 (March, 1955), 247-52.

35. *Ibid.*, p. 251.

should not rely on an old mental test score when a critical decision is being made. Some young people make substantial changes in mental performance over a three-year period.[36]

Renick's findings[37] support Cronbach's conclusions. He found that among persons who earned doctorates in the various disciplines, there were many who, as high-school students, appeared to have only average mental ability. Harmon[38] and Strauss[39] obtained essentially the same results. Renick concluded that, though intelligence test scores are useful in making immediate decisions, they must be viewed with distrust in making long-term predictions.

Since 1920, we have learned that mental ability measured by tests is not stable under all conditions. A learning climate that challenges and stimulates, but does not frustrate a child tends to increase I.Q., while a cold, forbidding educational climate operates in reverse for many children.[40]

Allen[41] obtained low correlations between measures of intelligence in Grade I and measures of achievement in Grade III. Her results may be accounted for in part by lack of stability in achievement test scores. Obviously, the students' scores are influenced by errors in measurement, the conditions under which the tests were administered, the students' attitudes toward themselves and testing, and the students' learning skills. If, for example, a student is handicapped by poor reading skills, he may do poorly even in an area like mathematics or science in which he is quite proficient. Upon repeated testing, following successful remedial reading in-

36. Cronbach, op. cit., pp. 179, 223.

37. T. F. Renick, "Early Identification of Potentially Successful Graduate Students." Unpublished doctor's dissertation, University of Illinois, 1961.

38. Lindsey R. Harmon, "High School Backgrounds of Science Doctorates," Science, CXXXIII (1961), 679-88.

39. Samuel Strauss, "High School Backgrounds of Ph.D.'s," Science Education, XLIV (1960), 45-51.

40. Warren G. Findley, "The Problem of Prediction: Two Views." A paper read at the American Personnel and Guidance Convention in Denver, 1961.

41. Mildred M. Allen, "The Relationship between Kuhlmann-Anderson Tests Grade I and Achievement in Grades III and IV," Educational and Psychological Measurement, IV (1944), 161-68.

struction, his scores in mathematics and science may improve markedly. Changes in either the school curriculum or in test batteries also change achievement test scores markedly. When the knowledge, concepts, and skills stressed by the test are very similar to those taught in the school it is obvious that students will do better than when the emphases differ. Furthermore, two tests may bear the same name but evaluate very different things. For example, some achievement tests evaluate primarily the mastery of knowledge, whereas others evaluate the ability to use knowledge. Findley[42] argues that these two differences in emphasis in testing could result in significant variations in scores of one type of gifted underachievers. This type of student is too indifferent and nonconforming to master the details, yet he pays enough attention to absorb the central ideas and he is bright enough to apply what he has learned to new situations. With much of the information often being provided in the newer type of test item, he is only slightly dependent on his organized fund of knowledge. If, on the other hand, he is called upon to recall facts, he is caught short. Consequently, it is logical to assume that his scores on these different types of tests would vary markedly.

There are several quite different explanations which may account for the variations in interest inventory scores. One is that some students do not recognize how they really feel and hence cannot accurately communicate their own feelings when they respond to the choices on the test items. Variation may also be accounted for by recognizing that prior to taking an interest test some youngsters have made a vocational choice or have selected models whom they admire very much. The latter students may develop a rather deep commitment to their model's occupation—sometimes with little awareness on their own part. Others want the prestige which they have associated with certain occupations. If, during one administration of the test, they unconsciously assume another person's role while taking the interest test and, then, on a later administration are able to respond in accordance with the way they really feel, one would expect significantly different scores in those instances in which the assumed self and real self were quite different. Where

42. Findley, *op. cit.*

students see little reason for taking the test, the variation in their test scores can often be accounted for by sheer indifference and carelessness. Finally, some of the basic differences between inventories certainly account for differences in scores.

Super[43] described another reason for lack of stability in interest test scores. He found that interests begin to manifest themselves vocationally in adult form in early adolescence and, although changing somewhat in ways which are systematic for groups, are still unpredictable for individuals during high-school years. He also noted that Kuder test scores changed more during high-school years than did Strong test scores.

> . . . we found that our typical ninth grade boys, in a typical small city high school, with a typical guidance program, were at a stage of vocational development which is characterized by readiness to consider problems of prevocational and vocational choice but also lacked readiness to make vocational choices. Ninth-graders are clearly in an exploratory stage, not in a decision-making stage, of vocational development.[44]

How accurate and stable are aptitude test and personality test scores? In most cases aptitude test scores are about as accurate and stable as intelligence test scores. Whenever one is called upon to interpret the scores for a specific test he should examine the research literature on that test and seek the data that he needs to define the limits within which he may expect estimated true scores to fall. Many of the same elements which influence interest test scores also influence personality test scores. Very likely the latter (especially projective tests) are influenced even more than interest tests by the conditions under which the tests are given and by the person who administers and scores the test.

As a result of this discussion of the accuracy and stability of test scores, one may be prompted to pose the question, "Are tests, then, completely useless?" The answer is, "No." Tests can be used to help teachers better understand their students and to help students better understand themselves. However, those who interpret the test must realize that a given score is not a precise measure. *Instead,*

43. Donald E. Super, "Critical Ninth Grade: Vocational Choice or Vocational Exploration," *Personnel and Guidance Journal*, XXXIX (January, 1960), 106-9.

44. *Ibid.*, p. 108.

*it is a useful estimate which must be interpreted in terms of its ac-
curacy and stability*—not a precise measure which should be given
to students and their parents. Counselors and teachers also must be
wary lest they infer that differences between scores are significant
when, in fact, they can be readily accounted for by chance.

Use of Graphic Devices

Recently test publishers have produced a number of graphic
devices to help test-users understand test data and to help them
interpret results to parents and students. Along with their graphic
devices, a few test publishers have introduced the idea of test bands
to help test interpreters take cognizance of measurement errors.
At least one publisher[45] has also developed a table from which
test-users can obtain standard errors of measurement for given
values of the reliability coefficient and standard deviation. A few
have also included contingency tables, accompanied by graphic
presentations of the data from the tables, to help users interpret
tests more effectively. This writer believes that these various
materials have helped test-users avoid common errors of interpretation and provide test information in meaningful language. However,
the success with which these devices are used should be evaluated
by research.

Unfortunately, these graphic devices have often been accompanied by suggestions for self-interpretation of tests by students.
The review of the literature presented earlier indicated why this
is a questionable practice. Furthermore, this practice is not consistent with the recommendations made in the section on test
interpretations in the bulletin on *Technical Recommendations for
Psychological Tests and Diagnostic Techniques:*

The problem of accuracy is not the only consideration related to
test interpretation. An equally important concern is the examinee's
reactions to interpretations of his test scores, if the interpretation is
made to him. Many educational and clinical uses of tests require reporting the interpretations to the person tested. The teacher who
interprets the results of academic achievement tests affects the student's
self-concept and future learning. The clinician, in making interpretations which bear upon the client's areas of conflict, may unwittingly

45. "How Accurate Is a Test Score?" *op. cit.*

intensify those conflicts. . . .B 3.11 The manual should not imply that the test is "self-interpreting" or that it may be interpreted by a person lacking proper training. B 3.12 The manual should point out the counseling responsibilities assumed when a tester communicates interpretations about ability or personality traits to the person tested.[46]

Another practice that all too frequently leads to undesirable effects is giving students either raw scores or percentile ranks and asking them to draw profiles. Usually they are given very good instructions on how to draw their profiles, but they are not prepared to use the data intelligently. Even when they are told about test bands, and why they are used, the fact still remains that students have scores which they can use in comparing themselves with their siblings and classmates. Consequently, they often treat differences which can be accounted for by irrelevant factors as differences in the behavior described by the test title. Furthermore, students often resent being given test scores in a setting in which classmates can learn their scores or coerce them into revealing their test scores. Such experiences cause students to question whether the staff can be trusted with confidential information.

Students and their parents have the right to know what schools learn about students through use of tests, and students should be informed periodically concerning their progress. This means that students, and their parents, should expect to have tests interpreted to them, but it does not mean that they should be given a student's test scores. It is not a matter of withholding information, but rather it is one of communicating what is known. With reference to this point, the writer would like to quote two of a group of six of the nation's leaders in tests and measurements who were asked to answer the question: Under what circumstances should test scores be reported to students and parents?

Test scores should be discussed with individual students and parents in a confidential conference or interview. The confidential nature of test scores should be stressed. In view of the fact that there are errors of measurement inherent in any test score, it is wise not to release the

46. *Technical Recommendations for Psychological Tests and Diagnostic Techniques*, pp. 10, 12. Prepared by a joint committee of American Psychological Association, American Educational Research Association, and National Council on Measurements Used in Education. Washington: American Psychological Association 1954.

obtained specific score. It is better to indicate that the student has aptitude or achievement that places him, for example, among the upper-fourth or upper-half of the students of his same age or grade; or to indicate that he is reading at fourth-grade, fifth-grade or sixth-grade level. (Wrightstone) [47]

Pupils and parents will derive maximal benefit from the tests when a trained counselor gives them information about the results in the context of other data and observation. (North) [48]

Although both have weaknesses, there are two graphic devices which seem to be of considerable value. One is a profile which uses the test-band idea. The other provides a five-point rating scale for each score on several types of test data on a single sheet, e.g., achievement test scores and intelligence test scores (and it can easily provide space to record relevant school grades for the purpose of making comparisons). Both are used most effectively in individual conferences in which the student is encouraged to participate in the test interpretation and to provide additional personal data to supplement the test data.

The profile with test score bands makes it easy for the test-interpreter to take account of measurement errors and to help a student see the relationship between various scores. It also makes it relatively easy for him to communicate which differences between scores are significant. When the profile sheet includes both achievement test scores and intelligence test scores, he can easily help the student make these comparisons and relate both to school grades. One of the major weaknesses is the misleading effect of profiles on which different tests are plotted, especially when the various tests are based upon different norm groups. Another weakness is that the profile sheets usually provide scores to students and their parents, some of whom may use these figures to make unjustified comparisons.

For the rating scale, all scores are divided into five categories, e.g., (a) bottom 10 per cent, (b) next 15 per cent, (c) middle 50 per cent, (d) the 15 per cent just above the middle, and (e) top 10 per cent. Each of these is then defined in terms which are appropriate for the students and the tests. In interpreting intelligence scores to

47. "Reporting Test Scores," *Education*, XXCI (October, 1960), 86.
48. *Ibid.*, p. 87.

junior high school students, the test-interpreter may say, "This test was developed to help students like you discover how easily you learn. I would like you to estimate about where you would fall, in comparison with others your own age, as I describe five groups of students: (*a*) learns with considerably greater difficulty than most (with great difficulty); (*b*) learns with greater difficulty than most (with difficulty); (*c*) learns as easily as most (like most); (*d*) learns more easily than most (easily); and (*e*) learns much, much more easily than most (very easily). (The words in parentheses appear on the scale.) Now you check where you think you would score on this test, and I will indicate whether the test describes you as you described yourself." Most students seem to understand these descriptions better than test bands. With test data from several tests recorded on a single sheet, it also is relatively easy to compare the various scores and to compare each with school grades. Moreover, fewer students will be in a position to make invidious comparisons than would be the case if they had scores. On the other hand, when one uses this technique it is more difficult to determine whether differences between scores are significant than when one uses profiles with test bands. Since there is a method for coping with the problem, this writer prefers the rating scale over the profile with test bands.

Test publishers who provide profiles with test bands use the standard error of measurement to lay off a percentile band on either side of specific scores. Such bands can also be computed by a test-interpreter who uses the rating scale. He follows these steps: (*a*) obtains either the standard error of measurement or data for computing it from the publisher (computed on the basis of raw scores), and (*b*) converts this figure into percentile bands for each of the following parts of the scale: one for the middle 50 per cent; another for the two 15 per cent parts on either side of the middle; and still another for the 10 per cent at each extreme. Since the raw score differences between percentiles gradually increases as one moves away from the mean in either direction, one must take account of this fact in computing estimated percentile bands for each of the five parts of the scale. Using this method, the writer found that for one test the percentile bands which were roughly equivalent to the standard error of measurement for the various parts of the scale were: 15 (middle), 9, and 4 (extremes). Therefore, a percentile rank of 46 had a band of roughly 31-61, but a percentile rank of 81 had a band of only about 72-90. Consequently, for this test a percentile rank of 81 is significantly different from one of 46, but not necessarily different from one of 70 (55-85). When the bands for two percentile ranks overlap, chance can account for the difference between the scores.

What Is Needed from Publishers

During the past decade test publishers' manuals have been improved markedly. As a matter of fact, many of the suggestions which follow have already been incorporated in some of the better manuals. It is suggested that test manuals should:

1. Indicate how teachers may use intelligence and achievement test results to understand their students and to improve their own teaching.
2. Indicate how students may use the test results to help them understand themselves better and to use the test data along with other data in making important decisions.
3. Explain how non-test data may be used to supplement test scores.
4. Discuss what a staff member needs to know in order to use results to improve teaching and to interpret scores for students and their parents.
5. Include information on the accuracy and stability of the test's scores and provide either test bands or some other devices for taking cognizance of measurement errors.
6. Provide contingency tables for appropriate tests and explain under what conditions it would be appropriate for members of the local staff to develop such tables on the basis of their own peculiar needs.
7. Alert test-interpreters to common errors that are made in interpreting the scores, especially warning them against making unjustified inferences concerning the precision of the test scores.
8. Encourage students and parents to participate in the interpretation of test scores.
9. Encourage students and parents to supplement the test data with other information.
10. Encourage students and parents to react to the test scores.
11. Take cognizance of the counseling responsibilities of the test-interpreter.
12. Explain how the test-interpreter can detect (and why he should take cognizance of) the pupil's and parents' emotional reactions to the test results.

13. Include more and better case materials.
14. Discourage self-interpretation of test scores.

Interpreting Achievement Test Scores

As the first step in interpreting an achievement test, the test-interpreter should review the notes which he made on the test during the in-service education session. Among other things, he should try to determine which subscores are valid for what and the extent to which test reliability is a factor in his use of test results. Next he should review the test manual, looking especially for ideas which he can use to diagnose learning problems and to describe the test in a meaningful way to a student or his parents. Some achievement tests will provide subtest scores which are based upon too few items to be reliable.

Whenever he interprets a test for the first time, a test-user would do well to write out what he expects to say about each score and obtain reactions from someone who knows the test better than he before attempting a test interpretation. Prior to interpreting the test to a student, he also should review relevant non-test data to determine how they agree and disagree with the test data.

If, for example, a test-user were called upon to interpret an achievement test (five scores: vocabulary, reading, language skills, work-study skills, and arithmetic skills) for a seventh-grader he might say: "About a month ago you took an achievement test. Perhaps you remember that it had five main parts. The first part was called a vocabulary test; compared with others in your grade, your score should give you some idea how well you understand words you read and hear others use. The second part should give you some idea how well you understand what you read. The third part tells how well you know and can use your language skills, e.g., spelling, punctuation, proper use of verbs, etc. The fourth part helps you find out how well you can use maps, graphs, tables, and such reference books as dictionaries and encyclopedias. Finally, the last part helps you discover how well you understand the main ideas in arithmetic and can use them in doing arithmetic problems. (The writer encourages test-interpreters to show the pupil samples from the various parts of the test as he describes them.) Here is a line on which parts are marked off to indicate how well you did on each test. There is a line here for each of the five parts of this achievement test, and one to indicate how well you did on the entire test. After I tell you what each part of this line means, I want you to put a check on that part of each line which describes how well you think you did.

VOCABULARY

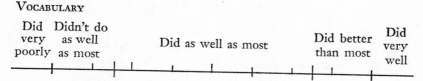

"This big space in the middle is the part where most pupils' scores fall, and if you think that you did about as well as most on the vocabulary test, you should put your check mark there. If you feel that you did better than most seventh-graders, you would put your check mark in this part just above the middle, or if you feel you did not do as well as most seventh-graders, you would put your check mark in this part on the left side of the middle. This part over here (point) to the extreme right describes those pupils who did a lot better than most seventh-graders and the one on the other side (point) describes those who did a lot less well than most seventh-graders. Do you have any questions (pause for questions)? Now you put your check marks where you think you fall on each of these five lines. As you put in these check marks, I wish you would tell me whatever you would like to say about the test and how you felt when you were taking it. After you have finished putting in your check marks I will tell you what the test said about you. Here, too, I hope you will feel that you can tell me how you feel about the results. When, for example, you like what you hear, or don't like what you hear, say so. Whenever you disagree with what the test says about you, tell me about it. All of this will help me to understand you and will help you make sense out of what we learn about you from these tests."

When the pupil's self-estimate agrees with the test estimate, the test-interpreter notes that they agree; then he can be reasonably certain that the pupil knows where he stands, and if he makes no negative comments about the results, or exhibits no negative non-verbal behavior, he may assume that the pupil has accepted himself as pictured by the test. When, however, either the non-test data from the cumulative folder or materials provided by the pupil suggest that the test estimate is questionable, this should be discussed further with the pupil (or the parent), and the test-interpreter may wish to arrange for further testing and/or counseling.

When a pupil's self-estimate disagrees with the test estimate, the test-interpreter indicates where the test estimate places the pupil and watches for any reactions which suggest that the pupil is having difficulty accepting the results. It's a common error to assume that a pupil will accept better scores than he expected, but not poorer ones. Some pupils have great difficulty accepting better scores than they expected. Whenever a pupil exhibits dissatisfaction with a test estimate, the test-interpreter should try to understand how the pupil feels and encourage him to talk about these feelings. Within this permissive relationship it is easier for him to re-evaluate his picture of himself, and even to change his self-estimate. This is especially true of adolescents; they are very sensitive to others' criticisms and judgments of their worth.[49]

Perhaps some readers, at this point, are posing various questions about disagreement of self-estimates and test estimates. For example, "Does this occur only when the estimates fall within different parts of the scale?" or, "Does falling within the same part of the scale necessarily indicate that there is no significant difference between the estimates?" To answer these questions, the test-interpreter must ask the pupil what was intended whenever he puts his check mark at the top or bottom of a part of the scale. Usually when a pupil does this he is trying to indicate that he is at the very top or bottom of that part of the scale. If that is not what was intended, the test-interpreter uses the median percentile rank for that part of the scale to determine whether the pupil's estimate is significantly different from the percentile rank for the test estimate. (See the earlier section of this chapter on "Use of Graphic Devices" to determine how to compute these differences.) When a pupil places himself

49. N. W. Ackerman, "Group Psychotherapy with a Mixed Group of Adolescents," *International Journal of Group Psychotherapy*, V (1955), 249-60.

at the top of one part of the scale and the test places him at the bottom of the scale above it (or vice versa), the test-interpreter does not suggest that there is disagreement; instead he merely notes that the pupil's scores falls at about the dividing line between the two parts of the scale.

The frame of reference for most pupils is their classmates. Therefore, when local norms differ from national norms, the test-interpreter should interpret the test first in terms of local norms, then in terms of national norms. For elementary-school pupils, the test-user may wish to supplement the rating scale information with grade equivalent scores. Where it seems appropriate to use achievement test data to predict future behavior (e.g., chances for success in college), the test-interpreter should request data for contingency tables from publishers when such tables are not provided in the manual. He also should seriously consider developing such tables on the basis of local data.

Even when the test interpretation has gone well up to this point, teachers and parents will often ask whether the student's scores were satisfactory, and they should be encouraged to do so. To determine whether a child's achievement test scores are satisfactory, one must have adequate data to answer three additional questions: (a) How easily does he learn? (b) Does he have any serious handicaps which have interfered with his school progress? (c) What progress has been made during the past year? For those who do as well as most in a typical school (the middle 50 per cent, or average group), the grade equivalents usually vary from approximately one grade below their grade placement to one grade above. Of course, this middle band varies with the achievement test. Hence, the teacher must consult the manual for the test in order to identify this middle group.

Finally, after the test has been interpreted, the rating scale should be filed in the student's folder with the test-interpreter's notes on pertinent non-test data, the pupil's and/or parents' reactions to the test results, suggestions for using results to improve learning, and, when necessary, suggestions of the test-interpreter for further testing and/or counseling. He also should note on the rating scale the name and form of the test used, norms used, pupil's age and grade, date administered, date interpreted, and to whom.

Interpreting Intelligence Test Scores

Statements made in the preceding section concerning preparation for test interpretation applies to intelligence tests and interest tests too. Perhaps the precautions on using subtest scores are even more relevant here. Before accepting the verbal and quantitative (or language and non-language) scores at face value, test-users should study with care the test reviews and the research literature on the test. Increasingly during the last three decades, intelligence tests have tended to provide users with separate scores for verbal and quantitative abilities, and the use of factor analysis in the study of intelligence has tended to support this trend. Recently, however, some of the measurement specialists have challenged this approach to intelligence testing and have presented a case for a single measure of general intelligence. Obviously, space cannot be provided in this chapter to review all the elements in this debate, but users of tests which provide these subscores should be thoroughly familiar with the research evidence on the test. It cannot be taken for granted that the scores predict that behavior which it appears they should predict.

DIFFERENCES BETWEEN ACHIEVEMENT AND INTELLIGENCE TESTS

Earlier this writer quoted from an issue of *Education* in which six measurement specialists were asked to answer some practical questions on testing. Now he should like to quote briefly from what three of them had to say about the differences between achievement tests and intelligence tests:

The achievement test differs from the intelligence test in that it is focused more precisely on the learnings that have taken place in the classroom. Naturally, there is a rather high positive relationship between intelligence tests and achievement tests, since we really are saying that, in general, learning in the classroom situation parallels learning in the total social situation, which includes the classroom. (Hastings) [50]

The typical achievement test usually deals with a narrower range of academic knowledge than the typical intelligence test and includes more items for a comprehensive measurement of that range. On the other hand, many parts of the typical intelligence test involve novel

50. "The Role of Intelligence Testing," *Education*, XXCI (October, 1960), 76.

situations not usually found in the typical achievement test. Thus the intelligence test's novelty and apparent unrelatedness to ordinary school subjects may create greater interest and better testing morale on the part of students who have antipathies toward one or more subjects than will the achievement test. . . (Rummel) [51]

An intelligence test should be regarded as only one of the many measures that schools use to assess the aptitudes and achievements of the individual. Proper use of tests involves continuous reassessment of the individual's abilities by means of a comprehensive review of all current data about the individual as he grows and develops. Intelligence and achievement measures should be regarded as dynamic, rather than static or fixed, indexes of the potential of an individual. (Wrightstone) [52]

The foregoing statements concerning achievement and intelligence tests should make the user better understand why these test scores are similar for most students but can differ markedly for some students. These quoted statements also help make the case for considering non-test data with test data in attempting to help students better understand themselves and their school behavior and to help them predict how they are apt to perform in the future. The remainder of this section will be devoted to illustrating how to interpret test scores and use results to improve learning.

A SAMPLE CASE

The twelfth-grade subject of this case study is a farmer's son. Neither of his parents graduated from high school. Throughout elementary school he did satisfactory work in all subjects, and exceptionally well in arithmetic. Early in the seventh grade his general-science teacher took special note of his work and encouraged him to study science. For the first three and a half years of high school he made almost all A's in mathmatics and science, but mostly C's in English and social studies. There was one exception in social studies; he earned an "A" in economics. He wanted to go to college, but was not sure he could measure up to the demands of college rhetoric. His ratings on an intelligence test which provides two subscores are presented graphically immediately following the next paragraph.

51. *Ibid.*, p. 79.
52. *Ibid.*, p. 78.

When the boy asked the counselor about his test results, the counselor encouraged him to estimate how well he did on the test. (In each instance the " √ " is his self-estimate, and the "X" is the test estimate, which was added by the counselor after the boy had made all three of his self-estimates.) The subscores and the parts of the scale were defined for the boy as follows: "This test was designed to help students like you discover how easily you learn. The verbal score tells how well you understand words and can use them to solve problems. The quantative score tells how well you use numbers and can deal with ideas which are expressed in numerical terms. The last score combines the two into a total score. The parts of this line are defined as follows: (*a*) the middle: you put a check mark here when you wish to indicate that you *learn as easily as most* of your classmates; (*b*) put your check mark in the part to the right of the middle when you wish to indicate that it is *easier for you* to learn than it is for most of your classmates; (*c*) a check mark in this part to the left of middle indicates that it is more *difficult for you to learn* than it is for most classmates; (*d*) a check in this part to your extreme right indicates it is *a lot easier for you to learn* than it is for most classmates; and (*e*) a check mark in this part to your extreme left indicates that it is *a lot more difficult for you* to learn than it is for most classmates.

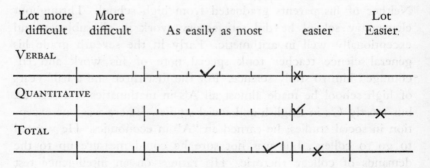

Lot more difficult   More difficult   As easily as most   easier   Lot Easier.

VERBAL

QUANTITATIVE

TOTAL

How did this boy react to the discrepancies between his self-estimates and the test estimates? When the counselor indicated that the boy had underrated himself, the boy said that he was pleased to learn that his scores were higher than he thought they were, but he did not appear to be convinced. Consequently, the counselor responded to the boy's inability to accept the new image of himself. This helped the boy to discuss his doubts about his chances for success in college. When he realized that the counselor could understand why he doubted his ability, he was able to examine his doubts more completely than he ever had before. He also discovered how these doubts had affected his school work—why he gave up too easily in some courses when perhaps he could have done better if he had had more confidence in himself. Moreover, the counselor suggested some things that he could do to correct certain deficiencies. This encouraged him too.

This boy's case was selected to illustrate how differences between these subscores can be meaningful. Achievement test scores, grades, and the boy's personal history not only supported but also tended to account for the scores. Whenever a test-user discovers such differences in "V" and "Q" scores, he should investigate the possibility of a reading problem. In this case, such an investigation revealed that the boy read as well as or a bit better than most seniors. That is not good enough for this boy to realize his full potential. Remedial reading instruction and a semester's work in vocabulary instruction improved significantly his achievement test scores in both reading and vocabulary. These experiences also increased his confidence in his ability to succeed in college.

THE UNDERACHIEVER

Often teachers discover another type of underachiever—pupils who are either educationally or culturally so deprived that they cannot exhibit their real ability on either subscore. Whenever a teacher discovers a pupil who seems to have *much* greater ability than he is able to exhibit on tests, the teacher should refer the child to a psychologist for an individual intelligence test and a diagnosis of learning skills. Even when a child knows more subject matter than his verbal skills permit him to exhibit on achievement tests, he cannot be expected to perform well in school until he receives the needed remedial instruction. Those factors which interfere with test performance also interfere with school success.

There also are underachievers who possess the learning skills to do well but lack the will to achieve. On the type of rating scale that has been described, their intelligence test scores usually fall in a part of the scale which is one or more steps above their grades. Their grades usually fall below their standardized achievement test scores too. Those in the top 10 per cent of the group may earn mostly A's and still be underachievers. Teachers usually recognize that, in spite of their superior performance, these students are not doing what they are capable of doing.

Some experts believe that underachievers' failure to achieve more merely reflects their antisocial attitudes. Another explanation which deserves careful study was developed by Gilmore.[53] He claimed that underachievement satisfies some of these students' unconscious needs, e.g., expression of hostility toward parents, acceptance by peers, belief that he is no good—that he does not deserve to do well.

Because gifted underachievers could help meet the nation's great current need for highly educated manpower, much has been written recently about them and methods which could be employed to salvage this manpower. Those who would like to achieve a better understanding of the gifted underachiever and to obtain suggestions for helping him would do well to study the new U.S. Office of Education bulletin,[54] and research reports by Karnes,[55] Pierce,[56] and Shaw.[57] Intellectually those selected for study have varied from the top 5 per cent to the top 25 per cent of the population. Of this group, Shaw said:

> It has been a typical research experience to find that students classified as underachievers on the basis of grades, characteristically

53. John V. Gilmore, "Clinical Counseling and Academic Achievement." A paper read at American Personnel and Guidance Association Convention in Chicago, March 30, 1953.

54. *Guidance for the Underachiever with Superior Ability.* Edited by Leonard M. Miller. Washington: U.S. Office of Education, Department of Health, Education, and Welfare, 1961.

55. Merle B. Karnes, "Factors Associated with Underachievement and Overachievement of Intellectually Gifted Children." Champaign, Illinois: Champaign Public Schools, 1961 (mimeographed).

56. James V. Pierce, "The Educational Motivation Patterns of Superior Students Who Do and Do Not Achieve in High School." Chicago: University of Chicago, 1960 (mimeographed).

57. Merville C. Shaw, "The Interrelationship of Selected Personality Factors in High Ability Underachieving School Children." Chico, California: Chico State College, 1961 (mimeographed).

are achieving at, or near, their true level of potential as indicated by the results of standardized achievement tests. The converse situation is not always true. Typically, if a high ability student has received high grades, his achievement test scores will reflect this. Only occasionally do high-ability students who have received high grades fall below their expected level of performance on standardized achievement tests.[58]

These gifted underachievers have certain characteristics which may help school personnel identify them. Shaw concluded that underachievement is predominantly a male problem. His review of the studies revealed that approximately half of all males with above-average ability were underachievers, whereas only approximately a fourth of such girls were underachievers. Shaw and McCuen[59] found that chronic male underachievers displayed underachieving behavior in primary grades, whereas most girls did not tend to exhibit this behavior until late elementary-school or junior high school grades. Shaw and Grubb[60] described underachievers as hostile, as did Gowan.[61] Gowan also described them as indifferent to their responsibilities, self-sufficient, and hard to reach. Compared to gifted achievers, Pierce[62] found that underachievers were less responsible and independent, less active in extracurricular activities, exhibited less leadership, and saw their fathers as less important to them. Karnes[63] reported that the following factors appeared to be associated with academic underachievement: "(1) a perceived lack of emotional support from parents; (2) poor peer relationships; (3) guardedness and lack of spontaneity in interpersonal relationships; (4) superficial self-reliance and independence used to mask feelings of inferiority; (5) unrealistic goals; (6) a high level of anxiety,

58. Merville C. Shaw, "Definition and Identification of Academic Under-achievers," in *Guidance for the Underachiever with Superior Ability, op. cit.,* chap. ii.

59. M. C. Shaw and J. T. McCuen, "The Onset of Academic Under-achievement in Bright Children," *Journal of Educational Psychology,* LI (June, 1960), 103-8.

60. M. C. Shaw and J. Grubb, "Hostility and Able High School Under-achievers," *Journal of Counseling Psychology,* V (Winter, 1958), 263-66.

61. J. C. Gowan, "The Underachievement Gifted Child—A Problem for Everyone," *Journal of Exceptional Children,* XXI (April, 1955), 247-49.

62. Pierce, *op. cit.*

63. Karnes, *op. cit.,* p. 37.

latent or manifest; (7) withdrawal tendencies in competitive areas; (8) difficulty in personal integration; and (9) lack of persistence in attaining goals." For Grades IV through X Shaw and Grubb[64] found that underachievers had a more negative outlook than achievers of the same sex and grade level; underachievers also had negative self-attitudes, and, though they seemed to be conforming, they displayed rather than suppressed their hostile feelings. Broedel, Ohlsen, Proff, and Southard[65] used a four-man observer team to analyze gifted underachieving ninth-graders' behavior during counseling. These observer teams noted that these adolescents were hostile, difficult to reach, and self-rejecting; they also noted that these underachievers questioned their giftedness. This tendency of the underachievers to reject their high-level learning aptitude may explain why intelligence test scores drop significantly for some underachievers between lower elementary grades and high school.

INTERPRETING THE I.Q.

Though more difficult to interpret than percentile ranks, intelligence quotients (I.Q.'s) are often recorded for intelligence test scores, and most test manuals provide tables for converting scores into I.Q.'s. In interpreting intelligence tests, teachers and counselors often need some general picture of a distribution of I.Q.'s. Cronbach[66] developed a very useful table (Table 1) on distribution of I.Q.'s based upon the research of Terman and Merrill,[67] Semans,[68] and Plant[69] and another table (Table 2) on expectancies at various

64. Shaw and Grubb, *op. cit.*

65. J. Broedel, M. Ohlsen, F. Proff, and C. Southard, "The Effects of Group Counseling on Gifted Underachieving Adolescents," *Journal of Counseling Psychology*, VII (Fall, 1960), 163-70.

66. Cronbach, *op. cit.*, pp. 172-74.

67. Louis M. Terman and Maud A. Merrill, *Measuring Intelligence*. Boston: Houghton Mifflin Co., 1959.

68. H. H. Semans, T. C. Holy, and L. H. Dunigan, "A Study of the June 1955 Graduates of Public High Schools in Certain California Counties," *California Schools*, XXVII (December, 1956), 417-30.

69. Walter T. Plant, "Mental Ability Scores for Freshmen in a California State College," *California Journal of Educational Research*, IX (March, 1958), 72-73.

I.Q. levels based upon the research of Beckman,[70] Havighurst and Janke, [71] Plant and Richardson, [72] Wolfle, [73] and the *Guide to Use of the General Aptitude Test Battery*. [74]

TABLE 1

PERCENTAGE OF DISTRIBUTION OF I.Q.'s

I.Q.	STANDARDIZING SAMPLE (N=2904)	H. S. GRADUATES (N=21,597)	COLLEGE GRADUATES (N=1,093)
	Per cent	*Per cent*	*Per cent*
120 & above	12.6	9.7	31.7
110 - 119	18.1	22.8	46.1
100 - 109	23.5	29.9	18.1
90 - 99	23.0	23.2	4.0
89 and below....	22.7	14.3	0.1

TABLE 2

EXPECTANCIES AT VARIOUS LEVELS OF MENTAL ABILITY

I.Q.	EXPECTANCIES
130	Mean of persons receiving Ph.D.
120	Mean of college graduates
115	Mean of freshmen in typical four-year college
	Mean of children from white-collar and skilled-labor homes
110	Mean of high-school graduates
	Has 50-50 chance of graduating from college
105	Has 50-50 chance of passing in academic high-school curriculum
100	Average for total population
90	Mean for children from low-income city homes or rural homes
	Adult can perform jobs requiring some judgment, e.g., operating sewing machine or assembling parts
75	About 50-50 chance of reaching high school
	Adult can operate small store, perform in orchestra
60	Adult can repair furniture, harvest vegetables, assist electrician
50	Adult can do simple carpentry, domestic work
40	Adult can mow lawns, do simple laundry

70. A. A. Beckman, "A Minimal Intelligence Level for Several Occupations," *Personnel Journal*, IX (June, 1930), 309-13.

71. Robert J. Havighurst and Leota L. Janke, "Relations between Ability and Social Status in Midwestern Community," *Journal of Educational Psychology*, XXXV (September, 1944), 357-68; XXXVI (November, 1945), 499-509.

72. Walter T. Plant and Harold Richardson, "The I.Q. of the Average College Student," *Journal of Counseling Psychology*, V (Fall, 1958), 229-31.

73. Dael Wolfle, *America's Resources of Specialized Talent*. New York: Harper & Bros., 1954.

74. *Guide to Use of the General Aptitude Test Battery*. Washington: Government Printing Office, 1958.

ERRORS IN INTERPRETING INTELLIGENCE TESTS

Inasmuch as certain mistakes are often made in interpreting intelligence test scores, it is well to call them to the attention of the reader:

1. Indiscriminate dissemination of test scores—consequently, the scores are not understood and parents and/or students often use them to make invidious comparisons.
2. Failure to recognize emotional reactions to test scores and to take cognizance of them.
3. Failure to communicate what the test scores mean and to help the student and/or parent accept and use test data in making decisions.
4. Treating scores as more precise measures than they are.
5. Failure to take cognizance of relevant non-test data.
6. Making either unwarranted predictions or failing to use scores to make reasonable predictions.
7. Making educational placements on only a single test score—e.g., selecting gifted students for advanced placement in a secondary-school subject on basis of scores from a single group test. For such decisions, group test data should be supplemented by scores from an individual intelligence test, achievement test scores in the subject area, previous grades in the subject, recommendations from former teachers in that subject, and a statement from the student on the relevance of the special course for him. When a bright under-achiever makes a good case for admission to such a course, and the person or persons responsible for selecting students demonstrates respect for his judgment by admitting him to the course, even if only on a trial basis, a turning point in his academic career may have been reached. In developing his case he often clarifies his goals and makes the commitments which he needs to succeed.

Interpreting Interest Inventory Scores

Earlier, the writer discussed various ways in which a student's aspirations, his models, his feelings about himself, and the extent to which his interests have matured can influence his scores on an interest inventory. His ability to comprehend items in the inventory also may influence his scores. For example, Johnson and Bond[75] concluded that, in order to insure that students comprehend the items in the *Kuder Preference Record—Vocational*, it should be

75. Ralph H. Johnson and Guy L. Bond, "Reading Ease of Commonly Used Tests," *Journal of Applied Psychology*, XXXIV (October, 1950), 319-24.

used cautiously below the ninth-grade level. All of these factors must be considered in interpreting interest test scores. The interpreter will, among other things, note when the student took the test, examine the cumulative folder for evidence on his maturity and reading level at that time, and point out to the student how all these factors can influence his scores. The test-interpreter also should encourage the student to comment on any of these factors which he believes influenced his scores. Interpretation of interest scores presents another problem: A student's failure to differentiate between interest in and aptitude for a vocation or avocation.

Since in its various forms the *Kuder Preference Record* is probably the most widely used interest inventory at the high-school level, an eleventh-grade girl's scores on the *Kuder* (vocational, Form C) will be used to illustrate interpretation of an interest inventory. Her scores are expressed in percentile ranks: 0-71, 1-2, 2-23, 3-78, 4-85, 5-12, 6-87, 7-18, 8-98, and 9-28. (The scale number is given with each percentile rank.) This girl is well-liked, unusually mature, learns as easily as most, did as well as most on an achievement test battery which was given in September when she took the intelligence test (all scores fell within the middle 50 per cent of national norms), and she has earned mostly C's although occasionally she has earned B's in English. Her father operates a small farm on the edge of town. She hopes to marry early, but also has given some thought to becoming an elementary teacher.

Prior to interpreting her interest inventory scores, the school counselor obtained the above information from the cumulative folder. He also used a table in the manual to convert raw scores into stanines and examined her "V" score (43); he concluded that he had no reason to question the validity of her scores. Nevertheless, he pointed out to her the extent to which her scores could be influenced by the conditions described above and gave her a chance to comment. Then he said: "These scores will help you discover how much more you seem to like some things than other things. Frequently, this kind of study of interests can help you become acquainted with broad areas of interests and job families; it may also help you discover occupations which you could enjoy, but it will not help you decide whether you have the ability to do the work. Now I shall define each of the scale's scores for you. If for any reason my definition doesn't make sense, please feel free to ask questions. After I define each I would like for you to indicate, with a check mark, where you think your score for the scale falls on the five parts of this line. When you have estimated your scores for all ten scales, I will go back over them and tell you where the test estimate agrees with your estimate and where it disagrees with your estimate. Where the test agrees with your estimate I will merely report that fact, but where it disagrees I will add an "x" to indicate how the test describes you." Listed below is an example.

OUTDOOR INTEREST

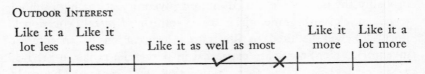

| Like it a lot less | Like it less | Like it as well as most | Like it more | Like it a lot more |

Obviously, her estimated score agreed with the test estimate on this scale. As a matter of fact, all of her estimates except those for Scales 3 and 4 agreed with the test estimates. In both of these instances she thought that she "liked it as well as most," whereas the test indicated that she "liked it more than most."

Next, the counselor suggested that she select, on the basis of their discussions of the results, those scales which she felt she should consider in a study of preferred occupations—namely, those in which she had most and least interest. She selected Scales 4, 6, and 8 for most interest and Scales 1 and 5 for least interest. Then they examined the list of occupations included in the manual for these combinations of interests (4, 6, and 8—also taking account of lack of interest in 1 and 5) in order to identify occupations for which she should achieve job satisfaction. From this list of occupations she selected bookstore salesman and telephone operator. She also decided to keep elementary-school teacher on her list of preferred occupations. Before he helped her locate occupational information for each of these occupations the counselor helped her compare her stanine scores for her entire inventory profile with the profiles for the 41 occupational families in the manual. This failed to reveal any additional occupations which she felt were worthy of further study.

This approach can be adapted for use with other interest inventories too. Obviously, what one can do over and beyond obtaining the student's self-estimate and comparing it with the inventory estimate of interest is determined by the data provided either by the inventory manual or by profiles and contingency tables which have been developed on the basis of local studies. The development of the latter certainly should be encouraged.

Ethics

Though teachers and counselors who interpret tests should know such standard references as the NEA *Code of Ethics, Ethical Standards of Psychologists,* and *Technical Recommendations for Psychological Tests and Diagnostic Techniques,* only those principles which apply to test interpretation will be reviewed here.

1. Tests and test scores should be released to only those persons who are qualified to use and interpret the tests.[76]

2. It is unethical for a supervisor to assign a staff member responsibility for interpreting a test for which he lacks adequate professional preparation.[77] Even when the test involved is one for which he may expect the staff member to have adequate professional preparation, he should provide supervision and appropriate in-service education.

3. Test scores should be interpreted to only appropriate individuals, e.g., students and their parents or legal guardians.[78] It also appears evident that they should be interpreted within a setting in which unauthorized persons cannot listen in on the interpretation or see the results.

4. Self-interpretation of test scores should not be encouraged.[79] However, it is appropriate for a qualified person to encourage a student or parent to participate in interpreting test scores.

76. *Ethical Standards of Psychologists,* p. 149. Washington: American Psychological Association, 1953.

77. *Ibid.,* 148-49.

78. *Ibid.,* p. 65.

79. *Technical Recommendations for Psychological Tests and Diagnostic Techniques,* p. 12. Washington: American Psychological Association, 1954.

5. The student's welfare should be the test-interpreter's first concern.[80] It follows, therefore, that the test-interpreter must be qualified to recognize and cope with emotional reactions to test data.[81] It is also essential that test scores be interpreted instead of merely being released or distributed.

6. The test-interpreter should understand test scores sufficiently well to communicate information on test results in a meaningful way to a student or his parents and be able to answer questions about the results.[82] This means that the test-interpreter must understand the limitations of the test as well as the ways its results can be used by the student and his parents.

7. The test-interpreter should know the relevant non-test data which he needs to supplement test data and to evaluate the accuracy of test data.[83]

8. To have confidence respected is important to everyone, but it is especially important to adolescents. In their struggle for independence, many adolescents have been unfairly judged by adults. When a school staff fails to keep test scores in a secure place, discusses test results where unauthorized persons can overhear the discussion, or releases test scores to unauthorized persons, it is breaking confidence with students, confidences which should be guarded by the entire staff as a trust.[84]

80. *Ibid.*, p. 164.

81. *Ibid.*, p. 10.

82. *Ibid.*

83. *Ibid.*, p. 11.

84. *Code of Ethics.* Washington: National Education Association, 1952.

INDEX

Index

Academic aptitude, need for evaluating achievement in relation to, 226-27

Accuracy of test scores, determination of, 267-68

ACE Psychological Examination, 108

Achievement, measurement of, essential to counseling, 142-43

Achievement and intelligence tests, differences between, 282-83

Achievement test scores: interpretation of, 278-81; need to study relationship of, to mental processes involved in attaining scores, 181-82

Adamek, Edward G., 257

Adams, Georgia Sachs, 27

Adapting testing to competence of student, 20

Administration: role of testing program in, 4; use of tests by, to check progress of schools, 9-10

Administration of tests, planning details of, 225

Administrative policies, major goals of, 79

Administrators' attitudes toward testing: discussion of, 112-16; recommendations based on, 115

Advanced Placement Program, 19

Aims of education: Aquinas, Aristotle, Hutchins, Maritain, Rousseau, and Sheen on, 30; Conant on, 30; Dewey on, 29; Huxley on, 29; Spencer on, 29; Whitehead on, 29-30

Allen, James E., 123

Allen, Mildred M., 270

Allport-Vernon-Lindzey Study of Values, 108, 174

American College Testing Program, 86, 136, 158, 194, 198

American Council Psychological Examination (ACE), 168, 218

American Educational Research Association, 217

American Psychological Association, 217

Anastasie, Anne, 50, 171, 174

Anderson, Robert H., 63, 74, 75

Appraisal of achievement: complexity of, 23; technical competence required for, 23-24

Appraisal devices, variety of, available for testing programs, 4-5

Aptitude and achievement tests, need for greater comparability of norms of, 187-88

Aptitude and personality, need for development of better measures of, 185-86

Arsenian, Seth, 259

Autumn vs. late-in-the-year testing, 9-10

Bechtoldt, Harold, 170

Beckman, A. A., 287

Behavioral goals, priority to be given among, 35-36

Behaviorally defined objectives, limitations of, 34

Bell Adjustment Inventory, 108, 184

Bell, H. M., 108

Bell Preference Inventory, 108

Belovsky, David B., 258

Bender-Gestalt Test, 174

Berdie, Ralph W., 146, 170, 263, 264

Bergmann, Gustav, 38

Betty Crocker Program, 158

Biersdorf, Kathryn R., 259

Billet-Starr Youth Problems Inventory, 174

Bingham, Walter V., 14

Bixler, Roy H., 265

Bloom, Benjamin S., 99, 100, 181

Bobbs-Merrill Company Test Division, 251

Bond, Guy L., 290

Bordin, Edward S., 265

Boroff, David, 95

Broder, Lois J., 181

Broedel, J., 288

Buros, Oscar, 191

California Achievement Tests, 160, 164, 176

CONSTITUTION AND BY-LAWS
OF
THE NATIONAL SOCIETY FOR THE
STUDY OF EDUCATION

(As adopted May, 1944, and amended June, 1945, February, 1949, and September, 1962)

ARTICLE I

NAME

The name of this corporation shall be "The National Society for the Study of Education," an Illinois corporation not for profit.

ARTICLE II

PURPOSES

Its purposes are to carry on the investigation of educational problems, to publish the results of same, and to promote their discussion.

The corporation also has such powers as are now, or may hereafter be, granted by the General Not For Profit Corporation Act of the State of Illinois.

ARTICLE III

OFFICES

The corporation shall have and continuously maintain in this state a registered office and a registered agent whose office is identical with such registered office, and may have other offices within or without the State of Illinois as the Board of Directors may from time to time determine.

ARTICLE IV

MEMBERSHIP

Section 1. *Classes.* There shall be two classes of members—active and honorary. The qualifications and rights of the members of such classes shall be as follows:

(*a*) Any person who is desirous of promoting the purposes of this corporation is eligible to active membership and shall become such on payment of dues as prescribed.

(*b*) Active members shall be entitled to vote, to participate in discussion, and, subject to the conditions set forth in Article V, to hold office.

(*c*) Honorary members shall be entitled to all the privileges of active

i

members, with the exception of voting and holding office, and shall be exempt from the payment of dues. A person may be elected to honorary membership by vote of the active members of the corporation on nomination by the Board of Directors.

(d) Any active member of the Society may, at any time after reaching the age of sixty, become a life member on payment of the aggregate amount of the regular annual dues for the period of life expectancy, as determined by standard actuarial tables, such membership to entitle the member to receive all yearbooks and to enjoy all other privileges of active membership in the Society for the lifetime of the member.

Section 2. *Termination of Membership.*

(a) The Board of Directors by affirmative vote of two-thirds of the members of the Board may suspend or expel a member for cause after appropriate hearing.

(b) Termination of membership for nonpayment of dues shall become effective as provided in Article XIV.

Section 3. *Reinstatement.* The Board of Directors may by the affirmation vote of two-thirds of the members of the Board reinstate a former member whose membership was previously terminated for cause other than nonpayment of dues.

Section 4. *Transfer of Membership.* Membership in this corporation is not transferable or assignable.

Article V

BOARD OF DIRECTORS

Section 1. *General Powers.* The business and affairs of the corporation shall be managed by its Board of Directors. It shall appoint the Chairman and Vice-Chairman of the Board of Directors, the Secretary-Treasurer, and Members of the Council. It may appoint a member to fill any vacancy on the Board until such vacancy shall have been filled by election as provided in Section 3 of this Article.

Section 2. *Number, Tenure, and Qualifications.* The Board of Directors shall consist of seven members, namely, six to be elected by the members of the corporation, and the Secretary-Treasurer to be the seventh member. Only active members who have contributed to the Yearbook shall be eligible for election to serve as directors. A member who has been elected for a full term of three years as director and has not attended at least two-thirds of the meetings duly called and held during that term shall not be eligible for election again before the fifth annual election after the expiration of the term for which he was first elected. No member who has been elected for two full terms as director in immediate succession shall be elected a director for a term next succeeding. This provision shall not apply to the Secretary-Treasurer who is appointed by the Board of Directors. Each director shall hold office for the term for which he is elected or appointed and until his successor shall have been selected and qualified. Directors need not be residents of Illinois.

Section 3. *Election.*

(*a*) The directors named in the Articles of Incorporation shall hold office until their successors shall have been duly selected and shall have qualified. Thereafter, two directors shall be elected annually to serve three years, beginning March first after their election. If, at the time of any annual election, a vacancy exists in the Board of Directors, a director shall be elected at such election to fill such vacancy.

(*b*) Elections of directors shall be held by ballots sent by United States mail as follows: A nominating ballot together with a list of members eligible to be directors shall be mailed by the Secretary-Treasurer to all active members of the corporation in October. From such list, the active members shall nominate on such ballot one eligible member for each of the two regular terms and for any vacancy to be filled and return such ballots to the office of the Secretary-Treasurer within twenty-one days after said date of mailing by the Secretary-Treasurer. The Secretary-Treasurer shall prepare an election ballot and place thereon in alphabetical order the names of persons equal to three times the number of offices to be filled, these persons to be those who received the highest number of votes on the nominating ballot, provided, however, that not more than one person connected with a given institution or agency shall be named on such final ballot, the person so named to be the one receiving the highest vote on the nominating ballot. Such election ballot shall be mailed by the Secretary-Treasurer to all active members in November next succeeding. The active members shall vote thereon for one member for each such office. Election ballots must be in the office of the Secretary-Treasurer within twenty-one days after the said date of mailing by the Secretary-Treasurer. The ballots shall be counted by the Secretary-Treasurer, or by an election committee, if any, appointed by the Board. The two members receiving the highest number of votes shall be declared elected for the regular term and the member or members receiving the next highest number of votes shall be declared elected for any vacancy or vacancies to be filled.

Section 4. *Regular Meetings.* A regular annual meeting of the Board of Directors shall be held, without other notice than this by-law, at the same place and as nearly as possible on the same date as the annual meeting of the corporation. The Board of Directors may provide the time and place, either within or without the State of Illinois, for the holding of additional regular meetings of the Board.

Section 5. *Special Meetings.* Special meetings of the Board of Directors may be called by or at the request of the Chairman or a majority of the directors. Such special meetings shall be held at the office of the corporation unless a majority of the directors agree upon a different place for such meetings.

Section 6. *Notice.* Notice of any special meeting of the Board of Directors shall be given at least fifteen days previously thereto by written notice delivered personally or mailed to each director at his business address, or by telegram. If mailed, such notice shall be deemed to be delivered when deposited in the United States mail in a sealed envelope so addressed, with postage thereon prepaid. If notice be given by telegram, such notice shall be deemed to be delivered when the telegram is delivered to the telegraph company. Any director may waive notice of any meeting. The attendance of a director at any meeting shall constitute a waiver of notice of such meeting, except where a director attends a meeting for the express purpose of objecting to the transaction of any business because the meeting is not lawfully called or convened. Neither the business to be transacted at, nor the purpose of, any regular or special meeting of the Board need be specified in the notice or waiver of notice of such meeting.

Section 7. *Quorum.* A majority of the Board of Directors shall constitute a quorum for the transaction of business at any meeting of the Board, provided, that if less than a majority of the directors are present at said meeting, a majority of the directors present may adjourn the meeting from time to time without further notice.

Section 8. *Manner of Acting.* The act of the majority of the directors present at a meeting at which a quorum is present shall be the act of the Board of Directors, except where otherwise provided by law or by these by-laws.

ARTICLE VI

THE COUNCIL

Section 1. *Appointment.* The Council shall consist of the Board of Directors, the Chairmen of the corporation's Yearbook and Research Committees, and such other active members of the corporation as the Board of Directors may appoint.

Section 2. *Duties.* The duties of the Council shall be to further the objects of the corporation by assisting the Board of Directors in planning and carrying forward the educational undertakings of the corporation.

ARTICLE VII

OFFICERS

Section 1. *Officers.* The officers of the corporation shall be a Chairman of the Board of Directors, a Vice-Chairman of the Board of Directors, and a Secretary-Treasurer. The Board of Directors, by resolution, may create additional offices. Any two or more offices may be held by the same person, except the offices of Chairman and Secretary-Treasurer.

Section 2. *Election and Term of Office.* The officers of the corporation shall be elected annually by the Board of Directors at the annual regular meeting of the Board of Directors, provided, however, that the Secretary-Treasurer may be elected for a term longer than one year. If the election of officers shall not be held at such meeting, such election shall be held as soon thereafter as conveniently may be. Vacancies may be filled or new offices created and filled at any meeting of the Board of Directors. Each officer shall hold office until his successor shall have been duly elected and shall have qualified or until his death or until he shall resign or shall have been removed in the manner hereinafter provided.

Section 3. *Removal.* Any officer or agent elected or appointed by the Board of Directors may be removed by the Board of Directors whenever in its judgment the best interests of the corporation would be served thereby, but such removal shall be without prejudice to the contract rights, if any, of the person so removed.

Section 4. *Chairman of the Board of Directors.* The Chairman of the Board of Directors shall be the principal officer of the corporation. He shall preside at all meetings of the members of the Board of Directors, shall perform all duties incident to the office of chairman of the Board of Directors and such other duties as may be prescribed by the Board of Directors from time to time.

Section 5. *Vice-Chairman of the Board of Directors.* In the absence of the Chairman of the Board of Directors or in the event of his inability or refusal to act, the Vice-Chairman of the Board of Directors shall perform the duties of the Chairman of the Board of Directors, and when so acting, shall have all the powers of and be subject to all the restrictions upon the Chairman of the Board of Directors. Any Vice-Chairman of the Board of Directors shall perform such other duties as from time to time may be assigned to him by the Board of Directors.

Section 6. *Secretary-Treasurer.* The Secretary Treasurer shall be the managing executive officer of the corporation. He shall: (*a*) keep the minutes of the meetings of the members and of the Board of Directors in one or more books provided for that purpose; (*b*) see that all notices are duly given in accordance with the provisions of these by-laws or as required by law; (*c*) be custodian of the corporate records and of the seal of the corporation and see that the seal of the corporation is affixed to all documents, the execution of which on behalf of the corporation under its seal is duly authorized in accordance with the provisions of these by-laws; (*d*) keep a register of the postoffice address of each member as furnished to the secretary-treasurer by such member; (*e*) in general perform all duties incident to the office of secretary and such other duties as from time to time may be assigned to him by the Chairman of the Board of Directors or by the Board of Directors. He shall also: (1) have charge and custody of and be responsible for all funds and securities of the corporation; receive and give receipts for moneys due and payable to the corporation from any source whatsoever, and deposit all such moneys in the name of the corporation in such banks, trust companies or other depositories as shall be selected in accordance with the provisions of Article XI of these by-laws; (2) in general perform all the duties incident to the office of Treasurer and such other duties as from time to time may be assigned to him by the Chairman of the Board of Directors or by the Board of Directors. The Secretary-Treasurer shall give a bond for the faithful discharge of his duties in such sum and with such surety or sureties as the Board of Directors shall determine, said bond to be placed in the custody of the Chairman of the Board of Directors.

ARTICLE VIII

COMMITTEES

The Board of Directors, by appropriate resolution duly passed, may create and appoint such committees for such purposes and periods of time as it may deem advisable.

ARTICLE IX

PUBLICATIONS

Section 1. The corporation shall publish *The Yearbook of the National Society for the Study of Education,* such supplements thereto, and such other materials as the Board of Directors may provide for.

Section 2. *Names of Members.* The names of the active and honorary members shall be printed in the Yearbook or, at the direction of the Board of Directors, may be published in a special list.

ARTICLE X

ANNUAL MEETINGS

The corporation shall hold its annual meetings at the time and place of the Annual Meeting of the American Association of School Administrators of the National Education Association. Other meetings may be held when authorized by the corporation or by the Board of Directors.

ARTICLE XI

CONTRACTS, CHECKS, DEPOSITS, AND GIFTS

Section 1. *Contracts.* The Board of Directors may authorize any officer or officers, agent or agents of the corporation, in addition to the officers so authorized by these by-laws to enter into any contract or execute and deliver any instrument in the name of and on behalf of the corporation and such authority may be general or confined to specific instances.

Section 2. *Checks, drafts, etc.* All checks, drafts, or other orders for the payment of money, notes, or other evidences of indebtedness issued in the name of the corporation, shall be signed by such officer or officers, agent or agents of the corporation and in such manner as shall from time to time be determined by resolution of the Board of Directors. In the absence of such determination of the Board of Directors, such instruments shall be signed by the Secretary-Treasurer.

Section 3. *Deposits.* All funds of the corporation shall be deposited from time to time to the credit of the corporation in such banks, trust companies, or other depositories as the Board of Directors may select.

Section 4. *Gifts.* The Board of Directors may accept on behalf of the corporation any contribution, gift, bequest, or device for the general purposes or for any special purpose of the corporation.

ARTICLE XII

BOOKS AND RECORDS

The corporation shall keep correct and complete books and records of account and shall also keep minutes of the proceedings of its members, Board of Directors, and committees having any of the authority of the Board of Directors, and shall keep at the registered or principal office a record giving the names and addresses of the members entitled to vote. All books and records of the corporation may be inspected by any member or his agent or attorney for any proper purpose at any reasonable time.

ARTICLE XIII

FISCAL YEAR

The fiscal year of the corporation shall begin on the first day of July in each year and end on the last day of June of the following year.

ARTICLE XIV

DUES

Section 1. *Annual Dues.* The annual dues for active members of the Society shall be determined by vote of the Board of Directors at a regular meeting duly called and held.

Section 2. *Election Fee.* An election fee of $1.00 shall be paid in advance by each applicant for active membership.

Section 3. *Payment of Dues.* Dues for each calendar year shall be payable in advance on or before the first day of January of that year. Notice of dues for the ensuing year shall be mailed to members at the time set for mailing the primary ballots.

Section 4. *Default and Termination of Membership.* Annual membership shall terminate automatically for those members whose dues remain unpaid after the first day of January of each year. Members so in default will be reinstated on payment of the annual dues plus a reinstatement fee of fifty cents.

ARTICLE XV

SEAL

The Board of Directors shall provide a corporate seal which shall be in the form of a circle and shall have inscribed thereon the name of the corporation and the words "Corporate Seal, Illinois."

ARTICLE XVI

WAIVER OF NOTICE

Whenever any notice whatever is required to be given under the provision of the General Not For Profit Corporation Act of Illinois or under the provisions of the Articles of Incorporation or the by-laws of the corporation, a waiver thereof in writing signed by the person or persons entitled to such notice, whether before or after the time stated therein, shall be deemed equivalent to the giving of such notice.

ARTICLE XVII

AMENDMENTS

Section 1. *Amendments by Directors.* The constitution and by-laws may be altered or amended at any meeting of the Board of Directors duly called and held, provided that an affirmative vote of at least five directors shall be required for such action.

Section 2. *Amendments by Members.* By petition of twenty-five or more active members duly filed with the Secretary-Treasurer, a proposal to amend the constitution and by-laws shall be submitted to all active members by United States mail together with ballots on which the members shall vote for or against the proposal. Such ballots shall be returned by United States mail to the office of the Secretary-Treasurer within twenty-one days after date of mailing of the proposal and ballots by the Secretary-Treasurer. The Secretary-Treasurer or a committee appointed by the Board of Directors for that purpose shall count the ballots and advise the members of the result. A vote in favor of such proposal by two-thirds of the members voting thereon shall be required for adoption of such amendment.

MINUTES OF THE ANNUAL MEETING OF THE SOCIETY

FEBRUARY 18, 1962

The 1962 meeting of the Society was held in the Traymore Room in Atlantic City at 3:30 p.m., Sunday, February 18, with Walter W. Cook, Chairman of the Board of Directors, presiding and some three hundred fifty members present.

The meeting of the Society is generally devoted to the presentation of Parts I and II of the yearbook. However, since it had been proposed that Part II, *Education for the Professions*, prepared by a committee of the Society under the chairmanship of G. Lester Anderson, Vice-Chancellor for Educational Affairs, University of Buffalo, be presented at the annual meeting of another national organization, only Part I, *Individualizing Instruction*, prepared by a committee under the chairmanship of Fred. T. Tyler, was presented at the Society's annual meeting.

The program of the presentation follows:

Individualizing Instruction

(Part I of the Society's Sixty-first Yearbook)

Joint meeting with the American Association of School Administrators and the American Educational Research Association

Introducing the Yearbook

Fred. T. Tyler, Professor of Education, University of California, Berkeley, and Chairman of the Yearbook Committee

Evaluation of the Yearbook

Paul Woodring, Editor, Education Supplement, *Saturday Review of Literature*, New York City

Informal Discussion

Mr. Fred. T. Tyler had previously addressed the annual meeting (Chicago, February 16) of the American Association of Colleges for Teacher Education on the subject, "Individualizing Instruction: A Foundation for Excellence."

ix

SYNOPSIS OF THE PROCEEDINGS OF THE
BOARD OF DIRECTORS OF THE SOCIETY FOR 1962

I. Meeting of February 18-19, 1962

The Board of Directors met at 9:00 A.M. on February 18 in the Dennis Hotel (Atlantic City) with the following members present: Walter W. Cook (Chairman), Edgar Dale, Laurence D. Haskew, Robert J. Havighurst, Ralph W. Tyler, and Herman G. Richey (Secretary).

1. The Secretary reported that the election of members of the Board of Directors held in November had resulted in the re-election of Ralph W. Tyler and Walter W. Cook, each for a term of three years beginning March 1, 1962.

2. Officers of the Board of Directors for the year beginning March 1, 1962, were elected as follows: Mr. Haskew, Chairman; Mr. Dale, Vice-Chairman; and Mr. Richey, Secretary.

3. The Secretary presented a report on activities designed to enlarge the membership, including the extremely successful efforts of Mr. Haskew in Texas and Mr. Cook in Minnesota.

4. Mr. Haskew proposed and the Board approved the award of a year's membership in the Society to persons receiving the Ph.D. or D.Ed. degree, the awards to be made on the recommendation of the Chairman of the Departments of Education of selected institutions.

5. It was moved that the Constitution be amended to provide that, upon direction of the Board, the names of members may be published in a special list rather than as an appendix to the yearbook. The motion was seconded and passed unanimously.

6. Dr. Melvin L. Barlow of the University of California, Los Angeles, appeared before the Board, on its invitation, to present a proposal for a yearbook on vocational education. The members of the Board made a number of suggestions and expressed general approval of the proposal. Mr. Haskew was appointed to represent the Board on the yearbook committee and was authorized to give final approval to the proposal. Publication of the proposed yearbook was tentatively scheduled for January, 1965.

7. The Board approved the proposal submitted last year by Professor Reid Hastie of the University of Minnesota for a yearbook on art education. Publication of the yearbook was tentatively scheduled for January, 1965.

8. Dr. Gerald Reed of Kent State University met with the Board, on its invitation, to discuss the possibilities of a yearbook on education in new and developing countries. Dr. Reed agreed to advise again with the Board on his return to this country.

9. Progress reports were submitted on the yearbooks in preparation and a number of proposals were presented for examination and discussion.

II. Meeting of September 28-29, 1962

The Board of Directors met at 6:00 P.M. on September 28 in the Conrad Hilton Hotel in Chicago with the following members present: Laurence D. Haskew (Chairman), Walter W. Cook, Stephen M. Corey, Edgar Dale, Ralph W. Tyler, and Herman G. Richey (Secretary).

1. The Board voted to schedule the annual meeting of the Society for Sunday, February 17, in Atlantic City. It was agreed that Part II, *The Impact and Improvement of School Testing Programs*, should be presented at the annual meeting. It was further agreed that Warren G. Findley, Theodore W. Clymer, and Merle M. Ohlsen should be asked to participate in the program.

2. The Board agreed that Mr. Cook should discuss with Dr. Pomeroy the possibility of a place on the program of the February meeting of the American Association of Colleges for Teacher Education in Chicago for discussion of Part I of the 1963 yearbook, *Child Psychology*, and inform the Chairman and Secretary of the results of the discussion. It was agreed that, if a place on the program was made available, the Society would ask Harold W. Stevenson (Director of the Institute of Child Development, University of Minnesota, and Chairman of the committee preparing the yearbook, *Child Psychology*) and Carson McGuire (Professor of Educational Psychology, University of Texas) to participate in the presentation of Part I of the yearbook. The Board approved the proposal of Mr. Cook that he ask to have Mr. Findley scheduled to discuss Part II, *The Impact and Improvement of School Testing Programs*, at a meeting in Chicago of the National Council on Measurement in Education.

3. The proposal for a yearbook on social maladjustment, submitted by Dr. William W. Wattenberg, Wayne State University, was discussed with a view to its approval at the February, 1963, meeting. The Secretary was directed to make available funds for any necessary expenses incurred by Dr. Wattenberg in completing his plan for the proposed publication.

4. Progress reports of the committees preparing the following yearbooks were presented: *Theories of Learning*, Ernest R. Hilgard, Chairman; *Educational Administration*, Daniel Griffiths, Chairman; *Art Education*, Reid Hastie, Chairman; *Vocational Education*, Melvin L. Barlow, Chairman.

5. Several new proposals for yearbooks were discussed at length. It was agreed that a decision on one proposal should be made no later than the February, 1963, meeting.

6. The Secretary reported on membership, finances, printing costs, and other matters of business.

REPORT OF THE TREASURER OF THE SOCIETY

1961-62

RECEIPTS AND DISBURSEMENTS

Receipts:

Membership dues	$34,069.30
Sale of yearbooks	40,716.47
Interest and dividends	106.50
Miscellaneous	601.85
	$75,494.12

Disbursements:

Yearbooks:

Manufacturing		$32,523.74
Reprinting		12,830.79
Preparation		1,975.71
Meetings of Society and Board		2,424.27

Secretary's Office:

Editorial, secretarial, and clerical services		14,320.65
Supplies		4,120.27
Repayment of loan		2,500.00

Miscellaneous:

Bank charges (N.S.F. checks, etc.)	108.50	
Refunds and transfer of commercial orders	159.50	
Chapter reprints (reclaimable from authors) and publications list	670.96	
Safe deposit box	4.40	
Filing fee, Not-for-Profit Corporation	1.00	
Insurance	506.54	1,450.90
		$72,146.33

Cash in bank at beginning of year	$ 6,934.90
Excess of receipts over disbursements	3,347.79
Total cash on hand	$10,282.69
Transfer to savings account, University National Bank, and purchase of stock, First National Bank of Boston	10,028.22
Cash in checking account, June 30, 1962	$ 254.47

STATEMENT OF CASH AND SECURITIES
As of June 30, 1962

Cash:

University National Bank, Chicago, Illinois—
Checking account . . . . $ 254.47
Savings account 15,125.75

Securities:

COST

38 shares First National Bank of Boston, capital stock. . . .   1,063.97

Total assets $16,444.19

MEMBERS OF THE NATIONAL SOCIETY FOR THE STUDY OF EDUCATION

[This list includes all persons enrolled December 1, 1962, whether for 1962 or 1963. An asterisk (*) indicates Life Members of the Society.]

Aarestad, Amanda B., 80 Kongsveien, Oslo, Norway
Aaron, Ira Edward, Col. of Educ., University of Georgia, Athens, Ga.
Abate, Harry, Board of Education, 607 Walnut Ave., Niagara Falls, N.Y.
Abbott, Frank C., Montana State University, Missoula, Mont.
Abbott, Samuel Lee, Jr., Plymouth Teachers College, Plymouth, N.H.
Abbott, Whitt K., Alice Robertson Junior High School, Muskogee, Okla.
Abelson, Harold H., Sch. of Educ., New York City College, New York, N.Y.
Abraham, Willard, Arizona State University, Tempe, Ariz.
Abrahamson, Stephen, University of Buffalo, Buffalo, N.Y.
Abramowitz, Mortimer J., Pub. Sch. 188, Queens, 218 Hartland Ave., Flushing, N.Y.
Acharlu, K. S., 1805 Temple Rd., Bangalore, India
Adams, Mrs. Daisy Trice, 2637 Park Ave., Kansas City, Mo.
Adams, Donald K., George Peabody College, Nashville, Tenn.
Adams, Gloria T., Box 479, Cut Off, La.
Adams, Robert G., 594 Capell St., Oakland, Calif.
Adams, Mrs. Ruth R., Sch. of Educ., New York City College, New York, N.Y.
Adamson, Oral Victor, R.R. 5, Princeton Rd., Evansville, Ind.
Adatto, Albert, 2244 Juniperberry Dr., San Rafael, Calif.
Adelberg, Arthur J., Sch. Dist. No. 3, N. Church Rd., Elmhurst, Ill.
Adell, James C., 16723 Fernway Rd., Shaker Heights, Ohio
Aden, Robert C., 2509 Glenwood Lane, Denton, Tex.
Adkisson, D. F., City Public Schools, Bristol, Tenn.
Adler, Mrs. Leona K., 101 Central Park W., New York, N.Y.
Adolphsen, Louis John, 2170 Carter Ave., St. Paul, Minn.
Aftreth, Orville, Sidney Pratt School, Minneapolis, Minn.
Ahee, Carl R., 30831 Casilina Dr., Palos Verdes Estates, Calif.
Ahrnsbrak, Henry C., 1121 Grand Ave., Wausau, Wis.
Akins, Harold S., 626 N. Mt. Carmel, Wichita, Kan.
Alberg, Gary L., 15 S. Lexington St., St. Paul, Minn.
Albohm, John C., 329 S. Lindbergh Ave., York, Pa.
Albrecht, Carl H., City Public Schools, Norwood, Ohio
Albrecht, Milton C., Col. of Arts and Sci., Univ. of Buffalo, Buffalo, N.Y.
Albright, Frank S., 37 Yale Terrace, West Orange, N.J.
Alcorn, Marvin D., 4808 Atlanta Dr., San Diego, Calif.
Aldrich, Julian C., Sch. of Educ., New York Univ., New York, N.Y.
Alexander, William M., George Peabody College, Nashville, Tenn.
Allen, Beatrice Ona, 5347 N. Wayne Ave., Chicago, Ill.
Allen, David, 8437 Truxton Ave., Los Angeles, Calif.
Allen, Dwight W., Sch. of Educ., Stanford University, Stanford, Calif.
Allen, Edward E., Akron Central School, Akron, N.Y.
Allen, James Robert, 1249 Lake Ave., Fort Wayne, Ind.
Allen, Ross L., State University College of Education, Cortland, N.Y.
Allen, Russell L., Clark County Schools, Jeffersonville, Ind.
Allen, Warren G., State Teachers College, Minot, N.D.
Allen, William H., 1355 Inverness Dr., Pasadena, Calif.
Allman, Reva White, Alabama State College, Montgomery, Ala.
Alm, Richard S., Dept. of Educ., University of Hawaii, Honolulu, Hawaii

Almcrantz, Mrs. Georgia, 402 Brown Circle, Knox, Ind.
Almroth, Frank S., 20 Hilltop Ter., Packanack Lake, Wayne, N.J.
Alt, Pauline M., Central Connecticut State College, New Britain, Conn.
Alt, Weston M., Rt. 5, Box 5174, Oroville, Calif.
Altman, Herbert H., 832 Ocean Ave., Brooklyn, N.Y.
Amar, Wesley F., Kelvyn Park High School, Chicago, Ill.
Ambrose, Edna V., 2124 N.E. 7th Ter., Gainesville, Fla.
Amidon, Edna P., Office of Education, Dept. of H.E.W., Washington, D.C.
Ammons, Margaret, Dept. of Educ., University of Wisconsin, Madison, Wis.
Anders, Mrs. Elizabeth M., 3601 Palm Dr., Riviera Beach, Fla.
Andersen, Dan W., 425 Merrill Crest Dr., Madison, Wis.
Andersen, Mrs. Flora, 5 Filbert St., Garden City, N.Y.
Anderson, Archibald W., Col. of Educ., Univ. of Illinois, Urbana, Ill.
Anderson, Bernard, John Spry Elementary School, Chicago, Ill.
Anderson, Clarence K., Amundsen High School, Chicago, Ill.
Anderson, Donald G., Oakland Public Schls., 1025 Second Ave., Oakland, Calif.
Anderson, Edmond C., George W. Carver Sch., 3701 Greenleaf St., Dallas, Tex.
Anderson, Edwin T., Mark Morris High School, Longview, Wash.
Anderson, Ernest M., Kansas State Teachers College, Pittsburg, Kan.
Anderson, Floydelh, West Virginia State College, Institute, W.Va.
Anderson, G. Lester, University of Buffalo, Buffalo, N.Y.
Anderson, Harold, Wausau Public Schools, Wausau, Wis.
Anderson, Harold A., Dept. of Educ., University of Chicago, Chicago, Ill.
Anderson, Harold H., 340 Wildwood Ave., East Lansing, Mich.
Anderson, Harold S., Southern State Tchrs. College, Springfield, S.D.
Anderson, Howard R., Houghton Mifflin Co., Boston, Mass.
Anderson, J. Paul, Col. of Educ., Univ. of Maryland, College Park, Md.
Anderson, Jack O., Civ. of Educ. and Psych., Chico State Col., Chico, Calif.
Anderson, James W., 742 Ashland Ave., St. Paul Park, Minn.
Anderson, Kenneth E., Sch. of Educ., Univ. of Kansas, Lawrence, Kan.
Anderson, Lester W., 4017 University High Sch., Ann Arbor, Mich.
Anderson, Marion A., Ginn & Co., Statler Office Bldg., Boston, Mass.
Anderson, Philip S., Wisconsin State College, River Falls, Wis.
Anderson, Robert H., Lawrence Hall, Harvard University, Cambridge, Mass.
Anderson, Ruth, 372 Central Park West, New York, N.Y.
Anderson, Stuart A., Niles Twp. High School, Skokie, Ill.
Anderson, Vernon E., Col. of Educ., University of Maryland, College Park, Md.
Anderson, Virginia, Col. of Educ., University of Arizona, Tucson, Ariz.
Anderson, Walter A., Sch. of Educ., New York University, New York, N.Y.
Andes, J. D., San Mateo City School District, San Mateo, Calif.
Andree, R. G., Rich Twp. High School, Park Forest, Ill.
Andregg, Neal B., 2553 Richmond Hill Rd., Augusta, Ga.
Andrews, Clay S., Dept. of Educ., San Jose State College, San Jose, Calif.
Andrews, Murray L., Montgomery County Board of Education, Rockville, Md.
Andrews, Stella F., 261 East Kingsbridge Rd., New York, N.Y.
Andrews, Wendell B., Public Schools, 108 Union St., Schenectady, N.Y.
Angelini, Arrigo L., University of Sao Paulo, Sao Paulo, Brazil
Angell, George W., State University College, Plattsburg, N.Y.
Angelo, Mark V., Siena College, Loudonville, N.Y.
Annis, Helen W., 6711 Conway Ave., Takoma Park, Md.
Ansel, James O., Western Michigan University, Kalamazoo, Mich.
Anselm, Karl R., State University College of Education, Geneseo, N.Y.
Anthony, Elsa J., 44 Mill St., New Britain, Conn.
Apple, Joe A., San Diego State College, San Diego, Calif.
Appleton, David, City Public Schools, Conway, N.H.
Archer, Clifford P., Col. of Educ., University of Minnesota, Minneapolis, Minn.
Archer, Marguerite P., 137 Highbrook Ave., Pelham, N.Y.
Archer, N. Sidney, Sch. of Educ., Univ. of Massachusetts, Amherst, Mass.
Armacost, Peter H., Augsburg College, Minneapolis, Minn.
Armstrong, Grace Orr, State Teachers College, Mankato, Minn.
Armstrong, Hubert E., 817 Fourth St., Myrtle Point, Ore.

Armstrong, J. Niel, Sch. of Educ., Agric. & Tech. College, Greensboro, N.C.
Arnaud, E. E., Our Lady of the Lake College, San Antonio, Tex.
Arndt, C. O., New York University, New York, N.Y.
Arnesen, Arthur E., 440 East First South St., Salt Lake City, Utah
Arnold, Dorothea, Western Michigan College, Kalamazoo, Mich.
Arnold, Earl A., North Texas State College, Denton, Tex.
Arnold, Eugene R., P.O. Box 1005, Springfield, Ohio
Arnold, Gala, 333 Silvergate Court, San Diego, Calif.
Arnold, J. E., Box 8540, University Station, Knoxville, Tenn.
Arnold, Marshall, 1921—21st St., Bowling Green, Ky.
Arnold, Phyllis D., 628 Patterson Ave., San Antonio, Tex.
Arnold, Roy W., Jr., Dept. of Educ., State University College, New Paltz, N.Y.
Arnold, William E., Sch. of Educ., Univ. of Pennsylvania, Philadelphia, Pa.
Arnsdorf, Val., Haviland Hall, University of California, Berkeley, Calif.
Arnstein, George E., NEA Journal, 1201—16th St., N.W., Washington, D.C.
Artley, A. Sterl., 213 Hill Hall, University of Missouri, Columbia, Mo.
Arveson, Raymond G., 38060 Logan Dr., Fremont, Calif.
Ashbaugh, H. B., Superintendent of Schools, Vermillion, S.D.
Ashe, Robert W., Dept. of Educ., Arizona State University, Tempe, Ariz.
Ashland, Homer B., Superintendent of Schools, Rutland, Vt.
Aslin, Neil C., Superintendent of Schools, Columbia, Mo.
Atkins, Neil P., Bedford Public Schls., Mount Kisco, N.Y.
Atkinson, William N., Jackson Junior College, Jackson, Mich.
Auer, B. F., 601 Cadiz Rd., Wintersville, Ohio
Aurand, Wayne O., 904 Columbia Dr., Cedar Falls, Iowa
Austin, David B., Tchrs. Col., Columbia University, New York, N.Y.
Austin, Martha Lou, 330 Anderson Ave., Winnipeg, Canada
Austin, Mary C., Grad. Sch. of Educ., Harvard University, Cambridge, Mass.
Ausubel, D. P., Col. of Educ., University of Illinois, Urbana, Ill.
Auzenne, Mrs. Anita D., Box 225, Grambling, La.
Avegno, T. Sylvia, Sch. of Educ., Fordham University, New York, N.Y.
Aycock, Howard A., Jefferson Interm. and Senior High School, El Paso, Tex.
Ayer, Joseph C., Box 111, Station B, Cincinnati, Ohio
Aylesworth, Thomas G., Div. of Educ., Michigan State Univ., East Lansing, Mich.

Babcock, Dorothy Boyeé, 2740 Alvingroom Ct., Oakland, Calif.
Bachar, James R., 6419 Kentucky Ave., Pittsburgh, Pa.
Bachman, Ralph V., South High School, Salt Lake City, Utah
Backus, Thomas A., 570—115th Ave., Treasure Island, Fla.
Bacon, William P., AF-ROTC, Kansas State University, Manhattan, Kan.
Baether, Theresa L., 3913 Beverly Dr., Toledo, Ohio
Bahn, Lorene A., 32 S. Elm Ave., Webster Groves, Mo.
Bahner, John M., 15 Duren Ave., Woburn, Mass.
Bailer, Joseph R., Dept. of Educ., Western Maryland College, Westminster, Md.
Bailey, Lucile, Wm. T. Machan Sch., 2140 E. Virginia St., Phoenix, Ariz.
Bair, Medill, Superintendent of Schools, Lexington, Mass.
Baird, Forrest J., San Jose State College, San Jose, Calif.
Baker, Bradley, 210 Ormond Ave., Indialantic, Melborne, Fla.
Baker, Charles R., 2084 Carmel Dr., Concord, Calif.
Baker, Eugene H., 6855 N. Crawford Ave., Lincolnwood, Ill.
Baker, G. Derwood, Sch. of Educ., New York University, New York, N.Y.
Baker, H. Leigh, 2040 Thackery Rd., Manhattan, Kan.
Baker, Harry J., 19050 Wiltshire, Lathrup Village, Mich.
Baker, I. D., Greenville College, Greenville, Ill.
Baker, Rebecca, Southern Illinois University, Carbondale, Ill.
Baker, Robert E., Sch. of Educ., George Washington Univ., Washington, D.C.
Baker, Russell C., Jr., P.O. Box 344, Fayette, Iowa
Balassi, S. J., Patersen College, Wayne, N.J.
Baldwin, Lee E., Superintendent, Union High Sch. Dist. No. 2, Burns, Ore.
Baldwin, Robert D., West Virginia University, Morgantown, W.Va.
Baldwin, Rollin, 924 West End Ave., New York, N.Y.

Balian, Arthur, Southern Colony and Training Sch., Union Grove, Wis.
Ball, George G., State College of Iowa, Cedar Falls, Iowa
Ballam, Oral L., Cache County School District, Logan, Utah
Ballantine, Francis A., San Diego State College, San Diego, Calif.
Baller, Warren R., University of Nebraska, Lincoln, Neb.
Ballou, Stephen V., Div. of Educ., Fresno State College, Fresno, Calif.
Baloun, Margaret, 4415 Sherman Blvd., Milwaukee, Wis.
Balzer, David M., Col. of Educ., Univ. of Minnesota, Minneapolis, Minn.
Bancroft, Roger W., State Univ. College of Education, Cortland, N.Y.
Banner, Carolyn, 409 Lafayette, Jefferson City, Mo.
Bannon, Michael F., Pennsylvania State College, West Chester, Pa.
Bany, Mary, 411 N. Third St., Alhambra, Calif.
Baratta, Anthony N., 38 Oak St., Nutley, N.J.
Barbe, Richard H., Research Foundation, 305 W. 12th St., Columbus, Ohio
Barbe, Walter B., Kent State University, Kent, Ohio
Barber, Anson B., 125 Alexander Ave., Nutley, N.J.
Barber, Grant W., 1251 Shipman St., Birmingham, Mich.
Barber, Joseph E., 1261—10th Court S.W., Largo, Fla.
Barber, Richard L., University of Louisville, Belknap Campus, Louisville, Ky.
Bardellini, Justin M., 121 Warwick Dr., Walnut Creek, Calif.
Barlow, Melvin L., Univ. of California, 405 Hilgard Ave., Los Angeles, Calif.
Barnard, J. Darrell, 16 Links Drive, Great Neck, N.Y.
Barnes, Cyrus W., Beachlake, Pa.
Barnes, Elinor A., 253 Bridge St., Corning, N.Y.
Barnes, Fred P., Col. of Educ., University of Illinois, Urbana, Ill.
Barnes, Melvin W., Superintendent of Schools, Portland, Ore.
Barney, E. Martin, Barrington College, Barrington, R.I.
Barr, Charlotte A., Chicago Teachers College, Chicago, Ill.
Barr, Dixon A., Laboratory Sch., Eastern Kentucky State Col., Richmond, Ky.
Barros, Raymond, Catholic University of Valparaiso, Valparaiso, Chile
Barry, Florence G., 5956 Race Ave., Chicago, Ill.
Bartel, Lorena, Franklin School, 401 Military Rd., Fond du Lac, Wis.
Bartels, Mrs. Isabella, 3224 Fairway Dr., Dayton, Ohio
Barter, Alice, 12 W. Withrow, Oxford, Ohio
Bartley, Imon, Drake University, Des Moines, Iowa
Barton, Carl L., Superintendent, Community Cons. Sch. Dist. 70, Freeburg, Ill.
Barton, George E., Jr., Tulane University, New Orleans, La.
Bartz, Amelia I., 2028 Webb St., Stockton, Calif.
Batho, Marshall G., 10236 S. Homan Ave., Evergreen Park, Ill.
Batinich, Mrs. Mary Ellen, 9215 S. Troy Ave., Evergreen Park, Ill.
Battle, John A., 11 Jones St., New Hyde Park, N.Y.
Baugher, James K., 132 W. 6th Ave., Roselle, N.J.
Baughman, Shirley, Westminster College, Salt Lake City, Utah
Baum, Paul B., La Verne College, La Verne, Calif.
Baumann, Margaret L., 1856 Sherman Ave., Evanston, Ill.
Baumgartner, Reuben A., Senior High School, Freeport, Ill.
Baumgartner, Rolla W., 1714 Bond St., Niles, Mich.
Baxter, Marlin B., Moline Public Schools, 1619 Eleventh Ave., Moline, Ill.
Bayer, Les, Concordia College, Austin, Tex.
Beach, Lowell W., 1408 Univ. Elem. Sch., Univ. of Michigan, Ann Arbor, Mich.
Beach, Norton L., Tchrs. Col., Columbia University, New York, N.Y.
Beachem, Katherine, 211 N. Manheim Blvd., New Paltz, N.Y.
Beadle, Laurena A., Lakeland College, Plymouth, Wis.
Beahm, W. I., Donegal Area Joint Sch. Sys., Mount Joy, Pa.
Beall, Harold, Monrovia Unified Sch. Dist., Monrovia, Calif.
Beamer, George C., North Texas State College, Denton, Tex.
Bear, David E., 3226 Brown St., Alton, Ill.
Beard, Richard L., 1621 Bruce Ave., Charlottesville, Va.
Beadley, Mrs. Eleanor C., 278 Ocean Ave., Portland, Me.
Beaton, Daniel W., Educ. Improv. Centre, 11669 Santa Monica, Los Angeles, Calif.
Beattie, Alfred W., 5501 Grubbs Rd., Gibsonia, Pa.

Beattie, George W., P.O. Box 100, Aptos, Calif.
Beatty, Walcott H., 209 Kensington Way, San Francisco, Calif.
Beaty, Betty, Tchrs. Col., University of Cincinnati, Cincinnati, Ohio
Beaubier, Edward W., 2431 Rockinghorse Rd., San Pedro, Calif.
Beauchamp, George A., Sch. of Educ., Northwestern University, Evanston, Ill.
Beaumont, Urville J., Tenney High School, Methuen, Mass.
Beaver, Eugene H., Roosevelt High School, 3436 Wilson Ave., Chicago, Ill.
Bebb, Randall R., State College of Iowa, Cedar Falls, Iowa
Bebell, Clifford S., State Dept. of Education, State Office Bldg., Denver, Colo.
Beck, Hubert Park, Sch. of Educ., City College, 523 W. 121st St., New York, N.Y.
Beck, John M., 5832 Stony Island Ave., Chicago, Ill.
Beck, Norman W., Supt., Monroe County Schls., Waterloo, Ill.
Beck, Ralph Lea, Bowling Green State University, Bowling Green, Ohio
Beck, Robert H., 233 Burton Hall, University of Minnesota, Minneapolis, Minn.
Becker, George, 1100 Elm Ave., Brooklyn, N.Y.
Becker, Harry A., Superintendent of Schools, Norwalk, Conn.
Becker, Millie A., 7637 S. Loomis Blvd., Chicago, Ill.
Bedell, Ralph, Office of Educ., Dept. of H.E.W., Washington, D.C.
Beebe, Nelson, Jr., Pennsville Memorial High School, Pennsville, N.J.
Berry, John R., Sch. of Educ., University of Miami, Coral Gables, Fla.
Beggs, David W., Lakeview High School, 1001 Brush College Rd., Decatur, Ill.
Behal, Rose, 9812 Broadview Rd., Brecksville, Ohio
Behrens, Herman D., 911 South Simon St., Ada, Ohio
* Behrens, Minnie S., 901 Sherman Ave., Denver, Colo.
Beitler, Roger T., Kent State University, 3129 State Rd., Ashtabula, Ohio
Belcher, Eddie W., Louisville Public Schls., 501 W. Hill St., Louisville, Ky.
Bell, Dorothy M., Bradford Junior College, Bradford, Mass.
Bell, Keith A., 3155 S.W. Grace Lane, Portland, Ore.
Bell, Millard D., Superintendent of Schools, 738 Tenth St., Wilmette, Ill.
Bell, Richard H., San Francisco State College, San Francisco, Calif.
Bell, Robert N., 2819 W. Sherwin Ave., Chicago, Ill.
Bell, Wilmer V., 702 Kingston Rd., Baltimore, Md.
Bellack, Arno A., Tchrs. Col., Columbia University, New York, N.Y.
Bemis, Eaton O., Millikan High School, 2800 Snowden Ave., Long Beach, Calif.
Bemis, James R., 1017 W. 36th St., Los Angeles, Calif.
Benben, John S., New York University, Washington Sq., New York, N.Y.
Bennett, Doris, Jacksonville State College, Jacksonville, Ala.
Bennett, Robert N., Greene Central School, Greene, N.Y.
Bennie, William A., 4803 Balcones Dr., Austin, Tex.
Bentall, Grace, 4712 S.E. River Dr., Portland, Ore.
Bentivegna, Joseph J., St. Francis College, Loretto, Pa.
Benz, Harry Edward, Col. of Educ., Ohio University, Athens, Ohio
Beran, D. L., 2118 Iris Lane, Madison, Wis.
Berg, Arthur D., 727 W. Capitol, Bellevue, Mich.
Berg, Pauline G., Odebolt, Iowa
Berg, Selmer H., Superintendent of Schools, Oakland, Calif.
Berge, Marvin L., Superintendent of Schools, DeKalb, Ill.
Bergen, Morris Carl, Citrus College, Azusa, Calif.
Berggren, T. N., Bd. of Educ., City School Dist., Shaker Heights, Ohio
Berkihise, Frances, Evangel College, Springfield, Mo.
Berkowitz, Edward, 2 Loretta Dr., Syosset, L.I., N.Y.
Berlin, Pearl W., 10634 Duprey, Detroit, Mich.
Berlin, Robert S., 383 Grand St., New York, N.Y.
Bernard, Alpha E., State Teachers College, Clarion, Pa.
Bernard, Harold W., 8405 S.W. Crestwood Lane, Portland, Ore.
Bernd, John M., Col. of Educ., Wayne State University, Detroit, Mich.
Bernstein, Abbot A., Children's Bureau, Columbia Ave. & Van Buren St., Passaic, N.J.
Bernstein, Abraham, Dept. of Educ., Brooklyn College, Brooklyn, N.Y.
Berry, Henry W., P.O. Box 158, Williamston, S.C.
Berryman, Charles, Col. of Educ., University of Georgia, Athens, Ga.

Berson, Mrs. Minnie, 311 Orchard Hills, S.E., Grand Rapids, Mich.
Bertermann, Helen A., 1339 Cryer Ave., Cincinnati, Ohio
Bertness, Henry J., 3701 N. Adams, Tacoma, Wash.
Bertrand, John R., Berry College, Mt. Berry, Ga.
Best, Mrs. Drusilla, 1148—8th Ave., S.W., Faribault, Minn.
Bettelheim, Bruno, 1365 E. 60th St., Chicago, Ill.
Bettencourt, Mildred, Dept. of Educ., Texas Tech. College, Lubbock, Tex.
Better, Morris, Los Angeles State College, Los Angeles, Calif.
Betts, Emmett A., Sch. of Educ., Universtiy of Miami, Coral Gables, Fla.
Beverly, Mrs. Mary Louise, 127 Highpoint Ave., Akron, Ohio
Beyer, Fred C., Superintendent of County Schools, Modesto, Calif.
Benyon, Robert P., Div. of Research, State Dept. of Education, Columbus, Ohio
Bickel, Lawrence G., Concordia Teachers College, Seward, Neb.
Bidstrup, Anna, Baker Ranch, Foresthill, Calif.
Bieber, Mrs. Ida P., 7357 Cornell Ave., University City, Mo.
Bigelow, Karl W., Tchrs. Col., Columbia University, New York, N.Y.
* Bigelow, M. A., Litchfield, Conn.
Bigelow, Roy G., Mississippi Southern College, Hattiesburg, Miss.
Biggs, Sarah Dorothy, 804 Court, Fulton, Mo.
Biggy, M. Virginia, 10 Alcott St., Acton, Mass.
Bigsbee, Earle M., Junior College of Connecticut, Bridgeport, Conn.
Bilhorn, J. Chester, 3846 N. Kedvale Ave., Chicago, Ill.
* Billig, Florence G., 2008 Melrose St., Rockford, Ill.
Bills, Mark W., Superintendent of Schools, Peoria, Ill.
Bilterman, Kathryn Smith, San Diego State College, San Diego, Calif.
Binford, George H., Central High School, Charlotte Courthouse, Va.
Binford, Linwood T., J. Andrew Bowler School, Richmond, Va.
Bingham, Alma, Portland State College, Portland, Ore.
Birch, Tom, 20 Alexander Ave., White Plains, N.Y.
Bird, A. O., Superintendent of Schools, Gonzales, Tex.
Bird, Charles A., 23 Fraser Pl., Hastings on Hudson, N.Y.
Birkmaier, Emma Marie, Col. of Educ., Univ. of Minnesota, Minneapolis, Minn.
Bishop, Clifford L., State College of Iowa, Cedar Falls, Iowa
Bishop, W. E., Superintendent of Schools, Englewood, Colo.
Bjork, Alton J., Dept. of Educ., Univ. of North Dakota, Grand Forks, N.D.
Black, Hugh C., 224 Anderson Hall, Rice University, Houston, Tex.
Black, Leo P., Office of Instructional Services, State Office Bldg., Denver, Colo.
Black, Mrs. Marian W., Sch. of Educ., Florida State Univ., Tallahassee, Fla.
Black, Millard H., 10031 Vecino Lane, La Habra, Calif.
Blackburn, Cleo W., Flanner House, 333 W. 16th St., Indianapolis, Ind.
Blackburn, Clifford S., North Texas College, Denton, Tex.
Blackledge, Mrs. Helen V., Southern Heights School, 950 Fairfax, Fort Wayne,
    Ind.
Blackman, Charles A., 361 Educ. Bldg., Michigan State University, East Lansing,
    Mich.
Blackshear, John S., 3066 Bethune Ave., Macon, Ga.
Blackwell, Lewis F., Jr., Box 1026, University, Ala.
Blaine, Russell K., 1816 Park Ave., S.E., Cedar Rapids, Iowa
Blanchard, Marion U., 190 E. Mosholy Pkwy., So., New York, N.Y.
Blandy, Gray M., 606 Rathervue Pl., Austin, Tex.
Blank, Stanley S., 2315 Grant St., Berkeley, Calif.
Blankenship, A. H., Superintendent of Schools, Gary, Ind.
Blanton, Roy R., Jr., Appalachian High School, Boone, N.C.
Bledsoe, Ernestine, Wesleyan College, Macon, Ga.
Bliesmer, Emery P., McGuffy Read. Clinic, Univ. of Virginia, Charlottesville, Va.
Bligh, Harold F., 100 Cedar St., Dobbs Ferry, N.Y.
Blodgett, Darrell R., Superintendent of Schools, Wheaton, Ill.
Blommers, Paul, East Hall, State University of Iowa, Iowa City, Iowa
Bloom, Royal F., Bethel College, St. Paul, Minn.
Bloomer, Richard H., Sch. of Educ., University of Connecticut, Storrs, Conn.
Blume, Robert A., Eastern Michigan University, Ypsilanti, Mich.

Boario, Dora A., 422 Third St., Leechburg, Pa.
Bockstruck, Else H., 159 Norris Gym, University of Minnesota, Minneapolis, Minn.
Bodkin, Raymond C., Southampton High School, Courtland, Va.
Boeck, Clarence H., 5101 Ewing Ave., So., Minneapolis, Minn.
Boenig, Robert W., State University College of Education, Fredonia, N.Y.
Boger, D. L., Morehouse College, Atlanta, Ga.
Boggs, Doyle W., Hartsville High School, Hartsville, S.C.
Bogle, Frank P., Superintendent of Schools, Millville, N.J.
Bohlander, Frank M., 109 S. Third St., Arkansas City, Kan.
Boland, Michael P., St. Joseph's College, 54th & City Line, Philadelphia, Pa.
Bolton, Dale L., DeKalb Community Schools, DeKalb, Ill.
* Bolton, Frederick E., 4514—16th Ave., N.E., Seattle, Wash.
Bond, George B., Robertsville Junior High School, Oak Ridge, Tenn.
Bond, George W., R.F.D. 2, Box 444B, New Paltz, N.Y.
Bond, Horace M., Sch. of Educ., Atlanta University, Atlanta, Ga.
Bond, Jesse A., University of California, 405 Hilgard Ave., Los Angeles, Calif.
Bondley, G. B., 1406 Griffith Ave., Las Vegas, Nev.
Bonk, Edward C., Box 5153, North Texas Univ. College, Denton, Tex.
Bonney, Virginia, 147-35—38th Ave., Flushing, N.Y.
Bonsall, Marcella Ryser, 137 Warwick Pl., South Pasadena, Calif.
Booker, Mrs. Ann, 1388 Prospect Ave., Bronx, N.Y.
Booker, Ivan A., N.E.A., 1201 Sixteenth St., N.W., Washington, D.C.
Bookwalter, Karl W., Indiana University, Bloomington, Ind.
Boos, John R., Hamilton Teachers College, Hamilton, Ont., Canada
Booth, Delores C., 6604 Tremont St., Oakland, Calif.
Borg, Robert L., Scott Hall, University of Minnesota, Minneapolis, Minn.
Bossard, Grace, Route 3, Box 6, Seaford, Del.
Bossier, Antonia M., 1661 No. Roman St., New Orleans, La.
Bossing, Nelson L., Sch. of Educ., Indiana University, Bloomington, Ind.
Bothell, John E., Colorado State College, Greeley, Colo.
Bottrell, Harold R., Col. of Educ., University of Houston, Houston, Tex.
Bouchard, John B., State Teachers College, Fredonia, N.Y.
Bougers, Marguerite B., Educ. Dept., Newcomb College, New Orleans, La.
Boula, James A., Office of Public Instrn., State Office Bldg., Springfield, Ill.
Bowen, Glenn K., Superintendent of Schools, River Rouge, Mich.
Bower, Robert K., 1905 E. Loma Alta Dr., Altadena, Calif.
Bower, Von Durbin, P.O. Box 806, Poughkeepsie, N.Y.
Bowers, Norman D., Sch. of Educ., Univ. of North Carolina, Chapel Hill, N.C.
Bowes, Paul E., 1237—28th St., Newport News, Va.
Bowman, George A., Kent State University, Kent, Ohio
Bowyer, Vernon, 225 Millbridge Rd., Riverside, Ill.
Boyajy, Robert J., 12 Tudor Court, Springfield, N.J.
Boyce, Floyd A., 3316 Scenic Dr., Austin, Tex.
Boyd, Laurence E., Sch. of Educ., Atlanta University, Atlanta, Ga.
Boyd, Rachel E., Cecil County Board of Education, Elkton, Md.
Boyer, C. E., Superintendent of Schools, 614 Main St., Boonton, N.J.
Boykin, Leander L., Florida A. & M. University, Tallahassee, Fla.
Boynton, Jason E., Superintendent of Schools, Wolfeboro, N.H.
Bozeman, Herman H., Virginia State College, Norfolk, Va.
Braam, L. S., Syracuse Univ. Reading Center, 508 Univ. Pl., Syracuse, N.Y.
Bracewell, George, Southern Illinois University, Carbondale, Ill.
Brady, Elizabeth H., 9218 Shoshone Ave., Northridge, Calif.
Brady, Florence A., 186 Oakland Rd., Maplewood, N.J.
Brady, John C., Bemidji State College, Bemidji, Minn.
Bragdon, Clifford R., 41 Harrison Ave., Northampton, Mass.
Brainard, Lois, San Jose State College, San Jose, Calif.
Brandsmeier, Elvira, 2236—4th St. "A", East Moline, Ill.
Brandt, Harry A., Menaul School, 301 Menaul Blvd., N.E., Albuquerque, N.M.
Brandt, Willard J., University of Wisconsin-Milwaukee, Milwaukee, Wis.
Branigan, Mary M., 5 Hamilton Ave., Bronxville, N.Y.

Branom, Wayne T., Superintendent of Schools, Hillside, N.J.
Brauer, Walter L., Rufus King High School, Milwaukee, Wis.
Braun, Frank, Burton Hall, University of Minnesota, Minneapolis, Minn.
Braum, Gertrude, Danbury State College, Danbury, Conn.
Breaux, Jerome E., 244 Aurora Ave., Metairie, La.
Breen, Lelwyn C., 205 Abert, Richland, Wash.
Bregman, Mrs. Sydell, 17 Bodnarik Dr., Fords, N.J.
Brehm, Mrs. Marie E., 10187 Toelle Lane, St. Louis, Mo.
Breihan, Edna, 920 Madison St., Lockport, Ill.
Brener, Mrs. Olga, Lincoln Elem. School, Shawano, Wis.
Brenholtz, Harold, North Texas College, Denton, Tex.
Brennan, A. F., Regina Regional High Schools, Corner Brook, Newfoundland, Canada
Brenner, Anton, Merrill-Palmer School, 71 Ferry E., Detroit, Mich.
Bresina, Bertha M., Arizona State University, Tempe, Ariz.
Bretsch, Howard S., Sch. of Educ., University of Michigan, Ann Arbor, Mich.
Bretz, Frank H., 1999 Arlington Ave., Columbus, Ohio
Bretz, Glen, Superintendent of Schools, Vincennes, Ind.
Breyfogle, Mary E., R. 1, Box G, Hazelwood, Mo.
Brickman, Benjamin, Dept. of Educ., Brooklyn College, Brooklyn, N.Y.
Brickman, William W., New York University, Washington Sq., New York, N.Y.
Bridges, C. M., Col. of Educ., University of Oklahoma, Norman, Okla.
Bridges, Mrs. Julia W., 110 West End Ave., Westwood, N.J.
Bridges, Lonnie H., Box 10194, Southern University, Baton Rouge, La.
Bridges, Raymond H., Box 10194, Southern University, Baton Rouge, La.
Bireland, Donald, Ill. Dept. of Mental Health, 160 N. LaSalle St., Chicago, Ill.
Brigham, Bruce W., 61 Llanfair Rd., Ardmore, Pa.
Bright, John H., 628 Cuesta Ave., San Mateo, Calif.
* Bright, Orville T., 516½ Prospect Ave., Lake Bluff, Ill.
Bright, Walter W., Superintendent of Schools, Escanaba, Mich.
Brimhall, Mrs. Alice, 111 Monticello Ave., Piedmont, Calif.
Briner, Conrad, Claremont University College, Claremont, Calif.
Brink, William G., Sch. of Educ., Northwestern University, Evanston, Ill.
Brinkman, A. John, 9929 S. Maplewood Ave., Chicago, Ill.
Brinkman, Albert R., Superintendent of Schools, Dobbs Ferry, N.Y.
Brinkmeier, Oria, 2203 Carter Ave., St. Paul, Minn.
Brish, William M., Superintendent of Schools, Washington County, Hagerstown, Md.
Brislawn, Maurice J., 1508—25th Ave., Longview, Wash.
Bristol, Stanley T., Joseph Sears School, Kenilworth, Ill.
Bristow, William H., Cur. of Curric. Res., Bd. of Educ., New York, N.Y.
Britt, Laurence V., University of Detroit, Detroit, Mich.
Brittain, Clay V., Div. of Tchr. Educ., Emory University, Atlanta, Ga.
Britton, Edward C., 6000 J St., Sacramento, Calif.
Britton, Ernest R., Superintendent of Schools, Midland, Mich.
Broderick, Catherine M., Girl Scouts of U.S.A., 830—3rd Ave., New York, N.Y.
Broening, Angela M., Baltimore Public Schls., 3 East 25th St., Baltimore, Md.
Bronars, Joseph C., 5200 Glennon Dr., St. Louis, Mo.
Bronson, Homer D., Chico State College, Chico, Calif.
Bronson, Moses L., 104 W. 70th St., New York, N.Y.
Brookover, Wilbur B., Michigan State University, East Lansing, Mich.
Brooks, Mary B., Georgia State Col. for Women, Milledgeville, Ga.
Brooks, Mary L., P.O. Box 129, Florida A. & M. College, Tallahassee, Fla.
Broome, Mrs. Jean N., Southeastern Louisiana Col., Hammond, La.
Brostoff, Theodore M., 3334 Bonnie Hill Dr., Hollywood, Calif.
Brother Adelbert James, Manhattan College, New York, N.Y.
Brother John M. Egan, Iona College, New Rochelle, N.Y.
Brother Julius Edgar, St. Mary's College, Winona, Minn.
Brother Luke, 2101 Maplewood Ave., Montreal, Canada
Brother Omer Cormier, St. Joseph's University, New Brunswick, Canada
Brother U. Cassian, St. Mary's College, St. Mary's College, Calif.

Brother William Mang, St. Edward's University, Austin, Tex.
Brottman, Marvin A., 8926 Bellefort, Morton Grove, Ill.
Brougher, John F., 304 S. West St., Carlisle, Pa.
Brower, George, Eastern Michigan University, Ypsilanti, Mich.
Brown, Aaron, Phelps-Stokes Fund, 101 Park Ave., New York, N.Y.
Brown, Alma, 6301 West 78th St., Overland Park, Kan.
Brown, Charles I., Bennett College, Greenboro, N.C.
Brown, Clark, 513 Myrtle St., Bellingham, Wash.
Brown, Clyde M., Col. of Engr., University of Wisconsin, Madison, Wis.
Brown, Cynthiana Ellen, 232 Chateau St., Playa Del Rey, Calif.
Brown, Douglas M., Superintendent of Schools, Shorewood, Wis.
Brown, Mrs. Edith F., Star Route, Erwinna, Pa.
Brown, Fred A., Col. of Educ., University of Maryland, College Park, Md.
Brown, George I., University of California at Santa Barbara, University, Calif.
Brown, George W., 127 Akenside Rd., Riverside, Ill.
Brown, Gerald W., Educ. Dept., University of California, Riverside, Calif.
Brown, Gerald William, 2009 Paseo del Sol, Palos Verdes Estates, Calif.
Brown, Gertrude E., 2835 Milan St., New Orleans, La.
Brown, Helen I., University of Maryland, College Park, Md.
Brown, Howard L., Schl. Admin. Center, 49 E. College Ave., Springfield, Ohio
Brown, I. C., 36 Bethune Court, Columbia, S.C.
Brown, Judith, 3017 N.E. 54th St., Portland, Ore.
Brown, Kenneth G., Mankato State College, Mankato, Minn.
Brown, Kenneth R., California Tchrs. Assn., 1705 Murchison Dr., Burlingame, Calif.
Brown, Lawrence L., Superintendent of Schools, Dedham, Mass.
Brown, Mahlon C., Marshall College, Huntington, W.Va.
Brown, Marjorie, Sch. of Home Econ., University of Minnesota, St. Paul, Minn.
Brown, Mrs. Marjorie D., 4455 West 64th St., Los Angeles, Calif.
Brown, Perry, 1101—93rd St., Niagara Falls, N.Y.
Brown, Roy A., Kutztown State College, Kutztown, Pa.
Brown, Thomas, Hofstra College, Hempstead, N.Y.
Brown, Walter R., 2001 Chowkeebin Nene, Tallahassee, Fla.
Browne, Rose Butler, North Carolina College at Durham, Durham, N.C.
Brownell, Samuel M., Superintendent of Schools, Detroit, Mich.
Brownell, W. A., 207 Haviland Hall, University of California, Berkeley, Calif.
Browning, Roy W., Ottawa University, Ottawa, Kan.
Brownrigg, Helen R., Dept. of Guid. & Res., Pub. Schls., Belmont, Mass.
Brubaker, Leonard A., 918 Pine Heights Rd., Wayne, Neb.
Bruce, William C., Bruce Publishing Co., Milwaukee, Wis.
Brueckner, Leo J., 10790 Clarmon Pl., Culver City, Calif.
Brunelle, Paul E., 31 Herring Ave., Biddeford, Me.
Brunning, Charles R., University of Minnesota-Morris, Morris, Minn.
Brunner, Henry S., U.S. Office of Educ., Dept. of H.E.W., Washington, D.C.
Brunson, Mrs. DeWitt, P.O. Box 237, Ellis Ave. School, Orangeburg, S.C.
Bryan, Ray, 220 Curtis Hall, Iowa State University, Ames, Iowa
Bryant, Hayden C., State Department of Education, Macon, Ga.
Bryant, Ira B., Kashmere Gardens High Sch., Houston, Tex.
Bryant, Merle L., Univ. of Minnesota Dem. Laboratory School, Duluth, Minn.
Bryner, James R., 1498 Galbraith Rd., Cincinnati, Ohio
Buchanan, Alfred K., Mulberry St., Plantsville, Conn.
Buchanan, Mrs. Juanita, 319 Avenue H., Dallas, Tex.
Buchanan, Paul G., 19 Elmdale St., Dorchester, Mass.
Buckley, J. L., Superintendent of Schools, Lockhart, Tex.
Buckner, John D., 4246 W. North Market St., St. Louis, Mo.
Buckner, William N., 2643—15th St., N.W., Washington, D.C.
Buda, Mrs. Mary C., Julia Richman High School, 317 E. 67th St., New York, N.Y.
Budde, Harold H., Southwestern State College, Weatherford, Okla.
Bueker, Armin H., Superintendent of Schools, Marshall, Mo.
Buelke, John A., Western Michigan University, Kalamazoo, Mich.
Buffie, Edward G., F113 Hoosier Courts, Bloomington, Ind.

Bullis, Ella, 2656 N. 68th St., Wauwatosa, Wis.
Bullock, Portia C., 408 Tea St., N.W., Washington, D.C.
Bullock, William J., Superintendent of Schools, Kannapolis, N.C.
Bunker, James G., Superintendent, Secondary Schools, Coalinga, Calif.
Bunnell, Robert, 331 Miami, Park Forest, Ill.
Burch, Charles H., 1602 S. Anderson St., Urbana, Ill.
Burdett, C. Fred., Burdett College, 160 Beacon St., Boston, Mass.
Burdette, Mrs. Elmyra, Box 231, Damascus, Md.
Burdick, A. E., Arkansas State Teachers College, Conway, Ark.
Burdick, Richard L., Educ. Dept., Carroll College, Waukesha, Wis.
Burdine, D. I., Prairie View A. & M. College, Prairie View, Tex.
Burg, Mrs. Mary, 2259 Wolfangle Rd., Cincinnati, Ohio
Burgdorf, Otto P., 40-30—77th St., Elmhurst, N.Y.
Burgess, Mrs. Evangeline, 714 W. California Blvd., Pasadena, Calif.
Burgess, Thomas C., Dept. of Psych., Montana State University, Missoula, Mont.
Burk, R. Burdett, 5940 E. Walton St., Long Beach, Calif.
Burke, Arvid J., New York State Tchrs. Assn., 152 Washington Ave., Albany,
    N.Y.
Burke, Eileen M., 649 Rahway Ave., Woodbridge, N.J.
* Burke, Gladys, 244 Outlook, Youngstown, Ohio
Burke, Henry R., 126 McGuire St., Menlo Park Terrace, Metuchen, N.J.
Burke, Thomas O., 424 Bayberry Dr., Plantation, Fla.
Burke, Thomas S., 6926 S. Wolcott Ave., Chicago, Ill.
Burkett, Mrs. Artie May, 1106 North Ave. G, Haskell, Tex.
Burkett, Mrs. Cecile C., Box 266, Arkansas Rd., West Monroe, La.
Burkholder, Kenneth, 4323 N. 37th St., Omaha, Neb.
Burks, Herbert M., Jr., 137 Burton Hall, Univ. of Minnesota, Minneapolis, Minn.
Burks, John B., Jersey City State College, Jersey City, N.J.
Burlingame, Anna Louise, 7148 Jeffery Ave., Chicago, Ill.
Burns, Hobert W., Sch. of Educ., Syracuse University, Syracuse, N.Y.
Buros, Francis C., 207 Davis Ave., White Plains, N.Y.
Burr, Elbert W., Monsanto Chemical Co., Lindbergh and Olive, St. Louis, Mo.
Burrell, E. William, 60-A Perkins Hall, Harvard University, Cambridge, Mass.
Burrell, Natelkka E., Oakwood College, Huntsville, Ala.
Burrough, Rudolph V., Louisiana Polytechnic Institute, Ruston, La.
Burrows, Alvina Treut, 117 Nassau Ave., Manhasset, N.Y.
Burt, Lucile, Lincoln School, 338 Forest Ave., Fond du Lac, Wis.
Burton, William H., Dedbroke Hall, 3512 Willamette Ave., Corvallis, Ore.
Bush, Clifford L., Newark State College, Union, N.J.
Bushnell, Allan C., Dept. of Educ., Pago Pago, Tutuila, American Samoa
Buswell, Guy T., 1836 Thousand Oaks Blvd., Berkeley, Calif.
Butler, Laurence, 630 Leonard St., Ashland, Ore.
Butler, Paul W., Roosevelt Junior College, West Palm Beach, Fla.
Butler, Thomas M., 1217 Madison Ave., Edwardsville, Ill.
Butler, Warren N., Superintendent of Schools, Metuchen, N.J.
Butts, Franklin A., Gov. George Clinton School, Poughkeepsie, N.Y.
Butts, R. Freeman, Tchrs. Col., Columbia University, New York, N.Y.
Buyse, R., Sch. of Educ., University of Louvain, Tournai, Belgium
Buzash, G. A., Baldwin-Wallace College, Berea, Ohio
Byas, Ulysses, P.O. Box 445, Gainesville, Ga.
Byerly, Carl L., 14213 Woodmont Ave., Detroit, Mich.
Byram, Harold M., Sch. of Educ., Michigan State Univ., East Lansing, Mich.
Byrne, John, Sullivan High School, 6631 N. Bosworth, Chicago, Ill.
Byrne, Richard Hill, Col. of Educ., Univ. of Maryland, College Park, Md.

Caccavo, Emil, 123 Willow St., Roslyn Heights, N.Y.
Cadwell, Herbert M., 265 N. San Rafael Ave., Pasadena, Calif.
Cahan. Mrs. Ruth, 1916 Overland Ave., Los Angeles, Calif.
Cain, Ralph W., 3408 Red River, Austin, Tex.
Caird, Mrs. Florence B., Joyce Kilmer Sch., 6700 N. Greenview Ave., Chicago,
    Ill.

Caldwell, Cleon C., Lewis-Clark Normal School, Lewiston, Idaho
Caldwell, O. K., Fostoria High School, Fostoria, Ohio
Califf, Stanley N., Augustana College, Rock Island, Ill.
Call, Mrs. Ardell, Utah Educ. Assn., Box 2159, Salt Lake City, Utah
Callahan, Carol, Creole Petrol. Corp., Cabimas, Edo, Zulia, Venezuela
Callahan, William T., Washington School, New Milford, N.J.
Callan, John H., Sch. of Educ., Seton Hall University, Newark, N.J.
Callas, Eliza E., 7080 Oregon Ave., N.W., Kensington, Md.
Callaway, Byron, Alabama Polytechnic Institute, Auburn, Ala.
Camhi, Paul S., Sch. Dept., Pacific St. Hospital, P.O. Box 100, Pomona, Calif.
Camien, Laiten L., P.O. Box 157, University Park, N.M.
Campbell, Bonham, Dept. of Engr., University of California, Los Angeles, Calif.
Campbell, Mrs. Eleanor L., State College, St. Cloud, Minn.
Campbell, Joe W., L. S. Rugg School, Alexandria, La.
Campbell, L. L., Knoxville College, Knoxville, Tenn.
Campbell, R. Lee, Campbellsville College, Campbellsville, Ky.
Campbell, Roald F., Midwest Adm. Center, Univ. of Chicago, Chicago, Ill.
Campbell, T. J., 109 Hughes Ave., Attalla, Ala.
Campbell, Thomas C., Superintendent, Sch. Dist., No. 834, Stillwater, Minn.
Campos, Mrs. M. A. Pourchet, Caixa Postal 8216, Sao Paulo S.P., Brazil
Canar, Donald A., Supt. Central YMCA Schls., 19 S. LaSalle St., Chicago, Ill.
Canfield, James K., Long Beach State College, Long Beach, Calif.
Cannon, Wendell E., Sch. of Educ., Univ. of Southern California, Los Angeles, Calif.
Cantrell, William P., Wesleyan College, Macon, Ga.
Canuteson, Richard L., State Univ. College of Education, Brockport, N.Y.
Capehart, Bertis E., Educ. Dept., Hill & Knowlton, Inc., New York, N.Y.
Caple, Mrs. Charlotte M., Maxwell, Iowa
Capocy, John S., 1113 W. 80th St., Chicago, Ill.
Cappa, Dan, Los Angeles State College, Los Angeles, Calif.
Cappalonga, Philip B., Sabine and Essex Aves., Narberth, Pa.
Capps, Lelon R., 6211 Monmouth Ave., Goleta, Calif.
Capps, Mrs. Marian P., Virginia State College, Norfolk, Va.
Capron, Clara, 301 Olive St., West Palm Beach, Fla.
Carbaugh, Gaile A., Campus Sch., State Univ. Tchrs. College, Geneseo, N.Y.
Cardina, Philip J., 6 Rustic Dr., Lakewood, N.J.
Cardwell, Robert H., Park Junior High School, Bertrand St., Knoxville, Tenn.
Carey, Clarence B., Jones Commerical High School, 607 Plymouth Ct., Chicago, Ill.
Carey, Elizabeth B., 489 State St., Albany, N.Y.
Carey, John W., Jr., 38 B Carpenter Ave., Mt. Kisco, N.Y.
Carey, Justin P., 110 Echo Ave., New Rochelle, N.Y.
Carey, Wendell, Dept. of Educ., Park College, Parkville, Mo.
Carico, Joseph V., George Wythe Junior High School, Hampton, Va.
Carline, Donald E., Read. Center, Kansas State Tchrs. Col., Emporia, Kan.
Carlson, Cecil V., 808 West 10th St., McCook, Neb.
Carlson, Mrs. Evelyn F., 6899 N. Wildwood, Chicago, Ill.
Carlson, F. Roy, Mt. Ida Junior College, Newton Centre, Mass.
Carlson, Mrs. Ruth K., 1718 LeRoy Ave., Berkeley, Calif.
Carlson, Thorston R., 415 Monte Vista Lane, Santa Rosa, Calif.
Carnahan, Eleanor, 11 Forest Rd., Oakmont, Wheeling, W.Va.
Carne, Vernon E., 1383 Dorothy Dr., Decatur, Ga.
Carney, Thomas, 2107 Morningside Dr., Mineral Wells, Tex.
Carney, Wilma B., 1479 S.W. 18th Ave., Fort Lauderdale, Fla.
Carnochan, John L., Jr., Kirby Lane, North Rye, N.Y.
Carpenter, Aaron C., P.O. Box 387, Grambling, La.
Carpenter, N. H., Superintendent, City Schools, Elkin, N.C.
Carper, M. L., Box 1311, Martinsville, Va.
Carr, Julian W., 205 West 15th St., New York, N.Y.
Carr, Louis D., Public School No. 23, 143 Romaine Ave., Jersey City, N.J.
Carrithers, Lura M., University of Wisconsin-Milwaukee, Milwaukee, Wis.

Carroll, Clifford, Gonzaga University, Spokane, Wash.
Carroll, John B., Grad. Sch. of Educ., Harvard University, Cambridge, Mass.
Carroll, John S., 3250 Oakes Dr., Hayward, Calif.
Carroll, Katherine M., Western Washington State College, Bellingham, Wash.
Carroll, Margaret L., 208 Fairmont Rd., DeKalb, Ill.
Carron, Malcolm, Col. of Arts and Sci., University of Detroit, Detroit, Mich.
Carsello, Carmen J., 2154 N. Nordica Ave., Chicago, Ill.
Carson, H. Maude, 6025 N. Mason, Chicago, Ill.
Carstater, Eugene D., 606 Jackson Dr., Falls Church, Va.
Carter, Gordon, Superintendent Sch. Dist. 501, Bellingham, Wash.
Carter, Harold D., Sch. of Educ., University of California, Berkeley, Calif.
Carter, Homer L. J., Western Michigan University, Kalamazoo, Mich.
Carter, Richard C., Box 1250, Fairbanks Public Schools, Fairbanks, Alaska
Carter, Sims, 401 Kelton Ave., Los Angeles, Calif.
Carter, Vincent, San Jose City Schools, San Jose, Calif.
Cartwright, William H., 106 Morningside Dr., New York, N.Y.
Carver, Velda, University of Toledo, Toledo, Ohio
Cash, Harry T., Hamilton High School, 1478 Wilson St., Memphis, Tenn.
Caskey, Helen C., Tchrs. Col., University of Cincinnati, Cincinnati, Ohio
Casserly, Catherine M., Public Schls., 170 Pond St., Providence, R.I.
Cassidy, Rosalind, University of California, 405 Hilgard Ave., Los Angeles, Calif.
Castelli, Albert, 2933 Shawnee Lane, Drayton Plains, Mich.
Caswell, Hollis L., Tchrs. Col., Columbia University, New York, N.Y.
Caton, W. Barnie, Superintendent, Gallup-McKinley County Schls., Gallup, N.M.
Catrambone, A. R., Superintendent of Schools, Camden, N.J.
Caudle, Jean I., Wisconsin State College, Oshkosh, Wis.
Caughran, Alex M., 93 N. Main St., Orono, Me.
Caulfield, Patrick J., Dept. of Educ., St. Peter's College, Jersey City, N.J.
Cavanaugh, Alfred D., Dept. of Educ., University of Detroit, Detroit, Mich.
Cawrse, Robert C., 40 Maple Hill Dr., Chagrin Falls, Ohio
Chadderdon, Hester, Home Econ. Div., Iowa State University, Ames, Iowa
Chaffee, Charles E., Superintendent of Schools, Bethlehem, Pa.
Chaikin, Milton, 224 East 28th St., New York, N.Y.
Chall, Jeanne, City College, 218 East 12th St., New York, N.Y.
Chambers, J. Richard, 5630 S.W. 76th St., Miami, Fla.
Chambers, M. M., Mich. Council of State Col. Presidents, Lansing, Mich.
Chambers, William M., 100th Div., 400th Regt., Co. L, Fort Chaffee, Ark.
Champlin, George R., P.O. Box 2219, Hartford, Conn.
Chandler, H. E., 1320 Haskell Ave., Lawrence, Kan.
Chang, Alvin K., 3642 S. Court St., Palo Alto, Calif.
Chang, Jen-chi, Florida Normal and Ind. Mem. College, St. Augustine, Fla.
Chao, Sankey C., 85 ½ Douglas Ave., St. Augustine, Fla.
Chapman, Carita A., 3001 S. Parkway, Chicago, Ill.
Chapman, Catherine, Weatherford College, Weatherford, Tex.
Chappell, Bartlett E. S., New York Military Academy, Cornwall-on-Hudson, N.Y.
Charles, Harvey, Dept. of Educ., John Carroll University, University Heights,
    Ohio
Charles, Ramon L., 327 Nickell Rd., Topeka, Kan.
Charters, Alexander N., 610 Fayette St., Syracuse, N.Y.
Chase, Francis S., Dept. of Educ., University of Chicago, Chicago, Ill.
Chase, Naomi C., University of Minnesota, Minneapolis, Minn.
Chasnoff, Robert, Newark State College, Union, N.J.
Cheeks, L. E., 213 McFarland St., Kerrville, Tex.
Chell, Elsie M., 2015 S. Sunnyslope Rd., New Berlin, Wis.
Chellevold, John O., Wartburg College, Waverly, Iowa
Chenault, R. N., 626 Russell St., Nashville, Tenn.
Chenoweth, Margaret, Admin. Center, 315 S. Jackson St., Janesville, Wis.
Chern, Mrs. Nona E., 492 Concord Rd., Broomall, Pa.
Cherry, J. H., Superintendent, Community Schls., 101 N. McCullough St., Urbana,
    Ill.
Chiara, Clara R., 945 Dobbin Dr., Kalamazoo, Mich.

Chidekel, Samuel J., 9124 Somoset Blvd., Skokie, Ill.
Chidester, Charles B., 6650 Jackson Ave., Hammond, Ind.
Chievitz, Gene L., Bldg. 12, University of New Mexico, Albuquerque, N.M.
Childress, Jack R., Sch. of Educ., Boston University, Boston, Mass.
Chiles, Doris E., 1552 N.W. 5th Ave., Pompano Beach, Fla.
Chinitz, Ben S., 15055 Hubbell Ave., Detroit, Mich.
Chipman, R. S., Superintendent of Schools, N. Summit Dist., Coalville, Utah
Chirhart, Mrs. Virginia, 608—6th St., North, St. Cloud, Minn.
Chitwood, R. B., Superintendent, Lakeside Schools, Lake Village, Ark.
Chivers, Naomi R., Spelman College, Atlanta, Ga.
Chiverton, William S., Moreland Sch. Dist., Murray Ave., Huntingdon Valley, Pa.
Choate, Ernest A., Germantown High School, Philadelphia, Pa.
Chow, Rita, American Journal of Nursing, 10 Columbus Circle, New York, N.Y.
Christenson, Bernice M., 5045 Alta Canyada Rd., La Canada, Calif.
Christie, Sarah C., 9 S. Stockton St., Trenton, N.J.
Christman, Paul S., Superintendent of Schools, Schuylkill Haven, Pa.
Chuck, Harry C., 265 Kanoelani Dr., Hilo, Hawaii
Chudler, Albert A., 3540 Summerfield Dr., Sherman Oaks, Calif.
Cianciolo, Patricia J., 211 Arps Hall, Ohio State University, Columbus, Ohio
Cioffi, Joseph M., 652 Doriskill Ct., River Vale, N.J.
Clabaugh, R. E., Superintendent of Schools, Arlington Heights, Ill.
Clark, Catherine, Middle Tennessee State College, Murfreesboro, Tenn.
Clark, David L., Col. of Educ., Ohio State University, Columbus, Ohio
Clark, Edward F., St. Peter's College, Hudson Blvd., Jersey City, N.J.
Clark, Elmer J., Laboratory Sch., Indiana State College, Terre Haute, Ind.
Clark, Mrs. Esmer Knudson, 2274 Cedar St., Berkeley, Calif.
Clark, Francis E., Dept. of Educ. Psych., Univ. of Hawaii, Honolulu, Hawaii
Clark, Franklin B., District Superintendent of Schools, Athens, N.Y.
Clark, John F., 1480 Summit Ave., Encinitas, Calif.
Clark, Leonard H., Pamrapo Court, Bayonne, N.J.
Clark, Lewis E., 3000 S.W. Flower Terrace, Portland, Ore.
Clark, Lois M., National Education Assn., 1201—16th St., N.W., Washington, D.C.
Clark, Maurice P., Superintendent of Schools, 4335 Howard Ave., Western
    Springs, Ill.
Clark, Max R., Superintendent of Schools, Dubuque, Iowa
Clark, Richard M., State University College of Education, Oneonta, N.Y.
Clark, Roy, Superintendent of Schls., 9526 S. Cook Ave., Oak Lawn, Ill.
Clark, Thomas H., 500B Pine St., Ketchikan, Alaska.
Clark, Mrs. Willa B., 1224—16th St., Parkersburg, W.Va.
Clark, Woodrow Wilson, 101 W. Leake St., Clinton, Miss.
Clarke, Albert T., Stephen F. Austin State College, Nacogdoches, Tex.
Clark, Stanley C. T., 11615—78th Ave., Edmonton, Alba., Canada
Clarkston, Emmerine A., 8216 Eberhart Ave., Chicago, Ill.
Classon, Marion E., 412 Harrison Ave., Highland Park, N.J.
Claxton, Clarence C., Steinmetz High School, Chicago, Ill.
Clayton, Harold, 109 N. Jackson, Americus, Ga.
Clayton, Thomas E., 7 Kelly Dr., Manlius, N.Y.
Clegg, Ambrose A., Jr., Sch. of Educ., Univ. of North Carolina, Chapel Hill, N.C.
Cleland, Donald L., Sch. of Educ., Univ. of Pittsburgh, Pittsburgh, Pa.
Cleveland, Ernest D., Superintendent of Schools, Palestine, Tex.
Clifford, Paul I., Sch. of Educ., Atlanta University, Atlanta, Ga.
Clift, Virgil A., Morgan State College, Baltimore, Md.
Cline, Marion, Jr., P.O. Box 746, Santa Fe., N.M.
Clinton, Robert, Jr., Snyder High School, Snyder, Tex.
Clopper, Mrs. Elizabeth, Bd. of Educ., Anne Arundel County, Annapolis, Md.
Clouser, John J., 200 N. Elm St., Mt. Prospect, Ill.
Clouthier, Raymond P., St. Norbert College, West DePere, Wis.
Clymer, Theodore W., Col. of Educ., University of Minnesota, Minneapolis, Minn.
Cobb, Beatrice M., Cambell Shore Rd., Gray, Me.
Cobb, Jacob E., Indiana State College, Terre Haute, Ind.
Cobban, Margaret R., 9 William St., Stamford, Conn.

* Cochran, J. Chester, 2413 Albans St., Houston, Tex.
Cochran, John R., Kalamazoo Public Schools, 1220 Howard St., Kalamazoo, Mich.
Cochran, Russell T., 27551 Drexel Way, Hayward, Calif.
Codwell, John E., Jack Yate Sr. High School, 3703 Sampson St., Houston, Tex.
Coen, Alban Wasson, II, Central Michigan University, Mt. Pleasant, Mich.
Coetzee, J. Christian, Potchefstroom University, Potchefstroom, South Africa
Cofell, William L., St. John's University, Collegeville, Minn.
Coffee, James M., Clark University, 950 Main St., Worcester, Mass.
Coffey, Thomas F., George Washington Sch., 3535 E. 114th St., Chicago, Ill.
Coffey, Warren, 1720 Bellamy Dr., Champaign, Ill.
Cohen, George, 8 Etheride Pl., Park Ridge, N.J.
Cohen, S. Alan, Jersey City State College, Jersey City, N.J.
Cohen, Samuel, 60 Everit Ave., Hewlett, N.Y.
Cohler, Milton J., 330 Diversey Parkway, Chicago, Ill.
Colbath, Edwin H., 101-40—117th St., Richmond Hill, N.Y.
Colburn, A. B., Rte. 5, Box 678E, Everett, Wash.
Cole, James C., USOM Port-au-Prince, State Department, Washington, D.C.
Cole, Mary I., Western Kentucky State College, Bowling Green, Ky.
Coleman, F. Basil, 435 W. 119th St., New York, N.Y.
Coleman, Mary E., Carver Intermediate Sch., 901 E. 133rd Place, Chicago, Ill.
Coleman, Mary Elizabeth, Univ. of Pennsylvania, 3944 Walnut St., Philadelphia,
    Pa.
Colla, Frances S., 1038 Maplewood Ave., Bridgeport, Conn.
Collier, Mrs. Anna K., 903 Fourth St., Liverpool, N.Y.
Collier, Calhoun C., Michigan State University, East Lansing, Mich.
Collier, Richard E., Montgomery County Public Schools, Rockville, Md.
Collings, Miller R., Cincinnati Public Schls., 608 E. McMillan St., Cincinnati, Ohio
Collins, James D., St. John's Prep. School, 82 Lewis Ave., Brooklyn, N.Y.
Collins, Helen C., 1203 Gilpin Ave., Wilmington, Del.
Collins, Kathleen M., 5410 Connecticut Ave., N.W., Washington, D.C.
Collins, Paul W., Box 119, Lucasville, Ohio
Collins, Robert E., Deephaven Junior High School, Excelsior, Minn.
Conan, Mrs. Beatrice, 2063—74th St., Brooklyn, N.Y.
Conaway, Mrs. Freda Yanit, West Liberty State College, West Liberty, W.Va.
Condon, Edward T., Tri Valley Central Sch., Grahamsville, N.Y.
Congreve, Willard J., Lab. Schls., University of Chicago, Chicago, Ill.
Conley, William H., Marquette University, Milwaukee, Wis.
Connor, E. Faye, Huntington College Library, Huntington, Ind.
Connor, Frances Partridge, Tchrs. Col., Columbia University, New York, N.Y.
Connor, William H., Washington Univ. Grad. Inst. of Education, St. Louis, Mo.
Conway, James A., 74 Bradford St., Albany, N.Y.
Conway, Marie M., Jefferson Court No. 31, 4925 Saul St., Philadelphia, Pa.
Cook, Ben J., Superintendent of Schools, South Plainfield, N.J.
Cook, Raymond M., Chicago Teachers College, 6800 Stewart Ave., Chicago, Ill.
Cook, Walter W., Col. of Educ., University of Minnesota, Minneapolis, Minn.
Cooke, Dan B., High Point College, High Point, N.C.
Cooke, Dorothy E., State Education Department, Albany, N.Y.
Cooling, Elizabeth, 93 Cottage Ave., North Providence, R.I.
Coon, Alice B., 303 W. North St., Manteca, Calif.
Cooper, Bernice, Peabody Hall, University of Georgia, Athens, Ga.
Cooper, George H., 2913 Washington Blvd., Chicago, Ill.
Cooper, Russell M., University of Southern Florida, Tampa, Fla.
Cooper, Shirley, Amer. Assn. of School Adm., 1201—16th St., N.W., Washington,
    D.C.
Cooper, William H., Col. of Educ., Ohio University, Athens, Ohio
Corbally, John E., 202D Educ. Hall, University of Washington, Seattle, Wash.
Corey, Stephen M., University of Miami Branch, Coral Gables, Fla.
Corley, Clifford L., Oregon College of Education, Monmouth, Ore.
Corman, Bernard R., Michigan State University, East Lansing, Mich.
Cornell, Francis G., Educ. Research Service, Inc., 124 E. 40th St., New York, N.Y.
Cornish, Dale, 5770 Dudley St., Arvada, Colo.

Cornish, Robert L., Sch. of Educ., Kansas University, Lawrence, Kan.
Cortage, Cecelia, 2053 Illinois Ave., Santa Rosa, Calif.
Cory, N. Durward, 908 W. North St., Muncie, Ind.
Coss, Mrs. Carrie B., Prairie View A. & M. College, Prairie View, Tex.
Coster, John K., Dept. of Educ., Purdue University, Lafayette, Ind.
Cotey, Helen G., 408 Idylwood Dr., S.E., Salem, Ore.
Cotter, Katharine C., South Main St., Osterville, Mass.
Cottone, Sebastian C., 2534 S. Colorado St., Philadelphia, Pa.
Couche, Martha E., Rust College, Holly Springs, Miss.
Coughlin, James H., Grad. Dept. of Educ., Fairfield University, Fairfield, Conn.
Coulson, John R., Parkside School, 6938 East End Ave., Chicago, Ill.
Coulson, Roger W., Col. of Educ., Butler University, Indianapolis, Ind.
Coulter, Myron L., Col. of Educ., Pennsylvania State Univ., University Park, Pa.
* Courtis, S. A., 9110 Dwight Ave., Detroit, Mich.
Courtney, Robert W., 10 Olcott St., Middlebush, N.J.
Cousins, E. H., 8 Upper Sandringham Ave., Half-way Tree P.O., Jamaica, B.W.I.
Cousins, John, High Street School, West Chester, Pa.
Covell, Merle O., California State College, California, Pa.
Cowan, Persis H., 1612 Fair Oaks Ave., South Pasadena, Calif.
Cowan, William A., San Francisco State College, San Francisco, Calif.
Coward, Gertrude, 401 East 9th St., Charlotte, N.C.
Cowles, Clifton V., Jr., 919 West H. St., Ontario, Calif.
Cowley, W. H., Cubberley Hall, Stanford University, Stanford, Calif.
Cox, Edwin A., Superintendent of Schools, North Parade, Stratford, Conn.
Cox, Johnnye, V., Col. of Educ., University of Georgia, Athens, Ga.
Cox, Velma V., Eastern Illinois University, Charleston, Ill.
Cozine, June, Oklahoma A. & M. College, Stillwater, Okla.
Crabtree, Charlotte, Sch. of Educ., University of California, Los Angeles, Calif.
Craddock, John R., 212 S. Celia Ave., Muncie, Ind.
* Craig, Gerald S., Tchrs. Col., Columbia University, New York, N.Y.
Craig, James C., 4302 Federal St., Rockville, Md.
Craig, Robert C., Dept. of Educ., Marquette University, Milwaukee, Wis.
Craig, Mrs. Ruth B., State Department of Education, Concord, N.H.
Cramer, Beatrice E., 1365 Weaver St., Scarsdale, N.Y.
Crandell, W. B., 301 W. Jackson St., Villa Park, Ill.
Craney, Wayne A., 926 Ferdinand Ave., Forest Park, Ill.
Craton, Edward J., 1777 Glenwood Ct., Bakersfield, Calif.
Crawford, Dorothy M., 212 W. Washington St., Ottawa, Ill.
Crawford, Ernest A., Sch. of Educ., University of Dublin, Dublin, Ireland
Crawford, Robert T., 713 Maple Ave., Rockville, Md.
Crawford, T. James, Sch. of Business, Indiana University, Bloomington, Ind.
Creason, Frank, Valley View School, 8101 W. 95th St., Overland Park, Kan.
Crescimbeni, Joseph, University of Bridgeport, 126 Park Ave., Bridgeport, Conn.
Creswell, Mrs. Rowena C., 305 Montclair Ave., So., College Station, Tex.
Crews, Roy L., Aurora College, Aurora, Ill.
Crocker, Richard F., Jr., Superintendent of Schools, Caribou, Me.
Crook, Robert R., Queens College, Flushing, N.Y.
Crosby, G. J., Queens College, Flushing, N.Y.
Cross, William C., New Mexico State University, University Park, N.M.
Crossley, John B., 1621 Keller Rd., Honolulu, Hawaii
Crosslin, Barbara, 14 N. 11th Ave., Yakima, Wash.
Crosson, Robert Henry, 4463 Clay St., Denver, Colo.
Crow, A. L., Superintendent of Schools, Kirkwood, Mo.
Crow, Lester D., Brooklyn College, Bedford Ave. and Ave. H., Brooklyn, N.Y.
Crowder, William W., Dept. of Educ., Whittier College, Whittier, Calif.
Crowe, James W., Chicago Vocational High School, 2100 E. 87th St., Chicago, Ill.
Crowell, R. A., Col. of Educ., University of Arizona, Tucson, Ariz.
Crowley, Mary C., 4636 Firestone No. 3, Dearborn, Mich.
Crowley, W. B., 823 Stebondale Rd., Columbia, S.C.
Crull, Howard D., Superintendent of Schools, Port Huron, Mich.
Crum, Clyde E., Div. of Educ., San Diego State College, San Diego, Calif.

Crumb, Frederick W., State University Tchrs. College, Potsdam, N.Y.
Culbertson, Jack A., Ohio State University, 65 S. Oval Dr., Columbus, Ohio
Culliton, Thomas E., Jr., 805 W. Pennsylvania St., Urbana, Ill.
Culver, Mrs. Erleen, 930 West Acres Rd., West Sacramento, Calif.
Cumbee, Carroll F., Col. of Educ., University of Florida, Gainesville, Fla.
Cummings, Mabel Anna, 6044 Linden St., Brooklyn, N.Y.
Cummings, Mrs. Reta, 120 S. Prospect St., Orange, Calif.
Cunningham, George S., State Department of Education, Concord, N.H.
Cunningham, L. R., 342 Webster St., Jackson, Tenn.
Cunningham, Luvern L., Col. of Educ., Univ. of Minnesota, Minneapolis, Minn.
Cunningham, Myron, Col. of Educ., University of Florida, Gainesville, Fla.
Currier, Mrs. Lynor O., 713 Giddings Ave., Annapolis, Md.
Currier, Richard R. D., Yardley-Newtown Rd., Yardley, Pa.
Curry, Mrs. Alma M., 3709—14th St., N.W., Washington, D.C.
Curry, John F., Box 6765, North Texas State College, Denton, Tex.
Curry, Robert, Sch. of Educ., Baylor University, Waco, Tex.
Curtin, James R., Col. of Educ., University of Minnesota, Minneapolis, Minn.
Curtin, Wylma R., 9600 Culver St., Kensington, Md.
Curtis, E. Louise, Macalester College, St. Paul, Minn.
Curtis, H. A., Florida State University, Tallahassee, Fla.
Curtis, James E., 720 Garland Dr., Palo Alto, Calif.
Cusick, Ralph J., 6443 N. Wayne Ave., Chicago, Ill.

Daddazio, Arthur H., Bd. of Educ., 98 Grand St., Newburgh, N.Y.
Dady, Milan B., Northwest Missouri State College, Maryville, Mo.
Dahl, Mrs. Barbara, 1330 Cedar St., Santa Monica, Calif.
Dahle, C. O., Superintendent of Schools, Highland Park, Ill.
Daines, Mrs. Delva, 554 E. 1864 South, Orem, Utah
Dale, Arbie Myron, Sch. of Commerce, New York University, New York, N.Y.
Dale, Edgar, Col. of Educ., 65 S. Oval Dr., Ohio State Univ., Columbus, Ohio
D'Alessio, Edward R., Sch. of Educ., Seton Hall University, South Orange, N.J.
Daly, Edmund B., Kelly High School, 4136 S. California Ave., Chicago, Ill.
D'Amelio, Guy R., Unity Drive School, Centereach, N.Y.
Daniel, A. A., Box 5451, North Texas Station, Denton, Tex.
Daniel, George T., 123 N. Wilbur St., Walla Walla, Wash.
Daniel, Sheldon C., Box 97, Bath, Ohio
Daniels, Paul R., 8411 Widener Rd., Philadelphia, Pa.
Danielson, Mrs. Hope F., Northeastern University, Boston, Mass.
Danielson, Paul J., Col. of Educ., University of Arizona, Tucson, Ariz.
Darcy, Natalie T., Dept. of Educ., Brooklyn College, Brooklyn, N.Y.
Darling, Richard, 12330 Middlebelt Rd., Livonia, Mich.
Darnell, Mrs. Myra C., P.O. Box 5811, Milwaukie, Ore.
Darroch, Frank W., 27 Princeton Rd., Toronto, Ont., Canada
Darte, Franck G., Dept. of Educ., Newark State College, Union, N.J.
D'Ascoli, Louis N., Roosevelt High School, 127 Park Ave., Yonkers, N.Y.
Davenport, William R., Col. of Educ., Butler University, Indianapolis, Ind.
Davey, Mrs. Elizabeth P., 5748 Harper Ave., Chicago, Ill.
Davidson, Mrs. Elizabeth W., Johnson Rd., Clarksburg, Md.
Davidson, Mrs. Evelyn K., Dept. of Educ., Kent State University, Kent, Ohio
Davidson, R. L., Texas Technological College, Lubbock, Tex.
Davies, Daniel R., Tchrs. Col., Columbia University, New York, N.Y.
Davies, Don, NCTEPS (NEA), 1201—16th St., N.W., Washington, D.C.
Davies, J. Leonard, Col. of Educ., State Univ. of Iowa, Iowa City, Iowa
Davies, Mrs. Lillian S., Dept. of Educ., Western Reserve Univ., Cleveland, Ohio
Davis, Benjamin F., 111-16—209th Pl., Queens Village, N.Y.
Davis, David Carson, 902 Cornell Ct., Madison, Wis.
Davis, Dwight M., 1110—17th St., Moline, Ill.
Davis, Floyd A., Superintendent of Schools, Knoxville, Iowa
Davis, Guy C., Trinidad State Junior College, Trinidad, Colo.
Davis, H. Curtis, 1605 Park Ave., San Jose, Calif.
Davis, Hazel A., Hofstra College, Hempstead, N.Y.

Davis, J. Pinckney, 516 N.W. 21st Ave., Fort Lauderdale, Fla.
Davis, J. Sanford, Box 646, Madison, Conn.
Davis, Joseph H., 8300 Jackson St., St. Louis, Mo.
Davis, Milton J., 725 West 18th St., North Chicago, Ill.
Davis, Nancy B., Sch. of Educ., Indiana University, Bloomington, Ind.
Davis, O. L., Jr., University of North Carolina, Chapel Hill, N.C.
Davis, Robert L., Wilmington Manor School, New Castle, Del.
Davis, Ron W., 1745 Hillside Rd., Southampton, Pa.
Davis, Warren C., 65 S. Plymouth Ave., Rochester, N.Y.
Davoren, David, Superintendent of Schools, Milford, Mass.
Dawald, V. F., Dept. of Educ., Millikin University, Decatur, Ill.
Dawkins, M. B., Philander Smith College, Little Rock, Ark.
Dawson, W. Read, Baylor University, Waco, Tex.
Day, James F., Dept. of Educ., Texas Western College, El Paso, Tex.
Deam, Calvin W., Boston University, 332 Bay State Rd., Boston, Mass.
Dease, E. Richard, McLean Co. Unit Sch. Dist. No. 5, Normal, Ill.
DeBernardis, Amo, 1814 Dekum St., N.E., Portland, Ore.
Debin, Louis, 83-37—247th St., Bellerose, N.Y.
DeBoer, Mrs. Dorothy L., DePaul University, 25 E. Jackson Blvd., Chicago, Ill.
DeBoer, John J., Col. of Educ., University of Illinois, Urbana, Ill.
DeBus, Raymond L., 666 Malabar Rd., Maroubra, N.S.W., Australia
DeClore, Beatrice Ann, 626 Pico Place, Santa Monica, Calif.
Deer, George H., Louisiana State University, Baton Rouge, La.
DeKeni, Sara L., State Education Department, Tallahassee, Fla.
DeKock, Henry C., Col. of Educ., State Univ. of Iowa, Iowa City, Iowa
Delaney, Eleanor C., Sch. of Educ., Rutgers University, New Brunswick, N.J.
Dell, Daryl L., Ball State Teachers College, Muncie, Ind.
Della-Dora, Delmo, County Bd. of Educ., City-County Bldg., Detroit, Mich.
DeLong, Arthur R., University of Delaware, Newark, Del.
Demming, John A., Bldg. S-502, Palm Beach Air Force Base, West Palm Beach, Fla.
DeMoraes, Maria P. Tito, WHO, Palais des Nations, Geneva, Switzerland
Denecke, Marie G., Col. of Educ., Univ. of Maryland, College Park, Md.
Denemark, George W., University of Wisconsin-Milwaukee, Milwaukee, Wis.
Denny, Mrs. Alma G., 7418 Poplar Ave., Baltimore, Md.
Denny, Terry, Sch. of Educ., Purdue University, West Lafayette, Ind.
Denson, Lucille D., 102 N. Saddle River Rd., Monsey, N.Y.
Derby, Orlo L., State University Teachers College, Brockport, N.Y.
DeShazo, Willard, 6117 Brookside Dr., Alexandria, Va.
Desjardins, Reno-Leo, St. Joseph's University, Moncton, N.B., Canada
Desoe, Hollis L., Board of Educ., 51 Route 100, Briarcliff Manor, N.Y.
Deutschman, Mrs. Marilyn L., 90-59—56th Ave., Elmhurst 73, Queens, L.I., N.Y.
DeVault, M. Vere, University of Texas, Austin, Tex.
Devine, Florence E., 515 E. Harding Ave., LaGrange Park, Ill.
Devine, Thomas F., College of Our Lady of the Elms, Chicopee, Mass.
Devine, Thomas G., Rhode Island College, Providence, R.I.
Devor, J. W., 6309 E. Holbert Rd., Bethesda, Md.
Deyell, J. Douglas, Provincial Teachers College, North Bay, Ont., Canada
Dezelle, Walter, Jr., 3205 Allison Ave., Groves, Tex.
D'Heurle, Adma, Spring Valley Rd., Ossining, N.Y.
Dickerson, James L., 180 South View Dr., Athens, Ga.
Dickey, Otis M., Superintendent of Schools, Birmingham, Mich.
Dickmeyer, Mrs. K. H., Fairfax, Minn.
Dickson, George E., Col. of Educ., University of Toledo, Ohio
* Diederich, A. F., St. Norbert College, West DePere, Wis.
Diefenderfer, Omie T., 828 Third St., Fullerton, Pa.
Diener, Russell E., Kent State University, Kent, Ohio
Dieterle, Louise E., 10700 S. Avenue F, Chicago, Ill.
Dietz, Elizabeth H., 1093 Northern Blvd., Baldwin, N.Y.
Diffley, Jerome, St. Bernard College, St. Bernard, Ala.
Diggs, Kermit H., St. Paul's College, Lawrenceville, Va.

DiGiacento, Mrs. Rose, 68 Pilgrim Ave., Yonkers, N.Y.
Dil, Anwar S., Educ. Extn. Service Center, Gulberg, Lahore, West Pakistan
DiLeonarde, Joseph H., 4316 S. Princeton Ave., Chicago, Ill.
DiLieto, Ray Marie, 4 Bayberry Lane, Westport, Conn.
Dillinger, Claude M., Illinois State Normal University, Normal, Ill.
Dillon, Frances H., Minnesota State College, Moorhead, Minn.
Dimond, Ray A., Jr., 4034 E. Cambridge, Phoenix, Ariz.
Dimond, Stanley E., 2012 Shadford Rd., Ann Arbor, Mich.
DiNapoli, Peter J., Public School 90, Sheridan Ave., New York, N.Y.
DiNardo, V. James, Massachusetts State College, Bridgewater, Mass.
DiPace, William, 316 Jordan Court, Martinez, Calif.
Disko, Michael, Box 394, Athens, Ohio
Dittmer, Daniel G., 1647 Francis Hammond Pkwy., Alexandria, Va.
Dittmer, Jane E., Kouts High School, Kouts, Ind.
DiVirgilio, James, 218 Middle Blvd., Salisbury, Md.
Dix, M. S., North Shore School, 1217 Chase Ave., Chicago, Ill.
Dixon, Mrs. Glendora M., Oregon College of Education, Monmouth, Ore.
Dixon, James T., 24 Arrow Wood Lane, Huntington Sta., L.I., N.Y.
Dixon, W. Robert, Sch. of Educ., University of Michigan, Ann Arbor, Mich.
Doak, Helen, 124—26th St., Santa Monica, Calif.
Doane, Kenneth R., Educ. Dept., Hamline University, St. Paul, Minn.
Dobbs, Louis H., 100 College St., Brookhaven, Miss.
Dodd, John M., State University College of Education, Buffalo, N.Y.
Dodds, A. Gordon, Superintendent of Schools, Edwardsville, Ill.
Dodson, Dan W., New York University, Washington Sq., New York, N.Y.
Dodson, Robert G., St. Gregory's College, Shawnee, Okla.
Doi, James I., 425—42nd St., Boulder, Colo.
Dolan, Francis, LaSalle-Peru Twp. High School, LaSalle, Ill.
Doll, Ronald C., 17 Rossmore Ter., Livingston, N.J.
Dolton, Leonard J., Southern Calif. State Dental Assn., Los Angeles, Calif.
Domian, E. O., 1595 Northrop, St. Paul, Minn.
Dominy, Mrs. Mildred, Ellenburg Center, N.Y.
Donovan, Egbert H., St. Vincent College, Latrobe, Pa.
Donchi, Mrs. Celia B., 118 Oakview Ave., Maplewood, N.J.
Donley, Donald T., State University Teachers College, Albany, N.Y.
Donner, Arvin N., Col. of Educ., University of Houston, Houston, Tex.
Donoghue, Mrs. Mildred R., Immaculate Heart College, Los Angeles, Calif.
Donohue, Francis J., Fordham University, New York, N.Y.
Donovan, Charles F., Sch. of Educ., Boston College, Chestnut Hill, Mass.
Doody, Louise E., 1697 Beacon St., Waban, Mass.
Dorricott, H. J., Western State College, Gunnison, Colo.
Doss, Paul, 12631 Fletcher Dr., Garden Grove, Calif.
Doster, Osie, 1945 N.W. 55th Ter., Miami, Fla.
Dotson, John M., 154 Jones Dr., Pocatello, Idaho
Douglass, Harl R., Col. of Educ., University of Colorado, Boulder, Colo.
Douglass, Malcolm P., Claremont Graduate School, Claremont, Calif.
Dowling, Thomas I., Superintendent, Dist. No. 50, Greenwood, S.C.
Downey, Joseph F., Col. of Arts and Sci., John Carroll Univ., Cleveland, Ohio
Downing, Mrs. Gertrude L., 87 Huron Rd., Bellerose Village, N.Y.
Doyle, Andrew McCormick, 1106 Bellerive Blvd., St. Louis, Mo.
Doyle, E. A., Loyola University, New Orleans, La.
Drag, Francis L., Chula Vista City Schools, Chula Vista, Calif.
Dragositz, Anna, 39-80—52nd St., Woodside, L.I., N.Y.
Dratz, Mrs. Eva M., Dept. of Educ., Keuka College, Keuka Park, N.Y.
Drees, Frank J., Dept. of Public Instr., P.O. Box 2360, Honolulu, Hawaii
Dreikurs, Rudolf, 6 N. Michigan Ave., Chicago, Ill.
Dressel, Paul L., Michigan State University, East Lansing, Mich.
Drew, Robert E., Steuben Elementary Sch., 520 S. Wildwood Ave., Kankakee, Ill.
Driver, Cecil E., Bushy Park Elem. Sch., APO 196, New York, N.Y.
Droney, Margaret L., Daley School, Fleming St., Lowell, Mass.
Dropkin, Stanley, Queens College, Flushing, N.Y.

Drotter, Stephen J., Drury High School, North Adams, Mass.
Drummond, Harold D., Hodgin Hall, University of New Mexico, Albuquerque, N.M.
Drummond, William H., 223 North 9th St., Cheney, Wash.
Ducanis, Alex J., 62 Grandview Ter., Albany, N.Y.
Duckers, Ronald L., 616 W. Central Rd., Arlington Heights, Ill.
Duckworth, Alice, Board of Education, Reef Rd., Fairfield, Conn.
Dudley, Margaret W., Natl. Book Committee, 58 West 40th St., New York, N.Y.
Duffey, Robert V., 611 Sheffield Dr., Springfield, Delaware County, Pa.
DuFour, Stuart, Hartnell College, Salinas, Calif.
Duker, Jan, 210 Pattee Hall, Univ. of Minnesota, Minneapolis, Minn.
Dumler, Marvin J., Concordia Teachers College, River Forest, Ill.
Dunathan, Homer, Libbey Hall, University of Toledo, Toledo, Ohio
Duncan, Neal, 810 No. Spring St., LaGrange, Ill.
Duncan, William B., Miami Edison Senior High School, Miami, Fla.
Dunham, Amelia K., 2340 Auburn Ave., Cincinnati, Ohio
Dunham, Darrell R., North Texas State College, Box 7261, Denton, Tex.
Dunham, Ralph E., 1302 Popkins Lane, Alexandria, Va.
Dunkel, Harold B., Dept. of Educ., University of Chicago, Chicago, Ill.
Dunkle, Maurice Albert, Superintendent, Calver Co. Schls., Prince Frederick, Md.
Dunlap, E. T., Eastern Oklahoma A. & M. College, Wilburton, Okla.
Dunlap, John T., Superintendent of Schools, Pueblo, Colo.
Dunlop, G. M., Div. of Educ., University of Alberta, Edmonton, Alba., Canada
Dunn, Ruth, 210 Breckinridge Lane, Louisville, Ky.
Dunning, Frances E., 125 Owre Hall, Univ. of Minnesota, Minneapolis, Minn.
Dunsmore, Philo C., 121 Southard, Toledo, Ohio
Dupee, C. W., 104 Smith St., East Stroudsburg, Pa.
Durant, Adrian J., Jr., 802 Monroe St., St. Charles, Mo.
Durante, Spencer E., Second Ward High School, Charlotte, N.C.
Durflinger, Glenn W., 5665 Cielo Ave., Goleta, Calif.
Durkee, Frank M., 183 Union Ave., Belleville, N.J.
Durost, Walter N., R.F.D. 2, Concord, N.H.
Durr, William K., Col. of Educ., Michigan State Univ., East Lansing, Mich.
Durrell, Donald D., Boston University, 332 Bay State Rd., Boston, Mass.
Dutton, Wilbur H., 1913 Greenfield Ave., Los Angeles, Calif.
Duval, Joan E., 3911 Argyle Ter., N.W., Washington, D.C.
Duyser, Emma, Highland Rd., New Hartford, Conn.
Dwyer, John E., Superintendent of Schools, Elizabeth, N.J.
Dwyer, Roy E., 3405 Corona St., Tampa, Fla.
Dyer, Frank E., 1331 Cecil Ave., Delano, Calif.
Dyke, Elwood E., Southport Elem. Sch., 723—76th St., Kenosha, Wis.
Dykes, Mrs. Alma, 9755 Cincinnati-Columbus Rd., Cincinnati, Ohio
Dykes, Mrs. Eunice, 119 Woodbine St., Kirkwood, Mo.
Dykstra, Robert, 248 Burton Hall, Univ. of Minnesota, Minneapolis, Minn.
Dypka, Jessie B., Univ. Sch., University of Michigan, Ann Arbor, Mich.
Dziak, Suzanne S., 2203—42nd St., N.W., Washington, D.C.

Earl, Rhea W., 1660 Shawnee Rd., Lima, Ohio
Early, Margaret J., 508 University Pl., Syracuse, N.Y.
Eash, Maurice J., Dept. of Educ., Ball State Tchrs. Col., Muncie, Ind.
Easley, Harriet, San Fernando State College, Northridge, Calif.
Ebel, Robert L., Educ. Testing Serv., 20 Nassau St., Princeton, N.J.
Eberle, August W., University of Chattanooga, Chattanooga, Tenn.
Everly, J. Wilgus, Texas Woman's Univ., University Hill Sta., Denton, Tex.
Eberman, Paul W., 404 Orchard Dr., Madison, Wis.
Eccles, Mrs. J. K., University of Alberta, Calgary, Alba., Canada
Echols, Jack, P.O. Box 660, Farmington, N.M.
Eckert, Ruth E., 219 Burton Hall, Univ. of Minnesota, Minneapolis, Minn.
Eckhardt, John W., 13 Panorama Gardens, Bakersfield, Calif.
Edelfelt, Roy A., Col. of Educ., Michigan State Univ., East Lansing, Mich.
Eden, Donald F., Adams State College, Alamosa, Colo.

Edgar, Robert W., Dept. of Educ., Queens College, Flushing, N.Y.
Edick, Helen, 55 Elizabeth St., Hartford, Conn.
Edmondson, Everett L., Div. of Educ., Little Rock Univ., Little Rock, Ark.
Edson, William H., 206 Burton Hall, Univ. of Minnesota, Minneapolis, Minn.
Edstrom, A. E., Senior High School, 1001 State Hwy., Hopkins, Minn.
Edwards, Arthur U., Eastern Illinois University, Charleston, Ill.
Edwards, Mrs. Barbara F., 310 W. Magnolia, Auburn, Ala.
Edwards, G. N., Board of Education, City Hall, Stratford, Ont., Canada
Edwards, Gerald F., Box 55A, Yellow Springs, Ohio
Edwards, Mrs. Inettie B., 2512 Orcutt Ave., Newport News, Va.
Edwards, Marcia, Burton Hall, University of Minnesota, Minneapolis, Minn.
Edwards, T. Bentley, Sch. of Educ., Univ. of California, Berkeley, Calif.
Effron, Michael P., John Adams High Sch., 3817 E. 116th St., Cleveland, Ohio
Egdorf, M. F., 1567 S. Spartan Village, Mich. State Univ., East Lansing, Mich.
Egge, Donald E., Hoquiam High School, 625 Emerson Ave., Hoquiam, Wash.
Eggert, Mary M., Box 489 Cedar City, Utah
Ehlers, Henry J., Duluth Branch, University of Minnesota, Duluth, Minn.
Ehrlich, Emanuel, 622 East 20th St., New York, N.Y.
Eichholz, Gerhard C., University of Southern Florida, Tampa, Fla.
Eikaas, Alf I., Dept. of Psych., West. Washington State Col., Bellingham, Wash.
Eikermann, G. C., Littleton Senior High School, Littleton, Colo.
Einolf, W. L., Birchrunville, Pa.
Eisenbise, Merlin E., Citrus Junior College, Azusa, Calif.
Eiserer, Paul E., Tchrs. Col., Columbia University, New York, N.Y.
Eklund, Paul A., Lake View School, 22nd and Bethesda Blvd., Zion, Ill.
Ekwall, Vera, 330 W. Legion Ave., Chico, Calif.
Elder, Richard D., 404 N. Huron St., Ypsilanti, Mich.
Elder, Ruth E., Univ. Sch., University of Oklahoma, Norman, Okla.
Elderson, Marquitta B., 15521 Oakbury, LaMirada, Calif.
Elkin, Sol, 17457 Manderson, Detroit, Mich.
Elland, A. H., Hutchinson Junior College, 1300 Plum, Hutchinson, Kan.
Ellerbrook, Louis W., Box 276, Stephen F. Austin Sta., Nacogdoches, Tex.
Ellingson, Mark, Rochester Institute of Technology, Rochester, N.Y.
Ellingson, Ruby, 216 Meray Blvd., Mankato, Minn.
Elliott, A. R., 520 Campbell Ave., Geneva, Ill.
Elliott, David L., Box 120, Tchrs. Col., Columbia Univ., New York, N.Y.
Elliott, Ella Mary, Northern Montana Col., 526—4th St., Havre, Mont.
Ellis, Mrs. Celia Diamond, 1125 S. LaJolla Ave., Los Angeles, Calif.
Ellis, Frederick E., University of British Columbia, Vancouver, B.C., Canada
Ellis, G. W., 724 Jackson St., Valdosta, Ga.
Ellis, John F., 4271 Highland Blvd., North Vancouver, B.C., Canada
Ellis, Joseph R., Dept. of Educ., Indiana State Tchrs. Col., Terre Haute, Ind.
Ellis, Robert L., 1125 S. LaJolla Ave., Los Angeles, Calif.
Ellis, U. Berkley, Delhaas High School, 1200 Rogers Rd., Bristol, Pa.
Ellison, Alfred, 1 Joseph St., New Hyde Park, N.Y.
Ellison, F. Robert, 1344 Laurel St., Casper, Wyo.
Ellsworth, Ruth E., 630 Merrick St., Detroit, Mich.
Elmer, Mrs. Marion Short, 131 Ullman St., Buffalo, N.Y.
Elsmere, Robert T., Manchester College, North Manchester, Ind.
Emmet, Thomas, 4001 W. McNichols Rd., Detroit, Mich.
Endres, Mary P., Purdue University, Lafayette, Ind.
Engelhardt, Jack E., 1214 Birk Ave., Ann Arbor, Mich.
Engelhardt, Nickolaus L., Jr., 221 West 57th St., New York, N.Y.
England, Byron, Box 1710, El Paso, Tex.
England, John L., Senior High School, Pittsburg, Kan.
Engle, Arthur W., Amherst Central Sch., 474 Church St., Amherst, Ohio
English, John W., 1418 W. Acre Rd., Joliet, Ill.
English, Marvin D., 23 West 270th St., St. Charles Rd., Glen Ellyn, Ill.
Enzinger, Philip, Jr., 5975 N. Points Blvd., St. Louis, Mo.
Epstein, Bertram, City College, 139th St. and Convent Ave., New York, N.Y.
Erbe, Wesley A., Western Reserve University, Cleveland, Ohio

Erdman, Robert L., Univ. of Wisconsin-Milwaukee, Milwaukee, Wis.
Erickson, Harley E., Dept. of Educ., Wisconsin State College, Superior, Wis.
Erickson, L. W., Sch. of Educ., Univ. of California, Los Angeles, Calif.
Erickson, Ralph, Box 56, State College, Mankato, Minn.
Erickson, Ralph W., College Sta., Columbus, Miss.
Erskine, Mrs. Mildred R., 2096 Watson Ave., St. Paul, Minn.
Ervin, John B., 5933 Enright St., St. Louis, Mo.
Ervin, William B., 1 Midland Pl., Newark, N.J.
Erxleben, Arnold C., 157 Bemis Dr., Seward, Neb.
Eson, Morris E., New York State College for Teachers, Albany, N.Y.
Ettinger, Mrs. Bernadette C., 474 Brooklyn Blvd., Brightwaters, L.I., N.Y.
Eurich, Alvin C., 477 Madison Ave., New York, N.Y.
Evans, Edgar Ernest, P.O. Box 111, Alabama State College, Montgomery, Ala.
Evans, Howard R., Col. of Educ., University of Akron, Akron, Ohio
Evans, John C., Jr., 6325 South, 550 East, Bountiful, Utah
Evans, John W., Superintendent of Schools, 1020—7th St., Lorain, Ohio
Evans, Mary C., 6970 Central, Hilltop Chateau, Lemon Grove, Calif.
Evans, Ralph F., Fresno State College, Fresno, Calif.
Evenson, Warren L., 1528 S. Douglas St., Springfield, Ill.
Everett, Millard S., Oklahoma State University, Stillwater, Okla.
* Ewigleben, Mrs. Muriel, 3727 Weisser Park Ave., Ft. Wayne, Ind.
Ewing, Parmer L., Sch. of Educ., New York Univ., Washington Sq., New York, N.Y.
Eyermann, Louis M., Niles East High School, Skokie, Ill.

Faddis, Mrs. Gabrielle J., Col. of Educ., Temple University, Philadelphia, Pa.
Faerber, Louis J., University of Dayton, Dayton, Ohio
Fairbanks, Gar, Div. of Educ., Hofstra College, Hempstead, L.I., N.Y.
Fairfield, Mrs. Ethel D., 6316 Riverview, Houston, Tex.
Falk, Conrad, Conception Seminary, Conception, Mo.
Falk, Philip H., 3721 Council Crest, Madison, Wis.
Fallon, Berlie J., Dept. of Educ., Texas Technological Col., Lubbock, Tex.
Farber, Evan I., Main Library, Emory University, Emory, Ga.
Fargen, J. Jerome, 329 Main Bldg., University of Notre Dame, Notre Dame, Ind.
Farley, Gilbert J., Sch. of Educ., University of Miami, Coral Gables, Fla.
Farley, John A., Univ. of Detroit, 4001 W. McNichols Rd., Detroit, Mich.
Farr, S. David, Educ. Res. Center, University of Buffalo, Buffalo, N.Y.
Fasan, Walter R., 7736 Sangamon St., Chicago, Ill.
Faulk, Charles J., McNeese State College, Lake Charles, La.
Fawley, Paul C., Dept. of Educ., University of Utah, Salt Lake City, Utah
Fay, Leo C., Sch. of Educ., Indiana University, Bloomington, Ind.
Fea, Henry Robert, University of Washington, Seattle, Wash.
Feelhaver, Carl T., Supt. of Schools, 5 North 16th St., Fort Dodge, Iowa
Feingold, S. Norman, 1640 Rhode Island Ave., N.W., Washington, D.C.
Feley, Ruth A., North Main St., East Granby, Conn.
Feller, Dan, 9951-B Robbins Dr., Beverly Hills, Calif.
Felton, Ralph D., 35 High St., Montrose, Pa.
Fenollosa, George M., Houghton Mifflin Co., 2 Park St., Boston, Mass.
Fenske, Arthur S., 2739 Lincoln Rd., Kenosha, Wis.
Ferguson, Donald G., Ball State Teachers College, Muncie, Ind.
Ferran, Rose M., 3515 Napoleon Ave., New Orleans, La.
Ferrier, William K., 6517 S.W. 35th Ave., Portland, Ore.
Ferris, Donald R., San Jose State College, San Jose, Calif.
Ferris, Newell D., Columbia Bible College, Columbia, S.C.
Fessier, Mrs. Margery, 3336 Josephine St., Lynwood, Calif.
Feuers, Stelle, 39 Sandra Lane, Pearl River, N.Y.
Ficken, Clarence E., Methodist College, Fayetteville, N.C.
Fiedler, E. L., Superintendent of Schools, Abilene, Kan.
Fiedler, William G., Superintendent of Schools, Union City, N.J.
Field, Robert L., 711 E. River Rd., Minneapolis, Minn.
Fields, Clarence J., Coppin State Teachers College, Baltimore, Md.

Fields, Ralph R., Tchrs. Col., Columbia University, New York, N.Y.
Fielstra, Clarence, Sch. of Educ., Univ. of California, Los Angeles, Calif.
Feilstra, Helen, San Fernando Valley State College, Northridge, Calif.
Figurel, J. Allen, 2430 Tanglewood Dr., Allison Park, Pa.
Filbeck, Orval, Abilene Christian College, Abilene, Tex.
Filosa, Mary G., Maple Lane, Mtd. Rte., Bound Brook, N.J.
Fina, Robert P., 522 Fourth St., Catasauqua, Pa.
Finch, F. H., 105 Gregory Hall, University of Illinois, Urbana, Ill.
Findlay, Stephen W., Delbarton School, Morristown, N.J.
Findley, Warren G., Col. of Educ., University of Georgia, Athens, Ga.
Findley, William H., Jr., 210—191st Ter., Miami Beach, Fla.
Fine, Huldah, 2970 Blaine Ave., Detroit, Mich.
Fink, Abel K., Educ. Dept., College of Education, Buffalo, N.Y.
Fink, Herbert J., Von Steuben High School, 5039 N. Kimball Ave., Chicago, Ill.
Fink, Martin B., 1557 Mendocino Dr., Concord, Calif.
Fink, Stuart D., Northern Illinois University, DeKalb, Ill.
Finlay, Mrs. Helen K., 4521 N. Dittmar Rd., Arlington, Va.
Finster, Mrs. Virginia, P.O. Box 714, Raceland, La.
Fischer, Mrs. Cora I., 1536 N. 51st St., Milwaukee, Wis.
Fischer, John H., Tchrs. Col., Columbia University, New York, N.Y.
Fischer, William G., Bd. of Educ., 228 N. LaSalle St., Chicago, Ill.
Fischoff, Ephraim, 15 Riverview Pl., Lynchburg, Va.
Fishback, Woodson W., Southern Illinois University, Carbondale, Ill.
Fishell, Kenneth N., Col. of Educ., University of Rochester, Rochester, N.Y.
Fisher, Hazel, Hartford Co. Bd. of Educ., 45 E. Gordon St., Bel Air, Md.
Fisher, James A., Boston University, 688 Boylston, Boston, Mass.
Fisher, Joseph T., University of South Dakota, Vermillion, S.D.
Fisher, Lawrence A., University of Illinois, 1853 W. Polk St., Chicago, Ill.
Fisher, Thomas K., Verde Valley School, Sedona, Ariz.
* Fisher, Mrs. Welthy H., Literacy Village, P.O. Singar Nagar, Lucknow, U.P., India
Fisk, Robert S., Sch. of Educ., University of Buffalo, Buffalo, N.Y.
Fitz, John Allen, c/o Amer. Consulate Genrl., P.O. Box 2895, Salisbury, Rhodesia
Fitzgerald, Eloise R., 135 Corey St., West Roxbury, Mass.
* Fitzgerald, James A., 1103 Pine St., Scranton, Pa.
Fitzgibbon, Walter C., 206 N. Lansing, Mt. Pleasant, Mich.
Fitzpatrick, E. D., Southern Illinois University, Carbondale, Ill.
Fitzsimons, Frank P., 2467 Ocean Ave., Brooklyn, N.Y.
Fitzwater, James P., 3333 West 31st St., Chicago, Ill.
Flagg, E. Alma, 44 Stengel Ave., Newark, N.J.
Flaggert, James J., Jr., USA Leghorn Genl. Depot, APO 19, New York, N.Y.
Flamand, Ruth K., 72 Goldenridge Dr., Levittown, Pa.
Flamme, Wayne H., Junior-Senior High School, Antigo, Wis.
Flanagan, John C., Amer. Inst. for Res., 410 Amberson Ave., Pittsburgh, Pa.
Flanagan, William F., 100 Tanner Ave., Warwick, R.I.
Flanders, Ned A., Sch. of Educ., Univ. of Mich., Ann Arbor, Mich.
Fleck, Henrietta, H.E. Dept., New York Univ., Washington Sq., New York, N.Y.
Fleming, Harold D., State Teachers College, Bemidji, Minn.
Fleming, Robert S., State Dept. of Educ., 175 W. State St., Trenton, N.J.
Flesher, Mrs. Marie A., 186 Arps Hall, Ohio State Univ., Columbus, Ohio
Flick, Doris L., 460 West "M" St., Benicia, Calif.
Fliegler, Louis A., Syracuse University, 805 S. Crouse Ave., Syracuse, N.Y.
Fligor, R. J., Southern Illinois University, Carbondale, Ill.
Flint, Jack M., Highland Junior College, Highland, Kan.
Floren, Marcella A., 308—4th Ave., N.E., Little Falls, Minn.
Flores, Vetal, Drawer M, Bronte, Tex.
Flower, George Edward, Ontario Col. of Educ., 371 Bloor St. W., Toronto, Canada
Flug, Eugene R. F., Box 727, Rt. 1, Excelsior, Minn.
Focht, James R., Educ. Dept., State Teachers College, Salisbury, Md.
Fonacier, Andres Medina, Ilocos Norte Normal Sch., Laoag, I. Norte, Philippines

Foote, Lawrence E., Superintendent, Allen County Schools, Fort Wayne, Ind.
Foran, Joseph A., Superintendent of Schools, Milford, Conn.
Foran, Mary Ellen, 2018 W. Greenleaf Ave., Chicago, Ill.
Foran, Thomas G., The Seigniory Club, Province of Quebec, Canada
Force, Dewey G., Jr., Pattee Hall, Univ. of Minnesota, Minneapolis, Minn.
Forcina, James J., 174 N. Main St., Yardley, Pa.
Ford, Harlan, Sul Ross State College, Alpine, Tex.
Ford, Roxana R., Sch. of Home Econ., Univ. of Minnesota, St. Paul, Minn.
Forrester, Carl M., Lake Park High School, Medinah, Ill.
Forrester, Gertrude, 71 Overpeck Ave., Ridgefield Park, N.J.
Fortess, Lillian, 96 Bay State Rd., Boston, Mass.
Fosback, Alta B., 5205 E. Burnside, Portland, Ore.
Foshay, Arthur W., Tchrs. Col., Columbia University, New York, N.Y.
Fossieck, Theodore H., Milne Sch., State Col. for Tchrs., Albany, N.Y.
Foster, Ashley, 13330 Bessemer St., Van Nuys, Calif.
Foster, E. M., Fresno State Col., 4021 Mt. Vernon Ave., Bakersfield, Calif.
Foster, Mrs. Mardis, 2368—16th Ave., San Francisco, Calif.
Foster, Zeph H., Evergreen Trailer Park, Rt. 1, Moscow, Idaho
Fournier, Edmond A., Sacred Heart Seminary, 2701 Chicago Blvd., Detroit, Mich.
Fowlkes, John Guy, 111 Educ. Bldg., Univ. of Wisconsin, Madison, Wis.
Fox, James H., 2556 N. Upland St., Arlington, Va.
Fox, Marion W., 705 Kensington Ave., Plainfield, N.J.
Fox, Richard E., 3000 Birch Ave., Boulder, Colo.
Fox, Robert S., 102 Univ. Sch., University of Michigan, Ann Arbor, Mich.
Francis, Ida L., P.O., Box 243, Somerville, N.J.
Frandsen, Arden N., Utah State University, Logan, Utah
Frankland, Elizabeth M., 612 Jackson St., Oshkosh, Wis.
Franklin, Jesse E., East Texas State Teachers College, Commerce, Tex.
Franklin, Ruby Holden, Roosevelt University, 430 S. Michigan Ave., Chicago, Ill.
Franson, Arthur H., 337 N. Brainard Ave., LaGrange Park, Ill.
Frantzen, Mrs. Carol A., 69 Woodland Ave., Summit, N.J.
Franz, Evelyn B., Trenton State College, Trenton, N.J.
* Franzen, Carl G. F., Dept. of Educ., Marycrest College, Davenport, Iowa
Franzen, William L., Sch. of Educ., New York Univ., Washington Sq., New York, N.Y.
Frase, H. Weldon, 1635 Hutchinson, S.E., Grand Rapids, Mich.
Fraser, Mrs. Dorothy McClure, Bd. of Higher Educ., 535 E. 80th St., New York, N.Y.
Frazier, James R., Superintendent of Schools, Okmulgee, Okla.
Fred, Bernhart G., 108 McCormick Dr., DeKalb, Ill.
Frederick, Pauline M., Kamahameha Schools, Honolulu, Hawaii
Frederick, Orie I., Western Michigan University, Kalamazoo, Mich.
Freeman, Kenneth H., 403 Christian College Ave., Columbia, Mo.
Freeman, Ruges Richmond, Jr., 4582 Aldine St., St. Louis, Mo.
French, Joseph L., Hill Hall, University of Missouri, Columbia, Mo.
French, William M., Muhlenberg College, Allentown, Pa.
Frenzel, Norman J., Wisconsin State College, Oshkosh, Wis.
Fretwell, Elbert K., Jr., State Education Dept., Albany, N.Y.
Freund, Evelyn, 5954 Guilford, Detroit, Mich.
Frieberg, Carter N., Loyola University, 820 N. Michigan Ave., Chicago, Ill.
Fristoe, Wallace H., Morgan Park High School, Chicago, Ill.
Fritts, J. Scott, Hunt Hall, LaGrande, Ore.
Fritzsche, Bertha M., Mississippi Southern College, Hattiesburg, Miss.
Froehlich, Gustave J., Bur. of Inst. Res., Univ. of Illinois, Urbana, Ill.
Frost, George E., Holyoke Junior College, 291 Pine St., Holyoke, Mass.
Frost, Ralph J., Jr., Maine Twp. High School East, Park Ridge, Ill.
Frost, S. E., Jr., Brooklyn Col., Bedford and Ave. H., Brooklyn, N.Y.
Frutchey, Fred P., U.S. Department of Agriculture, Washington, D.C.
Fujita, Shirley Y., 635B—12th Ave., Honolulu, Hawaii
Fulcher, Catherine, 3611 Beier St., Richmond, Mich.
Fulchino, Albert R., Revere High School, Revere, Mass.

Full, Harold, 30 Beekman Pl., New York, N.Y.
Fullagar, William A., Col. of Educ., Univ. of Rochester, Rochester, N.Y.
Fuller, Robert H., 35 Hickory Lane, Hanover, Mass.
Fullerton, Craig K., 2712 North 52nd St., Omaha, Neb.
Fulton, Helen, 9000 Westview Dr., Houston, Tex.
Fults, Dan A., 14815 Drummond, Pacific Palisades, Calif.
Fultz, Mrs. Jane N., Col. of Educ., Univ. of Hawaii, Honolulu, Hawaii
Furlow, Florine D., 1047 Simpson St., N.W., Atlanta, Ga.
Furness, Harry, R.F.D., Far Hills, N.J.
Futch, Olivia, Woman's College, Furman University, Greenville, S.C.

Gadbury, Mrs. Nada M., 2401 New York Ave., Muncie, Ind.
Gagon, Glen S., McKay Bldg., Brigham Young University, Provo, Utah
Gaines, Berthera E., 3418 S. Claiborne Ave., New Orleans, La.
Gaiser, P. F., 313 West 36th St., Vancouver, Wash.
Gall, Harold, Senior High School, Lancaster, Wis.
Gallagher, Dora Agnes, 400 S. Hauser Blvd., Los Angeles, Calif.
Gallen, Albert A., 54 Fern Hill Lane, West Chester, Pa.
Gallicchio, Francis A., 667 Madison Ave., Meadville, Pa.
Galloway, Geraldine, 111 Northwest Tenth St., Fairfield, Ill.
Gambert, Charles A., 607 Walnut Ave., Niagara Falls, N.Y.
Gambrill, Bessie Lee, 201 Armory St., New Haven, Conn.
Gamelin, F. C., 4054 Quail Ave., Robbinsdale, Minn.
Gammill, James R., Educ. Dept., Texas Technological Col., Tech Sta., Tex.
Gammon, Delore, 640 N. Emporia St., Wichita, Kan.
Gans, Leo, Bobbs-Merrill Co., 1720 East 38th St., Indianapolis, Ind.
Gansberg, Lucille, Superintendent of County Schools, Susanville, Calif.
Garbe, Lester, 2110 W. Marne Ave., Milwaukee, Wis.
Garbel, Marianne, 6732 Crandon Ave., Chicago, Ill.
Garber, Lee O., 3810 Walnut St., Philadelphia, Pa.
Garber, M. Delott, Burr Junior High School, 400 Wethersfield, Hartford, Conn.
Gardiner, Marian J., 415 N. Felton St., Philadelphia, Pa.
Garinger, Elmer H., Superintendent of Schools, Charlotte, N.C.
Garlich, Marvin O., 8901 McVicker Ave., Morton Grove, Ill.
Garoutte, Bill Charles, Univ. of California Medical Center, San Francisco, Calif.
Garrett, Charles G., 837 N. Cline St., Griffith, Ind.
Garrison, Mrs. Ann C., 1052 N.E. 2nd Ave., Homestead, Fla.
Garvey, Reba, Allegheny College, Meadville, Pa.
Garvin, Fannie, 606 Ohio St., Wichita, Kan.
* Gates, Arthur I., Tchrs. Col., Columbia University, New York, N.Y.
Gathercole, F. J., Superintendent of Schools, Saskatoon, Sask., Canada
Gauerke, Warren E., Wayne State University, Detroit, Mich.
Gauvey, Ralph E., Urbana Junior College, Urbana, Ohio
Gavin, Ann M., 27 Bourneside St., Dorchester, Mass.
Gayne, Clifton, 135 Wulling Hall, Univ. of Minnesota, Minneapolis, Minn.
Gazelle, Hazel N., 1255 N. Michillinda, Pasadena, Calif.
Gebbart, James, Montana State University, Missoula, Mont.
Geer, Owen C., Sch. of Educ., University of Bridgeport, Bridgeport, Conn.
Gelerinter, Alfred, 232 Linden Ave., Ithaca, N.Y.
Gemeinhardt, William C., Northern State Tchrs. College, Aberdeen, S.D.
Geng, George, Glassboro State College, Glassboro, N.J.
Gentry, George H., P.O. Box 30, Baytown, Tex.
Gentry, Ira A., Jr., Tennessee A. & I. State University, Nashville, Tenn.
George, Howard A., Northwest Missouri State College, Maryville, Mo.
George, Zale R., Jr., 309 Church Rd., Bethel Park, Pa.
Georgiades, William, 1009 Granvia Altamira, Palos Verdes Estates, Calif.
Georgiady, Nicholas P., 101 E. Birch Ave., Milwaukee, Wis.
Gephart, Woodrow W., Walton Acres, Toronto, Ohio
Geraty, T. S., 7422 Hancock Ave., Takoma Park, Md.
Gerberich, J. Raymond, University of Connecticut, Storrs, Conn.
Gerlach, Vernon, 2959 N. 53rd Pkwy., Phoenix, Ariz.

Gerletti, John D., USOM, APO 271, New York, N.Y.
Gerlock, D. E., Dept. of Educ., Valdosta State College, Valdosta, Ga.
Germann, Ruth Ann, 1964 Jeffords St., Clearwater, Fla.
Gernert, H. F., Jr., 522 North 24th St., Allentown, Pa.
Gesler, Harriet L., 70 Agnes Dr., Manchester, Conn.
Gest, Mrs. Viola S., P.O. Box 254, Seguin, Tex.
Getzels, J. W., Dept. of Educ., University of Chicago, Chicago, Ill.
Ghalib, Hanna, P.O. Box 5179, Beirut, Lebanon
Giannuzzi, John P., 482 Iris St., Los Alamos, N.M.
Gibbs, E. Delmar, College of Puget Sound, Tacoma, Wash.
Gibbs, Edward, III, 1145 Clinton Ter., South Plainfield, N.J.
Gibbs, Wesley, Superintendent, Dist. No. 68, 9300 N. Kenton, Skokie, Ill.
Gibert, James M., Randolph-Macon Woman's College, Lynchburg, Va.
Gibson, Mrs. Kathryn Snell, Prairie View A. & M. Col., Prairie View, Tex.
Gibson, Mrs. Norma Boyle, 902 S. Manhattan Pl., Los Angeles, Calif.
Gicquelais, Mae, 3418 Dogwood Pl., West Homestead, Pa.
Giertz, Margaret E., 816 Taylor St., Joliet, Ill.
Giesy, John P., 1017 Blanchard, Seguin, Tex.
Gilbert, Mrs. Doris Wilcox, 1044 Euclid Ave., Berkeley, Calif.
Gilbert, Floyd O., Minnesota State College, St. Cloud, Minn.
Gilbert, Jerome H., 11155 S. Depot St., Worth, Ill.
Gilbert, John H., Dept. of Educ., Monmouth College, West Long Branch, N.J.
Gilberts, Robert D., Superintendent of Schools, Oconomowoc, Wis.
Giles, LeRoy H., University of Dubuque, Dubuque, Iowa
Gilkey, Richard, Evermann Apts., No. 6, Bloomington, Ind.
Gill, Bernard I., Moorhead State Tchrs. College, Moorhead, Minn.
Gill, Margaret, ASCD, 1201 Sixteenth St., N.W., Washington, D.C.
Gilland, Thomas M., 327 Wood St., California, Pa.
Gillanders, Dorothy F., 752 Orange St., Tempe, Ariz.
Gillham, Vera M., Horace Mann School, 3345 Chicago Ave., Minneapolis, Minn.
Gilligan, Michael B., Jersey City State College, Jersey City, N.J.
Gilman, Alice, C. W. Post College, Greenvale, L.I., N.Y.
Gilmore, Mrs. Hulda G., 672 Wayne Dr. N., Salem, Ore.
Gingerich, Mrs. Julia B., Rte. 1, Box 193B, Bettendorf, Iowa
Gioia, Michael, 401 East 41st St., Paterson, N.J.
Glade, Melba, 2610 Highland Dr., Salt Lake City, Utah
Glaeser, Mrs. Louise M., 1409 Spaulding, Alton, Ill.
Glas, Marie, Thoheper Theme School, R.D. 2, Napier, New Zealand
Glasow, Ogden L., P.O. Box 143, Macomb, Ill.
Glenn, Edward E., 1130 E. Epler Ave., Indianapolis, Ind.
Glenn, J. Curtis, 1531 West 103rd St., Chicago, Ill.
Glock, Marvin D., Stone Hall, Cornell University, Ithaca, N.Y.
Glogau, Arthur H., Oregon College of Education, Monmouth, Ore.
Glover, Elmer T., Northwestern High Sch., 5200 E. Central, Zachary, La.
Gobetz, Wallace, 540 East 22nd St., Brooklyn, N.Y.
Goble, Robert I., McGuffey No. 360, Miami University, Oxford, Ohio
Godfrey, Mary E., Pennsylvania State University, University Park, Pa.
Goebel, Edmund J., Archdiocese of Milwaukee, 437 W. Galena St., Milwaukee, Wis.
Gold, Milton J., Hunter College, 695 Park Ave., New York, N.Y.
Goldberg, Miriam L., Tchrs. Col., Columbia University, New York, N.Y.
Goldberg, Nathan, 75-47—196th St., Flushing, N.Y.
Goldhammer, Keith, Sch. of Educ., University of Oregon, Eugene, Ore.
Goldman, Bert A., Dept. of Educ., Tufts University, Medford, Mass.
Goldstein, Mrs. Gertrude H., Woodward Sch., 321 Clinton Ave., Brooklyn, N.Y.
Goldstein, Herbert, 1003 W. Nevada St., Urbana, Ill.
Goltry, Keith, Dept. of Educ., Parsons College, Fairfield, Iowa
Gonnelly, Ellen M., James R. Lowell Sch., 3320 W. Hirsch, Chicago, Ill.
Gonzalez, Alice M., University of Puerto Rico, Rio Piedras, Puerto Rico
Gonzalez, Sarah M., University of Puerto Rico, Rio Piedras, Puerto Rico
Good, Carter V., Tchrs. Col., University of Cincinnati, Cincinnati, Ohio

Good, Richard M., 6814—10th Ave., Takoma Park, Md.
Good, Warren R., 1604 Stony Run Dr., Northwood, Wilmington, Del.
Goodlad, John I., Sch. of Educ., University of California, Los Angeles, Calif.
Goodman, Kenneth S., 11006 Arbuckle, Mission Hills, Calif.
Goodpaster, Robert L., University of Kentucky-Ashland Center, Ashland, Ky.
Goodside, Samuel, Ramaz Upper School, 22 East 82nd St., New York, N.Y.
Goodson, Max R., Sch. of Educ., Boston Univ., 332 Bay State Rd., Boston, Mass.
Goodwin, Helen J., 2403 Beverly Rd., Brooklyn, N.Y.
Googins, Duane G., 2964—116th Ave., N.W., Coon Rapids, Minn.
Goossen, Carl V., 220 Burton Hall, University of Minnesota, Minneapolis, Minn.
Gordon, Alice S., Einstein School, 3830 Cottage Grove Ave., Chicago, Ill.
Gordon, Ted E., 317 N. Lucerne, Los Angeles, Calif.
Gore, Joseph, Harris Tchrs. College, 5351 Enright, St. Louis, Mo.
Gore, Lillian L., U.S. Office of Education, Dept. of HEW, Washington, D.C.
Gorham, Marion, 10 Alcott St., Acton, Mass.
Gorman, Burton W., 1220 Lake Martin Dr., Kent, Ohio
Gorman, Frank H., Col. of Educ., University of Omaha, Omaha, Neb.
Gorman, William J., 219-40—93rd Ave., Queens Village, N.Y.
Gormley, Charles L., Dept. of Educ., Alabama College, Montevallo, Ala.
Gorn, Janice L., 255 East 176th St., New York, N.Y.
Gorton, Harry B., Rte. No. 1, New Cumberland, Pa.
Goslin, Willard E., George Peabody College, Nashville, Tenn.
Gossard, Paul, Superintendent of Schools, Quincy, Mass.
Gottfried, F. J., Superintendent of Schools, Elyria, Ohio
Gottschalk, G. R., 464 Brattle Rd., Syracuse, N.Y.
Gould, George, Cathedral of Learn., Univ. of Pittsburgh, Pittsburgh, Pa.
Gould, W. S., Graceland College, Lamoni, Iowa
Gowan, John Curtis, Educ. Div., State College, Northridge, Calif.
Gowin, D. Bob, Stone Hall, Cornell University, Ithaca, N.Y.
Graber, Eldon W., Dept. of Educ., Bluffton College, Bluffton, Ohio
Grabowski, A. A., 2512 Southport Ave., Chicago, Ill.
Grado, Louis M., USOM/Nicaragua, Dept. of State, Washington, D.C.
Grady, Joseph E., St. Bernard's Seminary, 2260 Lake Ave., Rochester, N.Y.
Graetz, Ralph C., 2532 Woodland Lane, Garden Grove, Calif.
Graff, George E., State Dept. of Educ., 41 Hale St., Rockville, Conn.
Graff, Orin B., Col. of Educ., University of Tennessee, Knoxville, Tenn.
Graffam, Donald T., Dickinson College, Carlisle, Pa.
Grandy, L. Munro, Superintendent of City Schools, Gloucester, Mass.
Granskog, Mrs. Dorothy, 1402 First Ave., So., Escanaba, Mich.
Grant, Eugene B., Northern Illinois University, DeKalb, Ill.
Grant, Wayman R. F., Booker T. Washington Junior High School, Mobile, Ala.
Grau, Mary, Montgomery County Schls., 12 W. Burke Ave., Towson, Md.
Grau, R. T., Clinton Public Schls., Box 110, Clinton, Iowa
Graves, Jack A., P.O. Box 4708, Carmel, Calif.
Graves, Linwood D., 51 Vine St., N.W., Atlanta, Ga.
Gray, Dorothy, Dept. of Educ., Queens College, Flushing, N.Y.
Gray, Susan C., Box 425, McArthur, Calif.
Graye, Mytrolene L., 825 Fairview St., High Point, N.C.
Grayson, William H., Jr., 21-71—34th Ave., Long Island City, N.Y.
Green, Donald Ross, 1419 Cornell Rd., N.E., Atlanta, Ga.
Green, John A., Educ. Field Service, Univ. of Idaho, Moscow, Idaho
Greenberg, Mrs. Gilda M., 5435 N. Kennebec Lane, Tucson, Ariz.
Greenberg, Mrs. Judith W., Sch. of Educ., City College, New York, N.Y.
Greenblatt, Edward L., 211 Calle de Arboles, Redondo Beach, Calif.
Greene, Bert I., 717 Charles St., Ypsilanti, Mich.
Greene, Charles E., P.O. Box 185, East Side Sta., Santa Cruz, Calif.
Greene, John G., 107 Chestnut St., Boston, Mass.
Greene, Mrs. Maxine, 108-27—70th Rd., Forest Hills, N.Y.
Greene, Mrs. Minnie S., 1121 Chestnut St., San Marcos, Tex.
Greenfield, Curtis O., P. L. Julian School, 1644 E. Adams St., Phoenix, Ariz.
Greenman, Mrs. Margaret H., Country Fair, Champaign, Ill.

Greenwood, Edward D., Menninger Clinic, Box 829, Topeka, Kan.
Greenwood, Roy, 462 Grand Ave., Johnson City, N.Y.
Greer, Evelyn, Fayette County Schls., 400 Lafayette Dr., Lexington, Ky.
Gregg, Russell T., Sch. of Educ., University of Wisconsin, Madison, Wis.
Greif, Ivo P., Illinois State Normal University, Normal, Ill.
Greivell, Richard, Fort Atkinson Public Schools, Fort Atkinson, Wis.
Grey, Mrs. Emylu D., 2565 Duke Ave., Richmond, Calif.
Griffith, Coleman R., 105 Gregory Hall, University of Illinois, Urbana, Ill.
Griffith, Harry E., P.O. Box 427, Arcata, Calif.
Griffiths, John A., Superintendent of Schools, Monongahela, Pa.
Griffiths, Ruth, 184 Middlesex St., North Andover, Mass.
Grigg, Charles B., Litchfield Junior-Senior High School, Litchfield, Ill.
Grimes, Leslie K., Superintendent of Schools, Greeley, Colo.
Grizzard, Mabel Youree, 711 W. Main St., Waxahachie, Tex.
* Grizzell, E. Duncan, 640 Maxwelton Ct., Lexington, Ky.
Groesbeck, Hulda, Fort Hays Kansas State College, Hays, Kan.
Groff, Frank E., New Hope-Solebury Joint School Dist., New Hope, Pa.
Grogan, M. Lucille, 7638 S. Wood St., Chicago, Ill.
Gronlund, Norman E., Col. of Educ., University of Illinois, Urbana, Ill.
Grose, Robert F., 46 Snell St., Amherst, Mass.
Gross, Lydia, Lock Haven State Tchrs. College, Lock Haven, Pa.
Gross, Marie L., 825 Main St., Evanston, Ill.
Gross, Neal, 8 Prescott St., Cambridge, Mass.
Gross, Richard Edmund, Sch. of Educ., Stanford University, Stanford, Calif.
Gross, Robert Dean, Sacramento State College, Sacramento, Calif.
Gross, Wilma, 3750 Harrison Blvd., Ogden, Utah
Grossman, Eileen, 2207 W. Rosemont Ave., Chicago, Ill.
Grossnickle, Foster E., 38 Elm Pl., Nutley, N.J.
Grotberg, Mrs. Edith H., Northern Illinois University, DeKalb, Ill.
Grote, Donald V., 2604 Central St., Evanston, Ill.
Grove, Robert N., Superintendent of Schools, Midland Park, N.J.
Grover, Burton L., Col. of Educ., University of Minnesota, Minneapolis, Minn.
Grubel, Muriel, 15 Washington Pl., New York, N.Y.
Gruber, Frederick C., Eisenlohr Annex, Univ. of Pennsylvania, Philadelphia, Pa.
Grudell, Regina C., 45 Chadwick Rd., Teaneck, N.J.
Guba, Egon G., Arps Hall, Ohio State University, Columbus, Ohio
Guillet, N. J., Midwest University, Wichita Falls, Tex.
Gulutsan, Metro, University of British Columbia ,Vancouver, B.C., Canada
Guss, Carolyn, R.R. 2, Box 139, Bloomington, Ind.
Gussner, William S., Superintendent of Schools, Jamestown, N.D.
Gustafson, A. M., Alice Vail Junior High Sch., 5350 E. 16th St., Tucson, Ariz.
Gustafson, Alma L., 1211 North 5th St., East Grand Forks, Minn.
Gwynn, J. Minor, 514 North St., Chapel Hill, N.C.

Haage, Catherine M., College of New Rochelle, New Rochelle, N.Y.
Haas, Richard J., Jr., 119 Stubbs Dr., Trotwood, Ohio
Hackmann, Jane, 38 Signal Hill Blvd., East St. Louis, Ill.
Hackney, Ben H., Jr., 400 Latimer Rd., Raleigh, N.C.
Haffner, Hyman, 6229 Nicholson St., Pittsburgh, Pa.
Hagarty, Edward M., 3908 Lancaster Pike, Wilmington, Del.
Hagen, Elizabeth, Tchrs. Col., Columbia University, New York, N.Y.
Hagenson, C. H., Mississippi Southern College, Hattiesburg, Miss.
Hager, Walter E., 1785 Massachusetts Ave., N.W., Washington, D.C.
Hagerman, Helen L., 1307 Newport Rd., Ann Arbor, Mich.
Haggerson, Nelson L., 132 W. Balboa Dr., Tempe, Ariz.
Haggerty, Helen Ruth, 110 N. George Mason Dr., Arlington, Va.
Haggerty, William J., State Univ. College of Education, New Paltz, N.Y.
Hagglund, Oliver C., Gustavus Adolphus College, St. Peter, Minn.
Hagstrom, Ellis A., 29 Madison St., Hamilton, N.Y.
Hahn, Albert R., Veterans' Administration Hospital, Phoenix, Ariz.
Hahn, Harry T., Bd. of Educ., 1025 N. Telegraph Rd., Pontiac, Mich.

Haight, Wilbur T., 314 S. DuPont Blvd., Milford, Del.
Haimbach, David, Lab. Sch., Fresno State College, Fresno, Calif.
Halbert, Bernice, East Texas Baptist College, Marshall, Tex.
Hale, Gifford G., Sch. of Educ., Florida State University, Tallahassee, Fla.
Hale, Jordan, 2267 Renfrew Rd., Elmont, L.I., N.Y.
Haley, Charles F., Col. of Educ., Northeastern University, Boston, Mass.
Haley, Elizabeth, 1938 Channing Ave., Palo Alto, Calif.
Haley, Gerald J., 161 Woodside Rd., Riverside, Ill.
Haley, Mrs. Margaret T., 1405 E. Grace St., Richmond, Va.
Halfter, Mrs. Irma Theobald, 134 W. St. Charles Rd., Elmhurst, Ill.
Hall, Barbara C., 2 Knollcrest Ct., Normal, Ill.
Hall, James A., Superintendent of Schools, Port Washington, N.Y.
Hall, Joseph I., Holt, Rinehart & Winston, Inc., 383 Madison Ave., New York, N.Y.
Hall, Leon P., Bd. of Educ., 1200 N. Telegraph Rd., Pontiac, Mich.
Hall, M. E., Music Dept., Michigan State Univ., East Lansing, Mich.
Hall, Thelma, R.D. No. 1, Fishkill, N.Y.
Hall, William Frank, Elem. Sch. Dist. No. 1, 125 E. Lincoln St., Phoenix, Ariz.
Hallenbeck, Edwin F., University of Rhode Island, Kingston, R.I.
Hallett, Mrs. Robert L., Jr., 8 Old Shawnee Rd., Milford, Del.
Halliwell, Joseph, 19 Bon Air Ave., New Rochelle, N.Y.
Hallman, George H., 434 Windermire Rd., Clarksville, Ind.
Halvorsen, H. M., Ginn & Co., Statler Bldg., Boston, Mass.
Hamalainen, Arthur E., 306 Third Ave., East Northport, N.Y.
Hamilton, DeForest S., 2406 Mendota Way, Santa Rosa, Calif.
Hamilton, Gene E., James Knoll Elem. School, Ortonville, Minn.
Hamilton, Herbert M., Sch. of Bus. Adm., Miami Univ., Oxford, Ohio
Hamilton, Homer H., Jackson State College, Jackson, Miss.
Hamilton, Lester L., Box 5285, North Charleston, S.C.
Hamilton, Robert J., Julian Curtiss School, Greenwich, Conn.
Hamlin, Elizabeth, 802 Semmes St., Memphis, Tenn.
Hammack, Mary L., 540 Norway St., N.E., Salem, Ore.
Hammel, John A., 740 Cadieux Ave., Grosse Pointe, Mich.
Hammer, Eugene L., Dept. of Educ., Wilkes College, Wilkes-Barre, Pa.
Hammer, Irwin A., Col. of Educ., Univ. of Florida, Gainesville, Fla.
Hammock, Robert C., 3812 Walnut St., Philadelphia, Pa.
Hammond, Granville S., USOM/Educ., Box 32, APO 143, San Francisco, Calif.
Hammond, Sarah Lou, Florida State University, Tallahassee, Fla.
Hand, Mrs. Doris Ruth, Antioch Dist. Schls., 9120 W. 75th St., Merriam, Kan.
Hand, Harold C., Col. of Educ., University of Illinois, Urbana, Ill.
Handley, W. Harold, Olympus High School, Salt Lake City, Utah
Hangartner, Carl A., 221 N. Grand St., St. Louis, Mo.
Hanigan, Levin B., Superintendent, Echobrook School, Mountainside, N.J.
Hantichak, John J., Sch. of Educ., Univ. of Kansas City, Kansas City, Mo.
Hankerson, M. R., Superintendent of Schools, Thief River Falls, Minn.
Hanley, James L., Superintendent of Schools, Providence, R.I.
Hanna, Alvis N., John Tyler High Schools, 331 S. College St., Tyler, Tex.
Hanna, Ben M., Baylor University, Waco, Tex.
Hanna, Geneva, University of Texas, Austin, Tex.
Hanna, Paul R., Stanford University, Stanford, Calif.
Hannifin, Mrs. Blanche B., 5259 Strohm Ave., North Hollywood, Calif.
Hansen, Mrs. Dorothy Gregg, 1913 Kitty Hawk Pl., Alameda, Calif.
Hansen, G. G., Superintendent of County Schools, Aurora, Neb.
Hansen, Helge E., Public Schools, 5757 Neckel St., Dearborn, Mich.
Hansen, Paul J., 1626 South 13th St., East, Salt Lake City, Utah
Hansen, R. G., 1333 West Maynard Dr., St. Paul, Minn.
Hansen, Robert E., Cherry Hill High School, Cherry Hill, N.J.
Hansen, Stewart R., St. John's University, Collegeville, Minn.
Hanson, Donald L., 1205 Normal Ave., Cape Girardeau, Mo.
Hanson, Earl H., Superintendent of Schools, Rock Island, Ill.
Hanson, Gordon C., University of Wichita, Wichita, Kan.

Hanson, Mrs. Mildred E., 923 W. Cavour Ave., Fergus Falls, Minn.
Hanway, Hannah F., 8011 Eastern Ave., Silver Spring, Md.
Harbo, L. S., Superintendent of Schools, Austin, Minn.
Hardee, Melvene D., Florida State University, Tallahassee, Fla.
Hardesty, Cecil D., 6401 Linda Vista Rd., San Diego, Calif.
Hardin, Mrs. Marjorie, 2421 El Camino, Turlock, Calif.
Hardy, J. Garrick, Alabama State College, Montgomery, Ala.
Hargett, Earl F., 1245 East 85th St., Chicago, Ill.
Hargrave, Ruth M., Div. of Educ., Central State College, Wilberforce, Ohio
Harkness, Donald E., Curriculum Service Center, Manhasset, N.Y.
Harlow, James G., Col. of Educ., University of Oklahoma, Norman, Okla.
Harmer, William R., Col. of Educ., Univ. of South. Florida, Tampa, Fla.
Harmon, Ruth E., 1720 Commonwealth Ave., West Newton, Mass.
Harnack, Robert S., Sch. of Educ., University of Buffalo, Buffalo, N.Y.
Harney, Paul J., University of San Francisco, San Francisco, Calif.
Harper, George Leslie, P.O. Box 310, Roxbard, N.C.
Harrington, Edmund Ross, 509 A St., Taft, Calif.
Harrington, Mrs. Edna B., 901 Savannah Rd., Lewes, Del.
Harrington, Frances J., 12½ Lafayette St., Attleboro, Mass.
Harrington, Johns H., 7615 McGroarty St., Tujunga, Calif.
Harris, Albert J., Educ. Clinic, Queens College, Flushing, N.Y.
Harris, Ben M., 325 Sutton Hall, University of Texas, Austin, Tex.
Harris, C. W., P.O. Box 1487, Deland, Fla.
Harris, Claude C., 201 North 15th St., Muskogee, Okla.
Harris, Dale B., Burrowes Bldg., Pennsylvania State Univ., University Park, Pa.
Harris, Fred E., Baldwin-Wallace College, Berea, Ohio
Harris, Janet C., 121 Allerton Rd., Newton Highlands, Mass.
Harris, Lewis E., 3752 N. Hight St., Columbus, Ohio
Harris, Mary Jo., Box 1523, University, Ala.
Harris, Mary Kate, 322 W. Vine St., Oxford, Ohio
Harris, Raymond P., Mt. Vernon Public Schools, Mt. Vernon, N.Y.
Harris, Ruby Dean, Univ. Hall, University of California, Berkeley, Calif.
Harris, Samuel D., Jr., 1108 Thomwal St., Valdosta, Ga.
Harris, Theodore L., Sch. of Educ., University of Wisconsin, Madison, Wis.
Harris, Wylie V., Superintendent of Schools, Shawnee Mission, Kan.
Harry, David P., Jr., Grad. Sch., Western Reserve University, Cleveland, Ohio
Harshman, Hardwick W., University of North Carolina, Chapel Hill, N.C.
Hart, Mrs. Lawrence W., P.O. Box 14, Rock Falls, Ill.
Hart, Richard H., 220 W. Forest St., Hillsboro, Ore.
Hart, Ruth M. R., 50 Willow St., Minneapolis, Minn.
Hartley, James R., Univ. Extn., University of California, Riverside, Calif.
Hartman, A. L., 104 Haddon Pl., Upper Montclair, N.J.
Hartsig, Barbara, Orange County State College, Fullerton, Calif.
Hartstein, Jacob I., Long Island University, 385 Flatbush Ave., Brooklyn, N.Y.
Hartung, Maurice L., Dept. of Educ., University of Chicago, Chicago, Ill.
Harwell, John Earl, State Teachers College, Kirksville, Mo.
Haskell, Charlotte L., 89 Royal Rd., Bangor, Me.
Haskew, Laurence D., Col. of Educ., University of Texas, Austin, Tex.
Hasman, Richard H., 61 Oakwood Ave., Farmingdale, N.Y.
Hassel, Carl W., Moorestown School Dist., Moorestown, N.J.
Hastie, Reid, 106 Jones Hall, University of Minnesota, Minneapolis, Minn.
Hatchett, Ethel L., Dept. of Educ., Hardin-Simmons University, Abilene, Tex.
Hatfield, Donald M., Dept. of Educ., University of California, Berkeley, Calif.
Haubrich, Vernon F., Dept. of Educ., Hunter College, New York, N.Y.
Hauer, William H., Hofstra College, Hempstead, N.Y.
Haupt, Leonard R., 2801 Glenview Rd., Glenview, Ill.
Hauschild, Mrs. J. R., 211 Bompart Ave., Webster Groves, Mo.
Hautzinger, Mrs. John, 10425 W. Meivina, Wauwatosa, Wis.
* Havighurst, Robert J., Dept. of Educ., University of Chicago, Chicago, Ill.
Hawkinson, Mabel, 11 Gregory St., Oswego, N.Y.
Hawley, Leslie R., 94 Walden Dr., RFD No. 1, Lakeview, Erie Co., N.Y.

Hawley, Ray C., Superintendent of County Schools, Ottawa, Ill.
Haws, Nina, 315 N. Lorraine, Wichita, Kan.
Hayden, Alice H., Miller Hall, University of Washington, Seattle, Wash.
Hayden, James R., 166 William St., New Bedford, Mass.
Hayden, Velma D., State Teachers College, Trenton, N.J.
Hayes, Allen P., 1504—4th Ave., Tuscaloosa, Ala.
Hayes, Mrs. Betty M., 725 Hawthorne Dr., Tiburon, Calif.
Hayes, Denis A., Paterson Diocesan Schls., 24 DeGrasse St., Paterson, N.J.
Hayes, Mary T., Aroostook State Tchrs. Col., Presque Isle, Me.
Hayes, Paul C., 3761 Mayfair Dr., Grove City, Ohio
Hays, Harry N., 407 Jesse St., Philipsburg, Pa.
Hays, Warren S., 3218 N. Reno Ave., Tucson, Ariz.
Hayward, Mrs. Lillian, 20 Spring Ridge Dr., Berkeley Heights, N.J.
Hayward, W. George, 27 Grant Ave., East Orange, N.J.
Hazan, Sam, 4930 Fulton Ave., Sherman Oaks, Calif.
Hazen, Oliver M., Renton School Dist. No. 403, Renton, Wash.
Hazleton, Edward W., 2143 West 107th Pl., Chicago, Ill.
Headd, Pearl Walker, Box 362, Tuskegee Institute, Ala.
Headley, Ross A., APO 164, c/o Hq. USA DEG, New York, N.Y.
Heagney, Genevieve, State Teachers College at Towson, Baltimore, Md.
Heald, James E., 112 Trieste Dr., St. Louis, Mo.
Healey, Margaret L., Rt. No. 1, Box 255, Taft, Calif.
Healy, Mary, 8459 Dante Ave., Chicago, Ill.
Heard, Charlsye Mae, 615 Jennette St., Memphis, Tenn.
Hearne, William P., 5630 S. Rockwell St., Chicago, Ill.
Heavenridge, Glen G., P.O. Box 836, Garden City, Mich.
Hebeler, Jean R., University of Maryland, College Park, Md.
Hecht, Irvin Sulo, Girls High School, 475 Nostrand Ave., Brooklyn, N.Y.
Heck, Theodore, St. Meinrad Seminary, St. Meinrad, Ind.
Hecker, Izora, 1486 Woodrow, Wichita, Kan.
Hedden, Gerald W., 3320 Jade Ave., Bakersfield, Calif.
Hedges, William D., Peabody Hall, University of Virginia, Charlottesville, Va.
Heding, Howard W., Col. of Educ., Univ. of Missouri, Columbus, Mo.
Heffernan, Helen, State Department of Education, Sacramento, Calif.
Heffernan, Mary, 296 Norwood Ave., Warwick, R.I.
Hegman, M. Marian, 332 South Ave., Medina, N.Y.
Heimann, Robert A., Arizona State University, Tempe, Ariz.
Heiney, John F., 14 Wollaston Rd., Wilmington, Del.
Heintzelman, Harvey A., 116 North 25th St., Camp Hill, N.J.
Heisner, H. Fred, P.O. Box 279, Redlands, Calif.
Held, John T., 707 Johns Ave., Gettysburg, Pa.
Helland, Philip C., Junior High School, 611 West 5th St., Willmar, Minn.
Heller, Melvin P., Sch. Dist. 234, 7500 W. Montrose Ave., Norridge, Ill.
Hellman, Walter H., 100 Reef Rd., Fairfield, Conn.
Helmick, Russell E., Peabody Hall, Louisiana State Univ., Baton Rouge, La.
* Helms, W. T., 1109 Roosevelt Ave., Richmond, Calif.
Heming, Hilton P., 12 Leonard Ave., Plattsburgh, N.Y.
Hemingway, W. C., 3402 Clarendon Rd., Cleveland Heights, Ohio
Hemink, Lyle H., State Univ. College of Education, Cortland, N.Y.
Henderson, Algo D., 4205 Univ. H.S., Univ. of Michigan, Ann Arbor, Mich.
Henderson, Edward, New York University, Washington Sq., New York, N.Y.
Hendrickson, Gordon, University of Cincinnati, Cincinnati, Ohio
Hendrix, Holbert H., Southern Reg. Div., Univ. of Nevada, Las Vegas, Nev.
Hengesbach, Alice R., Willoughby-Eastlake Schls., Center St., Willoughby, Ohio
Henion, Ethel S., 435 N. Central Ave., Ramsey, N.J.
Henle, R. J., 221 N. Grand Blvd., St. Louis, Mo.
Hennis, R. Sterling, Jr., 70 Hamilton Rd., Chapel Hill, N.C.
Henry, George H., Alison Hall, Univ. of Delaware, Newark, Del.
* Henry, Nelson B., Dept. of Educ., University of Chicago, Chicago, Ill.
Herbst, Leonard A., 11 Southdale Ave, Daly City, Calif.
Herge, Henry C., Sch. of Educ., Rutgers University, New Brunswick, N.J.

Herr, Ross, 3452 W. Drummond Pl., Chicago, Ill.
Herr, William A., 536 W. Maple St., Hazleton, Pa.
Herrick, Theral T., 306 E. Lovell St., Kalamazoo, Mich.
Herrick, Virgil E., Sch. of Educ., Univ. of Wisconsin, Madison, Wis.
Herrington, Mrs. Evelyn F., Sch. of Educ., Univ. of Texas, Austin, Tex.
Herriott, M. E., Air Port Junior High School, Los Angeles, Calif.
Herrmann, D. J., College of William and Mary, Williamsburg, Va.
Hertel, Robert, Illinois State Normal University, Normal, Ill.
Hertert, Patricia C., 2520 Hilgard Ave., Berkeley, Calif.
Hertzberg, Oscar E., State University College for Teachers, Buffalo, N.Y.
* Hertzler, Silas, 206 East "C" St., Hillsboro, Kan.
Hess, Clarke F., Marshall College, Huntington, W.Va.
Hess, Glenn C., 44 W. Wheeling St., Washington, Pa.
Hesse, Alexander N., 90 Salisbury Ave., Garden City, L.I., N.Y.
Hesla, Arden E., Mankato State College, Mankato, Minn.
Hetrick, J. B., Grove City Joint Consolidated Schools, Grove City, Pa.
Hetzel, Walter L., 1004 Murray Dr., Ames, Iowa
Heuer, Josephine C., 8444 Edna St., St. Louis, Mo.
Heusner, William W., Jr., Cooke Hall, Univ. of Minnesota, Minneapolis, Minn.
Heussman, John W., Concordia Seminary, Springfield, Ill.
Hewitt, Mrs. Sara F., 8 Bangert Ave., Perry Hall, Md.
Hibbs, M. Gregg, Superintendent of Schools, Red Bank, N.J.
Hickey, Philip J., Curriculum Lab., 1517 S. Theresa Ave., St. Louis, Mo.
Hicks, Mrs. Aline Black, 812 Lexington St., Norfolk, Va.
Hicks, Samuel I., Col. of Educ., Ohio University, Athens, Ohio
Hicks, Victor H., East Central State College, Ada, Okla.
Hidy, Mrs. Elizabeth Willson, Box 287, Gila Bend, Ariz.
Hieronymus, Albert N., East Hall, State Univ. of Iowa, Iowa City, Iowa
Hiers, Mrs. Turner M., 4260 S.W. 49th St., Fort Lauderdale, Fla.
Higgins, Mrs. Ardis, 1527 E. Mountain Dr., Santa Barbara, Calif.
Hightower, Emory A., 520 S. Pascack Rd., Spring Valley, N.Y.
Hilgard, Ernest R., Dept. of Psych., Stanford University, Stanford, Calif.
Hill, Alberta D., Office of Education, Dept. of H.E.W., Washington, D.C.
Hill, Charles E., 529 Fifth St., S.W., Rochester, Minn.
Hill, Elizabeth F., 647 N. Mayfield Ave., Chicago, Ill.
Hill, George E., Dept. of Educ., Ohio University, Athens, Ohio
Hill, Mrs. Ione A., 107 Filer St., Monroe, La.
Hill, Joseph K., Downstate Medical Center, Brooklyn, N.Y.
Hill, Katherine E., Press 23, New York Univ., Washington Sq., New York, N.Y.
Hill, Mrs. Margaret Ford, 32 S. Patterson Ave., Santa Barbara, Calif.
Hill, Mary C., 433 State St., Petoskey, Mich.
Hill, Mrs. Ruth E., 1255 Sandalwood Dr., El Centro, Calif.
Hill, W. W., P.O. Box 66, Cedartown, Ga.
Hill, Walker H., Michigan State University, East Lansing, Mich.
Hillerby, Ruth C., 212 E. Live Oak St., San Gabriel, Calif.
Hillerich, Robert L., 815 Glenwood Lane, Glenview, Ill.
Hilliard, Herbert S., Bates High School, Annapolis, Md.
Hillson, Maurie, Bucknell University, Lewisburg, Pa.
Hilton, M. Eunice, Dept. of Educ., University of Denver, Denver, Colo.
Himler, Leonard E., 1225 Fair Oaks Pkwy., Ann Arbor, Mich.
Himmele, Irvin H., Bd. of Education, 702 City Hall, Buffalo, N.Y.
Hinds, Jean, 1883 Morris Ave., Union, N.J.
Hines, Vynce A., 1220 S.W. Ninth Rd., Gainesville, Fla.
Hinkley, William C., Superintendent of Schools, Aurora, Colo.
Hitchcock, Catharine, 1837 E. Erie Ave., Lorain, Ohio
Hites, Christopher, 302 Portola Rd., Portola Valley, Calif.
Hitt, Harold H., 802 Lawson St., Midland, Tex.
Ho, Thomas C. K., 72 Distler Ave., West Caldwell, N.J.
Hobbs, Earl W., Mamaroneck Public Schools, Mamaroneck, N.Y.
Hobbs, Mrs. Edith E., 119 Parsonage St., Bennettsville, S.C.
Hobson, Cloy S., Fraser Hall, University of Kansas, Lawrence, Kan.

Hock, Louise E., Sch. of Educ., New York Univ., Washington Sq., New York, N.Y.
Hodgins, George W., Paramus High School, Paramus, N.J.
Hodgkins, George W., 1832 Biltmore St., N.W., Washington, D.C.
Hoeltgen, Alice, 4333 Benton Blvd., Kansas City, Mo.
Hoerauf, William E., 2701 W. Chicago Blvd., Detroit, Mich.
Hoffman, Charles L., East High School, 214 High St., Waterloo, Iowa
Hoffman, Joseph L., Chaminade College, 3140 Waialae Dr., Honolulu, Hawaii
Hofstrand, John M., San Jose State College, San Jose, Calif.
Hogan, Ursula, 2213-D Dresden Ct., Sacramento, Calif.
Hohl, George W., Superintendent of Schools, 189 Columbia Ave., Passaic, N.J.
Holland, Benjamin F., Sutton Hall, University of Texas, Austin, Tex.
Holland, Donald F., 11320 S. Prairie Ave., Chicago, Ill.
Holland, Gertrude I., 3160 E. Church St., Xenia, Ohio
Holley, Marian J., 120 Sexton St., Struthers, Ohio
Holliday, Jay N., P.O. Box 563, Canoga Park, Calif.
Hollis, Virgil S., Superintendent of County Schools, San Rafael, Calif.
Holloway, George E., Jr., Cooke Hall, Univ. of Buffalo, Buffalo, N.Y.
Holman, W. Earl, Jackson High School, 544 Wildwood Ave., Jackson, Mich.
Holmblade, Amy Jean, Dept. of H.E., University of Minnesota, St. Paul, Minn.
Holmer, Mrs. Helen, 515 Buchanan St., Gary, Ind.
Holmes, Daniel L., Scituate Public Schools, Scituate, Mass.
Holmes, Emma E., Orange County State College, Fullerton, Calif.
Holmes, Jack A., Sch. of Educ., Univ. of California, Berkeley, Calif.
Holmes, Jay William, 350 Castlewood, Dayton, Ohio
Holmquist, Emily, Indiana Univ. School of Nursing, Indianapolis, Ind.
Holmstedt, Raleigh W., Indiana State Teachers College, Terre Haute, Ind.
Holstein, Louise V., 7130 Union Ave., Chicago, Ill.
Holston, M. J., 1128 Valley Dr., Borger, Tex.
Holstun, Gordon, Superintendent of Schools, Thomaston, Ga.
Holt, Charles C., Proviso Township High School, Maywood, Ill.
Homburg, William, Union Grove High School, Union Grove, Wis.
Homer, Francis R., 4800 Conshohocken Ave., Philadelphia, Pa.
Honnen, Ruth Ann, 1363 Pierce, Denver, Colo.
Hood, Edwin Morris, The Claridge, 101 Old Mamaroneck Rd., White Plains, N.Y.
Hooper, George J., Sidney Lanier Sch., 1727 S. Harvard Ave., Tulsa, Okla.
Hoops, Robert C., Washington School, Bergen Ave., New Milford, N.J.
Hoover, Louis H., 1027 Dunlop Ave., Forest Park, Illinois
Hoover, Norman K., Pennsylvania State University, University Park, Pa.
Hopkins, Kenneth D., 12772 Oak Way Dr., Los Alamitos, Calif.
Hopkins, Monroe, Hannibal-LaGrange College, Hannibal, Mo.
Hopman, Anne B., 5935 Hohman Ave., Hammond, Ind.
Hopmann, Robert P., 210 N. Broadway, St. Louis, Mo.
Hoppock, Anne, State Department of Education, Trenton, N.J.
Horn, Ernest, East Hall, State University of Iowa, Iowa City, Iowa
Horn, Thomas D., Sutton Hall, University of Texas, Austin, Tex.
Hornburg, Mabel C., 118 Champlain Ave., Ticonderoga, N.Y.
Horowitz, Norman H., 3625 Purdue Ave., Los Angeles, Calif.
Horsman, Ralph D., Superintendent of Schls., 735 Washington Rd., Pittsburgh, Pa.
Horwich, Frances R., 10401 Wilshire Blvd., Los Angeles, Calif.
Hosford, Marian H., Stirling Rd., Warren Twp., Plainfield, N.J.
Hoskins, Glen C., Southern Methodist University, Dallas, Tex.
Hotaling, Mrs. Muriel P., 140 Jensen Rd., R.D. No. 1, Vestal, N.Y.
Hottenstein, Gerald G., Montgomery County Schls., Norristown, Pa.
Hough, John M., Jr., Mars Hill College, Mars Hill, N.C.
Hough, Robert E., Arthur L. Johnson Regional High School, Clark, N.J.
Houghton, John J., Superintendent of Schools, Ferndale, Mich.
Houlahan, F. J., Catholic University of America, Washington, D.C.
Houle, Cyril O., Dept. of Educ., University of Chicago, Chicago, Ill.
House, Ralph W., State Teachers College, Kirksville, Mo.
Houston, James, Jr., 300 Pompton Rd., Wayne, N.J.

Houston, W. Robert, 1104—16th St., Port Huron, Mich.
Hovet, Kenneth O., University of Maryland, College Park, Md.
Howard, Alexander H., Jr., Central Washington Col. of Educ., Ellensburg, Wash.
Howard, Daniel D., Pestalozzi-Froebel Tchrs. College, Chicago, Ill.
Howard, Elizabeth Z., 5550 S. Dorchester Ave., Chicago, Ill.
Howard, George, University of Alabama, University, Ala.
Howard, Glenn W., Queens College, Flushing, N.Y.
Howard, Marjorie M., 3201 Wisconsin Ave., N.W., Washington, D.C.
Howd, M. Curtis, 200 Winthrop Rd., Muncie, Ind.
Howe, Mrs. Flora S., 271 S. Tradewinds Ave., Lauderdale-by-the-Sea, Fla.
Howe, Walter, Box 6127, Lincoln, Neb.
Howland, Adelene E., Pennington School, Mount Vernon, N.Y.
Hoyle, Dorothy, Temple University, Philadelphia, Pa.
Hoyt, Cyril J., Burton Hall, Univ. of Minnesota, Minneapolis, Minn.
Hron, Joseph T., 2212 Lathrop Ave., North Riverside, Ill.
Huber, H. Ronald, 723 Portland Ave., Huntingdon, Pa.
Hubert, Frank W. R., Texas A. & M. College, College Station, Tex.
Huckaby, Arthur L., 1721 Damling, Houston, Tex.
Hucksoll, William J., 1332 Heather Hill Rd., Baltimore, Md.
Hudson, Bruce M., 9908 Fairfield Ave., Livonia, Mich.
Hudson, Douglas, 212 Brouse Dr., Wadsworth, Ohio
Hudson, L. P., Huddleston High School, Huddleston, Va.
Hudson, Margaret, P.O. Box 260, Bella Vista Rd., Watsonville, Calif.
Huebner, Mildred H., Southern Connecticut State College, New Haven, Conn.
Huehn, Kermith S., Superintendent of County Schools, Eldora, Iowa
Huelsman, Charles B., Jr., 203 Selby Blvd., West, Worthington, Ohio
Huff, Jack F., 19348 Glen Lyn Dr., Glendora, Calif.
Huffaker, Dixie, 4310 E. Lancaster, Fort Worth, Tex.
Hufford, G. N., Dept. of Educ., Lewis College, Lockport, Ill.
Hughes, James W., State University College of Education, Geneseo, N.Y.
Hughes, McDonald, 1715—32nd Ave., Tuscaloosa, Ala.
Hughes, Perra M., Kansas State College, Pittsburg, Kan.
Hughes, Thomas G., 1211 E. Bennett Ave., Glendora, Calif.
Hughes, Vergil H., San Jose State College, San Jose, Calif.
Hughson, Arthur, 131 East 21st St., Brooklyn, N.Y.
Hull, Marion, Northern Illinois University, DeKalb, Ill.
Hult, Esther, State College of Iowa, Cedar Falls, Iowa
Hultgren, Robert B., Culbertson Sch., Briggs and Washington Sts., Joliet, Ill.
Humelsine, Martha, Roberts Wesleyan College, North Chili, N.Y.
Humphrey, Charles, 6001 Berkeley Dr., Berkeley, Mo.
Hunsader, R. W., Senior High School, 409 S. High St., Fort Atkinson, Wis.
Hunt, Mrs. Anne Brown, Mahoning County Schools, Youngstown, Ohio
Hunt, Dorothy D., 2000 East 46th St., N., Kansas City, Mo.
Hunt, Elizabeth, Rt. No. 3, Johnson Rd., Oswego, N.Y.
Hunt, Herold C., Grad. Sch. of Educ., Harvard University, Cambridge, Mass.
Hunt, William A., Dept. of Psych., Northwestern University, Evanston, Ill.
Hunter, Eugenia, Woman's Col., Univ. of North Carolina, Greensboro, N.C.
Hunter, Harry W., P.O. Box 597, Ocala, Fla.
Hunter, James J., Jr., San Diego State College, San Diego, Calif.
Hunter, Lavinia, Western Kentucky State College, Bowling Green, Ky.
Hunter, Robert W., Grambling College, Grambling, La.
Hunter, William, P.O. Box 938, Tuskegee, Ala.
* Huntington, Albert H., 736 Fairview Ave., Webster Groves, Mo.
Huntington, Elizabeth A., 45 Morris Ave., Springfield, N.J.
Hurd, Blair E., 4900 Heatherdale Lane, Carmichael, Calif.
Hurd, Paul DeH., Sch. of Educ., Stanford University, Stanford, Calif.
Hurlburt, Allan S., Duke University, Col. Sta., Durham, N.C.
Hurlburt, Lydia Delpha, 1590 Hawthorne, Forest Grove, Ore.
Hurt, Mary Lee, Office of Education, Dept. of H.E.W., Washington, D.C.
Husmann, John L., 256 Ash St., Crystal Lake, Ill.
Huss, Francis G., North Penn Vocational School, Lansdale, Pa.

Husson, Chesley H., Husson College, 157 Park St., Bangor, Me.
Husted, Inez M., Luzerne County Schools, Wilkes-Barre, Pa.
Hutaff, Lucile W., Bowman Gray School of Medicine, Winston-Salem, N.C.
Hutchison, James M., 4231 West 59th St., Los Angeles, Calif.
Hutson, Darlene L., Col. of Educ., Univ. of Tennessee, Knoxville, Tenn.
Hutson, Percival W., University of Pittsburgh, Pittsburgh, Pa.
Hutto, Jerome A., Los Angeles State College, Los Angeles, Calif.
Hutton, Harry K., Pennsylvania State University, University Park, Pa.
Hybertson, Harriet, Augustana College, Sioux Falls, S.D.
Hyde, Edith I., University of California at L.A., Los Angeles, Calif.
Hyram, George H., Dept. of Educ., St. Louis University, St. Louis, Mo.

Iannaccone, Laurence, 424 Melville Ave., University City, Mo.
Iglesias-Borges, Ramon, P.O. Box 226, San Lorenzo, Puerto Rico
Ihara, Teruo, 111 Wist Hall, University of Hawaii, Honolulu, Hawaii
Imes, Orley B., 3985 La Cresenta Rd., El Sobrante, Calif.
Imhoff, Myrtle M., Orange County State College, Fullerton, Calif.
Inabnit, Darrell J., 5580 S.W. 63rd Ct., Miami, Fla.
Incardona, Joseph S., 325 Busti Ave., Buffalo, N.Y.
Ingebritson, Kasper I., 2790 Sunny Grove Ave., Arcata, Calif.
Ingram, Mrs. Mildred, Danville High School, Danville, Ill.
Ingrelli, Anthony V., University of Wisconsin-Milwaukee, Milwaukee, Wis.
Inlow, Gail M., Sch. of Educ., Northwestern University, Evanston, Ill.
Inskeep, James E., Jr., 6155 Lubbock Ave., La Mesa, Calif.
Ireland, Robert S., Superintendent of Schools, Stow St., Concord, Mass.
Irfan, Nancy M., Education Extension Centre, Lahore, India
Irish, Elizabeth, University of California, Santa Barbara, Goleta, Calif.
Ironside, Roderick A., College of William and Mary, Williamsburg, Va.
Irsfeld, H. L., Superintendent of Schools, Mineral Wells, Tex.
Irving, James Lee, 5713 Ogontz Ave., Philadelphia, Pa.
Irving, Mary Downing, 303 Crompton Rd., Waynesboro, Va.
Irwin, Alice M., Dept. of Spec. Classes, Public Schls, New Bedford, Mass.
Isaacs, Ann F., 409 Clinton Spring Ave., Cincinnati, Ohio
Isacksen, Roy O., Como Park Junior High School, 740 W. Rose Ave., St. Paul,
    Minn.
Isenberg, Robert M., N.E.A., 1201 Sixteenth St., N.W., Washington, D.C.
Isley, Thurston F., Dept. of Educ., William Jewell College, Liberty, Mo.
Iversen, Jack R., P.O. Box 447, Star Lake, N.Y.
Ivie, Claude, Public Schools, P.O. Box 470, Meridian, Miss.
Ivins, George H., Roosevelt College, 430 S. Michigan Ave., Chicago, Ill.
Ivok, Leo, Public Schools, Worcester, Mass.
Izzo, Raymond J., 12 Girard Rd., Winchester, Mass.

Jack, Maude E., P.O. Box 16, McLean, Ill.
Jackson, Lowell D., Dept. of Educ., University of Hawaii, Honolulu, Hawaii
Jackson, Philip W., Dept. of Educ., Univ. of Chicago, Chicago, Ill.
Jackson, Ronald, Taipei American School, APO 63, San Francisco, Calif.
Jackson, Mrs. Wilda S., 6403 Shoal Creek Blvd., Austin, Tex.
Jackson, William H., Hampton Junior College, Ocala, Fla .
Jacobs, Robert, 2041 N. Kinington, Arlington, Va.
Jacobsen, Carlyle, Upstate Medical Center, 766 Irving Ave., Syracuse, N.Y.
Jacobson, Irving, 16 Elm St., Westwood, N.J.
Jacobson, Marvin M., 6011 Hereford Dr., Los Angeles, Calif.
Jaeckel, Solomon, 13701 Bracken St., Pacoima, Calif.
Jaeger, Alan Warren, Rt. No. 1, Box 17B, Atwater, Calif.
Jaeger, Eloise M., Norris Gym., University of Minnesota, Minneapolis, Minn.
Jaeger, Herman F., 831 W. Park Ave., Pasco, Wash.
James, Mrs. Bernice O., 822 Avenue L., Galveston, Tex.
James, Carl A., Superintendent of Schools, Emporia, Kan.
James, J. I., Superintendent of Schools, Box 280, Eagle Pass, Tex.
James, Newton E., University of Arizona, Tucson, Ariz.

* James, Preston E., Dept. of Geog., Syracuse University, Syracuse, N.Y.
James, Viola, Administration Library, 1800 Grand Ave., Des Moines, Iowa
James, Virginia White, Box 1981, University, Ala.
James, W. Raymond, State University Teachers College, Plattsburgh, N.Y.
Jameson, Sanford F., Superintendent of Schools, Warren, Ohio
Jamrich, John X., 522 Cowley St., East Lansing, Mich.
Jansen, Udo H., Sch. of Educ., Miami University, Oxford, Ohio
* Jansen, William, 900 Palmer Rd., Bronxville, N.Y.
Jansic, Anthony F., Educ. Clinic, City College of New York, New York, N.Y.
Jardine, Alex, 228 S. St. Joseph St., South Bend, Ind.
Jarman, B. H., TC-ED, USOM Korea, APO 301, San Francisco, Calif.
Jarvis, Galen, Devonshire School, Skokie, Ill.
Jedrzejewski, Clement, 113 East 64th St., New York, N.Y.
Jeffers, Jay W., Box 551, Las Vegas, Nev.
Jefferson, James L., 866 Lincoln St., S.W., Birmingham, Ala.
Jelinek, James J., Col. of Educ., Arizona State University, Tempe, Ariz.
Jellins, Miriam H., 2849 Dale Creek Dr., N.W., Atlanta, Ga.
Jemison, T. H., Dept. of Educ., Andrews University, Berrien Springs, Mich.
Jenkins, Augusta, Hull, Ga.
Jenkins, Clara Barnes, Dept. of Educ., Shaw University, Raleigh, N.C.
Jenkins, David S., Anna Arundel County Schools, Annapolis, Md.
Jenkins, John F., Portland State College, Portland, Ore.
Jenks, William F., Holy Redeemer College, Washington, D.C.
Jennings, Wayne B., 1947 Malvern St., St. Paul, Minn.
Jensen, Arthur M., Tuttle School, 1042—18th Ave., Minneapolis, Minn.
Jensen, Gale E., 3055 Lakewood Dr., Ann Arbor, Mich.
Jensen, Grant W., South High School, 1101 Planz Rd., Bakersfield, Calif.
Jensen, Moroni L., Cyprus High Sch., 8623 West 3000 South, Magna, Utah
Jenson, T. J., Ohio State University, Columbus, Ohio
Jetton, Clyde T., 720 Amherst, Abilene, Tex.
Jewell, R. Ewart, Superintendent of Schools, 547 Wall St., Bend, Ore.
Jewett, Arno, Office of Education, Dept. of H.E.W., Washington, D.C.
Jex, Frank B., Dept. of Educ. Psych., Univ. of Utah, Salt Lake City, Utah
Johns, Edward B., Dept. of P.E., University of California, Los Angeles, Calif.
Johnson, Mrs. Alice N., 2635 Springfield Rd., Broomall, Pa.
Johnson, B. Lamar, Sch. of Educ., Univ. of California, Los Angeles, Calif.
Johnson, Carl E., 420 N. Elmhurst Ave., Mt. Prospect, Ill.
Johnson, Charles E., Col. of Educ., University of Illinois, Urbana, Ill.
Johnson, Charles E., 722 S. Van Ness, San Francisco, Calif.
Johnson, Mrs. Dorothea N., 670 Bell Ave., Elyria, Ohio
Johnson, Mrs. Dorothy K., 7 Dalston Circle, Lynbrook, N.Y.
Johnson, Douglas A., 3750 Esperanzo Dr., Sacramento, Calif.
Johnson, Eleanor M., Box 360, Middletown, Conn.
Johnson, Ellen V., State Teachers College, Minot, N.D.
Johnson, Evelyn Lawlah, Dept. of Soc., Kentucky State Col., Frankfort, Ky.
Johnson, G. Orville, 805 S. Crouse Ave., Syracuse, N.Y.
Johnson, Gladys V., 3229—4th Ave., South, Great Falls, Mont.
Johnson, Harry C., Duluth Branch, Univ. of Minnesota, Duluth, Minn.
Johnson, Harry O., 11411 Ingram, Livonia, Mich.
Johnson, Harry W. II, Municipal University of Omaha, Omaha, Neb.
Johnson, Helen L., Lab Sch., Central Michigan University, Mt. Pleasant, Mich.
Johnson, John N., 6191 Vereker Dr., Oxford, Ohio
Johnson, Leighton H., San Francisco State College, San Francisco, Calif.
Johnson, Leland I., 24—5th Ave., N.E., Osseo, Minn.
Johnson, Leonard E., L. H. Bugbee Sch., 1943 Asylum Ave., West Hartford, Conn.
Johnson, Mrs. Lois S., 29 S. Hillside Ter., Madison, Wis.
Johnson, Lois V., Los Angeles State College, Los Angeles, Calif.
Johnson, Margaret E., Alpine School District, American Fork, Utah
Johnson, Mrs. Marjorie Seddon, 61 Grove Ave., Flourtown, Pa.
Johnson, Minnie R., Crane Campus, Chicago Teachers College, Chicago, Ill.

Johnson, Philip G., Stone Hall, Cornell University, Ithaca, N.Y.
Johnson, Robert Leonard, 2500 South 118th St., West Allis, Wis.
* Johnson, Roy Ivan, 2333 Southwest Eighth Dr., Gainesville, Fla.
Johnson, Mrs. Olive L., 1925 Thornwood Ave., Wilmette, Ill.
Johnson, Mrs. Shiela K., Sixth Ave. and A. St., Taft, Calif.
Johnson, Theodore D., 5226 N. Spaulding Ave., Chicago, Ill.
Johnson, Walter F., Col. of Educ., Michigan State Univ., East Lansing, Mich.
Johnson, Walter R., Libertyville High School, Libertyville, Ill.
Johnson, Wynne E., 10261 Rinda Dr., Rancho Cordova, Calif.
Johnston, Aaron Montgomery, Col. of Educ., Univ. of Tennessee, Knoxville, Tenn.
Johnston, Edgar G., Waterford Twp. Schls., 3101 W. Walton Blvd., Pontiac, Mich.
Johnston, Lillian B., 538 W. Vernon Ave., Phoenix, Ariz.
Joll, Leonard W., Mulberry St., Plantsville, Conn.
Jonas, Russell E., Black Hills Teachers College, Spearfish, S.D.
Jones, A. Quinn, Lincoln High School, Gainesville, Fla.
Jones, Annie Lee, Sch. of Educ., Univ. of North Carolina, Chapel Hill, N.C.
* Jones, Arthur J., 407 Swarthmore Ave., Swarthmore, Pa.
Jones, Charles L., Gullett School, 6310 Treadwell Ave., Austin, Tex.
Jones, Clifford V., 189 Columbia Ave., Passaic, N.J.
Jones, Dilys M., 316 S. Fayette St., Shippensburg, Pa.
Jones, Donald W., 508 W. North St., Muncie, Ind.
Jones, Hildred B., Ohio Northern University, Ada, Ohio
Jones, Howard Robert, Sch. of Educ., University of Michigan, Ann Arbor, Mich.
Jones, Joseph, Burnett High School, Terrell, Tex.
Jones, Lewis C., Jr., P.O. Box 98, Langley, S.C.
Jones, Lloyd Meredith, University of Bridgeport, Bridgeport, Conn.
Jones, Mary Elliott, 131 Grand Ave., Englewood, N.J.
Jones, Olwen M., 5 Putnam Hill, Greenwich, Conn.
Jones, Richard N., Carroll Rd., Monkton, Md.
Jones, Ronald D., Dept. of Educ., Whitworth College, Spokane, Wash.
Jones, Samuel T., MacDonald Knolls School, Tenbrook Dr., Silver Spring, Md.
Jones, Vyron Lloyd, Route No. 2, Rosedale, Ind.
Jones, Wendell P., Sch. of Educ., Univ. of California, Los Angeles, Calif.
Joneson, Della, Washington School, Marseilles, Ill.
Jonsson, Harold, Div. of Educ., San Francisco State Col., San Francisco, Calif.
Jordan, A. B., 5811 Riverview Blvd., St. Louis, Mo.
Jordan, Benjamin W., Educ. Bldg., Wayne State Univ., Detroit, Mich.
Jordan, Laura, 1003 W. Nevada St., Urbana, Ill.
Jordan, Lawrence V., West Virginia State College, Institute, W.Va.
Jordan, Wayne, Antioch Public Schls., ABC Bldg., Antioch, Calif.
Joyce, Bruce R., Sch. of Educ., University of Delaware, Newark, Del.
Joyce, James M., O'Gorman High School, Sioux Falls, S.D.
Juan, K. C., 640 Middlefield Rd., Palo Alto, Calif.
Judenfriend, Harold, 23 Pleasant St., Colchester, Conn.
Julstrom, Eva, 7647 Colfax Ave., Chicago, Ill.
Junge, Charlotte W., Col. of Educ., Wayne University, Detroit, Mich.
Junge, Ruby M., Col. of Educ., Michigan State College, East Lansing, Mich.
Junker, Margaret, 9138 S. Claremont Ave., Chicago, Ill.
Jurjevich, J. C., Jr., Dept. of Educ., Mankato State College, Mankato, Minn.
Justice, Kenneth, Centralia Senior High School, Centralia, Wash.
Justman, Joseph, Board of Education, 110 Livingston St., Brooklyn, N.Y.
Juvancic, William A., Eli Whitney Elem. Sch., 2815 S. Komensky Ave., Chicago, Ill.

Kaar, Mrs. Galeta M., 7050 Ridge Ave., Chicago, Ill.
Kaback, Goldie Ruth, 375 Riverside Dr., New York, N.Y.
Kabrud, Margaret, State Teachers College, Ellendale, N.D.
Kahler, Carol, St. Louis University, St. Louis, Mo.
Kahrs, Mary V., Mankato State College, Mankato, Minn.

Kandyba, Bernard S., Lincoln Estates, Frankfort, Ill.
Kane, James L., Stratford School, Garden City, L.I., N.Y.
Kantor, Bernard R., 817 S. Windsor Blvd., Los Angeles, Calif.
Kaplan, Louis, 111 Via Monte de Oro Ave., Redondo Beach, Calif.
Karlin, Robert, Southern Illinois University, Carbondale, Ill.
Karr, Johnston T., Gary Public Schools, 620 E. 10th Pl., Gary, Ind.
Karrel, Oscar, Lord & Taylor, 424 Fifth Ave., New York, N.Y.
Karwiel, Mrs. Lela S., 723 Steves Ave., San Antonio, Tex.
Kasdon, Lawrence, Department of Public Instruction, Honolulu, Hawaii
Kata, Joseph J., Redbank Valley Joint Schools, New Bethlehem, Pa.
Katenkamp, Theodore W., Jr., Augsburg Home, Baltimore, Md.
Katz, Mrs. Florine, Educ. Clinic, City College, New York, N.Y.
Katz, Joseph, University of British Columbia, Vancouver, B.C., Canada
Kauffman, Merle M., Col. of Educ., Bradley University, Peoria, Ill.
Kawalek, Thaddens P., Superintendent of Schools, Brookfield, Ill.
Kaya, Esin, 520 Main Bldg., New York Univ., Washington Sq., New York, N.Y.
Kearl, Jennie W., State Department of Education, Salt Lake City, Utah
Kearney, George G., Rt. No. 1, Box 1108, Morgan Hill, Calif.
Keating, Barry J., 107 Somerset Ave., Garden City, N.Y.
Keaveny, T. Leo, 810 St. Germain St., St. Cloud, Minn.
Keck, Winston B., Superintendent of Schools, Springfield, Vt.
Keffer, Eugene R., 603 N. College Ave., Warrensburg, Mo.
Kegler, John, 7135th Sch. Group (GEN ED), APO 633, New York, N.Y.
Keleher, Gregory C., Dept. of Educ., St. Anselm's College, Manchester, N.H.
Keliher, Alice V., 2039 Hudson Blvd., Jersey City, N.J.
* Keller, Franklin J., 333 E. Mosholu Pkwy., New York, N.Y.
Keller, Robert J., Peik Hall, Univ. of Minnesota, Minneapolis, Minn.
Keller, Saul B., 957 Edgewood Rd., Elizabeth, N.J.
Kelley, Claude, Col. of Educ., University of Oklahoma, Norman, Okla.
Kelley, Mrs. Dorothy J., Willard Sch., 4915 St. Lawrence Ave., Chicago, Ill.
Kelley, H. Paul, University of Texas, Austin, Tex.
Kelley, Janet A., 88 Morningside Dr., New York, N.Y.
Kelley, Victor H., University of Arizona, Tucson, Ariz.
Kelley, William F., Marquette Univ., 1131 W. Wisconsin Ave., Milwaukee, Wis.
Kellogg, E. G., Superintendent of Schools, West Allis, Wis.
Kelly, Dean, 528 Lindberg Blvd., Berea, Ohio
Kelly, Edward J., 2215 Ninth Ave., Greeley, Colo.
Kelly, James A., 1665-B Catalpa Dr., Anaheim, Calif.
Kelly, Shaun, Jr., Central School Dist. No. 2, Box 192, Cold Spring Harbor, N.Y.
Kelner, Bernard G., 1804 Ashurst Rd., Philadelphia, Pa.
Kelsey, Roger R., Educ. Annex, University of Maryland, College Park, Md.
Kemp, Edward L., Sch. of Educ., New York Univ., Washington Sq., New York, N.Y.
Kendall, Betty Barker, Col. of Educ., Univ. of Arizona, Tucson, Ariz.
Kendall, Lloyd, Col. of Educ., San Diego State College, San Diego, Calif.
Kennard, Andrew J., 3511 Oakdale Ave., Houston, Tex.
Kennedy, Clephane A., Benjamin Franklin University, Washington, D.C.
Kentner, Harold M., Rochester Institute of Technology, Rochester, N.Y.
Kephart, Ruby G., Allen County Elementary Schools, Memorial Hall, Lima, Ohio
Keppers, George L., University of New Mexico, Albuquerque, N.M.
Kerns, LeRoy, Lab. Sch., Colorado State College, Greeley, Colo.
Kerr, Everett F., Superintendent of Schools, Blue Island, Ill.
Kersh, Bert Y., 260 Sacre Lane, Monmouth, Ore.
Kerst, Mrs. Marjorie, Campus Sch., Wisconsin State College, Stevens Point, Wis.
Keshian, Jerry G., 10 Kilburn Rd., Garden City, L.I., N.Y.
Kesselring, Ralph, Petaling, Jaya, Selanger, Malaya
Kevane, Eugene, 120 Curley Hall, Catholic University, Washington, D.C.
Kidder, William W., 216 Walton Ave., South Orange, N.J.
Kies, Michael S., Superintendent of County Schools, Milwaukee, Wis.
Kilbourn, Robert W., 4902 Argyle, Dearborn, Mich.
Kilburn, H. Parley, Evening Div., Bakersfield College, Bakersfield, Calif.

Kilpatrick, Arnold R., Northeastern Louisiana State College, Monroe, La.
* Kilpatrick, William H., 106 Morningside Dr., New York, N.Y.
Kincheloe, James B., University of Kentucky, Lexington, Ky.
Kind, Dan E., Ginn & Co., Statler Bldg., Boston, Mass.
Kindred, Leslie W., Temple University, Philadelphia, Pa.
King, Arthur R., Jr., Claremont Graduate School, Claremont, Calif.
King, Charles T., 374 Millburn Ave., Millburn, N.J.
King, Kent H., 103 Thayer Ave., Mankato, Minn.
King, Lloyd H., College of the Pacific, Stockton, Calif.
King, Paul E., 532 Sylvan Ave., Englewood Cliffs, N.J.
King, Thomas C., Col. of Educ. and Nursing, Univ. of Vermont, Burlington, Vt.
Kingdon, Frederick H., Kent State University, Kent, Ohio
Kingsley, Mrs. Iva Marie, Box 177, Kayehta, Ariz.
Kinsella, John J., Sch. of Educ., New York Univ., Washington Sq., New York, N.Y.
Kinsellar, Frances M., Rye St., Broad Brook, Conn.
Kinser, Mrs. Opha, 116 S. Walnut St., Bloomington, Ind.
Kinsman, Kephas Albert, 2009 Appleton St., Long Beach, Calif.
Kinzer, John R., 540 Harley Dr., Columbus, Ohio
Kirby, Frederick W., Baker High School, Columbus, Ga.
Kirchhoff, E. L., 29 Columbine Dr., Palatine, Ill.
Kirk, Samuel A., University of Illinois, Urbana, Ill.
Kirkland, Mrs. Eleanor R., 8707 Mohawk Way, Fair Oaks, Calif.
Kirkland, J. Bryant, North Carolina State College, Raleigh, N.C.
Kirkman, Ralph E., Concord College, Athens, W.Va.
Kirkpatrick, J. E., Black Hills Teachers College, Spearfish, S.D.
Kissinger, Doris C., 34 Roosevelt St., Glen Head, L.I., N.Y.
Kitch, Donald E., 721 Capitol Ave., Sacramento, Calif.
Kitts, Harry W., USOM, c/o U.S. Embassy, APO 146, San Francisco, Calif.
Klaus, Catherine, Box 9, Postville, Iowa
Klausmeier, Herbert J., Sch. of Educ., University of Wisconsin, Madison, Wis.
Klein, Philip, Harcum Junior College, Bryn Mawr, Pa.
Klein, Richard K., Department of Public Instruction, Bismarck, N.D.
Kleinpell, E. H., Wisconsin State College, River Falls, Wis.
Klevan, Albert, 9218 California St., Livonia, Mich.
Klevickis, Genevieve, 4311 Sheridan Rd., Kenosha, Wis.
Kleyensteuber, Carl J., University of Wisconsin-Milwaukee, Milwaukee, Wis.
Kline, Donald F., F. E. Compton & Co., 1000 N. Dearborn St., Chicago, Ill.
Kline, Frances F., 152—72nd St., Brooklyn, N.Y.
Kling, Martin, 1232 Sunset Loop, Walnut Creek, Calif.
Klofta, Norbert J., 2186 North 74th St., Milwaukee, Wis.
Klohr, Paul R., Arps Hall, Ohio State University, Columbus, Ohio
Klopf, Gordon, Tchrs. Col., Columbia University, New York, N.Y.
Klopfer, Leopold E., 151 Oxford St., Cambridge, Mass.
Kluwe, Mary Jean, 468 W. Hancock St., Detroit, Mich.
Knapp, Dale L., Los Angeles State College, Los Angeles, Calif.
Knapp, Royce H., Admin. Bldg., University of Nebraska, Lincoln, Neb.
Knight, George S., West 2nd St., St. Elmo, Fayette County, Ill.
Knight, R. W., 3909 East 5th Pl., Tulsa, Okla.
Knight, Reginald R., 4338 Heather Rd., Long Beach, Calif.
Knoeppel, LeRoy J., Proviso Township High School, Maywood, Ill.
Knowlden, Gayle E., 414 Strand, Manhattan Beach, Calif.
Knowles, Leone, 5 Pearl St., Camden, Me.
Knox, Stanley C., State College of Iowa, Cedar Falls, Iowa
Knuti, Leo Leonard, Montana State College, Bozeman, Mont.
Knutson, Helen A., 106 Second Ave., S.W., Austin, Minn.
Koch, Mrs. Sylvia L., 539 N. Highland Ave., Los Angeles, Calif.
Koehring, Dorothy, State College of Iowa, Cedar Falls, Iowa
Koenig, Adolph J., 612 Cedar Hill Rd., Ambler, Pa.
Koenig, Vernon H., 1318 S. Central Ave., Lodi, Calif.
Koerber, Walter F., Scarborough Board of Education, Scarborough, Ont., Canada

Koerner, Mrs. Winifred, 355 Smith Ave., Islip, L.I., N.Y.
Koester, George A., San Diego State College, San Diego, Calif.
Kohler, Lewis T., 7659 Whitsett Ave., North Hollywood, Calif.
Kohlmann, Eleanor L., 169 MacKay Hall, Iowa State University, Ames, Iowa
Kohn, Martin, 35 West 92nd St., New York, N.Y.
Kohn, Nathan, Jr., 9827 Clayton Rd., St. Louis, Mo.
Kohs, Samuel C., 620 Plymouth Way, Burlingame, Calif.
Komarek, Henrietta, 508 Rex Blvd., Elmhurst, Ill.
Konen, Robert C., 1535 Monroe Ave., River Forest, Ill.
Konsh, Adeline, 919 Park Pl., Brooklyn, N.Y.
Kontos, George, Jr., Superintendent of Elementary Schls., Sweet Home, Ore.
Koos, Leonard V., Route 2, Newago, Mich.
Kopel, David, Chicago Teachers College, 6800 S. Stewart Ave., Chicago, Ill.
Korey, Harold, 3750 Lake Shore Dr., Chicago, Ill.
Kornberg, Leonard, 137-30 Geranium Ave., Flushing, N.Y.
Korntheuer, Gerhard A., St. Johns College, Winfield, Kan.
Kough, Blachford, 1632 W. Wrightwood Ave., Chicago, Ill.
Koy, Arnold C., Little Fort School, 1775 Blanchard Rd., Waukegan, Ill.
Kraft, Milton Edward, Earlham College, Richmond, Ind.
Kramer, William A., Lutheran Church, Mo. Synod, 210 N. Broadway, St. Louis,
    Mo.
Krathwohl, David R., Michigan State University, East Lansing, Mich.
Kraus, Howard F., 512 Alameda de las Pulgas, Belmont, Calif.
Kraus, Philip E., 215 West 78th St., New York, N.Y.
Krautle, Hilda E., 3599 Werk Rd., Cincinnati, Ohio
Kravetz, Nathan, 328 Skyewiay Rd., Los Angeles, Calif.
Kravetz, Sol., 7642 Lena Ave., Canoga Park, Calif.
Krawitz, Harris, 431 Oakdale Ave., Chicago, Ill.
Kreitlow, Burton W., Dept. of Educ., University of Wisconsin, Madison, Wis.
Kress, Roy A., 925 W. Onondaga St., Syracuse, N.Y.
Krich, Percy, Univ. of California at Santa Barbara, University, Calif.
Krippner, Stanley, R.R. No. 1, Fort Atkinson, Wis.
Kroenke, Richard G., Valparaiso University, Valparaiso, Ind.
Krug, Edward, Dept. of Educ., University of Wisconsin, Madison, Wis.
Kruszynski, Eugene S., 360 Lakeside St., Redlands, Calif.
Kubik, Edmund J., 9741 S. Leavitt St., Chicago, Ill.
Kugler, Mrs. Ida C., Aiyepe Girls High School, Aiyepe via Odogbolu, W. Nigeria
Kuhn, Joseph A., 99 Buffalo Ave., Long Beach, N.Y.
Kuhnen, Mrs. Mildred, 2106 Park Ave., Chico, Calif.
Kullman, N. E., Jr., 153 Murray Ave., Delmar, N.Y.
Kumpf, Carl H., Sch. of Educ., Rutgers University, New Brunswick, N.J.
Kunimoto, Mrs. Tadako, 734—16th Ave., Honolulu, Hawaii
Kurtz, John J., Inst. for Child Study, Univ. of Maryland, College Park, Md.
Kusmik, Cornell J., 7400 Augusta St., River Forest, Ill.
Kutz, Frederick B., Newark High School, Newark, Del.
Kvaraceus, W. C., Boston University, 332 Bay State Road, Boston, Mass.
Kyle, Helen F., Sch. of Educ., University of Colorado, Boulder, Colo.

Labaj, J. J., Creighton Prep. School, 7400 Western Ave., Omaha, Neb.
Lacy, David W., Wilkinson, Ind.
Lacy, Susan M., W-215 Eddy Ave., Spokane, Wash.
LaFauci, Horatio M., 688 Boylston St., Boston, Mass.
Lafferty, Charles W., P.O. Box 1250, Fairbanks, Alaska
Lafferty, H. M., East Texas State Teachers College, Commerce, Tex.
LaForce, Charles L., 426 Malden Ave., LaGrange Park, Ill.
Lafranchi, W. E., Stabley Library, State College, Indiana, Pa.
LaGrone, Herbert F., Texas Christian University, Fort Worth, Tex.
Laidlaw, John, Laidlaw Bros., Inc., River Forest, Ill.
Laird, Byron F., Indiana University, Jeffersonville, Ind.
Lake, Mrs. Doris S., 145 East St., Oneonta, N.Y.
Lamb, George S., Burton Hall, University of Minnesota, Minneapolis, Minn.

Lambert, Pierre D., Sch. of Educ., Boston College, Chestnut Hill, Mass.
Lambert, Ronald T., Col. of Educ., University of Hawaii, Honolulu, Hawaii
Lambert, Sam M., N.E.A., 1201 Sixteenth St., N.W., Washington, D.C.
Lammel, Rose, Wayne State University, Detroit, Mich.
Lampard, Dorothy M., University of Alberta, Edmonton, Alba., Canada
Lampkin, Richard H., 205 Fayette Ave., Kenmore, N.Y.
Land, Adelle H., Dept. of Educ., University of Buffalo, Buffalo, N.Y.
Landskov, N. L., Mississippi Southern College, Station A., Hattiesburg, Miss.
Lane, Mrs. Elizabeth Miller, 4390 Hyland Ave., Dayton, Ohio
Lane, Frank T., 42 St. Clair Dr., Delmar, N.Y.
Lane, John J., Coolidge Junior High School, Natick, Mass.
Lane, Mrs. Mary B., 10 Lundy's Lane, San Mateo, Calif.
Lane, Olive, Sydney Teachers College, Newtown, Sydney, New South Wales,
    Australia
Lane, Ulysses S., Box 10062, Southern University Br. P.O., Baton Rouge, La.
Lange, Lorraine, State University College of Education, Buffalo, N.Y.
Lange, Phil C., Tchrs. Col., Columbia University, New York, N.Y.
Langenbach, Louise, P.O. Box 710, Diamond Springs, Calif.
Langeveld, M. J., Prins Hendriklaan 6, Bilthoven, Holland
Langland, Lois E., 235 Montana Ave., Santa Monica, Calif.
Langman, Muriel Potter, 913 Congress St., Ypsilanti, Mich.
Langston, Roderick G., 1451 S. Loma Verde St., Monterey Park, Calif.
Lanham, Frank W., Sch. of Educ., University of Michigan, Ann Arbor, Mich.
Lankton, Robert S., Detroit Public Schls., 5057 Woodward, Detroit, Mich.
Lansu, Walter J., 6036 Metropolitan Plaza, Los Angeles, Calif.
Lant, Kenneth A., Jericho Public Schools, Jericho, L.I., N.Y.
Laramy, William J., Haverford Junior High School, Havertown, Pa.
Larkin, Joseph B., San Jose State College, San Jose, Calif.
Larkin, Lewis B., 15818 Westbrook, Detroit, Mich.
Larsen, Arthur Hoff, Illinois State Normal University, Normal, Ill.
Larsen, Jack L., St. Joseph High School, St. Joseph, Mich.
Larson, Clifford E., Bethel College, St. Paul, Minn.
Larson, Eleanor E., Educ. Bldg., University of Wisconsin, Madison, Wis.
Larson, L. C., Audio-Visual Center, Indiana University, Bloomington, Ind.
Larson, Rolf W., Sch. of Educ., Western Illinois University, Macomb, Ill.
Larson, Vera M., 1331 N.E. 111th Ave., Portland, Ore.
Lassanske, Paul A., 1013 S. Robertson, Tyler, Tex.
Lasseigne, Russell E., Thibodaux Upper Elementary School, Thibodaux, La.
Lathrop, Irvin T., Long Beach State College, Long Beach, Calif.
Laudico, Minerva G., Centro Escolar University, Manila, Philippines
Lauria, Joseph L., 6401 Shoup Ave., Canoga Park, Calif.
Laurier, Blaise V., Les Clercs de Saint-Viateur, Montreal, Quebec, Canada
Lautenschlager, Harley, Lab. School, Indiana State College, Terre Haute, Ind.
La Venture, Robert, Morristown High School, Morristown, N.J.
Lavelle, Robert J., Xavier University, Cincinnati, Ohio
Lavenburg, F. M., Public Schls., 155 Broad St., Bloomfield, N.J.
Law, L. E., Superintendent of Schools, Alliance, Ohio
Lawhead, Victor B., Ball State Teachers College, Muncie, Ind.
Lawler, Marcella R., APO 143, Box ND, Tem, American Embassy, San Francisco,
    Calif.
Lawrence, Mrs. Bessie F., LeMoyne School, 851 Waveland Ave., Chicago, Ill.
Lawrence, Clayton G., Marion College, Marion, Ind.
Lawrence, Richard E., AACTE, 1201 Sixteenth St., N.W., Washington, D.C.
Lawrence, Ruth E., Board of Educ., 620 South 10th St., Fargo, N.D.
Laws, Billy Clyde, 300 E. Idaho St., Seymour, Tex.
Lawski, A. J., Edsel Ford High School, 20601 Rotunda Dr., Dearborn, Mich.
Lawson, John H., Hingham Public Schls., 229 North St., Hingham, Mass.
Lazar, Alfred L., Division of Schools, Box 542, Balboa, Canal Zone
Lazarus, Arnold, Purdue University Station, Lafayette, Ind.
Lazow, Alfred, 138 Asbury, Evanston, Ill.
Leach, Kent W., Sch. of Educ., University of Michigan, Ann Arbor, Mich.

Leach, Marian E., 744 Albemarle St., El Cerrito, Calif.
Leamy, Cora M., Gardner Junior High School, Gardner, Mass.
Leary, Mrs. Olive D., 9101 W. Wisconsin Ave., Milwaukee, Wis.
Leavitt, Jerome E., Portland State College, Portland, Ore.
Lee, Dorris May, Portland State College, Portland, Ore.
Lee, Ernest C., Rainbow High School, Victoria, Australia
Lee, Harold Fletcher, Box 38, Lincoln University, Jefferson City, Mo.
Lee, Howard D., Atwater School, Shorewood, Wis.
Lee, J. Murray, Southern Illinois University, Carbondale, Ill.
Lee, James Michael, Dept. of Educ., St. Joseph College, West Hartford, Conn.
Lee, John J., Col. of Educ., Wayne State University, Detroit, Mich.
Lee, William C., Box 327, Tusculum College, Greeneville, Tenn.
Leeds, Don S., 954 Harrison Ave., Niagara Falls, N.Y.
Leeds, Willard L., P.O. Box 824, San Carlos, Calif.
Leese, Joseph, New York State College for Teachers, Albany, N.Y.
Leeseberg, Norbert H., 663 Manor Rd., Staten Island, N.Y.
Lefcourt, Ann, Anthony Apartments, Muncie, Ind.
Lefever, David Welty, 4251 Don Felipe Dr., Los Angeles, Calif.
* Lefforge, Roxy, 1945 Fruit St., Huntington, Ind.
L'Heureux, Leon, Jr., Superintendent of Schools, Foster Center, R.I.
Lehman, James, Dryden Hall, Northwestern University, Evanston, Ill.
Lehmann, Irvin J., Michigan State University, East Lansing, Mich.
Lehmann, William, Jr., Concordia Teachers College, River Forest, Ill.
Leib, Joseph A., 2416 Summit Ter., Linden, N.J.
Leibert, Robert, 16 Danes St., Blue Point, N.Y.
Leiman, Harold I., 526 Clinton Ave., Newark, N.J.
Leiner, Barbara, Pennsylvania State University, University Park, Pa.
Leland, Simeon E., Col. of L.A., Northwestern University, Evanston, Ill.
Lemke, Donald A., Dept. of Educ., Lawrence College, Appleton, Wis.
Lemons, Bonnie, 2314 Mariposa St., Fresno, Calif.
Lennon, Joseph L., Providence College, Providence, R.I.
Lennon, Lawrence J., 310 N. Webster Ave., Scranton, Pa.
Lensmire, Warren J., Wood County Teachers College, Wisconsin Rapids, Wis.
Lentz, Dorothy R., 1972 West 73rd Ave., Philadelphia, Pa.
Lepera, Alfred G., 33 Grenville Rd., Watertown, Mass.
LePere, Jean M., Michigan State University, East Lansing, Mich.
Lepthien, Emilie V., 4019 N. Long Ave., Chicago, Ill.
Lesh, Ethel P., 110 North 2nd St., Paterson, N.J.
Letson, Charles T., 315 Whitney Ave., New Haven, Conn.
Letson, John W., Superintendent of Schools, 224 Central Ave., Atlanta, Ga.
Levin, J. Joseph, 5142 S. Kimbark Ave., Chicago, Ill.
Levine, Stanley L., 158 S. Westgate, Los Angeles, Calif.
Levit, Martin, University of Kansas City, Kansas City, Mo.
Lewis, Arthur J., 5025 Garfield, So., Minneapolis, Minn.
Lewis, Edward R., 6254 Bernhard Ave., Richmond, Calif.
Lewis, Elizabeth V., University of Alabama Center, Mobile, Ala.
Lewis, Gertrude M., U.S. Office of Education, Dept. of H.E.W., Washington, D.C.
Lewis, Mrs. J. R., Batesville, Miss.
Lewis, Maurice S., Col. of Educ., Arizona State University, Tempe, Ariz.
Lewis, Philip, 6900 S. Crandon Ave., Chicago, Ill.
Lewis, Robert, 915 N. Union St., Natchez, Miss.
Lewis, Roland B., Eastern Washington State College, Cheney, Wash.
Leyton, Mario, 1318 E. Hyde Park Blvd., Chicago, Ill.
Libby, Mildred P., 7 Riverside Rd., Simsbury, Conn.
Lichty, E. A., Illinois State Normal University, Normal, Ill.
Lichty, John C., Paradise Township Elementary School, Paradise, Pa.
Light, Alfred B., 93 Bailey Ave., Plattsburgh, N.Y.
Ligon, Mary Gilbert, Hofstra College, Hempstead, N.Y.
Liljeblad, Maynard T., P.O. Box 1067, Hanford, Calif.
* Lincoln, Edward A., Thompson St., Halifax, Mass.

Lind, Arthur E., 1422 Johnston Ave., Richland, Wash.
Lindberg, Lucile, Queens College, Flushing, N.Y.
Lindeman, Richard H., Tchrs. Col., Columbia University, New York, N.Y.
Lindemann, Erich, Massachusetts General Hospital, Fruit St., Boston, Mass.
Lindgren, Henry Clay, 1975—15th Ave., San Francisco, Calif.
Lindley, Mrs. Esther C., Rea School, Hamilton and Meyer Pl., Costa Mesa, Calif.
Lindvall, C. Mauritz, Sch. of Educ., University of Pittsburgh, Pittsburgh, Pa.
Linehan, Mrs. Louise W., 4 Bolton Pl., Fair Lawn, N.J.
Linthicum, J. B., P.O. Box 1719, Albuquerque, N.M.
Lipham, James M., Dept. of Educ., University of Wisconsin, Madison, Wis.
Lippold, Paul C., 21 S. Smith St., Aurora, Ill.
Lipscomb, William A., Box 505, Wilder, Idaho
Lipsitz, Herbert J., Asst. Superintendent of Schls., Paterson, N.J.
Lisle, Mrs. H. G., 1559 Kinney Ave., Cincinnati, Ohio
Litin, Annette, 5218 North 18th Pl., Phoenix, Ariz.
Little, J. Kenneth, Bascom Hall, University of Wisconsin, Madison, Wis.
Little, Lawrence C., Cath. of Learn., Univ. of Pittsburgh, Pittsburgh, Pa.
Littlefield, Lucille J., State Teachers College, Indiana, Pa.
Litzky, Leo, 11 Pomona Ave., Newark, N.J.
Livingston, Mrs. Esta H., 1747—48th St., Brooklyn, N.Y.
Livingston, Thomas B., Box 4060, Texas Tech. Station, Lubbock, Tex.
Lizotte, Mrs. Oneita B., 126 N. East St., Medina, Ohio
Llewellyn, Mrs. Urban B., 743 Gumnock Rd., Olympia Fields, Ill.
Lloyd, Francis V., Jr., Superintendent of Schools, Clayton, Mo.
Lloyd-Jones, Esther, 525 West 120th St., New York, N.Y.
Lobdell, Lawrence O., Union Free School Dist. 30, Valley Stream, N.Y.
LoBuglio, Armand Steven, 24 Audrey Ct., Malverne, L.I., N.Y.
Lockett, B. T., 1848 Tiger Flowers Dr., N.W., Atlanta, Ga.
Lodeski, Frank J., 212 S. Harvey Ave., Oak Park, Ill.
Loew, Climmont C., 1733 North 76th Ct., Elmwood Park, Ill.
Lofgren, Mrs. Marie Luise S., 687 Cambridge, Santa Clara, Calif.
Logan, Jack M., Superintendent of Schools, 214 High St., Waterloo, Iowa
Logdeser, Mrs. Thomas, 11616 Woodview Blvd., Parma Heights, Ohio
Lohmann, Mrs. Ethel, R.D. No. 1, Monroeville, Ohio
Lohmann, Victor L., State Teachers College, St. Cloud, Minn.
Lomax, James L., Lomax Junior High School, Valdosta, Ga.
London, Jack, 2328 Derby St., Berkeley, Calif.
Long, F. P., Jr., R. D. No. 1, Valencia, Pa.
Long, Isabelle, 4343 Harriet Ave., S., Minneapolis, Minn.
Lonsdale, Mrs. Maxine deLappe, 1405 Campbell Lane, Sacramento, Calif.
Lonsdale, Richard C., 1339 Westmoreland Ave., Syracuse, N.Y.
Loomis, Arthur K., 400 S. Marion St., Denver, Colo.
Loomis, Chester M., 15443 Grandville, Detroit, Mich.
Looney, William F., State Teachers College, 625 Huntington Ave., Boston, Mass.
Loop, Alfred B., 2619 Franklin St., Bellingham, Wash.
Loree, M. Ray, Box 742, University of Alabama, University, Ala.
Lorenz, Donald Walter, Concordia College, 2811 N.E. Holman, Portland, Ore.
Loretan, Joseph O., Bd. of Educ., 110 Livingston St., Brooklyn, N.Y.
Lorusso, Rocco E., 2386 Knapp Dr., Rahway, N.J.
Loudon, Mrs. Mary Lou, 1408 Stephens Ave., Baton Rouge, La.
Loughlin, Leo J., 257 Rolfe Rd., DeKalb, Ill.
Loughrea, Mildred, 716 City Hall and Court House, St. Paul, Minn.
Lourie, Samuel, 185 Hall St., Brooklyn, N.Y.
Lovell, O. E., Jr., Dept. of Educ., Louisiana State Univ., New Orleans, La.
Lowe, A. J., University of Virginia, Charlottesville, Va.
Lowe, Alberta L., Col. of Educ., University of Tennessee, Knoxville, Tenn.
Lowe, Paul F., Southern Connecticut State College, New Haven, Conn.
Lowe, R. N., Sch. of Educ., University of Oregon, Eugene, Ore.
Lowe, William T., Stone Hall, Cornell University, Ithaca, N.Y.
Lowers, Virginia Belle, 322 N. Flores St., Los Angeles, Calif.
Lowes, Ruth, 2004 Seventh Ave., Canyon, Tex.

Lowry, Carmen, Huston-Tillotson College, Austin, Tex.
Lowry, V. A., General Beadle State Teachers College, Madison, S.D.
Lowther, William L., Superintendent of Schools, Glassboro, N.J.
Lubbock-Evans, Catherine, P.O. Box 57, Houston, Tex.
Lubell, Richard M., 2 Stoddard Pl., Brooklyn, N.Y.
Lucas, Ernest A. J., P.O. Box 842, St. Joseph's College, Collegeville, Ind.
Lucas, J. H., 121 Warren Ave., Oxford, N.C.
Lucas, Mrs. May, Oregon College of Education, Monmouth, Ore.
Lucash, Benjamin, 1219 Robbins Ave., Philadelphia, Pa.
Lucio, William H., Sch. of Educ., University of California, Los Angeles, Cailf.
Lucito, Leonard J., George Peabody College for Tchrs., Nashville, Tenn.
Luck, Thelma D., 3005 Clinton St., N.E., Washington, D.C.
Luckey, Bertha M., 1310 West 104th St., Cleveland, Ohio
Lucy, Herbert E., 1100 South 28th Ave., Hattiesburg, Miss.
Ludes, Titus H., Quincy College, Quincy, Ill.
Ludwig, Adela E., 2453 N. Grant Blvd., Milwaukee, Wis.
Luebke, Martin F., 1508 Whittier, Springfield, Ill.
Luecke, Mrs. Carl, 411 Sergeant Ave., Joplin, Mo.
Luhmann, Philip R., 5752 Maryland Ave., Chicago, Ill.
Luihn, Mrs. Martha Bruckner, 1027 N.E. Schuyler, Portland, Ore.
Lukas, John, Crestwood School, Northbrook, Ill.
Luke, Arno H., Colorado State College, Greeley, Colo.
Lund, S. E. Torsten, Haviland Hall, University of California, Berkeley, Calif.
Lundquest, Mrs. Alma, 422 Allegheny St., Boswell, Pa.
Lunney, Gerald H., 1070 E. County Rd. D., White Bear Lake, Minn.
Lunt, Robert, Superintendent, School Union Ten, Cape Elizabeth, Me.
Luther, Vincent A., Bishop Guilfoyle High School, Altoona, Pa.
Lutz, Frank W., 14824 Larchburr, Bridgeton, Mo.
Luvaas, Clarence B., 2326 Bever Ave., S.E., Cedar Rapids, Iowa
Lynch, James M., Superintendent of Schools, Rt. No. 9, East Brunswick, N.J.
Lynch, Katherine D., 224 East 28th St., New York, N.Y.
Lynch, Mary Elizabeth, 23 Winborough St., Mattapan, Boston, Mass.
Lynch, Patrick D., Hodgin Hall, University of Albuquerque, N.M.
Lynch, Viola M., 8329 S. Langley Ave., Chicago, Ill.
Lyons, Mrs. Cora E., 25 N. Jefferson St., Amboy, Ill.
Lyons, John H., Box 216, Thompsonville, Conn.
Lyons, John Wesley, 349 Angell St., Providence, R.I.

Maag, Raymond E., 3553 Hennepin Ave., Minneapolis, Minn.
Mabry, Mrs. Robert P., 1697 Oak St., Baldwin, N.Y.
Macbeth, Ruby, 69 Cannon St., Charleston, S.C.
MacGown, Paul C., 3128 N. Ash St., Spokane, Wash.
MacDonald, M. Gertrude, 78 Sheffield Rd., Melrose, Mass.
Mack, Esther, San Jose State College, San Jose, Calif.
Mackay, G. Gordon, 2121 Staunton Ct., Palo Alto, Calif.
* MacKay, James L., 2205 W. Mistletoe, San Antonio, Tex.
MacKay, Vera A., Col. of Educ., Univ. of British Columbia, Vancouver, B.C.
MacKay, William R., 4067 Wesley Way, El Sobrante, Calif.
Mackenzie, Donald M., Lindenwood College, St. Charles, Mo.
MacKenzie, Elbridge G., Anderson College, Anderson, Ind.
Mackenzie, Gordon N., Tchrs. Col., Columbia University, New York, N.Y.
Mackintosh, Helen K., U.S. Office of Education, Dept. of H.E.W., Washington, D.C.
MacVicar, Robert, Oklahoma State University, Stillwater, Okla.
Madden, Richard, Sonoma State College, Cotati, Calif.
Maddox, Clifford Rhea, Cedarville College, Cedarville, Ohio
Madore, Normand William, Illinois State Normal University, Normal, Ill.
Maehara, Oei, 3535 Pinao St., Honolulu, Hawaii
Magary, James F., University of Southern California, Los Angeles, Calif.
Magoon, Thomas M., 9521 Woodley Ave., Silver Spring, Md.
Mahar, Robert J., Col. of Educ., Wayne State University, Detroit, Mich.

Maher, Trafford P., St. Louis University, 15 N. Grand Blvd., St. Louis, Mo.
Maia, Celeste, 3244 Louise St., Oakland, Calif.
Mailey, James H., Midland Ind. School Dist., 702 North N St., Midland, Tex.
Mains, Mrs. Susie T., 4 Fern St., Auburn, Me.
Malan, Russell, Superintendent of Schools, Harrisburg, Ill.
Mallery, Adele, 801 Kirby Pl., Shreveport, La.
Mallery, Kenneth P., Superintendent of Schools, Centralia, Wash.
Mallory, Berenice, Office of Education, Dept. of H.E.W., Washington, D.C.
Malmquist, M. L., Superintendent, School Dist. 318, Grand Rapids, Minn.
Malone, James J., Sumner School, 715 S. Kildare Ave., Chicago, Ill.
Malone, James W., Diocese of Youngstown, 144 W. Wood St., Youngstown, Ohio
Maloof, Mitchell, 63 Main St., Williamstown, Mass.
Malsky, Stanley J., 85-09—167th St., Jamaica Hills, L.I., N.Y.
Mangum, G. C., P.O. Box 494, Darlington, S.C.
Manley, Francis J., Frontier Central Sch., Bay View Rd., Hamburg, N.Y.
Mann, Maxine, Eastern Illinois University, Charleston, Ill.
Mann, Vernal S., Box 266, State College, Miss.
Mannello, George, 26 Regis Pl., Hempstead, N.Y.
Manning, Edward, Superintendent of Schools, Pearl River, N.Y.
Manning, Harvey, 5305 Tilden Ave., Brooklyn, N.Y.
Manone, Carl, Abington Township Schools, Abington, Pa.
Mantor, Lyle E., State Teachers College, Kearney, Neb.
Manuel, Herschel T., University of Texas, Austin, Tex.
Manwiller, Lloyd V., Glassboro State College, Glassboro, N.J.
Mapes, Cecil S., 29 Payne Ave., Chatham, N.Y.
Mapes, Elmer S., Superintendent of Schools, East Weymouth, Mass.
Marable, Mrs. Florence, Spring Avenue School, 1001 Spring Ave., LaGrange, Ill.
Marburger, Carl L., 17430 Denby St., Detroit, Mich.
Marc-Aurele, Paul, 162 Marois Blvd., Laval-des-Rapids, Montreal, Quebec
Margolin, Mrs. Edythe, 12013 Rose Ave., Los Angeles, Calif.
Margolis, Isidor, Yeshiva University, 1495 Morris Ave., New York, N.Y.
Marinaccio, Anthony, Superintendent of Schools, Davenport, Iowa
Mark, Mrs. Retha D., Edmunds High School, Haynsworth St., Sumter, S.C.
Markarian, Robert E., Springfield College, Springfield, Mass.
Markle, David H., Ohio Northern University, Ada, Ohio
Marksberry, Mary Lee, Sch. of Educ., Univ. of Kansas City, Kansas City, Mo.
Marksheffel, Ned D., Oregon State University, Corvallis, Ore.
Marni, Mrs. Alma L., 202 Lafayette Circle, Cincinnati, Ohio
Marquis, Francis Norwood, Apartado Aereo 1689, Cali, Colombia, South America
Marquis, R. L., Jr., Box 5282, North Texas Station, Denton, Tex.
Marsden, W. Ware, 2217 West 5th St., Stillwater, Okla.
Marsh, Mrs. Augusta B., 30 Bronner Ave., Prichard, Ala.
Marsh, Marian, 616 Sheridan Ave., Nampa, Idaho
Marshall, B. F., Pleasantville Jt. Schools, Pleasantville, Pa.
Marshall, Beth, 1526 Catherine Dr., Anaheim, Calif.
Marshall, Daniel W., North Hall, Tufts University, Medford, Mass.
Marshall, Marvin L., 10121 Palms Blvd., Los Angeles, Calif.
Marshall, Thomas O., 2 Davis Ct., Durham, N.H.
Marshall, Wayne P., 2013—13th Ave., Kearney, Neb.
Marston, Mrs. Marjorie, 860 Lake Shore Dr., Chicago, Ill.
Martin, Edwin D., 2341 Quenby, Houston, Tex.
Martin, Elaine, 608 S. Norwood Ave., Green Bay, Wis.
Martin, Frieda, 2428½ Wabash, Terre Haute, Ind.
Martin, George Berry, Salem Public Schools, P.O. Box 87, Salem, Ore.
Martin, Ignatius A., Supt., Diocese of Lafayette, Drawer E., Lafayette, La.
Martin, Jackson J., 41 Ardmore Rd., Berkeley, Calif.
Martin, John Henry, Superintendent of Schools, Freeport, N.Y.
Martin, Kathryn J., 2208 Fairhill Ave., Glenside, Pa.
Martin, Mrs. Mary M., Gulf Coast Junior College, Panama City, Fla.
Martin, R. J., Ballard-Hudson Senior High School, Macon, Ga.
Martin, R. Lee, State University Teachers College, Oswego, N.Y.

Martin, William R., 320 N.W. 19th Ave., Fort Lauderdale, Fla.
Martini, Angiolina A., 2524 Benvenue Ave., Berkeley, Calif.
Martinson, Ruth A., 7614 Brunache, Downey, Calif.
Martire, Harriette A., Loyola University, New Orleans, La.
Martorana, Sebastian V., Office of Education, Dept. of H.E.W., Washington, D.C.
Marvin, John H., 101 Manchester, Arlington, Va.
Marvin, R. Paul, 208 Horticulture, Univ. of Minnesota, St. Paul, Minn.
Marzolf, Stanley S., Illinois State Normal University, Normal, Ill.
Masiko, Peter, Dade County Junior College, Miami, Fla.
Mason, George E., 138 Sims Rd., Syracuse, N.Y.
Mason, John M., Michigan State University, East Lansing, Mich.
Massey, William J., 427 University Blvd. E., Silver Spring, Md.
Massingill, Richard A., 15905 Harrison, Livonia, Mich.
Masters, Harry V., Albright College, Reading, Pa.
Masterson, John A., Selma Public Schools, 917 Lapsley St., Selma, Ala.
Mathews, C. O., Ohio Wesleyan University, Delaware, Ohio
Mathias, C. Wilbur, State Teachers College, Kutztown, Pa.
Mathias, John A., Moorefield High School, Moorefield, W.Va.
Mathiasen, O. F., Antioch College, Yellow Springs, Ohio
Mathis, Claude, Sch. of Educ., Northwestern University, Evanston, Ill.
Matson, Margaret G., 218 N. Dunlap St., St. Paul, Minn.
Matthew, Eunice Sophia, 860 West End Ave., New York, N.Y.
Matthews, Ethel B., Box 83, Bowling Green, Ky.
Mattila, Mrs. Ruth Hughes, 2702 E. Drachman St., Tucson, Ariz.
Mattison, Robert James, Plymouth Teachers College, Plymouth, N.H.
Matzner, G. C., Eastern Illinois University, Charleston, Ill.
Maucker, James William, State College of Iowa, Cedar Falls, Iowa
Mauk, Gertrude, 2880 S.W. First St., Ft. Lauderdale, Fla.
Mauk, Mrs. R. I., 623-A E. South Broadway, Lombard, Ill.
Maurer, Marion V., 1119 Bonnie Brae, River Forest, Ill.
Maurer, Robert L., California State Polytechnic College, Pomona, Calif.
Mauth, Leslie J., Ball State Teachers College, Muncie, Ind.
Maw, Wallace H., Sch. of Educ., University of Delaware, Newark, Del.
Maxwell, Ida E., Box 34, Cheyney, Pa.
May, John B., State Teachers College, Salisbury, Md.
Mayer, Lewis F., 4507 West 213th St., Cleveland, Ohio
Mayfield, L. B., Superintendent of Schools, 500 Monroe St., Medford, Ore.
Maziraz, Edward A., St. Joseph's College, Collegeville, Ind.
Mazyck, Harold E., Jr., 1521 Cunningham St., Greensboro, N.C.
McAbee, Harold V., Superintendent of Schools, LaGrande, Ore.
McAdam, J. E., State University of Iowa, Iowa City, Iowa
McAllister, David, USOM—Field, APO 205, New York, N.Y.
McArthur, L. C., Jr., Drawer 1191, Sumter, S.C.
McAuliffe, M. Eileen, 3251 Belle Plaine Ave., Chicago, Ill.
McBirney, Ruth, Boise Junior College, Boise, Idaho
McBride, James H., Superintendent of Schools, Norwalk, Ohio
McBride, William B., Ohio State University, Columbus, Ohio
McBurney, Mrs. Doris, 1641 West 105th St., Chicago, Ill.
McCaffrey, Austin J., Amer. Textbook Publ. Inst., 432 Fourth Ave., New York, N.Y.
McCain, Paul M., Arkansas College, Batesville, Ark.
McCallum, Gladys, 207 W. Wesley, Jackson, Mich.
McCann, Thomas W., 19 Jeffery Pl., Trumbull, Conn.
McCartin, William B., Superintendent, Catholic Schools, Tucson, Ariz.
McCartney, Hilda, 2916 Redwood Ave., Costa Mesa, Calif.
McCartney, Mrs. Virginia, Stonehouse Farm, R.F.D., Colon, Mich.
McCarty, Henry R., San Diego County Bd. of Educ., San Diego, Calif.
McClain, Warren J., Superintendent of Schools, Woodbury, N.J.
McClean, Donald E., P.O. Box 702, Menlo Park, Calif.
McClendon, LeRoy, Box 715, Stephen F. Austin Station, Nacogdoches, Tex.
McClintock, James A., Drew University, Madison, N.J.

McCluer, V. C., Superintendent of Schools, Ferguson, Mo.
McClure, L. Morris, Col. of Educ., Univ. of Maryland, College Park, Md.
McClure, Robert M., 22838 Epsilon St., Woodland Hills, Calif.
McClurkin, W. D., George Peabody College for Teachers, Nashville, Tenn.
McClusky, Howard Yale, Elem. Sch., University of Michigan, Ann Arbor, Mich.
McCollum, Elinor C., 619 Ridge Ave., Evanston, Ill.
McConnell, Gaither, 254 Pine St., New Orleans, La.
McConnell, John C., Windward School, Inc., White Plains, N.Y.
McConnell, T. R., Center for Study of Higher Educ., Univ. of Calif., Berkeley,
    Calif.
McCook, T. Joseph, 32 Spring St., Springfield, Mass.
McCorkle, C. Howard, Superintendent of Schools, Johnson City, Tenn.
McCrimmon, James M., Altgeld Hall, University of Illinois, Urbana, Ill.
McCue, L. H., Jr., E. C. Glass High School, Lynchburg, Va.
McCue, Robert E., 715½ W. Locust St., Davenport, Iowa
McCullen, John M., Route 1, Box 519, Mound, Minn.
McCullough, Constance M., San Francisco State College, San Francisco, Calif.
McCully, Clyde C., Antelope Valley College, Lancaster, Calif.
McCurdy, Charles M., 933 S.W. Avenue B., Belle Glade, Fla.
McDaniel, Ernest D., Univ. Test. Service, Univ. of Kentucky, Lexington, Ky.
McDavit, H. W., South Orange-Maplewood Public Schools, South Orange, N.J.
McDermott, John C., 165 Chapel Road, Manhasset, N.Y.
McDonald, Arthur S., Reading Center, Marquette University, Milwaukee, Wis.
McDonald, L. R., Woodruff Senior High School, Peoria, Ill.
McElroy, Mrs. Kathryn Mohr, Kensington Foundry Rd., Arlington Heights, Ill.
McEwen, Colin, 1776 N. Highland Ave., Hollywood, Calif.
McEwen, Gordon B., 545 E. Walnut St., Whittier, Calif.
McFarland, Donald F., Jr., Wayne State University, Detroit, Mich.
McFeaters, Margaret M., 608 Brown's Lane, Pittsburgh, Pa.
McGavern, John H., Hillyer College Library, 315 Hudson St., Hartford, Conn.
McGeoch, Dorothy M., Tchrs. Col., Columbia University, New York, N.Y.
McGinnis, Frederick A., Wilberforce University, P.O. Box 22, Wilberforce, Ohio
McGinnis, James H., Univ. Apts. E-01, Indiana University, Bloomington, Ind.
McGlasson, Maurice A., Sch. of Educ., Indiana University, Bloomington, Ind.
McGrath, Earl J., 525 West 120th St., New York, N.Y.
McGrath, G. D., Col. of Educ., Arizona State University, Tempe, Ariz.
McGuire, George K., 7211 Merrill Ave., Chicago, Ill.
McGuire, J. Carson, Col. of Educ., University of Texas, Austin, Tex.
McHugh, Walter J., Alameda County State College, Hayward, Calif.
McIlfatrick, Mrs. Edna M., 130 Walnut St., Paterson, N.J.
McInerney, George K., 88-42—210th St., Jamaica, N.Y.
McIntire, Imogene, Pennsylvania State University, University Park, Pa.
McIntosh, Lucy J., McNeil Hall, University of Minnesota, St. Paul, Minn.
McIntosh, William Ray, Superintendent of Schools, Rockford, Ill.
McIntyre, Richmond E., 809 Carver St., Burlington, N.C.
McIsaac, John S., 2829 Fourth Ave., Beaver Falls, Pa.
McKay, Jean W., Board of Education, Manassas, Va.
McKean, Robert C., Col. of Educ., University of Colorado, Boulder, Colo.
McKee, Richard C., Ball State Teachers College, Muncie, Ind.
McKelpin, Joseph P., Southern University Laboratory School, Baton Rouge, La.
McKenna, John J., Superintendent, Princeton Twp. Schls., Princeton, N.J.
McKenney, James L., Grad. Sch. of Business, Harvard Univ., Boston, Mass.
McKenzie, Francis W., Board of Educ., 1025 Post Rd., Darien, Conn.
McKercher, Mrs. Berneth N., 1600 Dryden Rd., Metamora, Mich.
McKillop, Anne S., Tchrs. Col., Columbia University, New York, N.Y.
McKinley, Mrs. Elva, 219 Oak St., Fond du Lac, Wis.
McKinley, S. Justus, Emerson College, 130 Beacon St., Boston, Mass.
* McKinney, James, American School, Drexel Ave. and 58th St., Chicago, Ill.
McKinney, Lorella A., 504 Eastmoor Blvd., Columbus 9, Ohio
McKown, George W., 2603 S. Forest Ave., Palatine, Ill.
McKune, Esther J., State University Teachers College, Oneonta, N.Y.

McLaren, Dallas C., 3240 Manoa Rd., Honolulu, Hawaii
McLaughlin, Kenneth F., 871 N. Madison, Arlington, Va.
McLaughlin, Rita E., 242 Marlborough St., Boston, Mass.
McLean, Harvard W., 1100 Finkbine Park, Iowa City, Iowa
McLean, Mary Cannon, 909 Roosevelt Rd., Springfield, Mass.
McLendon, Jonathon C., Sch. of Educ., Northwestern Univ., Evanston, Ill.
McMahan, F. J., St. Ambrose College, 518 W. Locust St., Davenport, Iowa
McMahan, John Julia, State Univ. of Agric., Engr., and Sci., State College, N.M.
McMahon, Charles W., 22439 Gregory, Dearborn, Mich.
McMahon, Edna T., Bennett Sch., 10115 S. Prairie Ave., Chicago, Ill.
McMahon, Frances E., 6233A Loran, St. Louis, Mo.
McManamon, James, Quincy College, Quincy, Ill.
McManus, William E., Supt. of Catholic Schls., 205 Wacker Dr., Chicago, Ill.
McMaster, Blanche E., 102 Hull St., Bristol, Conn.
McMath, James G., Box 3912, Odessa, Tex.
McMillan, Linda Lee, Arizona State University, Tempe, Ariz.
McMillian, Nathaniel B., 242 Tarragona Way, Daytona Beach, Fla.
McMullen, Charles B., Sakonnet Point Rd., Little Compton, R.I.
McMurtrey, Violet, 3365 S.W. 103rd, Beaverton, Ore.
McNally, Harold J., Teachers Col., Columbia University, New York, N.Y.
McNally, Wayne W., N. Bishop Junior High School, Providence, R.I.
McNamee, L. V., Waco Independent School Dist., P.O. Drawer 27, Waco, Tex.
McNeil, Alvin J., P.O. Box 66, Grambling, La.
McNelis, Francis A., Supt., Diocesan Schools, 1406—12th Ave., Altoona, Pa.
McNutt, C. R., 116 Ridge Rd., Woodbridge, Va.
McPheeters, Alphanso A., Clark College, Atlanta, Ga.
McPherson, Virgil L., Adams State College, Alamosa, Colo.
McPherson, W. N., Darke County Superintendent of Schools, Greenville, Ohio
McSharry, John T., Vailsburg High School, Newark, N.J.
McSwain, E. T., Sch. of Educ., Northwestern University, Evanston, Ill.
McTeer, Blanche R., 1705 Bay St., Beaufort, S.C.
McWilliams, Earl M., Winchester-Thurston Sch., 4721—5th Ave., Pittsburgh, Pa.
* Mead, Arthur R., 1719 N.W. 6th Ave., Gainesville, Fla.
Meador, Bruce, Arizona State University, Tempe, Ariz.
Mease, Clyde D., Superintendent of Schools, Humboldt, Iowa
Mecham, George P., Texas Technological College, Lubbock, Tex.
Meder, Elsa M., 176 Marlborough St., Boston, Mass.
Medsker, Leland L., Ctr., Study of Higher Educ., Univ. of Calif., Berkeley, Calif.
Medved, A. A., Cherry Lawn School, Darien, Conn.
Meer, Samuel J., 631 Lafayette Ave., Mt. Vernon, N.Y.
Meier, Frederick A., State Teachers College, Salem, Mass.
Meissner, Harley W., 13 Devonshire, Pleasant Ridge, Mich.
Melberg, Merritt E., 1222 W. 22nd St., Cedar Falls, Iowa
Melby, Ernest O., Michigan State University, East Lansing, Mich.
Mellott, Malcolm E., Prentice-Hall, Inc., P.O. Box 900, Englewood Cliffs, N.J.
Melnick, Curtis C., Supt., Dist. 14, Chicago Public Schls., Chicago, Ill.
Melnik, Amelia, Col. of Educ., University of Arizona, Tucson, Ariz.
Melnyk, Maria, 4432 S. Christiana Ave., Chicago, Ill.
Melvin, Keith L., Peru State College, Peru, Neb.
Mendenhall, Alan D., 5205 Sunny Point Pl., Palos Verdes, Calif.
Mendenhall, C. B., Col. of Educ., Ohio State University, Columbus, Ohio
Mendoza, Romulo Y., 17 Iba, Sta. Mesa Heights, Quezon City, Philippines
Menge, Carleton P., University of New Hampshire, Durham, N.H.
Menge, Joseph W., Wayne University, Detroit, Mich.
Meno, Lionel, 291 E. First St., Corning, N.Y.
Merchant, Vasant V., 1629—6th St., S.E., Minneapolis, Minn.
Meredith, Cameron W., Southwestern Illinois Campus, Alton, Ill.
Merenda, Peter F., 258 Negansett Ave., Warwick, R.I.
Merideth, Howard V., Central Sch. Dist. No. 2, Syosset, L.I., N.Y.
Merkle, Paul M., Phoenixville Area High School, Phoenixville, Pa.
Merkley, Marion G., 440 E. First St., South, Salt Lake City, Utah

Merrill, Dale O., 1002 N. Indian Hill Blvd., Claremont, Calif.
Merritt, C. B., Col. of Educ., Univ. of Arizona, Tucson, Ariz.
Merritt, Frances L., Div. of Educ., Howard Payne College, Brownwood, Tex.
Merry, Mrs. Frieda Kiefer, 2108 Kanawha Ave., S.E., Charleston, W.Va.
Mersand, Joseph, Jamaica High Sch., 168th St. and Gothic Dr., Jamaica, N.Y.
Metcalf, Harold H., Bloom Township High School, Chicago Heights, Ill.
Metzner, William, John B. Stetson Junior High School, Philadelphia, Pa.
Meyer, Ammon B., Route 1, Fredericksburg, Pa.
Meyer, George A., University of Hawaii, Honolulu, Hawaii
Meyer, Lorraine V., 4501 N. 41st St., Milwaukee, Wis.
Meyer, Mrs. Marie, Douglass Col., Rutgers Univ., New Brunswick, N.J.
Meyer, Warren G., 5829 Portland Ave., So., Minneapolis, Minn.
Meyer, William T., Adams State College, Alamosa, Colo.
Meyers, Max B., 324 E. 59th St., Brooklyn, N.Y.
Michael, Calvin B., Col. of Educ., East. Mich. Univ., Ypsilanti, Mich.
Michael, Lloyd S., Evanston Township High School, Evanston, Ill.
Michael, Lois, 10967 Roebling Ave., Los Angeles, Calif.
Michaelis, John U., Sch. of Educ., Univ. of California, Berkeley, Calif.
Micheels, William J., Stout State College, Menomonie, Wis.
Michelson, John M., Sch. of Educ., Temple University, Philadelphia, Pa.
Mickelson, I. T., Superintendent of Schools, Austin, Minn.
Middleton, Mildred L., 1944 Park Ave., S.E., Cedar Rapids, Iowa
Middleton, Ray F., 327 Ashbourne Rd., Elkins Park, Pa.
Miles, Arnold A., 11500 Hamilton Ave., Detroit, Mich.
Miles, Mrs. V. G., Baylor Station, Belton, Tex.
Milheim, Robert Porter, 925 Cedar Dr., Oxford, Ohio
Millar, Allen R., Mankato State College, Mankato, Minn.
Miller, Arthur L., 5625 Rosa Ave., St. Louis, Mo.
Miller, Benjamin, 251 Ft. Washington Ave., New York, N.Y.
Miller, Carroll H., Dept. of Educ., Northern Illinois Univ., DeKalb, Ill.
Miller, Carroll L., Howard University, Washington, D.C.
Miller, Charles, 1 Essex Ave., Maplewood, N.J.
Miller, Doris I., Sch. of Nursing, University of California, San Francisco, Calif.
Miller, Edna Caroline, Univ. of Kentucky, North Ctr., Covington, Ky.
Miller, Ethel Beryl, Box 332, Peabody College, Nashville, Tenn.
Miller, G. Harold, Gastonia City Schools, Gastonia, N.C.
Miller, George E., Univ. of Illinois Col. of Medicine, Chicago, Ill.
Miller, Harold E., Westmont College, Santa Barbara, Calif.
Miller, Mrs. Helen H., 1471 Westhaven Rd., San Marino, Calif.
Miller, Henry, Sch. of Educ., City College of New York, New York, N.Y.
Miller, Howard G., North Carolina State College, Raleigh, N.C.
Miller, Ingrid O., Edina-Morningside Senior High School, Edina, Minn.
Miller, Ira E., Eastern Mennonite College, Harrisonburg, Va.
Miller, Mrs. Ivy, 4280 Van Slyke Rd., Flint, Mich.
Miller, Mrs. J. Winona, 1961 Center St., Salem, Ore.
Miller, Jack W., Div. of Surveys, Peabody College, Nashville, Tenn.
Miller, Jacob W., Brooke Rd., Saybrooke Park, Pottstown, Pa.
Miller, John L., 345 Lakeville Rd., Great Neck, N.Y.
Miller, Leon F., Northwest Missouri State College, Maryville, Mo.
Miller, Lyle L., Col. of Educ., University of Wyoming, Laramie, Wyo.
Miller, Mrs. Mildred T., Box 215, Mooresville, N.C.
Miller, Paul A., Superintendent of Schools, Omaha, Neb.
Miller, Ralph, Superintendent of Schools, Georgetown, Ill.
Miller, Ward I., Board of Public Education, 511 W. 8th St., Wilmington, Del.
Millhollen, Lloyd F., Board of Education, Dist. No. 4, Eugene, Ore.
Millikin, R. M., 301 South State St., Geneseo, Ill.
Milling, Euleas, 227 N. Spring St., Concord, N.C.
Mills, Charles L., Superintendent of Schools, Box 2017, Hobbs, N.M.
Mills, Donna M., 530 Taft Place, Gary, Ind.
Mills, Forrest L., Racine Public Library, Racine, Wis.
Mills, Henry C., University of Rochester, Rochester, N.Y.

Mills, Marjorie F., Flower Vocational High School, Chicago, Ill.
Mills, Robert E., Mills Center, 1512 E. Broward Blvd., Fort Lauderdale, Fla.
Mills, William H., Univ. School, Univ. of Michigan, Ann Arbor, Mich.
Milner, Ernest J., Sch. of Educ., Syracuse University, Syracuse, N.Y.
Miner, George D., 1108 Bissel Ave., Richmond, Calif.
Miniclier, Gordon E., 1965 Laurel Ave., St. Paul, Minn.
Minnis, Roy B., U.S. Office of Education, Dept. of H.E.W., Washington, D.C.
Minock, Mrs. Daniel F., 5520 Donna Ave, Tarzana, Calif.
Minogue, Mildred M., 612 Ridge Ave., Evanston, Ill.
Misner, Paul J., Superintendent, Glencoe Public Schools, Glencoe, Ill.
Mitchell, Donald P., 58 Woodridge Rd., Wayland, Mass.
Mitchell, Guy Clifford, Dept. of Educ., Mississippi College, Clinton, Miss.
Mitchell, Mrs. Leona, 3310 S.W. 192nd St., Aloha, Ore.
Mitchell, Mrs. Marian A., 1331 Bernard St., N.W., Atlanta, Ga.
Mitchell, Mary Frances, 9305 Ewing Dr., Bethesda, Md.
Mitchell, Ronald, Burton Hall, University of Minnesota, Minneapolis, Minn.
Mitzel, Harold E., 928 S. Sparks St., State College, Pa.
Mobley, M. D., 1010 Vermont Ave., N.W., Washington, D.C.
Modiste, Charles J., 3221 Southmore Blvd., Houston, Tex.
Moffatt, Maurice P., Montclair State College, Upper Montclair, N.J.
Moffitt, John C., Superintendent of Schools, Box 309, Provo, Utah
Mohney, Mary, DuBois Central Junior High School, Falls Creek, Pa.
Mohr, Raymond E., 2050 South 108th St., Milwaukee, Wis.
Mohr, Robert L., University of Tampa, Tampa, Fla.
Molenkamp, Alice, 5 Homeside Lane, White Plains, N.Y.
Moll, Boniface E., St. Benedict's College, Atchison, Kan.
Monahan, Belle, 3114 W. Edgerton Rd., Cuyahoga Falls, Ohio
Monell, Ira H., 2714 Augusta Blvd., Chicago, Ill.
Monell, Ralph P., Superintendent of Schools, Canon City, Colo.
Mongon, John E., Superintendent of Schools, Levittown, N.J.
Monroe, Blythe F., 22311—3rd Ave., South Laguna, Calif.
Monroe, Charles R., Wilson Junior College, 6800 S. Stewart Ave., Chicago, Ill.
Monroe, Shelby H., Georgia Southern College, Statesboro, Ga.
Montean, John J., Col. of Educ., University of Rochester, N.Y.
Montesano, Edmund J., Carteret School No. 6, Bloomfield, N.J.
Montgomery, John F., Greenbrier College, Lewisburg, W.Va.
Montz, Doyle F., 2532 Sierra Way, LaVerne, Calif.
Moore, Alexander M., 1140 Northwest St., Indianapolis, Ind.
Moore, Arnold J., Dept. of Educ., Creighton University, Omaha, Neb.
Moore, Cecil L., 1704 E. 14th St., Austin, Tex.
Moore, Clyde B., Sch. of Educ., Cornell University, Ithaca, N.Y.
Moore, Fletcher, Dept. of Fine Arts, Box 313, Elon College, N.C.
Moore, H. Kenton, Arkansas A. & M. College, College Heights, Ark.
Moore, Harold E., Superintendent of Schools, Littleton, Colo.
Moore, Hollis A., Jr., Col. of Educ., University of Arizona, Tucson, Ariz.
Moore, Mrs. Patricia S., 2119 Guilford Rd., Hyattsville, Md.
Moore, Robert Ezra, 26 Bercareli Dr., San Francisco, Calif.
Moore, W. J., Eastern Kentucky State College, Richmond, Ky.
Moore, Wilhelmina E., C. D. Hine Library, State Office Bldg., Hartford, Conn.
Moorhead, Sylvester A., Sch. of Educ., Univ. of Mississippi, University, Miss.
Moran, John F., Pittsfield, Mass.
Moreau, Jules L., Seabury-Western Theological Seminary, Evanston, Ill.
Morehead, Charles G., North Carolina State College, Raleigh, N.C.
Moreland, Kenneth O., Box 119, McLean, Ill.
Moreskine, Wallace R., 7802 Burns Ct., El Cerrito, Calif.
Moretz, Elmo E., Col. of Educ., Univ. of Southern Florida, Tampa, Fla.
Morgan, Raymond W., 1110 Milford St., Johnstown, Pa.
Morgan, Roland R., Superintendent, Mooresville City Schls., Mooresville, N.C.
Morgenstern, Mrs. Anne, 2037 Olivia Way, Merrick, L.I., N.Y.
Moriarty, Margaret C., 1220 Powderhorn Ter., Minneapolis, Minn.
Moriarity, Mary J., 57 Spring Hill Ave., Bridgewater, Mass.

Morley, Franklin P., 597 Harper Ave., Webster Groves, Mo.
Moroney, Joseph P., Col. of Arts and Sciences, Duquesne Univ., Pittsburgh, Pa.
Morris, Harold W., Dept. of Educ., University of Portland, Portland, Ore.
Morris, James L., 577 W. College St., Yellow Springs, Ohio
Morris, M. B., 1133 Westridge, Abilene, Tex.
Morris, Mrs. Marjorie S., 16225 Moorpark, Encino, Calif.
Morrison, Coleman, 32 Hillcrest Circle, Watertown, Mass.
Morrison, D. A., East York Bd. of Educ., 670 Cosburn Ave., Toronto, Ont.
* Morrison, J. Cayce, 13 Cherry Tree Rd., Loudonville, N.Y.
Morrison, Leger R., 16 Brown St., Warren, R.I.
Morrison, Louis E., Superintendent of Schools, Alliance, Neb.
Morrison, Robert H., 16 Farm Rd., Trenton, N.J.
Morse, Horace T., Nicholson Hall, University of Minnesota, Minneapolis, Minn.
Morse, Richard N., 16154 Via Lupine, San Lorenzo, Calif.
Morton, Harold L., Cowen High School, Cowen, W.Va.
Morton, R. Clark, 210 Drummond St., Wattensburg, Mo.
Mosbo, Alvin O., Colorado State College, Greeley, Colo.
Moseley, S. Meredith, 424 N.W. 15th Way, Fort Lauderdale, Fla.
Moser, William G., 95 Concord Rd., Chester, Pa.
Moses, Morgan, 310 Garland Ave., Garland, Tex.
Mosher, Frank K., 2 Haskell Ave., Suffern, N.Y.
Mosier, Earl E., 28 Woodhampton Dr., Trenton, N.J.
Moss, Theodore C., 88 Sixth Ave., Oswego, N.Y.
Mother Anne Martina, St. Joseph Provincial House, Crookston, Minn.
Mother Beth Nothomb, San Francisco Col. for Women, San Francisco, Calif.
Mother Margaret Burke, Barat Col. of the Sacred Heart, Lake Forest, Ill.
Mother Marie Louise Martinez, Duchesne College, Omaha, Neb.
Mother Mary Aimee Rossi, San Diego Col. for Women, San Diego, Calif.
Mother M. Gonzaga, Blessed Sacrament College, Cornwells Heights, Pa.
Mother M. Gregory, Marymount College, Palos Verdes Estates, Calif.
Mother Mary Inez, Dept. of Educ., Holy Family College, Manitowoc, Wis.
Mother M. Irene Cody, Marymount College, 331 E. 71st., New York, N.Y.
Mother Mary McQueeny, Duchesne College, Omaha, Neb.
Mother St. Lawrence, Rosemont College, Rosemont, Pa.
Mother St. Rita Marie, Notre Dame College, Staten Island, N.Y.
Motyka, Agnes L., 6311 Utah Ave., N.W., Washington, D.C.
Moulton, Gerald L., 600 S. Ruby St., Ellensburg, Wash.
Moyer, James H., Pennsylvania State University, University Park, Pa.
Muck, Mrs. Ruth E. S., 1091 Stony Point Rd., Grand Island, N.Y.
Mudge, Evelyn L., Box 842, Hood College, Frederick, Md.
Muellen, T. K., 3606 Spruell Dr., Silver Spring, Md.
Mulhern, Joseph C., Spring Hill College, Mobile, Ala.
Muller, Philippe, Reulle Dofeyronz, Neuchatel, Switzerland
Mulliner, John H., 1885 Willow Hill Ct., Northfield, Ill.
Mulrooney, Thomas W., Board of Public Education, Wilmington, Del.
Mulroy, Mary D., South Shore High School, 7627 S. Constance, Chicago, Ill.
Mulry, Verna, 701 Dopp St., Waukesha, Wis.
Muns, Arthur C., Superintendent of Schools, Sycamore, Ill.
Munshaw, Carroll, 555 Byron St., Plymouth, Mich.
Munster, T., 2219 N. Kenmore Ave., Chicago, Ill.
Muntyan, Milosh, Michigan State University, East Lansing, Mich.
Murdick, Olin J., Superintendent, Diocesan Schools, Saginaw, Mich.
Murdock, Mrs. Ruth, Andrews University, Berrien Springs, Mich.
Murphy, Anne P., 1909 Dahlia St., Denver, Colo.
Murphy, Mrs. Carol M., 1117 McDaniel St., Evanston, Ill.
Murphy, Daniel A., Seton Hall University, South Orange, N.J.
Murphy, Forrest W., Sch. of Educ., University of Mississippi, University, Miss.
Murphy, Helen A., Boston University, 332 Bay State Rd., Boston, Mass.
Murphy, John A., 21-10—33rd Rd., Long Island City, N.Y.
Murphy, Loretta, 303 Lime St., Joliet, Ill.
Murray, Beatrice E., 40335 Pacific St., Fremont, Calif.

Murray, C. Merrill, State University Col. of Educ., Geneseo, N.Y.
Murray, Robert E., 1916 S. Signal Hill Dr., Kirkwood, Mo.
Myer, Marshall E., Jr., 2329 S. Rose St., Kalamazoo, Mich.
Myers, Donald A., Pattonville R-3 School Dist., St. Ann, Mo.
Myers, Garry Cleveland, 968 Main St., Honesdale, Pa.

Nafziger, Mary K., Goshen College, Goshen, Ind.
Nagel, Roberta F., 3207—54th St., Moline, Ill.
Nagel, Wilma I., 1849 Warwick Ave., Warwick, R.I.
Nagle, Robert J., 289 Rock St., Fall River, Mass.
Nagy, Richard, North Junior High School, Bloomfield, N.J.
Nahm, Helen, Sch. of Nursing, University of Calif., Med. Center, San Francisco,
    Calif.
Nahshon, Samuel, Bureau of Jewish Educ., 2030 S. Taylor Rd., Cleveland, Ohio
Nally, Thomas P., University of Rhode Island, Kingston, R.I.
Nance, Mrs. Afton Dill, State Educ. Bldg., 721 Capitol Ave., Sacramento, Calif.
Nance, Helen M., 6 Donna Dr., Normal, Ill.
Nardelli, Robert, Campus Lab. Sch., San Diego State Col., San Diego, Calif.
Narkis, William F., 4921 W. Ferdinand St., Chicago, Ill.
Naslund, Robert A., Sch. of Educ., Univ. of So. California, Los Angeles, Calif.
Nason, Doris E., University of Connecticut, Storrs, Conn.
Nason, Leslie J., 216 Euclid Ave., Long Beach, Calif.
Nasser, Sheffield, Sarasota County Schls., 2405 Hatton St., Sarasota, Fla.
Nault, William H., Field Enterprises Educational Corp., Chicago, Ill.
Naus, Grant, 911 Seventh St., Coronado Unified Schl. Dist., Coronado, Calif.
Neal, Mrs. Bernice E., 7510 Richmond Dr., Omaha, Neb.
Neale, Daniel C., Col. of Educ., University of Minnesota, Minneapolis, Minn.
Nees, Ruth, 1220 N. Reymond St., Las Cruces, N.M.
Neff, Laura, Hotel Albert, Albert Lea, Minn.
Neiderhiser, F. J., Superintendent of Schools, McClure, Ohio
Nelligan, William J., Sch. of Educ., St. John's University, Jamaica, N.Y.
Nelson, Carl B., New York State University College, Cortland, N.Y.
Nelson, Edith I., 8 Waterford St., Edinboro, Pa.
Nelson, Ethel C., 692 Des Plaines Ave., Des Plaines, Ill.
Nelson, Florence A., Univ. of South Carolina, 825 Sumter St., Columbia, S.C.
Nelson, Harvey D., 1473 Queen City Ave., Tuscaloosa, Ala.
Nelson, John M., Dept. of Educ., Purdue University, Lafayette, Ind.
Nelson, Kenneth G., 511 Glasgow Rd., Alexandria, Va.
Nelson, Mrs. Lois Ney, 13506 Rye St., Sherman Oaks, Calif.
Nelson, Margaret B., State College of Iowa, Cedar Falls, Iowa
Nelson, Orville W., Route No. 1, Stanchfield, Minn.
Nelson, Pearl Astrid, Boston University, 332 Bay State Rd., Boston, Mass.
Nelson, Sylvia, 415 W. 8th St.,Topeka, Kans.
Nemzek, Claude L., Univ. of Detroit, 4133 W. McNichols Rd., Detroit, Mich.
Nerbovig, Marcella, Northern Illinois University, DeKalb, Ill.
Nesi, Carmella, 906 Peace St., Pelham Manor, N.Y.
Netsky, Martin G., Dept. of Path., University of Virginia, Charlottesville, Va.
Neuner, Elsie Flint, 2 Atlas Place, Mt. Vernon, N.Y.
Neville, Donald, Child Study Center, Peabody College, Nashville, Tenn.
Newman, Herbert M., Educ. Dept., Brooklyn College, Brooklyn, N.Y.
Newman, Louis, Milton Res. Ctr., 3080 Broadway, New York, N.Y.
Newsom, A. Carolyn, Louisiana State University, Baton Rouge, La.
Newsom, Herman A., P.O. Box 5243, North Texas Station, Denton, Tex.
Newton, Eunice S., Howard University, Washington, D.C.
Niblock, W. Howard, Winchester Senior High School, Winchester, Mass.
Nicholas, William T., 609 Nevada St., Susanville, Calif.
Nichols, J. Herbert, Frankfort, Del.
Nicholson, Alice, 1009 E. Hatton St., Pensacola, Fla.
Nicholson, Lawrence E., Harris Teachers Col., 5351 Enright Ave., St. Louis, Mo.
Niehaus, Philip C., Sch. of Educ., Duquesne University, Pittsburgh, Pa.
Niemeyer, John H., Bank Street College of Education, New York, N.Y.

Nigg, William J., Superintendent of Schools, Litchfield, Minn.
Nikoloff, Sayra B., 234 Woodmere Dr., Tonawanda, N.Y.
Niland, William P., 1858 Tacoma Ave., Berkeley, Calif.
Nimroth, William T., Sch. of Educ., Stanford University, Stanford, Calif.
Nix, J. Gordon, Jr., Harlingen Senior High School, Harlingen, Tex.
Nixon, Arne John, Dept. of Educ., Fresno State College, Fresno, Calif.
Nixon, Clifford L., East Carolina College, Greenville, N.C.
Nixon, John Erskine, Sch. of Educ., Stanford University, Stanford, Calif.
Nixon, W. D., Sch. of Educ., Univ. of South Carolina, Columbia, S.C.
Noar, Gertrude, 195 Adams St., Brooklyn, N.Y.
Noe, Samuel V., 506 West Hill St., Louisville, Ky.
Noll, Frances E., 1810 Taylor St., N.W., Washington, D.C.
Noll, Victor H., Col. of Educ., Michigan State Univ., East Lansing, Mich.
Nonnamaker, Eldon R., 153 Student Services Bldg., East Lansing, Mich.
Noonan, Joseph D., Jr., 34 Holden St., Worcester, Mass.
Norcross, Claude E., 301 E. Lucard, Taft, Calif.
Nordberg, H. Orville, Sacramento State College, Sacramento, Calif.
Norem, Grant M., State Teachers College, Minot, N.D.
Norman, Ralph Paul, 18395 Clemison Ave., Saratoga, Calif.
Norman, Robert H., 315—4th Ave., N.W., Faribault, Minn.
Norris, Forbes H., Supt. of Schools, Briarcliff Manor, Westchester County, N.Y.
Norris, Ralph C., 216 S.W. First St., Des Moines, Iowa
Northey, Ethel May, 224 Iowa Ave., Muscatine, Iowa
Northrup, Sunbeam Ann, Off. of Supt. of Sch. Dist. VI, c/o USAREUR (rear)
    Com. Z, APO 58, New York, N.Y.
Norwick, Mrs. Terese D., 1820 Page Ave., East Cleveland, Ohio
Nosofsky, William, Junior High School 178, 2163 Dean St., Brooklyn, N.Y.
Now, H. O., Findlay College, Findlay, Ohio
Nowell, Mrs. Lillian D., 2500—25th Ave., San Francisco, Calif.
Nunnally, Nancy, 5916 Monticello Ave., Cincinnati, Ohio
Nutter, H. E., Norman Hall, University of Florida, Gainesville, Fla.
Nutterville, Catherine, 1618 Third Ave., N., Great Falls, Mont.
Nutting, William C., University of Utah, Salt Lake City, Utah
Nye, Robert E., Sch. of Music, University of Oregon, Eugene, Ore.
Nystrom, J. W., Jr., American University of Beirut, Beirut, Lebanon

Oaks, Ruth E., B-104 Haverford Villa, Haverford, Pa.
Oberholtzer, Kenneth E., Superintendent of Schools, Denver, Colo.
Obourn, L. C., Superintendent of Schools, East Rochester, N.Y.
O'Brien, Cyril C., 2568 N. Summit Ave., Milwaukee, Wis.
O'Brien, John W., Ridley Township School Dist., Folsom, Delaware County, Pa.
O'Connor, Clarence D., Lexington School for Deaf, 904 Lexington Ave., New
    York, N.Y.
O'Connor, John D., Maple Park, Ill.
O'Connor, Joseph F., Spring Gardens Institute, Philadelphia, Pa.
O'Connor, Mrs. Marguerite O., Maple Park, Ill.
Odland, Norine, Burton Hall, University of Minnesota, Minneapolis, Minn.
O'Donnell, Beatrice, Michigan State University, East Lansing, Mich.
O'Donnell, John F., Box 1086, Tupper Lake, N.Y.
O'Fallon, O. K., Sch. of Educ., Kansas State University, Manhattan, Kan.
O'Farrell, John J., Loyola University, 7101 W. 80th St., Los Angeles, Calif.
Ogden, Lowell K., Bakersfield Center, Fresno State College, Bakersfield, Calif.
O'Hara, Charles M., Marquette University, Milwaukee, Wis.
Ohlsen, Merle M., Col. of Educ., University of Illinois, Urbana, Ill.
Ohnmacht, Fred W., Col. of Educ., University of Maine, Orono, Me.
Ojemann, R. H., Child Welfare Res. Sta., State Univ. of Iowa, Iowa City, Iowa
Olander, Herbert T., University of Pittsburgh, Pittsburgh, Pa.
* Oldham, Mrs. Birdie V., 621 W. Silver St., Lakeland, Fla.
O'Leary, Timothy F., Dept. of Educ., Archdiocese of Boston, Boston, Mass.
Olivari, Irene M., 80 LaSalle St., New York, N.Y.
Olivas, Romeo A., 2005 Fruit St., Huntington, Ind.

Oliver, George J., Richmond Professional Institute, Richmond, Va.
Olmsted, M. D., Geneseo Central School, Geneseo, N.Y.
Olphert, Warwick Bruce, University of New England, Armidale, New South Wales
Olsen, George L., Wessels Library, Newberry College, Newberry, S.C.
Olsen, Hans C., Jr., Col. of Educ., Wayne State University, Detroit, Mich.
Olsen, Marion G., 462 Grider St., Buffalo, N.Y.
Olson, Norma M., 1207 S. Linden Ave., Park Ridge, Ill.
Olson, Ove S., Wisconsin State College, Superior, Wis.
Olson, R. A., Ball State Teachers College, Muncie, Ind.
* Olson, Willard C., Sch. of Educ., University of Michigan, Ann Arbor, Mich.
Olson, William L., 1946 Sharondale Ave., St. Paul, Minn.
O'Malley, Sarah, 1130 Washington Blvd., Oak Park, Ill.
O'Mara, Arthur P., Lane Tech. High School, Chicago, Ill.
O'Mara, J. Francis, 29 Snowling Rd., Uxbridge, Mass.
O'Neal, John F., Dept. of Educ., Lehigh University, Bethlehem, Pa.
O'Neal, Thomas A., 10331 Bretton, Houston, Tex.
O'Neill, John H., Dept. of Educ., DePaul University, Chicago, Ill.
O'Neill, John J., State College of Boston, 625 Huntington Ave., Boston, Mass.
O'Neill, Leo W., Jr., Col. of Educ., University of Maryland, College Park, Md.
O'Neill, Patrick J., Superintendent, Diocesan Schools, Fall River, Mass.
Oppenheim, Alan, 5200 Blackstone Ave., Chicago, Ill.
Oppenheimer, J. J., Belknap Campus, University of Louisville, Louisville, Ky.
Oppleman, Dan L., Iowa Wesleyan College, Mt. Pleasant, Iowa
Ore, Malvern L., Div. of Educ., Huston-Tillotson Col., Austin, Tex.
Orear, Margaret Louise, 16703 S. Clark Ave., Bellflower, Calif.
O'Reilly, Robert C., Morningside College, Sioux City, Iowa
Orlovich, Joseph, 554 Clax St., Joliet, Ill.
Ormsby, Lelia Ann, Sacramento State College, Sacramento, Calif.
O'Rourke, J. Mel, Englewood High School, 6201 S. Stewart Ave., Chicago, Ill.
O'Rourke, Joseph, 3197 Gerbert Rd., Columbus, Ohio
Orr, Beryl, 308 Stanley St., Middletown, Ohio
Orr, Louise, 925 Crockett St., Amarillo, Tex.
Ort, Lorrene Love, Bowling Green State University, Bowling Green, Ohio
Orton, Don A., Lesley College, Cambridge, Mass.
Orton, Kenneth D., Southern Illinois University, Carbondale, Ill.
Osborn, Wayland W., 2701 Hickman Rd., Des Moines, Iowa
O'Shea, John T., 3233 Main St., Buffalo, N.Y.
Osibov, Henry, Oregon Educ. Assn., 1530 S.W. Taylor St., Portland, Ore.
Ostlie, Selmer, Los Angeles State College, Los Angeles, Calif.
Ostrander, Raymond H., 15 Winter St., Weston, Mass.
Ostrom, Gerald, 215 Prospect Ave., Highland Park, Ill.
Ostwalt, Jay H., P.O. Box 387, Davidson, N.C.
Osuch, A. E., 3844 Wrightwood, Chicago, Ill.
Osuna, Pedro, Sch. of Educ., College of the Pacific, Stockton, Calif.
Oswalt, Edna Rickey, Dept. of Spec. Educ., Westminster Col., New Wilmington, Pa.
Oswalt, Howard C., 1518 N. McAllister Ave., Tempe, Ariz.
Oswalt, William W., Jr., Lehigh County Schools, 445 Hamilton St., Allentown, Pa.
Otterness, June, Public Schools, Hutchinson, Minn.
Otto, Henry J., University of Texas, Austin, Tex.
Otts, John, University of North Carolina, Chapel Hill, N.C.
Overfield, Ruth, State Educ. Bldg., 721 Capitol Ave., Sacramento, Calif.
Overstreet, George Thomas, 811 S. Frances St., Terrell, Tex.
Owen, Jason C., P.O. Box 537, Tech. Station, Ruston, La.
Owen, John, Dept. of Educ., Paterson State College, Wayne, N.J.
Owen, Mary E., F. A. Owen Publishing Co., Dansville, N.Y.
Owens, John, Roslyn Public Schools, Roslyn, N.Y.
Owens, Robert G., Webster Hill School, West Hartford, Conn.
Owings, Ralph S., Mississippi Southern College, Hattiesburg, Miss.

Pace, C. Robert, Sch. of Educ., University of California, Los Angeles, Calif.
Packer, C. Kyle, 629 Deerfield Dr., Tonawanda, N.Y.
Padget, Mattie Bell, 704 N. Chestnut St., Carlsbad, N.M.
Page, Ellis B., Bur. of Educ. Res., Univ. of Connecticut, Storrs, Conn.
Pagel, Betty Lou, 304 E. 5th Ave., Cheyenne, Wyo.
Paine, Harry W., 5436 North Woods Lane, Norwood, Cincinnati, Ohio
Painter, Fred B., Superintendent, Brighton School Dist. No. 1, Rochester, N.Y.
Palliser, G. C., Central P.O. Box 1525, Wellington, New Zealand
Palmer, Albert, Stockton College, Stockton, Calif.
Palmer, Anne M. H., 22277 Cass Ave., Woodland Hills, Calif.
Palmer, Frank J., 208 Church St., North Syracuse, N.Y.
Palmer, James B., Ginn & Co., Statler Bldg., Boston, Mass.
Palmer, John C., Tufts University, Medford, Mass.
Palmer, Lulu, State Department of Education, Montgomery, Ala.
Pangburn, Margaret C., 104 Glenwood Ave., Leonia, N.J.
Papanek, Ernst, 1 West 64th St., New York, N.Y.
Pappas, George, 26 Keith St., Parkdale S. 12, Victoria, Australia
Paquin, Laurence G., Board of Education Bldg., New Haven, Conn.
Parisho, Eugenia G., 709 West 11th St., Cedar Falls, Iowa
Park, Maxwell G., 44 Clayton Ave., Cortland, N.Y.
Parke, Margaret B., 430 West 118th St., New York, N.Y.
Parker, Don H., Science Research Associates, Chicago, Ill.
Parker, James R., 210 Thornbrook Rd., DeKalb, Ill.
Parker, Marjorie H., 4919 Sixteenth St., N.W., Washington, D.C.
Parkinson, Daniel S., 725 Melissa Dr., Oxford, Ohio
Parkyn, George William, Southern Cross Bldg., Wellington, New Zealand
Parmelee, Elizabeth, Calhoun School, 309 West 92nd St., New York, N.Y.
Parr, Kenneth E., Box 1348, c/o Tapline, Beirut, Lebanon
Parry, O. Meredith, William Penn Senior High School, York, Pa.
Parsey, John M., 305 Droste Circle, East Lansing, Mich.
Parsons, Brooks A., Superintendent of Schools, Norwood, Ohio
Parsons, Seth Hamilton, 1114 Seventh St., Las Vegas, N.M.
Parton, Daisy, Box 1882, University, Ala.
Partridge, Deborah C., 62 S. Union Ave., Cranford, N.J.
Paschal, Harland L. R., 5675 Carr St., Arvada, Colo.
Pascoe, David D., LaMesa Spring Valley Sch. Dist., LaMesa, Calif.
Pasquale, Vincent C. D., Superintendent, Valley Central School System, Montgomery, N.Y.
Passow, Aaron Harry, Teachers College, Columbia University, New York, N.Y.
Paster, G. Nicholas, 117 W. Center College St., Yellow Springs, Ohio
Patacsil, Gregorie C., Sec. Educ. Div., Bur. of Public Schools, Manila, Philippines
Patch, Robert B., 4 Carleton Dr., Glens Falls, N.Y.
Pate, Mildred, 1806 East 6th St., Greenville, N.C.
Paterson, John J., 1008 Happy Hollow, West Lafayette, Ind.
Patrick, Robert B., 433 W. Park Ave., University Park, Pa.
Patt, Jack M., Soc. Sci. Div., San Jose State College, San Jose, Calif.
Pattee, Howard H., Rt. 1, Box 102, Carmel, Calif.
* Patterson, Herbert, 406 S. Stallard Ave., Stillwater, Okla.
Pattison, Mattie, Home Econ. Hall, Iowa State University, Ames, Iowa
Patton, Earl D., 703 S. New St., Champaign, Ill.
Paul, Marvin S., 6743 N. California Ave., Chicago, Ill.
Paulsen, Gaige B., 36 Fairview Ave., Athens, Ohio
Paulson, Alice T., 125 W. Eighth St., Blue Earth, Minn.
Pautz, Wilmer, Dept. of Educ., Northern Illinois University, DeKalb, Ill.
Pavel, Mrs. Harriet M., 6343 N. Kildare Ave., Chicago, Ill.
Pavelich, Thomas A., 208 Dudley Ave., Coleraine, Minn.
Paxton, J. Hall, 1405 Pine St., St. Louis, Mo.
Payne, Donald T., 221 East 7th St., Bloomington, Ind.
Payne, Joe D., 2217—48th St., Lubbock, Tex.
Payne, W. K., Savannah State College, Savannah, Ga.
Paynovich, Nicholas, Rt. 4, Box 840, Tucson, Ariz.

Peacock, A. E., Superintendent of Schools, Moose Jaw, Sask., Canada
Pearson, Jim, 4350 Neo St., Pierrefonds, Que., Canada
Pearson, Millie V., 215 S. Monroe St., Stillwater, Okla.
Peavey, Samuel B., Educ. Dept., University of Louisville, Louisville, Ky.
Pebley, Wilson A., 310 Lincoln Way East, McConnellsburg, Pa.
Peccola, Charles, 2456 Hobbs Dr., Manhattan, Kan.
Pederson, Arne K., Pacific Lutheran University, Tacoma, Wash.
Pederson, Clara A., Dept. of Educ., Univ. of North Dakota, Grand Forks, N.D.
Pedigo, Louise, Lynchburg College, Lynchburg, Va.
Peiffer, Paul D., 5902 Jonestown Rd., Harrisburg, Pa.
Pell, Richard E., 409 S. Swain Ave., Bloomington, Ind.
Pella, Milton O., Wisconsin High School, Univ. of Wisconsin, Madison, Wis.
Pellegrin, Lionel, 945 E. River Oaks Dr., Baton Rouge, La.
Pelton, Frank M., Dept. of Educ., Univ. of Rhode Island, Kingston, R.I.
Pendleton, James N., Jr., Kiona-Benton Cons. Sch. Dist. 52, Benton City, Wash.
Penn, Floy L., Mt. Lebanon Public Schls., 735 Washington Rd., Pittsburgh, Pa.
Pennetta, Gerardo, 841—80th St., North Bergen, N.J.
Penta, A. H. Della, Superintendent of Schools, Lodi, N.J.
Perdew, Philip W., Sch. of Educ., University of Denver, Denver, Colo.
Peregoy, C. G., Woodrow Wilson High School, Beckley, W.Va.
Perry, James Olden, 2919 Wheeler St., Houston, Tex.
Perry, Leland M., 3180 W. Rome Ave., Anaheim, Calif.
Perry, T. Edward, 2080 Alton Rd., East Cleveland, Ohio
Perry, W. D., University of North Carolina, Chapel Hill, N.C.
Pescosolido, John R., Central Connecticut State College, New Britain, Conn.
Peterkin, A. Gordon, Superintendent of Schools, Westport, Conn.
Peters, J. V., Dept. of Educ., Walla Walla College, College Place, Wash.
Peters, Jon S., State Col. for Alameda County, Hayward, Calif.
Peters, Mary Magdalene, 950 West "D" St., Ontario, Calif.
Petersen, Clarence E., 19 Fulton St., Redwood City, Calif.
Petersen, Fred J., University of South Dakota, Vermillion, S.D.
Peterson, Basil H., Orange Coast Col., 2701 Fairview Rd., Costa Mesa, Calif.
Peterson, Carl H., 9807 S. Seeley Ave., Chicago, Ill.
Peterson, Donald W., 1817—16th St., Rock Island, Ill.
Peterson, Douglas W., Dept. of Educ., Kalamazoo College, Kalamazoo, Mich.
Peterson, Elmer T., Col. of Educ., State Univ. of Iowa, Iowa City, Iowa
Peterson, Evelyn F., East High School Bldg., Waterloo, Iowa
Peterson, Grace, Nebraska State Teachers College, Kearney, Neb.
Peterson, LeRoy, University of Wisconsin, Madison, Wis.
Peterson, Miriam E., 5422 Wayne Ave., Chicago, Ill.
Peterson, Vianna, 300 Humphrey St., Logansport, Ind.
Pethick, Wayne M., 6136 Northwest Hwy., Chicago, Ill.
Petor, Andrew, East Dear-Frazer Union High School, Creighton, Pa.
Pettersch, Carl A., 200 Southern Blvd., Danbury, Conn.
Petterson, Mrs. Muriel, County Schls. Serv. Center, San Luis Obispo, Calif.
Pettinga, R. C., North Fourth St. Christian School, Paterson, N.J.
Pettiss, J. O., Dept. of Educ., Louisiana State University, Baton Rouge, La.
Petty, Edgar L., Jr., Eastern New Mexico University, Portales, N.M.
Petty, Mary Clare, Col. of Educ., University of Oklahoma, Norman, Okla.
Petty, Walter T., 3632 Tolenas Ct., Sacramento, Calif.
Pezzullo, Thomas J., 268 Greenville Ave., Johnston, R.I.
Phay, John R., Bur. of Educ. Res., University of Mississippi, University, Miss.
Phearman, Leo Thomas, Long Beach State College, Long Beach, Calif.
Phelan, William F., 95 Ryder Ave., North Babylon, N.Y.
Phelps, H. Vaughn, 8727 Shamrock Rd., Omaha, Neb.
Phelps, Roger P., 4 Barnes Ave., Baldwin, L.I., N.Y.
Phillips, Cecil K., State College of Iowa, Cedar Falls, Iowa
Phillips, Don O., 1158 S. Harris Ave., Columbus, Ohio
Phillips, James A., Jr., Col. of Educ., Kent State University, Kent, Ohio
Phillips, Paul, 520 W. Palmer Ave., Morrisville, Pa.
Phillips, Richard C., 1570 Oak Ave., Evanston, Ill.

Phillips, Thomas Arthur, 1536 S. Sixth St., Terre Haute, Ind.
Philp, William A., 440 Williams Ave., Natchitoches, La.
Phipps, Mrs. H. W., 133 Summit Ave., Summit, N.J.
Phoenix, William D., 28 W. Winthrope Rd., Kansas City, Mo.
Piazza, Frank, Board of Education, 51 Aldine Ave., Bridgeport, Conn.
Pickett, Louis L., County Supt. of Schools, Court House, Davenport, Iowa
Piekarz, Josephine A., Sch. of Educ., New York University, New York, N.Y.
Pierce, Arthur E., Hanover School District, Hanover, N.H.
Pikunas, Justin, Psych. Dept., University of Detroit, Detroit, Mich.
Pilch, Mrs. Mary M., State Dept. of Education, Centennial Bldg., St. Paul, Minn.
Pinkston, Dow G., 105 E. Madison, Yates Center, Kan.
Pitkin, Royce, Goddard College, Plainfield, Vt.
Pitts, F. N., 435 S. Fifth St., Louisville, Ky.
Pittillo, Robert A., Jr., Raleigh Public Schools, Raleigh, N.C.
Pittman, DeWitt Kennieth, 6800 Monroe Rd., Charlotte, N.C.
Pitts, Clara L., 4700 Upton St., N.W., Washington, D.C.
Piucci, V. L., Campus School, Oswego State Teachers College, Oswego, N.Y.
Pivnick, Isadore, 135 Van Ness Ave., San Francisco, Calif.
Plana, Juan F., Andrés Sánchez 306, Vigía. Camagüey, Cuba
Plantz, Nina, East Street School, Hicksville, N.Y.
Pledger, Maude M., 3481 College Station, Commerce, Tex.
Plimpton, Blair, Superintendent of Schools, 400 S. Western Ave., Park Ridge, Ill.
Pliska, Stanley R., 1022 Hanover Ave., Norfolk, Va.
Plotnick, Morton, 31860 Beverly St., Oak Park, Mich.
Plowman, Paul D., 1152 Fernwood St., West Sacramento, Calif.
Plumb, Mary Louise, Bennington High School, Bennington, Vt.
Plumb, Valworth R., University of Minnesota, Duluth Branch, Duluth, Minn.
Plummer, Violin G., Oakwood College, Huntsville, Ala.
Podell, Mrs. Harriett A., Dept. of Educ., Univ. of California, Berkeley, Calif.
Podlich, William F., Jr., 1630 College Ave., Tempe, Ariz.
Poehler, W. A., Concordia College, St. Paul, Minn.
Pogue, E. Graham, Ball State Teachers College, Muncie, Ind.
Pogue, Pauline C., Colorado State College, Greeley, Colo.
Polansky, Leon, 33-47 Fourteenth St., Long Island City, N.Y.
Polglase, Robert J., 10 Army Dr., Westfield, N.J.
Pond, Millard Z., Superintendent of Schools, Dist. No. 4, Eugene, Ore.
Poole, Albert E., 214 N. Washington Cir., Lake Forest, Ill.
Pooley, Robert C., Baxom Hall, University of Wisconsin, Madison, Wis.
Porter, M. Roseamonde, University of Hawaii, Honolulu, Hawaii
Porter, R. H., The Steck Co., Box 16, Austin, Tex.
Porter, Willis P., Sch. of Educ., Indiana University, Bloomington, Ind.
Potell, Herbert, 1719—48th St., Brooklyn, N.Y.
Potter, Willis N., University of the Pacific, Stockton, Calif.
Potts, John F., Voorhees Junior College, Denmar, S.C.
Poulos, Thomas H., Michigan School for the Deaf, Flint, Mich.
Poulter, James R., Superintendent of Schools, Aplington, Iowa
Pound, Clarence A., Educ. Bldg., Purdue University, Lafayette, Ind.
Pounds, Ralph L., Tchrs. Col., University of Cincinnati, Cincinnati, Ohio
Pourchot, Leonard L., 2490 Simms Circle, Sparks, Nev.
Powell, Mrs. Ruth Marie, 611 Young's Lane, Nashville, Tenn.
Powell, William R., Ball State Teachers College, Muncie, Ind.
Powers, F. R., 262 Cornell Ave., Amherst, Ohio
Powers, Francis P., Sch. of Educ., Boston College, Chestnut Hill, Mass.
Powers, Philander, Ventura College, 4667 Telegraph Rd., Ventura, Calif.
Prasch, John, Superintendent of Schools, Racine, Wis.
Preil, Joseph J., 189 Shelley Ave., Elizabeth, N.J.
Prentice, Warren L., Sacramento State College, Sacramento, Calif.
Preseren, Herman J., Box 7266, Reynolds Sta., Winston-Salem, N.C.
Preston, Ralph C., Sch. of Educ., University of Pennsylvania, Philadelphia, Pa.
Prestwood, Elwood L., 426 Righters Mill Rd., Gladwyne, Pa.
Pricco, Ernest, Melrose Park School, Melrose Park, Ill.

Price, Reuben Holleman, University of Mississippi, University, Miss.
Price, Robert Diddams, 7819 Pinemeadow Lane, Cincinnati, Ohio
Price, Ruth Evert, 3455 Englewood St., Philadelphia, Pa.
Prince, Mrs. Virginia Faye, P.O. Box 4015, St. Louis, Mo.
Pringle, Glenn L., Wheaton College, Wheaton, Ill.
Prior, Francis X., St. John's Preparatory School, 82 Lewis Ave., Brooklyn, N.Y.
Pritchard, Ruth B., 2205 Park Ave., Des Moines, Iowa
Pritchett, John P., Trenton Junior College, 101 W. State St., Trenton, N.J.
Pritzkau, Philo T., University of Connecticut, Storrs, Conn.
Procunier, Robert W., 600 N. Elmhurst Ave., Mt. Prospect, Ill.
Profeta, Philip, 2021 Sheridan St., West Hyattsville, Md.
Prosser, Raymond A., 300 Berryman Dr., Snyder, N.Y.
Prouse, Peter, 414 Aliso, S.E., Albuquerque, N.M.
Pruitt, Robert E., Superintendent of Schools, Dist. 91, Forest Park, Ill.
Prutzman, Stuart E., County Superintendent of Schools, Jim Thorpe, Pa.
Pugmire, Jean, Edith Bowen Sch., Utah State University, Logan, Utah
Pulliam, A. Lloyd, Knox College, Galesburg, Ill.
Purdy, Ralph D., Miami University, Oxford, Ohio
Puryear, Ada P., P.O. Box 1243, Tuskegee Institute, Ala.
Puryear, Royal W., Florida Normal and Ind. Mem. College, St. Augustine, Fla.
Putnam, John F., Office of Education, Dept. of H.E.W., Washington, D.C.

Quall, Alvin B., Whitworth College, Spokane, Wash.
Quanbeck, Martin, Augsburg College, Minneapolis, Minn.
Quanbeck, Thor H., Augustana College, Sioux Falls, S.D.
Quesenberry, Virginia C., Fresno County Schls., 2314 Mariposa St., Fresno, Calif.
Quick, Henry E., 293 Main St., Box 279, Oswego, Tioga County, N.Y.
Quick, Otho J., Northern Illinos University, DeKalb, Ill.
Quiller, Gordon F., Colorado State University, Fort Collins, Colo.
Quinn, Villa H., State Department of Education, Augusta, Me.
Quish, Bernard A., 2601 W. 81st Pl., Chicago, Ill.

Rabb, Willynne, Kingsville Public Schools, Kingsville, Tex.
Rabin, Bernard, Bowling Green State University, Bowling Green, Ohio
Raciti, C. Stephen, Pennington-Titusville Rd., Pennington, N.J.
Radhakrishna, K. S., Seveagram via Wardha (Mohroashtra), India
Raffone, Alexander M., 44 Paramount Ave., Hamden, Conn.
Ragan, William Burk, University of Oklahoma, Norman, Okla.
Ragsdale, Elva Mae, Dept. of Educ., Anderson College, Anderson, Ind.
Ragsdale, Ted R., 301 W. College St., Carbondale, Ill.
Ramer, Earl M., University of Tennessee, Knoxville, Tenn.
Ramos, John P., Jr., Morris Ave., Union, N.J.
Ramsey, J. W., Superior-Maitland School, Northfork, W.Va.
Ramsey, Wallace, 425 Malabu Dr., Lexington, Ky.
Ramseyer, John A., 13 Page Hall, Ohio State University, Columbus, Ohio
Ramseyer, Lloyd L., Blufften College, Blufften, Ohio
Rand, E. W., Texas Southern University, Houston, Tex.
Randall, Edwin H., Western State College, Gunnison, Colo.
Randall, William M., Wilmington College, 1220 Market St., Wilmington, N.C.
Rankin, Earl F., Jr., 3921 Lynncrest Dr., Fort Worth, Tex.
Rankin, Paul T., 16823 Plainview Rd., Detroit, Mich.
Rappaport, David, 2747 Coyle Ave., Chicago, Ill.
Rappaport, Mary B., State Education Department, Albany, N.Y.
Rasmussen, Elmer M., Dana College, Blair, Neb.
Rasmussen, Glen R., Southern Illinois University, Southwest Campus, Alton, Ill.
Rasmussen, H. L., 427 S.W. Bade Ave., College Place, Wash.
Raubinger, F. M., State Dept. of Educ., 175 W. State St., Trenton, N.J.
Rauch, Louise T., 1330 Carlisle Ave., Dayton, Ohio
Rausch, Richard G., Webster Hill School, West Hartford, Conn.
Rawson, Kenneth O., Superintendent of Schools, Clintonville, Wis.
Ray, Rolland, State University of Iowa, Iowa City, Iowa

Read, Edward M., St. Paul Academy, 1712 Randolph Ave., St. Paul, Minn.
Reak, Jack E., Ball State Teachers College, Muncie, Ind.
Reas, Herbert D., Sch. of Educ., Seattle University, Seattle, Wash.
Red, S. B., University of Houston, 3801 Cullen Blvd., Houston, Tex.
Reddin, Estoy, Trenton State College, Trenton, N.J.
* Reddy, Anne L., 117 E. 34th St., Savannah, Ga.
Rediger, Milo A., Taylor University, Upland, Ind.
Reed, Bernard W., Sch. of Cont. Prof. Studies, Pratt Institute, Brooklyn, N.Y.
Reed, Earl J., Superintendent of Schools, Longview, Wash.
Reed, Flo, Department of Education, Carson City, Nev.
Reed, Lula B., County Superintendent of Schools, Red Oak, Iowa
Reed, William S., 3105 W. University Ave., Gainesville, Fla.
Reed, Zollie C., Birmingham Southern College, Birmingham, Ala.
Reeves, Glenn D., Superintendent of Schools, Littlefield, Tex.
Reeves, James H., University of Minnesota, Minneapolis, Minn.
Reeves, Wilfred, Washington Junior High School, Olympia, Wash.
Regner, Olga W., 116 South 4th St., Darby, Pa.
Rehage, Kenneth J., Dept. of Educ., University of Chicago, Chicago, Ill.
Reid, C. E., Jr., 6225 N. Circuit Dr., Beaumont, Tex.
Reid, Jackson B., University of Texas, Austin, Tex.
Reid, L. Leon, 517 Clemson Dr., Pittsburgh, Pa.
Reilley, Albert G., 28 Long Ave., Framingham, Mass.
Reiner, William B., Board of Educ., 110 Livingston St., Brooklyn, N.Y.
* Reinhardt, Emma, Eastern Illinois University, Charleston, Ill.
Reisman, Diana J., 223 N. Highland Ave., Merion Station, Pa.
Reisman, Morton, Anshe Emet Day Sch., 3760 N. Pine Grove Ave., Chicago, Ill.
Reiter, Mrs. Anne, 51 Buchanan Pl., Bronx, N.Y.
Reitz, Donald J., Loyola College, 4501 N. Charles St., Baltimore, Md.
Reitz, Louis M., St. Thomas Seminary, 7101 Brownsboro Rd., Louisville, Ky.
Reitze, Arnold W., 3 Lienau Pl., Jersey City, N.J.
Remmers, Herman H., Purdue University, West Lafayette, Ind.
Rempel, P. J., State College of Washington, Pullman, Wash.
Renard, John N., Oxnard Evening High School, Oxnard, Calif.
Rendel, Dorothy, 1111 Minnie St., Port Huron, Mich.
Reneau, James C., 3607 S. Pleasant, Independence, Mo.
Renouf, Edna M., 116 Yale Square, Swarthmore, Pa.
Resek, E. Frederick, 913 Garden St., Park Ridge, Ill.
Reuter, George S., Jr., 1806 E. Lilac Ter., Arlington Heights, Ill.
Reuther, Carolyn A., Mills College, Oakland, Calif.
Reuwsaat, Emily A., Col. of Educ., Univ. of New Mexico, Albuquerque, N.M.
Rex, Ronald G., Michigan State University, East Lansing, Mich.
Reynolds, Charlotte, 154 Centre Ave., New Rochelle, N.Y.
Reynolds, Dorothy S., 414—14th St., Denver, Colo.
Reynolds, James Walton, Box 7998, University of Texas, Austin, Tex.
Reynolds, M. C., University of Minnesota, Minneapolis, Minn.
Rhoads, Jonathan E., 3400 Spruce St., Philadelphia, Pa.
Rhodes, Gladys L., State University College, Geneseo, N.Y.
Ricciardi, Richard S., Dept. of Education, 100 Reef Rd., Fairfield, Conn.
Riccio, Anthony C., Sch. of Educ., Ohio State University, Columbus, Ohio
Rice, Arthur H., The Nation's Schools Pub. Co., Chicago, Ill.
Rice, David, Ball State Teachers College, Muncie, Ind.
Rice, J. C., Superintendent of Schools, Elkhart, Ind.
Rice, John E., Jenkintown High School, Jenkintown, Pa.
Rice, Lloyd M., Jr., Box 426, Port Orford, Ore.
Rice, Roy C., Arizona State University, Tempe, Ariz.
Rice, Theodore D., 33963 N. Hampshire, Livonia, Mich.
Richards, Eugene, Sol R. Crown Elem. School, 2123 S. St. Louis, Chicago, Ill.
Richards, Henry M. M., Muhlenberg College, Allentown, Pa.
Richardson, Canute M., Paine College, Augusta, Ga.
Richardson, George M., 1422 S. Queen St., Arlington, Va.
Richardson, John S., 4079 Overlook Dr., East., Columbus, Ohio

Richardson, L. S., 1615 West 4th St., Freeport, Tex.
Richardson, Orvin T., Washington University, St. Louis, Mo.
Richardson, Thomas H., 200 Summitt Rd., Elizabeth, N.J.
Richey, Herman G., Dept. of Educ., University of Chicago, Chicago, Ill.
Richey, Robert W., Sch. of Educ., Indiana University, Bloomington, Ind.
Richmond, John D., P.O. Box 1311, Martinsville, Va.
Ricketts, Robert E., 490 Park Ave., Paterson, N.J.
Riddle, William T., Box 4007, Tech. Station, Lubbock, Tex.
Riedel, Mark T., 210 S. Edgewood, LaGrange, Ill.
Riederer, L. A., 3114—14th Ave., Regina, Sask.
Riegel, Samuel A., Biddle Street Area School, West Chester, Pa.
Riegle, H. Edgar, Superintendent of Schools, Gettysburg, Pa.
Riehm, Carl L., 8531 Devon St., Norfolk, Va.
Riese, Harlan C., 511 North Ave., East, Missoula, Mont.
Riethmiller, Gorton, Olivet College, Olivet, Mich.
Riggio, Ines, 2967 Perry Ave., New York, N.Y.
Riggle, Earl L., 160 E. Main St., New Concord, Ohio
Riggs, Edwon L., 2702 E. Flower St., Phoenix, Ariz.
Riggs, William J., East 38 Hoffman, Spokane, Wash.
Righter, Charles L., 419 Lee Pl., Frederick, Md.
Rigney, Mrs. Margaret G., Hunter College, Park Ave. and 68th St., New York,
    N.Y.
Rikkola, V. John, Dept. of Educ., State Teachers College, Salem, Mass.
Riley, Garland G., 910 Colby Ct., DeKalb, Ill.
Rinehart, John, Oakfield Rd., St. James, L.I., N.Y.
Ripple, Richard E., Stone Hall, Cornell University, Ithaca, N.Y.
Risinger, Robert G., Col. of Educ., University of Maryland, College Park, Md.
Risk, Thomas M., 319 Elm St., Vermillion, S.D.
Ritchie, Harold L., Superintendent of Schools, West Paterson, N.J.
Ritchie, Harold S., 725 E. 26th St., Paterson, N.J.
Ritscher, Richard C., 47 W. Hyatt Ave., Mt. Kisco, N.Y.
Ritsema, Louise, 231 Wildwood, Ann Arbor, Mich.
Ritter, William E., 2910 E. State St., Sharon, Pa.
Rivard, Thomas L., Superintendent of Schools, Chelmsford, Mass.
Rivlin, Harry N., 535 East 80th St., New York, N.Y.
Roaden, Arliss, Dept. of Education, Ohio State University, Columbus, Ohio
Robbins, Edward T., Alamo Heights Sch. Dist., San Antonio, Tex.
Robbins, Melvyn Paul, 6500 W. Irving Park, Chicago, Ill.
Robbins, Rintha, Office of County Supt. of Schools, Madera, Calif.
Roberson, James A., 1802 Lincoln Dr., Abilene, Tex.
Roberts, Dodd Edward, Oakland County Schools, Pontiac, Mich.
Roberts, Francis J., Central School Dist. No. 2, Cold Spring Harbor, N.Y.
Roberts, Jack D., Dept. of Educ., Queens College, Flushing, N.Y.
Roberts, James B., Dept. of Educ., West Texas State Col., Canyon, Tex.
Roberts, Ralph M., Box 1198, University, Ala.
Robertson, Robert L., 101 Virginia Ave., Springfield, Kan.
Robin, Holly, 6331 N. Washtenaw Ave., Chicago, Ill.
Robinette, Walter R., University of Louisiana, Lafayette, La.
Robinson, Alice, Board of Educ., 115 E. Church St., Frederick, Md.
Robinson, Alvin E., 255 Palm Drive, Oxnard, Calif.
Robinson, Charles R., County Admin. Center, 2555 Mendocina Ave., Santa Rosa,
    Calif.
Robinson, H. Alan, Dept. of Educ., University of Chicago, Chicago, Ill.
Robinson, Mrs. Helen M., Dept. of Educ., University of Chicago, Chicago, Ill.
Robinson, Phil C., 8635 Dexter Blvd., Detroit, Mich.
Robinson, Richard M., 6808—16th St., N.E., Seattle, Wash.
Robinson, Thomas L., 3224 McElvy St., Montgomery, Ala.
Robinson, W. L., Norfolk City Schools, Norfolk, Va.
Roche, Lawrence A., Duquesne University, Pittsburgh, Pa.
Rockwell, Perry J., Jr., Sch. of Educ., Indiana University, Bloomington, Ind.
Rodgers, John O., 6402 Wilbur Dr., Austin, Tex.

Rodgers, Margaret, Lamar State College of Technology, Beaumont, Tex.
Rodgers, Paul R., Board of Education, Dist. No. 102, LaGrange Park, Ill.
Rodriguez-Diaz, Manlo, Alfred University, Alfred, N.Y.
Roemmich, Herman, San Diego State College, San Diego, Calif.
Roenigk, Elsie Mae, R.D. No. 1, Box 311, Cabot, Pa.
Roens, Bert A., Superintendent of Schools, Arlington, Mass.
Roeper, George A., City and Country School, Bloomfield Hills, Mich.
Roers, James P., Appleton-Century-Crofts, Inc., New York, N.Y.
Roff, Mrs. Rosella Zuber, 4410 S. 148th St., Seattle, Wash.
Rogers, John D., 735 Washington Rd., Pittsburgh, Pa.
Rogers, Virgil M., Sch. of Educ., Syracuse University, Syracuse, N.Y.
Rogers, William R., San Jose State College, San Jose, Calif.
Rohan, William, 5683 N. Rogers Ave., Chicago, Ill.
Rolens, Robert E., 295 S. Arcade St., Ventura, Calif.
Rolfe, Howard C., 1344 Studebaker Rd., Long Beach, Calif.
Rollins, William B., Jr., 7772 Otto St., Downey, Calif.
Romano, Frank E., 588 Broadway, Newark, N.J.
Romano, Louis, 1701 E. Capitol Dr., Shorewood, Wis.
Rome, Samuel, 9852 Cerritos Ave., Anaheim, Calif.
Rondinella, Orestes R., 106 Louis St., North Massapequa, L.I., N.Y.
Rooney, Edward B., Jesuit Educ. Assn., 49 E. 84th St., New York, N.Y.
Roossinck, Esther P., Alameda State College, Hayward, Calif.
Rosamilia, M. T., 183 Union Ave., Belleville, N.J.
Roschy, Mrs. Bertha B., 1807 Gildner Rd., Hampton, Va.
Rose, Gale W., Dept. of Educ., University of Chicago, Chicago, Ill.
Rose, Mrs. Ruth R., 1251 S.W. 42nd Ave., Fort Lauderdale, Fla.
Roseberry, Minnie, Box 545, Flagstaff, Ariz.
Rosebrock, Allan F., State Dept. of Educ., 175 W. State St., Trenton, N.J.
Rosecrance, Francis C., Col. of Educ., Wayne State University, Detroit, Mich.
Rosen, Sidney, Col. of Educ., University of Illinois, Urbana, Ill.
Rosenberg, Marguerite G., 216 Conroy Ave., Scranton, Pa.
Rosenberger, David S., 5827 Garden Park Dr., Sylvania, Ohio
Rosenberger, Russell S., Dept. of Educ., Gettysburg Col., Gettysburg, Pa.
Rosenbloom, Alfred A., Jr., 6829 S. Crandon Ave., Chicago, Ill.
Rosenbluh, Benjamin J., Central High School, Bridgeport, Conn.
Rosenfeld, Babette F., 22 Prospect Park, West, Brooklyn, N.Y.
Rosenstein, Pearl, 124 Sheldon Ter., New Haven, Conn.
Rosenthal, Alan G., 18 Homeside Lane, White Plains, N.Y.
Rosenthal, Lester, 94 Stirling Ave., Freeport, N.Y.
Rosenthal, Samuel, 5213 N. Moody Ave., Chicago, Ill.
Rosenzweig, Celia, 6239 N. Leavitt St., Chicago, Ill.
Ross, Mrs. Alice M., 1446 Wilbraham Rd., Springfield, Mass.
Ross, John G., Haviland Hall, University of California, Berkeley, Calif.
Rossmiller, Richard, Sch. of Educ., University of Wisconsin, Madison, Wis.
Rost, Nellie, Tabor College, Hillsboro, Kan.
Roswell, Florence G., 38 Bon Air Ave., New Rochelle, N.Y.
Roth, Bernice, 401 College Ave., DeKalb, Ill.
Roth, Mrs. Frances, 21598 Ellacott Pkwy., Cleveland, Ohio
Roth, Lois H., Midland College, Fremont, Neb.
Roth, Robert E., Joel Barlow High School, Black Rock Tnpk., Redding, Conn.
Rothenberg, William, 600 West 239th St., Riverdale, N.Y.
Rothstein, Arnold M., 27 Rellim Dr., Glen Cove, N.Y.
Rothstein, Jerome H., San Francisco State College, San Francisco, Calif.
Rothwell, Angus B., State Superintendent of Public Instruction, Madison, Wis.
Roush, Donald C., New Mexico State University, University Park, N.M.
Rousseve, Charles B., 2040 Humanity St., New Orleans, La.
Rousseve, Ronald J., Prairie View A. and M. College, Prairie View, Tex.
Row, Howard E., 207 Orchard Ave., Dover, Del.
Rowe, Ernest Ras, 512 East Flower St., Phoenix, Ariz.
Rowland, Sydney V., 420 E. Lancaster Ave., Wayne, Pa.
Rubie, Harry C., 1130 Fifth Ave., Chula Vista, Calif.

Rubke, Walter C., 6325 Camden St., Oakland, Calif.
Ruch, Mary A. R., R.F.D. No. 1, Tower City, Pa.
Ruckman, Stanley Van, 394 S. Monmouth Ave., Monmouth, Ore.
Ruddell, Arden K., Sch. of Educ., Univ. of California, Berkeley, Calif.
Rudman, Herbert C., Col. of Educ., Michigan State Univ., East Lansing, Mich.
Rudolph, Mrs. Jean, 12211 W. Lincoln Ave., West Allis, Wis.
Rudolf, Kathleen Brady, 53 Cook St., Rochester, N.Y.
Ruffier, Mrs. Joseph P., 429 Highland Ave., Mt. Vernon, N.Y.
Rugen, Mabel E., Sch. of Pub. Health, Univ. of Michigan, Ann Arbor, Mich.
Rugen, Myrtle L., 2240 Pfingsten Rd., Northbrook, Ill.
Rule, Philip, East Otero School Dist., Rt. 1, LaJunta, Colo.
Rulon, Phillip J., Harvard Grad. School of Education, Cambridge, Mass.
Rummel, J. Francis, Sch. of Educ., University of Oregon, Eugene, Ore.
Runyan, Charles S., Marshall University, Huntington, W.Va.
Rusch, Reuben R., State University Teachers College, Oneonta, N.Y.
Rushdoony, Haig A., Stanislaus State College, Turlock, Calif.
Russel, John H., Office of Educ., Dept. of H.E.W., Washington, D.C.
Russell, Mrs. Audrey B., Admin. Bldg., 228 W. Franklin St., Elkhart, Ind.
Russell, David H., Sch. of Educ., Univ. of California, Berkeley, Calif.
Russell, Earle Stone, Superintendent of Schools, Windsor, Conn.
* Russell, John Dale, R.R. 10, Russell Rd., Bloomington, Ind.
Russo, Anthony J., Dept. of Public Schools, 211 Veazie St., Providence, R.I.
Ruthenberg, Donald B., 2185 S. Vine St., Denver, Colo.
Rutledge, James A., Univ. High School, Univ. of Nebraska, Lincoln, Neb.
Ryan, Carl J., 5418 Moeller Ave., Cincinnati, Ohio
Ryan, J. Joseph, Dept. of Educ., College of the Holy Cross, Worcester, Mass.
Ryan, Margaret R., 23-22—36th St., Long Island City, N.Y.
Ryan, Thomas A., 719 Bullock Ave., Yeadon, Pa.
Ryan, W. Carson, 1303 Mason Farm Rd., Chapel Hill, N.C.
Rye, Howard H., 6 Kent Dr., Normal, Ill.
Rzepka, Louis, DePaul University, Chicago, Ill.

Sabik, Adolph J., Franklin School, 4215 Alder St., East Chicago, Ind.
Sachs, Moses B., Congregation B'nai Abraham, St. Louis Park, Minn.
Sack, Saul, Grad. Sch. of Educ., Univ. of Pennsylvania, Philadelphia, Pa.
Sacks, Ethel, 10601 Cavalier Dr., Silver Spring, Md.
Sadler, Vera J., 15587 Inverness, Detroit, Mich.
Sagen, H. Bradley, Bur. of Inst. Res., Univ. of Illinois, Urbana, Ill.
Sain, Leonard F., Eastern High School, 770 E. Grand Blvd., Detroit, Mich.
Saine, Lynette, Atlanta University, Atlanta, Ga.
Salen, George P., 300 Hollowood Dr., West Lafayette, Ind.
Salinger, Herbert E., 3740 Hamilton Ave., Napa, Calif.
Sallee, Mrs. Mozelle T., 4401 North Ave., Richmond, Va.
Salisbury, Arnold W., Superintendent of Schools, Cedar Rapids, Iowa
Salmons, George B., Plymouth Teachers College, Plymouth, N.H.
Salsbury, Jerome C., 557 Bernard St., Costa Mesa, Calif.
Salser, G. Alden, 207 S. Sheridan St., Wichita, Kan.
Salten, David G., 10 The Esplanade, New Rochelle, N.Y.
Saltz, Martin, Broad Brook School, Broad Brook, Conn.
Sample, William J., 45 Van Ethel Dr., Matawan, N.J.
Samson, Gordon E., Dept. of Educ., Fenn College, Cleveland, Ohio
Samson, Ruth D., 20641 Sandpiper Lane, Huntington Beach, Calif.
Sand, Ole, Natl. Educ. Assn., 1201 Sixteenth St., N.W., Washington, D.C.
Sander, Paul J., 3139 E. Monterosa, Phoenix, Ariz.
Sanders, Dannetta M., Hunter College, 695 Park Ave., New York, N.Y.
Sanders, David C., Sutton Hall, University of Texas, Austin, Tex.
Sanders, Richard H., 10639 Drew St., Chicago, Ill.
Sanders, Mrs. Ruby, P.O. Box 1956, Waco, Tex.
Sanderson, Jesse O., Superintendent of Schools, Raleigh, N.C.
Sandilos, James C., Hopewell Twp. Board of Education, Pennington, N.J.
Sandilos, Peter C., Superintendent of Schools, West Long Branch, N.J.

Sandin, Adolph A., Sch. of Educ., University of Oregon, Eugene, Ore.
Sando, Wilbur B., Bethel College, 1000 W. McKinley Ave., Mishawaka, Ind.
Santigian, Marty, 2624 University Ave., Fresno, Calif.
Sapp, Mrs. Undine Cathcart, 201 N. Arkansas St., Springhill, La.
Sarafian, Armen, Pasadena City College, Pasadena, Calif.
Sarner, David S., Keene Teachers College, Keene, N.H.
Sartain, Harry W., Falk Lab. Schls., Univ. of Pittsburgh, Pittsburgh, Pa.
Sarto, Angeline, 1210 Superior Ave., Sheboygan, Wis.
Satterfield, Martha A., 40 N. Summit Ave., Gaithersburg, Md.
Saunders, Alden C., Superintendent of Schools, Foster Center, R.I.
Saunders, Jack O. L., New Mexico Western College, Silver City, N.M.
Saunders, Margaret, Colorado College, Colorado Springs, Colo.
Sauvain, Walter H., R.D. No. 2, Buffalo Rd., Lewisburg, Pa.
Savage, Russell H., 4409 Pomona, La Mesa, Calif.
Sawin, Ethel, Shrewsbury Junior-Senior High School, Shewsbury, Mass.
Sax, Gilbert, Dept. of Educ., University of Hawaii, Honolulu, Hawaii
Saxe, Richard W., 11351 S. Fairfield St., Chicago, Ill.
Saylor, Charles F., Superintendent of Schools, New Wilmington, Pa.
Saylor, Galen, Tchrs. Col., University of Nebraska, Lincoln, Neb.
Scally, Mary Irene, 2722 Cheswolde Rd., Baltimore, Md.
Scanlan, William J., Wilson High School, 631 N. Albert, St. Paul, Minn.
Scanlon, Kathryn I., Sch. of Educ., Fordham University, New York, N.Y.
Schaadt, Mrs. Lucy G., Cedar Crest College, Allentown, Pa.
Schaefer, Frances M., 9946 S. Campbell Ave., Chicago, Ill.
Schaefer, Reed N., Sch. of Educ., Parsons College, Fairfield, Iowa
Schaefer, Robert J., Dept. of Educ., Washington University, St. Louis, Mo.
Schaefer, Wilbert S., 194 Hillside Ave., Mineola, L.I., N.Y.
Schaibly, Colon L., Waukegan Township High School, Waukegan, Ill.
Schardein, Raymond C., Arkansas Polytechnic College, Russellville, Ark.
Scharf, Louis, 350 Sterling St., Brooklyn, N.Y.
Scharf, Mary C., St. Cloud State College, St. Cloud, Minn.
Schenke, Lahron H., Dept. of Educ., Drury College, Springfield, Mo.
Schiavone, James, 17410 N.W. 37th Court, Opa-locka, Fla.
Schiffilea, Doris, Mount St. Mary's College, Los Angeles, Calif.
Schifreen, Edward B., 314 Iris Rd., Cherry Hill, N.J.
Schiller, Mrs. Bertha, 34 Bellevue St., Willimantic, Conn.
Schlegel, Miriam A., 1610 Moore St., Huntingdon, Pa.
Schleif, Mabel, 1908 Hennepin Ave., Minneapolis, Minn.
Schlessinger, Fred R., 1945 N. High St., Columbus, Ohio
Schmidt, Florence, 785 Temple St., Long Beach, Calif.
Schmidt, L. G. H., J. J. Cahill Mem. Sch., Mascot P.O., Rosebery, New So. Wales
Schmidt, Ralph L. W., 568 Magnolia Wood Dr., Baton Rouge, La.
Schmidt, William S., County Superintendent of Schools, Upper Marlboro, Md.
Schmitt, Irvin H., 4808 S. 30th St., Arlington, Va.
Schnabel, Robert V., 6902 S. Calhoun St., Fort Wayne, Ind.
Schneider, Erwin H., Sch. of Music, Ohio State University, Columbus, Ohio
Schneider, Samuel, 126 Pine St., Woodmere, N.Y.
Schnell, Fred, 1625 Wilson Ave., Sheboygan, Wis.
Schnell, Rodolph L., Educ. Dept., University of Detroit, Detroit, Mich.
Schnepf, Virginia, 428 Park Blvd., Glen Ellyn, Ill.
Schneyer, J. Wesley, 7454 Ruskin Rd., Philadelphia, Pa.
Schnitzen, Joseph P., University of Houston, Houston, Tex.
Schnitzer, Mrs. Eunice E., 3223 East First St., Wichita, Kan.
Schoeller, Arthur W., 8626 W. Lawrence Ave., Milwaukee, Wis.
Schooler, Virgil E., Sch. of Educ., Indiana University, Bloomington, Ind.
Schooling, Herbert W., Superintendent of Schools, Webster Groves, Mo.
Schor, Theodore, 149 N. Fifth Ave., Highland Park, N.J.
Schott, Marion S., Central Missouri State College, Warrensburg, Mo.
Schramm, John S., 201 Third Ave., New Town Square, Pa.
Schreiber, Herman, 80 Clarkson Ave., Brooklyn, N.Y.
Schroeder, Carl N., 6 Atkins Ave., Cortland, N.Y.

Schroeder, Marie L., 3125 N. Spangler St., Philadelphia, Pa.
Schueler, Herbert, Hunter College, 295 Park Ave., New York, N.Y.
Schuker, Louis A., Jamaica High School, 168-01 Gothic Dr., Jamaica, N.Y.
Schuller, Charles F., Michigan State University, East Lansing, Mich.
Schultz, Frederick, Box 931, G.P.O., New York, N.Y.
Schulze, Herbert, 12102 Gilbert St., Garden Grove, Calif.
Schumann, Myrtle G., Orono School Dist. 278, Long Lake, Minn.
Schumann, Victor, 3355 N. 23rd St., Milwaukee, Wis.
Schuyler, Helen K., Kansas State College of Pittsburg, Pittsburg, Kan.
Schwanholt, Dana B., Valparaiso University, Valparaiso, Ind.
Schwartz, Alfred, Drake University, Des Moines, Iowa
Schwartz, Emanuel, 193 Sullivan St., Brooklyn, N.Y.
Schwartz, Sheila, Dogwood Drive., Kings Point, L.I., N.Y.
Schwartz, William P., 273 Ave. P., Brooklyn, N.Y.
Schwarz, A. R., J. D. Pierce Lab. Sch., Northern Mich. College, Marquette, Mich.
Schwarzenberger, Alfred J., 5943 North 42nd St., Milwaukee, Wis.
Schwertfeger, Mary Jane, 6 Parkview Pl., Ann Arbor, Mich.
Schwisow, Lauren L., Superintendent of Schools, Scottsbluff, Neb.
Scobey, Mary-Margaret, San Francisco State College, San Francisco, Calif.
Scott, Cecil Winfield, Rutgers University, New Brunswick, N.J.
Scott, Guy, Larned State Hospital, Larned, Kan.
Scott, Helen E., 385 Bullocks Point Ave., Riverside, R.I.
Scott, Waldo I., 21 Second Ave., Port Washington, N.Y.
Scott, Walter E., Dept. of Educ., State Univ. Col. of Educ., Potsdam, N.Y.
Scott, Walter W., 340 Pine Ave., Holland, Mich.
Scott, William Owen Nixon, 275 Milledge Terrace, Athens, Ga.
Schritchfield, Floyd C., South Div., University of Nevada, Las Vegas, Nev.
Seaberg, Dorothy I., 119 Stadium, Stockton, Calif.
Seagoe, May V., Sch. of Educ., University of California, Los Angeles, Calif.
Sear, C. E., General Beadle State Teachers College, Madison, S.D.
Searle, Herbert A., 761 Mt. Vernon Ave., Haddonfield, N.J.
Searles, Mrs. Anna Hawley, Univ. of Southern California, Los Angeles, Calif.
Searles, Warren B., 97 Surrey Lane, Hempstead, L.I., N.Y.
Sears, Jesse B., 40 Tevis Pl., Palo Alto, Calif.
Seaton, Donald F., Superintendent of Schools, Boone, Iowa
Seay, Maurice F., Kellogg Foundation, Battle Creek, Mich.
Sebaly, A. L., Western University of Michigan, Kalamazoo, Mich.
Sechler, Hazel B., 800 West 8th St., Silver City, N.M.
Seckinger, Richard K., Sch. of Educ., University of Pittsburgh, Pittsburgh, Pa.
Seedor, Marie M., 1401 Lincoln Ave., Prospect Park, Pa.
Seely, Gordon M., Jr., P.O. Box 533, Redwood City, Calif.
Sehmann, Henry R., 6101 East 7th St., Long Beach, Calif.
Seifert, George G., 1719 East 116th Pl., Cleveland, Ohio
Seifert, Leland B., Haverstraw-Stony Point School Dist., Stony Point, N.Y.
Selleck, Eugene R., Superintendent, School Dist. No. 98, Berwyn, Ill.
Sellery, Austin R., 344 Sunset Way, Palm Springs, Calif.
Selzer, Edwin, 168-06 Jewel Ave., Flushing, N.Y.
Sengstock, David K., Summy-Birchard Pub. Co., 1834 Ridge Ave., Evanston, Ill.
Sentman, Everette E., United Educators, Inc., Lake Bluff, Ill.
Sentz, Erma, Burton Hall, University of Minnesota, Minneapolis, Minn.
Service, Randolph G., Los Angeles State College, Los Angeles, Calif.
Serviss, Trevor K., L. W. Singer Co., 249 W. Erie Blvd., Syracuse, N.Y.
Seubert, Eugene E., Washington University, St. Louis, Mo.
Severson, Eileen E., 6701 N. Port Washington Rd., Milwaukee, Wis.
Severson, John, 249 Douglas Ave, Salinas, Calif.
Seville, George C., 134 Newcomb Rd., Tenafly, N.J.
Sexton, Besse G., Box 43, Navy 127, c/o Postmaster, Seattle, Wash.
Seyfert, Warren C., 6423 N. Santa Monica, Milwaukee, Wis.
Shack, Jacob H., 127 Remsen St., Brooklyn, N.Y.
Shafer, B. Henry, 1885 Grand Blvd., Wyomissing, Pa.
Shafer, Robert E., Tchrs. Col., Columbia University, New York, N.Y.

Shaffer, John R., 75 Port Watson St., Cortland, N.Y.
Shane, Harold G., Sch. of Educ., Indiana University, Bloomington, Ind.
Shankman, Mrs. Florence, 20 Garner St., South Norwalk, Conn.
Shannon, MacRae, Ottawa Twp. High School, 211 E. Main St., Ottawa, Ill.
Shaplin, Judson T., 182 Upland Rd., Cambridge, Mass.
Shattuck, George E., Norwich Free Academy, Norwich, Conn.
Shaw, Frances, 4717 Central Ave., Indianapolis, Ind.
Shaw, M. Luelle, 1126 N.W. Eighth Ave., Miami, Fla.
Shaw, Robert C., Superintendent of Schools, Columbia, Mo.
Shea, James T., San Antonio Ind. School Dist., 141 Lavaca St., San Antonio, Tex.
Sheerin, James S., Sarah D. Ottiwell Sch., Diman St., New Bedford, Mass.
Sheffield, Lester H., Juneau County Teachers College, New Lisbon, Wis.
Sheldon, Dorothy R., Bethany Nazarene College, Bethany, Okla.
Sheldon, Muriel Inez, Los Angeles City Board of Educ., Los Angeles, Calif.
Sheldon, William Denley, 508 University Pl., Syracuse, N.Y.
Shelton, Nollie W., 328 Blowing Rock Rd., Boone, N.C.
Shemky, Robert W., St. Joseph's College, Rensselaer, Ind.
Shepard, Samuel, Jr., 4633 Moffitt Ave., St. Louis, Mo.
Shepherd, Gerald Q., 501 N. Segovia Ave., San Gabriel, Calif.
Sheppard, Lawrence E., Antioch Unified School Dist., Antioch, Calif.
Sherbondy, Freda J., 470 McPherson Ave., Akron, Ohio
Sherer, Lorraine, 1109 Magnolia Ave., Los Angeles, Calif.
Sherman, Mrs. Helene, 350 Central Park West, New York, N.Y.
Sherman, Neil, School Dist. No. 1, 125 E. Lincoln, Phoenix, Ariz.
Shiflet, R. B., Lamar Elementary School, Mineral Wells, Tex.
Schimmel, Ethel, 157 Bulkley St., Kalamazoo, Mich.
Shinaberry, Charles G., Box 114, Slippery Rock, Pa.
Shive, Mrs. Mae L., 600 Michael Rd., Newton, Kan.
Shoemaker, F. L., 15 Woodside Dr., Athens, Ohio
Shohen, Samuel S., 229 Friends Lane, Westbury, L.I., N.Y.
Sholund, Milford, Gospel Light Press, 725 E. Colorado, Glendale, Calif.
Shope, Nathaniel H., Superintendent of Schools, Goldsboro, N.C.
Shores, J. Harlan, 805 W. Pennsylvania Ave., Urbana, Ill.
Short, D. Robert, Wessington Springs College, Wessington Springs, S.D.
Short, Robert Allen, 17059 Fifth N.E. St., Seattle, Wash.
Shrum, John W., 97 E. Lane Ave., Columbus, Ohio
Shuff, Robert V., Burton Hall, University of Minnesota, Minneapolis, Minn.
Shultz, Mrs. Dona, R. R. 1, Grabill, Ind.
Shuman, Elsie, 4819 Magoun Ave., East Chicago, Ind.
Shyryn, E. Layne, Queen Elizabeth High School, Calgary, Alberta
* Sias, A. B., Route 3, Box 459B, Orlando, Fla.
Sica, Morris G., 11-13 West View Ave., White Plains, N.Y.
Siebert, Edna M., 5742 N. Kingsdale Ave., Chicago, Ill.
Siebrecht, Elmer B., 3019 Queen Anne Ave., Seattle, Wash.
Siegel, Martin, 1807 Randolph Rd., Schenectady, N.Y.
Siegfried, Paul V., 892 W. Boston Blvd., Detroit, Mich.
Siemers, Allan A., Wisconsin State College, River Falls, Wis.
Siemons, Alice E., San Francisco State College, San Francisco, Calif.
Sieswerda, David E., 1001 W. Fairmont Ave., Phoenix, Ariz.
Sievert, Erich H., 31 Waldheim Dr., New Ulm, Minn.
Sieving, Eldor C., Concordia Teachers College, River Forest, Ill.
Siewers, Karl, 2301 Estes Ave., Chicago, Ill.
Sikorski, Harold R., Superintendent of Schls., Diocese of Saginaw, Saginaw, Mich.
Silas, Gordon, Roanoke College, Salem, Va.
Silvern, Leonard Charles, 979 Teakwood Rd., Los Angeles, Calif.
Silverstein, Paul C., 364 Sackman St., Brooklyn, N.Y.
Simmons, Marian Alice, 2118 East 50th St., Kansas City, Mo.
Simmons, Patricia Caldwell, 1018—45th Way, Long Beach, Calif.
Simmons, Virginia Lee, 1207 Essex House, Indianapolis, Ind.
Simms, Naomi, 333 College Ct., Kent, Ohio
Simms, Thelma, 80 Waddell Ave., Elm Grove, W.Va.

Simon, Dan, Superintendent of Schools, East Chicago, Ind.
Simon, Eric, Sherman, Conn.
Simpson, Mrs. Elizabeth A., 5627 Blackstone Ave., Chicago, Ill.
Simpson, Elisabeth P., 140 Evergreen Dr., Dover, Del.
Simpson, Frederick W., University of Tulsa, Tulsa, Okla.
Simpson, Mrs. Hazel D., Col. of Educ., University of Georgia, Athens, Ga.
Simpson, Ray H., Col. of Educ., University of Illinois, Urbana, Ill.
Sims, H. H., Superintendent of Schools, Bristow, Okla.
Sims, Harold W., 9423 Harvard Ave., Chicago, Ill.
Singer, Harry, Div. of Soc. Sci., Univ. of California, Riverside, Calif.
Singh, Mrs. Kirpal T., 2994/4 Ranjeet Nagar, New Delhi, India
Singletary, James Daniel, USOM/Kabul, State Dept. Mail Room, Washington, D.C.
Singleton, Stanton J., Col. of Educ., University of Georgia, Athens, Ga.
Sipay, Edward R., 173 Franklin St., Ansonia, Conn.
Sires, Ely, 5018 LaCrosse Lane, Madison, Wis.
Sister Agnes Cecilia, Nazareth Academy, 1001 Lake Ave., Rochester, N.Y.
Sister Ann Augusta, 400 The Fenway, Boston, Mass.
Sister Anna Clare, College of St. Rose, Albany, N.Y.
Sister Barbara Geoghegan, Col. of Mt. St. Joseph-on-the-Hudson, Mt. St. Joseph, Ohio
Sister Celine, 57 Lincoln Ave., Port Chester, N.Y.
Sister Charles Edward, Annhurst College, Putnam, Conn.
Sister Clare Mary, Xavier University, Palmetto and Pine Sts., New Orleans, La.
Sister Dorothy Marie Riordan, College of St. Elizabeth, Convent Station, N.J.
Sister Elizabeth Ann, Immaculate Heart College, Los Angeles, Calif.
Sister Eugenia Marie, Mercy College, 8200 W. Outer Dr., Detroit, Mich.
Sister Magdalita, Marymount College, Salina, Kan.
Sister Irene Elizabeth, 1 Main St., Groton, Mass.
Sister James Edward, Brescia College, Owensboro, Ky.
Sister Justa McNamara, Dept. of Educ., St. Joseph College, Emmitsburg, Md.
Sister Margaret Eucharia, St. Mary's High School, Rutherford, N.J.
Sister Margaret Mary O'Connell, College of Notre Dame of Maryland, Baltimore, Md.
Sister Marie Claudia, Barry College, Miami Shores, Fla.
Sister Mary Agnes Hennessey, Mount Mercy College, Cedar Rapids, Iowa
Sister Mary Alma, St. Mary's College, Notre Dame, Ind.
Sister M. Angela Betke, Cantalician Ctr. for Child., 3233 Main St., Buffalo, N.Y.
Sister Mary Antonius, St. Mary College, Hooksett, N.H.
Sister Mary Basil, Good Counsel College, White Plains, N.Y.
Sister Mary Basil, Notre Dame of the Lake, Nequon, Wis.
Sister Mary Benedict Phelan, Clarke College, Dubuque, Iowa
Sister Mary Bernice, St. John College, Cleveland, Ohio
Sister M. Brideen Long, Holy Family College, Manitowoc, Wis.
Sister M. Camille Kliebhan, Cardinal Stritch College, Milwaukee, Wis.
Sister Mary Celestine, College Misericordia, Dallas (Luzerne Co.), Pa.
Sister Mary Chrysostom, College of Our Lady of the Elms, Chicopee, Mass.
Sister Mary Clarissa, Dominican College of Blauvelt, Blauvelt, N.Y.
Sister Mary Conleth, Mount Alvernia College, Chestnut Hill, Mass.
Sister M. Consolata, St. Hedwig High School, 5680 Konkel St., Detroit, Mich.
Sister Mary David, College of St. Benedict, St. Joseph, Minn.
Sister Mary de Lourdes, Saint Joseph College, West Hartford, Conn.
Sister Mary Dolores, College of St. Francis, Joliet, Ill.
Sister Mary Dorothy, Educ. Dept., Siena Heights College, Adrian, Mich.
Sister Mary Dorothy, Queen of Apostles Library, Harriman, N.Y.
Sister Mary Edward, College of St. Catherine, St. Paul, Minn.
Sister Mary Edward, Comstock Hall, University of Minnesota, Minneapolis, Minn.
Sister Mary Edwina, 5286 South Park Ave., Hamburg, N.Y.
Sister Mary Elaine, College of St. Mary, 1901 S. 73rd St., Omaha, Neb.
Sister Mary Elizabeth, Sister Mary's High School, Rutherford, N.J.

Sister M. Felicitas, Regina Heights, 4830 Salem Ave., Dayton, Ohio
Sister Mary Fidelia, Immaculata College, 5531 S. Karlov Ave., Chicago, Ill.
Sister M. Francis Regis, 444 Centre St., Milton, Mass.
Sister Mary Fridian, Dept. of Educ., St. Francis College, Fort Wayne, Ind.
Sister Mary Gabrielle, Nazareth College, Nazareth, Mich.
Sister Mary Giles, Mariam College, Indianapolis, Ind.
Sister M. Harriet Sanborn, Aquinas College, Grand Rapids, Mich.
Sister Mary Hugh, Fontbonne College, St. Louis, Mo.
Sister Mary Imeldine, Marylhurst College, Marylhurst, Ore.
Sister Mary Innocenta, The Felician College, 3800 Peterson Ave., Chicago, Ill.
Sister Mary Irmina Saelinger, Villa Madonna College, Covington, Ky.
Sister Mary James, Mt. St. Vincent College, Rockingham, Nova Scotia
Sister Mary Joachim, Benedictine Heights College, Tulsa, Okla.
Sister Mary John Francis, Mount Mary College, Milwaukee, Wis.
Sister M. Josephina, Xavier University, 7325 Palmetto St., New Orleans, La.
Sister Mary Judith, Dept. of Educ., Briar Cliff College, Sioux City, Iowa
Sister Mary Kathleen, Mt. St. Agnes College, Mt. Washington, Baltimore, Md.
Sister M. Laurina, Mount Mary College, Yankton, S.D.
Sister Mary Lawrence, Mary Manse College, Toledo, Ohio
Sister Mary Lawrence Huber, Mt. St. Joseph Teachers College, Buffalo, N.Y.
Sister Mary Leo, Immaculata College, Immaculata, Pa.
Sister M. Leonella, St. Mary of the Wasatch, Salt Lake City, Utah
Sister Mary Liguori, Mercyhurst College, Erie, Pa.
Sister Mary Lucille, Mercy College, 8200 W. Outer Dr., Detroit, Mich.
Sister M. Margarita, Rosary College, River Forest, Ill.
Sister M. Matthew, Sacred Heart Dominican College, Houston, Tex.
Sister Mary Mercita, St. Mary College, Xavier, Kan.
Sister M. Merici, Educ. Dept., Ursuline College, Louisville, Ky.
Sister Mary Muriel, Marian College, Fond du Lac, Wis.
Sister M. Muriel Gallagher, Mt. Mercy College, Pittsburgh, Pa.
Sister Mary Muriel Hogan, Ottumwa Heights College, Ottumwa, Iowa
Sister Mary Nila, Cardinal Cushing Education Clinic, Boston, Mass.
Sister M. Petrine, 1205 Louisiana Ave., New Orleans, La.
Sister M. Philomene Schiller, Webster College, Webster Groves, Mo.
Sister Mary Priscilla, Notre Dame College, Cleveland, Ohio
Sister M. Ronalda, St. Margaret Hospital, Hammond, Ind.
Sister Mary Rose Agnes, Our Lady of Cincinnati College, Cincinnati, Ohio
Sister M. Rose Alice, St. Paul's Priory, 301 Summit Ave., St. Paul, Minn.
Sister M. Roselyn, 45 Sixth Ave., Le Mars, Iowa
Sister M. Rosine, Dunbarton College, Washington, D.C.
Sister Mary of St. Michael, College of the Holy Names, Oakland, Calif.
Sister Mary Teresa Francis McDade, St. Joseph Convent, Dubuque, Iowa
Sister Mary Theodine, Viterbo College, LaCrosse, Wis.
Sister M. Theodore, Educ. Dept., Dominican College, Racine, Wis.
Sister Mary Vianney, St. Xavier College, 103rd and Central Park, Chicago, Ill.
Sister Mary Vincent Therese Tuohy, 245 Clinton Ave., Brooklyn, N.Y.
Sister Mary Zeno, Notre Dame College, 320 E. Ripa Ave., St. Louis, Mo.
Sister Maureen, College of Great Falls, Great Falls, Mont.
Sister Nesta Feldman, 136 West 75th St., New York, N.Y.
Sister Rosemarie Julie, Éduc. Dept., College of Notre Dame, Belmont, Calif.
Sittler, Mrs. Fannie Ruth, 1000 W. Rollins St., Box 458, Moberly, Mo.
Sizemore, Robert A., 2602 Glendale Ave., Toledo, Ohio
Skaggs, Darcy A., 3699 N. Holly Ave., Baldwin Park, Calif.
Skalski, John M., Sch. of Educ., Fordham University, New York, N.Y.
Skard, Mrs. Aase Gruda, Fjellvn 2, Lysaker, Norway
Skatzes, D. H., P.O. Box 105, Old Washington, Ohio
Skawski, John, 20 Curtis Rd., Vernon, N.Y.
Skibbens, Charles P., 3732 N. Kildare Ave., Chicago, Ill.
Skinner, Richard C., Clarion State College, Clarion, Pa.
Skipper, Mrs. Dora Sikes, Florida State University, Tallahassee, Fla.
Skogsberg, Alfred H., Bloomfield Junior High School, Bloomfield, N.J.

Skonberg, Mrs. Madelon, 2601 Sunnyside Ave., Chicago, Ill.
Slater, Margaret Ruth, 84 W. Washington St., Painesville, Ohio
Sligo, Joseph R., 102 N. Lancaster St., Athens, Ohio
Slobetz, Frank, St. Cloud State College, St. Cloud, Minn.
Slocum, Helen M., 202 Morris Gym, University of Minnesota, Minneapolis, Minn.
Slutter, Earl J., 90 Lackawanna Ave., East Stroudsburg, Pa.
Smail, Robert W., USOM, APO 153, San Francisco, Calif.
Small, Lowell A., Superintendent of Schools, Hutchinson, Kan.
Small, Mrs. Turie T., 554 S. Campbell St., Daytona Beach, Fla.
Smallenburg, Harry W., County Schools, 808 N. Spring St., Los Angeles, Calif.
Smedstad, Alton O., Superintendent, Elem. Schools, Hillsboro, Ore.
Smerling, William H., 709 Gephart Dr., Cumberland, Md.
Smith, A. Edson, East Alton–Wood River High School, Wood River, Ill.
Smith, Mrs. Adean M., 2519 North 41st St., Milwaukee, Wis.
Smith, Alice Brown, Box 312, Grambling, La.
Smith, Ara K., 609 Lafayette St., Michigan City, Ind.
Smith, Arthur E., National Merit Scholarship Corp., Evanston, Ill.
Smith, B. Othanel, Col. of Educ., University of Illinois, Urbana, Ill.
Smith, C. C., 4801 Tremont St., Dallas, Tex.
Smith, Calvin S., 5705 South 1700 West, Murray, Utah
Smith, Dorothy D., 1721 E. Third St., Duluth, Minn.
Smith, Emmitt D., Box 745, West Texas Station, Canyon, Tex.
Smith, Garmon B., Austin College, Sherman, Tex.
Smith, Gary R., 14520 Asbury Park, Detroit, Mich.
Smith, H. Hayes, 326 Tower Dr., East Alton, Ill.
Smith, Hannis S., State Office Annex, 117 University Ave., St. Paul, Minn.
Smith, Henry P., Sch. of Educ., University of Kansas, Lawrence, Kan.
Smith, Ida T., Col. of Educ., Oklahoma State University, Stillwater, Okla.
Smith, Inez L., New York University, Washington Square, New York, N.Y.
Smith, J. Edward, Westminster College, New Wilmington, Pa.
Smith, James O., R.R. 2, Wilson St., Rising Sun, Ind.
Smith, Joseph M., 283 Lloyd St., Newington, Conn.
Smith, Lawrence J., Central Michigan University, Mt. Pleasant, Mich.
Smith, Leslie F., 705 N. Killingsworth, Portland, Ore.
Smith, Lloyd L., Col. of Educ., State University of Iowa, Iowa City, Iowa
Smith, Lloyd N., Dept. of Educ., Indiana State Teachers Col., Terre Haute, Ind.
Smith, Mary Alice, State College, Lock Haven, Pa.
Smith, Menrie M., Rte. 4, Hamilton, Ala.
Smith, Nila B., Sch. of Educ., New York University, Wash. Sq., New York, N.Y.
Smith, Paul E., Board of Educ., 13 S. Fitzhugh St., Rochester, N.Y.
Smith, Paul M., 7271 East Ave., U-3, Littlerock, Calif.
Smith, Philip John, Box 13, P.O. Cottesloe, Western Australia
Smith, Sara E., Western Maryland College, Westminster, Md.
Smith, Sisera, 115 South 54th St., Philadelphia, Pa.
* Smith, Stephen E., East Texas Baptist College, Marshall, Tex.
Smith, W. D., P.O. Box 2587, Lafayette, La.
Smith, W. Holmes, El Camino College, El Camino College, Calif.
Smith, Walter Douglas, Winthrop College, Rock Hill, S.C.
Smith, Winifred W., Chicago Read. and Speech Clinic, 116 S. Michigan, Chicago, Ill.
Snader, Daniel W., State University Col. of Education, Fredonia, N.Y.
Snider, Glenn R., Col. of Educ., University of Oklahoma, Norman, Okla.
Snider, Hervon Leroy, Sch. of Educ., University of Idaho, Moscow, Idaho
Sniderman, S. M., Barber School, 45 E. Buena Vista, Highland Park, Mich.
Snowden, Terrence J., Sch. of Educ., University of Wisconsin, Madison, Wis.
Snyder, Agnes, 50 Central Ter., Clifton Park, Wilmington, Del.
Snyder, Harvey B., Pasadena College, 1539 E. Howard St., Pasadena, Calif.
Snyder, Jerome R., 1114 Mogford St., Midland, Tex.
Snyder, Mrs. Marjorie Sims, Col. of Educ., Univ. of Florida, Gainesville, Fla.
Snyder, Ralph E., 50 Howell Ave., Larchmont, N.Y.
Snyder, Robert D., Superintendent of Schools, Wayzata, Minn.

Snyder, Ruth C., 1217 Walnut St., Utica, N.Y.
Snyder, Walter E., 362 N. Craven St., Monmouth, Ore.
Snyder, Wayne T., 8707 Ward Parkway, Kansas City, Mo.
Soares, Anthony T., 617 Central Ave., Needham Heights, Mass.
Sobel, Morton J., Suite 300, 515 Madison Ave., New York, N.Y.
Sobel, Stuart W., 135 Hawthorne St., Brooklyn, N.Y.
Sobin, Gloria A., 370 Seymour Ave., Derby, Conn.
Soeberg, Mrs. Dorothy, 106 Ridge Rd., Whittier, Calif.
Soles, Stanley, San Francisco State College, San Francisco, Calif.
Solomon, Ruth H., 91 N. Allen St., Albany, N.Y.
Sommers, Mildred, Board of Educ., 290 W. Michigan Ave., Jackson, Mich.
Sommers, Wesley S., 820 Sixth St., Menomonie, Wis.
Sonntag, Ida May, 5101 Norwich Rd., Toledo, Ohio
Sonstegard, Manford A., State College of Iowa, Cedar Falls, Iowa
Sorenson, A. Garth, Moore Hall., University of California, Los Angeles, Calif.
Sorensen, Helmer E., Oklahoma A. and M. College, Stillwater, Okla.
Sorenson, Katherine, Burton Hall, University of Minnesota, Minneapolis, Minn.
Sorgatz, Walter C., 1845 E. Hubbell St., Phoenix, Ariz.
Soucy, Leo, Central School, Dist. No. 1, 27 Cayuga St., Union Springs, N.Y.
Southall, Maycie K., Peabody College for Teachers, Nashville, Tenn.
Sowards, G. Wesley, Sch. of Educ., Stanford University, Stanford, Calif.
Spalding, Willard B., 1620 S.W. Park Ave., Portland, Ore.
Spalke, E. Pauline, P.O. Box 405, Salem Depot, N.H.
Sparks, J. E., Beverly Hills High School, Beverly Hills, Calif.
Sparling, Edward J., Roosevelt University, 430 S. Michigan Ave., Chicago, Ill.
Spaulding, Seth, 1701 Sixteenth St., N.W., Washington, D.C.
Spaulding, William E., Houghton-Mifflin Co., 2 Park St., Boston, Mass.
Spear, William G., 7233 W. Lunt Ave., Chicago, Ill.
Spears, William, Superintendent of Schools, Appleton, Wis.
Speer, Hugh W., University of Kansas City, Kansas City, Mo.
Spence, Morris E., 1320—41st St., Des Moines, Iowa
Spence, Ralph B., Tchrs. Col., Columbia University, New York, N.Y.
Spencer, Doris U., Johnson State College, Johnson, Vt.
Spencer, Edward M., Fresno State College, Fresno, Calif.
Spencer, James E., 261 Sea Vale St., Chula Vista, Calif.
Spencer, Lyle M., Science Research Associates, Inc., 259 E. Erie, Chicago, Ill.
Spencer, Peter L., 5550 Gravois Ave., Los Angeles, Calif.
Sperber, Robert I., 278 A-1 Cherry Valley Ave., Garden City, N.Y.
Sperry, Mrs. Florence, 10560 Lemoran Ave., Downey, Calif.
Spieseke, Alice W., Tchrs. Col., Columbia University, New York, N.Y.
Spigle, Irving, Superintendent of Schools, Park Forest, Ill.
Spinola, A. R., Superintendent, Denville School Dist. No. 1, Denville, N.J.
Spitz, Thomas A., Sch. of Educ., City College, New York, N.Y.
Spitzer, Herbert F., Col. of Educ., State University of Iowa, Iowa City, Iowa
Spooner, Donald William, Educational Research Council, Cleveland, Ohio
Sprietsma, Lewis R., 1031 Princeton Ave., Modesto, Calif.
Springer, Robert L., Superintendent of Schools, Rochester, N.Y.
Springman, John H., 1215 Waukegan Rd., Glenview, Ill.
Spruill, Betty Anne, 241 Langdon St., Madison, Wis.
Squire, James R., 805 W. Indiana Ave., Urbana, Ill.
Staats, Pauline G., Chas. Hay Elem. Sch., 3185 S. Lafayette, Englewood, Colo.
Stabler, Ernest, Wesleyan University, Middletown, Conn.
Stachenfeld, Emanuel, Marine Park Junior High School, Brooklyn, N.Y.
Stack, Eileen C., 937 N. Linden Ave., Oak Park, Ill.
Stack, Mrs. Thelma D., 2209 E. Park Pl., Milwaukee, Wis.
Stafford, H. D., P.O. Box 610, Langley, British Columbia
Staggs, Jack, Sam Houston Teachers College, Huntsville, Tex.
Stahlecker, Lotar V., Kent State University, Kent, Ohio
Stahly, Harold L., 1401 Randol Ave., Cape Girardeau, Mo.
Staiger, Ralph C., 701 Dallam Rd., Newark, Del.
Staiger, Roger P., Dept. of Chem., Ursinus College, Collegeville, Pa.

Stalnaker, John M., 1580 Sherman Ave., Evanston, Ill.
Stanchfield, Jo M., Occidental College, Los Angeles, Calif.
Stanford, Madge, 3336 Rankin, Dallas, Tex.
Stanley, Charles J., Jr., Florida A. and M. University, Tallahassee, Fla.
Stanley, W. O., 1406 W. Green St., Champaign, Ill.
Stanton, Louella M., Wheaton High School, Wheaton, Md.
Stanton, William A., 3037 Garfield Ave., Costa Mesa, Calif.
Stapleton, Mary Ellen, Jonathan Maynard Training School, Framingham, Mass.
Stapley, Howard A., Jr., State University College of Education, Oneonta, N.Y.
Starner, Norman Dean, Wyalusing Valley Joint High School, Wyalusing, Pa.
Stathopulos, Peter H., Elem. School, Second Ave. and Manavon St., Phoenixville, Pa.
Stauffer, Richard F., Horton Watkins High School, St. Louis, Mo.
Stauffer, Russell G., University of Delaware, Newark, Del.
Staven, LaVier L., 1304 MacArthur Rd., Hays, Kan.
Steadman, E. R., 277 Columbia, Elmhurst, Ill.
Stedje, Raynard L., 3146 Minnehaha Ave., So., Minneapolis, Minn.
Stedman, Edith, 600 University Ave., S.E., Minneapolis, Minn.
Steel, Wade A., Leyden High School, Franklin Park, Ill.
Steele, Lysle H., Beloit College, Beloit, Wis.
Steeves, Frank L., University of Vermont, Burlington, Vt.
Steg, Mrs. Loreen E., 4114 Fountain Green, Lafayette Hill, Pa.
Stegeman, William H., Educ. Ctr., San Diego City Schools, San Diego, Calif.
Steigelman, Mrs. Vivian R., 1544 Oxford St., Berkeley, Calif.
Stein, Jay W., Drake University, Des Moines, Iowa
Stein, Michael W., New Lebanon School, Byram, Conn.
Steinberg, Paul M., Hebrew Union Sch. of Educ., 40 W. 68th St., New York, N.Y.
Steinberg, Walter F., Luther High School South, 3130 W. 87th St., Chicago, Ill.
Steinberg, Warren L., 4418 Corinth Ave., Culver City, Calif.
Steininger, Earl W., 535 West 5th St., Dubuque, Iowa
Steinkellner, Robert H., Southern Illinois Univ., S.W. Campus, East St. Louis, Ill.
Stephens, A., 1936 Carlotta Dr., Concord, Calif.
Stephens, Bertha L., 1765 Gilpin St., Denver, Colo.
Stephens, Coral, 919 Orchard Ave., Chariton, Iowa
Stephens, J. M., Dept. of Educ., University of California, Berkeley, Calif.
Stephens, Kenton E., Dept. of Educ., University of Chicago, Chicago, Ill.
Stephens, Lester D., Sch. of Educ., University of Miami, Coral Gables, Fla.
Stephenson, Mrs. Drubelle, 310 N. Meridian St., Lebanon, Ind.
Sterling, A. M., P.O. Box 213, Northville, N.Y.
Sternberg, William N., Public Sch. 114, 1155 Cromwell Ave., New York, N.Y.
Stetson, Ethel A., 94 E. Valley Stream Blvd., Valley Stream, N.Y.
Steudler, Mary Margaret, 70 Grove Hill, New Britain, Conn.
Stevens, J. H., 320 S. Highland St., Murfreesboro, Tenn.
Stevens, Paul C., Rapid City Public Schools, Rapid City, S.D.
Stewart, C. E., Grant School, 21131 Gardenlane, Ferndale, Mich.
Stewart, Frederick H., P.O. Box 3, Jarrettown, Pa.
Stibbs, R. B., Supt., School Dist 43, New Westminster, British Columbia
Stickler, W. Hugh, Florida State University, Tallahassee, Fla.
Stiemke, Eugenia A., Valparaiso University, Valparaiso, Ind.
Stier, Lealand D., 14675 Aloha St., Saratoga, Calif.
Stigall, Clarence C., 6327 Ingleside Ave., Chicago, Ill.
Stiles, Mrs. Cordelia L., 401 East Ninth St., Charlotte, N.C.
Stiles, Grace Ellen, Box 34, Kingston, R.I.
Stirzaker, Norbert A., 323 South 32nd St., Terre Haute, Ind.
Stitt, Sam C., Superintendent of Schools, Ellinwood, Kan.
Stoddard, George D., 14 Washington Mews, New York, N.Y.
Stofega, Michael E., 271 State St., Perth Amboy, N.J.
Stokes, Maurice S., Savannah State College, Savannah, Ga.
Stokes, Rembert, Wilberforce University, Wilberforce, Ohio
Stolee, Michael J., Burton Hall, University of Minnesota, Minneapolis, Minn.
Stoller, Nathan, Hunter College, 695 Park Ave., New York, N.Y.

Stolurow, Lawrence M., 809 Dodds Dr., Champaign, Ill.
Stone, Chester D., 549 Westwood Ct., Vacaville, Calif.
Stone, Franklin D., Superintendent of Schools, Keokuk, Iowa
Stone, George P., Union College, Lincoln, Neb.
Stone, Gladys, Superintendent, Monterey County Schools, Salinas, Calif.
Stone, Mode L., Sch. of Educ., Florida State University, Tallahassee, Fla.
Stone, Paul T., Huntingdon College, Montgomery, Ala.
Stone, Samuel B., Sch. of Educ., University of Denver, Denver, Colo.
Stone ,Wilson M., Western Illinois University, Macomb, Ill.
Stonebraker, W. Chester, 1439 N.E. Brooklyn Ave., Roseburg, Ore.
Stoneking, Lewis W., George Peabody College for Teachers, Nashville, Tenn.
Stonehocker, D. Doyle, 1515 Oakdale St., Burlington, Iowa
Stoneman, Mrs. Nora C., Lincoln School, 1821 Lincoln Rd., Wickliffe, Ohio
Stoops, John A., Dept. of Educ., Lehigh University, Bethlehem, Pa.
Stordahl, Kalmer E., 264 N. Broad St., Monmouth, Ore.
Storen, Helen F., Dept. of Educ., Queens College, Flushing, N.Y.
Storlie, Theodore R., 3400 Rose St., Franklin Park, Ill.
Storr, Mrs. Maude L., 2001 N.W. Third Ct., Fort Lauderdale, Fla.
Stottler, Richard H., University of Maryland, College Park, Md.
Stoughton, Robert W., State Department of Education, Hartford, Conn.
Straight, Mrs. Madeline J., 312 S. Scoville Ave., Oak Park, Ill.
Strain, Mrs. Sibyl M., 2236 Los Lunas St., Pasadena, Calif.
Strand, Helen A., Luther College, Decorah, Iowa
Strand, William H., 170 Mimosa Way, Menlo Park, Calif.
* Strang, Ruth, Col. of Educ., University of Arizona, Tucson, Ariz.
Stratemeyer, Florence B., Tchrs. Col., Columbia University, New York, N.Y.
Strathairn, Pamela L., Women's Phy. Ed. Dept., Stanford Univ., Stanford, Calif.
Strauch, Arnold, Elon College, P.O. Box 726, Elon College, N.C.
Strauss, John F., Jr. College of St. Thomas, St. Paul, Minn.
* Strayer, George D., 6 Mercer St., Princeton, N.J.
Strayer, George D., Jr. Col. of Educ., University of Washington, Seattle, Wash.
Strebel, Jane D., Bd. of Educ., 807 N.E. Broadway, Minneapolis, Minn.
Strem, Bruce E., 222 W. Gardner St., Long Beach, Calif.
Streng, Alice, University of Wisconsin-Milwaukee, Milwaukee, Wis.
Strickland, C. G., Sch. of Educ., Baylor University, Waco, Tex.
Strickland, Mrs. Helen B., Arlington High School, Arlington, Tex.
* Strickler, Robert E., 3815 Flod, St. Louis, Mo.
Strickling, Cloria Ann, 6904 Calverton Dr., Hyattsville, Md.
Strohbehn, Earl F., 12151 Mellowood Dr., Saratoga, Calif.
Strole, Lois E., R.R. No. 2, West Terre Haute, Ind.
Strong, Ethel, 815 East St., Iola, Kan.
Stroud, James B., Col. of Educ., State University of Iowa, Iowa City, Iowa
Stuardi, J. Edwin, 550 Dauphin St., Mobile, Ala.
Stuart, Alden T., 81 Rose Ave., Patchogue, L.I., N.Y.
Stuart, Chester J., Canisius Hall, Fairfield University, Fairfield, Conn.
Stuenkel, Walter W., Concordia College, 3126 W. Kilbourn Ave., Milwaukee,
    Wis.
Sturke, Ralph C., Superintendent of Schools, Attleboro, Mass.
Suber, James W., Woodrow Wilson High School, Washington, D.C.
Sugden, W. E., Superintendent of Schools, 7776 Lake St., River Forest, Ill.
Sullivan, Daniel C., Sch. of Educ., St. John's University, Jamaica, N.Y.
Sullivan, F. W., 1012 Lena St., N.W., Atlanta, Ga.
Sullivan, Helen Blair, 106 Elm St., Belmont, Mass.
Sullivan, Joyce, 125 E. Lincoln St., Phoenix, Ariz.
Sullivan, Ruth E., 885 Easton Rd., Glenside, Pa.
Sullivan, Sheila R., Ohio State University, Columbus, Ohio
Sun, Huai Chin, 3837 Simpson Stuart Rd., Dallas, Tex.
Suskowitz, Min, 81-31—188th St., Jamaica, N.Y.
Sutherland, J. K., Col. of Educ., Univ. of Saskatchewan, Saskatoon, Sask.
Sutherland, Jack W., San Jose State College, San Jose, Calif.
Sutherland, Margaret, Col. of Educ., University of California, Davis, Calif.

Sutter, Belva, Friends University, 732 Beverly Dr., Wichita, Kan.
Sutton, Elizabeth, Montgomery Co. Public Schools, Rockville, Md.
Sutton, Mrs. Grace L., Ridgeway Elementary School, White Plains, N.Y.
Swann, Mrs. A. Ruth, 2713 Mapleton Ave., Norfolk, Va.
Swann, Reginald L., Central Connecticut State College, New Britain, Conn.
Swanson, Mrs. Arlene, Box 288, Ossining, N.Y.
Swanson, Gordon L., Dept. of Agric. Educ., Univ. of Minnesota, St. Paul, Minn.
Swanson, J. Chester, Sch. of Educ., University of California, Berkeley, Calif.
Swanson, Reynold A., Board of Education, 100 N. Jefferson, Green Bay, Wis.
Swartout, Sheridan G., State University College of Education, Brockport, N.Y.
Swartzmiller, Jean, 90 Ridge Ave., North Plainfield, N.J.
Swauger, Velora V., 1314 Potomac Ave., Hagerstown, Md.
Swearingen, Mildred E., 930 N. Wildwood Dr., Tallahassee, Fla.
Sweet, Harmon C., Rochester Business Inst., 172 Clinton Ave., Rochester, N.Y.
Swenson, Esther J., Box 1942, University, Ala.
Swertfeger, Floyd F., Route 3, Box 16, Farmville, Va.
Swindall, Wellington, Palmdale School, 3000 E. Wier Ave., Phoenix, Ariz.

Taba, Hilda, San Francisco State College, San Francisco, Calif.
Tabachnick, B. Robert, Dept. of Educ., University of Wisconsin, Madison, Wis.
Tackman, Mary C., P.O. Box 6, Damascus, Md.
Tadena, Tomas, Philippine Normal College, Manila, Philippines
Tag, Herbert G., University of Connecticut, Storrs, Conn.
Tajima, Yuri, 1918 N. Bissell, Chicago, Ill.
* Tallman, Russell W., 2024 Avalon Rd., Des Moines, Iowa
Tallmon, Mrs. Violet, P.O. Box 644, Hughson, Calif.
Tamura, Kunihiko, No. 16, 2 Chome, Hachimandori, Sibuya-ku, Tokyo, Japan
Tancil, Sallie E., 5823 Dix St., N.E., Washington, D.C.
Tanger, Frederick, Media Borough School District, Media, Pa.
Tanner, B. William, 650 S. Detroit Ave., Toledo, Ohio
Tanner, Daniel, Northwestern University, Evanston, Ill.
Tanner, Wilbur H., Northwestern State College, Alva, Okla.
Tanruther, Edgar M., Indiana State Teachers College, Terre Haute, Ind.
Tant, Norman, Morehead State College, Morehead, Ky.
Tarbox, Florence H., D'Youville College, Buffalo, N.Y.
Tardif, Fernand R., La Salette Seminary, Enfield, N.H.
Tarver, K. E., John P. Odom School, 3445 Fannett Rd., Beaumont, Tex.
Tate, Virginia, 1440—7th St., Charleston, Ill.
Tauber, Mildred C., 825 Sheridan Rd., Glencoe, Ill.
Taylor, Charles H., Board of Education, Columbus Ave., Thornwood, N.Y.
Taylor, Mrs. Emily C., Mayo Elementary School, Edgewater, Md.
Taylor, Faith, 3681B Alabama Ave., S.E., Washington, D.C.
Taylor, Kenneth I., West Leyden High School, Northlake, Ill.
Taylor, L. O., 4314 Dodge St., Omaha, Neb.
Taylor, M. Ruth, Hillcrest School, Drexel Hill, Pa.
Taylor, Marvin J., St. Paul School of Theology, 5110 Cherry, Kansas City, Mo.
Taylor, Marvin T., Div. of Educ., Queens College, Flushing, N.Y.
Taylor, Mrs. Mary C., Box 164, Rt. No. 1, New Lenox, Ill.
Taylor, Robert E., 1835 Riverhill Rd., Columbus, Ohio
Taylor, Sara B., 5 Procter Court, Bowling Green, Ky.
Taylor, Wayne, 160 Kenberry, East Lansing, Mich.
Teague, Carroll, Pasadena Ind. School District, Pasadena, Tex.
Teal, Stanton M., 1425-B Spartan Village, East Lansing, Mich.
Teare, B. R., Jr., Carnegie Institute of Technology, Pittsburgh, Pa.
Tegner, Olaf H., 1121 West 79th St., Los Angeles, Calif.
Teigen, B. W., Bethany Lutheran College, Mankato, Minn.
Tempero, Howard E., Teachers Col., University of Nebraska, Lincoln, Neb.
Temple, F. L., Box 2185, University, Ala.
Templin, Mildred C., Inst. of Child Welfare, Univ. of Minnesota, Minneapolis, Minn.
Tennessee, Mrs. Hyacinth B., 1123—28th St., Newport News, Va.

Tenny, John W., 7745 Pinehurst, Dearborn, Mich.
Terrill, Maymie I., 2477 Overlook Rd., Cleveland Heights, Ohio
Tetz, Henry E., Oregon College of Education, Monmouth, Ore.
Thevaos, Deno G., 575 Westview Ave., State College, Pa.
Thiede, Wilson B., Educ. Bldg., University of Wisconsin, Madison, Wis.
Thomann, Don F., Dept. of Educ., Ripon College, Ripon, Wis.
Thomas, Cleveland A., Francis Parker School, 330 Webster Ave., Chicago, Ill.
Thomas, Donald R., 25102½ Malibu Rd., Malibu Beach, Calif.
Thomas, Granville S., Superintendent of Schools, Salem, N.J.
Thomas, Harold P., Dept. of Educ., Lehigh University, Bethlehelm, Pa.
Thomas, Helen C., 18 Third Ave., Ettrick, Va.
Thomas, Mrs. M. C., 1306—22nd St., Columbus, Ga.
Thomas, R. Irene, Col. of Educ., Kent State University, Kent, Ohio
Thomas, Ruth H., Van Rensselaer Hall, Col. of Home Economics, Ithaca, N.Y.
Thomas, Wade F., Santa Monica City College, Santa Monica, Calif.
Thomassen, Henry S., Webster Pub. Co., 1154 Reco Ave., St. Louis, Mo.
Thompson, Mrs. Annie B., 705 Apple St., Burlington, N.C.
Thompson, Anton, Long Beach Public Schls., 715 Locust Ave., Long Beach,
    Calif.
Thompson, Charles H., Grad. Sch., Howard University, Washington, D.C.
Thompson, Elton Noel, City Schools, 133 Mission St., Santa Cruz, Calif.
Thompson, Franklin J., South Pasadena High School, South Pasadena, Calif.
Thompson, Helen M., Chapman College, Orange, Calif.
Thompson, J. M., Elgin Academy, Elgin, Ill.
Thompson, James H., 135 Larkins St., Findlay, Ohio
Thompson, John D., Box 635 Seminole Public Schools, Seminole, Tex.
Thompson, Olive L., 1541 Iroquois Ave., Long Beach, Calif.
Thompson, Orrin G., Superintendent of Schools, Elgin, Ill.
Thompson, Ralph H., Western Washington College of Education, Bellingham,
    Wash.
Thompson, Ray, North Carolina College, Durham, N.C.
Thomson, Procter, Pitzer Hall, Claremont Men's College, Claremont, Calif.
Thornblad, Carl E., 1204 W. California Ave., Urbana, Ill.
Thorndike, Robert L., Tchrs. Col., Columbia University, New York, N.Y.
Thorne, Edmund H., 7 Whiting Lane, West Hartford, Conn.
Thornton, James W., Jr., San Jose State College, San Jose, Calif.
Thorp, Mary T., 84 Eleventh St., Providence, R.I.
Thorpe, Louis P., Sch. of Educ., University of California, Los Angeles, Calif.
Threlkeld, A. L., Jamaica, Vt.
Throne, Elsie M., 306 Lincoln Ave., Avon-by-the-Sea, N.J.
Thursby, Mrs. Ruth, 310 W. Francis St., Corona, Calif.
Thurston, Edmund W., Superintendent of Schools, Westwood, Mass.
Thyberg, Clifford S., 1717 W. Merced Ave., West Covina, Calif.
Tidrow, Joe, Dept. of Educ. and Phil., Texas Tech. College, Lubbock, Tex.
Tidwell, R. E., Stillman College, Tuscaloosa, Ala.
Tiedeman, Herman R., Illinois State Normal University, Normal, Ill.
Tiedt, Sidney W., Educ. Div., San Jose State College, San Jose, Calif.
Tierney, Marie, Chicago Teachers College, 6800 Stewart Ave., Chicago, Ill.
Tiffany, Burton C., Superintendent of Schools, Chula Vista, Calif.
Tillan, Lynn, 417 Hillsboro Pkwy., Syracuse, N.Y.
Tillman, Rodney, George Peabody College for Teachers, Nashville, Tenn.
Timberlake, Walter B., Jr., 715 N.W. Military Dr., San Antonio, Tex.
Timko, Irene H., 6153 Fletcher St., Chicago, Ill.
Timmons, F. Alan, 230 East 12th St., Long Beach, Calif.
Tinari, Charles, Shackamaxon School, Scotch Plains, N.J.
Tingle, Mary J., Col. of Educ., University of Georgia, Athens, Ga.
Tink, Albert K., 18 Wendall Pl., DeKalb, Ill.
Tinker, Miles A., 991 Winther Way, Santa Barbara, Calif.
Tipton, Elis M., 941 East Bel Air, Merced, Calif.
Tisdall, William J., Pennsylvania State University, University Park, Pa.
Todd, G. Raymond, R.D. No. 3, Bethlehem, Pa.

Toepfer, Conrad F., Jr., 383 Hewitt Ave., Buffalo, N.Y.
Toles, Caesar F., Bishop Junior College, 4527 Crozier St., Dallas, Tex.
Tollinger, William P., Superintendent, Wilson Borough Schls., Easton, Pa.
Tomes, Cornelia A., 1584 Koch Lane, San Jose, Calif.
Toops, Herbert A., 1430 Cambridge Blvd., Columbus, Ohio
Topp, Robert F., Col. of Educ., Northern Illinois University, DeKalb, Ill.
Torbet, David P., Butler University, Indianapolis, Ind.
Torchia, Joseph, State Teachers College, Millersville, Pa.
Torkelson, Gerald M., Pennsylvania State University, University Park, Pa.
Torrance, E. Paul, Bur. of Educ. Res., Univ. of Minnesota, Minneapolis, Minn.
Tostberg, Robert E., Dept. of Educ., University of Washington, Seattle, Wash.
Totten, W. Fred, Mott Sci. Bldg., 1401 E. Court St., Flint, Mich.
Toussaint, Isabella H., 101 Olive Dr., Level Green, Trafford, Pa.
Towles, Lena Ruth, 2104 Murray Ave., Louisville, Ky.
Trabue, M. R., 306 Strathmore Rd., Lexington, Ky.
Tracy, Edward, Easton-Forks and Easton Area Joint Sch. System, Easton, Pa.
Tracy, Elaine M., St. Olaf College, Northfield, Minn.
Traeger, Carl, 375 N. Eagle St., Oshkosh, Wis.
Traiber, Frank, USAID Mission, Guatemala, Dept. of State Mail Rm., Washington, D.C.
Traill, Robert R., 84 Argyle Rd., KEW, Victoria, Australia
Travelstead, Chester C., Col. of Educ., Univ. of New Mexico, Albuquerque, N.M.
Travers, John F., Sch. of Educ., Boston College, Chestnut Hill, Mass.
Travis, Vaud A., Dept. of Educ., Northeastern State College, Tahlequa, Okla.
Traxler, Arthur E., Educational Records Bureau, 21 Audubon Ave., New York, N.Y.
Treece, Marion B., Southern Illinois University, Carbondale, Ill.
Tremaine, Donahue L., Roosevelt University, 430 S. Michigan Ave., Chicago, Ill.
Trice, Mrs. E. R., 3220 Guilford Ave., Baltimore, Md.
Trice, J. A., Superintendent of Schools, Pine Bluff, Ark.
Triggs, Frances, Mountain Home, N.C.
Tripp, Philip A., Washburn University of Topeka, Topeka, Kan.
Trippe, Matthew J., George Peabody College for Teachers, Nashville, Tenn.
Trippensee, Arthur E., Col. of Educ., University of Bridgeport, Bridgeport, Conn.
Trow, William Clark, Sch. of Educ., University of Michigan, Ann Arbor, Mich.
Trubov, Herman, 13B Page Hall, Ohio State University, Columbus, Ohio
Trueblood, Inabell, 2002 E. Main St., Decatur, Ill.
Truher, Helen Burke, 803 Morada Pl., Altadena, Calif.
Truitt, John W., Michigan State University, East Lansing, Mich.
Trumble, Verna J., 42 West St., Johnson City, N.Y.
Trump, J. Lloyd, National Educ. Assn., 1201 Sixteenth St., N.W., Washington, D.C.
Trump, Paul L., Bascom Hall, University of Wisconsin, Madison, Wis.
Truncellito, Louis, P.O. Box 366, Portville, N.Y.
Tsugé, Haruko, 5570 Tsujido, Fujisawa, Kanagawa, Japan
Tucker, Mrs. Sylvia B., 30929 Rue Langlois, Palos Verdes Estates, Calif.
Tudyman, Al, 9333 Murillo Ave., Oakland, Calif.
Tully, Glover E., Educ. Dept., Florida State University, Tallahassee, Fla.
Turansky, Isadore, Western Michigan University, Kalamazoo, Mich.
Turner, C. Adam, Western Illinois University, Macomb, Ill.
Turner, Delia F., 3310 Edgemont, Tucson, Ariz.
Turner, Howard, Southern Louisiana Institute, Lafayette, La.
Turner, James W., Box 5431 North Texas Station, Denton, Tex.
Turner, Mrs. Nell B., 3431 Sangamon Ave., Dayton, Ohio
Turney, David T., George Peabody College for Teachers, Nashville, Tenn.
Tuseth, Alice, 1500 N. Washburn, Minneapolis, Minn.
Tuttle, Edwin A., Jr., 3620 Woodbridge Lane, Wantagh, N.Y.
Twohig, Patricia, Cedarburg Public Schools, Cedarburg, Wis.
Twombly, John J., Northern Illinois University, DeKalb, Ill.
Tyler, Fred. T., Sch. of Educ., University of California, Berkeley, Calif.
Tyler, I. Keith, Ohio State University, Columbus, Ohio

Tyler, Louise L., University of California, Los Angeles, Calif.
Tyler, Priscilla, Harvard Graduate School of Education, Cambridge, Mass.
Tyler, Ralph W., 202 Junipero Serra Blvd., Stanford, Calif.
Tyler, Robert, Educ. Dept., Southwestern State College, Weatherford, Okla.
Tyrell, Francis M., Immaculate Conception Seminary, Huntington, N.Y.
Tyson, Ivernia M., Arizona State College, Flagstaff, Ariz.
Tystad, Edna, Thoreau Public Schools, Thoreau, N.M.

Uehara, Betty K., 336-A N. Kuakini St., Honolulu, Hawaii
Ulmer, T. H., Superintendent of Schools, Hartville, S.C.
Umansky, Harlan L., Emerson High School, Union City, N.J.
Umholtz, Mrs. Anne K., 292 N. Fifth Ave., Highland Park, N.J.
Umstattd, James G., Sutton Hall, University of Texas, Austin, Tex.
Underwood, Mrs. Anna, Box 72, Southard, Okla.
Underwood, Mrs. Frances A., P.O. Box 3093, Pensacola, Fla.
Underwood, Helen B., 1920 Madrona, Napa, Calif.
Underwood, William J., 116 Madison, Lee's Summit, Mo.
Ungaro, Daniel, Saratoga Union Elementary Schools, Saratoga, Calif.
Unger, Mrs. Dorothy Holberg, 99 Lawton Rd., Riverside, Ill.
Unruh, Adolph, Washington University, St. Louis, Mo.
Utley, Mrs. Faye L., 11158 Ebert Dr., St. Louis, Mo.

* Vakil, K. S., 119, Marzbanabad, Andheri, Bombay, India
Valentine, Mrs. M., 138 Highland, Highland Park, Mich.
Van Bruggen, John A., 549 Benjamin Ave., Grand Rapids, Mich.
Van Dam, Thomas E., 204th and Keeler, R.R. No. 1, Matteson, Ill.
Vandenberg, E. M., Hirsch High School, 7740 S. Ingleside Ave., Chicago, Ill.
Vanderford, John A., 2817 Virginia Rd., Augusta, Ga.
Vander Horck, Karl J., 1853 N. Pascal, St. Paul, Minn.
Vander Linde, Louis F., 163 Parker Ave., Alpena, Mich.
Vanderlinden, J. S., Whiting Community Schools, Whiting, Iowa
Vander Meer, A. W., 627 W. Hamilton, University Park, Pa.
Vanderpol, Jeanette A., 10 Huron Ave., Jersey City, N.J.
Vanderpool, J. Alden, 1125 West 6th St., Los Angeles, Calif.
Vander Werf, Lester S., Col. of Educ., Northeastern University, Boston, Mass.
Van Devander, Donald M., Superintendent of Schools, Overland Park, Kan.
Van Ness, Paul H., 140 Roseville Ave., Newark, N.J.
Van Slyke, Valerie R., 4130 Monteith Dr., Los Angeles, Calif.
Van Vrancken, Charles, Ponchatoula Elem. School, Ponchatoula, La.
Van Wagenen, Marvin J., 1729 Irving Ave., South, Minneapolis, Minn.
Van Zanten, Mrs. Hazel, 4822 Division Ave., Grand Rapids, Mich.
Van Zwoll, James A., Col. of Educ., University of Maryland, College Park, Md.
Varn, Guy L., Superintendent of Schools, 1311 Marion St., Columbia, S.C.
Vasey, Hamilton G., Superintendent of Schools, Fargo, N.D.
Vaughan, Elaine P., 1433 Teller Ave., Bronx, N.Y.
Vaughan, Verdry D., Gallaudet College, Washington, D.C.
Vaughan, W. Donald, Centennial Joint Schools, Johnsville, Pa.
Veach, Jeannette, Pennsylvania State University, University Park, Pa.
Veltman, Peter, 600 College Ave., Wheaton, Ill.
Venable, Douglas, 665—45th St., Los Alamos, N.M.
Verseput, Robert Frank, 8 South St., Dover, N.J.
Vesper, Jean N., 1721 Penbrooke Trail, Dayton, Ohio
Veto, John M., 4820 W. Walton St., Chicago, Ill.
Vett, John George, State University Teachers College, New Paltz, N.Y.
Vigilante, Nicholas J., 181 Cornell Ct., Westerville, Ohio
Vignos, Dorothy Z., 718 Hermosa Ave., Hermosa Beach, Calif.
Vikner, Carl F., Gustavus Adolphus College, St. Peter, Minn.
Villano, George R., 1415 Pearl St., Denver, Colo.
Vineyard, Jerry J., Superintendent of Schools, Arkansas City, Kan.
Vinson, Mrs. Etta Mary, 434 Newman Ave., Huntsville, Ala.
Vitalo, Nicholas F., Jr., 262 Blacksmith Rd., Levittown, N.Y.

Vocalis, James C., Jersey City State College, Jersey City, N.J.
Voelker, Paul Henry, Detroit Public Schools, 453 Stimson Ave., Detroit, Mich.
Voigt, Harry R., St. Paul's College, Concordia, Mo.
Voigt, Virginia E., 9 East Clark Pl., South Orange, N.J.
Voland, Bernice H., 2020-A Folger St., Sheboygan, Wis.
Vonk, Paul Kenneth, 9065 S.W. 82nd Ave., Miami, Fla.
Vopni, Sylvia, Col. of Educ., University of Washington, Seattle, Wash.
Votava, Arthur J., 5401 S. Nordica Ave., Chicago, Ill.
Votaw, Daniel C., 3535 Sterne St., San Diego, Calif.

* Waddell, Charles W., 1365 Midvale Ave., Los Angeles, Calif.
Wade, D. E., 73 Second St., Geneseo, N.Y.
Waggoner, Sherman G., Teachers College of Connecticut, New Britain, Conn.
Wagner, Carl E., 7421 Zephyr Pl., Maplewood, Mo.
Wagner, Eva, 6 Barberry Rd., Convent, N.J.
Wagner, Mazie Earle, State University of New York, Buffalo, N.Y.
Wagner, Robert W., 1885 Neil Ave., Ohio State University, Columbus, Ohio
Wagner, Victor H., 21 Minetta Ct., Huntington, N.Y.
Waimon, Morton D., Illinois State Normal University, Normal, Ill.
Waine, Sidney I., 312 West 24th St., Deer Park, N.Y.
Wainscott, Carlton O., 301 Hawthorne, Abilene, Tex.
Walby, Grace S., 330 Anderson Ave., Winnipeg, Manitoba
Walcott, Fred G., University High School, Univ. of Michigan, Ann Arbor, Mich.
Waldron, Margaret L., St. Mary-of-the-Woods College, St. Mary-of-the-Woods, Ind.
Walker, Charles Lynn, San Jose State College, San Jose, Calif.
* Walker, Ernest T., Bigfork, Mont.
Walker, John S., Storer Junior High School, 3111 W. Euclid Ave., Muncie, Ind.
Walker, K. P., Superintendent of Schools, Jackson, Miss.
Walker, Mary Louise, 502 Rio Vista Dr., Daytona Beach, Fla.
Walker, Robert N., 2629 Pocomoke St., North, Arlington, Va.
Walker, Thomas N., P.O. Box 175, Philadelphia, Miss.
Wall, John L., North Texas State College, Denton, Tex.
Wall, T. H., Jr., Lowndes County High School, Valdosta, Ga.
Wall, William M., 536 Blair House, 43 Roslyn Rd., Winnipeg, Manitoba
Wallace, Donald G., Col. of Educ., Drake University, Des Moines, Iowa
Wallace, Elsie H., Florida State University, Tallahassee, Fla.
Wallace, James O., 1300 San Pedro Ave., San Antonio, Tex.
Wallace, Morris S., Dept. of Educ., Texas Tech. College, Lubbock, Tex.
Wallar, Gene A., San Jose State College, San Jose, Calif.
Wallen, Carl J., Sch. of Educ., Oregon State University, Corvallis, Ore.
Waller, Raymond L., 31 S. Penn St., Allentown, Pa.
Wallis, C. Lamar, 258 McLean Blvd., Memphis, Tenn.
Walsh, J. Hartt, Col. of Educ., Butler University, Indianapolis, Ind.
Walter, Ralph, 28 College Ave., Upper Montclair, N.J.
Walter, Raymond L., Box 201, Millbrook, Ala.
Walter, Robert B., 434 N. DelMar Ave., San Gabriel, Calif.
Walters, Mrs. Maxine Oyler, 12 S. High St., Mt. Sterling, Ohio
Walther, Herbert K., USOM/Education, American Embassy, APO 143, San Francisco, Calif.
Walvoord, Anthony C., Box 2845, University Hill Station, Denton, Tex.
Walz, Garry R., 1718 Arbordale, Ann Arbor, Mich.
Wampler, W. Norman, Superintendent of Schools, Bellflower, Calif.
Wantling, G. K. Dale, TCM/American Embassy, New Delhi, India
Wantoch, Mrs. Ardell H., McNeal Hall, University of Minnesota, St. Paul, Minn.
Ward, Mrs. Annie W., Volusia County Schools, DeLand, Fla.
Ward, John Henry, Texas College, Tyler, Tex.
Ward, Ted, Michigan State University, East Lansing, Mich.
Ward, Virgil S., Sch. of Educ., University of Virginia, Charlottesville, Va.
Wardeberg, Helen L., Stone Hall, Cornell University, Ithaca, N.Y.
Ware, Mrs. Dorothy, 109 Touraine Rd., Grosse Pointe Farms, Mich.

Wark, John, Yale Public Schools, Yale, Mich.
Warner, Doris E., 4C Sandra Ct., Niagara Falls, N.Y.
Warren, John Howard, 405th Air Base Group, Box 278, APO 74, San Francisco, Calif.
Warriner, Clell C., Okmulgee High School, Okmulgee, Okla.
Warriner, David A., 514 Division St., East Lansing, Mich.
Warshavsky, Mrs. Belle, 35 Cooper Dr., Great Neck, N.Y.
Warshavsky, Bernard, 910 West End Ave., New York, N.Y.
Warwick, Raymond, 627 Elm Terrace, Riverton, N.J.
Washburne, Carleton W., Michigan State University, East Lansing, Mich.
Washington, B. T., Williston School, 401 South 10th St., Wilmington, N.C.
Washington, Walter, Utica Junior College, Utica, Miss.
Wasserman, Mrs. Lillian, 1684 Meadow Lane, East Meadow, N.Y.
Wasson, Margaret, 3705 University Blvd., Dallas, Tex.
Wasson, Roy J., 1115 N. El Paso St., Colorado Springs, Colo.
Waterman, Floyd T., 540 West 122nd St., New York, N.Y.
Waters, E. Worthington, Maryland State College, Princess Anne, Md.
Waters, Rudolph E., Alcorn A. and M. College, Lorman, Miss.
Watkins, Lillian M., 351 South Hudson Ave., Pasadena, Calif.
Watkins, Ralph K., Hill Hall, University of Missouri, Columbia, Mo.
Watkins, Ray H., Decatur Baptist College, 1401 S. Trinity, Decatur, Tex.
Watkins, Thomas W., South Lehigh School District, Coopersburg, Pa.
Watson, David Roland, Elm Place School, 2031 Sheridan Rd., Highland Park, Ill.
Watson, N. E., Northfield Township High School, Northbrook, Ill.
Watson, Norman E., Orange Coast College, Costa Mesa, Calif.
Watson, Mrs. Robert, 22 Burlington St., Bordentown, N.J.
Watson, William Crawford, 29 Woodstock Rd., Mt. Waverly, Victoria, Australia
Watt, John Stewart, Col. of Educ., University of Akron, Akron, Ohio
Watt, Ralph W., 1206 Parker Ave., Hyattsville, Md.
Wattenberg, William W., Wayne University, Detroit, Mich.
Watters, Velma V., Savannah State College, Savannah, Ga.
Watts, Ann Rorem, 1508 N.W. 37th St., Oklahoma City, Okla.
Watts, Morrison L., Dept. of Educ., Province of Alberta, Edmonton, Alberta
Waxwood, Howard B., Jr., Witherspoon School, Quarry St., Princeton, N.J.
Way, Gail W., 1232 Henderson St., Chicago, Ill.
Wayson, William W., 5659 S. Drexel Ave., Chicago, Ill.
Weakley, Mrs. Mary L., 1426 Center St., Geneva, Ill.
Weaks, R. H., 22 Heather Hill Lane, St. Louis, Mo.
Weaver, Gladys C., Dept. of Educ., Juniata College, Huntingdon, Pa.
Weaver, James Frederick, Sch. of Educ., Boston University, Boston, Mass.
Webb, Mrs. E. Sue, 216 W. Fifth St., Shawano, Wis.
Webb, Holmes, Dept. of Educ., Texas Tech. College, Lubbock, Tex.
Webber, Warren L., Music Dept., Cedarville College, Cedarville, Ohio
Weber, Clarence A., N. Eagleville Rd., Storrs, Conn.
Weber, Martha Gesling, Bowling Green State University, Bowling Green, Ohio
Weddington, Rachel T., Queens College, 65-30 Kissena Blvd., Flushing, N.Y.
Wedul, Melvin O., Minnesota State College, Winona, Minn.
Wegener, Frank C., 1916 Montair Ave., Long Beach, Calif.
Wegrzyn, Helen A., 5240 W. Newport Ave., Chicago, Ill.
Wegstein, Mrs. Joseph L., 3027 Morehead Ave., El Paso, Tex.
Wehner, Freda, 723 Woodland Ave., Oshkosh, Wis.
Wehrer, Charles Siecka, Jr., 1800 Watrous Ave., Des Moines, Iowa
Weidig, Phyllis D., 33 North St., Ramsey, N.J.
Weilbaker, Charles R., Tchrs. Col., University of Cincinnati, Cincinnati, Ohio
Weinrich, Ernest F., Board of Coop. Educ. Services, P.O. Box 338, Huntington, N.Y.
Weintraub, Sam, Dept. of Educ., University of Chicago, Chicago, Ill.
Weis, Harold P., 437—23rd Ave., Moline, Ill.
Weisberg, Patricia H., 9411 S. Pleasant Ave., Chicago, Ill.
Weisiger, Louise P., 312 N. Ninth St., Richmond, Va.
Weiss, George D., Kutztown State College, Kutztown, Pa.

Weiss, M. Jerry, Jersey City State College, Jersey City, N.J.
Weiss, Morris H., Public School 215, Ave. S. and East 2nd St., Brooklyn, N.Y.
Welcenbach, Frank J., Trombly School, Grosse Pointe, Mich.
Welch, Cornelius A., St. Bonaventure University, St. Bonaventure, N.Y.
Weld, Mary D., 9407 Corsica Dr., Bethesda, Md.
Welker, Latney C., Jr., 3704 Eastbrook Rd., Natchez, Miss.
Wellck, A. A., 724 Solano Dr., N.E., Albuquerque, N.M.
Welling, Helen F., 333 E. McWilliams, Fond du Lac, Wis.
Welliver, Paul W., 508 University Dr., Greensboro, N.C.
Welsh, Walter C., School of Indust. Art, 211 E. 79th St., New York, N.Y.
Wendt, Paul R., Southern Illinois University, Carbondale, Ill.
Wenger, Roy E., Kent State University, Kent, Ohio
Wenner, Harry W., 40 Mills St., Morristown, N.J.
Wenrich, Ralph C., Sch. of Educ., University of Michigan, Ann Arbor, Mich.
Wente, Walter H., Concordia Senior College, Fort Wayne, Ind.
Wentz, Howard A., Nether Providence School District, Wallingford, Pa.
Wernick, Leo J., 3500 W. Douglas Blvd., Chicago, Ill.
Wesley, Emory Jones, 1314 S. First St., Louisville, Ky.
West, L. Clinton, Sch. of Educ., University of Wisconsin, Madison, Wis.
West, Mrs. Lorraine W., Bakersfield Ctr., Fresno State Col., Bakersfield, Calif.
West, William H., County Union Schools, 7 Bridge St., Elizabeth, N.J.
Westbrook, Charles Hart, 17 Towana Rd., Richmond, Va.
Westbrooks, Sadye Wylena, 1433 Sharon St., N.W., Atlanta, Ga.
Westby-Gibson, Dorothy, San Francisco State College, San Francisco, Calif.
Westlund, Hildur L., 920 North 22nd St., Superior, Wis.
Wetter, Allen H., Superintendent of Schools, 21st and Parkway, Philadelphia, Pa.
Wetzel, Alma E., R.D. No. 1, Green Lane, Pa.
Wewer, William P., 638 Buttonwood St., Anaheim, Calif.
Wharton, William P., Allegheny College, Meadville, Pa.
Whayland, Charles W., Glen Burnie High School, Glen Burnie, Md.
Wheat, Leonard B., Southern Illinois University, Alton, Ill.
Wheeler, Eldon G., East Alton-Wood River Community High School, Wood
    River, Ill.
Wheeler, Elizabeth, University of Wisconsin-Milwaukee, Milwaukee, Wis.
Wheeler, Mrs. Olive Boone, Box 818, Austin, Tex.
Whelhan, Amelia, State University College of Education, Oswego, N.Y.
Whetton, Mrs. Betty B., 1810 N. Mitchell St., Phoenix, Ariz.
Whigham, E. L., Oak Ridge Board of Education, P.O. Box Q, Oak Ridge, Tenn.
Whilt, Selma E., 49 Norfolk Rd., Island Park, N.Y.
Whipple, Carl E., 28 Franklin St., Warren, Pa.
Whipple, Gertrude, 14505 Mettetal Ave., Detroit, Mich.
Whitcomb, Charles L., Superintendent of Schools, Haverhill, Mass.
White, Andrew William, St. Michael's College, Cerrillos Rd., Sante Fe, N.M.
White, Edwin R., 5555 West 71st St., Indianapolis, Ind.
White, George L., Harcourt, Brace & Co., 383 Madison Ave., New York, N.Y.
White, John C., Edison School, Mesa, Ariz.
White, Kenneth B., New Jersey State Teachers College, Paterson, N.J.
White, Kenneth E., Central Michigan College, Mt. Pleasant, Mich.
White, Vern A., 26720 Grayslake Rd., Palos Verdes Estates, Calif.
Whitehead, Willis A., 3692 Traynham Rd., Shaker Heights, Ohio
Whitener, Joy E., Superintendent of Schools, Dist. 229, Kewanee, Ill.
Whiteside, Mrs. I .H., County Superintendent of Education, Ashland, Miss.
Whitten, James M., 118 School St., Gorham, Me.
Whittier, C. Taylor, Rt. 3, Box 285, Gaithersburg, Md.
Whorton, W. W., Valley High School, Fairfax, Ala.
Wickenden, Roma C., 542 N. Main St., Ada, Ohio
Wickes, Mrs. Una Southard, 141 N. Bonnie, Pasadena, Calif.
Wickstrom, Rod A., 2505 Cairns Ave., Saskatoon, Saskatchewan
Wiebe, Joel A., 1717 S. Chestnut St., Fresno, Calif.
Wieden, Clifford O. T., 181 Main St., Presque Isle, Me.
Wieder, Beth Joyce, 161 West 86th St., New York, N.Y.

Wiggin, Gladys A., Col. of Educ., University of Maryland, College Park, Md.
Wiggin, Richard G., 1426 N. Quincy St., Arlington, Va.
Wildebush, Sarah W., 125 Hobart Ave., Rutherford, N.J.
Wiley, Russell, Board of Public Instruction, Sarasota, Fla.
Wilkerson, Bernice, 2726 Wauwatosa Ave., Milwaukee, Wis.
Wilkes, Robert R., Benedictine High School, 2900 East Blvd., Cleveland, Ohio
Wilkinson, H. A., Station ACC, Box 565, Abilene, Tex.
Wilkinson, Virginia, Middle Tennessee State College, Murfreesboro, Tenn.
Willard, Robert L., Utica College, Utica, N.Y.
Willcockson, Max E., Coachella Valley Joint Union High School, Coachella,
    Calif.
Willey, Lawrence V., Jr., 259 E. Erie St., Chicago, Ill.
Williams, Aimee, 1136 East 48th St., Chicago, Ill.
Williams, Alma V., Educ. Dept., University of California, University, Calif.
Williams, Arloff L., St. John's Military Academy, Delafield, Wis.
Williams, Arthur E., Dillard Comprehensive High School, Fort Lauderdale, Fla.
Williams, Byron B., University of Rochester, Rochester, N.Y.
Williams, Catharine M., 1945 N. High St., Columbus, Ohio
Williams, Charles C., North Texas State College, Denton, Tex.
Williams, Chester Spring, 1800 Argentia Dr., Dallas, Tex.
Williams, Clarence M., Col. of Educ., University of Rochester, Rochester, N.Y.
Williams, Cyrus Paul, 903 Peach St., El Campo, Tex.
Williams, Emmet D., 1261 Highway 36, St. Paul, Minn.
Williams, Fannie C., 1633 St. Bernard Ave., New Orleans, La.
Williams, Fountie N., 505 Pennsylvania Ave., Clarksburg, W.Va.
Williams, Frances I., Lab. Sch., Indiana State Teachers Col., Terre Haute, Ind.
Williams, G. A., Walnut Hill High School, Shreveport, La.
Williams, Harold A., Flat Top, W.Va.
Williams, Herman, 40 Elmwood St., Tiffin, Ohio
Williams, Howard Y., Jr., 2298 Doswell Ave., St. Paul, Minn.
Williams, Jacob T., 804 Eighth St., North, Gadsden, Ala.
Williams, James Harry, Armstrong High School, Richmond, Va.
Williams, John D., Long Beach State College, Long Beach, Calif.
Williams, Mrs. Lois, 200 North 18th St., Montebello, Calif.
Williams, Malcolm, Sch. of Educ., Tennessee A. & I. University, Nashville, Tenn.
Williams, Nat, Superintendent of Schools, Lubbock, Tex.
Williams, Richard H., 380 Moseley Rd., Hillsborough, Calif.
Williams, Robert Bruce, 122 East 6th Ave., Roselle, N.J.
Williams, W. Morris, USOM/K, TC ED, APO 301, San Francisco, Calif.
Williams, Wilbur A., Moorhead State College, Moorhead, Minn.
Williamson, Jane, Morehead State College, Morehead, Ky.
Wills, Benjamin G., 1550 Bellamy St., Santa Clara, Calif.
Willson, Gordon L., Superintendent of Schools, Baraboo, Wis.
Wilson, Alan S., Hillyer Col., University of Hartford, Hartford, Conn.
Wilson, David H., Lodi, N.Y.
Wilson, Dustin W., Community Cons. School District 10, Rt. 2, Woodstock, Ill.
Wilson, Harold M., 3006 N. Trinidad St., Arlington, Va.
Wilson, Herbert B., University of Arizona, Tucson, Ariz.
Wilson, Irma B., 809 Catalina Ave., Redondo Beach, Calif.
Wilson, J. A. R., University of California, Goleta, Calif.
Wilson, James W., Rochester Institute of Technology, Rochester, N.Y.
Wilson, Jean Alice, 715 Tidball Ave., Grove City, Pa.
Wilson, Joseph E., 2635—79th Ave., Baton Rouge, La.
Wilson, Lytle M., Geneva College, Beaver Falls, Pa.
Wilson, Merle A., 2800—62nd St., Des Moines, Iowa
Wilson, Ulrey K., Dept. of Educ. and Psych., Univ. of Chattanooga, Chattanooga,
    Tenn.
Wilson, Vera S., Virginia State College, Norfolk, Va.
Wilson, William G., Briar Wood, Wolf Road, Mokena, Ill.
Wilstach, Mrs. Ilah M., 2127 N. Eastern Ave., Los Angeles, Calif.
Wiltse, Earl W., Superintendent of Schools, H.S. Dist. 207, Park Ridge, Ill.

Wimpey, John A., The Citadel, Charleston, S.C.
Winfield, Kenneth, Superintendent of Schools, Clark, N.J.
Wing, Richard L., North. Westchester Tech. and Educ. Center, Yorktown Heights, N.Y.
Wingerd, Harold H., Superintendent of Schools, West Chester, Pa.
Winkley, Mrs. Carol K., 1815 Kenilworth Pl., Aurora, Ill.
Winsor, Mrs. Charlotte B., Bank Street College, 4 East 74th St., New York, N.Y.
Winston, Bertha H., 730 Oakwood Blvd., Chicago, Ill.
Winter, Stephen S., Sch. of Educ., University of Buffalo, Buffalo, N.Y.
Winters, Mrs. Harry E., 38841 Willodale, Willoughby, Ohio
Wiseman, Rex M., 808 Genoa St., Monrovia, Calif.
Wishart, James S., 1638 Ridge Rd., West, Rochester, N.Y.
Witherspoon, W. H., P.O. Box 527, Rockhill, S.C.
Witt, Paul W. F., Tchrs. Col., Columbia University, New York, N.Y.
Witte, Cyril M., Loyola College, 4501 N. Charles St., Baltimore, Md.
Witter, Sanford C., Superintendent of Schools, Dist. 202, Kansas City, Kan.
Wittick, Mildred Letton, 300 Pompton Rd., Wayne, N.J.
Wittmer, Arthur E., 2112 Broadway, Rm. 401, New York, N.Y.
Witty, Paul A., Sch. of Educ., Northwestern University, Evanston, Ill.
Wixon, John L., 6519 Knott Blvd., El Cerrito, Calif.
Wixted, William G., Hunter College, 695 Park Ave., New York, N.Y.
Wochner, Raymond E., Arizona State University, Tempe, Ariz.
Woerdehoff, Frank J., Dept. of Educ., Purdue University, Lafayette, Ind.
Woestehoff, Orville W., Oak Park Elementary Schls., 122 Forest Ave., Oak Park, Ill.
Wolbrecht, Walter F., 316 Parkwood, Kirkwood, Mo.
Wolf, Dan B., P.O. Box 367, Bloomington, Ind.
Wolf, Irvin G., Denby High School, 12800 Kelly Rd., Detroit, Mich.
Wolf, Lloyd L., 605 N. McLean Ave., Lincoln, Ill.
Wolf, William C., Jr., Arps Hall, Ohio State University, Columbus, Ohio
Wolfe, Josephine B., 793B Erford Rd., Camp Hill, Pa.
Wolfram, Donald J., 7125 E. Colfax Ave., Denver, Colo.
Wolfson, Bernice J., University of Wisconsin-Milwaukee, Milwaukee, Wis.
Wolinsky, Gloria F., 69-52 Groton St., Forest Hills, N.Y.
Wong, William T. S., 1640 Paula Dr., Honolulu, Hawaii
Wood, Donald I., Dept. of Educ., Houston, Tex.
Wood, Harvey, Dimondale Area Schools, Dimondale, Mich.
Wood, Helen A., Dept. of Educ., Brooklyn College, Brooklyn, N.Y.
Wood, Joseph E., 18 Duryea Rd., Upper Montclair, N.J.
Wood, Roi S., Superintendent of Schools, Joplin, Mo.
Wood, W. H., Dept. of Educ., Emmanuel Missionary College, Berrien Springs, Mich.
Woodard, Prince B., Col. of Educ., Temple University, Philadelphia, Pa.
Woodburn, A. C., Alamogordo Public Schools, Alamogordo, N.M.
Woodburn, John H., Walter Johnson High School, Rockville, Md.
Wooden, Maurice L., West Covina High School, West Covina, Calif.
Woodhull, James E., USAID to Colombia, American Consulate, Cali, Colombia
Woodruff, Olive, Kent State University, Kent, Ohio
Woods, Robert Keith, 103 W. Hickory St., Platteville, Wis.
Woodson, C. C., 435 S. Liberty St., Spartanburg, S.C.
Woodson, Grace I., West Virginia State College, Institute, W.Va.
Woodward, Mrs. Etta K., 927 Cayuga Heights Rd., Ithaca, N.Y.
Woodworth, Denny, Col. of Educ., Drake University, Des Moines, Iowa
Woodworth, William O., 999 Kedzie Ave., Flossmoor, Ill.
Woofter, James, 412 S. Union St., Ada, Ohio
Woolbright, William J., 820—11th St., Huntington Beach, Calif.
Woolf, Kenneth A., Hunterdon County Schools, Flemington, N.J.
Woolson, Edith L., Box 203, Imperial, Calif.
Wozencraft, Marian, State University College of Education, Geneseo, N.Y.
Wrenn, C. Gilbert, Burton Hall, University of Minnesota, Minneapolis, Minn.
Wright, Adele J., 275 S. Glencoe St., Denver, Colo.

Wright, C. O., Kansas State Teachers Assn., Topeka, Kan.
Wright, C. P., Guthrie High School, Guthrie, Okla.
Wright, Eleanore B., Little Silver Public Schools, Little Silver, N.J.
Wright, Floyd K., 1432 Price Dr., Cape Girardeau, Mo.
Wright, John R., San Jose State College, San Jose, Calif.
Wrightstone, J. Wayne, Board of Educ., 110 Livingston St., Brooklyn, N.Y.
Wronski, Stanley P., Col. of Educ., Michigan State Univ., East Lansing, Mich.
Wubben, Horace J., Mesa County Junior College, Grand Junction, Colo.
Wulfing, Gretchen, 1025 Second Ave., Oakland, Calif.
Wuolle, Mrs. Ethel, P.O. Box 173, Pine City, Minn.
Wyeth, E. R., 18111 Nordhoff St., Northridge, Calif.
Wyllie, Eugene D., Sch. of Bus., Indiana University, Bloomington, Ind.
Wynn, Cordell, 3018 Bethune Ave., Macon, Ga.
Wynn, Willa T., 1122 N. St. Clair St., Pittsburgh, Pa.

Yamashiro, Margaret H., 1720 Ala Moana Blvd., Honolulu, Hawaii
Yaple, Graydon W., 664 Timber Lane, Wilmington, Ohio
Yates, Mrs. Flora R., R.F.D. 1, Box 43, Elkton, Va.
Yates, J. W., Curric. Lab., Kansas University, Lawrence, Kan.
Yates, Virginia D., 5318 Troost, Kansas City, Mo.
Yauch, Wilbur A., Northern Illinois University, DeKalb, Ill.
Yavicoli, Mildred,, 3067 Orleans Ave., Niagara Falls, N.Y.
Yeager, Paul M., Sheridan School, Second and Liberty Sts., Allentown, Pa.
Yoshimori, Alice S., 1801 University Ave., Honolulu, Hawaii
Young, Albert T., Jr., National Science Foundation, Washington, D.C.
Young, Gordon Mawson, Sine Nomine, Hempstead Lane, Hailsham, Sussex,
    England
Young, Harold L., Central Missouri State College, Warrensburg, Mo.
Young, Horace A., Jr., Texas Southern University, Houston, Tex.
Young, J. E. M., Macdonald College Post Office, Quebec
Young, Jean A., San Francisco College for Women, San Francisco, Calif.
Young, John J., 519 Clay St., Mishawaka, Ind.
Young, Lloyd P., Keene Teachers College, Keene, N.H.
Young, William E., New York State Education Department, Albany, N.Y.
Young, William Howard, 1460 Tampa Ave., Dayton, Ohio
Youngblood, Chester E., P.O. Box 413, College, Alaska
Younglund, Donald E., 3831 S. Fees St., Wichita, Kan.
Yourd, John L., 1104—2nd Ave., Fargo, N.D.
Yuhas, Theodore Frank, Educ. Dept., Ball State Teachers College, Muncie, Ind.
Yunghans, Ernest E., 1145 S. Barr St., Fort Wayne, Ind.

Zahm, Bernice S., 5033 Biloxi Ave., North Hollywood, Calif.
Zahn, D. Willard, Col. of Educ., Temple University, Philadelphia, Pa.
Zahorsky, Mrs. Metta, San Francisco State College, San Francisco, Calif.
Zakrzewski, Aurelia R., 4806 Chovin St., Dearborn, Mich.
Zambite, Stephen C., 616 North River, Ypsilanti, Mich.
Zawadski, Bohdan, 106 East 85th St., New York, N.Y.
Zbornik, Joseph J., 3219 Clarence Ave., Berwyn, Ill.
Zdanowicz, John Paul, 71 Spring Hill Ave., Bridgewater, Mass.
Zebrowski, Kenneth M., USA DEG, Dist. V., APO 58, New York, N.Y.
Zeiler, E. J., Superintendent of Schools, Whitefish Bay, Wis.
Zepper, John Thomas, Hodgin Hall, University of New Mexico, Albuquerque,
    N.M.
Ziebold, Edna B., 6401 Linda Vista Rd., San Diego, Calif.
Ziemba, Walter J., St. Mary's College, Orchard Lake, Mich.
Zim, Herbert Spencer, Box 34, Tavernier, Fla.
Zimmerman, Katherine A., 619½ East 3rd St., Northfield, Minn.
Zimmerman, William G., Jr., Sch. of Educ., University of Miami, Coral Gables,
    Fla.
Zimnoch, Frances J., West Tresper Clark High School, Westbury, L.I., N.Y.
Zinn, Lawrence A., 312 "A" S. Poplar, Oxford, Ohio

Zintz, Miles V., 3028 Marble Ave., N.E., Albuquerque, N.M.
Zipper, Joseph H., 1569 West 41st St., Erie, Pa.
Zucker, Alfred, Moore Hall, University of California, Los Angeles, Calif.
Zweig, Richard L., Reading Guid. Center, Inc., 9200 Colima Rd., Whittier, Calif.

INFORMATION CONCERNING THE NATIONAL SOCIETY FOR THE STUDY OF EDUCATION

1. PURPOSE. The purpose of the National Society is to promote the investigation and discussion of educational questions. To this end it holds an annual meeting and publishes a series of yearbooks.

2. ELIGIBILITY TO MEMBERSHIP. Any person who is interested in receiving its publications may become a member by sending to the Secretary-Treasurer information concerning name, title, and address, and a check for $8.00 (see Item 5), except that graduate students, on the recommendation of a faculty member, may become members by paying $6.00 for the first year of their membership. Dues for all subsequent years are the same as for other members (see Item 4).

Membership is not transferable; it is limited to individuals, and may not be held by libraries, schools, or other institutions, either directly or indirectly.

3. PERIOD OF MEMBERSHIP. Applicants for membership may not date their entrance back of the current calendar year, and all memberships terminate automatically on December 31, unless the dues for the ensuing year are paid as indicated in Item 6.

4. DUTIES AND PRIVILEGES OF MEMBERS. Members pay dues of $7.00 annually, receive a cloth-bound copy of each publication, are entitled to vote, to participate in discussion, and (under certain conditions) to hold office. The names of members are printed in the yearbooks.

Persons who are sixty years of age or above may become life members on payment of fee based on average life-expectancy of their age group. For information, apply to Secretary-Treasurer.

5. ENTRANCE FEE. New members are required the first year to pay, in addition to the dues, an entrance fee of one dollar.

6. PAYMENT OF DUES. Statements of dues are rendered in October for the following calendar year. Any member so notified whose dues remain unpaid on January 1, thereby loses his membership and can be reinstated only by paying a reinstatement fee of fifty cents.

School warrants and vouchers from institutions must be accompanied by definite information concerning the name and address of the person for whom membership fee is being paid. Statements of dues are rendered on our own form only. The Secretary's office cannot undertake to fill out special invoice forms of any sort or to affix notary's affidavit to statements or receipts.

Cancelled checks serve as receipts. Members desiring an additional receipt must enclose a stamped and addressed envelope therefor.

7. DISTRIBUTION OF YEARBOOKS TO MEMBERS. The yearbooks, ready prior to each February meeting, will be mailed from the office of the distributors, only to members whose dues for that year have been paid. Members who desire yearbooks prior to the current year must purchase them directly from the distributors (see Item 8).

8. COMMERCIAL SALES. The distribution of all yearbooks prior to the current year, and also of those of the current year not regularly mailed to members in exchange for their dues, is in the hands of the distributor, not of the Secretary. For such commercial sales, communicate directly with the University of Chicago Press, Chicago 37, Illinois, which will gladly send a price list covering all the publications of this Society. This list is also printed in the yearbook.

9. YEARBOOKS. The yearbooks are issued about one month before the February meeting. They comprise from 600 to 800 pages annually. Unusual effort has been made to make them, on the one hand, of immediate practical value, and, on the other hand, representative of sound scholarship and scientific investigation.

10. MEETINGS. The annual meeting, at which the yearbooks are discussed, is held in February at the same time and place as the meeting of the American Association of School Administrators.

Applications for membership will be handled promptly at any time on receipt of name and address, together with check for $8.00 (or $7.50 for reinstatement). Applications entitle the new members to the yearbook slated for discussion during the calendar year the application is made.

5835 Kimbark Ave.　　　　　HERMAN G. RICHEY, *Secretary-Treasurer*
Chicago 37, Illinois

PUBLICATIONS OF THE NATIONAL SOCIETY FOR THE STUDY OF EDUCATION

NOTICE: Many of the early Yearbooks of this series are now **out of print.** In the following list, those titles to which an asterisk is prefixed are not available for purchase.

c   PUBLICATIONS

Distributed by
THE UNIVERSITY OF CHICAGO PRESS, CHICAGO 37, ILLINOIS
1963